LOEB CLASSICAL LIBRARY

FOUNDED BY JAMES LOEB 1911

EDITED BY

JEFFREY HENDERSON

AUGUSTINE

THE TEACHER

TEACHING CHRISTIANITY

LCL 560

AUGUSTINE

THE TEACHER

TEACHING CHRISTIANITY

EDITED AND TRANSLATED BY

CAROLYN J.-B. HAMMOND

HARVARD UNIVERSITY PRESS
CAMBRIDGE, MASSACHUSETTS
LONDON, ENGLAND
2025

First published 2025

Library of Congress Control Number 2025000797
CIP data available from the Library of Congress

ISBN 978-0-674-99772-1

*Composed in ZephGreek and ZephText by
Technologies 'N Typography, Merrimac, Massachusetts.
Printed on acid-free paper and bound by
Maple Press, York, Pennsylvania*

CONTENTS

PREFACE ix

ABBREVIATIONS xvii

GENERAL BIBLIOGRAPHY xxiii

THE TEACHER

INTRODUCTION 2

TESTIMONIA 20

TEXT AND TRANSLATION 22

TEACHING CHRISTIANITY

INTRODUCTION 152

TEXT AND TRANSLATION

PROEM 192

BOOK I 208

BOOK II 278

BOOK III 400

BOOK IV 498

INDEX OF PERSONS AND PLACES 635

INDEX OF SUBJECTS 639

For Stephen Farr—

corde et digitis tangis arcana dei

PREFACE

Titles can be misleading. *The Teacher* (*TT*) says little about the one person it acknowledges as truly a teacher, Christ. *Teaching Christianity* (*TC*) says more about that one true teacher, but equally little about how readers might learn to teach Christianity.[1] Yet Augustine gave both works their titles; to him at least they were descriptive of the contents. The Latin title of *TT* is *De magistro*, and *magister*[2] came to mean "teacher" in a sense close to its English derivative, "master."[3] *TC* in Latin is *De doctrina christiana*: but *doctrina* had not then acquired its later Christian meaning, referring to the propositional content of Christianity. It is the noun form cognate with the verb *docere*, "teach." So the "teach-" part of these two book titles comes from different Latin words. It is not unreasonable, therefore, to ask whether *doctor* and *magister* are synonymous. *Magister* has no cognate verb; the verb Augustine uses with it in *TT* is *docere.* He mostly uses *magister* for an instructor in

[1] He covers these Christian basics elsewhere, in e.g., *Cat. Rud.* and *Ench.*

[2] A noun formed from a comparative adverb *magis* and comparative ending *-ter.*

[3] His use of *magister* rather than *doctor* is influenced by the Bible text he cites: in Matthew 23:10 the word is *magister* in both the Vulgate and the Old Latin translations.

some subject for study. When he uses the term *doctor*, on the other hand, he applies it to Christians on a higher level of intellectual and spiritual achievement. The two words, then, are not perfectly synonymous, but they are close enough.

Alongside these two works, one from the beginning and the other from the end of his scholarly career, Augustine's extraordinary *Confessions* provide invaluable context. They disclose reflections and remembrances drawn from his own experiences of learning and teaching and allow the reader to trace the development of his mature understanding of what teaching is, or should be. His personal experiences doubtless played a part in forming him as a teacher; but this volume is testament to the fact that they formed him as a theorist and thinker too, constantly interrogating and evaluating motivations and assumptions—his own, and other people's—about the processes of teaching and learning. When he wrote *Confessions*, he had begun *TC* but not completed it. Questions about teaching must have been fresh in his mind; and what he says about it there should be read in the light of both *TT* and *TC*.

In *Confessions* he described how he learned. At home he imitated what he saw and progressed in language (and in other ways) by being praised and encouraged (1.14.23). At primary school, the place where his learning was paid for, rather than being the fruit of affection (1.16.26), he shifted between fear of and contempt for his teachers. He acquired knowledge, but not from their teaching, not even obliquely from their example of life or instruction of manners. Instead, his learning was self-driven, motivated by his dread of his teachers' brutal punishments (*Conf.* 1.9.15).

Even at that early stage he was beginning to question the point of learning at all, given that his teachers "never paid any attention to the use I made of what they forced me to learn" (1.12.19). To God he expresses his disgust at having for his masters men whose use of language was immaculate, but whose morality and behavior were not:

> The knowledge of letters is definitely not imprinted as deeply as the graven sense that it is wrong to inflict on another what one does not wish to endure oneself. (*Conf.* 1.18.29)

When he looked back at the time he spent in Carthage for the secondary stage of his education, it was his own arrogance that disgusted him:

> How great is the blindness of those who even boast about their being blind! I was top of the class in the rhetor's schoolroom. I reveled in my arrogance, I was puffed up with pride. (*Conf.* 3.3.6)

This unpromising territory, though, was the setting for his first conversion—not to Christianity as yet, but to the pursuit of wisdom. The reader is invited to observe this as a first stage of his soul's return to God. Once more the impulse comes from within himself, not from the guidance or instruction of a human teacher.[4] He depicts it as the

[4] The failure of his mother's constant pressure to effect his Christian conversion is a recurring theme in the early books of *Confessions*. The person whom he loved most, and whom he held in the highest intellectual as well as emotional honor ("a woman in appearance, she had faith strong as a man's," *Conf.* 9.4.8), could not transfer her faith into him. Not that this stopped her trying.

first time he became aware of learning as something worth pursuing for its own sake:

> At that vulnerable age, I was mastering works of rhetoric. I was desperate to excel on account of the pleasures of human vanity—what a conceited, damnable course of action! In the ordinary course of my studies I had arrived at a work by a certain person called Cicero, whose use of language is almost universally admired even if his character is not. One of his works contains a call to philosophy: it is called *Hortensius*. That same work effected a change in my feelings, and also changed my prayers to you, Lord. It altered the substance of my supplications and desires. All of a sudden every one of my vain hopes became worthless to me, and with an extraordinary passion of the heart I began to long for immortal wisdom, and I started to arise so as to return to you. Not to sharpen my style of delivery (which was what my mother's payments were ostensibly for, now that I had reached the age of nineteen and my father had died two years back), no, not to sharpen my style was I applying myself to this work: and it was not the style of speaking but the content of what was said, that I found persuasive. (*Conf.* 3.4.7)

Both here and in *TC* Augustine was cautious about treating Cicero as a model: but the juxtaposition of this conversion to wisdom (*Conf.* 3.4.7) with his first serious attempt to fix his mind on the holy Scriptures and "see what kind of thing they really were" (3.5.9) makes it clear how he regarded the great statesman as a positive influ-

ence. This first "conversion" marks the point when he begins to ask himself questions about what learning is, and how it happens. It is easy to see how he would be dissatisfied with an "information-transfer" understanding of learning.

Dissatisfaction played a part, then, in forwarding his intellectual formation. But neither as an uncommitted youth, nor as a Manichaean, nor even as a catholic Christian did he attempt to find his way entirely alone. He always wanted to be part of a like-minded group and to find a person of intellectual stature and renown to attach himself to.[5] So when he discovered that Faustus the Manichaean was a fraudulent windbag, Augustine denounced him as "that man who dared to pass himself off as the teacher (*doctor*)" (*Conf.* 5.5.9).

His next candidate proved to be a more successful model, for Ambrose, bishop of Milan, was a man of real intellectual stature, and—still crucially at this stage in Augustine's progress—a brilliant orator as well as an intelligent thinker. Ambrose, he decided, *did* deserve the title of "teacher," but he admits that back then he was more in love with the eloquence than the content of Ambrose's words. The following passage reveals Augustine's reverence for what a real teacher could be, as he describes the process by which he himself learned his faith from Ambrose:[6]

[5] Being part of a group: *Conf.* 2.3.7–8; 3.3.6; 4.1.1, 4.7, 8.13–9.14; 6.7.11–10.17, 14.24; 8.1.1–2.3, 6.14; 9.3.5–4.7. Finding a "guru": 5.3.3, 6.10–7.13 (Faustus); 5.13.23 (Ambrose).

[6] As almost throughout *Confessions*, he is addressing his words here to God.

I began to love him in return, not initially as a teacher of truth (*doctor veri*)—I despaired of finding any such in your church—but as a human being who looked kindly upon me. I listened carefully to his debates among the people, not as attentively as I should, but as it were making trial of his eloquence, whether it matched his reputation or whether it was more or less fluent than I had been told. I hung upon his words, listening carefully, but I cared little for the subject matter and stood looking on scornfully. Yet I was delighted by his attractive way of speaking, for though it was better-informed, it was still, as far as style of delivery goes, less crowd-pleasing and charming than that of Faustus. Yet there was no comparison when it came to actual content: for Faustus kept wandering off into Manichaean inconsistencies, while Ambrose was teaching wholesome salvation. . . . I put no effort into learning what he was saying but only into hearing how he was saying it . . . Even so, while the words which I loved kept coming into my mind, some actual facts, to which I usually paid no attention, came with them, for I could not keep them separate. Thus while I was opening my heart to absorb how eloquently he was speaking, at the same time the true subject matter of which he spoke was entering too, though only gradually. First I began to see that such views were defensible; and then I began to believe that the catholic faith, which I had thought had nothing to be said for it against the attacks of the Manichaeans, could be proclaimed without embarrassment. (*Conf.* 5.13.23–14.24)

It was listening to Ambrose that made him decide to join the catechumenate.[7]

Confessions, therefore, is a valuable witness to how Augustine ordinarily spoke and thought about the business of teaching and learning. He became disillusioned with teaching as a profession because students were either badly behaved (as at Carthage, 5.8.14) or dishonest about paying for the teaching they received (as in Rome, 5.12.22). No wonder the idea of a civic appointment in Milan as a teacher of rhetoric (*rhetoricae magister*) appealed (5.13.23): it would provide the recognition of status that he craved and insulate him from irregularity of income.

Loeb translators can be expected to have decades-long involvement in teaching. All of them have been pupils (*discipuli*), whose job was to learn (*discere*), before they became teachers, tasked with—what? Passing on that knowledge? The reader must read Augustine first, and adjudicate afterward. The best teachers go on learning, not least from their pupils: as Augustine did from both his son and his mother. Anatomizing how teaching works may lead into some challenging philosophical territory; but somehow knowledge still achieves its *traditio*, that "handing-over" from one generation to the next. If teachers do not teach facts, they can and do teach the love of a subject through personal witness and testimony. And they do not have to be Christians like Augustine to recognize his experience of inner illumination, even if the subtle mechanics of the teaching/learning process remain a mystery.

7 Persons preparing for baptism were called "catechumens."

PREFACE

Once more my thanks are due to the Master and Fellows of Gonville and Caius College, Cambridge, for kindly granting me sabbatical leave so that I could complete this volume. During my absence from college duties, the combined talents and labors of the Rev. Canon Dr. Megan Daffern, the Rev. Canon Dr. Nicholas Thistlethwaite, Mr. Matthew Martin, and Mrs. Claire Wheeler have meant that my absence was entirely unproblematic, and I take the opportunity to thank them here, from the heart, for all that they have done. When I was at a loss how to access information about the beautiful Leningrad codex of *TC* (on account of a breakdown in international relations following the Russian invasion of Ukraine), Professors John Mollon and Marina Danilova came to my aid, as did Professor Peter Saenger, so I record here my gratitude for all their generous help. No one but myself is to blame for whatever errors readers may detect.

For the debt I owe to Graham, Lizzie, and Jonny, what can I say? You give me strength to carry on.

Gonville & Caius College
July 2023

Yma o hyd.

ABBREVIATIONS

BIBLE VERSIONS

MT/HB	Masoretic Text/Hebrew Bible
LXX	Septuagint
Vulg.	Latin Vulgate Bible
VL	Old Latin Bible
AV (= KJV)	Authorized Version ("King James" Version 1611)
RSV	Revised Standard Version

ANCIENT

For more common abbreviations, consult the *Oxford Classical Dictionary*.

Ambr.	Ambrose
De fug. saec.	*De fuga saeculi/ On Flight from the World*
Virg.	*De virginibus/On Virgins*
Ans. *Pros.*	Anselm, *Proslogion*
Apoc. M.	*Apocalypsis Mosis/Apocalypse of Moses*
Arn.	Arnobius
Aug.	Augustine
An. et or.	*De anima et eius origine* (also known as *De natura et origine animae*)/ *On the Soul and Its Origin*

Cat. Rud.	*De catechizandis rudibus/ On the Instruction of Beginners*
Civ.	*De civitate dei contra paganos/ City of God*
Con. Acad.	*Contra academicos/ Against the Academicians*
Conf.	*Confessiones/Confessions*
Cont.	*De continentia/On Continence*
C. Jul. imp.	*Contra Iulianum opus imperfectum/ Against Julian, an Unfinished Work*
Cur. mort.	*De cura pro mortuis gerenda/ On the Care to be Taken for the Dead*
De lib. arb.	*De libero arbitrio voluntatis/ On Free Choice of the Will*
Div. quaest.	*De diversis quaestionibus octoginta tribus/Eighty-three Different Questions*
Doctr./TC	*De doctrina christiana/ Teaching Christianity*
Ench.	*Enchiridion/On Faith, Hope, and Love*
En. Ps.	*Enarrationes in psalmos/ Explanations of the Psalms*
Ep.	*Epistulae/Letters*
Gen. Man.	*De Genesi contra Manichaeos/ On Genesis against the Manichees*
Haer.	*De haeresibus/On Heresies*
Io. Ev. Tr.	*In Iohannis evangelium tractatus/ Tractates on the Gospel of John*
Mag./TT	*De magistro/The Teacher*
Mor.	*De moribus ecclesiae catholicae et de moribus Manichaeorum/ On the Catholic and Manichaean Ways of Life*

Mus.	*De musica/On Music*
Qu.	*Quaestiones in Heptateuchum/ Questions on the Heptateuch*
Retr.	*Retractationes/Retractations*
Simpl.	*Ad Simplicianum/de diversis quaestionibus ad Simpl.* (not to be confused with *De diversis quaestionibus octoginta tribus*)
Spir. et litt.	*De spiritu et littera/ On the Spirit and the Letter*
Trin.	*De trinitate/On the Trinity*
Cypr.	Cyprian
De dom. orat.	*De domini oratione/ On the Lord's Prayer*
Disc.	*De disciplina et habitu virginum/ On the Dress of Virgins*
Ep.	*Epistulae/Epistles*
Ep. ad Don.	*Epistula ad Donatum/Letter to Donatus*
Unit.	*De unitate ecclesiae/ On the Unity of the Church*
Diom.	Diomedes Grammaticus, *Ars grammatica*
Euseb.	Eusebius of Caesarea
Iren. *Haer.*	Irenaeus of Lyons, *Adversus haereses/ Against Heresies*
Jer.	Jerome
Justin	Justin Martyr
Apol.	*Apologia/Apology*
Dial. Tryph.	*Dialogus cum Tryphone/ Dialogue with Trypho*
Mar. Vict.	Marius Victorinus
Adv. Ar.	*Adversus Arium/Against Arius*

ABBREVIATIONS

Socrates, *Hist. eccl.*	Socrates of Constantinople, *Historia ecclesiastica/Church History*
Tert.	Tertullian
Apol.	*Apologeticus/Defense*
Mar.	*Adversus Marcionem/Against Marcion*
Prax.	*Adversus Praxean/Against Praxeas*
Thphl. *Autol.*	Theophilus of Antioch, *Apology to Autolycus*
Tic.	Ticonius, *Liber regularum/ Book of Rules*

MODERN

Arnold and Bright	Arnold, Duane W. H., and Pamela Bright, eds. *De doctrina christiana: A Classic of Western Culture*. Christianity and Judaism in Antiquity 9. Notre Dame: University of Notre Dame Press, 1995.
Aug&Witt	Paffenroth, K., A. R. Eodice, and J. Doody, eds. *Augustine and Wittgenstein*. Lexington Books: Fortress Academic, 2018.
AugStud	*Augustinian Studies*
August.	*Augustiniana*
Brown	Brown, Raymond. *The Gospel According to John*. Yale: Yale University Press, vol. 1, 1966; vol. 2, 1970.
CCSL	Corpus Christianorum Series Latina
ChHist	*Church History*

CSEL	Corpus Scriptorum Ecclesiasticorum Latinorum
Enos and Thompson	Enos, Richard Leo, and Roger Thompson, eds. *The Rhetoric of St Augustine of Hippo: de doctrina christiana and the Search for a Distinctly Christian Rhetoric.* Waco, TX: Baylor University Press, 2008.
Gr.	Green, William M., ed. *Sancti Aureli Augustini Opera 6.6: de doctrina christiana*. CSEL 80,.Vienna, 1963.
HThR	*The Harvard Theological Review*
JTh	*Journal of Thought*
JThS	*The Journal of Theological Studies*
Mart.	Martin, Joseph, ed. *Sancti Aurelii Augustini De doctrina christiana; de vera religione.* CCSL 32. Turnholt: Brepols, 1982.
MBM	Bibliothèque Augustinienne. Oeuvres de Saint Augustin, 11/2: *La doctrine chrétienne. De doctrina christiana*. Texte critique du CCSL, revu et corrigé. Introduction et traduction de Moreau, Madeleine. Annotation et notes complémentaires d'Bochet, Isabelle et Madec, Goulven. Paris: Institut d'Etudes Augustiniennes, 1997.
Metaph	*Metaphilosophy*
Phil	*Philosophy*
PMLA	*Journal of the Modern Language Association of America*

REAug	*Revue des Études Augustiniennes et Patristiques*
RGr.	Green, R. P. H. *De doctrina christiana*. Oxford Early Christian Texts. Oxford: Clarendon Press, 1995.
StudPatr	*Studia Patristica*

GENERAL BIBLIOGRAPHY

Ando, C. "Augustine on Language." *REAug* 40 (1994).

Babcock, William. "*Caritas* and signification in *de doctrina christiana* 1–3." In Arnold and Bright, 145–63.

Baehrens, Emil. *Fragmenta poetarum Romanorum.* Teubner: Leipzig, 1886.

Baer, Helmut. "The Fruit of Charity: Using the Neighbor in *de doctrina christiana.*" *The Journal of Religious Ethics* 24 (1996).

Bearsley, Patrick. "Augustine and Wittgenstein on Language." *Phil* 58 (1983).

Blaise, Albert. *Dictionnaire latin-français des auteurs chrétiens*. Revised by P. Tombeur. Turnhout: Brepols, 2005. [Paris: Libraire des méridiens 1954, 1967; Turnhout: Brepols, 1997].

Bochet, Isabelle. "De l'exégèse à l'herméneutique augustinienne." *REAug* 50 (2004).

———. "Reflexions sur l'exégèse figurative d'Augustin." *AugStud* 45 (2014).

Bonner, Gerald. *Freedom and Necessity: St Augustine's Teaching on Divine Power and Human Freedom.* Washington, DC: The Catholic University of America Press, 2007.

Bright, Pamela. "Biblical Ambiguity in African Exegesis." In Arnold and Bright, 25–32.

Burnaby, John. *Amor Dei: A Study in the Religion of St Augustine*. London: Hodder and Stoughton, 1947.

Burnyeat, M. F. "The Inaugural Address: Wittgenstein and Augustine *de magistro*." *Proceedings of the Aristotelian Society* (*suppl*) 61 (1987). Reproduced in *Aug&Witt*.

Cary, Phillip. "How Words Became Signs: The Development of Augustine's Expressionist Semiotics." In *Outward Signs: The Powerlessness of External Things in Augustine's Thought*." Oxford University Press: Oxford, 2008.

Chidester, David. "The Symbolism of Learning in St. Augustine." *HThR* 76 (1983).

Courtney, Edward. *The Fragmentary Latin Poets*. Clarendon Press: Oxford, 1993.

Crosson, Frederick. "The Structure of the *de magistro*." *REAug* 35 (1989).

Crystal, David. "Some Current Trends in Translation Theory." *Bible Translator* 27 (1976).

———. "A Liturgical Language in a Sociolinguistic Perspective." In *Language and the Worship of the Church*, edited by D. Jasper and R. C. D. Jasper. Macmillan: Basingstoke, 1990.

Darrell Jackson, B. "The Theory of Signs in St. Augustine's *de doctrina christiana*." *REAug* 15 (1969).

DeVitis, Joseph L. "The Interiorized Self: Augustinian Epistemology and Existential Education." *JTh* 6 (1971).

Doignon, Jean. "Nos bons hommes de foi: Cyprien, Lactance, Victorin, Optat, Hilaire (Augustin, *de doctrina christiana*, 4.[*sic*: *lege* 2]61)." *Latomus* 22 (1963).

Eden, Kathy. "Hermeneutics and The Ancient Rhetorical Tradition." *Rhetorica: A Journal of the History of Rhetoric* 5 (1987).

———. "The Rhetorical Tradition and Augustinian Hermeneutics in *de doctrina christiana*." *Rhetorica: A Journal of the History of Rhetoric* 8 (1990).

Eggsdorfer, F. X. *Der heilige Augustinus als Padadoge und seine Bedeutung fur die Geschichte der Bildung*. Freiburg im Breisgau, 1917.

Eller, Meredith F. "The *Retractationes* of Saint Augustine." *ChHist* 18 (1949).

Engelland, Chad. "Learning by Ostension in Augustine and Wittgenstein." In *Aug&Witt*.

Evangeliou, Christos C. "Man as the Most Mimetic Animal According to Aristotle." In *The Many Faces of Mimesis: Selected Essays from the 2017 Symposium on the Hellenic Heritage of Western Greece*, edited by Heather L. Reid and Jeremy C. DeLong. Parnassos Press: Fonte Aretusa, 2018.

Ferretter, Luke. "The Trace of the Trinity: Christ and Difference in Saint Augustine's Theory of Language." *Literature and Theology* 12 (1998).

Fortin, Ernest L. "Augustine and the Problem of Christian Rhetoric." *AugStud* 5 (1974): 85–100. In Enos and Thompson, 219–33.

Glowasky, Michael. "the Author Is the Meaning: Narrative in Augustine's Hermeneutics." *Scottish Journal of Theology* 71 (2018).

Gorman, Michael M. "The Diffusion of the Manuscripts of Saint Augustine's *de doctrina christiana* in the Early Middle Ages." Revue Bénédictine 95 (1985).

Green, William M. "A fourth century ms. of Saint Augustine." *Revue Bénédictine* 69 (1959).

———. "Textual Notes on Augustine's *de doctrina christiana*." *REAug* 8 (1962).

Hagendahl, Harald. *Augustine and the Latin Classics*. Studia Graeca et Latina Gothoburgensia 20. Vol. 1, Testimonia; vol. 2, Augustine's Attitude. Goteborg: Almquist and Wiksell, 1967.

Hammond, Cally [Carolyn]. *The Sound of the Liturgy: How Words Work in Worship*. SPCK: London, 2014.

Hill, Edmund. "*De doctrina christiana*: A Suggestion." *StudPatr* 6 (1962).

———. *The Trinity: De trinitate. The Works of Saint Augustine: A Translation for the 21st Century*. New York: New City Press, 1991.

———. *Teaching Christianity: De doctrina christiana*. The Works of Saint Augustine: a Translation for the 21st Century. New York: New City Press, 1996.

Jordan, Mark D. "Words and Word: Incarnation and Signification in Augustine's *de doctrina christiana*." *AugStud* 11 (1980).

Kannengiesser, Charles. "The Interrupted *de doctrina christiana*." In Arnold and Bright, 3–13.

Kenyon, Erik. "Platonic Pedagogy in Augustine's Dialogues." *Ancient Philosophy* 34 (2014).

Kevane, Eugene. "Augustine's *de doctrina christiana*: A Treatise on Christian Education." *REAug* 4 (1966).

———. "Paideia and Anti-paideia. The *prooemium* of Saint Augustine's *de doctrina christiana*." *AugStud* 1 (1970).

Kicey, Michael. "Hard Saying: Language and Teaching in Augustine and Kierkegaard." *Diacritics* 41 (2013).

Kidd, Erica. "In the Beginning. Wittgenstein Reads Augustine." In *Aug&Witt*.

King, Peter. "Augustine on The Impossibility of Teaching." *Metaph* 29 (1998).

Knauer, G. N. "*Sarabara.*" *Glotta* 33 (1954).

Küpper, Joachim. "*Uti* and *frui* in Augustine and the Problem of Aesthetic Pleasure in the Western Tradition (Cervantes, Kant, Marx, Freud)." *Modern Language Notes* 127 (2012).

Lardinois, A. P. M. H., J. H. Blok, and M. G. M. van der Poel, eds. *Sacred Words: Orality, Literacy and Religion*. Leiden: Brill, 2011.

Louth, Andrew. "Augustine on Language." *Literature and Theology* 3 (1989).

Machiavelli, Niccolo. *The Prince*. Florence, 1513.

Mackey, Louis H. "The Mediator Mediated: Faith and Reason in Augustine's *de magistro.*" *Franciscan Studies* 42 (1982).

Markus, R. A. "St. Augustine on Signs." *Phronesis* 2 (1957).

———. *Augustine: A Collection of Critical Essays*. Garden City, NY: Anchor Books, 1972.

———. "Augustine on Magic: A Neglected Semiotic Theory." *REAug* 40 (1994).

———. "Signs, Communication and Communities in Augustine's *de doctrina christiana.*" In Arnold and Bright, 97–108.

Marrou, Henri-Irene. *Saint Augustin et la fin de la culture antique.* Paris: Editions E. de Boccard, 1958.

Mayer, Cornelius. "Res per signa: der Grundgedanke des Prologs in Augustins Schrift *de doctrina christiana* und das Problem seiner Datierung." *REAug* 20 (1974).

Moore, Dwayne. "Truth and Image in Augustinian Epistemology." *August.* 61 (2011).

Murphy, James J. "St Augustine and the Debate about a Christian Rhetoric," *Quarterly Journal of Speech* 46 (1960). In Enos and Thompson, 205–18.

Oberhelman, S. "The History and Development of the *cursus mixtus* in Latin Literature." *The Classical Quarterly* 38 (1988).

O'Donovan, Oliver. *The Problem of Self-Love in St Augustine.* New Haven: CT, 1980.

———. "*Usus* and *fruitio* in Augustine, *de doctrina christiana* I." *JThS* 33 (1982).

Peperzak, Adriaan T. "Teachers Without and Within." In *Augustine Our Contemporary: Examining the Self in Past and Present*, edited by Willemien Otten and Susan E. Schreiner. Notre Dame: University of Notre Dame Press, 2018.

Ployd, Adam. "The Place of *de magistro* in Augustine's Theology of Words and the Word." *AugStud* 54 (2023).

Pollman, Karla. *Doctrina Christiana. Untersuchungen zu den Anfängen der christlichen Hermeneutik unter besonderer Berücksichtigung von Augustinus: de doctrina christiana*. Paradosis 41. Universitätsverlag Freiburg Schweiz, 1996.

Press, Gerald A. "The Subject and Structure of Augustine's *de doctrina christiana*." *AugStud* 11 (1980).

———. "The Content and Argument of Augustine's *de doctrina christiana*." *August.* 31 (1981).

———. "*Doctrina* in Augustine's *de doctrina christiana*." *Philosophy & Rhetoric* 17 (1984).

Primmer, Adolf. "The Function of the *genera dicendi* in *de doctrina christiana* 4." In Arnold and Bright, 68–86.

Rosén, H. B. "Arrius' Speech Again (Catullus 84)." *Mnemosyne* 14 (1961).

Russell, Donald, and Michael Winterbottom. *Ancient Literary Criticism: The Principal Texts in New Translations.* Oxford: Clarendon Press, 1972.

Saenger, Paul. "Augustine as Reader: Prospects for Col-

laboration between Palaeography and the Neurosciences." In *Textual Communities, Textual Selves: Essays in Dialogue with Brian Stock*, edited by Sarah Powrie and Gur Zak. Papers in Mediaeval Studies 37. Toronto, 2023.

Sayers, Dorothy L. *Gaudy Night.* London: Gollancz, 1935.

Schaeffer, John D. "The Dialectic of Orality and Literacy: The Case of Book 4 of Augustine's *de doctrina christiana.*" *PMLA* 111 (1996). In Enos and Thompson, 289–307.

Schäublin, Christoph. "Augustin, *de utilitate credendi*: Über das Verhältnis des Interpreten zum Text." *Vigiliae Christianae* 43 (1989).

———. "*De doctrina christiana*: A Classic of Western Culture?" In Arnold and Bright, 47–67.

Schildgen, Brenda Deen. "Augustine's Answer to Jacques Derrida in the *de doctrina christiana.*" *New Literary History* 25 (1994).

Schindel, Ulrich. "Textkritisches zu lateinischen Figurenlehren (Anecdoton Parisinum, Cassiodor, Quintilian)." *Glotta* 52 (1974).

Schlier, Heinrich. *Der Brief an die Galater.* Kritisch-exegetischer Kommentar über das Neue Testament 7. Göttingen: Vandenhoeck and Ruprecht, 1962.

Schopenhauer, Arthur. "On the Vanity of Existence." §4 in *Parerga and Paralipomena*. Berlin, 1851.

Smith, Brett W. "Complex Authorial Intention in Augustine's Hermeneutics." *AugStud* 45 (2014)

Spurrell, George James. *Notes on the Hebrew Text of the Book of Genesis: With Two Appendices.* Oxford: Clarendon Press, 1896 [1887].

Steinhauser, K. B. "Codex Leningradensis Q.v.I.3: Some Unsolved Problems." In Arnold and Bright, 33–43.

Stock, Brian. *Augustine the Reader: Meditation, Self-Knowledge, and the Ethics of Interpretation*. Cambridge, MA: Harvard University Press, 1998.

———. *After Augustine: The Meditative Reader and the Text*. Philadelphia: University of Pennsylvania Press, 2001.

Sullivan, Thérèse. *Latin Text, Translation and Commentary of Book IV of "de doctrina christiana."* Washington: Catholic University of America, 1930. In Enos and Thompson, 33–183.

Tambiah, S. J. "The Magical Power of Words." *Man: New Series* 3 (1968).

Teske, Roland. "Criteria for Figurative Interpretation in St Augustine." In Arnold and Bright, 109–22.

Thériault, Patrick. "La destination communautaire de l'interprétation, le *de doctrina christiana* d'Augustin." *Dialogue* 45 (2006).

Ticciati, Susannah. "The Human Being as Sign in Augustine's *de doctrina christiana*." *Neue Zeitschrift für Systematicsche Theologie und Religionsphilosophie* 55 (2013).

———. *On Signs: Christ, Truth and the Interpretation of Scripture*. London: Bloomsbury Press, 2022.

Toom, Tarmo. *Thought Clothed with Sound: Augustine's Christological Hermeneutics in "de doctrina christiana."* Bern: Peter Lang, 2002.

———. "Augustine on the 'Communicative Gaps' in Book Two of *de doctrina christiana*." *AugStud* 34 (2003).

———, ed. *Patristic Theories of Biblical Interpretation: The Latin Fathers*. Cambridge: Cambridge University Press, 2016.

Tracy, David W. "Charity, Obscurity, Clarity: Augustine's

Search for a True Rhetoric." In *Morphologies of Faith*, edited by Mary Gerhart and Anthony C. Yu. Atlanta, GA: Scholars Press, 1990.

Tyndale, William. *The New Testament*. Worms, 1530.

Van der Lof, L. J. "Verbricht Augustin das Schweigen des klassischen Altertums um Ps.-Longinus?" *Vigiliae Christianae* 16 (1962).

Van Fleteren, Frederick. "St Augustine, Neoplatonism, and the Liberal Arts: The Background to *de doctrina christiana*." In Arnold and Bright, 14–24.

———. "Augustine's Principles of Biblical Exegesis, *de doctrina christiana* Aside: Miscellaneous Observations." *AugStud* 27 (1996).

———. "Comments on a Recent Edition of *de doctrina christiana/La Doctrine Chrétienne*." *AugStud* 34 (2003).

Verheijen, Lucas. "Le *de doctrina christiana* de Saint Augustin." *August.* 24 (1974).

Wagemakers, Bart. "Incest, Infanticide, and Cannibalism: Anti-Christian Imputations in the Roman Empire." *Greece & Rome* 57 (2010).

Watson, Gerard. "St. Augustine's Theory of Language." *The Maynooth Review/Revieú Mhá Nuad* 6 (1982). In Enos and Thompson, 247–65.

Wilkins, Eliza G. "ΜΗΔΕΝ ΑΓΑΝ in Greek and Latin Literature." *Classical Philology* 21 (1926).

Williams, Rowan, "Language, Reality and Desire in Augustine's *de doctrina*." *Literature and Theology* 3 (1989).

Wittgenstein, Ludwig. *Philosophical Investigations*. New York: Wiley-Blackwell, 1953.

Wogan, Peter. *Magical Writing in Salasaca: Literacy and Power in Highland Ecuador:* Westview Case Studies in Anthropology. Boulder, CO: Westview Press, 2004.

DE MAGISTRO

THE TEACHER

INTRODUCTION

POSTLUDE AND PRELUDE

We rack our brains about the nature of actual signs. Is it the concept of the sign? Or the concept at a particular moment? It is difficult to . . . stay focused on things in terms of everyday thinking, so as not to go astray because we suppose that we have to describe things using the finest of fine distinctions—even though we have no such capacity with the means at our disposal. It feels like having to fix a ruined spider-web with our fingers.

Philosophical Investigations 105–6

Wittgenstein began his *Philosophical Investigations* (1953) with a quotation from Augustine.[1] It is good to repay the compliment on Augustine's behalf, for as philosophers of language they have more in common than Wittgenstein apparently thought. Just as scholars dispute how much Augustine knew of the Greek background to his philosophical subject matter, so too they argue how well Wittgenstein was acquainted with Augustine's thinking on words, language, and signification. The fact that Augustine

[1] *Conf.* 1.8.13: "a highly self-conscious contribution to theological understanding." Burnyeat, "Inaugural Address," 4.

had chosen the dialogue form suggests a degree of sympathy with Plato, or at least neoplatonism, and also with Cicero. The fact that within the text the dialogue form is first worked and then abandoned hints that the African theologian was not averse from the odd language game of his own.

Wittgenstein took care to select a passage that maximized his opportunity for challenging common conceptions of words and language against which he was to argue. Perhaps he knew he was misrepresenting Augustine's views by oversimplifying them or distorting the context. Perhaps it seemed unimportant given that, when shorn of context within *Confessions* and isolated from developments in Augustine's thinking over the thirty more years of writing and reflection that followed that work, the selected passage was a perfect foil for his own investigations into language. *The Teacher* (*TT*) may be an early work (it was written only three years after he became a Christian, in AD 389), but it is already witnessing to a sophisticated sensitivity to words in practical usage and theoretical interpretation. Augustine anticipates Wittgenstein's spiderweb when he says:

> Listen more carefully to what I'm saying—if, that is, I can even find an effective way to express what I want. Using words to discuss words runs the risk of causing a tangle of confusion, like when we interlock fingers and rub them together; which makes it almost impossible for anyone but the person doing the scratching to tell which fingers are itching and which are relieving the itch. (*TT* 5.14)

Both thinkers resort to figurative language, using simile to express the difficulty of pinning down verbal meaning[2] in a way that is still communicable to others, without developing infinite degrees of nuance in terminology that will obscure, not facilitate, explication. Both will have recognized the attraction added to their writing by the use of these vivid images for the fragility and frustration involved in human attempts at communication.[3]

Wittgenstein is far from unique in having quoted selectively from Augustine's oeuvre what suited his own view of a subject at issue. Taking a sentence here, a remark there, as somehow representative of the bishop of Hippo, either within the work quoted[4] or across the whole extant corpus—whether on language, teaching, predestination, original (birth) sin, free will, just war theory, human sexuality—is virtually guaranteed to mislead. Since words as signs are the matter at issue in *TT*, it is important for the reader to be clear that, for example, Augustine claimed to have taught himself to speak, rather than having linguistic knowledge inserted into him in the form of names for objects. Even in the early work *TT* (never mind in *Teaching Christianity* [*TC*] taken in its final form), Augustine did not hold what Watson calls "a naive object-bound

[2] Though Augustine did not pursue the nature of meaning like Wittgenstein: "For a large class of examples (though not for every usage) in which the word 'meaning' is used we can explain it thus: the meaning of a word is its use in the language." *Philosophical Investigations* 43.

[3] See also *TC* 2.7.11–12 on the power of imagery.

[4] *City of God*, for example, took more than a decade to write.

theory of meaning."[5] Had Wittgenstein taken account of *TT* and/or *TC* as well as *Confessions*, he might have been more nuanced in his criticisms.

Augustine's first publication had been an attempt at philosophical inquiry, "The Beautiful and the Fitting" (*De pulchro et apto*). By then he had been "a practitioner of the art of words"[6] for some time. In *Confessions* he refers to his first publication as already lost and forgotten. By the time he finished *TT*, he had completed a number of Christian writings that bear witness to his first intellectual expressions of his new faith. These were composed during the only prolonged period of peaceful withdrawal from public engagement that he was to enjoy in his long life, at Cassiciacum, outside Milan, where his friend Verecundus had a villa. Friends and family joined him there, including his mother (Monnica), his son (Adeodatus), and Alypius, his companion in the garden of conversion (*Conf.* 8.8.19, 12.29–30).

Some of the Cassiciacum works were completed before his baptism; they show relatively little of his later depth of knowledge of what he called the "holy writings" (the Bible). By the time he composed *Confessions*, his thinking was saturated with scripture, which was becoming for him a kind of special language for his "private" communications with God.

Augustine doubtless chose philosophical dialogue as the genre for most of these early writings because he had found it helpful in the texts that had the most intellectual

5 Watson, "St. Augustine's Theory," 16–17.

6 Watson, "St. Augustine's Theory," 5.

impact on him, such as Cicero's lost dialogue *Hortensius* (*Conf.* 3.4.7).[7] In the final years of his writing career, when he composed a set of retrospective summaries of all his works, which he called *Retractations*, he drew attention to what he by then regarded as shortcomings in all of those early dialogues, elements in their theology that he had come to regard as unsatisfactory. Except for *TT*. Although he referred to this work in *Confessions*, and again, much later, in *Retractations*, he does not suggest any correction or redirection of argument.[8] This makes it reasonable to conclude that even after decades he remained content with the content and manner of the arguments he had presented there.

The first Christian work produced during his time at Cassiciacum was *Contra academicos*, "Against the Academicians." In it he argued that acquiring knowledge was possible, thus challenging the skepticism of Plato's successors.[9] By 389 he was beginning to fuse two initially separate intellectual interests: (1) the theory and practice of words; (2) the imparting of Christian knowledge and belief.[10] The passing on of correct belief ("ortho-doxy") was of particular importance to Christianity, which as an ideological movement, and a social identity, lacked a national, linguistic, or racial means of defining the group and trans-

[7] Cicero's dialogues are themselves modeled on those of Plato.

[8] See Testimonia to *TT* in this volume (p. 20).

[9] It is clear from *Confessions* (5.10.19, 14.25; 8.2.3) that he had discarded an earlier allegiance to the new Academy.

[10] In a looser sense than the technical Platonist one, of fundamental disjuncture between knowledge and opinion.

mitting its characteristics down the generations. Perhaps stimulated to further inquiry by *TT*, he also began *TC*, which was eventually to set the problem of words and communication within a deeper and broader intellectual framework.

THE TEACHER

Why was the nature of teaching such a perplexing theological question for Augustine in those early days? In practical terms, he must have recognized that however great his expertise and intelligence, he himself was a learner in this new object of inquiry (Christianity) and that it did not map perfectly onto his familiar classical paradigms for learning. During his previous teaching career in Carthage, and later in Rome and Milan, he had been paid to impart his expertise in rhetoric (the skills and arts of public persuasive speech). That consisted of two levels of communication: first, between teachers and the words that formed and informed them; second, between teachers and their pupils. A third was located in Christianity, which had made both written texts and speech acts into privileged categories of communication between human beings and God. On all these levels, communication[11] was a pearl beyond price, such that every intellectual endeavor to make sense of it was worthwhile. Words were the means to overcome what would otherwise be an inescapable isolation in every human life:

[11] Augustine does not give much attention yet to noninformative speech categories.

> To be an outsider means being a foreigner in the land. Outsiders are people who live in a country not their own. In this life, every person is an outsider: you can see how, in this life, we are clothed in flesh, and that flesh conceals our heart from view. Therefore the apostle says, "Judge nothing before the proper time, when the Lord comes, and will illuminate the darkness of concealment, and make plain the thoughts of the heart, and then God will bestow praise on each." Until that happens, we all bear our own heart as outsiders in this earthly life: and every heart is closed off from every other heart.[12]

TT responds to this problem of communication, as Augustine tries to persuade his son that all speech acts are a form of teaching, even a question from an ignorant person (which teaches the teacher what that person wants to learn). But it soon becomes a discussion about how words mean things, in other words, how they signify.

The underlying paradox of *TT*, well-known from antiquity, derives from Plato's dialogue *Meno*; it is sometimes referred to as "Meno's paradox." In that dialogue, Socrates summarized it like this:

> A man cannot inquire either about what he knows or about what he does not know. For he cannot inquire about what he knows, because he knows it, and in that case is in no need of inquiry; nor again can he inquire about what he does not know, since

[12] *En Ps.* 55$^{\text{Vulg.}}$.9 (on Psalm 56:7): *omne cor omni cordi clausum est.*

he does not know about what he is to inquire. (*Meno* 80e, LCL translation)

If this were straightforwardly true, it would mean that the verse of scripture from which Augustine's argument springs was incapable of conveying, from book to reader/listener, the very information on which his conclusions depend. Perhaps that is why he delays quoting it until the final phase of his argument.[13] The argument takes place entirely on the level of mind or intellect: neither the Platonic solution to the Meno paradox (that learning is a form of recollection)[14] nor the Augustinian one (that Christ the inner Teacher causes moments of illumination in which learning occurs) works adequately when applied to the teaching of practical skills rather than intellectual material.[15] One of the reasons why this puzzle was of more than passing interest to Augustine is clarified in *Conf.* 1.1.1–5.6: a prelude to the shift from infancy to boyhood, it tests a tumbling succession of options for how a

13 Matthew 23:10; *TT* 14.46.

14 Plato's Greek term is *anamnesis*. This is a compound of the verb "remember" (*mimnēskō/μιμνήσκω*) and a preposition, *ana/ἀνά*, meaning (among other things) "from the top" or "over again." A fallacy that it derives from the verb plus a doubled alpha-privative prefix (supposedly meaning "un-forget") is persistent in some secondary literature.

15 It does not work for learning to read and write, or play the piano, or drive. In *Confessions* he contrasted his pleasure in reading stories from Latin literature (its "poetic fictions," 1.13.22) with the tedium of learning practical skills like reading and writing, or chanting his times tables as he learned them by rote.

human being can make any kind of connection with God at all.

The Meno paradox in its starkest form acquires a degree more subtlety from an exploration of the interstice between absolute ignorance and absolute knowledge. Socrates may have misled some readers when he claimed[16] that he questioned the slave in such a way that the boy "recollected" the answer to the question (as if he had always known it and needed only to jog his memory): but as a master of the leading question in dialectic, he was unlikely to have misled himself.

The recollection theory of learning had been driven by Platonic ontology. It might have led in another direction if Socrates had encouraged the slave to go on from that beginning and look for further applications of this new intelligence, for the experience of teaching and learning entails an element of "see how you could take this further, look for ways to apply it to new situations!" Even if Socrates has not really taught the slave to "recollect" mathematical truths, he has shown him that an argumentative process, in the shape of a connected series of questions applied to a problem, may lead one to uncover potential solutions to that problem. In *TT* 11.36 Augustine suggests as much when he remarks:

> The importance of words (to give them the best acknowledgment I can) has lain in their giving us directions to seek out things.

[16] By not giving due weight to the influence and effect of leading questions.

LANGUAGE, SIGNS, AND SIGNIFYING

In *TT* Augustine was quick to establish that words, in their capacity to signify, are both the theme and the building blocks of his argument:

> When a person speaks, they utter coherent sounds externally as a sign of what they want. (*TT* 1.2)

Already in *De musica* (AD 387), he had explored the puzzle of words as signs, which in *TC* he would develop into a fundamental distinction between realities ("things," *res*) and pointers to realities (*signa*: words being the most important form of sign):

> Things exist alike in the minds of everyone. Words, though, are set there as each decides, and their force depends on authority and convention. Hence there is a diversity of languages, but there cannot be a like diversity of things as they subsist in actual reality. (*Mus.* 3.3)

In Greek philosophical thought, inquiry into language was represented at two extremes by the schools of the Stoics and the Epicureans, both of them materialist. Epicureans focused on the language sign as "perceptible" (*aisthēton*/*αἰσθητόν*), Stoics on its being "intelligible" (*noēton*/*νοητόν*). The skeptic philosopher Sextus Empiricus (second century AD) pointed to a link between perceptible sounds and perceived meanings, expressing the uniqueness of human language not only in its capacity to produce articulate sounds but also in its capacity to com-

bine sounds in sequences in such a way as both to transmit meaning from speaker to hearer and also to enable a hearer (by grasping the nature of the sequence) to carry the process further:

> Man does not differ in respect of uttered reason from the irrational animals (for crows and parrots and jays utter articulate sounds), but in respect of internal reason; nor <does he differ> in respect of the merely simple impression (for the animals, too, receive impressions), but in respect of the transitive and constructive impressions. Hence, since he has a conception of logical sequence, he immediately grasps also the notion of sign because of the sequence; for in fact the sign in itself is of this form—"If this, then this." (*Against the Logicians* 2.275–77, LCL translation)

When father and son scrutinize a line of Virgil's *Aeneid* in *TT* 2.3, they investigate how the words of which it is made up function and how their function can be described. Working through the parts of speech, they reveal the scope for ambiguity—and in the case of *nihil* for downright paradox—in human speech acts. This leads to a further puzzle: how, despite such linguistic stumbling blocks, the line as a whole remains perfectly intelligible to people reading even on a surface level.

If using words, with their capacity to signify, made human beings unique in the created order, it was no great leap for Augustine to connect that with the Christian belief in Christ as the incarnate Word, as described in the prologue to the gospel of John 1:1–14. He explains the

difference between words and "the Word" in a commentary on John 8:19–20:[17]

> You recall your ordinary way of speaking, and say to yourself, "What is a word? How is a word something important? It sounds and passes away. It vibrates the air and strikes the ear; and then it is no more." Now hear this: "The Word was with God." It existed continually, it did not sound and then vanish. Maybe you still undervalue it: "the Word was God." . . . You have no understanding of human words, you who do not respect the Word of God!

Augustine's instinct would be to privilege the intelligible over the perceptible.[18] Such selectivity would begin with the utterance of a word: if, for example, we hear the word "head" (*caput*) for the first time, we cannot tell if it is meaningless noise or meaningful signifier except by using our eyes and ears to attend to the circumstances in which the sound is produced (*TT* 10.34).

TT 11.38 delineates both the power and the limitations of words as signs, bringing forward Christ the Teacher in such a way as to provide the means by which learning happens, and also to explain why not all human beings learn the same things in the same ways or to the same extent:

[17] *Io. Ev. Tr.* 37.4. By a modern convention, "Word" is capitalized to indicate the second person of the Christian Trinity; in an ancient manuscript, only context determines whether "word" or "Word" is meant.

[18] *Conf.* 10.27.38 is a *locus classicus*.

> We don't consult truth like some speaker making a sound external to ourselves, but rather as an inner presence that holds sway over our own mind—though perhaps it was words that urged us to consult it. That being whom we consult, who teaches us, who is said to abide deep in the inner person, is Christ, in other words, the unchangeable "power of God and the eternal wisdom." And indeed every rational soul consults this wisdom, but it reveals itself to each only insofar as each can grasp it, in accordance with their own will, whether good or bad.

Christ teaches, according to Augustine, by illuminating our understanding to interpret aright the realities to which signs (supremely words) have directed our attention. Knowledge of a reality comes before recognition of the sign that stands for that reality: as, say, our observation that a rose is red (irrespective of what label we use for the concept "red") is what allows us to understand, and later apply, that sign (the word "red") to other roses, yet not to all flowers of the species. Belief,[19] that grade-two epistemological category of Plato, "is useful because it enables us to move from sign to reality without understanding. So moving us, faith makes understanding possible."[20]

TT is mostly straightforward dialectic with only an occasional seasoning of scripture. In *TC*, Augustine was to speak in his own magisterial voice, without an inter-

[19] Or "opinion."

[20] Mackey, "The Mediator Mediated," 142.

locutor, and to provide detailed interpretations of Bible passages. By the time of its completion, he had a much broader conception of scripture as a form of signifying akin to the category of the sacramental (an outward sign of an inward truth). The Bible, insofar as it signifies a divine reality, is rather a means to an end, than an end in itself. He makes a similar case at the end of *City of God* for words as signifiers giving way to the realities for which they stand:

> So we shall know God and see him clearly, so that by the Spirit he will be visible to one individual in another individual; he will be visible to one person in another person; and he will be visible in himself, and he will be visible in a new heaven and a new earth, and in the entire creation as it will then appear; and he will be visible through the means of the physical body in every physical body—wherever the eyes of the spiritual body look, as far as their gaze can reach. Then our thoughts will lie open to one another. (22.29.6)

ILLUMINATION

At *TT* 12.40 Augustine provides his solution to his puzzle about how teaching and learning work. Dismissing that common understanding known as “information transfer,” on the grounds that he cannot make sense of the mechanism by which it takes place, he argues instead that our coming to know something happens through the inner person being enlightened by the “inner light of truth.” He

identifies this internal power as Christ the Teacher.[21] Augustine's "illumination" does for learning what the concept of "revelation" does for theology: for illumination (in the case of teaching/learning) and revelation (in the case of theology) provide an alternative to the standard way of finding the truth (the information-transfer account) or God (natural theology). Both phenomena can be cooperated with, by means of human openness to the experience (of illumination or revelation) but cannot be engineered or guaranteed. Appearing to be generated from within, illumination is rather (like revelation) imparted from without. So to the conclusion:

> If the teacher doesn't cause the student to understand—and it's clear that the teacher cannot literally *cause* the student to understand, since otherwise everyone in the class room would get it, or nobody would—then what is it that takes place? What is learning, if not a mysterious inner episode of awareness?[22]

In a later sermon Augustine contextualized this as a paradoxical irony of the search for truth:

> Some people, in search of God, read books. But the whole spectacle of the creation is a kind of great book: observe what goes before, and what follows after, pay heed to it, read it! God has not written his text in ink for you to come to know him. He has set

21 Who "abides deep in the inner person" and whom "every rational soul consults" (*TT* 11.38).

22 King, "Augustine on the Impossibility of Teaching," 1.94.

> before your eyes this very creation, which he made. Why do you ask for a greater voice? Heaven and earth are crying out loud to you, "God made me!"[23]

CONCLUSION

TT is a stage on the way to the full maturity of Augustine's language theory. But that theory, presented in a more developed form in *TC*, was still embedded in the sense-bound category that is rhetoric, which explored and exploited the practical affect of language, and drew its materials from usage in context rather than isolated rhetorical features. Wittgenstein's torn spiderweb and Augustine's itching, scratching fingers show that ancient theologian and modern philosopher alike knew the power of figurative speech to encapsulate what no infinite regress of linguistic definition can express. In *TC* Augustine went on to analyze not words, but whole passages: a tacit acknowledgment, perhaps, that both teaching/learning and meaning need to be understood in terms of the word-in-context, not the word-in-isolation. As a fictional Tudor historian once expressed it:

> I entirely agree that a historian ought to be precise in detail; but unless you take all the characters and circumstances into account, you are reckoning without the facts. The proportions and relations of things are just as much facts as the things themselves.[24]

23 *Sermo* 68.6, frequently misidentified and quoted in secondary material as 126.6.

24 Helen de Vine; in Sayers, *Gaudy Night*, ch. 10.

Which could be applied to *TT*, and *TC*, thus:

> The proportions and relations of words are just as much things as the words themselves.

HISTORY AND CONSTITUTION OF THE TEXT

Sigla (up to 10th century)

B *Bernensis* (fr. AA 90) (9th c.)
H *Monacensis* 6331 (10th c.)
J *Monacensis* 6322 (10th–11th c.)
M *Monacensis* 18 540[b] (10th–11th c.)
R *Remensis* 392 (9th c.)
S *Sangallensis* 140 (early 10th c.)
S[1] marginal and interlinear glosses to S
T *Londinensis Royal* 8 C III (late 10th c.)
V *Vaticanus Latinus* 515 (9th–10th c.)

Editions

Six printed editions antedate that of the Maurists, which was based on manuscripts later than the twelfth century. In 1841 it was substantially reproduced by Migne in *Patrologia Latina*, vol. 32.

μ *Maurini* (Parisiis, 1679)
Weig. Corpus Scriptorum Ecclesiasticorum Latinorum (CSEL) 77 = G. Weigel (1961)

Günther Weigel argues that the work is intended as a monument to Augustine's son Adeo-

datus.[25] He did not identify any single manuscript as preeminent in accuracy and quality, but instead highlighted twelve as "primary" and thirteen as "secondary," all from the ninth to twelfth centuries.

Daur Corpus Christianorum Series Latina (CCSL) 29 = K.-D. Daur (1970)[26]

Klaus-Detlef Daur claimed to be responsible only for the punctuation of this critical edition, the rest of the text being the unpublished work of M. Skutella. He used *Weig.*, but based his critical text on a larger number of manuscripts.

25 AD 372–ca. 389.

26 "A highly professional piece of work," P.G Walsh, in *JThS* 23.1 (1972): 253.

DE MAGISTRO

TESTIMONIA

1 *Conf.* 9.6.14 (ca. AD 397)

Est liber noster qui inscribitur "De magistro": ipse ibi mecum loquitur. tu scis illius esse sensa omnia quae inseruntur ibi ex persona conlocutoris mei, cum esset in annis sedecim. multa eius alias mirabiliora expertus sum: horrori mihi erat illud ingenium.

2 *Retr.* 1.2 (ca. AD 426)

Per idem tempus scripsi librum cuius est titulus de magistro, in quo disputatur et quaeritur et invenitur magistrum non esse qui docet hominem scientiam nisi deum, secundum illud etiam quod in evangelio scriptum est, unus est magister vester Christus. Hic liber sic incipit: quid tibi videmur efficere velle cum loquimur?

THE TEACHER

TESTIMONIA

1 *Conf.* 9.6.14 (ca. AD 397)

There is a book of mine entitled, "The Teacher": in it Adeodatus has a conversation with me. You know that all the views introduced there in the character of my interlocutor were really his, when he was sixteen years old. I experienced many attributes of his that were even more remarkable: I was in awe of his intelligence.

2 *Retr.* 1.2 (ca. AD 426)

At the same time[1] I wrote a book entitled "The Teacher" which debates, and questions, and discovers that there is no teacher but God who teaches people knowledge; following what is written in the gospel, "you have one teacher, that is Christ." This book begins, "In your opinion, when we speak, what are we trying to achieve?"

[1] As he was writing his six books *De musica* (*Retr.* 1.11).

DE MAGISTRO

1. AUGUSTINUS: Quid tibi videmur efficere velle cum loquimur?

ADEODATUS: Quantum quidem mihi nunc occurrit, aut docere, aut discere.

AU. Unum horum video et assentior: nam loquendo nos docere velle manifestum est; discere autem quomodo?

AD. Quo tandem censes, nisi cum interrogamus?

AU. Etiam tunc nihil aliud quam docere nos velle intellego, nam quaero abs te utrum ob aliam causam interroges, nisi ut eum quem interrogas doceas quid velis?

AD. Verum dicis.

AU. Vides ergo iam nihil nos locutione nisi ut doceamus appetere.

AD. Non plane video: nam si nihil est aliud loqui quam verba promere, video nos id facere cum cantamus. Quod cum saepe soli facimus, nullo praesente qui discat, non puto nos docere aliquid velle.

AU. At ego puto esse quoddam genus docendi per commemorationem, magnum sane, quod in hac nostra

---

[1] This term describes a solemn liturgical formula of recalling or remembering, including, in church Latin, the speaking aloud of the names of departed saints within the liturgy. See Aug. *Cur. mort*. 4.6.

THE TEACHER

1. AUGUSTINE: In your opinion, when we speak, what are we trying to achieve?

ADEODATUS: Well, what comes to mind at this moment is, either to teach or to learn.

AU. One of these two seems right to me, and I agree with it, for it is clear that by the act of speaking we want to teach something. But how does that act entail learning?

AD. How can you come to a point of view, except when we ask you questions?

AU. Even then it's my understanding that the only thing we want is to teach, because what I want to know from you is whether you ask questions for any purpose other than teaching the person you're asking what it is that you want.

AD. You're right.

AU. So now you can see how, when we speak, the only thing we're after is to teach.

AD. I'm not perfectly clear about it; for if speaking means simply uttering words, I see that we do this when we sing. As we often sing when alone, there's no one present to learn from us. So I don't think we can be intending to teach something.

AU. Despite this, I think that there's a specific type of teaching that happens through acts of commemoration;[1]

sermocinatione res ipsa indicabit. Sed si tu non arbitraris nos discere cum recordamur, nec docere illum qui commemorat, non resisto tibi: et duas iam loquendi causas constituo, aut ut doceamus, aut ut commemoremus vel alios vel nosmetipsos; quod etiam dum cantamus, efficimus: an tibi non videtur?

AD. Non prorsus: nam rarum admodum est, ut ego cantem commemorandi me gratia, sed tantummodo delectandi.

AU. Video quid sentias. Sed nonne attendis id quod te delectat in cantu modulationem quandam esse soni? quae quoniam verbis et addi et detrahi potest, aliud est loqui, aliud est cantare? Nam et tibiis et cithara cantatur, et aves cantant, et nos interdum sine verbis musicum aliquid sonamus, qui sonus cantus dici potest, locutio non potest: an quidquam est quod contradicas?

AD. Nihil sane.

2 AU. Videtur ergo tibi, nisi aut docendi, aut commemorandi causa non esse institutam locutionem?

AD. Videretur nisi me moveret quod dum oramus utique loquimur; nec tamen deum aut doceri aliquid a nobis, aut commemorari fas est credere.

---

2 See Quint. *Inst.* 9.2.31: "there are those who prefer fictitious conversations between people to be called 'dialogues,' though some Latin writers call this *sermocinatio.*"

3 The verb (*commemorat*) is cognate with *commemoratio*, rendered here as "recall" and "commemoration."

4 Latin *cantare* can embrace instrumental as well as vocal music.

5 Such as humming, or singing to "la."

6 Too limited a list for the functions of language, but his categories are broader than they sound to us. For "teaching," he has in mind forms of communication; for "commemorating," liturgi-

it is undoubtedly important, a fact that the subject matter of this dialogue[2] of ours will prove. But if you don't believe that when we remember we're learning, and that when someone is commemorating[3] something they're teaching, I will not oppose you, and I still suggest two reasons for our speaking: either so that we can teach, or to commemorate others or ourselves. This is something we also achieve when we sing. Or do you disagree?

AD. Not entirely: but it's quite unusual for me to sing in order to commemorate something for myself, rather than just for pleasure.

AU. I see what you mean. But surely you're aware that the source of your pleasure in singing is the sound of a particular melody? Given that the words of songs can be added or removed, isn't speaking one kind of activity, while singing[4] is quite another? For there's music for woodwind and stringed instruments too; and birdsong, and occasionally we make a kind of musical sound without words, and we can call this sound singing, but we can't call it speaking.[5] Or do you want to make a case to the contrary?

AD. No, I don't.

AU. Does it look to you, then, as if speaking has be- 2
come established purely for the purposes of teaching and commemorating?[6]

AD. It would, but for the consideration that we are undoubtedly speaking when we pray; but despite this, we are not teaching God something, nor is it right to believe that we are recalling anything.

cal speech and prayer. David Crystal lists six functions: informative, identifying, expressive, performative, historical, and aesthetic. See Hammond, *Sound of the Liturgy*, 7.

AU. Nescire te arbitror, non ob aliud nobis praeceptum esse ut in clausis cubiculis oremus, quo nomine significantur mentis penetralia, nisi quod deus, ut nobis quod cupimus praestet, commemorari aut doceri nostra locutione non quaerit. Qui enim loquitur, suae voluntatis signum foras dat per articulatum sonum: deus autem in ipsis rationalis animae secretis, qui homo interior vocatur, et quaerendus et deprecandus est; haec enim sua templa esse voluit. An apud apostolum non legisti, "nescitis quia templum dei estis, et spiritus dei habitat in vobis"; et, "in interiore homine habitare Christum"? Nec in propheta animadvertisti, "dicite in cordibus vestris, et in cubilibus vestris compungimini: sacrificate sacrificium iustitiae, et sperate in domino"? Ubi putas sacrificium iustitiae sacrificari, nisi in templo mentis, et in cubilibus cordis? Ubi autem sacrificandum est, ibi et orandum. Quare non opus est locutione cum oramus, id est sonantibus verbis, nisi forte, sicut sacerdotes faciunt, significandae mentis suae causa, non ut deus, sed ut homines audiant, et consensione

---

[7] It is unlikely that Adeodatus was unaware of the text; the remark is ironic.

[8] First appearance of the verb *significare*.

[9] He states elsewhere that people pray "in order to fortify their own mind, not in order to inform God" (*Ep*. 140.29.69). See Hammond, *Sound of the Liturgy*, 65.

[10] First appearance of the noun *signum*.

[11] This "inner person" reappears toward the end of *TT* at 11.38–13.45.

[12] 1 Corinthians 3:16. This is the first quotation from scripture in *TT*, which is distinctively sparing with such references.

AU. I reckon this has slipped your mind:[7] we're instructed to go into a room and shut the door to pray—and the room, with its closed door, signifies[8] the innermost recesses of the mind—precisely because God doesn't require any speech from us either to recall for him, or to teach him, what we long for him to provide to us.[9] When a person speaks, they utter coherent sounds externally as a sign[10] of what they want: but God must be looked for, and prayed to, in the secret places of the rational soul, which we call the "inner person."[11] He wanted these secret places to be temples dedicated to himself. Or haven't you read in Paul's writings, "do you not know that you are God's temple, and that God's spirit abides in you?"[12] and, "Christ abides in the inner person"?[13] And haven't you noticed in the prophet, "speak in your own hearts, and feel remorse in your own chambers: offer a sacrifice of righteousness, and put your hope in the Lord."[14] Where else do you think the sacrifice of righteousness takes place but in the temple of the mind, and in the chambers[15] of the heart? After all, wherever sacrifice takes place, there prayer is offered also. So there's no need for speech when we're praying, not for words spoken aloud, I mean—except perhaps as priests speak, to signify what is in their own mind, not so that God hears them, but so that other people do. And so that the act of commemoration, by their

13 Ephesians 3:16–17.

14 Psalm 4:4–5

15 Metaphor, not the modern medical "chambers" of the heart.

quadam per commemorationem suspendantur in deum: an tu aliud existimas?

AD. Omnino assentior.

AU. Non te ergo movet quod summus magister cum orare doceret discipulos, verba quaedam docuit? In quo nihil aliud videtur fecisse, quam docuisse quomodo in orando loqui oporteret.

AD. Nihil me omnino istud movet. Non enim verba, sed res ipsas eos verbis docuit, quibus etiam seipsi commonefacerent, a quo et quid esset orandum, cum in penetralibus, ut dictum est, mentis orarent.

AU. Recte intellegis: simul enim te credo animadvertere, etiamsi quisquam contendat, quamvis nullum edamus sonum, tamen quia ipsa verba cogitamus, nos intus apud animum loqui, sic quoque locutione nihil aliud agere quam commonere, cum memoria cui verba inhaerent, ea revolvendo facit venire in mentem res ipsas quarum signa sunt verba.

AD. Intellego ac sequor.

3 2. AU. Constat ergo inter nos verba signa esse?

AD. Constat.

AU. Quid? signum, nisi aliquid significet, potest esse signum?

AD. Non potest.

---

[16] See 13.42 for liturgical speaking as a separate category.

[17] Who appears again at 14.46.

[18] Anticipating the *signum/res* dichotomy of *TC*.

experiencing it together, lifts them up toward God.[16] Or do you disagree?

AD. I completely agree with you.

AU. Doesn't it cause you to waver then, the fact that when he was teaching his disciples to pray, our ultimate Teacher[17] taught them a particular set of words? And that by this means what he actually achieved was to teach them how to speak when they prayed?

AD. No, that doesn't make me waver at all. For it wasn't words that he taught, but rather the actual things that his words described,[18] and the words were for them to impress upon themselves who it was who had prayed them, and the substance of what he prayed, when (as you suggested) they themselves were praying in the innermost recesses of their mind.

AU. Your understanding is correct. For even if someone were to challenge us, I believe that you're noticing two things happening at once: we make no external sound, but because we are thinking actual words, within our mind we're still speaking internally. So too, when we speak aloud, what we are doing is making an impression upon ourselves: when the act of remembrance, which the words are part of, makes the actual realities that the words signify come into our mind, by the repeating of those words over and over.

AD. I understand, and I follow you.

2. AU. We are agreed, then, that words are signs? 3

AD. Agreed.

AU. What next? Can a sign be a sign without signifying something?

AD. Impossible.

AU. Quot verba sunt in hoc versu, "si nihil ex tanta superis placet urbe relinqui"?

AD. Octo.

AU. Octo ergo signa sunt.

AD. Ita est.

AU. Credo te hunc versum intellegere.

AD. Satis arbitror.

AU. Dic mihi quid singula verba significent.

AD. Video quidem quid significet "si"; sed nullum aliud verbum, quo id exponi possit, invenio.

AU. Saltem illud invenis, quicquid significatur hoc verbo, ubinam sit?

AD. Videtur mihi quod dubitationem significet: iam dubitatio, ubi nisi in animo est?

AU. Accipio interim; persequere cetera.

AD. "Nihil," quid aliud significat, nisi id quod non est?

AU. Verum fortasse dicis, sed revocat me ab assentiendo quod superius concessisti, non esse signum nisi aliquid significet; quod autem non est, nullo modo esse aliquid potest. Quare secundum verbum in hoc versu non est signum, quia non significat aliquid; et falso inter nos constitit, quod omnia verba signa sint, aut omne signum aliquid significet.

AD. Nimis quidem urges; sed quando non habemus quid significemus, omnino stulte verbum aliquod promimus: tu autem nunc mecum loquendo, credo quod nullum sonum frustra emittis, sed omnibus quae ore tuo erum-

---

[19] Verg. *Aen.* 2.659. [20] Misleading. To mean "nothing" is not the same as to have no meaning.

[21] A vivid expression with a military flavor. On the mouth as a barrier restraining speech, see Hom. *Od.* 1.64, 5.22.

AU. How many words are there in this line of poetry:[19] "If nothing from this city remains, gods decree."

AD. Eight.

AU. So here are eight signs.

AD. Correct.

AU. I believe you understand this line.

AD. Well enough, I think.

AU. Tell me what the individual words mean.

AD. I'm certainly clear what "if" signifies; but I can't find another word so that I can explain it.

AU. Well, whatever the word signifies, here's something I'm sure you can determine—where does it exist?

AD. It seems to me that it signifies uncertainty: now where else does uncertainty exist but in the mind?

AU. That answer will do for now. Now go on with the other words.

AD. "Nothing": what does "nothing" signify, except for what does not exist?

AU. You may be right; but what keeps me from agreeing is the point you accepted just now, that something that does not signify anything[20] is not a sign at all: then what does not exist can by no means be anything. Therefore the second word in this line of verse is not a sign, because it does not signify something. So we were wrong to agree that either all words are signs, or every sign signifies something.

AD. You're pressuring me too much. But when we have nothing to signify, it's completely stupid to utter some word. By speaking with me now, I believe you're not making a single sound to no purpose. Rather, with every sound that breaks free from your mouth[21] you're giving me a sign

punt, signum mihi das ut aliquid intellegam;[1] quapropter non te oportet istas duas syllabas enuntiare dum loqueris, si per eas non significas quicquam. Si autem vides necessariam per eas enuntiationem fieri, nosque doceri vel commoneri cum auribus insonant, vides etiam profecto quid velim dicere, sed explicare non possum.

AU. Quid igitur facimus? An affectionem animi quandam, cum rem non videt, et tamen non esse invenit, aut invenisse se putat, hoc verbo significari dicimus potius quam rem ipsam quae nulla est?

AD. Istud ipsum est fortasse quod explicare moliebar.

AU. Transeamus ergo hinc, quoquo modo se habet, ne res absurdissima nobis accidat.

AD. Quae tandem?

AU. Si "nihil" nos teneat, et moras patiamur!

AD. Ridiculum hoc quidem est, et tamen nescio quomodo video posse contingere; immo plane video contigisse.

4 AU. Suo loco genus hoc repugnantiae, si deus siverit, planius intellegemus: nunc ad illum versum te refer, et conare, ut potes, cetera eius verba quid significent pandere.

AD. Tertia praepositio est "ex," pro qua "de" possumus, ut arbitror, dicere.

AU. Non id quaero, ut pro una voce notissima aliam

[1] mihi das ut aliquid intellegam *S*: signum das aliquid intellegi *T*

---

[22] In the sense of "physical object."

[23] That is, what physical sight cannot perceive can still be a something without being a physical something.

that I need to understand something. Then you shouldn't utter those two syllables, "no-thing," when you speak, if there isn't something that you're signifying by them. But if you perceive that by saying them an utterance necessarily comes into being, and that we're being taught or reminded when they sound in our ears, you certainly also perceive what I would want to say, but am unable to explain.

AU. So what do we do? When someone cannot see a thing[22] and then finds out that it doesn't exist (or thinks that they've found this out), are we saying that what the word "nothing" signifies is a certain mental association, rather than the actual thing that does not exist?[23]

AD. Maybe this is just what I was trying to express.

AU. In that case let's move on from this point about how it subsists, in case we tumble into a ludicrous situation.

AD. What, exactly?

AU. If "nothing" is holding us back, but still we're being held up!

AD. That's certainly absurd: even though I don't know how it can turn out that way, I can plainly see, all the same, that it just has.

AU. God willing, we shall understand this kind of contradiction more clearly in its proper place. Now turn back to that line of poetry, and try, if you can, to unpack what the rest of its words are signifying. 4

AD. The third word is a preposition, "from." I reckon we can say "out of" for this.

AU. That's not what I'm after. Don't use one familiar

vocem aeque notissimam, quae idem significet dicas—si tamen idem significat, sed interim concedamus ita esse. Certe si poeta iste non "ex tanta urbe" sed "de tanta" dixisset, quaereremque abs te quid "de" significaret, diceres "ex," cum haec duo verba essent, id est signa unum aliquid, ut tu putas, significantia. Ego autem idipsum nescio quid unum quod his duobus signis significatur inquiro.

AD. Mihi videtur secretionem quandam significare ab ea re in qua fuerat aliquid, quod ex illa esse dicitur, sive illa non maneat, ut in hoc versu non manente urbe poterant aliqui ex illa esse Troiani: sive maneat, sicut ex urbe Roma dicimus esse negotiatores in Africa.

AU. Ut concedam tibi haec ita esse, nec enumerem quam multa fortasse praeter hanc tuam regulam reperiantur, illud certe tibi attendere facile est, exposuisse te verbis verba, id est signis signa, eisdemque notissimis notissima. Ego autem illa ipsa quorum haec signa sunt, mihi si posses vellem ut ostenderes.

5 3. AD. Miror te nescire, vel potius simulare nescientem, responsione mea fieri quod vis omnino non posse, siquidem sermocinamur, ubi non possumus respondere nisi verbis. Tu autem res quaeris eas quae, quodlibet sint, verba certe non sunt, quas tamen ex me tu quoque verbis quaeris! Prior itaque tu sine verbis quaere, ut ego deinde ista condicione respondeam.

---

[24] In Latin: *ex* (from) and *de* (out of). [25] Thus risking criticism for circular reasoning. [26] *TC* 2.8.15.

[27] Cicero remarks of reply or retort as an aspect of rhetoric that "quick wits are more important, as retorting shows—and to retort is human nature." He notes it as a figure of rhetoric (answering one's own question; *De or.* 2.230, 3.207).

term in place of another, equally familiar, which signifies the same thing. That's if it actually does signify the same thing—but let's accept for now that it does. Undoubtedly, if that poet had said "out of that great city" instead of "from that great," and I were to ask you what the "out of" signified, you would say "from," since these were two words,[24] that is, signs that both signify a single something, as you think. But what I'm looking for is this same single something that those two words signify.

AD. To me they seem to signify a kind of separation from a particular entity in which something had once been present that is said to be "from" it: this hold true whether the entity no longer exists (as in this verse: some men from that city could still be men of Troy even though the city itself was no more), or does still exist, as when we say that there are traders from the city of Rome in Africa.

AU. Insofar as I go along with your view that this is so, and don't count up how many cases may perhaps be found that go against your rule, it's certainly easy to notice that you've used words to explain words,[25] specifically signs to explain signs, and familiar things to explain the same familiar things.[26] But I'd like you, if you can, to show me those actual things of which these words are signs.

3. AD. I'm surprised that you don't know—or rather 5
that you're pretending not to know—my reply[27] can't possibly achieve what you want while we are engaging in dialogue, for this does not allow us to reply by any means but words. Yet you're asking about things that, whatever else they may be, are certainly not words: and yet you yourself are questioning me about them—using words! So first of all you ask without words, so that I can reply on your terms.

AU. Iure agis, fateor: sed si quaererem tres istae syllabae quid significent, cum dicitur "paries," nonne posses digito ostendere, ut ego prorsus rem ipsam viderem, cuius signum est hoc trisyllabum verbum, demonstrante te, nulla tamen verba referente.

AD. Hoc in solis nominibus quibus corpora significantur, si eadem corpora praesentia sint, fieri posse concedo.

AU. Num colorem corpus dicimus, ac non potius quandam corporis qualitatem?

AD. Ita est.

AU. Cur ergo et hic digito demonstrari potest? An addis corporibus etiam corporum qualitates, ut nihilominus etiam istae cum praesentes sunt, doceri sine verbis possint?

AD. Ego cum corpora dicerem, omnia corporalia intellegi volebam, id est omnia quae in corporibus sentiuntur.

AU. Considera tamen, utrum etiam hinc[2] aliqua tibi excipienda sint.

AD. Bene admones: non enim omnia corporalia, sed omnia visibilia dicere debui. Fateor enim sonum, odorem, saporem, gravitatem, calorem, et alia quae ad ceteros sensus pertinent, quamquam sentiri sine corporibus nequeant, et propterea sint corporalia, non tamen digito posse monstrari.

AU. Nunquamne vidisti ut homines cum surdis gestu quasi sermocinentur, ipsique surdi non minus gestu, vel quaerant vel respondeant vel doceant vel indicent aut omnia quae volunt, aut certe plurima? Quod cum fit, non

[2] etiam hinc *J M*: etiam vel hinc nunc *B R V H S T*

AU. That's a fair point, I admit. But if I were asking what is the significance of the three syllables that are heard in the word "barrier," surely you could point with your finger, so that I spotted the actual thing directly—that thing whose sign is the three-syllable word—by your act of pointing, even without any words referring to it.

AD. I admit that this is possible but only for nouns that refer to physical entities, and when those physical entities are present.

AU. Surely we don't call color a physical entity; isn't it rather a certain property of a physical entity?

AD. True.

AU. So why can we use a finger to point to it? Or are you including properties of physical entities as well as the entities themselves, so that they can equally be taught without using words, when they are before us?

AD. When I was referring to physical entities, I meant it to be understood as including everything related to such an entity, in other words everything observable by our sense perceptions.

AU. But think—should some exceptions be made, even with this qualification?

AD. That's a fair criticism. I should have said all visible, not all physical, entities. I admit that we can't point with our finger to sound, scent, taste, weight, heat, and other things to do with the senses, even though we need physical bodies if we are to sense them at all.

AU. Have you never noticed how people hold a sort of dialogue with the deaf through gestures, while the deaf likewise use gestures to ask a question, or reply, or teach, or indicate anything they want, or at any rate a large proportion of it? When this happens, it certainly isn't only

utique sola visibilia sine verbis ostenduntur, sed et soni et sapores, et cetera huiusmodi. Nam et histriones totas in theatris fabulas sine verbis saltando plerumque aperiunt et exponunt.

AD. Nihil habeo quod contradicam, nisi quod illud "ex" non modo ego, sed nec ipse quidem saltator histrio tibi sine verbis quid significet posset ostendere.

6 AU. Verum fortasse dicis, sed fingamus eum posse; non ut arbitror dubitas, quisquis ille motus corporis fuerit, quo mihi rem quae hoc verbo significatur, demonstrare conabitur, non ipsam rem futuram esse, sed signum. Quare hic quoque non quidem verbo verbum, sed tamen signo signum nihilominus indicabit, ut et hoc monosyllabum "ex," et ille gestus unam rem quandam significent, quam mihi ego vellem non significando monstrari —

AD. Qui potest quod quaeris, oro te?—

AU. —quomodo paries potuit.

AD. Ne ipse quidem, quantum ratio progrediens docuit, ostendi sine signo potest. Nam et intentio digiti non est utique paries, sed signum datur per quod paries possit videri. Nihil itaque video quod sine signis ostendi queat.

AU. Quid si ex te quaererem quid sit ambulare, surgeresque et id ageres? nonne re ipsa potius quam verbis ad me docendum, aut ullis aliis signisutereris?

AD. Fateor ita esse, et pudet me rem tam in promptu positam non vidisse: ex qua etiam mihi milia rerum iam

---

[28] Performed by *pantomimi*, actors who used bodily movement and dance to perform stories on stage, combining elements of ballet and mime. An actor might speak lines for the dancer. See Lucian, *The Dance* 67.

[29] See *TC* 2.3.4 for "visible words."

[30] *rem*: but not part of the technical analysis of *res/signum*.

visible things that are being shown without words, but also sounds and tastes and other such things. Again, in theaters, actors commonly launch into whole stories and tell them without words, through pantomime.[28]

AD. I've no means of contesting this, except that neither I—nor the pantomime actor for that matter—could show you what that word "from" means, without using words.[29]

AU. What you're saying is probably correct. But let's 6
imagine that he can. I reckon you're in no doubt that whatever that bodily gesture may be, which he uses to try and show me the thing that this word "from" signifies, it will not in itself be that thing, but rather a sign of that thing. He too, therefore, will not use a word to explain a word, but he will still use a sign to explain a sign, so that both this monosyllable, "from," and that gesture signify one particular thing, and I would like to have it shown to me without the use of any signifying—

AD. I ask you! Who can do what you request?—

AU. —in the same way as the barrier was able to function as a sign.

AD. Not even that barrier can be indicated without using a sign, as our argument thus far has taught us. For finger-pointing is definitely not a barrier, it simply gives a sign for the barrier to be recognized by. I don't see that anything can be shown without signs.

AU. What if I was asking you what walking is, and you got up and did it? Surely you would be using the actual thing, the walking, rather than words (or any other signs), to teach me?

AD. That's a fair point. I'm embarrassed that I didn't see something[30] so obvious. It means that thousands of

occurrunt, quae ipsae per se valeant, non per signa monstrari, ut edere, bibere, sedere, stare, clamare, et innumerabilia cetera.

AU. Age, nunc dic mihi, si omnino nesciens huius verbi vim, abs te ambulante quaererem quid sit ambulare, quomodo me doceres?

AD. Idipsum agerem aliquanto celerius, ut post interrogationem tuam aliqua novitate admonereris; et tamen nihil aliud fieret, quam id quod deberet ostendi.

AU. Scisne aliud esse ambulare, aliud festinare? Nam et qui ambulat, non continuo festinat; et qui festinat, non continuo ambulat: dicimus enim et in scribendo et in legendo, aliisque innumerabilibus rebus festinationem. Quare cum illud quod agebas, celerius ageres post interrogationem meam, putarem ambulare nihil esse aliud quam festinare: id enim novi addideras; et ob hoc fallerer.

AD. Fateor rem non posse nos monstrare sine signo, si cum id agimus interrogemur: si enim nihil addamus, putabit qui rogat, nolle nos ostendere, contemptoque se, in eo quod agebamus perseverare. Sed si de his roget quae agere possumus, nec eo tamen tempore quo agimus roget, possumus post eius interrogationem id agendo, re ipsa potius quam signo demonstrare quod rogat: nisi forte loquentem me interroget quid sit loqui. Quidquid enim

---

[31] Actions, in other words, that are signified by *verba* (general meaning: "words") that are also *verba* (grammatical meaning: "verbs").

things now occur to me that have meaning within themselves, and are not revealed by signs, for example eating, drinking, sitting, standing, shouting, and countless others.[31]

AU. Right, now tell me this: if I were completely ignorant of the meaning of this word, and I asked you, while you were actually walking, what "walking" means, how would you teach me?

AD. I would keep doing the same thing, walking, but somewhat faster, so that after you had asked your question an element of change would catch your attention, while nothing would be happening except for the thing that needed to be demonstrated.

AU. Do you know that walking is one thing, and hurrying is something else? For one thing, a walker does not begin by hurrying. For another, someone hurrying is not necessarily walking too: we refer to hurrying in writing and in reading, and countless other things. So after I asked my question, when you speeded up what you were doing, I would think that walking was no different from hurrying. For you had added a new element, which misled me.

AD. I'll concede that we cannot show a thing without using a sign, if we are being questioned while we are enacting that sign. For if we add nothing, our questioners will think that we don't want to show the answer, and that, by continuing with what we were doing, we are disregarding them. But if they ask about things that we have the ability to do (even though at the moment when they ask we're not actually doing them), after they've made their inquiry we can show them what they are asking about, using the thing itself rather than a sign for it. The exception is if they happen to ask me what "speaking" is, while

dixero, ut eum doceam, loquar necesse est. Ex quo securus docebo, donec ei planum faciam quod vult, non recedens a re ipsa quam sibi voluit demonstrari, nec signa quaerens quibus eam ostendam praeter ipsam.

7 4. AU. Acutissime omnino: quare vide utrum conveniat iam inter nos ea posse demonstrari sine signis, quae aut non agimus cum interrogamur, et tamen statim agere possumus, aut ipsa signa forte agimus; cum enim loquimur, signa facimus, de quo dictum est significare.

AD. Convenit.

AU. Cum ergo de quibusdam signis quaeritur, possunt signis signa monstrari: cum autem de rebus quae signa non sunt, aut eas agendo post inquisitionem si agi possunt, aut signa dando per quae animadverti queant.

AD. Ita est.

AU. In hac igitur tripartita distributione prius illud consideremus, si placet, quod signis signa monstrantur: num enim sola verba sunt signa?

AD. Non.

AU. Videtur ergo mihi loquendo nos aut verba ipsa signare verbis, aut alia signa, velut gestum cum dicimus aut litteram; nam his duobus verbis quae significantur, nihilominus signa sunt: aut aliquid aliud quod signum non sit, velut cum dicimus "lapis"; hoc enim verbum signum

---

[32] *significare* from *signum* (sign) and *facio* (do/make): in Classical Latin, *signum* is more likely to refer to a Roman military standard than to a tool of semiotics.

I am actually speaking. In that case, whatever I can say with the intention of teaching, I will have to use speech. It follows that my teaching will be unproblematic until I show them clearly what they want: I will not avoid the very thing they wanted to have explained, nor will I be hunting for signs (apart from the thing itself) to use in showing this to them.

4. AU. That's pretty perceptive. Now let's see whether 7
we're in agreement. These are the things that can be indicated without using signs: (a) things that we are not enacting when being asked but that we have the capacity to enact immediately; (b) those same signs when we are enacting them; for when we speak, we are making signals, hence the word "signification."[32]

AD. Agreed.

AU. So when we're asking a question about certain signs, we can use other signs to illustrate them. But when it is a question of things that are not signs, we can either enact them following on from the question (if they are the kind of things one can enact); or we can provide signs for drawing attention to them.

AD. That's right.

AU. Then if you approve, should we divide this matter into three parts, and consider what are the signs which can be illustrated by signs? Or are words the only signs?

AD. No, they aren't.

AU. Then it seems to me that when we are speaking, we either use words themselves to signify words, or we use other signs; for example when we say "gesture" or "letter." For the things which are signified by these two words are still themselves signs. Or take something else which is not itself a sign, for example when we say "stone." The word

est, nam significat aliquid, sed id quod eo significatur, non continuo signum est: quod tamen genus, id est cum verbis ea quae signa non sunt significantur, non pertinet ad hanc partem quam discutere proposuimus. Suscepimus enim considerare illud, quod signis signa monstrantur, et partes in eo duas comperimus, cum aut eadem aut alia signa signis docemus vel commemoramus: an non tibi videtur?

AD. Manifestum est.

8 AU. Dic ergo signa quae verba sunt, ad quem sensum pertineant.

AD. Ad auditum.

AU. Quid gestus?

AD. Ad visum.

AU. Quid, cum verba scripta[3] invenimus? num verba non sunt, an signa verborum verius intelleguntur? ut verbum sit quod cum aliquo significatu articulata voce profertur; vox autem nullo alio sensu quam auditu percipi potest. Ita fit ut cum scribitur verbum, signum fiat oculis, quo illud quod ad aures pertinet, veniat in mentem.

AD. Omnino assentior.

AU. Id quoque te arbitror assentiri, cum dicimus "nomen," significare nos aliquid.

[3] verba non sunt scripta *B R V*

---

[33] "that are signs" supplied: e.g., waving, beckoning, etc.

[34] Highlighting how "word" is applied both to what is written and to what is spoken. *Vox* (utterance), on the other hand, refers only to the spoken.

[35] *Nomen* can be any kind of name, including a personal name. It is also the grammatical term for a noun, so *dicimus nomen* could be translated as "say a noun," or "say someone's name."

"stone" is a sign, because it signifies something. But the thing that it signifies is not straightforwardly a sign too. This whole category (consisting of things that are not signs but which are signified by words) is not relevant to the proposed distribution of our argument into sections. For this is the matter we have undertaken to investigate, specifically, signs being illustrated by means of signs; and we have established two elements within that undertaking. These are using signs in teaching or commemorating either the same signs or other signs. Do you agree?

AD. That's clear.

AU. Now tell me, these signs which are words, what 8
sense do they relate to?

AD. To hearing.

AU. What about gestures that are signs?[33]

AD. To sight.

AU. What about when the words we encounter are written down? Surely they aren't actual words, or at least are more precisely understood as signs of words? "Word"[34] is something produced by an articulate utterance, which has a particular meaning; but "utterance" cannot be perceived by any other sense than hearing. It follows, therefore, that when a word is written down, it becomes a sign to the eyes that brings to mind what actually relates to hearing.

AD. I completely agree.

AU. I think this too will win your approval: when we speak the "name-word"[35] for something, we are signifying it.

It is here translated "name-word," to avoid obscuring how, in the Latin, one term does duty for both "name" and "noun."

AD. Verum est.

AU. Quid tandem?

AD. Id scilicet quod quidque appellatur, velut Romulus, Roma, virtus, fluvius, et innumerabilia cetera.

AU. Num ista quattuor nomina nullas res significant?

AD. Immo aliquas.

AU. Num nihil distat inter haec nomina, et eas res quae his significantur?

AD. Immo plurimum.

AU. Vellem abs te audire, quidnam id sit.

AD. Hoc vel in primis, quod haec signa sunt, illa non sunt.

AU. Placetne appellemus significabilia ea quae signis significari possunt et signa non sunt, sicut ea quae videri possunt, visibilia nominamus, ut de his deinceps commodius disseramus?

AD. Placet vero.

AU. Quid? illa quattuor signa quae paulo ante pronuntiasti, nullo alio signo significantur?

AD. Miror quod iam mihi excidisse arbitraris, quod ea quae scribuntur, eorum quae voce proferuntur signorum signa esse comperimus.

AU. Dic inter ista quid distet?

---

36 *Significabilia*: a very rare technical word, which points to the novelty of Augustine's thinking. He surely took it from Varro, *Ling.* 6.52: "the first person to speak is someone who sends forth from his lips a signifying utterance."

37 In sequence: (1) thing, (2) name of thing written down, (3) name of thing written down being spoken aloud.

AD. That's true.

AU. So what is it?

AD. Obviously it's what each thing is called: for example "Romulus," "Rome," "virtue," "river," and countless other instances.

AU. Now take those four name-words, surely there are things that they signify?

AD. Certainly there are.

AU. And surely these name-words are not indistinguishable from the things that they signify?

AD. Of course they aren't.

AU. I would like to hear from you what the distinction between them is.

AD. Well, to begin with, there's the fact that the name-words are signs, but the things are not.

AU. Concerning those things that can be signified, but that are not themselves signs, will you assent to our calling them "signifiable"?[36] On the analogy of calling things we can see "visible"? This will allow us to discuss them more easily.

AD. Certainly I will.

AU. What next? Those four signs that you just spoke of, are they signified by no other sign?

AD. I'm amazed at you thinking it has already escaped me that we found that things that are written down are signs of those signs that are utterances produced by the voice.[37]

AU. State what it is that separates them.

AD. Quod illa visibilia sunt, haec audibilia. Cur enim et hoc nomen non admittas, si admisimus significabilia?

AU. Prorsus admitto, et gratum habeo. Sed rursus quaero, quattuor haec signa nullo alio signo audibili significari queant, ut visibilia recordatus es?

AD. Hoc quoque recentius dictum recordor. Nam nomen responderam significare aliquid, et huic significationi quattuor ista subieceram; et illud autem et haec, si quidem voce proferuntur, audibilia esse cognosco.

AU. Quid ergo inter audibile signum et audibilia significata, quae rursus signa sunt, interest?

AD. Inter illud quidem quod dicimus, "nomen," et haec quattuor quae significationi eius subiecimus, hoc distare video, quod illud audibile signum est signorum audibilium: haec vero audibilia quidem signa sunt, non tamen signorum, sed rerum partim visibilium, sicut est Romulus, Roma, fluvius; partim intellegibilium, sicut est virtus.

9 AU. Accipio et probo. Sed scisne omnia quae voce articulata cum aliquo significatu proferuntur verba appellari?

AD. Scio.

AU. Ergo et nomen verbum est, quandoquidem id vi-

---

[38] *Nomen*. Unless generalized beyond "name-word," the singular reads oddly as a reference to both *visibilia* and *audibilia*.

[39] He asks because in Latin these adjectives (*visibilis* and *audibilis*) are rare, though their equivalents in English are not: see *Ep.* 169.10; *C. Jul. imp.* 4.14.73. He may have borrowed both from Ambrose, *De Noe* 15.52.

[40] The noun "significate" is a technical term of semiotics for the things that signs signify.

[41] Here not *significatio* but an alternative term, *significatus*, for either the meaning of a word (e.g., Gell. *NA* 5.12.9) or an appellation (see Arn. 1.3).

AD. The fact that the written name-words are visible signs, while the spoken name-words are audible signs. Why would you not accept this terminology[38] now that we have accepted "signifiable"?[39]

AU. I do accept it, by all means, thank you. But I ask again, these four signs, is there no other audible sign that can signify them, just like the visible signs you mentioned?

AD. I recollect that this too was mentioned just now. I'd answered that a name-word is a signifier of something, and I'd added those four name-words to this category of signification. I know that both written and spoken forms are audible, provided that a voice produces them.

AU. What, then, is the difference between an audible sign on the one hand, and on the other, audible significates[40] that are also signs?

AD. Here is the distinction that I perceive between what we call a "name-word" and these four things that we have added to that signification: "name-word" is an audible sign of audible signs; and these things that are audible are definitely signs, but not signs of signs, rather of things some of which are visible, like "Romulus," "Rome," and "river"; and others are discernible, such as "virtue."

AU. Yes, I agree. But do you know that all things that 9
can be produced by articulate utterance, and that carry some signification[41] with them, are called "words"?

AD. I do know.

AU. So a name-word[42] is also a word,[43] for we observe

[42] *nomen*.

[43] *verbum*. Just as *nomen* does duty for "word," "name," and "noun," *verbum* refers to "words" or "verbs." Here Augustine makes the ambiguity explicit.

demus cum aliquo significatu articulata voce proferri; et cum dicimus disertum hominem bonis verbis uti, etiam nominibus utique utitur; et cum seni domino apud Terentium servus rettulit, "bona verba quaeso!" multa ille etiam nomina dixerat.

AD. Assentior.

AU. Concedis igitur his duabus syllabis quas edimus, cum dicimus, "verbum," nomen quoque significari, et ob hoc illud huius signum esse.

AD. Concedo.

AU. Hoc quoque respondeas velim: cum verbum signum sit nominis, et nomen signum sit fluminis, et flumen signum sit rei quae iam videri potest, ut inter hanc rem et flumen, id est signum eius, et inter hoc signum et nomen, quod huius signi signum est dixisti quid intersit, quid interesse arbitraris inter signum nominis, quod verbum esse comperimus, et ipsum nomen cuius signum est?

AD. Hoc distare intellego, quod ea quae significantur nomine, etiam verbo significantur—ut enim nomen est verbum, ita et flumen verbum est—quae autem verbo significantur, non omnia significantur et nomine. Nam et illud "si," quod in capite habet abs te propositus versus, et hoc "ex," de quo iam diu agentes in haec duce ratione

---

[44] *An.* 204.

[45] *bona verba* suggests words that are propitious.

[46] *duabus syllabis*: the Latin word for "word," *verbum*, has two syllables.

[47] *rem.*

[48] This complicated summary struggles to express the difference between words and names (*verba, nomina*) that in Latin is also a difference between verbs and nouns.

it being produced in an articulate utterance that has some meaning. Also, when we say that someone who is an able speaker uses "good words," they are certainly also using "name-words." And when the slave in a play of Terence[44] replies to his elderly master, "good words,[45] please!" that master too had spoken many name-words.

AD. I agree.

AU. So do you admit that in the one syllable that we enunciate when saying "word,"[46] a name-word is being signified as well, and thus that "word" is a sign of the term "name-word"?

AD. Agreed.

AU. I would like you to reply to this too: when "word" is a sign for a name-word, and "name-word" is a sign for a river, and "river" is a sign of a real observable thing, and so you have stated what the difference is between this real physical thing[47] and the word "river" (i.e., its sign), and between this sign and "name-word" (which is a sign of that first sign, "river"); what do you think is the difference between the sign for "name-word" (which we have found is itself "word"), and the term "name-word" itself, which "word" is a sign of?[48]

AD. I understand that this is where the difference comes in. Things that are signified by a name-word are also signified by a word—for as "name-word" is a type of word, so too "river" is a type of word—but not everything which is signified by a word is signified by a name-word. For that word "if," which began the line of poetry you suggested, and the word "from" have led on—with reason

pervenimus, verba sunt, nec tamen nomina; et talia multa inveniuntur. Quam ob rem cum omnia nomina verba sint, non autem omnia verba nomina sint, planum esse arbitror quid inter verbum distet et nomen, id est inter signum signi eius quod nulla alia signa significat, et signum signi eius quod rursus alia signa significat.

AU. Concedisne omnem equum animal esse, nec tamen omne animal equum esse?

AD. Quis dubitaverit?

AU. Hoc ergo inter nomen et verbum, quod inter equum et animal interest. Nisi forte ab assentiendo id te revocat, quod dicimus et alio modo verbum, quo significantur ea quae per tempora declinantur, ut scribo scripsi, lego legi, quae manifestum est non esse nomina.

AD. Dixisti omnino quod me dubitare faciebat.

AU. Ne te istud moveat. Dicimus enim et signa universaliter omnia quae significant aliquid, ubi etiam verba esse invenimus. Dicimus item signa militaria, quae iam proprie signa nominantur, quo verba non pertinent. Et tamen si tibi dicerem, ut omnis equus animal, non autem omne animal equus est, ita omne verbum signum, non autem omne signum verbum est, nihil, ut opinor, dubitares.

AD. Iam intellego, et prorsus assentior, hoc interesse inter universale illud verbum et nomen, quod inter animal et equum.

---

49 They inflect according to their tense, in other words. This is the key aspect of the difference between nouns and verbs that suggests itself to Augustine.

50 *Signa*: banners or tokens such as an eagle, *aquila*, used to lead armies.

directing us in this lengthy discussion—to our conclusion: they are words, but not name-words, and we find many similar examples. For this reason, since all name-words are words, but not all words are name-words, I consider it obvious what the difference is between "word" and "name-word." That is, between a sign of this sign that signifies no other signs; and a sign of this sign that further signifies other signs.

AU. Do you admit that every horse is an animal, but that not every animal is a horse?

AD. Who can argue with that?

AU. This difference between name-word and word is like that between horse and animal. Unless maybe something holds you back from agreeing to this, namely the fact that we say "word" with another meaning, to signify things which change in accordance with time, for example "I write/I wrote," "I gather/I gathered":[49] it's obvious that these are not name-words.

AD. What you have said is precisely what was causing me to waver.

AU. Don't let it bother you. We speak of signs in a general way as being all the things which signify something, and here is where we find words included. Likewise we speak of signs that are military standards:[50] it is right to call them "signs," but they are irrelevant to this matter of words. And yet if I were to say to you that every horse is an animal, but that not every animal is a horse, in the same way as every word is a sign, but not every sign is a word, you would, I think, agree with that.

AD. Now I understand, and yes, I agree, the difference between the general terms "word" and "name-word" is like that between "animal" and "horse."

10 AU. Scisne etiam cum dicimus "animal," aliud esse hoc trisyllabum nomen, quod voce prolatum est, aliud id quod significatur?

AD. Iam hoc supra concessi de omnibus signis et significabilibus.

AU. Num omnia signa tibi videntur aliud significare quam sunt, sicut hoc trisyllabum, cum dicimus, "animal," nullo modo idem significat quod est ipsum?

AD. Non sane: nam cum dicimus "signum," non solum signa cetera quaecumque sunt, sed etiam seipsum significat; est enim verbum, et utique omnia verba signa sunt.

AU. Quid? in hoc disyllabo cum dicimus "verbum," nonne tale aliquid contingit? Nam si omne quod cum aliquo significatu articulata voce profertur, hoc disyllabo significatur, etiam ipsum hoc genere includitur.

AD. Ita est.

AU.[4] Quid? nomen nonne similiter habet? Nam et omnium generum nomina significat, et ipsum nomen generis neutri nomen est. An si ex te quaererem quae pars orationis nomen, posses mihi respondere recte nisi nomen?

AD. Verum dicis.

AU. Sunt ergo signa quae inter alia quae significant, et seipsa significent.

AD. Sunt.

AU. Num tale tibi videtur hoc quadrisyllabum signum, cum dicimus "coniunctio"?

AD. Nullo modo: nam ea quae significat, non sunt nomina; hoc autem nomen est.

[4] *Hic incipit fr. B*

AU. Do you know too that when we say "animal," this 10
trisyllabic word is one thing (which is produced by the voice), and what it signifies is something else?

AD. I already agreed to this earlier with reference to all signs and signifiable things.

AU. But can you see that all signs signify something other than what they are, as that three-syllable word, when we say "animal," by no means signifies what it itself is?

AD. Not entirely. When we say "sign," it signifies not just other signs of all kinds, but also signifies itself: for it is a word, and unquestionably all words are signs.

AU. Right, when we say this monosyllable "word," surely something of this sort happens? For if every thing that is produced by articulate utterance, and has some kind of significance, is signified by that monosyllable, it too belongs in this category.

AD. That's right.

AU. Then what? Doesn't the term "name-word" work the same way?—given that it signifies name-words of every kind, and "name" is itself a name-word of neuter gender. Or if I were to ask you what part of speech "name-word" is, could you answer correctly with anything but "'name-word' is a name-word"?

AD. You're right.

AU. There are signs, then, which, among the other things which they signify, also signify themselves.

AD. There are.

AU. You surely don't think that when we say "conjunction" this trisyllabic word is that kind of a sign?

AD. No way. Because although it is itself a name-word, the things that it signifies are not name-words.

11 5. AU. Bene attendisti! Nunc illud vide, utrum inveniamus signa quae se invicem significent, ut quemadmodum hoc ab illo, sic illud ab hoc significetur. Non enim ita sunt inter se hoc quadrisyllabum, cum dicimus "coniunctio," et illa quae ab hoc significantur, cum dicimus, "si," vel "nam," "namque," "nisi," "ergo," "quoniam," et similia; nam haec illo uno significantur, nullo autem horum unum illud quadrisyllabum significatur.

AD. Video, et quaenam signa sint se invicem significantia, cupio cognoscere.

AU. Tu ergo nescis, cum dicimus "nomen" et "verbum," duo verba nos dicere?

AD. Scio.

AU. Quid? illud nescis, cum dicimus "nomen" et "verbum," duo nomina nos dicere?

AD. Id quoque scio.

AU. Scis igitur tam nomen verbo, quam etiam verbum nomine significari.

AD. Assentior.

AU. Potesne dicere, excepto eo quod diverse scribuntur et sonant, quid inter se differant?

AD. Possum fortasse; nam id esse video quod paulo ante dixi. Verba enim cum dicimus, omne quod articulata voce cum aliquo significatu profertur, significamus; unde omne nomen, et ipsum cum dicimus "nomen," verbum est: at non omne verbum nomen est, quamvis nomen sit, cum dicimus "verbum."

12 AU. Quid, si quisquam tibi affirmet et probet, ut omne

5. AU. You've been paying attention! Now consider whether we may discover signs that are mutual signs of each other in such a way that as one signifies the other, so the other also signifies the one. This will not be the case between our saying that three-syllable word "conjunction" and the other words that it signifies, when we say, "if," "or," "for," "for sure," "unless," "therefore," "since," and the like. For all of these are signified by that one word "conjunction"; but not one of them conversely signifies that trisyllabic word. 11

AD. I get it, and now I want to know what are these signs which signify each other.

AU. So don't you know that when we say "name-word" and "word," we are saying two words?

AD. I know that.

AU. What then? Don't you know this, that when we say "name-word" and "word," we are saying two name-words?

AD. I know that too.

AU. So do you know, then, that "name-word" is signified by "word," just as "word" is signified by "name-word"?

AD. Agreed.

AU. Can you say what the difference between them is, except for the fact that they are written and pronounced differently?

AD. Maybe I can, for I see this is what I spoke of just now. When we say "words," we're signifying everything produced as articulate utterance that carries some signifier of meaning with it. It follows that every name-word, including when we say the word "name-word" itself, is a word. But not every word is a name-word, although when we say "word" that is a name-word.

AU. What if someone asserted and endorsed the idea 12

nomen verbum est, ita omne verbum nomen esse? poterisne invenire quid distent, praeter diversum in litteris sonum?

AD. Non potero, nec omnino distare aliquid puto.

AU. Quid, si omnia quidem quae voce articulata cum aliquo significatu proferuntur, et verba sunt et nomina; sed tamen alia de causa verba, et alia de causa nomina sunt? nihilne distabit inter nomen et verbum?

AD. Quomodo istud sit non intellego.

AU. Hoc saltem intellegis, omne coloratum visibile esse, et omne visibile coloratum, quamvis haec duo verba distincte differenterque significent.

AD. Intellego.

AU. Quid si ergo ita et omne verbum nomen, et omne nomen verbum est, quamvis haec ipsa duo nomina, vel duo verba, id est nomen et verbum, differentem habeant significationem?

AD. Iam video posse id accidere: sed quomodo id accidat, exspecto ut ostendas.

AU. Omne quod cum aliquo significatu articulata voce prorumpit animadvertis, ut opinor, et aurem verberare, ut sentiri; et memoriae mandari, ut nosci possit.

AD. Animadverto.

AU. Duo ergo quaedam contingunt, cum aliquid tali voce proferimus.

AD. Ita est.

AU. Quid si horum duorum ex uno appellata sunt

that as every name-word is a word, so every word is a name-word? Would you be able to discover what the difference is between them, apart from the different sound of their letters?

AD. I wouldn't. In any case, I don't think they are completely different.

AU. What if all the things that articulate speech produces, and that have some meaning, are both words and name-words; but they are words according to one usage, and name-words according to another? Will there then be no distinction between name-word and name?

AD. I don't understand how that can be.

AU. Well, I'm sure you'll understand this: everything that is visible has a color, and everything that has a color is visible; although these two words are separate, meaning different things.

AD. I understand that.

AU. What, then, if just as every word is a name-word, and every name-word is a word—although the actual things are two name-words, or two words (i.e., "name-word" and "word")—they were to signify different things?

AD. I can see now that it's possible: but I'm waiting for you to tell me how it's possible.

AU. In my view, you notice every sound that emerges by articulate utterance and has some capacity to signify: it strikes your ear, making you sense it; and is committed to memory, so that you can know it.

AD. I do notice, yes.

AU. Therefore two particular things happen when we produce some form of articulate speech.

AD. That's right.

AU. What if "words" are so called after one of these

verba, ex altero nomina; verba scilicet a verberando, nomina vero a noscendo, ut illud primum ab auribus, hoc autem secundum ab animo vocari meruerit?

13 AD. Concedam, cum ostenderis quomodo recte possimus omnia verba nomina dicere.

AU. Facile est: nam credo te accepisse ac tenere pronomen dictum, quod pro ipso nomine valeat, rem tamen notet minus plena significatione quam nomen. Nam, ut opinor, ita definivit ille, quem grammatico reddidisti: pronomen est pars orationis, quae pro ipso posita nomine, minus quidem plene, idem tamen significat.

AD. Recordor et probo.

AU. Vides igitur secundum hanc definitionem nullis nisi nominibus servire, et pro his solis poni posse pronomina, velut cum dicimus, hic vir, ipse rex, eadem mulier, hoc aurum, illud argentum: hic, ipse, eadem, hoc, illud pronomina esse; vir, rex, mulier, aurum, argentum, nomina, quibus plenius quam illis pronominibus res significatae sunt.

AD. Video et assentior.

AU. Tu ergo nunc mihi paucas coniunctiones quaslibet enuntia.

AD. Et, que, at, atque.

---

[51] *verbum* and *verbero*; *nomen* and *nosco*.

[52] In an etymology *ab* can indicate derivation.

[53] Exegetical translation of *res*.

[54] Mentioned twice because the first "this" is grammatically masculine, the second neuter.

two things, and "name-words" from the other? Surely "words" comes from the word for beating, and "name-words" from the word for knowing,[51] so have the former earned their name from[52] their effect on the ears, and the latter from their effect on the mind?

AD. I'll agree to this once you've shown me how we can 13
properly call all words "name-words."

AU. That's easy. I think you acknowledge, and maintain, that we call something a "pronoun" when it does the job of the actual name-word, though it denotes the thing it stands for[53] with a less complete form of signification than the name-word itself does. I think the man who was your grammar teacher defined it thus, and you repeated it back to him: pronouns are the part of speech that are used in place of actual name-words, and they signify the same thing, albeit less fully.

AD. I remember, you're right.

AU. So you see that according to this definition pronouns do the work of name-words only, and can only be used in place of name-words. For example when we say "this man," "the king himself," "the same woman," "this gold," "that silver"; "this," "himself," "the same," "this,"[54] and "that" are pronouns, while "man," "king," "woman," "gold," and "silver" are name-words, and so can signify things more fully than those pronouns.

AD. I see. I agree with you.

AU. Now you express a few conjunctions for me—any ones you like.

AD. "Also," "and," "but," "plus."

AU. Haec omnia quae dixisti, nonne tibi videntur esse nomina?

AD. Non omnino.

AU. Ego saltem tibi recte locutus videor, cum dicerem, haec omnia quae dixisti?

AD. Recte prorsus, et iam intellego quam mirabiliter ostenderis me nomina enuntiasse: non enim aliter de his recte dici potuisset, "haec omnia." Sed vereor adhuc, ne propterea mihi recte locutus videaris, quod has quattuor coniunctiones etiam verba esse non nego; ut ideo de his recte dici potuerit, "haec omnia," quoniam recte dicitur, "haec verba omnia." Si autem a me quaeras quae sit pars orationis, verba; nihil aliud respondebo quam nomen. Quare huic nomini fortasse pronomen adiunctum est, ut illa recta esset locutio tua.

14 AU. Acute quidem falleris, sed ut falli desinas, acutius attende quod dicam, si tamen dicere id, ut volo, valuero. Nam verbis de verbis agere tam implicatum est, quam digitos digitis inserere et confricare; ubi vix dignoscitur, nisi ab eo ipso qui id agit, qui digiti pruriant, et qui auxilientur prurientibus.

AD. En toto animo adsum, nam ista haec similitudo me intentissimum fecit.

AU. Verba certe sono et litteris constant.

---

55 By referring to the conjunctions using a pronoun (*haec*), Augustine sets up the paradox that because all pronouns refer to nouns, the conjunctions must also be nouns. Adeodatus is right to be skeptical.

56 *omnia haec*: adjective plus pronoun.

57 Perhaps recalling Luke 6:1[Vulg.]: *confricare* is a *hapax* in Vulg.

AU. All these[55] you've mentioned, surely they seem to you to be name-words?

AD. Not at all.

AU. But surely you think I was talking sense when I referred to "all these things you've mentioned"?

AD. You're absolutely right—and now I understand the remarkable way you showed that I was expressing name-words: for otherwise it would not have been possible to say correctly "all these things."[56] But I'm still worried that this is why in my view you spoke accurately: because I do not deny that these four conjunctions are also words, so therefore "all these" could correctly be said of them, since it is correct to say "all these words." But if you ask me what part of speech "words" is, I will only be able to reply, "it is a name-word." Perhaps it was for this reason that a pronoun was attached to the name-word, to make the way you referred to it be correct.

AU. That's a clever mistake you make there. But to stop 14
being mistaken, listen more carefully to what I'm saying—if, that is, I can even find an effective way to express what I want. Using words to discuss words runs the risk of causing a tangle of confusion, like when we interlock fingers and rub them together;[57] which makes it almost impossible for anyone but the person doing the scratching to tell which fingers are itching and which are relieving the itch.

AD. Well, go on—I'm all attention, your comparison has me on tenterhooks.

AU. Words definitely consist of[58] sounds and letters.

[58] *constant*: as yet making no distinction between the sound (*sonus*) of whole words when spoken aloud (*verba/voces*), the sounds, when articulated, of individual written characters (*litterae*), and whole words on the page (also *verba*).

AD. Ita est.

AU. Ergo ut ea potissimum auctoritate utamur, quae nobis carissima est, cum ait Paulus apostolus, *Non erat in Christo "est" et "non," sed est in illo erat*, non opinor putandum est tres istas litteras, quas enuntiamus cum dicimus, *est*, fuisse in Christo, sed illud potius quod istis tribus litteris significatur.

AD. Verum dicis.

AU. Intellegis igitur eum qui ait, "'est' in illo erat," nihil aliud dixisse quam, "est appellatur quod in illo erat"; tamquam si dixisset, "virtus in illo erat," non utique[5] dixisse acciperetur nisi "virtus appellatur quod in illo erat," ne duas istas syllabas quas enuntiamus, cum dicimus, "virtus," et non illud quod his duabus syllabis significatur, in illo fuisse arbitraremur.

AD. Intellego ac sequor.

AU. Quid? illud nonne intellegis etiam nihil interesse utrum quisque dicat, "virtus appellatur," an "virtus nominatur"?

AD. Manifestum est.

AU. Ergo ita manifestum est nihil interesse utrum quis dicat, "est appellatur," an "est nominatur quod in illo erat."

AD. Video et hic nihil distare.

AU. Iamne etiam vides quid velim ostendere?

AD. Nondum sane.

[5] utique *S T*: utique aliud *M* μ

---

[59] 2 Corinthians 1:19: the first direct quotation from scripture since 1.2.

AD. That's right.

AU. So let's use the best authority of all, the one we hold most dear. When the apostle Paul says, "in Christ there was no 'yes' and 'no,' but in him all was 'yes,'"[59] I do not think we are to imagine it was actually those three letters, which we enunciate when we say "yes," that were in Christ, but rather that thing that is signified by those three letters.

AD. You're right.

AU. You understand, therefore, that the person who is saying "in him was 'yes,'" is not saying anything other than "what was in him was what is called 'yes.'" Just as if, had he said "virtue was in him," we would certainly not have taken it as saying anything other than "what was in him was what we call 'virtue.'" So we should not think that those two syllables which we enunciate when we say "virtue" were in him, rather than that quality which is signified by the two syllables.

AD. I understand, and I agree.

AU. What next? I'm sure you understand too that there is no difference between someone saying "it is called virtue" and "it is named virtue," don't you?

AD. Obviously.

AU. So is it likewise obvious that there is no difference whether a person says "what was in him is called 'yes,'" or "what was in him is named 'yes'"?

AD. I see no difference in this case either.

AU. Now do you see what I want to show you?

AD. Not yet, I don't.

AU. Itane tu non vides nomen esse id quo[6] res aliqua nominatur?

AD. Hoc plane nihil certius video.

AU. Vides[7] ergo, "est" nomen esse, siquidem illud, quod erat in Christo, "est" nominatur.

AD. Negare non possum.

AU. At si ex te quaererem quae sit pars orationis, "est," non opinor nomen, sed verbum esse diceres, cum id ratio etiam nomen esse docuerit.

AD. Ita est prorsus ut dicis.

AU. Num adhuc dubitas alias quoque partes orationis eodem modo, quo demonstravimus, nomina esse?

AD. Non dubito, quandoquidem fateor ea[8] significare aliquid. Si autem res ipsae quas significant, quid singulae appellentur, id est nominentur, interroges, respondere non possum, nisi eas ipsas partes orationis, quas nomina non vocamus, sed, ut cerno, vocare convincimur.

AU. Nihilne te movet, ne quis existat qui nostram istam rationem labefactet dicendo, apostolis non verborum sed rerum auctoritatem esse tribuendam? Quam ob rem fundamentum persuasionis huius non tam esse firmum quam putamus; fieri enim posse ut Paulus, quamquam vixerit praeceperitque rectissime, minus tamen recte locutus sit cum ait, "est in illo erat," praesertim cum se ipse imperitum sermone fateatur. Quo tandem modo istum refellendum arbitraris?

[6] quo *V*: quod *B R* [7] vides *A F*: vide *R V S T*
[8] eas *coni. Weig.* {*scr. "correxi"*}

---

60 Expressed as paradox: the Latin translated as "yes" is a verb.

61 Not *res* here but *illud*, a neuter pronoun.

62 2 Corinthians 11:6.

AU. So you don't see that a name-word is something by which any given thing is named?

AD. I see this as completely clear.

AU. So, you see, "yes" is a name-word,[60] if indeed that thing[61] which was in Christ is named as "yes."

AD. I can't deny that.

AU. Yet if I asked you what part of speech "yes" is, I don't think you would call it a name-word. But our reasoning has taught us that it is also a name-word.

AD. You're exactly right.

AU. You can't still be in doubt, can you, that other parts of speech are name-words in the same way as we have just established?

AD. No, I've no doubts, because I am conceding that they are signifying something. But if you were to ask what the actual things are that they signify, what each one of them is called (in other words, what their names are), I can only answer by saying that they are these very parts of speech which we do not call name-words, but—as I now perceive the matter—name-words is what we have now been prevailed upon to call them.

AU. Aren't you worried that someone may come for- 15
ward and undermine this line of reasoning we're taking, by saying that what we attribute to the apostles should be authority over things, not words? This would mean that the basis for our convictions is more unstable than we think. It's possible that even though his way of life, and his teachings, were of supreme integrity, Paul's mode of speech was less so when he says "in him was 'yes'"—especially when he himself confesses to a lack of expertise in public speaking.[62] What's your opinion, then, on how to refute this?

AD. Nihil habeo quod contradicam, et te oro ut aliquem de illis reperias, quibus verborum notitia summa conceditur, cuius auctoritate potius id quod cupis efficias.

AU. Minus enim tibi videtur idonea remotis auctoritatibus ipsa ratio, qua demonstratur omnibus partibus orationis significari aliquid et ex eo appellari;[9] si autem appellari, et nominari; si nominari, nomine utique nominari: quod in diversis linguis facillime iudicatur. Quis enim non videat, si quaeram[10] quid Graeci nominent quod nos nominamus "quis," responderi mihi[11] *τίς*; quid Graeci nominent quod nos nominamus "volo," responderi mihi, *θέλω*; quid Graeci nominent quod nos nominamus "bene," responderi[12] *καλῶς*; quid Graeci nominent quod nos nominamus "scriptum," responderi mihi *τὸ γεγραμμένον*; quid Graeci nominent quod nos nominamus "et," responderi *καί*; quid Graeci nominent quod nos nominamus "ab" responderi *ἀπό*; quid Graeci nominent, quod nos nominamus "heu," responderi *οἴ*: atque in his omnibus partibus orationis quas nunc enumeravi, recte loqui eum qui sic interroget, quod nisi nomina essent fieri non posset. Hac ergo ratione Paulum apostolum recte locutum esse, cum remotis omnium eloquentium auctoritatibus obtinere possimus. Quid opus est quaerere cuius persona sententia nostra fulciatur?

9 appellari . . . appellari et nominari *S*: si autem appellari {*ante* et nominari} *om. B S T μ*

10 quaeram *V R*: quaeras *μ*

11 mihi *om. μ et tria sequ.*

12 responderi] *B S T*: responderi <mihi> *Weig.*

---

63 Pronoun, verb, adverb, adjective/participle, conjunction,

AD. I've nothing to counter this with. Please find someone from among those whose supreme expertise in words is recognized. Their authority will best achieve your objective.

AU. If we set aside such authorities, do you think that pure reason is a less effective way to prove that in all the parts of speech something is being signified, and is called after this? But if it is called, it is also named; if named, then it is undoubtedly a name-word that names it. This is easy to determine in different languages. Surely it is obvious that if I ask what name Greeks give to the word we name as "who?," I will get this answer: *tis*? If I ask what name Greeks give to the word we name as "I want," I will get this answer: *thelō*. If I ask what name Greeks give to the word we name as "well," I will get this answer: *kalōs*. If I ask what name Greeks give to the word we name as "writing," I will get this answer: *to gegrammenon*. If I ask what name Greeks give to the word we name as "and," this will be the answer: *kai*. If I ask what name Greeks give to the word we name as "from," this will be the answer: *apo*. If I ask what name Greeks give to the word we name as "alas," this will be the answer: *oi*. And when it comes to all these parts of speech[63] that I have just listed, a person who asks questions like this is speaking correctly; because they would be unable to do so, unless all these words were name-words. According to this argument the apostle Paul has spoken correctly, since we can prevail even if we dispense with the authority of eloquent speakers. Why would we need some personage to bolster our view?

preposition, interjection, respectively. Only "noun" (already *passim*) is omitted from his list.

16 Sed ne quis tardior aut impudentior nondum cedat, asseratque nisi illis auctoribus, quibus verborum leges consensu omnium tribuuntur, nullo modo esse[13] cessurum, quid in Latina lingua excellentius Cicerone inveniri potest? At hic in suis nobilissimis orationibus quas "Verrinas" vocant, "coram," praepositionem, sive illo loco adverbium sit, nomen appellavit. Verumtamen quia fieri potest ut, cum[14] ego illum locum minus bene intellegam, exponatur[15] alias aliter vel a me vel ab alio; est ad quod responderi posse nihil puto. Tradunt enim nobilissimi disputationum magistri, nomine et verbo plenam constare sententiam, quae affirmari negarique possit. Quod genus idem Tullius quodam loco pronuntiatum vocat. Et cum verbi tertia persona est, nominativum cum ea casum nominis aiunt esse oportere. Et recte aiunt, quod mecum si consideres velut[16] cum dicimus "homo sedet," "equus currit," agnoscis, ut opinor, duo pronuntiata esse.

AD. Agnosco.

AU. Cernis in singulis singula esse nomina, in uno "homo," in altero "equus"; et verba singula, in uno "sedet," in altero "currit"?

AD. Cerno.

13 esse <se> *fortasse coni. Weig.* 14 cum ego *B R V T*: ut cum lego *H S*: cum *om.* *μ* 15 expugnatur *Weig.*: expugnaturque] *S T B μ* 16 velim *B R V S*

---

64 Meaning "in the presence of." There is no single-word English equivalent.

65 *Verr.* 2.104 (cf. *Verr.* 2.94). Whether Augustine really thinks Cicero called *coram* a noun (or was taking advantage of the ambiguity to further his argument) is another question.

If someone is too slow-witted or high-handed to back 16
down, insisting that they will only yield when faced with those authorities who are universally credited with establishing the laws of language, what standard can we find in the Latin tongue that is more exemplary than Cicero? Yet this man, in his most distinguished speeches known as the *Verrines*, called *coram*[64] (which is a preposition, or in that context an adverb) a name-word.[65] It's possible that although I am interpreting that passage less well, in some other time and place either I or someone else may succeed in explaining it: so here, I think, is something beyond dispute. The most accomplished teachers of argument instruct that a name-word and a verb[66] constitute a sentence, which can be affirmative or negative. Somewhere Cicero—again[67]—calls this a proposition.[68] They state that when the verb is in the third person, the case of the name-word ought to be nominative. And they're right. After all, if you consider with me, by way of example, when we say "a person sits," "a horse runs," I think you recognize that here are two propositions.

AD. Agreed.

AU. Do you see that if we take them individually the name-words are singular—in the one, "person," in the other, "horse"; and the verbs are in the singular—in the one "sits," in the other, "runs"?

AD. Yes, I see.

66 *verbo*: not in its more general sense, "word."

67 Augustine is cautious about treating Cicero as an authority.

68 Or "axiom." Cicero uses it to translate Greek (*Tusc*. 1.7.14). Gellius proposes *proloquium* as an alternative translation into Latin (*NA* 16.8.8).

AU. Ergo si dicerem "sedet" tantum aut "currit" tantum, recte a me quaereres quis vel quid, ut responderem "homo," vel "equus," vel "animal," vel quodlibet aliud, quo[17] possit nomen redditum verbo implere pronuntiatum, id est illam sententiam quae affirmari et negari potest.

AD. Intellego.

AU. Attende cetera, et finge nos videre aliquid longius et incertum habere utrum animal sit an saxum, vel quid aliud, meque tibi dicere, "quia homo est, animal est"; nonne temere dicerem?

AD. Temere omnino, sed non temere plane diceres "si homo est, animal est."

AU. Recte dicis. Itaque in locutione tua placet mihi "si," placet et tibi: utrique autem nostrum in mea displicet "quia."

AD. Assentior.

AU. Vide iam utrum istae duae sententiae plene pronuntiatae sint: "placet si," "displicet quia."

AD. Plena omnino.

AU. Age nunc dic mihi quae ibi sint verba, quae nomina.

AD. Verba ibi video esse "placet" et "displicet": nomina vero quid aliud quam "si" et "quia"?

AU. Has ergo duas coniunctiones etiam nomina esse satis probatum est.

AD. Prorsus satis.

AU. Potesne ipse per te in aliis partibus orationis hoc idem ad eandem regulam docere?

AD. Possum.

[17] quo S^1 μ: quod *V B R S T*

AU. So if I only said "sits," or "runs," you would be right to ask me, "who?" or "what," prompting me to answer, "a person" or "a horse," or "a living creature," or whatever you like, so that the name-word you supplied for the verb could complete the proposition—in other words a sentence, which can be affirmative or negative.

AD. I understand.

AU. Now listen to what follows. Imagine that I see something quite a way off, and I'm unsure whether it is a living creature or a rock, or something else, and I say to you, "because it is a person, it is a living creature"; wouldn't I be speaking carelessly?

AD. Yes, very carelessly. But you certainly wouldn't be careless if you said, "if it is a person, it is a living creature."

AU. That's right. So when you say "if," you and I both agree. Whereas both of us disagree with my "because."

AD. Agreed.

AU. Now see whether these two sentences have formed complete propositions: "I am pleased if"; "I disagree because."

AD. Absolutely not.

AU. Now then, tell me which are the verbs in that speech act, and which are the name-words.

AD. The verbs I see there are "agree" and "disagree": the name-words can only be "if" and "because."

AU. I think we have adequately proved that these two conjunctions are also name-words.

AD. Undoubtedly.

AU. On the same principle, can you produce this same outcome in the other parts of speech on your own?

AD. I can.

17 6. AU. Transeamus[18] hinc et iam dic mihi utrum sicut omnia verba nomina, et omnia nomina verba esse comperimus, ita tibi et omnia nomina vocabula, et omnia vocabula nomina esse videantur.

AD. Plane inter haec quid distet praeter diversum syllabarum sonum non video.

AU. Nec ego interim resisto, quamquam non desint qui etiam significatione ista discernunt, quorum sententiam modo considerare non opus est. Sed certe animadvertis ad ea iam signa nos pervenisse, quae se invicem significent, nulla praeter sonum distantia, et quae seipsa significent cum ceteris omnibus partibus orationis.

AD. Non intellego.

AU. Non ergo intellegis et nomen vocabulo et vocabulum nomine significari; et ita ut praeter sonum litterarum nihil intersit, quantum ad generale nomen pertinet: nam et speciale nomen dicimus, quod inter octo partes orationis ita est, ut alias septem non contineat.

AD. Intellego.

AU. At hoc est quod dixi, se invicem significare vocabulum et nomen.

18 AD. Teneo, sed quaero quid dixeris: cum etiam seipsa significant cum aliis partibus orationis.

[18] transeamus ergo μ

---

[69] This could be the sound difference between a three- and a four-syllable word (*nomina*, *vocabula*); or of the units of sound/rhythm that are syllables composed of differing letter sounds. Artistic Latin used syllables as units of measurement that could be arranged to fulfill the function performed, in English, by punctuation.

6. AU. Let's move on from this. Now tell me whether, 17
just as we have established that all words are name-words and all name-words are words, you think that likewise all name-words are appellations, and all appellations are name-words.

AD. I really don't see any difference, apart from the different sound of the syllables.[69]

AU. For now, then, I'm making no objection, though there are those who differentiate what they refer to. There's no need to give consideration here to their view. But you must have noticed that we've finally come to those signs that mutually signify each other, differing in nothing except their sound,[70] and that signify themselves along with all the other parts of speech.

AD. I don't understand.

AU. So you don't understand that on the one hand "name-word" is signified by "appellation," and, on the other hand, "appellation" is signified by "name-word," in such a way that nothing, apart from the sound of the letters, separates them?—at least insofar as general meaning of "name-word" is concerned. For we also use "name-word" in a technical sense,[71] which is one of the eight parts of speech, and which excludes the other seven.

AD. I understand.

AU. That's what I said, though: appellation and name-word each signify the other.

AD. I get that. But I'm asking why you said, "when 18
they also signify themselves along with the other parts of speech."

[70] Synonyms.
[71] That is, as "noun."

AU. Nonne superior ratio docuit nos omnes partes orationis, et nomina posse dici et vocabula, id est et nomine et vocabulo posse significari?

AD. Ita est.

AU. Quid? ipsum nomen, id est sonum[19] istum duabus syllabis expressum, si ex te quaeram quid appelles, nonne recte mihi respondebis, "nomen"?

AD. Recte.

AU. Num ita se significat hoc signum quod quattuor syllabis enuntiamus cum dicimus "coniunctio"? Hoc enim nomen inter illa quae significat numerari non potest.

AD. Accipio.

AU. Id est quod dictum est nomen seipsum significare cum aliis quae significat; quod etiam de vocabulo per teipsum licet intellegas.[20]

AD. Iam facile est: sed illud mihi nunc venit in mentem, nomen et generaliter et specialiter dici; vocabulum autem inter octo partes orationis non accipi. Quare hoc quoque ‹non› nihil[21] inter se praeter diversum sonum differre arbitror.

AU. Quid? nomen et *ὄνομα* distare inter se aliquid putas praeter sonum, quo etiam linguae discernuntur Latina atque Graeca?

AD. Hic vero nihil aliud intellego.

[19] sonum *B*: nomen *S T*

[20] Id est . . . intellegas *om. V*

[21] nihil *del μ Daur*: ‹non› nihil *suppl.* {*sic: vere coni.*} *Weig.*: quoque nihil *MSS*

AU. Hasn't higher reasoning taught us that all the parts of speech can be called name-words and appellations—in other words that they can be signified by a name-word and by an appellation?

AD. Yes.

AU. Right: if I ask you what you call "name-word" itself—that two-syllable utterance, in other words—won't you correctly answer me, "name-word"?

AD. That's right.

AU. What about the sign that we articulate with three syllables when we say "conjunction"—that doesn't signify itself in this way, does it? This name-word can't be counted as an example of what it signifies.

AD. Granted.

AU. That's what's been said, that "name-word" signifies itself along with the other things which it signifies. You can also understand for yourself the same point in the case of "appellation."

AD. Now it's simple. But something just occurred to me: "name-word" is spoken both with a meaning that is general and with one that is precise. "Appellation," though, is not included among the eight parts of speech.[72] For this reason, I judge that they differ somewhat in this respect too, besides their different sound.

AU. Right, do you think that there is some distinction between "name-word" and *onoma*,[73] apart from their sound, by which we tell the Greek and Latin languages apart?

AD. I perceive no other distinction, no.

[72] That is, not a technical term for describing a grammatical category. [73] The Greek equivalent of "name-word/noun."

AU. Perventum est ergo ad ea signa quae et seipsa significent; et aliud ab alio invicem significetur; et quidquid ab uno hoc et ab alio; et nihil praeter sonum inter se differant: nam hoc quartum[22] modo invenimus; tria enim superiora et de nomine et verbo intelleguntur.

AD. Omnino perventum.

19 7. AU. Iam quae sermocinando invenerimus, velim recenseas.

AD. Faciam quantum possum. Nam primo omnium recordor aliquamdiu nos quaesisse quam ob causam loquamur, inventumque esse docendi commemorandive gratia nos loqui, quandoquidem nec cum interrogamus aliud agimus quam ut ille qui rogatur discat quid velimus audire; et in cantando, quod delectationis causa facere videmur, non sit proprium locutionis; in orando deo,[23] quem doceri aut commemorari existimare non possumus, id verba valeant, ut vel nos ipsos commonefaciamus, vel alii commemorentur doceanturve per nos. Deinde cum satis constitisset verba nihil aliud esse quam signa, ea vero quae non aliquid significent signa esse non posse, proposuisti versum, cuius verba singula quid significarent, conarer ostendere: is autem erat:

Si nihil ex tanta superis placet urbe relinqui.

22 quartum] quarto *H S T*
23 deo *B* μ: *om. S*

---

74 Getting Adeodatus to summarize the argument's progress marks a shift in the dialogue, but it is also a likely reflection of Augustine's teaching method.

AU. So we have reached a conclusion: there are signs which signify themselves; signs which signify each other reciprocally; signs where whatever is signified by the one is signified also by the other; and signs where the only difference between them is one of sound. This fourth one we have only just discovered, for the first three are also understood apropos to name-words and verbs.

AD. Yes, that's our conclusion.

7. AU. Now I would like you to review what we have 19
discovered in our dialogue.[74]

AD. I will do my best. The first thing I recall is our spending some time investigating the reason why we speak, and we found that we speak as a means of teaching or commemorating. This is because when we're asking questions, all that we're really doing is to teach the person we're asking what we want to hear. As for singing, which we apparently do purely for pleasure, this is not strictly anything to do with speaking. When it comes to our prayers to God, we can't believe that he needs to be taught anything, or have anything commemorated for him, so then the power that our words possess is either to tell ourselves to be mindful of something, or to commemorate others, or to teach them.[75] Next, after it was pretty well established that words are nothing other than signs, while whatever does not signify anything cannot be a sign, you suggested a line of poetry, and I tried to show what its individual words signified. This is the line:

If nothing from this city remains, gods decree.[76]

[75] These three possibilities are all purposes of prayer distinct from information-transfer to God. [76] Above, 2.3.

Cuius secundum verbum quamvis notissimum et manifestissimum, quid tamen[24] significaret, non reperiebamus. Cumque mihi videretur non frustra nos id in loquendo interponere, sed quod eo aliquid doceamus audientem, ipsam mentis affectionem, cum rem quam quaerit non esse invenit vel invenisse se putat, hoc verbo fortasse indicari respondisti tu quidem, sed tamen nescio quam profunditatem quaestionis ioco evitans in aliud tempus illustrandam distulisti: ne me debiti quoque tui oblitum putes!

Inde tertium in versu verbum cum satagerem exponere, urgebar verbum pandere.[25] Urgebar abs te ut non verbum aliud quod idem valeret, sed rem ipsam potius quae verbo[26] significaretur ostenderem; cumque id sermocinantibus nobis fieri non posse dixissem, ventum est ad ea quae interrogantibus digito monstrantur. Haec ego corporalia esse omnia arbitrabar, sed invenimus sola visibilia.

Hinc nescio quomodo ad surdos et histriones devenimus, qui non quae sola videri possunt, sed multa praeterea ac prope omnia quae loquimur, gestu sine voce significant; eosdem tamen gestus signa esse comperimus. Tunc rursus quaerere coepimus, quomodo res ipsas quae signis significantur, sine ullis signis valeremus ostendere, cum et ille paries et color et omne visibile quod intentione digiti ostenditur, signo quodam convinceretur ostendi. Hic ego[27] errans cum inveniri tale nihil posse dixissem, tandem inter nos constitit, ea posse demonstrari sine signo,

24 tandem *Daur*
25 urgebar verbum pandere *B R V S H T*: *del.* μ
26 verbo] per verba μ
27 ego *B* μ *r*: ergo *S T J M*

Its second word is particularly familiar and ubiquitous, but we could not determine what it signified. And just when I began to think that we don't insert it into our speech acts to no purpose, but that we do use it to teach something to the person listening, I'm sure that you replied that this word perhaps indicates that state of mind when you look for something, but find—or think you've found—that it doesn't exist. Still you avoided that element of philosophical thought, and used a joke to postpone explaining it for another day. Don't think I have forgotten your obligation!

Next I did my best to explain the third word of the line, "from." You encouraged me to unpack the word. But what you were encouraging me to do was not to produce some other word with the same meaning, but rather the actual thing that that word was signifying. And when I said that I couldn't do so while we were still engaged in our dialogue, we moved on to things we can use a finger to point to when someone asks us something. I used to think that all these things are physical; but we discovered that only the things we can see are.

From here we somehow ended up on deaf people and actors, who use gesture without speech, to signify not only visible things but many others, and in fact almost everything we speak of. We found those same gestures to be signs. After that we began to ask once more how, without signs of any kind, we might have the capacity to point out the actual things which are signified by signs: for we established that the barrier there, and color, and everything we see, which can be indicated by a pointing finger, was being made known by some kind of sign. At this point I made a mistake by saying that such a thing couldn't be found, and in the end we came to an agreement that point-

quae cum a nobis quaeruntur, non agimus, et post inquisitionem agere possumus; locutionem tamen ex eo non esse genere, siquidem et loquentes cum interrogamur quid sit locutio ipsa per seipsam demonstrare facile esse satis apparuit.

20 Ex quo admoniti sumus aut signis signa monstrari, aut signis alia quae signa non sunt, aut etiam sine signo res quas agere post interrogationem possumus: horumque trium primum diligentius considerandum discutiendumque suscepimus.

Qua disputatione declaratum est partim esse signa, quae ab his signis quae significarent significari vicissim non possent, ut est hoc quadrisyllabum cum "coniunctio," dicimus; partim quae possent, ut cum dicimus "signum," etiam verbum significamus, et cum dicimus "verbum," etiam signum significamus; nam signum et verbum et duo signa et duo verba sunt. In hoc autem genere, quo invicem se signa significant, quaedam non tantum, quaedam tantum, quaedam vero etiam idem valere monstratum est. Etenim hoc disyllabum, quod sonat cum dicimus "signum," prorsus omnia quibus quidque significatur significat: non autem omnium signorum signum est cum dicimus "verbum," sed tantum eorum quae articulata voce proferuntur. Unde manifestum est, quamvis et verbum signo, et signum verbo, id est et duae istae syllabae illis et illae

---

77 In the Latin a disyllable, *signum*.

78 Namely, syllable (two each in Latin).

ing things out without signs is possible, if we are not doing them at the point when we're being asked (but then we can do them after being questioned). Even so, we agreed, speech is not in this category, since it was fairly obvious that if we are speaking in reply, when being asked what speech itself is, it is a simple matter to manifest the thing itself.

Following on from this, we were reminded that either 20
signs are demonstrated by signs, or some things that are not signs are demonstrated by signs; or that things that we are able to enact after we've been questioned about them can also be demonstrated without a sign. Of these three possibilities, we set about investigating and analyzing the first in greater depth.

This debate led to the conclusion that on the one hand there are signs that cannot be conversely signified by these signs that they signify—for example the trisyllabic word "conjunction"; and on the other there are those that can—for example, when we say "sign," we are also signifying a word; and when we say "word," we are also signifying a sign; for "sign" and "word" are two signs and also two words. But in this category in which signs signify one another conversely, it became evident that some do not have an equivalent range of meaning, others do, while yet others have precisely the same range of meaning. Indeed the syllable which resounds when we say "sign"[77] certainly signifies all the things by which each thing is signified: but when we say "word," that is not a sign of every sign; it signifies only those things that are given vocal utterance. From this is it apparent that although "word" is signified by "sign" and vice versa—to be precise, the sound unit[78] of the first term is signified by that of the second and vice

istis significentur, plus tamen signum valere quam verbum, plura scilicet illis duabus syllabis, quam istis significantibus.

Tantundem autem valet generale verbum, et generale nomen. Docuit enim[28] ratio omnes partes orationis etiam nomina esse, quod et pronomina his addi possunt, et de omnibus dici potest quod aliquid nominent, et[29] nulla earum sit quae non verbo adiuncto pronuntiatum possit implere. Sed cum tantundem valeant nomen et verbum, eo quod omnia quae verba sunt, sint etiam nomina; non tamen idem valent. Alia quippe de causa verba, et alia nomina nuncupari, satis probabiliter disputatum est. Siquidem alterum horum ad auris verberationem, alterum ad animi commemorationem notandam[30] esse compertum, vel ex hoc intellegi potest, quod in loquendo rectissime dicimus "quod est huic rei nomen," rem memoriae mandare cupientes; "quod est autem huic rei verbum," dicere non solemus. Quae vero non solum tantundem, sed etiam idem omnino significent, et inter quae nihil praeter litterarum distet sonum, nomen et *ὄνομα* invenimus. Illud sane mihi elapsum erat in hoc genere, in quo invicem se significant, nullum nos signum comperisse, quod non inter cetera quae significat, se quoque significet. Haec quantum

[28] enim *S*: ergo *B* [29] et *B S T μ*: ut *J M*
[30] notandam *μ*: notandum *B R*^{1} *V S T*

---

[79] 5.13. [80] 5.13–16.

[81] The shift between *verbum* meaning "word" (when coupled with "sign") to *verbum* meaning "verb" (when associated with "name-word" in the sense of "noun") is potentially confusing.

[82] The Greek and the Latin terms for "name": like Latin,

versa—"sign" still has a greater range of meaning than "word": for the sound-unit "sign" signifies more things than the sound-unit "word" does.

Still, "word," used generally, has the same force as "name-word" generally does. Reason has taught us that all the parts of speech are also name-words, because pronouns can be applied to them;[79] and because we can say of all of them that they are naming something; and because every one of them can be combined with a verb to complete a proposition.[80] But although "name-word"[81] and "word" have the same degree of meaning, insofar as everything that is a word is also a name-word, they don't have the same actual meaning. We calculated that it is fairly likely they are termed "words" for one purpose, and "name-words/nouns" for another. If we found that one of them denotes a sound striking the ear, while the other denotes a mental commemoration, we could perhaps understand why it is that when speaking with precision we say "what is the name for this thing?" because we want to commit it to memory; we don't tend to say "what is the word for this thing?" We discovered that "name-word" and *onoma*[82] not only signify to the same extent but also signify exactly the same thing; and that nothing distinguishes them but the sound of their component letters. Admittedly one point did escape me: in the category of things that signify one another reciprocally, we didn't find a single sign which (amid the other things it signifies) doesn't also signify itself. This is as much as I have managed to remember. Now you can see whether I've described these

Greek *onoma* can mean "noun" (the Greek equivalent of "verb"/ *verbum* is *rhēma*).

potui recordatus sum. Tu iam videris, quem nihil puto in hoc sermone nisi scientem certumque dixisse, utrum ista bene ordinateque digesserim.

21 8. AU. Satis tu quidem memoriter omnia quae vellem recoluisti, et, ut tibi fatear, multo evidentius mihi nunc videntur ista distincta, quam cum ea inquirendo ac disserendo de nescio quibus latebris ambo erueremus.

Sed quonam tantis ambagibus tecum pervenire moliar, difficile dictu est hoc loco. Tu enim fortasse aut ludere nos, et a seriis rebus avocare animum, quasi quibusdam puerilibus quaestiunculis, arbitraris, aut parvam vel mediocrem aliquam utilitatem requirere; aut si magnum quiddam parturire istam disputationem suspicaris, iamiamque id scire sive saltem audire desideras. Ego autem credas velim neque me vilia ludicra hoc instituisse sermone, quamvis fortasse ludamus, idque ipsum tamen non puerili sensu aestimandum sit, neque parva bona vel mediocria cogitare. Et tamen si dicam vitam esse quandam beatam, eandemque sempiternam, quo nos deo duce, id est ipsa veritate, gradibus quibusdam infirmo gressui nostro accommodatis perduci cupiam, vereor ne ridiculus videar, qui non rerum ipsarum quae significantur, sed signorum consideratione tantam viam ingredi coeperim.

Dabis igitur veniam si praeludo tecum non ludendi gratia, sed exercendi vires et mentis aciem, quibus regionis illius, ubi beata vita est, calorem ac lucem non modo sustinere, verum et amare possimus.

---

[83] *quaestiuncula*, ae, *f.*, a dimininutive of *quaestio*; probably borrowed from Cic. *De or.* 1.22.102, *Leg.* 2.20.51; cf. Sen. *Ep.* 117.1; Suet. *Gram. et rhet.* 24.

matters properly, and in the right order; because I don't think you said anything in this discussion that you weren't firmly convinced of.

8. AU. Your recollection of all that I wanted you to 21
remember is pretty good, and to tell the truth, all those distinctions seem far clearer to me now than when the two of us together were using questioning and discussion to unearth them from wherever they were lurking.

But at this point it's difficult to explain where I am trying to get to with you, by means of these long digressions. Perhaps you think that we're messing around, and distracting our minds from serious matters, with supposedly childish and trivial questions;[83] or that what we seek is something worthwhile, but hardly momentous. Or if you suppose that our argument is laboring to give birth to something significant, you're already longing to know what it is, or at least to hear about it. I would like you to trust me not to use our conversation to work out some silly triviality, for even if there is an element of playfulness in it, the subject itself is still not to be esteemed as a childish notion, reflecting on insignificant or marginal benefits. Yet if I were to state that there is such a thing as the blessed life, and that it is everlasting, and that I long for us to be led there, with God to guide us—in other words with Truth itself—step by step, adapted to our faltering pace, I'm afraid of sounding like a fool: because I began my journey on this noble path by reflecting on signs, and not on the realities that they signify.

So you will forgive me if I play out this scenario with you, not merely for playing's sake but as a way of training our mental strength and focus. This way, we won't only be able to experience the warmth and brightness of that realm where life is blessed, but also to love it.

AD. Perge potius ut coepisti: nam numquam ego contemnenda putem quae tu dicenda vel agenda putaveris.

22 AU. Age iam ergo illam partem consideremus, cum signis non alia signa significantur, sed ea quae significabilia vocamus. Et primum dic mihi utrum homo, homo sit.

AD. Nunc vero an ludas[31] nescio.

AU. Quid ita?

AD. Quia quaerendum ex me censes, utrum homo aliud sit quam homo.

AU. Ita credo te illudi arbitrareris, si etiam quaererem utrum prima huius nominis syllaba aliud sit quam "ho-," et aliud secunda quam "-mo."

AD. Ita omnino.

AU. At istae duae syllabae coniunctae homo est: an negabis?

AD. Quis neget?

AU. Quaero ergo, num tu duae istae syllabae coniunctae sis.

AD. Nullo modo: sed video quo tendas.

AU. Dicito ergo, ne me contumeliosum putes.

AD. Concludi existimas quod homo non sim.

AU. Quid? tu non idem existimas, qui omnia superiora ex quibus hoc confectum est, vera esse concedis?

AD. Non tibi ego dicam quid existimem, nisi prius abs te audiero, cum quaereres utrum homo homo sit, de dua-

[31] ludas *B*: laudas *T*: inludas me *S H*: illudas me *S*[1]

---

[84] See 4.8, 10.

[85] Translating *homo* thus provides two syllables rather than the one in "man," and also embraces both noun and adjective.

AD. Please keep going as you began. I would never think of undervaluing anything you thought was worth saying or doing.

AU. Right then, let's reflect on that group of signs 22
which do not signify other signs but instead what we call signifiables.[84] Now first, tell me whether "human" is human.

AD. I can't tell now if you are joking.

AU. How so?

AD. Because you are proposing to inquire of me whether a human is something other than "a human."[85]

AU. Is that so? Then I believe you would think you were being made a fool of if I asked you whether the first syllable of this name-word is anything other than "hu-," and the second anything but "-man."

AD. Frankly, I would.

AU. But join them together and these two syllables make "hu-man": don't you agree?

AD. Who wouldn't?

AU. Right: so I'm asking whether you are these two syllables joined together.

AD. By no means! But I can see where you're going with this.

AU. Tell me, then, so you don't think I'm insulting your intelligence.

AD. You reckon the answer is that I am not human.

AU. And? Don't you reckon the same thing? Don't you admit that everything we dealt with already is true, and that this argument was constructed from it?

AD. I shan't tell you what I reckon, unless I first hear this from you: when you were asking whether a human is

bus istis syllabis, an de re ipsa quam significant, me interrogaveris?

AU. Tu potius responde ex qua parte acceperis interrogationem meam: nam si est ambigua, prius hoc cavere debuisti, neque mihi respondere antequam certus fieres quonam modo rogaverim.

AD. Quid enim me impediret haec ambiguitas, cum ego ad utrumque responderim; homo enim prorsus homo est: nam et istae duae syllabae nihil[32] aliud sunt quam istae duae syllabae; et id quod significant, nihil aliud est, quam id quod est.

AU. Scite hoc quidem! Sed cur hoc solum quod dictum est homo, non etiam cetera quae locuti sumus, ad utrumque accepisti?

AD. Unde enim convincor quod et cetera non sic acceperim?

AU. Ut alia omittam, eam ipsam primam rogationem meam si totam ex ea parte accepisses, qua syllabae sonant, nihil mihi respondisses; possem tibi enim videri nihil etiam interrogasse. Nunc vero cum tria verba sonuerim, quorum unum in medio repetivi dicens "utrum homo homo sit," primum et ultimum verbum, non secundum ipsa signa, sed secundum ea quae his significantur te accepisse, vel hoc solo manifestum est quod statim certus ac fidens rogationi respondendum putasti.

AD. Verum dicis.

AU. Cur ergo id tantum quod in medio positum est, et secundum id quod sonat, et secundum id quod significat, te accipere libuit?

[32] nihil . . . syllabae *om. S*

---

[86] In Latin, "middle."

"human," was your question to me referring to those two syllables ("hu-" and "-man") or to the actual thing which they signify?

AU. No, first you reply in what sense you are taking my questioning. For if it is ambiguous, you should have been careful first, and not replied before you were sure of how I meant the question.

AD. Why should this ambiguity stand in the way of my responding to both senses? A human is certainly "human": for its two syllables are nothing other than two syllables; and what they signify is nothing but what actually is.

AU. That's a good one! But why only this example we spoke: "human"? Why not also take the other terms we mentioned in both senses?

AD. Where did you prove that I didn't take the other terms both ways?

AU. Here's one example: if you had accepted that very first question of mine wholly in terms of the sound of its syllables, you would not have given me an answer. I could have seemed to you as if I was asking nothing at all. Now, though, I have given voice to three words, and repeated the second[86] one, saying "whether human is 'human,'" and it's perhaps apparent just from this that you accepted the other two words[87] not as signs in and of themselves, but as the things which they signify; because you were instantly certain and confident that the question had to be answered.

AD. You're right.

AU. So why were you willing to take only the word that was in the middle ("human") in its dual sense—both the sound it makes and the thing it signifies?

[87] In Latin, "the first and last" ("whether" and "is").

AD. Ecce iam totum ex ea tantum parte qua significatur accipio. Assentior enim tibi sermocinari nos omnino non posse, nisi auditis verbis ad ea feratur animus, quorum ista sunt signa. Quare ostende nunc, quomodo ista ratiocinatione deceptus sim, qua me hominem non esse concluditur.

AU. Immo eadem rursus interrogabo, ut ipse invenias ubi lapsus sis.

AD. Bene facis.[33]

23 AU. Illud ergo quod primo quaesieram, quia iam[34] dedisti, non quaeram. Vide igitur diligentius utrum syllaba "ho-," nihil aliud sit quam "ho-," et utrum "-mo" nihil aliud sit quam "-mo."

AD. Hic prorsus nihil aliud video.

AU. Vide etiam num istis[35] duabus iunctis "homo" fiat.

AD. Nequaquam hoc concesserim; placuit enim et recte placuit signo dato id quod significatur attendere, et ex eius consideratione vel dare vel negare quod dicitur. Illae autem separatim enuntiatae syllabae, quia sine ulla significatione sonuerunt, hoc eas esse quod sonuere concessum est.

AU. Placet igitur[36] firmumque animo tenes non respondendum esse interrogationibus, nisi ex his rebus quae verbis significantur.

[33] facis *B*: facies *S H T* [34] iam ‹non› *Daur*

[35] istis *J M*: his *B R V S H T*

[36] placet igitur *B S^1*: Ad. placet Ag igitur *S T*

---

[88] In philosophy, *dare* refers to granting a proposition (e.g., Cic. *Fin*. 5.28.83; *Tusc*. 1.11.25; *Inv. rhet.* 1.31).

AD. Look: now I'm going to take the whole thing only in the sense of what's signified. I agree with you that we cannot hold a rational dialogue at all unless our minds are carried to those things that are signified when we hear their corresponding words. So tell me now how I was tricked by your Socratic method into concluding that I am not a human.

AU. No, but I will ask the same questions again, so that you discover for yourself where you went astray.

AD. Thanks.

AU. I shan't reiterate what I first asked, since you have 23
already ceded the point.[88] So look more carefully: are the syllables "hu-" and "-man" anything other than "hu-" and "-man"?

AD. I really can't detect anything else.

AU. Now look—can a "human" come into being when the two syllables are joined together?

AD. I should never have agreed to that. It was acceptable—and rightly so—to pay attention to what is being signified when a sign is used, and, in accordance with that scrutiny, to approve or reject what is being said. But because those syllables, when sounded separately, signify no meaning, we accepted the point that they are sounds, nothing more.[89]

AU. You agree, therefore, and are entirely convinced, that we should give no answer to questions except in accordance with those things that the words signify.

[89] That is, the first syllable of *homo* can only be part of a word, whereas saying "hu" in English is a homophone for "hew" and for the name "Huw/Hugh," i.e., it can be a complete sense unit.

AD. Non intellego cur displiceat si modo verba sint.

AU. Vellem scire quomodo illi resisteres, de quo iocantes solemus audire, quod ex eius ore cum quo disputabat, leonem processisse concluserit. Cum enim quaesisset utrum ea quae loqueremur nostro ore procederent, atque ille non potuisset negare, quod facile fuit, egit cum homine ut in loquendo leonem nominaret. Hoc ubi factum est, ridicule insultare coepit et premere, ut quoniam quicquid loquimur, ore nostro exire confessus erat, et leonem se locutum esse nequibat abnuere, homo non malus tam immanem bestiam vomuisse videretur!

AD. Minime vero erat arduum scurrae huic resistere; non enim concederem[37] ore nostro exire quaecumque loquimur. Nam quae loquimur, ea significamus; non autem res quae significatur, sed signum quo significatur loquentis ore procedit, nisi cum ipsa signa[38] significantur, quod genus paulo ante tractavimus.

24 AU. Bene tu quidem hoc modo adversus illum esses paratus. Verumtamen mihi quid respondebis, utrum homo nomen sit requirenti?

AD. Quid, nisi esse nomen?

AU. Quid? cum te video, num nomen video?

AD. Non.

AU. Visne igitur dicam quod sequitur?

AD. Ne quaeso; nam mihi ipse renuntio me hominem non esse, qui nomen esse responderim, cum homo utrum

[37] concederem . . . loquimur ea *B*: condere ore nostro exire quae loquimur ea *S T* [38] signa *om.* *B S T*

---

[90] That is, speak words for things.

AD. I don't see why this would be unacceptable—so long as they really are words.

AU. I would like to know how you would counter the man we commonly hear about by way of a joke; because when he was in an argument with someone, he concluded that a lion had issued from their mouth. For after he had asked the other person whether the things that we say issue from our mouths, and his interlocutor was unable to disagree, he took the next step, an easy one, and engineered a way to make them say the name-word, "lion." Once this was achieved, he began to jeer, and pressure them, so after they admitted that whatever we speak issues from our mouth (and they could not deny that they had said "lion") a perfectly decent person apparently spewed out a savage beast!

AD. It was hardly difficult to counter this comedian, as I would not admit that whatever we speak comes out of our mouth. That's because when we say things[90] we are signifying them: what issues from our mouth is not the thing being signified, but a sign to signify that thing—except when signs themselves are being signified, and we dealt with that category just now.

AU. That way you were certainly well-prepared to face 24
him. Nevertheless how will you answer me, if I ask you whether "human" is a name-word?

AD. What else but "yes, it is"?

AU. What if I look at you, am I really looking at a name word?

AD. No.

AU. Now do you want me to say what comes next?

AD. Please don't. I freely admit I'm not a human, because I answered "name-word" when you asked if "hu-

nomen esset inquireres. Iam enim placuerat ex ea re quae significaretur aut assentiri aut negare quod dicitur.

AU. At mihi videtur non te frustra in hanc responsionem decidisse; nam vigilantiam tuam mentibus nostris indita[39] ipsa lex rationis evicit. Nam si quaererem quid esset homo, responderes fortasse "animal"; si autem quaererem quae pars orationis esset homo, nullo modo posses recte respondere nisi "nomen." Quam ob rem cum homo et nomen et animal esse inveniatur, illud dicitur ex ea parte qua signum est, hoc[40] qua[41] significat.[42] Qui ergo quaerit utrum homo nomen sit, nihil ei aliud quam esse respondeam: satis enim significat ex ea parte se velle audire, qua signum est. Si autem quaerit utrum animal sit, multo proclivius adnuam: quoniam si tacens et nomen et animal, tantum quid esset[43] homo requireret, placita illa loquendi regula ad id quod duabus syllabis significatur, animus curreret; neque quicquam responderetur nisi animal, vel etiam tota definitio diceretur, id est animal rationale mortale: an tibi non videtur?

AD. Prorsus videtur. Sed cum esse nomen concesserimus, quomodo illam conclusionem nimis contumeliosam evitabimus, qua nos homines non esse conficitur?[44]

[39] indita *S T*: inditam *J M*: indicia *B*

[40] *post* hoc *suppl.* ex parte rei *μ*

[41] qua *B*: quia *S*: quasi *T*

[42] significat *B S H μ*: significatur *Daur*: *vel* quam significat *vel* quae significatur *coni. Weig.*

[43] T *f.102v hinc m. al.*

[44] conficitur *J M μ*: convincitur *B R V S T*

man" is a "name-word." After all, we'd already agreed either to affirm or deny what is said in accordance with the thing that signified it.[91]

AU. Even so I think there was something positive about your stumbling into this reply. The law of reason itself, bestowed upon our minds, has overcome your caution. For if I asked what a human was, you would perhaps answer "a living creature"; but if I asked what part of speech "human" was, the only correct answer you could give would be "name-word." When "human" is found to be both a name-word and a living creature, therefore, the former is a statement applied to its being in the category of signs; while the latter is about how it functions as a sign. So when someone asks if "human" is a name-word, the only reply I could give would be "yes": for they are signifying adequately that they want to hear in what respect, precisely, it is a sign. But if they ask whether it's a living creature, I can much more readily assent, for as they made no mention of "name-word" or "living creature," and asked only what "human" was, in agreement with an established rule in speaking their mind jumps to what is signified by the two syllables. The only possible answer would be "a living creature," or, to give the fuller definition, "a living creature that is rational and mortal." Or do you disagree?

AD. I agree completely. But once we've ceded the point that "human" is a name-word, how shall we avoid the totally objectionable conclusion which makes us out not to be human?

91 *TT* 8.23.

AU. Quomodo putas, nisi docendo non ex ea parte illatam, qua interroganti assentiebamur? Aut si ex ea parte illam se fatetur inferre, nullo modo est formidanda. Quid enim metuam hominem, id est tres istas syllabas non esse me confiteri?

AD. Nihil est verius. Cur ergo animum offendit, cum dicitur "non es igitur homo," cum secundum illa concessa nihil verius dici potuerit?

AU. Quia non possum[45] non putare ad id conclusionem referri, quod his duabus syllabis significatur, simul atque ista verba sonuerint, ea scilicet regula, quae naturaliter plurimum valet, ut auditis signis ad res significatas feratur intentio.

AD. Accipio quod dicis.

9. AU. Proinde[46] intellegas volo, res quae significantur pluris quam signa esse pendendas. Quicquid enim propter aliud est, vilius sit necesse est quam id propter quod est; nisi tu aliud existimas.

AD. Videtur mihi non temere hic esse assentiendum: nam cum dicimus "caenum," longe hoc nomen arbitror rei quam significat antecellere. Quod enim nos offendit audientes non ad ipsius verbi pertinet sonum; caenum enim nomen, mutata una littera caelum est. Inter illa vero quae his nominibus significantur quantum distet videmus. Quam ob rem nequaquam huic signo tribuerim, quod in

45 possum *B S T* μ: possumus *S*[1]
46 proinde *B S T*: iam ergo μ

---

92 *ho-mo* in the accusative case has three syllables, *ho-mi-nem.*
93 *Caenum/caelum.* "Filth/faith" comes close.

AU. How do you think? By proving that it has not been inferred in accordance with the sense in which we gave assent to the questioner. But if they then claim that they were inferring it in that sense, it won't bother us at all. After all, why would I be afraid of admitting that I am not those two syllables?[92]

AD. Exactly. Why would it trouble our thinking if someone says, "therefore you are not human," when according to the alternative meaning no truer word could be said?

AU. Because I have to believe that the moment those words sound aloud, we are brought back to that conclusion, namely what is being signified by the two syllables. Surely there's a naturally dominant principle at work here, that when signs are audible, they draw our attention to the things which are signified.

AD. I agree with you.

9. AU. Now then, I want you to understand this: things 25
which are being signified must be regarded as more important than the signs that signify them. This is because anything that exists on account of something else has to be less valuable that the thing for which it exists—or do you disagree?

AD. I don't think I should agree to that too rashly. For when we say "filth," I judge this name-word is far superior to than the thing that it signifies. After all, what disgusts us when we hear it is nothing to do with the actual sound of the word; "filth" is a name-word, but change a single letter and there you have "heaven."[93] Certainly there is a yawning gap plain to see between the realities these two name-words signify. That's why there's no way I could ever apply to the sign what disgusts us in the reality it signifies.

re quam significat odimus; et propterea hoc illi iure antepono: libentius enim hoc audimus, quam ullo sensu illud attingimus.

AU. Vigilantissime omnino. Itaque falsum est omnes res pluris quam earum signa esse pendendas.

AD. Ita videtur.

AU. Dic ergo mihi quid arbitreris eos secutos esse qui huic rei tam foedae atque aspernabili nomen indiderunt; vel utrum eos probes an improbes.

AD. Ego vero illos nec probare nec improbare audeo, nec quid fuerint secuti scio.

AU. Potesne saltem scire quid tu sequaris, cum hoc nomen enuntias?

AD. Hoc plane possum: nam significare volo, ut eum cum quo loquor[47] doceam vel admoneam de re illa, quod eum doceri vel admoneri oportere arbitror.

AU. Quid? ipsum docere aut admonere (sive doceri aut admoneri) quod vel tu exhibes commode per hoc nomen vel exhibetur tibi; nonne carius quam ipsum nomen habendum est?

AD. Concedo ipsam scientiam quae per hoc signum evenit eidem signo esse anteponendam; sed non ideo etiam rem ipsam[48] puto.

26 AU. In illa igitur sententia nostra, quamquam sit falsum res omnes signis suis praeponi oportere, non tamen falsum est omne quod propter aliud est, vilius esse quam

[47] loquor] loquar *B R V S T*
[48] rem ipsam *B T*: ipsius rei *S H*

And that's why I'm right to prefer the word for filth to the reality it signifies: for we are happier to hear the word than to have contact—by any of our senses—with the reality.[94]

AU. That's certainly ultracautious. So it is incorrect to consider all things as more positive than what they signify.

AD. It looks like it.

AU. Now tell me what you judge was the aim of those who applied this name-word to something so foul and repellent—and whether you approve or disapprove of them.

AD. I don't presume to approve or disapprove of them, and I have no idea what may have been their aim.

AU. But you surely can know what you are aiming at when you speak this name-word aloud?

AD. Certainly I can: I want to use a sign for something so as to teach or remind whoever I'm talking to about the thing itself, because I judge that they ought to be taught or reminded of it.

AU. What about the actual content of the teaching or reminding (or being taught or reminded), which you perhaps use this name-word to show (or be shown)? Surely it should be taken as more valuable than the actual name-word?

AD. I accept that the actual knowledge that proceeds from this sign is more important than the sign itself; but that doesn't convince me that the actual thing is too.

AU. Although it may be wrong that all things ought to 26
be more important that the signs that signify them, it is still not wrong, in our opinion, that everything that exists on account of some other thing is less valuable than the

94 Adeodatus is now on high alert for his father's Socratic traps.

id propter quod est. Cognitio quippe caeni, propter quam hoc nomen est institutum, pluris habenda est ipso nomine, quod eidem caeno praeponendum esse comperimus. Non enim ob aliud ista cognitio signo, de quo agimus, antelata est nisi quia illud propter hanc, non haec propter illud esse convincitur. Nam ita cum quidam vorator ventrisque, ut ab apostolo dicitur, cultor, diceret ideo se vivere, ut vesceretur; non tulit qui audiebat frugi homo, et "quanto," inquit, "melius ideo vescereris ut viveres"? Uterque tamen ex eadem ista regula locutus est, nam neque alia de causa ille displicuit, nisi quod vitam suam tam parvi penderet, ut eam duceret gutturis voluptate viliorem, dicendo se propter epulas vivere: neque hic ob aliud iure laudatur, nisi quod in his duobus quid propter quid fieret, hoc est quid cui subiectum esset intellegens, cibandum potius ut vivamus quam vivendum ut cibemur admonuit.

Similiter et tu fortasse, et quilibet hominum non imperite res aestimantium, dicenti cuipiam loquaci amatorique verborum, "ideo doceo ut loquar," responderetis, "homo, cur non potius ideo loqueris ut doceas?" Quod si haec vera sunt, sicuti esse cognoscis, vides profecto quanto verba minoris habenda sint, quam id propter quod utimur verbis, cum ipse usus verborum iam sit verbis anteponendus: verba enim sunt ut his utamur; utimur autem his ad docendum. Quanto est igitur melius docere quam loqui, tanto

95 Called Augustine's rule: G. Wijdeveld, *Aurelius Augustinus De Magistro, ingeleid, vertaald en toegelicht door* (Amsterdam 1937), 163. 96 Romans 16:18.

97 *Melius* and *melior* in 9.26–27 evoke good of various kinds, including ethical.

thing on account of which it exists.[95] Certainly knowledge of what filth is (on account of which it was given its name) is more worthwhile than the name-word itself, which we found to be more important than actual filth. This knowledge has been preferred to the sign we are discussing for no other reason than that we have proved the sign exists because of the knowledge: the knowledge does not exist because of the sign. There was once a certain glutton, "devoted to his stomach" as the apostle puts it,[96] who claimed that he lived in order to fill his belly. Someone heard this, and being a person of moderate appetites they said, "How much better[97] to fill your belly so that you may live." Nevertheless, both of them spoke in accordance with this same rule. For the first one aroused disapproval for precisely this reason: counting their own life as so worthless that they reckoned it less important than hedonistic gluttony, saying that they lived to feast. As for the second person, they are praiseworthy precisely because of their counsel as to which activity of the two ought to depend on the other; in other words, because they understood what should come first and what second, whether eating should depend on living or vice versa.

Likewise, when some garrulous person who loves talking remarks, "This is why I teach—so I can talk," you, perhaps, and anyone with experience in making value judgments, would reply, "Hey, why don't you try talking so that you can teach instead?" But if these things are true, as you know they are, you surely see how much less valuable words are than the realities to which we apply those words; when even the way we use words is more important than the words are. Words exist for us to use them; and what we use them for is teaching. How much better, then,

melior est quam verba locutio. Multo enim[49] melior doctrina quam verba. Sed cupio audire quid forte contradicendum putes.

27 AD. Assentior quidem meliorem quam verba esse doctrinam, sed utrum adversus istam regulam qua dicitur omne quod propter aliud est inferius esse quam id propter quod est nihil sit quod obici possit ignoro.

AU. Alias hoc opportunius diligentiusque tractabimus. Nunc illud quod concedis, satis est ad id quod conficere studeo. Das enim cognitionem rerum quam signa rerum esse cariorem. Quam ob rem cognitio rerum quae significantur, cognitioni signorum anteferenda est: an tibi non videtur?

AD. Num ego[50] cognitionem[51] rerum[52] cognitione[53] signorum[54] ac non signis ipsis praestantiorem esse concessi? quare vereor ut hic tibi assentiar. Quid? si enim ut caenum nomen melius est ea re quam significat, ita et huius nominis[55] cognitio cognitioni quoque illius rei est anteponenda, quamvis ea cognitione sit ipsum nomen inferius? Quattuor quippe sunt: nomen, et res, cognitio nominis, et cognitio rei. Sicut ergo primum secundo, cur non

49 enim *B M*: ergo *S T* *μ*
50 ego *S*[1]: ergo *S T*
51 cognitionem *B S*[1] *μ*: cogitationem *S T*
52 rerum *μ*: signorum *B S T*
53 cognitione *μ*: cognitioni *B*: cogitationi *T*
54 signorum *μ*: rerum *B S T*
55 nominis *om. H V B R*

to teach than to talk, and correspondingly how much better talking is than words! So teaching[98] is better than words by far. But I'm eager to hear what you may be thinking of saying by way of an answer.

AD. I do agree that teaching is better than words; but 27
I don't know whether there is any possible argument against that rule which says that everything that exists for something else's sake is inferior to the thing for which it exists.

AU. This is a subject we'll have more time to investigate carefully another day. For now, what you've granted will be enough for what I'm eager to accomplish. After all, you allow that knowledge of things is more valuable than signs of things. Consequently knowledge of things that are signified ought to take priority over knowledge of signs—or do you disagree?

AD. Have I really conceded that knowledge of things is superior to knowledge of signs, but not superior to the signs themselves? This is why I'm nervous of disagreeing with you. Look, the name-word "filth" is better than the actual thing it signifies, so what if knowledge of this name-word is similarly preferable to knowledge of that actual thing?—although the actual name-word is inferior to this knowledge. There are four categories: (1) name-word; (2) thing; (3) knowledge of a name-word; and (4) knowledge of a thing. Just as (1) is superior to (2), then, why shouldn't

98 *doctrina*: the abstract noun (cognate verb: *doceo*) appears in *TT* only here and in Adeodatus' immediate reply.

et tertium quarto antecellat? si non[56] antecellat, num etiam subiciendum est?

28 AU. Mire omnino te video et tenuisse quid concesseris et explicasse quid senseris. Sed, ut opinor, intellegis, hoc trisyllabum nomen, quod sonat cum dicimus "vitium," melius esse quam id quod significat; cum ipsius cognitio nominis multo sit inferior cognitione vitiorum. Licet itaque constituas etiam ista quattuor atque consideres, nomen et rem, cognitionem nominis et cognitionem rei; primum secundo iure praeponimus. Hoc enim nomen positum in carmine, cum ait Persius, "sed stupet hic vitio," non modo nihil vitii fecit in versu, sed nonnihil etiam ornati dedit: cum tamen res ipsa quae significatur hoc nomine, in quocumque inest, cogit esse vitiosum.

At non ita et tertium quarto, sed quartum tertio videmus excellere. Huius enim cognitio nominis vilis est prae cognitione vitiorum.

AD. Etiamne cum ista cognitio miseriores facit censes esse praeferendam? Nam idem Persius omnibus poenis, quas tyrannorum vel crudelitas excogitavit vel cupiditas pendit, hanc unam anteponit, qua cruciantur homines qui vitia quae vitare non possunt, coguntur agnoscere.

56 si non R^2: sed non *B R V S H T M*: ut non *μ*: ne *coni. Weig.*

---

99 The subjunctive verb (*antecellat*[2]) has encouraged scribes and editors to supply a conjunction: "since (*cum*)," "that (*ut*)," and "that not (*ne*)" have all been suggested in later manuscripts and early editions. Of these, "if (*si*)" is a scribal correction in an early (ninth century) manuscript. 100 Three syllables in Latin, *vi-ti-um.* 101 Approximating to the neat oxymoron, *vitia* (wickednesses)/*vitare* (avoid).

(3) be superior to (4) as well? But even if (3) were not superior,[99] it surely shouldn't be made inferior to (4)?

AU. I see that you've done a quite remarkable job of 28
keeping in mind what you've accepted, and of explaining what you've perceived. Next, in my opinion you understand that this monosyllabic[100] word which resounds when we say "vice" is preferable to the reality it signifies, since knowledge of the actual name-word is far less relevant than knowledge of vice. So it's acceptable for you to posit these four categories—name-word; thing; knowledge of a name-word, and knowledge of a thing—and scrutinize them. We are right to prefer the first to the second. For example: the name-word "vice" has been used in a poem, when Persius says, "but he is stunned by vice": yet he not only did nothing vicious in this verse, he instead added an element of embellishment. This is despite the fact that the actual thing being signified by the name-word "vice" compels anyone in whom it subsists to be vicious.

When it comes to categories (3) and (4), we don't find that (3) is superior to (4), but rather the opposite; for knowledge of the name-word in this case is not as worthless as knowledge of vices.

AD. Do you consider this knowledge preferable even when you judge that it makes people more pitiable? After all, out of all the penalties which despots in their cruelty have dreamed up, or have dished out in their covetousness, this same Persius gave preference to one alone: the one which torments those who are forced to admit to the vices which they have failed to vitiate.[101]

AU. Potes hoc modo cognitioni huius nominis ipsam quoque virtutum cognitionem negare praeferendam: quia virtutem videre nec tenere, supplicium est: quo[57] idem ille satyricus tyranni ut puniantur optavit.

AD. Deus hanc avertat amentiam! Iam enim intellego non ipsas cognitiones quibus animum imbuit optima omnium disciplina esse culpandas, sed eos omnium miserrimos iudicandos, sicut et Persium iudicasse arbitror, qui tali morbo affecti sunt, cui nec tanta medicina subveniat.

AU. Bene intellegis: sed quoquo modo se habeat Persiana sententia, quid ad nos? Non enim horum auctoritati subiecti sumus in talibus rebus. Deinde si qua cognitio cognitioni praeferenda sit, non hic facile est explicare. Satis habeo quod effectum est cognitionem rerum quae significantur, etsi non cognitione signorum ipsis tamen signis esse potiorem. Quare iam illud magis magisque discutiamus, quale sit genus rerum quas sine signis monstrari posse dicebamus per seipsas, ut loqui, ambulare, sedere, iacere, atque huiusmodi cetera.

AD. Iam recolo quid dicas.

29 10. AU. Omniane tibi videntur, quae interrogati mox agere possumus, sine signo posse monstrari, an aliquid excipis?

AD. Ego vero etiam atque etiam genus hoc totum considerans, nihil adhuc invenio quod sine signo valeat doceri, nisi forte locutionem, et si forte idipsum quispiam

[57] quo *B* μ: quod *S H*

---

102 Augustine does not want to imply that he regards "pagan" writings as providing worthwhile guidance in the same way as scripture. 103 *omnia*: because he is referring to verbs.

AU. In the same way, you can argue that actual knowledge of virtues is not preferable to knowledge of the name-word "virtue," because to look upon virtue, yet not possess it, is a form of torture, by which this same satirist determined that despots should be disciplined.

AD. God preserve us from that insanity! Now I understand: it isn't the individual items of knowledge themselves, which the very finest education has filled the mind with, that are blameworthy; rather, as I reckon Persius decided, the most pitiable people of all are the ones who are afflicted with this disease which not even a drug as strong as this can cure.

AU. You've grasped the point. But what do we care how Persius' opinion is meant? In such matters we are not answerable to such writers as if they were authoritative.[102] Also, if one form of knowledge is to be preferred to another, this isn't the place for explaining it in straightforward terms. I'm content with what we've achieved: that knowledge of things being signified is at least more positive than the signs themselves, even if it isn't more positive than knowledge of the signs. So let's discuss that in much greater detail; this category of things that we were saying can in themselves be expressed without signs—such as speaking, walking, sitting, reclining, and the like—what is its nature?

AD. Now I recall what you're referring to.

10. AU. All these actions[103] which we are directly able 29
to perform when asked, do you think they can be analyzed without recourse to a sign, or do you make an exception?

AD. I keep thinking over this entire category, and I find nothing so far which can be taught without use of a sign, expect perhaps for speaking; and perhaps the very act of

quaerat, quid sit docere. Video enim me, quicquid post eius interrogationem fecero ut discat, ab ea ipsa re non discere[58] quam sibi demonstrari cupit. Nam si me cessantem, ut dictum est, vel aliud agentem roget quispiam quid sit ambulare, et ego statim ambulando, eum quod rogavit sine signo coner docere; unde cavebo ne id tantum putet esse ambulare, quantum ego ambulavero? quod si putaverit, decipietur: quisquis enim plus minusve quam ego ambulaverit, hunc ille ambulasse non arbitrabitur. Et quod de hoc uno verbo dixi, transit in omnia quae sine signo monstrari posse consenseram, praeter duo illa quae excepimus.

AU. Accipio quidem istud: sed nonne tibi videtur aliud esse loqui, aliud docere?

AD. Videtur sane: nam si esset idem, non doceret quisquam nisi loquens; cum vero et aliis signis praeter verba multa doceamus, quis de ista differentia dubitaverit?

AU. Quid? docere et significare nihilne interest? an aliquid differunt?

AD. Idem puto esse.

AU. Nonne recte dicit, qui dicit ideo nos significare ut doceamus?

AD. Recte prorsus.

AU. Quid, si dicat alius ideo nos docere ut significemus? nonne facile superiore sententia refelletur?

58 discere *R V S T μ*: discedere *B J M*

---

104 *verbum*, with the meaning "verb" uppermost.

teaching, if someone were to ask what teaching is. This latter is because I see that after they've asked that question, whatever I do to make them learn, they aren't learning from the actual thing which they want to have shown to them. If I've stopped doing something, as we said, or if I'm doing something else, at the moment when someone asks me what "walking" means, and I try to teach them the answer without a sign by immediately walking about, how shall I prevent them from thinking that "walking" means how far I have walked? If they thought that, they would be mistaken: for if someone else were to walk a longer or shorter distance, our questioner will conclude that this is not "walking." And this point, which I have applied to the one word,[104] also applies to all the actions which I previously agreed could be demonstrated without a sign, apart from the two exceptions we made.

AU. I agree with that: but don't you think that speaking 30
and teaching are two different things?

AD. It certainly looks like it. After all, if they were the same, no one would be teaching except when speaking. Given that there are many things we teach by means of other signs apart from words, who would have doubts about this distinction?

AU. So then, is there or isn't there any difference between teaching and signifying?

AD. I think they are the same.

AU. It's true, isn't it, if someone says that the reason why we signify things is in order to teach?

AD. Definitely.

AU. What about if someone were to say that this is why we teach things: in order to signify? Surely our earlier decision proves them wrong?

AD. Ita est.

AU. Si ergo significamus ut doceamus, non docemus ut significemus, aliud est docere, aliud significare.

AD. Verum dicis nec recte idem esse utrumque respondi.

AU. Nunc illud responde, utrum qui docet quid sit docere, significando id agat, an aliter.

AD. Non video quomodo aliter possit.

AU. Falsum igitur paulo ante dixisti, doceri rem posse sine signis, cum quaeritur quid sit ipsum docere; quando ne hoc quidem videmus[59] sine significatione agi posse, cum aliud esse significare, aliud docere concesseris. Si enim diversa sunt, sicut apparet, neque hoc nisi per illud ostenditur, non per se utique ostenditur, sicut tibi visum erat. Quam ob rem nihil adhuc inventum est, quod monstrari per seipsum queat praeter locutionem, quae inter alia se quoque significat: quae tamen cum etiam ipsa signum sit, nondum prorsus exstat quod sine signis doceri posse[60] videatur.

AD. Nihil habeo cur non assentiar.

31 AU. Confectum est igitur et nihil sine signis doceri, et cognitionem ipsam signis quibus cognoscimus cariorem nobis esse oportere: quamvis non omnia quae significantur possint signis suis esse potiora.

AD. Ita videtur.

AU. Quanto tandem circuitu res tantilla peracta sit,

[59] videmus *B S T μ*: vidimus *J M*

[60] posse videatur . . . signis doceri *om. T i.t., in marg. scr. ead. manu*

AD. Yes.

AU. If we use signs in order to teach, then, but don't use teaching to signify, teaching must be one thing, and signifying another.

AD. True. I was wrong to answer you that they were the same.

AU. Now answer this. If someone is teaching what "teaching" is, do they do that by using signs, or by some other means?

AD. I can't see how it could be otherwise.

AU. So when we asked what "teaching" really is, what you just said is untrue, that it's possible to teach a thing without signs: in fact we find that even this cannot be done without signifying, now that you've admitted signifying to be one thing, and teaching something else. But if they are different (as seems to be the case), and if teaching can only be done by means of using signs, then it certainly isn't (as you thought) self-disclosing. So far, therefore, we haven't found anything which can be proved, in and of itself, except for speaking, which signifies itself, among other things. Nevertheless, although speaking is also itself a sign, nothing is yet apparent that can, it seems, be taught without the use of signs.

AD. I have to agree with you.

AU. So now we have established first that nothing is 31
taught without the use of signs; and second that we ought to value knowledge itself more highly, compared with signs as a means of knowing; although not every thing that is signified can be more important than the signs which point to it.

AD. That seems to be the case.

AU. What a long digression it has taken for us finally to

meministine, quaeso?[61] Nam ex quo inter nos verba iaculamur, quod tam diu fecimus, haec tria ut invenirentur laboratum est: utrum nihil sine signis possit doceri, et utrum sint quaedam signa rebus quas significant praeferenda, et utrum melior quam signa sit rerum ipsa cognitio. Sed quartum est, quod breviter abs te vellem cognoscere, utrumnam ista inventa sic putes, ut iam de his dubitare non possis.

AD. Vellem quidem tantis ambagibus atque anfractibus esset ad certa perventum, sed et ista rogatio tua nescio quomodo me sollicitat, et ab assensione deterret. Videris enim mihi non hoc[62] de me fuisse quaesiturus, nisi haberes quod contradiceres; et ipsa rerum implicatio totum me inspicere, ac securum respondere non sinit, verentem ne quid in tantis involucris lateat, quod acies mentis meae lustrare non possit.

AU. Dubitationem tuam non invitus accipio, significat enim animum minime temerarium, quae custodia tranquillitatis est maxima. Nam difficillimum omnino est non perturbari, cum ea quae prona et procliva approbatione

61 quaeso S^1 μ: Ad. ne quaeso S
62 hoc] haec μ

---

105 *Tantus* is an adjective meaning "great." The diminutive form, *tantulus* (used by Cicero), is already oxymoronic, before this further diminutive, *tantillus*, is factored in. Cf. *Conf.* 1.12.19 (*tantillus puer et tantus peccator*: "so small a boy, yet so great a sinner"); *Sermo* 225.3 (*esse potuit tantus in loco tantillo*: "so great a being in a place so small"; a reference to *deus in utero*). The perplexing contradictory effect is akin to the paired English modifier, "Yes, no, but . . ."

achieve our *bijou*[105] main objective—you remember, don't you? From the moment we started this verbal fencing, which we've kept going for quite some time, our effort has gone into ascertaining these three points: (1) can we teach anything without the use of signs? (2) are there some signs that are more worthwhile than the actual things they signify: and (3) is knowledge of things, in and of itself, better than the signs that signify them? But there is a fourth point, and I would like—briefly—to know from you whether you believe what we have found out in a way that means you no longer have any doubts about them?

AD. If only our roundabout digressions had finally reached some firm conclusions! But your question troubles me, I'm not sure why; and also discourages me from simply agreeing with you. It seems to me that you would not have gone asking me about this unless you had grounds for telling me I'm wrong.[106] Also, the very intricacy of these matters as a whole stops me from contemplating it and answering with confidence; I'm afraid of what's lurking beneath the layers of wrapping, which my mind's eye can't penetrate.

AU. I'm delighted to get this doubting reply! it's the sign of an ultracautious brain, and that's the best protection for our peace of mind. After all, it's incredibly difficult not to be disturbed when things that we were once inclined to regard with favor start to crumble in the cut and

106 Words of learned experience as much logical insight.

tenebamus contrariis disputationibus labefactantur, et quasi extorquentur e manibus. Quare, ut aequum est bene consideratis perspectisque rationibus cedere, ita incognita pro cognitis habere periculosum. Metus est enim ne cum saepe subruuntur quae firmissime statura et mansura praesumimus, in tantum odium vel timorem rationis incidamus ut ne ipsi quidem perspicuae veritati fides habenda videatur.

32 Sed age nunc expeditius retractemus utrum recte ista dubitanda[63] putaveris. Nam quaero abs te si quisquam ignarus deceptionis avium, quae calamis et visco affectatur,[64] obviam fieret aucupi, armis quidem suis instructo non tamen aucupanti, sed iter agenti, quo viso premeret[65] gradum secumque, ut fit, admirans cogitaret et quaereret quidnam sibi hominis ille vellet ornatus; auceps autem cum in se videret attentum, ostentandi[66] se studio cannas expediret, et prope animadversam aliquam aviculam fistula et accipitre figeret, subigeret et caperet: nonne illum spectatorem suum doceret nullo significatu, sed re ipsa, quod ille scire cupiebat?

AD. Metuo ne quid hic tale sit, quale de illo dixi, qui

[63] dubitanda *T*: disputanda *S*: disputata S^1

[64] affectatur *M* μ: affectantur *recc.*: effectatur *R V S H T*: efficitur *coni. Weig.*

[65] viso premeret] *recc.* μ: visu premeret *J M N*: vis oppremeret *R V*: quo vis opprimeret *S H T*

[66] ostentandi *Weig. Daur*: ostendi R^1: ostentendi *V S H T*

---

107 *Viscum* is a sticky substance made from mistletoe berries. Augustine is fond of this image from nature: *Conf.* 6.12.22, 10.30.42; *Trin.* 8.1.3; *Sermo* 255.7.

thrust of debate, and are wrenched (as it were) from our grasp. For this reason, just as it's proper to yield to arguments that are well thought out and properly scrutinized, so too it's risky to treat matters we know nothing about as if we did know about them. For it's a worry if things which we take it for granted as being established and enduring keep being demolished: then we sink into such a distaste for argument, or fear of it, that even trust in self-evident truth can't be sustained.

For now, though, let's crack on with tackling whether 32
you're right to suspect that these matters are open to doubt. I'm asking you this: imagine someone who knew nothing about how to trap birds (which is done with sticks and birdlime[107]) coming across a fowler who, though equipped with the tools of his trade, was not catching birds just then, but merely on his way somewhere. On seeing the fowler he sped up, asking himself (as people do) and wondering what the fowler's rig-out might be for. But when the fowler became aware of this scrutiny, he was eager to show his skill, so got out his reeds, and used his rod and his hawk to pin down, conquer, and capture[108] some small bird[109] he had noticed nearby. Didn't the fowler teach the person watching him? And without using any kind of signifying, but with the real thing itself, which that observer wanted to know about?

AD. I'm afraid this looks like an example of the kind

108 The three verbs have a military flavor, bathetic in the context of catching an *avicula*.

109 The deprecating diminutive calls to mind the British birdwatcher's "LBJ," or "little brown job."

quaerit quid sit ambulare. Neque enim video et hic totum illud aucupium esse monstratum.

AU. Facile est hac cura te exuere; addo enim, si ille[67] intellegens esset, ut ex hoc quod vidit totum illud genus artis agnosceret: satis est namque ad rem[68] et de quibusdam rebus tametsi non omnibus, et quosdam homines doceri posse sine signo.

AD. Hoc etiam ego possum illi addere; si enim sit bene[69] intellegens, paucis passibus ambulatione monstrata, totum quid sit ambulare cognoscet.

AU. Facias per me licet, nec tantum nihil resisto, verum etiam faveo: vides enim ab utroque nostrum id effici, ut quaedam quidam doceri sine signis queant, falsumque illud sit quod nobis paulo ante videbatur, nihil esse omnino quod sine signis possit ostendi. Iam enim ex his non unum aliquid aut alterum, sed milia rerum animo occurrunt, quae nullo signo dato per seipsa monstrentur. Quid enim dubitemus, oro te? Nam ut hominum omittam innumerabilia spectacula in omnibus theatris sine signo ipsis rebus exhibentium, solem certe istum lucemque haec omnia perfundentem atque vestientem, lunam et cetera sidera, terras et maria, quaeque in his innumerabiliter gignuntur, nonne per seipsa exhibet atque ostendit deus et natura cernentibus?

67 ille ita *μ* 68 namque ad rem *μ*: namque addet *R*: namque ad *V*: namque *S T*

69 sit bene *Daur*: sit tibi bene *R V S H T*

---

110 Adeodatus' last intervention before the final words of the dialogue, 14.46. The rest is rather a lecture than a dialogue.

111 Readers are to imagine accompanying gestures here, a

which I mentioned, the person who asked what "walking" is. And even here I don't see that the art of bird catching has been fully revealed.

AU. I can easily relieve you of this concern. I will go so far as to say that if the person were intelligent enough they could understand this skill as a whole from the part of it which they've seen. It's enough for our purpose if it's the case with certain things (though not all) that particular people can be taught without signs.

AD. I can factor something else in here. If someone is reasonably intelligent, observing walking for just a few steps can show them everything that's relevant to what "walking" is.[110]

AU. It's fine by me for you to do so. In fact, not only am I not resistant to it, I actually support your doing so. You see that we have both of us established that certain people can be taught certain things without using signs, and what we thought just a moment ago is incorrect—namely that nothing whatever exists that can be demonstrated without using signs. In fact, it is not one or two examples from these cases that come to mind, it is thousands, which are proven in and of themselves without the use of a sign. Why should we doubt it, do you think? I needn't mention the countless public spectacles men perform in all the theaters, performing using actual things without any sign. Surely God and nature of themselves lay out for display—to those who look—the sun there, and its light which pours out on all of this and clothes it,[111] the moon and the rest of the stars, the seas and lands, and all the countless creatures spawned there.

pointing hand, and sweep of the arm. For the clothing/light metaphor, see Psalm 104:2.

33 Quod si diligentius consideremus, fortasse nihil invenies quod per sua signa discatur. Cum enim mihi signum datur, si nescientem me invenit cuius rei signum sit, docere me nihil potest: si vero scientem, quid disco per signum? Non enim mihi rem quam significat ostendit verbum cum lego, "Et sarabarae[70] eorum non sunt commutatae."[71] Nam si quaedam capitum tegmina nuncupantur hoc nomine, num ego hoc audito aut quid sit caput aut quid sint tegmina didici? Ante ista noveram; neque cum appellarentur ab aliis, sed cum a me viderentur, eorum est mihi facta notitia. Etenim cum primum istae duae syllabae, cum dicimus "caput," aures meas impulerunt, tam nescivi quid significarent, quam cum primo audirem legeremve "sarabaras." Sed cum saepe diceretur "caput," notans atque animadvertens quando diceretur, repperi vocabulum esse rei quae mihi iam erat videndo notissima. Quod priusquam repperissem, tantum mihi sonus erat hoc verbum: signum vero esse didici, quando cuius rei signum esset inveni; quam quidem ut dixi non significatu sed aspectu didiceram. Ita magis signum[72] re cognita quam signo dato ipsa res discitur.

[70] sarabarae] saraballae *μ* [71] commutatae *S T*: immutatae *J M μ* [72] signum *om.* *R*[1] *V S H T*

---

[112] Cf. Cic. *Acad.* 2.26, *Quid quod si ista vera sunt* ("What about the fact that . . .).

[113] *Sarabara* (an Aramaic word) is chosen for its obscurity. It has been variously translated as "trousers" (Lewis and Short); "coat" or "tunic" (following translations of Daniel 3:94[Vulg.] [= 3.27 MT/HB]); "shoe" (LXX, demonstrating that the three youths in the furnace were unharmed "from head to toe"). Jer. *Comm. Dan.* 3.21 (written twenty years after *TT*) shows how the confusion may

If we reflect[112] more carefully, though, you will maybe find nothing that is learned by means of its own signs. When I'm given a sign, if it finds me ignorant as to what thing it signifies, it cannot teach me anything. But if it finds that I know, what am I learning by means of this sign? When I read, "and their turbans were not changed,"[113] the word "turbans" does not show me the actual thing that it signifies. For if some head coverings are called by this name-word, surely hearing that name-word has not taught me what a "head" is, or what "coverings" are? I already knew both things, and knowledge of them both came into being in me, not when other people called them by their names, but when I saw them for myself. Thus the first time that monosyllable,[114] "head," resounded in my ears, I was as ignorant of what it signified, as when I first heard (or read) "turbans." But when the word "head" was repeated over and over, I observed and took note of when it was said, and discovered it to be the term for a thing that was already completely familiar to me from my having seen it before. Before I had found it out, though, this word was nothing more than noise to me: I learned it as a sign when I discovered what the thing which it signified was; and—as I said—I had learned that, not by means of its capacity for signifying, but by the act of observing it. Therefore we learn a sign through coming to know a thing, rather than learning the thing itself through its sign being given. 33

have come about: "those three men, wearing their trousers and head-gear, and footwear, and clothing, were sent into the midst of the burning fiery furnace." Knauer suggests that Augustine may have been influenced by knowledge gained as a Manichee to hit upon the correct meaning: Knauer, "*Sarabara*," 100–118.

114 Disyllable in Latin, *ca-put*.

34 Quod ut apertius intellegas, finge nos primum nunc audire quod dicitur "caput," et nescientes utrum vox ista sit tantummodo sonans an aliquid etiam significans, quaerere quid sit caput (memento nos non rei quae significatur, sed ipsius signi velle habere notitiam, qua caremus profecto, quamdiu cuius signum est ignoramus): si ergo ita quaerentibus res ipsa digito demonstratur, hac conspecta discimus[73] signum quod audieramus tantum, nondum noveramus. In quo tamen signo cum duo sint, sonus et significatio, sonum certe non per signum percipimus, sed eo ipso aure pulsata; significationem autem re quae significatur aspecta. Nam illa intentio digiti significare nihil aliud potest, quam illud in quod[74] intenditur digitus: intentus est autem non in signum, sed in membrum quod caput vocatur. Itaque per illam neque rem possum nosse quam noveram, neque signum in quod intentus digitus non est.

Sed de intentione digiti non nimis curo, quia ipsius demonstrationis signum mihi videtur potius quam rerum aliquarum quae demonstrantur, sicut adverbium quod "ecce," dicimus; nam et cum hoc adverbio digitum solemus intendere, ne unum demonstrandi signum non sit satis.[75] Et id maxime tibi nitor persuadere si potero, per ea signa quae verba appellantur, nos nihil discere; potius enim ut dixi vim verbi, id est significationem quae latet in

[73] discimus S^1: dicimus *R V S H T* [74] in quod S^1: quo *R V*: *om. S H T* [75] satis S^1: satius *R V S H T*

---

[115] *vim* has a wide lexical range: "force/power/meaning/nature."

To help you understand more clearly, imagine that we hear "head" spoken now for the first time. We don't know whether that utterance is only a sound, or whether it is also signifying something. So we ask what "head" is (remember that we don't want to have an idea of the thing being signified, only of the actual sign: and we certainly lack this as long as we don't know what it is the sign for). So if, when we ask the question, a finger points the thing itself out to us, and we observe this, then we learn the sign that until then we had heard, but not yet known. Yet this sign has two aspects to it, a sound and a signification: we certainly don't become aware of the sound by means of the sign, but by its actual striking of our ear, whereas we become aware of its capacity to signify through observing the thing that is being signified. For that pointing finger cannot signify anything other than the object at which the finger is pointed: and it is pointed not toward a sign but to that part of the body which we call the head. The act of pointing, then, can't make me know a thing which I knew already, or a sign which the finger was not pointed at. 34

Anyway, I'm not too bothered about the pointing finger. I reckon it is a sign for the act of pointing something out, rather than a sign of the individual things being pointed out. Take saying the adverb "here!": even when we say "here" we tend to point a finger too, in case one sign for pointing something out is not enough. This is what I am doing my utmost to persuade you of, if possible: that we learn nothing by means of the signs which we call "words." Rather, as I said, we are learning the meaning[115] of a word, to be specific, what it signifies, which lies hidden in the sound, once we know the actual thing being signi-

sono, re ipsa quae significatur cognita discimus, quam illam tali significatione percipimus.

35 Et quod dixi de capite, hoc etiam de tegminibus deque aliis rebus innumerabilibus dixerim: quas tamen cum iam noverim, sarabaras illas adhuc usque non novi; quas mihi si gestu quispiam significarit aut pinxerit, aut aliquid cui similes sunt ostenderit, ne[76] dicam non me docuerit, quod facile obtinerem, si paulo amplius loqui vellem, sed dico id quod proximum est, non verbis docuerit. Quod si eis forte conspectis cum simul adero me admonuerit, dicens "ecce sarabaras!" discam rem quam nesciebam, non per verba quae dicta sunt, sed per eius aspectum, per quem factum est ut etiam nomen illud quid valeret, nossem ac tenerem. Non enim cum rem ipsam didici, verbis alienis credidi, sed oculis meis: illis tamen fortasse ut attenderem credidi, id est ut aspectu quaererem quid viderem.[77]

36 11. Hactenus verba valuerunt, quibus ut plurimum tribuam, admonent tantum ut quaeramus res, non exhibent ut norimus. Is me autem aliquid docet, qui vel oculis, vel ulli corporis sensui, vel ipsi etiam menti praebet ea quae cognoscere volo. Verbis igitur nisi verba non discimus, immo sonitum strepitumque verborum: nam si ea quae signa non sunt, verba esse non possunt, quamvis iam auditum verbum[78] nescio tamen verbum esse, donec quid

[76] ne *S T*: non μ
[77] credidi id . . . quid viderem] *om. H S T*
[78] verbum *om. H S T*

---

[116] *credidi* encompasses "have/put faith in" and "believe."

fied—rather than becoming aware of the meaning through this kind of signifying.

What I've said about "head" I might just as well have said about "coverings" and countless other things: but although I already knew what these things are, I still don't know what those "turbans" are. If someone were to use a gesture to signify them for me, or do a drawing, or show me something like them, I mustn't say that they didn't teach me, though I could easily maintain this if I were willing to develop the argument a little further. But I'm saying what comes closest to that: they didn't use words to teach me. If, on the other hand, they catch sight of them at a time when I am present, and they advise me in these words, "look here, turbans!"; then I shall learn something I was hitherto unaware of, not through the words they spoke, but by the act of looking at them. This is how it would come about that I knew and remembered what that name-word meant. For when I learned the thing itself, I didn't put my faith[116] in someone else's words, but in my own eyesight: though perhaps I did put my faith in the words insofar as I turned my attention to them, so that looking would prompt me to ask what it was that I saw. 35

11. Up until now, the importance of words (to give them the best acknowledgment I can) has lain in their giving us directions to seek out things. They don't set the things before us, for us to know them. But the person who teaches me something is one who sets before my eyes, or another bodily sense, or even my mind, what I want to know. So the only thing we learn from words is words, or rather the sound and noise of words. For if things which aren't signs can't be words, then even if I've heard a word, I still don't know that it's a word, until I know what it 36

significet sciam. Rebus ergo cognitis, verborum quoque cognitio perficitur; verbis vero auditis, nec verba discuntur. Non enim ea verba quae novimus discimus; aut quae non novimus, didicisse nos possumus confiteri, nisi eorum significatione percepta, quae non auditione vocum emissarum, sed rerum significatarum cognitione contingit. Verissima quippe ratio est, et verissime dicitur, cum verba proferuntur, aut scire nos quid significent, aut nescire: si scimus, commemorari potius quam discere; si autem nescimus, ne commemorari quidem, sed fortasse ad quaerendum admoneri.

37 Quod si dixeris tegmina quidem illa capitum, quorum nomen sono tantum tenemus, non nos posse nisi visa cognoscere, neque nomen ipsum plenius nisi ipsis cognitis nosse: quod tamen de ipsis pueris accepimus, ut regem ac flammas fide ac religione superaverint, quas laudes deo cecinerint, quos honores ab ipso etiam inimico meruerint,[79] num aliter haec nisi per verba didicimus? Respondebo cuncta quae illis verbis significata sunt in nostra notitia iam fuisse. Nam quid sint tres pueri, quid fornax, quid ignis, quid rex, quid denique illaesi ab igne, ceteraque omnia iam tenebam quae verba illa significant. Ananias vero, et Azarias et Misael tam mihi ignoti sunt quam illae sarabarae; nec ad eos cognoscendos haec me nomina[80] quicquam adiuverunt aut adiuvare iam potuerunt. Haec

[79] inimico meruerint] inimicum eruerint *R V S H T*
[80] nomina] omnia *V S H T*

---

[117] Daniel 3.
[118] Zeugma.

signifies. Thus when we've come to know things, we have achieved knowledge of words: whereas hearing words doesn't teach us that they are words. For we don't learn the words we know; nor can we declare that we have learned things we didn't know unless we've recognized their signification, which happens not by the act of hearing words spoken aloud, but by coming to know the actual things that are signified. The most accurate account, the most accurate way of putting it, is that when words are mentioned, we either know what they signify or we don't. If we do know, then what they do is to bring things to mind, rather than to teach; if we don't know, they can't even bring things to mind, though perhaps they can encourage us to look for answers.

Now of course you might say that we cannot come to 37
know those head coverings—the name-word for which is just a noise to us—unless we've seen them; and that we can't know the name-word itself more fully unless we've come to know the actual head coverings. But still we have heard about those youths,[117] how by their devout faith they triumphed over king and flames[118] alike, the praises they sang to God, the rewards they earned even from their enemy: how else have we learned about them if not by means of words? I shall reply that all the things signified by those words were already known to us. For I already had a grasp of what "three youths," "furnace," "fire," "king," and finally "unharmed by fire," were, and of all the other things that those words signified. After all, Ananias, and Azarias, and Misael were as unfamiliar to me as those "turbans" of theirs: these name-words gave me no help in recognizing them, indeed it was impossible for them to do so. But I admit that I have faith, rather than know objec-

autem omnia quae in illa leguntur historia, ita illo tempore facta esse, ut conscripta[81] sunt, credere me potius quam scire confiteor: neque istam differentiam idem ipsi quibus credimus nescierunt. Ait enim propheta "nisi credideritis, non intellegetis;" quod non dixisset profecto, si nihil distare iudicasset. Quod ergo intellego, id etiam credo; at non omne quod credo etiam intellego. Omne autem quod intellego scio: non omne quod[82] credo scio. Nec ideo nescio quam sit utile credere etiam multa quae nescio; cui utilitati hanc quoque adiungo de tribus pueris historiam: quare pleraque rerum cum scire non possim, quanta tamen utilitate credantur scio.

38 De universis autem quae intellegimus non loquentem qui personat foris, sed intus ipsi menti praesidentem consulimus veritatem, verbis fortasse ut consulamus admoniti. Ille autem qui consulitur, docet, qui in interiore homine habitare dictus est Christus, id est incommutabilis dei virtus[83] atque sempiterna sapientia: quam quidem omnis rationalis anima consulit, sed tantum cuique panditur, quantum capere propter propriam sive malam sive

[81] conscripta *R V J M*: scripta *S H T μ*

[82] quod . . . nec ideo *μ*: quod scio etiam credo non omne quod credo scio nec ideo *V T* [83] virtus *om. S T*

---

[119] For this Platonic epistemological distinction, see also *Mus.* 4.16.30: "we cannot know this, but only, by listening and reading, believe it."

[120] Isaiah 7:9, with *Trin.* 8.5.8, cf. *TC* 2.17.39 with note. Christians counted the book of Daniel as part of the prophetic canon, though in Judaism it is counted among the writings.

[121] The first appearance of *homo interior* since 1.2.

tively,[119] that all the things written in that history took place at that time just as they have been written up: nor were those same authors, in whom we put our trust, unaware of that distinction. For a prophet says "unless you have faith, you will not understand";[120] and he certainly wouldn't have said that if he thought there was no such distinction. What I understand, therefore, that I also believe; but I do not understand everything that I believe. Everything that I understand, though, I know; but I do not know everything that I believe. And I am not ignorant of how useful it is to believe in many things that I don't know; and I put the story about the three youths into that "useful" category. Therefore although there's a vast number of things I cannot know about, I still know how useful it is to believe them.

Taking together all the things which we understand, we 38
don't consult truth like some speaker making a sound external to ourselves, but rather as an inner presence that holds sway over our own mind—though perhaps it was words that urged us to consult it. That being whom we consult, who teaches us, who is said to abide deep in the inner person,[121] is Christ, in other words, the unchangeable "power of God and the eternal wisdom."[122] And indeed every rational soul consults this wisdom, but it[123] reveals itself to each only insofar as each can grasp it, in

122 Ephesians 3:16–17; 1 Corinthians 1:24. Closest to "unchangeable" (*incommutabilis*) in the New Testament is James 1:17. "Wisdom" is a personified title of God/Christ.

123 Wisdom in Latin (as in Hebrew) is grammatically feminine; the incarnate Christ is physically as well as grammatically masculine.

bonam voluntatem potest. Et si quando fallitur, non fit vitio consultae veritatis, ut neque huius, quae foris est, lucis vitium est, quod corporei oculi saepe falluntur; quam lucem de rebus visibilibus consuli fatemur, ut eas nobis quantum cernere valemus ostendat.

39 12. Quod si et de coloribus lucem, et de ceteris quae per corpus sentimus elementa huius mundi, eademque corpora quae sentimus, sensusque ipsos quibus tamquam interpretibus ad talia noscenda mens utitur, de his autem quae intelleguntur, interiorem veritatem ratione consulimus, quid dici potest unde clareat verbis nos aliquid discere praeter ipsum qui aures percutit sonum?

Namque omnia quae percipimus, aut sensu corporis, aut mente percipimus. Illa sensibilia, haec intellegibilia; sive, ut more auctorum nostrorum loquar, illa carnalia, haec spiritalia nominamus. De illis cum[84] interrogamur respondemus si praesto sunt ea quae sentimus, velut cum a nobis quaeritur intuentibus lunam novam, qualis aut ubi sit. Hic ille qui interrogat, si non videt, credit[85] verbis, et saepe non credit: discit autem nullo modo, nisi et[86] ipse quod dicitur videat, ubi iam non verbis sed rebus ipsis et sensibus discit. Nam verba eadem sonant videnti, quae non videnti etiam sonuerunt.

84 cum] dum *μ*
85 credit] credet *R V*: credat *S H T*
86 et *om. R V H S T*

---

124 In other words, "coming to know."

accordance with their own will, whether good or bad. And if ever a soul is misled, it is not because the truth is faulty, any more than the fact that our physical sight is often misled is the fault of the light that is external to us. We admit to consulting this light where visible things are concerned, so that it shows them to us in proportion to our capacity to perceive them.

12. Now if it's a matter of colors, we consult light; 39
and for other things which our bodily senses show us we consult the scientific principles of this world, and those material phenomena which we perceive through physical senses, and the senses themselves which the mind uses as translators when it comes to know things: but when it comes to things that are understood, we use our capacity for reason to consult the truth within. So what can we say to prove that we learn anything, by using words, apart from the actual sound that strikes our ears?

Everything that we perceive, we perceive through a physical or a mental sense. The former are perceived by the senses, the latter by the intellect; or, to speak in the terms used by our forebears in the faith, we name the former "of the flesh," the latter "of the spirit." When we're questioned about the former, we reply if those sense-perceptible objects are before us: for example, if we're looking at a new moon, and we're asked what sort of thing it is, or where it is. In this case, the person asking, if unable to see the moon, does believe my words—or, frequently, does not believe them. But they can't possibly be learning[124] this unless they see for themselves what we are speaking of, for then they're learning by means of real things and sense perceptions, not by words. After all, the sound of the words was the same for the person who could see as for the one who didn't.

Cum vero non de his quae coram sentimus, sed de his quae aliquando sensimus quaeritur, non iam res ipsas, sed imagines ab eis impressas memoriaeque mandatas loquimur: quae omnino quomodo vera dicamus, cum falsa intueamur,[87] ignoro, nisi quia non nos ea videre ac sentire, sed vidisse ac sensisse narramus. Ita illas imagines in memoriae penetralibus rerum ante sensarum quaedam documenta gestamus, quae animo contemplantes bona conscientia non mentimur cum loquimur. Sed nobis sunt ista documenta; is enim qui audit, si ea sensit atque adfuit, non discit meis verbis, sed recognoscit ablatis secum et ipse imaginibus: si autem illa[88] non sensit, quis non eum credere potius verbis quam discere intellegat?

Cum vero de his agitur quae mente conspicimus, id est intellectu atque ratione, ea quidem loquimur quae praesentia contuemur in illa interiore luce veritatis, qua ipse qui dicitur homo interior, illustratur et fruitur: sed tum quoque noster auditor, si et ipse[89] illa[90] secreto ac simplici oculo videt, novit quod dico sua contemplatione, non verbis meis. Ergo ne hunc quidem doceo vera dicens vera[91] intuentem; docetur enim non verbis meis, sed ipsis rebus, deo intus pandente, manifestis. Itaque de his interrogatus respondere posset.

87 falsa intueamur] falsum intuemur *S H T*
88 illa *μ*: ille *cett.*
89 ipse S^1: ipso *R V S H T*
90 illa *μ*: illo *S T cett.*
91 vera *om.* *S H T*

---

125 *coram* is used in its normal sense, unlike in 5.16.

When we investigate things that we're not perceiving before us[125] at that moment, but that were perceptible to us in time past, we don't speak of actual things but of imprints left by them as likenesses, which have been committed to memory. Since we are analyzing things that are not real, I can't see that we can call these things "true"—unless we're referring to things that we aren't seeing and sensing, but which we did see and sense on a previous occasion. In the furthest corners of our memory, we carry about with us, like proofs, those imprinted likenesses of actual things that we once knew through our senses: when we reflect upon them in our minds, in good faith, we are not lying if we speak of them. But those proofs are for us alone. Anyone who hears them, if they experienced them and were present at the time, does not learn about them by my words, but recognizes them by those impressions that they themselves took away from that experience. On the other hand, if someone has no experience of those things, who wouldn't understand that they were believing my words, rather than learning from them?

So when we are discussing things that we perceive with 40
our minds, which is to say with our understanding and reason, we speak of what we see before us in that inner light of truth. What we call our "inner person" is enlightened by this, and enjoys it. Here too, though, if the person who's listening to us also sees those things with sight that is pure, and theirs alone, their own reflections, not my words, make them know what I'm referring to. That's why I'm not teaching such a person; no, not even when what I'm speaking of is true. Not my words, but the reality of things themselves, made clear by a disclosure from God within, is what does the teaching. This is how they would be able to respond if questioned.

Quid autem absurdius quam eum putare locutione mea doceri, qui posset, antequam loquerer, ea ipsa[92] interrogatus exponere? Nam quod saepe contingit, ut interrogatus[93] aliquid neget, atque ad id fatendum aliis interrogationibus urgeatur, fit hoc imbecillitate cernentis, qui de re tota illam lucem consulere non potest: quod ut partibus faciat, admonetur, cum de istis partibus interrogatur, quibus illa summa constat, quam totam cernere non valebat. Quo si verbis perducitur eius qui interrogat, non tamen docentibus verbis, sed eo[94] modo inquirentibus, quo modo est ille a quo quaeritur, intus discere idoneus; velut si abs te quaererem hoc ipsum quod agitur, utrumnam verbis doceri nihil possit, et absurdum tibi primo videretur non valenti totum conspicere: sic ergo quaerere oportuit, ut tuae sese vires habent ad audiendum illum intus magistrum, ut dicerem[95] "Ea quae me loquente vera esse confiteris, et certus[96] es et te illa nosse confirmas, unde didicisti?"[97] responderes fortasse quod ego docuissem. Tum ego subnecterem, "quid si me hominem volantem vidisse dicerem, itane te certum verba mea redderent, quemadmodum si audires sapientes homines stultis esse meliores?" Negares profecto et responderes illud te non

[92] ipse *coni. Weig.*
[93] exponere . . . interrogatus *om. T*
[94] eo S^1: quo *S H T*
[95] dicerem *μ*: docerem R^1 *V S H T*
[96] certus R^2 S^1: certius *V S T*
[97] et certus . . . didicisti *om.* R^1

Now, what is more ridiculous than thinking they have been taught by my speaking, when even before I spoke they had the ability to explain a thing if questioned? For it often happens that a person being questioned disagrees with something, but further questioning pressures them into affirming it:[126] this is down to the weakness of this person's judgment, for they are only able to consult the light on that subject in a piecemeal fashion. Instead, when questioned bit by bit about those same elements that make up the whole, they are directed to tackle it piecemeal because they haven't the capacity to scrutinize the whole. Even if the words of the questioner are directing them, still the words aren't doing the teaching; but they do ask questions in a way which suits the ability of that person to look within. It's as if I were to ask you about the subject of our present discussion, whether it's the case that nothing can be taught by words; and at first it seemed ridiculous to you because you had not the capacity to see it in the round. Then I would have to do my questioning in a way adapted to your ability to hear that teacher within.[127] I might ask you, "Those things which, while I'm speaking, you declare to be true, and you're convinced and confirm that you know them, where did you learn them from?" Perhaps you would reply that I had taught you. Then I would follow up with, "what if I were to say that I'd seen a human being fly—would my words then make you convinced in the same way as if you heard that wise people are better than fools?" Undoubtedly you would say "no,"

126 As happens to Adeodatus in *TT*.

127 The first appearance of the term "teacher" (*magister*) since 5.16. The divine "inner teacher" (*intus magister*) is a counterpart to the human "inner self" (*homo interior*).

credere, aut etiamsi crederes ignorare, hoc autem certissime scire.

Ex hoc iam nimirum intellegeres, neque in illo quod me affirmante ignorares, neque in hoc quod optime scires, aliquid te didicisse verbis meis; quandoquidem etiam interrogatus de singulis, et illud ignotum, et hoc[98] tibi notum esse iurares. Tum vero totum illud quod negaveras fatereris, cum haec ex quibus constat, clara et certa esse cognosceres: omnia scilicet quae loquimur, aut ignorare auditorem utrum vera sint, aut falsa esse non ignorare, aut scire vera esse. Horum trium in primo aut credere aut opinari aut dubitare; in secundo adversari[99] atque renuere; in tertio attestari: nusquam igitur discere. Quia et ille qui post verba nostra rem nescit, et qui se falsa novit audisse, et qui posset interrogatus eadem respondere quae dicta sunt, nihil verbis didicisse convincitur.

41 13. Quam ob rem in his etiam quae mente cernuntur, frustra cernentis loquelas audit quisquis ea cernere non potest, nisi quia talia quamdiu ignorantur utile est credere. Quisquis autem cernere potest, intus est discipulus veritatis, foris iudex loquentis, vel potius ipsius locutionis. Nam plerumque scit illa quae dicta sunt, eo ipso nesciente

[98] hoc . . . negaveras *μ*: hoc illud tibi notum esse iuraris profecto et responderis illud tum vero totum illud quod negaveras *T*: hoc illud tibi notum esse iuraris profecto et responderis {responderes *S*[1]} illud tum vero totum illud quodquod negaveras *S*

[99] adversari *Daur*: aversari *M*: aversare *R V S H*

---

[128] Reinforcing the point made at the beginning of 12.40.

and would reply that you don't believe the second point, or that though you believe it you don't know it for sure, whereas you know the other thing is indisputably true.

Now this would surely make you understand that you'd learned nothing from my words, either in the first example, where you knew nothing (but I was speaking in support of it); or in the second where you were well-informed. Indeed if you'd been questioned about them one at a time, you would have sworn that you did have knowledge of the latter, but not the former. Then you would have to admit what you had just denied, for now you would know clearly and for certain what was at issue: that of course with reference to every thing we speak, our hearer either does not know whether what we are speaking is true or not; or knows that it is untrue; or knows that it is true. The first is a matter of belief, or opinion, or doubt; the second is a matter of debate or denial; the third is all about corroboration. Learning has nothing to do with it. For this reason, it is proven that the person who, after our words, doesn't know the truth of a thing, and who knows that what they have heard is untrue, and who could respond with the same words if questioned, has learned nothing from my words.

13. For this reason, when it comes to matters which the 41
mind discerns, it's futile for someone who is unable to discern those matters to hear them described by someone who is able to—except for when it's useful to believe such things while not having knowledge of them.[128] But anyone who can discern them is a student of the truth internally, and externally is a judge of the person speaking—or of their actual words, to be more precise. For they often know the things that are spoken, even when the actual

quae dixit; velut si quisquam Epicureis credens et mortalem animam putans, eas rationes quae de immortalitate eius a prudentioribus tractatae sunt, eloquatur, illo audiente qui spiritalia contueri potest iudicat iste[100] eum vera dicere. At ille qui dicit utrum vera dicat ignorat, immo etiam falsissima existimat: num igitur putandus est ea docere[101] quae nescit? Atqui eisdem verbis utitur, quibus uti etiam sciens posset.

42 Quare iam ne hoc quidem relinquitur verbis, ut his saltem loquentis animus indicetur, si quidem incertum est utrum ea quae loquitur, sciat. Adde mentientes atque fallentes, per quos facile intellegas non modo non aperiri, verum etiam occultari animum verbis. Nam nullo modo ambigo id conari verba veracium, et quodam modo profiteri, ut animus loquentis appareat; quod obtinerent omnibus concedentibus, si loqui mentientibus non liceret. Quamquam saepe experti fuerimus et in nobis et in aliis non earum rerum quae cogitantur, verba proferri: quod duobus modis posse accidere video, cum aut[102] sermo memoriae mandatus[103] et saepe decursus, alia cogitantis ore funditur; quod nobis cum hymnum canimus saepe contingit: aut cum alia pro aliis verba praeter voluntatem nostram linguae ipsius errore prosiliunt; nam hic quoque non earum rerum signa quas in animo habemus, audiuntur. Nam mentientes quidem cogitant etiam de his rebus quas loquuntur, ut tametsi nesciamus an verum dicant, sciamus

100 ista *S T* 101 docere *S*[1]: doceri *R B V S H T*
102 aut] et *R V S H T* 103 mandatus] mandatur *R V S H T*

---

129 A liturgical or ritual formula, for example.
130 Hammond, *Sound of the Liturgy*, 81–82.

speaker doesn't know what they have said. It's like someone who believes the Epicureans, and thinks that the soul is subject to death, declaring arguments which wiser thinkers have used in favor of its immortality; then another person, who can discern spiritual matters, listens and determines that they are speaking the truth. Yet the one doing the talking has no idea whether what they say is true, or even reckons that it is utterly false: should we conclude that the ignorant person is teaching? And yet they're using the same words as the person who had knowledge could.

Words, then, don't even retain the role of illustrating 42
a speaker's thought processes—if, indeed, it's unclear whether they know what they're talking about. You have to factor in liars, and fraudsters, and it's easy to see that not only do they not make their thinking plain by their words, they actually cover it up. I'm wholly convinced that honest people's words are an attempt, a kind of declaration, to make the speaker's mind transparent; and everyone agrees that they would succeed, if liars were not allowed to speak. We have often found, though, in ourselves and in other people, that words are pronounced which don't reflect what people are really thinking. I see this happening in two ways. In the first, when a speech is memorized and delivered repeatedly,[129] it gushes out of the mouth of the person, whose mind is on other things. We often experience this when we're singing hymns.[130] The other is when the wrong words are unintentionally blurted out by a slip of the tongue; in this case, too, people aren't hearing the signs of the actual things that we have in mind. Liars, you see, are thinking about things they're referring to, but in such a way that even if we don't know whether they're speaking the truth, we still know what they say is

tamen eos in animo habere quod dicunt, si non eis aliquid duorum quae dixi accidat.

Quae si quis et interdum accidere contendit, et cum accidit apparere, quamquam saepe occultum est, et saepe
43 me fefellit audientem, non resisto tamen: sed his accedit[104] aliud genus, sane late patens, et semen innumerabilium dissensionum atque certaminum, cum ille qui loquitur eadem quidem significat quae cogitat, sed plerumque tantum sibi et aliis quibusdam; ei vero cui loquitur et item aliis nonnullis, non idem significat. Dixerit enim aliquis audientibus nobis, ab aliquibus beluis hominem virtute superari: nos ilico[105] ferre non possumus, et hanc tam falsam pestiferamque sententiam magna intentione refellimus. Cum ille fortasse virtutem, vires corporis vocet, et hoc nomine id quod cogitavit enuntiet, nec mentiatur, nec erret in rebus, nec aliud aliquid volvens[106] animo mandata memoriae verba contexat,[107] nec linguae lapsu aliud quam volebat[108] sonet; sed tantummodo rem quam cogitat, alio quam nos nomine appellat. De qua illi statim assentiremur, si eius cogitationem possemus inspicere, quam verbis

[104] accedit *T*: accidit *cett.*
[105] ilico ferre *Weig.*: illic offerre *S H T J M*
[106] volens *R V S H T*
[107] contexat *S¹*: contexit *S*
[108] volvebat *R V* μ

---

[131] It could include the deceit that they are attempting to perpetrate.

[132] Repeated texts and slips of the tongue.

[133] This could embrace "restricted code" language (among groups using it to reinforce a common identity while remaining

something they have in their mind[131]—provided that neither of the two possibilities I just mentioned[132] happens to them.

If someone claims that this occurs only rarely, and that when it does it's obvious, I'm not going to argue with them; but it's often covered up, and has often deceived me as I
listened: but there's another category to add to those two. 43
It is certainly widespread, and causes countless disagreements and clashes to spring up. It happens when speakers use words that signify what they are thinking, but do so chiefly to themselves and a select group of others.[133] To the people they're addressing, though, and likewise to some others listening, their words do not have the same signification. For example, imagine someone saying to us, their listeners, that wild animals are superior to human beings in virtue. We are instantly outraged. We do our utmost to disprove such a misguided and noxious opinion—but they are using "virtue" in the sense of "strength,"[134] and are expressing the thing they have in mind using this name-word. They are not lying, or factually incorrect, or pondering anything else in their mind while they cobble together words committed to memory, nor are they uttering a word unintentionally, by a slip of the tongue. All they are doing is to call the thing they're thinking of by name that's different from the one we use. If we could see into their thinking, we would agree with

opaque to outsiders) as well as the example he selects, of a word with multiple significations.

134 *virtus*, formed from *vir*, refers to qualities associated with manliness, such as "excellence" or "strength." It regularly occurs in Cicero as something akin to English "virtue."

iam prolatis explicataque sententia sua, nondum nobis pandere valuit.

Huic[109] errori definitiones mederi posse dicunt,[110] ut in hac quaestione si definiret[111] quid sit virtus eluceret, aiunt, non de re sed de verbo esse controversiam: quod ut concedam ita esse, quotus quisque bonus definitor inveniri potest? et tamen adversus disciplinam definiendi multa disputata sunt; quae neque hoc loco tractare opportunum est, nec usque quaque a me probantur.

44 Omitto quod multa non bene audimus,[112] et quasi de auditis diu multumque contendimus, velut tu nuper verbo quodam punico, cum ego misericordiam dixissem, pietatem significari te audisse dicebas ab eis quibus haec lingua magis nota esset. Ego autem resistens, quid acceperis tibi omnino excidisse asserebam; visus enim mihi eras non pietatem dixisse sed fidem, cum et coniunctissimus mihi assideres, et nullo modo haec duo nomina similitudine soni aurem decipiant. Diu te tamen arbitratus sum nescire quid tibi dictum sit, cum ego nescirem quid dixeris: nam si te bene audissem, nequaquam mihi videretur absurdum pietatem et misericordiam uno vocabulo punice nominari.

Haec plerumque accidunt; sed ea, ut dixi, omittamus, ne calumniam verbis de audiendi[113] neglegentia, vel etiam de surditate hominum videar commovere. Illa magis an-

109 huic *T*: hunc S^1 110 dicunt S^1 μ: dicuntur *B R V T* 111 definiretur *coni. Weig.* 112 audimus *Daur*: audivimus *S* 113 audientis μ

135 See Cic. *Fin.* 2.2.4, "Definition is the clarification of obscure matters, disclosing what each thing is," referring to Plato on definition as a prerequisite for argument (*Phdr.* 237b–c).

them at once; but as yet they have not succeeded in unpacking it for us in the words they uttered to explain their opinion.

It is said that definitions can correct this type of error, in this case, if someone were to define the meaning of "virtue." They would make it clear, they say, that this is a debate about words, not things: but even allowing this, look how few people can be found who are good at definition. What's more, there have been many objections to definition as a branch of learning,[135] though this is not the place to discuss them. In any case I don't altogether approve of it.

I'm not including the fact that we mishear many things, 44
and dispute them long and hard as if we had heard correctly. After I'd said recently that a certain Punic word meant "mercy," you began to say that you'd heard from people who were more fluent in this language that its meaning was actually "devotion." But I held out against you, insisting that you'd misremembered what you heard. It seemed to me that you'd said the word for "faith," not "devotion"; even though you were sitting right beside me, and those two name-words are by no means so similar in sound as to confuse to the ear. For a while I thought you didn't know what had been said to you; though it was I who didn't know what you said! If I'd heard you properly, it would never have seemed ridiculous to me that a single term is used in Punic to identify "devotion" and "mercy."

This is a common enough occurrence; so let's leave such matters, as I said, so I don't look like I'm stirring up an unfair criticism of words out of carelessness in listening, or even people's inability to hear. The examples I gave

gunt quae superius enumeravi, ubi verbis liquidissime aure perceptis et Latinis non valemus, cum eiusdem linguae simus, loquentium cogitata cognoscere.

Sed ecce iam remitto atque concedo, cum verba eius auditu cui nota sunt, accepta fuerint, posse illi esse notum de his rebus quas significant, loquentem cogitavisse: num ideo etiam quod nunc quaeritur, utrum vera dixerit, discit? 14. Num hoc magistri profitentur, ut cogitata eorum ac non ipsae disciplinae quas loquendo se tradere putant, percipiantur atque[114] teneantur? Nam quis tam stulte curiosus est qui filium suum mittat in scholam, ut quid magister cogitet discat?

At istas omnes disciplinas quas se docere profitentur, ipsiusque virtutis atque sapientiae, cum verbis explicaverint, tum illi qui discipuli vocantur utrum vera dicta sint apud semetipsos considerant, interiorem scilicet illam veritatem pro viribus intuentes. Tunc ergo discunt. Et cum vera dicta esse intus invenerint laudant, nescientes non se doctores potius laudare quam doctos, si tamen et illi quod[115] loquuntur sciunt. Falluntur autem homines, ut eos qui non sunt magistros vocent, quia plerumque inter tempus locutionis et tempus cognitionis nulla mora interponitur; et quoniam post admonitionem sermocinantis cito intus discunt, foris se ab eo qui admonuit, didicisse arbitrantur.

[114] atque ad quem *S H T*
[115] quod qui *S H T M*

---

[136] *doctores*: used here for the first time, it is an agent-noun from *docere*, "teach," rather than a precise synonym for *magister*.
[137] *magistros*.

just now cause more trouble when—even though words are caught with perfect clarity by the ear, and they are in Latin—we lack the capacity to know speakers' thoughts, despite sharing the same language.

Now look, I'm giving in and making a concession. 45
When words are heard by someone familiar with them, it is possible for that person to know that the speaker has been thinking of the things that those words signify. But can it really be the case that they likewise learn whether what the speaker has said is true—which is what we're now investigating? 14. And can teachers really be claiming that what their pupils learn and retain is their teachers' ideas, rather than those of the branch of learning which they think their speaking is passing on? Whose eagerness for knowledge is so absurd that they send their own son to school to learn what the teacher thinks?

Yet when they have used words to explain all the branches of learning that they profess to teach, even virtue and wisdom, then those who are called pupils reflect in their own mind whether what they've said is true, undoubtedly by scrutinizing that inner truth according to their ability. Then, and only then, do they learn. And when they discover for themselves that they have heard the truth, they praise him, not realizing that that they are not so much praising those who teach[136] as praising those who've been taught (always supposing that their teachers know what they're talking about). But people are mistaken in naming them "teachers"[137] when they are no such thing: because on the whole there is no interval of time between the moment of speaking and the moment of knowing; and because the moment of inner learning follows so fast upon the instructions of the person doing the talking that they think they have learned it externally from that instructor.

46 Sed de tota utilitate verborum quae si bene consideretur non parva est, alias, si deus siverit, requiremus. Nunc enim ne[116] plus eis quam oportet tribueremus, admonui te, ut iam non crederemus tantum, sed etiam intellegere inciperemus quam vere scriptum sit auctoritate divina, ne nobis quemquam magistrum dicamus in terris, quod unus omnium magister in caelis sit. Quid sit autem in caelis, docebit ipse a quo etiam per homines signis admonemur et[117] foris, ut ad eum intro conversi erudiamur:[118] quem diligere ac nosse beata vita est, quam se omnes clamant quaerere, pauci autem sunt qui eam vere se invenisse laetentur. Sed iam mihi dicas velim, quid de hoc toto meo sermone sentias. Si enim vera esse quae dicta sunt nosti, etiam de singulis sententiis interrogatus ea te scire dixisses. Vides ergo a quo ista didiceris; neque enim a me, cui roganti omnia responderes. Si autem vera esse non nosti, nec ego nec ille te[119] docuit; sed ego, quia numquam possum docere, ille, quia tu adhuc non potes discere.[120]

AD. Ego vero didici admonitione verborum tuorum, nihil aliud verbis quam admoneri hominem ut discat, et perparum esse quod per locutionem aliquanta cogitatio

[116] ne] si *R V S T J M*
[117] et μ: *om. S T*
[118] erudiamur S^1
[119] te *T*: *om. S*
[120] discere S^1 *T* μ: dicere *S H T*

God willing, we shall find another occasion for investigating the functions of words as a whole, since it will be a substantial topic if it's done properly. For now, I've advised you not to allow words more importance than they deserve. This will mean that at last we shouldn't just believe, but also begin to understand, how truly it is written by divine decree that we should call no one on earth our teacher, because there is one Teacher of all, and he is in heaven.[138] He himself will teach us the meaning of "in heaven," for he even instructs us externally by signs from human beings, so that we are directed to turn to him within ourselves. To love him, and know him, is eternal life,[139] which all people claim to be searching for, though those who rejoice that they have truly discovered it are few. But now I would like you to tell me what you think of my argument as a whole. If you've realized that the things I've said are true, then you could be questioned about individual parts of the argument and be able to reply that you knew those things were right. So you see who you learned them from: it wasn't from me, for you could have answered all my questions. If you've not realized that they're true, neither I nor the Teacher has taught you. But I haven't, because I cannot teach; whereas the Teacher hasn't, because you are still unable to learn. 46

AD. I have certainly learned from the direction of your words that words can only direct a person to learn; and that the degree to which a speaker's thinking is disclosed through what they say is minimal. When it comes to

138 Matthew 23:10: Augustine leaves right to the end quotation of the scripture text that underpins the dialogue.

139 John 17:3.

loquentis apparet: utrum autem vera[121] dicantur, eum docere solum, qui se intus habitare cum foris loqueretur admonuit, quem iam favente ipso tanto ardentius diligam, quanto ero in discendo provectior. Verumtamen huic orationi tuae, qua perpetua usus es, ob hoc habeo maxime gratiam, quod omnia quae contradicere paratus eram, praeoccupavit atque dissolvit; nihilque omnino abs te derelictum est, quod me dubium faciebat, de quo non ita mihi responderet[122] secretum illud oraculum, ut tuis verbis asserebatur.

121 vera] verba R^1 *V* S^1 *H T*
122 responderet] respondere] *R* V^1 *S H T*

whether people are speaking the truth, the only one who teaches is he who, when he was speaking to us outwardly, told us that he dwells within. With his help, the more advanced in learning I become, the more passionately I shall love him. But I am particularly appreciative of how you have conducted this argument of yours free from interventions, because you have anticipated everything that I had been ready to disagree with, and resolved each point. You didn't neglect a single one of the matters which were causing me to doubt. That hidden voice of divine truth[140] answered me about them, exactly as your words promised it would.

[140] *oraculum* is used of "pagan" oracles like Delphi, and prophetic texts of the Hebrew Bible/Old Testament.

DE DOCTRINA CHRISTIANA
TEACHING CHRISTIANITY

INTRODUCTION

> *The Greeks (and the Romans after them) always seem to have been primarily concerned with the element of persuasiveness or convincingness in literature—its reference not to the writer's needs nor to the subject's, but to the impact on the audience . . . It seems doubtful whether self-release and self-expression were ever thought of as impulses to write.*
>
> Russell and Winterbottom, *Ancient Literary Criticism*, xv

This summary statement of one key coordinate of ancient literary criticism highlights a commonality between "pagan" and Christian texts, namely, a focus on persuasion. Like the delivery of speeches in public, the writing of text is a tool for pressing a point of view, arguing a case, besmirching an enemy, defending a friend. Even when a piece of speaking or writing is produced in self-defense, it is not self-expression in the modern sense of a disclosure of the interior self. Speaking and writing as ways to record and disseminate teaching fit this same paradigm of persuasion, rather than disclosure, even for Augustine, whose *Confessions* are a rare exception to this general rule.

Teaching Christianity, then, is just such a work of rhetoric, aimed at persuading the reader/hearer of a point of view. Like many books by early Christian theologians of both East and West, it follows a compositional model that

is primarily oral, rather than written. The way it presents arguments and addresses points of view may seem repetitive, discursive, even occasionally digressive to a modern reader. But it is not in the nature, or within the technical constraints, of ancient book writing for authors to go back and forth within the text, editing and shifting sections.

TC does for the new religion what Plato and Aristotle, Cicero and Tacitus and Quintilian had done for the intellectual environment of the past, by exploring how to argue and communicate effectively and (to some extent) ethically:[1]

> Surely [Christians] should learn, without pride, whatever they can learn through human instruction; and let that person who teaches another communicate what they have received, without pride and without envy. (*Proem* 5.11)

The proem[2] does not introduce the key themes of the first two books[3] at all. Instead it is an apologia for teaching as effective communication, defending it against claims from Christians that such knowledge has become otiose in the brave new world of biblical revelation.[4]

[1] See A. Louth, *JThS* 50 (1999): 345–47, on the ethical function of rhetoric, to make the process of hermeneutics converge on the central Christian emphasis on love of God and neighbor.

[2] I have followed the convention of separating the proem from Book 1, as in some ninth- and tenth-century manuscripts, though not in the earliest manuscript (L), from the late fourth century.

[3] Namely, the distinction between "things" and "signs," and, to a lesser extent, "using" and "enjoying."

[4] In theology, "revelation" constitutes a special epistemological category that is set apart from Platonic "opinion" and "knowl-

AUGUSTINE'S WRITINGS

It is easy to doubt that a book written in two stages, with a gap of decades between those stages, could genuinely work as a coherent whole. Yet this is the objective *TC* tries to achieve. The two parts (1.1.1–3.35.78, 3.36.79–4.64.166) have each their own thematic integrity; but it is the fourth book, which presents a defense of rhetoric in the service of Christianity, that ties the whole together. "Rhetoric" refers to the subject as a field of intellectual theory and endeavor; "eloquence" refers to the end product of that expertise.

Augustine is remarkable in so many ways that his decision, later in life, to complete a summary survey of all his writings, in chronological order, comes as less of a surprise than it otherwise might. From that comprehensive review, the *Retractations*, comes vital information about *TC*. He lists *TC* at the point when he began it (AD 397), not when he completed it (426). Without the witness of *Retractations*, the join would not be apparent:

> *Retr.* 2.4, On Teaching Christianity, Four Books
>
> 1. When I found that the books on teaching Christianity were incomplete, I preferred to complete them rather than abandon them and instead go on to take up some other, new, subjects. So I finished the third book, which had been written up to the place where I recorded the witness of the gospel-

edge," by virtue of its being unmediated: a direct revealing of knowledge to individuals (authors of biblical books, e.g.) or communities (of Christians).

writer, "about a woman who covered up yeast in three measures of flour, until all the dough was leavened." I also added a new book, so completing the work in four books: the first three help people to understand scripture, while the fourth shows how to communicate what we understand.

2. True, what I said in the second book about the author of the book which most people call "Wisdom of Solomon" (on the grounds that Jesus ben Sirach wrote it, as he did Ecclesiasticus), is not the common view. I later learned that he was, in all likelihood, not the author of that book. When I said, "the canon of the Old Testament consists only of these forty-four books" (2.26), I was calling it the "Old Testament" as the Church currently uses the term. The apostle Paul, though, seems to have used "old testament" only for the law that was given on mount Sinai (Galatians 4.24). As for what I also said, as though Plato and Jeremiah were contemporaries, "saint Ambrose solved a problem of chronology" (2.107); my memory deceived me. For what that bishop said on the subject can be read in his book on the sacraments, or the one on philosophy (see *Civ.* 8.11). This work begins, "there are certain principles."

So we learn that Augustine stopped writing part way through the third book, and that later (he makes no remark on the length of the interval) he completed that book and added a fourth. His summary of the books' purposes states that three teach hermeneutics (the principles of text interpretation) and the fourth, delivery. As usual in *Re-*

tractations, he corrects anything with which he has come to disagree or which has been superseded. Finally, he records the *incipit*, or opening words, of the work.

Like his other works, then, *TC* has two forms of title: one consists of those opening words, the other is a thumbnail sketch of the contents. The title is often translated as "On Christian Doctrine," but that is highly misleading, for *doctrina* is a word for the process of communication between teacher and learner. Once Augustine moves on, moreover, from his necessary preliminaries about "things" and "signs," it is plain that he is not giving any kind of summary of the nature and content of Christian belief, which is what "doctrine" now means in English. His concern is communicating the faith, not itemizing it. But *TC* is not a treatise on Christian education in general, either,[5] only on one aspect of it, namely learning and teaching the Bible. Those who read it expecting a practical guide to preaching and exegesis will be disappointed.

The summary in *Retractations* gives more information than is available for describing the genesis of most ancient books. But it has led to more, not less, debate. Augustine could have chosen to leave the work in its unfinished form, as he did with other works.[6] He could have begun afresh. That he chose continuation, taken with the information of *Retractations*, confirms that he was content with what he

[5] It is nearly a century since H.-I. Marrou (1958) demolished the idea that *TC* is a manual for the formation of Christian clergy.

[6] For example, on the literal meaning of Genesis (393/4), a commentary on Romans (394/5), and a refutation of the Pelagian Julian of Eclanum (his last book, presumably cut short by his death, 429/30).

had already written and confident that the join (which he describes in *Retractations* but passes over in *TC* itself) would not be noticeable.

Given the quantity and range of Augustine's extant works, it is helpful to provide some context for *TC* not only chronologically but also thematically. Augustine was sometimes an experimental writer: nothing could be more original than *Confessions*, a uniquely self-expressive piece of writing in which the drive to persuade, though certainly present, is not so much concealed as rendered near invisible by the unparalleled laying out of his interior thought world. More often he was a traditional one (dialogue, letter, and speech—in the form of sermon—are mainstream genres). With Plato and Cicero in mind, he tackled the ideology of statehood (*City of God*). He was energetic and prolific in written contributions to disputes with rival ideologies like Donatism and Pelagianism. The weapons for such contests were theological (grace, free-will, predestination) and exegetical or hermeneutical (his many writings on biblical texts). Ethical questions concerned with Christian living were also prominent in his writings.

Augustine the monk secluded from the world, the man of prayer, had come to life in his early dreams of what the Christian life could be. That dream died daily, though, in the reality of his life as a bishop, which was packed with public speaking and with administrative and judicial functions. Reading, writing, study, and prayer had to be fitted in around these. The visionary servant of God, to whom declarations of love and faithfulness ring out in *Confessions*, disappears from his later writings. This makes it impossible to know whether he went on having visions or dreaming dreams. Sometimes the gloomy tenor of

his theology of grace and predestination hints at a disillusion (perhaps better unillusion) with human capacities for goodness. All that preaching and praying was not solving political affairs in which he was caught up. Nor did it render his congregation in Hippo noticeably improved in Christian virtue and devotion. His last written work has been criticized as "lamentable" and "melancholy" by one reputable scholar, and as a rehash with "added bitterness" by another.[7]

In *TC*, however, a glimpse of the first raptures of a man in love with God does resurface. Augustine's passionate enthusiasm for scripture has all the zeal of the convert and more besides. In the early sections of the text, composed around the same time as *Confessions*, it might be reasonable to expect that. But eagerness and passion are apparent in book four too, albeit with a different focus. Late in life, but not too late, the rediscovery of this unfinished work gave him an opportunity to develop a daring argument on a sensitive subject: he is aware that it will be controversial, but he has become convinced of the Church's need to heed what he proposes, for the sake of the Church's earthly future. For the task of teaching Christianity, a deep and wide knowledge of the Bible is indispensable. But so too, he reveals, are the skills in communication that will enable that knowledge to be imparted to others.

EXPLAINING TEXT

This situation requires a new kind of intellectual theory to underpin it, because the boundaries are different from

[7] Burnaby, *Amor Dei*, 231; Bonner, *Freedom and Necessity*, ix.

those that governed the philosophical presentations of ideal polities in the classical past. Plato's *Republic* was built on an Athenian foundation. Cicero's was likewise essentially Roman. Augustine completed *TC* 4 in 426/7, perhaps immediately after finishing his monumental *De civitate dei contra paganos* ("City[8] of God against the Pagans"). That had been, in places, a different kind of struggle against the positive elements in "pagan" literature, and certainly a rejection of the belief that humankind could advance toward wisdom through education and philosophy. But it must have brought some of the old "pagan" authors to the forefront of his thinking. In particular, as he grew old, and (one must imagine) felt his powers of mind and memory beginning to weaken, he had to ask himself a question that had never bothered Plato or Cicero: how was his God to be entrusted effectively by one generation to the next?

Plato and Cicero had not been preoccupied with this matter because their ideal republics, like their views of their several divinities, were not primarily founded upon a shared ideology, but upon a common racial and political identity, speaking the same language, sharing the same history. Christianity had by now taken on some aspects of such a shared cultural identity, but without the racial and linguistic underpinnings that enabled the smooth transmission of an entire cultural oeuvre from one generation to the next. The advantage of the Christian approach had been the flexibility of portable religion, for Christianity

8 "Polity," a closer translation of *civitas* (which means "state" or "body politic"), will never supersede the traditional title. The regular Latin word for a city is *urbs*.

was not tied to a particular building, land, nation, or language. The drawback was that every generation had to reconstitute itself afresh.

This was sensitive ground. Two centuries earlier, a fellow north African theologian, Tertullian, who had also been trained in the arts of argument and communication, had stated a dichotomy as if it were God-given and eternal:

> [9] What does Athens have to do with Jerusalem? What does philosophy have to do with the Church? What do heretics have to do with Christians? [11] Let those who promote Stoic or Platonic or dialectic Christianity deal with what concerns them. [12] We have no need of intellectual inquiry after we have Christ Jesus; and no more need for searching after we have received the gospel. [13] When we become believers, there is nothing more that we long to believe; for the first thing that we believe is that there is nothing further that we must believe.

That hostility to "pagan" learning hardened over the intervening years. Christianity was not just radical in its locus of religious expression (shared text as well as shared ritual; freedom from geographical or racial boundaries). It was also radical in the way that it offered an education in a framework of ethical precepts that was not the preserve of an educated elite. No one had to pay to listen to Christian teaching (in the form of sermons), as they did when attending lectures by a "pagan" philosopher. If they were curious about how the world was thought to work, they needed an expert in natural philosophy; if they were inter-

ested in ethics, or politics, a teacher of Aristotle or Stoicism might do; if metaphysical speculation on things unseen preoccupied them, there was Plato to guide them. The attraction of one book, and one structure, was not nugatory.

Amid the several disciplines of ancient "pagan" education, one stood out because it was essentially vocational. It occupied a place in the heart of educational practice, but at the periphery of educational ideals. It was rhetoric; the art and skill of persuasive public speaking, as indispensable a tool for use in public life as the internet is today. It had its theoretical underpinning, naturally. No less a philosopher than Aristotle himself had taken up the topic, arguing from the first for rhetoric as a natural counterpart of dialectic (logic). He followed on from Plato, in whose dialogues we can observe the beginnings of a separation between philosophy proper and sophism. Both employed rhetoric to further their arguments. Both claimed to be paths to wisdom. But rhetoric's purpose in the minds of men with ambitions for public office, whether in the military, politics, or the law (all these categories overlap), was pragmatic. If you could persuade, you could succeed. This was the path the young Augustine had himself embarked upon, though he abandoned it for another that he found more satisfying.

Rhetoric was morally suspect, from a Christian perspective, for a number of reasons. First, it taught objectives over principles, and effects over ideals. Second, it was associated with style rather than substance (a dichotomy in which the influence of Plato seems to have been undying). And third, most important of all for the Chris-

tians of Augustine's time, it seemed to imply that Jerusalem stood in need of the expertise of Athens. What no Christian theorist could admit was that the theory of inspiration by the Holy Spirit was all very well in Bible days, when the apostles were apparently remarkable for their rhetorical skill and practical eloquence, but that in their own time, it was remarkable how dull and even incompetent a public speaker could be who relied wholly on the Spirit, and made no effort at all to cooperate with the divine design by preparing arguments, mustering an army of supportive and corroborative texts from scripture, and paying close attention to the audience he was trying to persuade.

Plato had argued that the sense-perceptible world was inferior to an ideal world wherein true knowledge was to be found. Sense-perceptible phenomena were imitations of the true realities. His idea of *mimesis*, "imitation," as secondary and derivative was to become the Japanese knotweed of ancient literary theory. It associated the ideal and the perfect with what is at a remove from humankind. Works of art of all kinds (painting, sculpture, literature) were seen likewise as derivative and secondary, not innovative or aboriginal. Two works of critical theory stand out against this generally accepted association of artistic representation with what is inferior. The first is Aristotle's *Poetics*, in which *mimesis* is morphed into a creative, nuanced and, above all, positive feature. The more mimetic a representation is, Aristotle argued, the better. Hence drama comes out in his scheme ahead of epic, history, and other literary forms.

No direct influence from Aristotle's *Poetics* is detect-

able in *TC*. Nor is there any trace of the other critical work that demands an honorable mention in this context, *On the Sublime*, by pseudo-Longinus.[9] It too sought to locate literary excellence elsewhere than in imitativeness regarded negatively. Neither of these works had any influence on Augustine's mind or method. The Platonist hierarchy, privileging the unseen over the seen, and the ideal over the concrete, made sense to him in the first enthusiasm of his search for wisdom (discovering Cicero's work, *Hortensius*, now lost) and in the nine years of his Manichaeism (a sub-Christian version of the orthodox faith). After he became an orthodox Christian, its appeal remained for a while undimmed, as his early writings, including elements of *Confessions*, attest.

But Platonist ideal truth could never coexist comfortably with one of the staples of rhetorical theory and practice in which Augustine had been trained to a high standard: learning how to present and argue both sides of a case. Teaching people how to argue what they did not believe to be true, or knew to be false, was (and is) as practically necessary as it was (and is) difficult to defend morally. So advocates and other public speakers who sought to acquire rhetorical expertise as a way to improve their oratorical power were instead obliged to take refuge in the hope of an ideal: that a person of eloquence be a *vir bonus dicendi peritus*.[10]

[9] Though the search has been undertaken, by Van Der Lof, "Verbricht Augustin das Schweigen," 21–33.

[10] "A good person, skilled in public speaking." The famous vignette is attributed to Cato: see Quint. *Inst.* 12.1.

PROEM

Augustine introduces *TC* as a book about principles (*praecepta*) for handling the scriptures, thus identifying it from the start as a work of hermeneutics. It is not the first work to survive from antiquity to aim at systematizing the principles of scriptural interpretation. That distinction belongs to Ticonius, whose "Book of Rules"[11] Augustine makes extensive use of in *TC* 3.42.92–56.134. More than a century earlier, Origen had discussed some of the same ideas and problems in book four of his *De principiis*; but he did so as part of a wider theological work. *TC* is the first work of such a kind to survive from the hand of a mainstream (orthodox/catholic) Christian, which makes a major difference to how it has been treated by posterity.

The rest of the proem is a proleptic response to a series of imagined critics, the third group of which, consisting of those who regard hermeneutics as unnecessary, is his real target. His answer is that the Church cannot rely wholly on direct divine revelation when interpreting scripture, because scripture itself reveals that God's preferred mode of self-disclosure is person-to-person.

[11] Or *liber regularum*, ca. AD 382/3: Augustine remarks that "all these laws [except the third] use one thing to make some other thing understood" (*TC* 3.56.133), which was his short definition of figurative discourse. Cicero noted, "Of literal words we should choose the most polished; and in the case of figurative language we should aim for straightforward comparisons, and be cautious about metaphors with no clear point of contact" (*Opt. gen.* 4).

TEACHING CHRISTIANITY

BOOK 1: SIGNS AND THINGS, USING AND ENJOYING

Book 1 can be read mainly for the philosophical problems it identifies, particularly the distinction between "things" and "signs [of things]," and that between using and enjoying. But that would not reflect the book as a whole. Augustine begins by reiterating his themes of how to understand scripture and how to present it, taking understanding first. By applying the term *inventio* (finding material; a rhetorical category) he indicates that "understanding" scripture will consist of establishing the meaning of what it says, so preparing readers for books full of puzzles and problems.

So far so pertinent. But what follows is the groundwork for an analysis of relevant material in terms of "things" and "signs." He seems to be defining terms in this way so that he can deal first with concrete and meaning-free realities.[12] This concern for evaluation also directs his distinction between using things and enjoying them, and between different levels of enjoyment. The distinction between enjoyment of God's creation and enjoyment of God the creator is one that must have preoccupied him at the time, for it also surfaces in *Confessions*, most lyrically at 10.27.38. It naturally embraces the incarnation of the Word, that characteristic Christian belief, rooted in John

[12] A possible (but not ideal) alternative translation to "things" for the Latin term *res*. He wants to get the discussion of material reality out of the way so that he can move on to words, which are the real subject matter of his *doctrina*.

1, that the second person of the holy Trinity was made a human being, in the person of Jesus Christ. That draws him into a brief account of how salvation works theologically and how human beings should respond to the divine initiative that is the incarnation, by learning and imitating divine love.

Use and enjoyment are treated as ways of getting to the heart of human motivation and the proper direction of human loving. These are both characteristic preoccupations of Augustine. By 1.39.84 he reaches the conclusion of the first phase of his argument:

> Of everything, then, that has been said since we began our discussion of these matters, this one is the chief: that we understand that love is the fullness and purpose of the law, and of all of holy scripture—love of the thing we ought to enjoy, and love of any thing that can share our enjoyment of that thing.

This leads him to an equally characteristic conclusion on how building up love relates to his hermeneutic quest:

> If anyone, therefore, considers that they have understood the holy scriptures, or some part of them, but does so in a way that fails to build up that double love—of God and neighbor—then they have not yet understood it. (1.40.86)

Only when Book 1 is ending does he begin to tackle scripture in earnest, suggesting what he will go on to make plain: that scripture itself, however divinely inspired, is for use, rather than enjoyment, as being a means to an end, not an end in itself.

BOOK 2: UNKNOWN SIGNS

At *TC* 1.2.4, Augustine had stated that "things are learned by means of the signs" (*res per signa discuntur*). It seems odd to begin with what he has implied is secondary.[13] One explanation lies in Platonist ideas of reality and imitation; another possibility is that the form/content dichotomy is at work (see below, p. 173), making clothing secondary to the body that it clothes. Or it could be because in chronological terms things that happen in history (*res*) come before the meanings that those things acquire (*signa*).

His definition of signs is straightforward: they signify something to someone; and they can be natural, or intentional (i.e., produced with the aim of communicating X to Y). All the same, this is not the prelude to a comprehensive theory of signs. The focus stays on the practicalities of signifying; the content of the book is the groundwork for preaching scripture.[14]

After a brief sketch of ways of signifying, Augustine moves on to his main subject—words as the principal signs. Letters are signs for sounds, while words are signs, composed of one or more sounds, for things (whether concrete, like "food," or abstract, like "hunger" [my example]). Figurative (i.e., metaphorical, symbolic) use of words (he takes an example from the Song of Songs, 2.6.11–8.15) is part of the complex attraction of scripture.

Next come seven stages in the acquisition of scriptural fluency, which is a spiritual as well as an intellectual state, culminating in the attainment of wisdom. *TC* is most in-

13 Babcock, "*Caritas* and Signification," 145.

14 Hill, "*De doctrina christiana,*" 446.

sistent about level three, knowledge, not as abstract reasoning but in the form of familiarity with the scriptures. So the foundation necessary for teaching Christianity is knowing which books are canonical (universally authoritative) and what they contain ("guidance for living or rules of belief," 2.14.30). Sometimes scripture addresses us in literal terms; but in other places it speaks figuratively: thus the next requirement is understanding of languages. This is a collective endeavor in pursuit of truth, in which communication is more important than absolute linguistic precision (a point he returns to in Book 4).

Expertise in biblical languages[15] is vital, as is knowledge of the Bible's world (plants, animals, even stones may have the power to signify if we are familiar with their properties). Numerology, the pseudoscience of number, makes for links between Old and New Testaments and can carry hidden meanings. In contrast, Augustine is scathing about what he regards as superstitious apotropaeic and necromantic practices. In his references to demons and angels, he takes their reality for granted as part of divine communication with humankind. Signifying systems of human origin, such as currency, calendars, chronology, and weights and measures (proper standards in such systems, taken for granted now, were of the highest importance in underpinning social stability in ancient times) may be morally neutral or even beneficial. Above all, the alphabet (2.40.102) is not to be shunned just because it is of human origin. History too has its value, as does logic,

[15] That is, Hebrew, Aramaic, Greek. Augustine is not concerned with Aramaic, but he has plenty to say about the many Latin versions circulating in his day.

which, despite the fact that it was developed by "pagans," is endorsed by scripture (2.50.122–23).

Toward the end of the book, Augustine turns to eloquence, which, at its best, is logic (the application of reason to the end of persuasion) in action. This is his way of preparing the ground for the sensitive matter of how (if at all) Christians should approach "pagan" learning.

BOOK 3: AMBIGUOUS SIGNS

This takes the argument a stage further: ambiguous signs need to be interpreted with accuracy and authority, so as not to undermine faith. An example from John's gospel shows how small tweaks to a scriptural text can have major impact on orthodoxy and meaning. One from Paul (usually referred to as "the apostle") shows that when nothing within the statement allows for a decision one way or another, context may be the only decisive factor in resolving an ambiguity. Phrasing, punctuation, vowel length, and accidence can all create and resolve ambiguities. In his investigation of ambiguity in relation to sign and signified, Augustine has been succeeded by Rahner, Ricoeur, and, more recently Derrida.[16] His view of language and signification is shaped by the constraints of his milieu: only one medium—writing—was available for the recording of language-acts, and some of the inherent ambiguity in human language use can be attributed to that fact. Even writings of the highest authority are only approximations to reality; hence all writings may admit of ambiguity.

16 Schildgen, "Augustine's Answer to Jacques Derrida," 383–97.

Often a choice must be made whether something being said is meant literally or figuratively. "Sacrifice" is given as an example of a lower meaning being literal (an animal sacrifice) but the higher being figurative (the death of Christ, for example). This introduces typology (a signifying system in which the old covenant prefigures the new) as a way of explaining Christianity's emergence from its Jewish matrix (3.9.20–11.25). It is with that Jewish matrix that he engages when he refers to gods as "idols," for this is a conceptual category that is meaningless to "pagans" (3.11.27–12.29). In place of the figurative meanings of the Jewish law, a small number of special signs has been established among Christians, called "sacraments" (3.13.31–32). These are pointers to what they signify (as, e.g., bread "signifies" the Lord's body).

Augustine marks his distance from the freewheeling allegorism of Origen by insisting on a universal criterion for deciding whether a text is literal or figurative: if, when applied literally to scripture, it leads to integrity and faith, there is no need to look for other meanings. But if, applied literally, it says anything unworthy of God, a figurative meaning is present (for him it is not an option to say that a scripture is meaningless): because "scripture insists on nothing that is not love, and condemns nothing that is not appetite" (3.15.36, 3.24.55).[17] Again he resists reinterpreting scripture just because it is found to be unpalatable (3.17.39); a resistance all the more necessary because the Bible is full of material that is apparently wrong or unworthy (3.18.42–29.66).

[17] See *Gen. Man.* 2.2.3; and Teske, "Criteria for Figurative Interpretation," 109.

Augustine takes an unusual (for the time) step toward contextual ethics when he argues that different ways of life "look wrong to other peoples in other historical eras" (3.22.51). His cautious approach to allegory removes the only possible way in which every verse of scripture could be said to be applicable to every believer. That leads, of necessity, to his conclusion that some texts are universal, others particular (3.59), which becomes a way of explaining variation in social customs like marriage. He analyzes an example of it, the case of King David (3.30.68–31.72). At 3.33.75 he even provides a metanarrative for the Bible as a whole: "there is scarcely a page of the holy books in which that principle does not resound: 'God resists the proud, but gives grace to the lowly.'" Just after this (*TC* 3.35.78; in AD 397), he leaves his text "poised over the abyss of the ever-shifting referent of figurative language,"[18] right where he needs to make sense of how a scriptural sign (leaven is his chosen example) may mean X in one place and Y in another.[19]

In 426, he takes up *TC* from where he left off by giving more examples of signs (lion, snake, bread) having multiple significance. He introduces here a factor that is more innovative than it may appear to modern readers: making authorial intention a part of hermeneutics (3.38.84). This

[18] Bright, "Biblical Ambiguity," 28: in an argument linking African exegesis and ecclesiology she points to "double typology" in African exegesis

[19] Kannengiesser, "The Interrupted *de doctrina christiana*," argues that the break happens because Augustine realized he did not yet have an adequate exegetical methodology; he needed to master Ticonius's "rules" first.

relates to his reluctance to let scripture be treated merely as a backdrop to theological imagination. For one thing, the text is always there to challenge and test an interpretation. By treating authors as contributing participants in the creation of scriptural writings, he answers the difficulty of how divine communications are created and embedded in scripture. Inspiration does not, for Augustine, mean that God moved the pen in the hand of an automaton author. Neither does he argue that the meaning of scripture must be restricted to what the author intended, which is certainly radical for its time, but he never follows it up in detail (3.38.85–39.86).

After further examples of figurative language (3.40.87–41.91), Augustine closes Book 3 by bringing forward the text in which he had found the answers that enabled him to complete *TC*. The *Book of Rules* of the fourth-century schismatic and heretic Tyconius provided a method and structure for understanding the language of scripture. Some of his rules were theological (1–3, 7), others concerned with language (4–6). Augustine takes the reader through these rules, showing how principles of language and rhetoric can elucidate the sacred text, before concluding that "all these laws . . . use one thing to make some other thing understood. This is the proper function of the metaphorical mode of expression" (3.56.133).

BOOK 4: A PROGRAM AND A VISION

The final book of *TC* showcases the expert orator giving, in effect, a master class on presentation, in order to clinch his case for Christian teachers needing to learn eloquence. He demonstrates how scriptural words impart truth syn-

thetically (constructing an assemblage of materials) rather than analytically (taking text apart), so that teachers of the Bible can embark on the hermeneutical quest toward their exegetical goal by gathering information, scrutinizing the selection and arrangement of words, and detecting relationships between the different parts of the canon. Teaching Christianity entails mastering the content and presentation of the sacred text, always with a view to communicating it to others. This is confirmed at the end of *TC* as the purpose of the work as a whole.

The skills that Augustine and others had learned in their rhetorical education were honed and polished tools of the speaker's art. It is not his intention to argue that these tools were indispensable for Christians; but he does insist that in themselves they are morally neutral and practically useful, and that without them, theology and preaching alike would be the poorer, in both form and content. Augustine's passion for communicating to his Christian audiences relied on a foundation of "pagan" education. In his old age, he came to reassess the value of the skills he had long deployed in Christianity's service and to realize the importance of teaching people, for the faith's future, how precious an educational asset the art of persuasive speech really was. *TC* 4 was the result.

Underpinning most ancient literary theory is the assumption of a dichotomy between form and content. "Content" encompasses the semantic element in communication, that is, the information contained in, or conveyed by, the words. "Form" covers the techniques applied to putting that information across, whether generic (the genre or type of literature to which the text belongs) or stylistic (its usage of figures of rhetoric, arrangement of

material, etc). A body and its clothing; a container and its contents: these are the interpreter's parameters. Augustine has been regarded as associating rhetoric with style, but his attitude is not straightforward, and it fluctuates over time. In this paradigm, rhetoric is a matter of form, not content, and belongs, therefore, to the category of the decorative: as a type of embellishment, it is nonessential. This paradigm surfaces in *TC*, and it offers some defense against the charge of depending on "pagan" wisdom, at 4.2.3.

Centuries before, Cicero had reflected on the separation of rhetoric and philosophy making perfect eloquence unattainable:

> To express these many important ideas one must use innumerable stylistic ornaments; which at that time comprised the sole instruction given by those accounted teachers of rhetoric. As a consequence no one attains to that true and perfect eloquence, because there is one course of training in thought, and another in expression; from one group of teachers we seek instruction in facts, from others instruction in language. (*Orat.* 17)

Augustine, unlike Cicero, needs to defend the value of inelegant texts; and as a preacher, for whom persuasion mattered more than good Latinity, he is prepared to disregard the linguistic flaws that had formerly repelled him. But that did not stop him thinking of them as flaws, even though he made the case for clarity mattering more.

In any case, Augustine's own arguments point to a different conclusion. At the start of Book 4, he constructs an extended series of questions that impel the reader to agree with his own estimation of the value of rhetoric: in rapid

succession he unrolls the disastrous consequences flowing from neglecting it. Four times antithesis and anaphora intensify the divide between "them" and "us" (*illi . . . isti*); clusters of evaluative terminology draw the reader toward Augustine's assessment of the situation, setting *illi . . . falsas/falsa/fallacibus/falsitatem/errorem* against *isti vera/vera/veritate* and using irony to emphasize the folly of leaving so powerful a tool (or weapon) in the hands of Christianity's opponents. A triumphant rhetorical question clinches the argument before it has been developed in the rest of Book 4, by implying that only the foolish and ignorant could think Christians neglecting rhetoric was a good idea: "Who is so stupid as to see any sense in that?" (4.3.4).

That passionate defense of the value of rhetoric does not mean that he has an uncritical attitude to practitioners of his former profession. Motivation is, characteristically, his primary evaluative criterion. Deployed for the purpose of self-advancement, rhetoric is pernicious. Spread at Christ's feet to serve his purposes, rhetoric can be a handmaiden of truth. The logic of his position on this subject is inconsistent. Just as he cannot allow for the possibility of scripture being "wrong," so he also cannot allow himself to argue that Jerusalem needs Athens. Any suggestion that pagan learning could contribute positively to something in which Christianity must be deficient implied a flaw in the faith, while Christian scholars were always eager to find ways of showing that even the finest "pagan" minds were in fact imitative of, and derived from, biblical history and literature. Augustine displayed just such a sensitivity when he reported how "our own Ambrose" proved that Plato had filched his teachings from Jeremiah (*TC* 2.43.107).

By the time he came to write Book 4, Augustine had

come to believe that rhetoric ought to be a part of the Christian teacher's equipment. In 4.2.3, he warns readers not to expect him to impart the subject he once taught in the schools of "pagan" education. "This is not because such stuff has no use, but because, if it has any, it should be a separate educational subject for any worthy person who has the free time to learn it," he remarks. Only a few lines later, he commends rhetoric more straightforwardly as a necessary, not just a valuable, tool: "Independently of these writings of mine, anyone with the capacity to learn fast, when they have reached an appropriate maturity, should set aside a proper period of time for mastering this subject" (4.4.6).

The first main section of Book 4 approaches rhetoric less from the technical point of view and more in conceptual terms, looking at how speakers acquire eloquence through attentive listening and imitation. When it comes to detecting rhetoric in scripture, Augustine has to expand the meaning of the term "eloquence" to make it apply, so that what appears to be lacking in eloquence (the practical end product of theoretical rhetoric) turns out to be full of a better kind of eloquence:

> When I do not understand [biblical] authors, their eloquence is harder for me to recognize, but I have no doubt that it is of the same quality as what I do understand. Indeed, this very obscurity in sacred and salvific pronouncements had to be mixed in with a commensurate amount of eloquence, . . . which obliges us not only to discover meaning, but also to wrestle with it. (4.9.27)

This tension is never resolved. The most he feels justified in doing is to set the case in favor of rhetoric side by side

with the idea of inspiration rendering it unnecessary, in the hope that readers would draw the correct conclusion (that acquiring eloquence is of the first importance to teachers of the faith). His later elaboration of how there is a kind of natural rhetoric at work in scripture and his concession that men of leisure may pursue those studies in addition to the more important one of interpreting scripture were never going to be sufficient to secure for teachers of Christianity an education in the art of persuasive speech. Once his generation of teachers, the last to be brought up in a world where "pagan" education was an unquestionable good, was gone, rhetoric's place in Christian teaching would inevitably decline.

If goodness and virtue were not part of the factual contents of rhetoric, another source for those qualities needed to be identified. Augustine found what he was looking for, in a person he does not name in Book 4, but whose influence is evident: Cicero. Cicero figures more prominently in Augustine's many references to classical literature than any other "pagan" writer; and the way in which he refers to him in this late work is more cautious than the enthusiasm with which he commended him in *TT*:

> What standard can we find in the Latin tongue that is more exemplary than Cicero . . . in his most distinguished speeches known as the *Verrines*? (5.16)

Describing those speeches as *nobilissimae* is high praise indeed. In this instance, as in another of the speeches (rather, a series of speeches) that he alludes to often[20]—the *Catilinarian Orations*—what seems to attract his ap-

[20] Hagendahl counts eleven references (*Augustine and the Latin Classics*, 2:481).

proval is Cicero's high moral tone in condemning the malefactors Verres and Catiline. The influence on the young Augustine of Cicero's lost work *Hortensius* is often observed by scholars; but what saves Cicero from the wastepaper basket of "pagan" texts is his noble ideal of the public speaker as a person of good character. Not that Cicero was naïve about the reasons for ascribing virtue to a public speaker:

> The character, habits, actions, and way of life of forensic orators have a powerful impact on their success. (*De or.* 2.182)

> A degree of good sense, and an organized way of speaking are so effective that a speech can apparently illustrate the speaker's good character. (*De or.* 2.184)

> I am always very nervous at the start of a speech. Whenever I speak, I always seem to be inviting a judgment upon not only my talent, but also my honor and duty. (*Clu.* 51)

No less than Augustine was Cicero aware of the dangers of eloquence unmoderated by morality:

> Eloquence is one among the supreme virtues . . . It uses words to reveal the impressions and intentions of the mind in such a way that it can drive listeners to whatever conclusion it has thrown its weight behind. Therefore the more powerful it is the more it has to be bound together with good morals and supreme wisdom: for if we transmit eloquence to those who have no virtue, we will not be making

> them into orators but actually handing weapons to people who lack all self-regulation. (*De or.* 3.55)

Augustine cautiously commends Cicero as a worthwhile object of study for those eager to become proficient persuaders in the Latin language. In this, as on other matters, he was at odds with Jerome, who was the better linguistic exegete, but whose rebarbative personality suggests that he may have fallen far short of Augustine in persuasive skill. Jerome's abhorrence from Cicero is that of the recovering addict:

> Many years ago, when I was setting out for Jerusalem as a soldier for Christ, I simply could not do without the library that I had taken such care and trouble to build up back in Rome. I used to fast—wretch that I was!—whenever I was planning to read Cicero.[21] Whenever I came to my senses and started to read the prophets, I found their uneducated speech repellent: because my eyes were blinded and could not see the light, I blamed the sun, not my own capacity for vision. While I was the plaything of that ancient serpent, Satan, half-way through Lent I became racked with fever that attacked my body in its weakened state. My funeral was being prepared. Suddenly I was carried away in the spirit, and dragged, resisting, before the Judge in his court. Asked who and what I was, I replied that I was a Christian. The Judge replied, "Liar! you are a Ciceronian, not a Christian: for where your treasure is, there will your heart be also." I was

21 As a proleptic penance.

> dumbstruck . . . but then began to cry out, saying, "have mercy on me, Lord, have mercy on me." I began to swear, and call upon his name, saying, "Lord, if I ever again possess pagan books, or if I read them, I have denied you!" (Jer. *Ep.* 22.30)

After setting out a cautious defense of teaching rhetoric (4.1.1–10.28), Augustine launches into a series of analyses of biblical texts to show not just *that* they are eloquent but also *how* they are. These include minute observations on textual structure across both Testaments. Though he regards all scripture as inspired, he does not teach that it is all equally useful in teaching. Instead, he concedes that it can be incomprehensible at times (4.22.61–23.63). He makes practical suggestions for preaching in such circumstances, including the need to be flexible, so that the vital goal of changing people's thoughts and actions can take place (4.22.61–30.83).

At 4.31.84–34.96, Augustine again draws on Cicero, recalling his instructions on the purposes of eloquent speech, combining them with prayer and self-examination: this is his response to those who claim to rely only on the Holy Spirit for their eloquence. He analyzes a series of Pauline texts to illustrate Cicero's plain, middle, and grand styles (4.35.97–45.125), before moving on to Cyprian and Ambrose as post-biblical examples of eloquence (4.45.126–50.33), showing how the best Christian speakers have repurposed their rhetorical expertise to fit new subject matter. Sounding like a teacher of rhetoric as much as a bishop, he concludes that "by constant reading and listening, combined with some training also, students can become adept in [the] use [of the three styles]" (4.50.133).

From 4.51.134–56.45 his affirmation of the value of

rhetoric begins to be delivered without any admixture of Christianity to contextualize it. Only a choice of example (4.53.139) identifies the instruction as being of Christian origin. At 4.55.142 he makes reference to "those who want to speak wisely and eloquently in public," also in a way that recalls his first, rather than his final, teaching career. Scriptures does finally reemerge (4.56.146) as the object of that eloquence: but still the Ciceronian framing does not recede, for at last Augustine is able to bring forward the person of the Christian teacher, who is Cicero's ideal orator baptized: *ecclesiasticus eloquens*—the "Christian orator." Once again, the "good person, skilled in public speaking" is before the reader, such that a preacher about to address his congregation is distinguishable from the politician delivering a speech *apud populum*, "before the people" (4.63.164), only by the prayer they must offer to God. The *orator* (= "speaker in public") and the *orator* (= "the pray-er") have finally become one and the same.

BIBLICAL EXEGESIS IN THE TIME OF AUGUSTINE

Literary texts are mostly (though not exclusively)[22] written to be read. The act of writing presupposes an audience, whether of many, as in the case of speeches, drama, and the like, or of a select few, as in poetry "published" by invited performance or of one individual, as in a private letter. The literary text without an audience does not exist in ancient literary theory.

[22] See, e.g., Numbers 5:11–31. Also Wogan, *Magical Writing in Salasaca*; Tambiah, "The Magical Power of Words," 175–208 (https://doi.org/10.2307/2798500).

The business of scrutinizing texts is almost as old as the process of writing them, for copying by hand made errors inevitable, as did readers and scribes with opinions and objectives of their own. Attention to the detail of texts, and acquiring expertise in the style of an author, was a way of life for some professional scholars, such as Aristophanes of Byzantium (ca. 257–ca. 185/80 BC); and it enabled them to debate questions of authorship, and consequently authenticity, through minute attention to words. Christian attitudes to textual scholarship came to be equally scrupulous; for they too were exercised by authenticity, and hence authority, as a criterion of inclusion during the years in which the canon of scripture was forming.

There was more to ancient criticism than establishing a text. Greek and Latin scholars before Augustine had developed theories of argument, presentation, and meaning too. Plato distinguished between different ways of meaning ("semantic" and "dianoetic": in *Cratylus*, a dialogue about naming), as did Aristotle (in *Rhetoric* and *Poetics*).[23] Keeping his focus on style, Cicero investigated words having literal (*propria*) and metaphorical (*translata*) meanings, and Augustine adopted both his terminology and his preference for clarity over complexity.

Attention to form in "pagan" rhetorical instruction could go all the way down to the microcosmic level of individual words. But Christian textual scholarship at its extreme held that not only the individual words but also the individual strokes of the individual letters of the individual words had been divinely inspired. Origen had said, "even the smallest letter, or even a fraction of a letter,

23 Eden, "Hermeneutics"; Eden, "Rhetorical Tradition."

written in scripture has something to offer those who understand how it works . . . Taking account, from the holy writings, of each iota and each particle as it occurs, reveals the power of the letter, that it has been written to be useful, never superfluous."[24] The authority attributed to the biblical books was so great as to stimulate the development of a new genre, the commentary. Its generic label might vary,[25] but the scrutiny of individual words and phrases did not: once again Origen provided the example that others followed. Examples from Augustine include his expositions of the Psalms and his tractates on the gospel of John.

In antiquity, textual scrutiny of the two major Homeric poems (plus a number of lesser works whose authenticity was debated) was a relatively simple matter. The Bible consisted of either sixty-six or seventy-three separate compositions[26] produced in three different languages over a period of (roughly) a thousand years. This made exegesis and hermeneutics much more problematic, for from the Christian standpoint, every biblical book must be related theologically, and in some sense historically, to every other. Intertextuality, therefore, could be both objective and obstacle.[27]

24 In *Philocalia* 10.1–2 (= *Homily on Jeremiah* 39); following Matthew 5:18.

25 Augustine's scriptural writings include *enarratio*, *tractatus*, *annotatio*, *expositio*, *locutio*, and *quaestio*.

26 Depending on whether the deuterocanonical works are counted.

27 See Frances Young, "Christian Teaching," in *The Cambridge History of Early Christian Literature*, ed. F. Young, L. Ayres, and A. Louth (Cambridge, 2004), 464–84.

The establishment of an authentic text was not an end in itself but a first step in identifying secure texts to support disputed theological and ecclesiological positions. *TC* presupposes theories of language and signification; but the theories are the means to a different end, so philosophers of language must acquaint themselves thoroughly with Augustine's milieu if they are not to misunderstand and misrepresent him.[28]

Long before Augustine, Origen had identified the problem of texts that could have no palatable literal meaning for Christians.[29] There was general agreement that the Bible had content that could be absorbed straightforwardly, and also content that was cloaked or figurative of something else, which needed revealing or explaining. The question was where and on what grounds to draw the distinction. By reading meaning microcosmically (at the level of individual letters, words, or phrases), Origen could construct exegesis that was infinitely flexible. But to others it appeared that this was a free-floating exercise in creative imagination.

A macrocosmic sense of the message of scripture, as indicated by the idea of a "rule of faith" or "rule of truth" (a common shorthand for the whole package of authentic Christianity), seemed to promise a more secure way of accessing the divine will as revealed both in the texts and

[28] For more about language and signification, see the introduction to *TT*.

[29] Narratives of the patriarchs, on moral grounds; laws on food, on logical grounds (why forbid eating a creature that does not exist? 4.17); the creation narrative of Genesis 1, on scientific grounds (how can light be created before sun, moon, and stars?).

in the history and message that they related. But this too risked a circularity of self-authentication that was essentially arbitrary. As well as by writing commentaries, Origen was also an innovator in proposing the "difficulty hypothesis," a conviction that obscurities in scripture (which he calls "stumbling blocks," *scandala*) were intentional, to stimulate readers.[30]

The hermeneutical assumption underlying every Christian interpreter's method was the same. Because scripture is sacred, the words, phrases, sentences, and books that it contains cannot be meaningless or wrong. Augustine follows Paul (2 Corinthians 3:6; *TC* 3.9.20) in using the language of "letter" and "Spirit" as equivalents for the classical dichotomy between written text (*scriptum*) and intended meaning (*voluntas*). But he goes a stage further into language and meaning by making his fundamental antithesis one between things and signs,[31] and identifying words as a type of sign that (with other signs) have an intention or will (*voluntas*) to signify.

LANGUAGE, SIGNS, AND COMMUNICATION

Like the individual word, language can be a barrier or a key to human flourishing, for the divine communications

[30] *De principiis* 4.2.9. See Tarmo Toom, "Early Christian Handbooks on Interpretation," in *The Oxford Handbook of Early Christian Biblical Interpretation*, ed. Paul M. Blowers and Peter W. Martens (Oxford, 2022), 109–25.

[31] On classical Latin definitions of signs, see Cic. *Inv. rhet.* 1.30.48; Quint. *Inst.* 5.9.9.

of scripture, which depend on language in order to be shared, are mediated by fallible human beings. Augustine's interest in matters of language and signification is really part of a broader fascination with communication. How do knowledge and understanding pass from one mind to another? How does one person go about participating in the language act of another person? Just as his interest in morality is focused on individual human motivation, so his interest in communication (person to person, text to person, and vice versa; God to humankind and vice versa) stems from curiosity about the origin, nature, and locus of human understanding. Without the modern discipline of psychology to give him words and a conceptual framework for making sense of the phenomenon, he has to rely on physical metaphors (the mind being a place, for example) when expressing communications of thoughts and ideas.

This conceptual constriction is one reason why his own theory of language acquisition is not as straightforward as the nominalist position that has been attributed to him by philosophers like Wittgenstein.[32] Augustine describes a child's progress out of infancy in terms that resemble learning the rules of language games by observation and imitation; like his story of the illiterate monk, Antony, who learned to read (as well as memorize) scripture by repeated acts of observation (*TC* Proem 4.8). For most of

[32] Wittgenstein probably had not read either *TT* or *TC*. His views are based on *Conf.* 1.6.10, 8.13, and do not fully take into account how Augustine was reasoning from observation of his son Adeodatus's infancy (1.7.12).

TC, Augustine is concerned with language as a means of signifying, a subject that had captured his attention early on in his Christian life, as *TT* attested. He regards all instances of communication between human and divine as signs of the divine initiative exercised toward humanity. Scripture, as it were, is a "sign," of which God is the *res*, or "thing/reality" being made known.

Augustine gives two definitions of the term "sign":

> Signs "are those things that we call into service to signify something." (*TC* 1.2.5)
>
> "A sign is a thing that, apart from the impression it makes on our senses, makes something other than itself come to mind." (*TC* 2.1.1)

Both owe something to earlier tradition:[33] what seems to be innovative about *TC*, at least in the Latin tradition, is the application of sign terminology to words and language.[34]

HISTORY AND CONSTITUTION OF THE TEXT

Among Augustine's extant works, *De doctrina christiana* is unique in two ways. First, it survives in the textual his-

33 For example, [Arist.] *Rh. Al.* 13.1430b; Cic. *Inv. rhet.* 1.48; Quint. *Inst.* 5.9.

34 Darrel Jackson, "The Theory of Signs," 30, 49; he also argues that Augustine's originality was most marked in using signification in biblical hermeneutics.

tory in two editions. Second, one of those manuscripts is unique in being a copy made in his own lifetime: on the clear balance of probabilities (though not beyond reasonable doubt), this was made from the archetype, copied on the orders of Augustine himself, to be sent to his friend Simplicianus.[35] The first edition, which is referred to by Augustine in *Retractations*, survives only in that late fourth-century code. It is the basis of all modern critical editions of Books 1 and 2. The manuscript was probably produced at Carthage, and it may have been handled by Augustine himself, for we know that he liked to keep an eye on the publication of his work. He subsequently forgot about completing the composition during the intervening decades of duty as a bishop in Hippo.

This codex Leningradensis, formerly known as Corbeiensis (kept in the monastery at Corbie before it found its way to Catherine the Great's National Library in St. Petersburg), is a luxury edition on fine white vellum. It incorporates the latest scribal techniques to aid reading: with quotations indented, and book incipits written in red ink.[36] At the time of this writing, the codex is inaccessible to scholars following the invasion of Ukraine (2022). Nevertheless, it (in the case of *Gr.* using photographs) has been central to the production of two major critical editions of

[35] Steinhauser, "Codex Leningradensis Q.v.I.3," 33–43, argues that the Leningrad Codex was a gift from Augustine to Simplicianus; Hill argues that it was for Bishop Aurelius of Carthage (*De doctrina christiana*, 444).

[36] See Saenger, "Augustine as Reader," 43–73. Plates 1–5 show folios of L.

the last century. The 1963 edition of William Green (*Gr.*) is not to be confused with the R. P. H. Green (*RGr.*) who produced a text and translation in 1995 for Clarendon Press (which includes a number of interesting readings, but no critical apparatus);. The edition of Joseph Martin (*Mart.*) followed *Gr.*, in 1982. The apparatus of *Gr.* is generally succinct, while that of *Mart.* is cluttered with detail. They are both based on that codex Leningradensis (siglum L) in combination with a small number of principal manuscripts common to both, and a great many more used by one editor or the other but not both. The result is sometimes a wider divergence between these major editions than could be wished for.

For this volume, I have relied on *Gr.*, *Mart.*, and *RGr.*, as well as systematically consulting three ninth-century manuscripts. Two of these, P and K, were common to *Gr.* and *Mart.*; the third, *Lond.*, is not a complete text, for several folios are missing. *Gr.* nevertheless made use of it (with the *siglum* L), though not *Mart.* All three of these manuscripts are available online in a high-quality digital form. In 1885, Pius Knöll (Kn.) produced a critical edition of an anthology of Augustine's writings that had been compiled in the sixth century by one Eugippius:[37] this preserves an important early witness for portions of *TC*, and it has been referenced where relevant. The magisterial seventeenth-century Maurist edition (here μ) of Augustine has been influential on later generations of editors; I have made reference to that also, as appropriate.

Older editions of *TC* are divided by chapter number-

[37] CSEL 9.

ing, then paragraph numbering. *Gr.* in his 1963 edition followed smaller subdivisions of text (which are more convenient when cross-referring), as suggested by Vinzenz Bulhart ("Ille . . . numeros crassos addidit, quibus textus in minimas partes nunc distinguitur"). This edition follows suit.

Since the most detailed, and most recent, critical text is *Mart.*, his *sigla* have been adopted here; so, for example, the Leningrad codex appears as L, not—as in *Gr.*—C.[38] I have also made use of occasional suggestions by Edmund Hill in the notes to his translation (*sans* Latin). The Latin text presented here rests, therefore, on a fifth-to-ninth century foundation, consisting of L + P K Lond. Reference is also made to other manuscripts where helpful in giving an indication of the range and dissemination of difficulties through the tradition. I have used Greek letters for the consensus of these principal manuscripts (ϕ) and recent editions (γ).

Sigla

L	Leninopolitanus Q v. I 3 (4th or 5th c.)
Mon.	Monacensis 3824 (9th c.)
G	codex papyraceus Genevensis (7th c.)
P	Palatinus Vaticanus 188 (late 8th–early 9th c.)
B	Parisinus acq.1595 (9th c.)
Bam.	Bambergensis Patr. 21 (9th c.)
D	Parisinus 2704 (9th c.)
Par.	Parisinus 13359 (late 8th–early 9th c.)

[38] Though perhaps it should now be *SP*, for St. Petersburg.

F Monacensis 6301 (9th c.)
K Oxon Laud misc. 121 (9th c.)
Col. Coloniensis 74 (9th c.)
Lond. Brit. Mus. Add. 11873 (9th c.)
M Monacensis 6407 (9th c.)
Cam. Cameracensis 473 (9th c.)
R codex Vaticanus Reginensis 259 (9th c.)
San. Sangallensis 147 (9th c.)

Editions

μ editio Maurinorum (1680)
Kn. Eugippi textus institutus a Pio Knöll (1885)
Sull. (Book 4 only): T. Sullivan (1930)
Gr. W. M. Green, CSEL (1963)
Mart. Joseph Martin, CCSL (1962)[39]
RGr. R. H. P. Green (1995)

39 "Unimportant material . . . clogs Martin's apparatus . . . and sometimes Green's": *RGr.*

DE DOCTRINA CHRISTIANA

PROOEMIUM[1]

1. (1) Sunt praecepta quaedam tractandarum scripturarum, quae studiosis earum video non incommode posse tradi, ut non solum legendo alios, qui divinarum litterarum operta aperuerunt, sed etiam[2] ipsi[3] aperiendo proficiant. Haec tradere institui volentibus et valentibus discere, si dominus ac deus noster ea, quae de hac re cogitanti solet suggerere, etiam scribenti mihi non deneget. (2) Quod antequam exordiar, videtur mihi respondendum esse his qui haec reprehensuri sunt aut reprehensuri essent, si eos non ante placaremus. Quod si nonnulli etiam

[1] *vid. §19; 4.1.1* prologus] μ [2] et alia *F*: et aliis] *R* μ
[3] ipsi] *P*[1] *om. P F*

---

[1] On arguments for a late date of composition (AD 426/7), see Ulrich Duchrow, "Zum Prolog von Augustins De doctrina christiana," *Vigiliae Christianae* 17, no. 3 (1963): 165–72.

[2] *scriptura* (sing.) means a passage of scripture; *scripturae* (pl.), as here, means "writings" (see also Greek *ta biblia*, "the books"), usually in a specifically Christian sense, "scripture."

[3] The verb *trado, -ere* (3) appears ten times in the proem in this sense. At its core is the idea of handing or passing something on (hence, "tradition"), the means of transmitting Christian faith

TEACHING CHRISTIANITY

PROEM[1]

1. (1) There are certain principles for handling the scriptures[2] which in my view can easily be communicated[3] to anyone who is eager to learn about them. As a result, not only through reading other writers who have clarified obscurities in the holy texts, but also through the act of opening them up for others, they become competent themselves.[4] I have decided to communicate these principles to those who are willing and able to learn them, if our Lord and God consents to supply me, in my writing, with the assistance he usually gives me in my thinking on this subject. (2) But before I begin, I feel I must reply to those who are going to be critical of this undertaking—or who would be critical but for our[5] assuaging their fears beforehand. If, even after this, some still remain critical, at least

from generation to generation. It also helps Augustine by depersonalizing his chosen task; as he had said in *TT*, no human really teaches another. 4 A statement of objectives: to show people how to read the Bible themselves and how to pass on that expertise to others. He knew from experience that the best way to learn a subject is to teach it. 5 The first use of a plural for singular. The distinction is present from the beginning between Augustine the person (*ego*) and Augustine the teacher (*nos*).

post ista reprehenderint, saltem alios non movebunt nec ab utili studio ad imperitiae pigritiam revocabunt, quos movere possent nisi praemunitos praeparatosque invenirent.

2. (3) Quidam enim reprehensuri sunt hoc opus nostrum, cum ea quae praecepturi sumus non intellexerint. Quidam vero cum intellectis uti voluerint conatique fuerint scripturas divinas secundum haec praecepta tractare neque valuerint aperire atque explicare quod cupiunt, inaniter me laborasse arbitrabuntur; et quia ipsi non adiuvabuntur hoc opere, nullum adiuvari posse censebunt. (4) Tertium genus est reprehensorum qui divinas scripturas vel re vera bene tractant vel bene tractare sibi videntur. Qui quoniam nullis huiusmodi observationibus lectis quales nunc tradere institui, facultatem exponendorum sanctorum librorum se assecutos vel vident vel putant, nemini esse ista praecepta necessaria, sed potius totum quod de illarum litterarum obscuritatibus laudabiliter aperitur, divino munere fieri posse clamitabunt.

3. (5) Quibus omnibus breviter respondens, illis qui haec quae scribimus non intellegunt hoc dico: ita me non esse reprehendendum, quia haec non intellegunt. Tamquam si lunam vel veterem vel novam sidusve aliquod minime clarum vellent videre, quod ego intento digito demonstrarem, illis autem nec ad ipsum digitum meum

---

[6] 1 Corinthians 15:58.

[7] That is, by revelation rather than by reason—a fundamental theological dichotomy in debates about how God discloses himself to humanity.

they will not disturb others, or divert them from worthwhile study to slothful ignorance—though they could have done so, had they not found them forewarned and forearmed.

2. (3) Some people are going to be critical of this work of ours, because they have misunderstood what we are going to be teaching. Some, moreover, will want to make use of what they have understood, and will try to handle the divine scriptures according to these principles: but they will not have the capacity to clarify and expound what they want to, so they will reckon that my labor has been in vain.[6] Because my work has been no help to them, they will conclude that it cannot help anyone. (4) There is a third group of critics, those who handle the divine scriptures properly (either in reality, or in their own estimation). Since they see, or at least believe, that they have acquired their ability to expound the sacred books without reading any of the type of precepts which I have decided to communicate, they will keep on insisting that no one needs such principles, but rather that everything from the obscurities of those texts that is worth revealing can be achieved by divine gift.[7]

3. (5) My response to all of them is brief. To those who do not understand what we have written, I say this: they should not be criticizing me because they fail to understand these things. It is as if they wanted to see a new moon, or a fading moon, or some barely visible star, and I was pointing to it with my finger, but the beam of their eye

videndum sufficiens esset acies oculorum, num[4] propterea mihi succensere deberent. (6) Illi vero, qui etiam istis praeceptis cognitis atque perceptis ea, quae in divinis scripturis obscura sunt, intueri nequiverint, arbitrentur se digitum quidem meum videre posse, sidera vero, quibus demonstrandis intenditur, videre non posse. Et illi ergo et isti me reprehendere desinant et lumen oculorum divinitus sibi praeberi deprecentur. Non enim si possum membrum meum ad aliquid demonstrandum movere, possum etiam oculos accendere quibus vel ipsa demonstratio mea vel etiam illud, quod volo demonstrare, cernatur.

4. (7) Iam vero eorum qui divino munere exsultant et sine talibus praeceptis, qualia nunc tradere institui, se sanctos libros intellegere atque tractare gloriantur, et propterea me superflua voluisse scribere existimant, sic est lenienda commotio ut, quamvis magno dei dono iure laetentur, recordentur se tamen per homines didicisse vel litteras. (8) Nec propterea sibi ab Antonio sancto et perfecto aegyptio monacho insultari debere, qui sine ulla scientia litterarum scripturas divinas et memoriter audiendo tenuisse et prudenter cogitando intellexisse praedicatur; aut ab illo servo barbaro christiano, de quo a gravissimis fideique dignissimis viris nuper accepimus, qui litteras quoque ipsas nullo docente homine in plenam notitiam

[4] non *D F* μ

---

[8] Sight being understood as a beam reaching from the eye of the viewer to the object viewed.

[9] A point developed at length in *TT.*

[10] He implies (but does not state) that learning letters was

was not strong enough[8] even to see that finger of mine: that would not give them the right to reproach me. (6) As for those who have become familiar with my principles and mastered them, but who have still been unable to gain insight into the obscurities within the holy scriptures, well, they should conclude that they can see my finger, but they still cannot see the stars it indicates by pointing them out. These two groups should stop criticizing me, and pray for divine inspiration to impart enlightenment to their eyes. Even if I can move my finger to point something out, I cannot also illuminate their eyes to let them perceive either the action of presenting, or the material which I am trying to present.[9]

4. (7) Now for those who glory in their divine gift, and who—without such principles as I have now decided to communicate—boast that they understand the sacred books and how to handle them, and so consider that what I have chosen to write is redundant. They need to temper their enthusiasm, for although there is reason to celebrate such a great gift from God, they ought to remember that even when they learned their letters they had teachers[10] for the task. (8) They should not take offense at Antony, that saintly and impeccable Egyptian monk, who, it is said, did not know his letters, but first by listening memorized the holy scriptures, and then by wise reflection came to understand them. Or that barbarian slave who was a Christian (we learned of this recently from trustworthy men in good standing) and who had no one to teach him, so he prayed to receive full knowledge by revelation, and

akin to learning to use tools, a manual, functional task not relevant to the true teaching and learning, which is his subject matter here.

orando ut sibi revelarentur, accepit triduanis precibus impetrans, ut etiam codicem oblatum, stupentibus qui aderant, legendo percurreret.

5. (9) Aut si haec quisque falsa esse arbitratur, non ago pugnaciter. Certe enim quoniam cum christianis nobis res est, qui se scripturas sanctas sine duce homine gaudent nosse et, si ita est, vero et non mediocri gaudent bono, concedant necesse est unumquemque nostrum et ab ineunte pueritia consuetudine audiendi linguam suam didicisse et aliam aliquam vel Graecam vel Hebraeam vel quamlibet ceterarum aut similiter audiendo aut per hominem praeceptorem accepisse.

(10) Iam ergo, si placet, moneamus omnes fratres, ne parvulos suos ista doceant, quia momento uno temporis adveniente spiritu sancto repleti apostoli omnium gentium linguis locuti sunt? aut cui talia non provenerint, non se arbitretur esse christianum aut spiritum sanctum accepisse se dubitet? (11) Immo vero et quod per hominem discendum est, sine superbia discat, et per quem docetur alius, sine superbia et sine invidia tradat quod accepit; neque temptemus eum cui credidimus, ne talibus inimici versutiis et perversitate decepti ad ipsum quoque audien-

---

[11] *Codex*—a book in the modern form, not a roll (*volumen*), so probably a Bible. [12] That is, fellow Christians.

[13] Acts 2: "nations" translates *gentes* (Greek, *ethnē*); older translations English this as "gentiles" (Hebrew, *gōyīm*: foreigners, non-Jewish peoples). That is, there is no need to work to acquire language skills if they are bestowed by divine gift.

[14] Satan ("Adversary": see Job 2:1, etc.; Matthew 4:10, etc.). For "Enemy," see Matthew 13:39, "but the Enemy who sowed

learned his alphabet—and after three days of prayer, to the amazement of those present, he read fluently from start to finish a book[11] which was given to him.

5. (9) All the same, if someone decides that these tales are false, I am not going to go on the attack. We take issue with Christians who pride themselves on knowing the sacred scriptures without human guidance—and if that is so, then they are taking pride in a good which is beyond dispute, and hardly insignificant—but they must still admit that each and every one of us, from the beginnings of childhood, learned our own language through the constant practice of listening; and any other language, perhaps Greek or Hebrew, or one of the other languages, we acquired either in the same way, by listening, or by having someone teach us.

(10) So—can you believe it—are we now to advise all our brothers[12] not to teach these things to their children, because, when a particular moment of time came, the apostles were filled with the Holy Spirit, and spoke in the languages of all the nations?[13] Or should those who have not received such gifts consider themselves not to be Christian, or doubt whether they have received the Holy Spirit? (11) Surely they should learn, without pride, whatever they can learn through human instruction; and let that person who teaches another communicate what they have received, without pride and without envy. We must not put to the test the one in whom we have believed, lest the snares and wrongdoing of the Enemy[14] deceive us into

them is the Devil." This appellation stems from early Christianity: see Cyprian of Carthage (ca. AD 210–258), *Unit.* 1, "beware of the Enemy."

dum evangelium atque discendum nolimus ire in ecclesias aut codicem legere aut legentem praedicantemque hominem audire; et exspectemus rapi usque in tertium caelum sive in corpore sive extra corpus, sicut dicit apostolus, et ibi audire ineffabilia verba quae non licet homini loqui, aut ibi videre dominum Iesum Christum et ab illo potius quam ab hominibus audire evangelium.

6. (12) Caveamus tales temptationes superbissimas et periculosissimas magisque cogitemus et ipsum apostolum Paulum, licet divina et caelesti voce prostratum et instructum, ad hominem tamen missum esse, ut sacramenta perciperet atque copularetur ecclesiae; et centurionem Cornelium, quamvis exauditas orationes eius elemosinasque respectas ei angelus nuntiaverit, Petro tamen traditum imbuendum, per quem non solum sacramenta perciperet, sed etiam quid credendum, quid sperandum, quid diligendum esset audiret. (13) Et poterant utique omnia per angelum fieri, sed abiecta esset humana condicio,[5] si per homines hominibus deus verbum suum ministrare nolle videretur. Quomodo enim verum esset quod dictum est: templum enim dei sanctum est, quod estis vos; si deus

[5] conditio] *P F R C μ*

---

[15] Latin, *codex*. [16] 2 Corinthians 12:2–4.

[17] In other words, not on his mysterious words about the third heaven or trying to replicate his mystical experience.

[18] In classical Latin, a military oath or solemn undertaking; in ecclesiastical Latin, a type that signifies a reality (Cypr. *De dom. orat.* 9; *Ep.* 63.12), hence a sacrament in the modern sense (a physical sign of a metaphysical grace), particularly of the bread and wine of the eucharist.

being unwilling to go to our churches and hear and learn the gospel itself, or to read the Bible,[15] or pay attention to the person who is reading and preaching, waiting instead to be carried up into the third heaven ("whether in the body or out of the body") as the apostle says,[16] and to hear there "inexpressible words which no person may utter," or to see there the Lord Jesus Christ, and to hear the gospel directly from him, rather than from mere human beings.

6. (12) We must avoid such arrogant and perilous temptations, and instead focus our attention on the apostle Paul himself.[17] For despite being cast to the ground and told what to do by a voice from heaven, he was still sent to a fellow human being to learn about the sacraments[18] and to be made a member of the church.[19] As for the centurion Cornelius, even though an angel had told him that his prayers had been heard, and his acts of kindness had not gone unnoticed, yet he was handed over[20] to Peter to be initiated—and through Peter he not only learned about the sacraments, but also heard what should be the objects of his faith, his hope, his love.[21] (13) To be sure, all these things could have been accomplished by the angel, but the human condition would have been contemptible indeed if God were to seem unwilling to impart his Word to humanity by means of humanity. How would it be true to say that the temple of God is sacred, and "that temple is you,"[22] if

[19] Acts 9:3–8.

[20] *traditum*: here, in its literal sense, not of transmission of information.

[21] Acts 10; Augustine adds the gloss on faith, hope, and love.

[22] 1 Corinthians 3:17.

de humano templo responsa non redderet et totum, quod discendum hominibus tradi vellet, de caelo atque per angelos personaret? Deinde ipsa caritas, quae sibi homines invicem nodo unitatis astringit, non haberet aditum refundendorum et quasi miscendorum sibimet animorum, si homines per homines nihil discerent. 7. (14) Et certe illum spadonem, qui Esaiam prophetam legens non intellegebat, neque ad apostolum angelus misit[6] nec ei per angelum id quod non intellegebat expositum aut divinitus in mente sine hominis ministerio revelatum est. Sed potius suggestione divina missus est ad eum seditque cum eo Philippus, qui noverat Esaiam prophetam, eique humanis verbis et lingua quod in scriptura illa tectum erat aperuit. (15) Nonne cum Moyse deus loquebatur et tamen consilium regendi atque administrandi tam magni populi a socero suo, alienigena scilicet homine, et maxime providus et minime superbus accepit? Noverat enim ille vir, ex quacumque anima verum consilium processisset, non ei sed illi qui est veritas incommutabili deo esse tribuendum.

8. (16) Postremo quisquis se nullis praeceptis instructum divino munere quaecumque in scripturis obscura sunt intellegere gloriatur, bene quidem credit, et verum est, non esse illam suam facultatem quasi a se ipso ex-

[6] neque . . . misit] *L Gr. Mart.* neque ad angelum apostolus misit] μ ad quem apostolum non angelum misit instruendum] *K*

[23] The language is evocative of consulting a "pagan" oracle.

[24] Acts 8:27.

[25] See W. Green, "Textual Notes," 226. For Augustine, teaching is a proper calling for human beings.

God delivered no replies from that human temple,[23] but rather proclaimed from heaven, and by means of angels, the entirety of what he wanted to be communicated to human beings, for them to learn? Then even love itself, which binds people to itself in a bond of mutual unity, would have no opportunity to make minds overflow and mingle, as it were, with one another, if human beings learned nothing from one another. 7. (14) Surely, too, it was no angel who sent that eunuch, who was reading the prophet Isaiah without understanding him,[24] to the apostle Philip; and it was no angel who explained to him what he did not understand.[25] Nor was it revealed to his mind by some divine means without any human help. Instead Philip was sent to him by divine instigation, and sat with him. Now Philip knew the prophet Isaiah, and disclosed to the eunuch in human words and language what was hidden in that passage of scripture. (15) After all, when God used to talk with Moses, Moses certainly also took advice from his father-in-law (even though he was a foreigner) on governing and managing so great a people—and did so with maximum foresight and minimum pride.[26] That man knew that from whatever soul true advice proceeded, it should not be ascribed to the person concerned but to the unchanging God who is truth.[27]

8. (16) In conclusion, whoever boasts that they understand everything that is obscure in the scriptures by divine gift, without being instructed in any principles, does well to believe (for this is the truth) that this is not some power of their own, something originating as it were within

[26] Jethro: Exodus 18:1–9.
[27] John 14:6; cf. 17:7.

sistentem, sed divinitus traditam; ita enim dei gloriam quaerit et non suam. Sed cum legit et nullo sibi hominum exponente intellegit, cur ipse aliis affectat exponere ac non potius eos remittit deo, ut ipsi quoque non per hominem sed illo intus docente intellegant? (17) Sed videlicet timet ne audiat a domino: serve nequam, dares pecuniam meam nummulariis. Sicut ergo hi ea quae intellegunt produnt ceteris vel loquendo vel scribendo, ita ego quoque, si non solum ea quae intellego, sed etiam in intellegendo[7] ea quae observent, prodidero, culpari ab eis profecto non debeo. Quamquam nemo debet aliquid sic habere quasi suum proprium, nisi forte mendacium. Nam omne verum ab illo est qui ait: Ego sum veritas. Quid enim habemus quod non accepimus? Quod si accepimus, quid gloriamur quasi non acceperimus?

9. (18) Qui legit audientibus litteras, utique quas agnoscit enuntiat; qui autem ipsas litteras tradit, hoc agit ut alii quoque legere noverint; uterque tamen id insinuat quod accepit. Sic etiam qui ea quae in scripturis intellegit exponit audientibus, tamquam litteras quas agnoscit, pro-

[7] *L R Lond. Gr* intellegendo] *μ Mart.*

---

[28] See *TT* 12.40, 14.46, on the "teacher within."

[29] Matthew 25:26–27.

[30] Alluding to John 8:44 which in Vulg. reads *cum loquitur mendacium ex propriis loquitur* (when he speaks untruth he speaks of what belongs to him); but in VL (Augustine's preferred version) the text is closer to what Augustine writes here: *qui loquitur mendacium ex suis* [or *suo*] *propriis loquitur* (he who speaks untruth speaks of what belongs to himself).

[31] John 6:55, 14:6, 15:1.

themselves, but rather something communicated by divine providence: in this way they seek God's glory, not their own. But when they read it and understand it without anyone explaining it to them, why do they presume to interpret it for other people, instead of sending those people back to God, so that they too may understand not through human instruction but with God as our inner teacher?[28] (17) Obviously they are afraid of hearing from the Lord, "you good-for-nothing slave, you should have given my money to the bankers."[29] Just as these people provide their interpretations to others, either orally or in writing, so it follows that I do not deserve to be criticized by them because I provide people not only with my interpretation, but also with rules for them to follow when they attempt an interpretation of their own. All the same, no one should treat anything as belonging to themselves, except perhaps for a lie.[30] For everything that is true comes from him who says, "I am Truth."[31] What do we own that we have not been given? But if we have been given it, why do we boast as if we have not been given it?[32]

9. (18) Anyone who reads out letters before listeners is surely declaring something they know; but someone who teaches others their letters does this so that others too can know how to read.[33] In either case they are inculcating something which they themselves have received. So too the person who understands what is in the scriptures explains it to those listening, as if he has the office of a

32 Romans 11:18.

33 Exploiting the semantic range of *litterae* (pl.), which can mean a written text (here translated "letters" to reproduce the Latin wordplay), and also the letters of the alphabet.

nuntiat lectoris officio. Qui autem praecipit quomodo intellegendum sit, similis est tradenti litteras, hoc est praecipienti quomodo legendum sit, ut, quomodo ille qui legere novit alio lectore non indiget, cum codicem invenerit, a quo audiat quid ibi scriptum sit, sic iste, qui praecepta quae conamur tradere acceperit, cum in libris aliquid obscuritatis invenerit, quasdam regulas velut litteras tenens intellectorem alium non requirat, per quem sibi quod opertum est retegatur, sed quibusdam vestigiis indagatis ad occultum sensum sine ullo errore ipse perveniat aut certe in absurditatem pravae sententiae non incidat.

(19) Quapropter, quamquam et in ipso opere satis apparere possit huic officioso labori nostro non recte aliquem contradicere, tamen, si huiusmodi proemio quibuslibet obsistentibus convenienter videtur esse responsum, huius viae quam in hoc libro ingredi volumus, tale nobis occurrit exordium.[8]

[8] exordium] *in codd. al. prooemium continuat ad fin. lib. 1.1.3* gaudeamus

reader[34] in proclaiming the text which he is familiar with. But the person who teaches how to understand the scripture is like someone teaching the alphabet, in other words, teaching how to read: thus anyone who knows how to read, when they come across a book, has no need of another reader from whom to hear what the text contains. In the same way, if anyone who comprehends these principles which we are trying to communicate finds some obscurity in the books, they do not need anyone else to understand the text, because they keep to those particular rules (just as with knowing the letters of the alphabet). They can uncover what had been cloaked, following the trail to arrive at the hidden sense without losing their way—or at any rate avoiding stumbling into the folly of a distorted interpretation.

(19) In the main text of this work, therefore, it may be sufficiently obvious that no one ought to be condemning this task we have undertaken in the service of others. But still, if it is helpful to provide a response to those who are critical of introductions like this, here you have before you the kind of preface which suggests itself to us.

[34] Latin, *lectoris officio*. *Officium* can mean a service of worship ("divine office") or general duty; *lector* is either, general, any person who reads, or, specific, one tasked with reading scripture in public worship, "Reader."

LIBER I

1. (1) Duae[1] sunt res quibus nititur omnis tractatio scripturarum, modus inveniendi quae intellegenda sunt, et modus proferendi quae intellecta sunt. De inveniendo prius, de proferendo postea disseremus. Magnum opus et arduum, et si ad sustinendum difficile, vereor ne ad suscipiendum temerarium; ita sane si de nobis ipsis praesumeremus. Nunc vero cum in illo sit spes peragendi huius operis, a quo nobis in cogitatione multa de hac re iam tradita tenemus, non est metuendum ne dare desinat cetera, cum ea quae data sunt coeperimus impendere. (2) Omnis enim res quae dando non deficit, dum habetur et non datur, nondum habetur, quomodo habenda est. Ille enim ait, "qui habet, dabitur ei." Dabit ergo habentibus—id est, cum benignitate utentibus eo quod acceperunt—adimplebit atque cumulabit quod dedit. Illi quinque et illi

[1] duae] *in F R hic incipit liber primus*: *scr. in mg.* *P¹ INCIPIT*

---

[1] In rhetorical theory *inventio* is "the devising of materials either true or apparently true to yield a plausible explanation" (Cic. *Inv. rhet.* 1.7.9), the first of the five subjects into which he divides rhetoric. Augustine takes it as a way of finding out what is true within a text.

[2] Christ, surely, rather than (as *RGr.*) God; cf. *ille* repeated two sentences later.

[3] *Res*: a concrete or physical reality, object, item, or phenomenon, a category of thought.

BOOK I

1. (1) All handling of scripture depends on two factors: how to discover what we need to understand; and how to present it once we have understood it. We shall consider discovery[1] first, and presentation afterward. It is a substantial task, and a demanding one. Difficult though it may be to carry it through, my worry is that even undertaking it may seem rashly presumptuous. That would certainly be true if we did so relying upon ourselves alone. As it is, our hope of completing this work rests upon him[2] through whom we hold fast to much that has been handed down to us in our frequent reflection on this subject. So, now that we are starting to apply what we have received, we need not be afraid that he will withhold what remains. (2) For when every thing[3] that does not dwindle to nothing by being given away[4] is kept hold of, rather than being given away, we are not yet keeping hold of it in the way that we ought to. For he says, "To the one who has, more will be given."[5] So he will give to those who have—that is, to those who make a benevolent use of what they have received—he will supply and increase[6] what he has given. Someone once had five loaves, and someone else had

[4] Knowledge, e.g., or love.

[5] Matthew 13:12, 25:29; Mark 4:25; Luke 8:18, 19:26.

[6] Luke 6:38.

septem erant panes, antequam inciperent dari esurientibus; quod ubi fieri coepit, cophinos et sportas satiatis hominum tot milibus impleverunt. (3) Sicut ergo ille panis dum frangeretur accrevit, sic ea quae ad hoc opus aggrediendum iam dominus praebuit, cum disputari[2] coeperint, eo ipso suggerente multiplicabuntur, ut in[3] hoc nostro ministerio, non solum nullam patiamur inopiam, sed de mirabili abundantia gaudeamus.[4]

2. (4) Omnis[5] doctrina vel rerum est vel signorum, sed res per signa discuntur. Proprie autem nunc res appellavi, quae non ad significandum aliquid adhibentur, sicuti est lignum, lapis, pecus, atque huiusmodi cetera: sed non illud lignum quod in aquas amaras Moysen misisse legimus, ut amaritudine carerent; neque ille lapis quem Iacob sibi ad caput posuerat; neque illud pecus quod pro filio immolavit

[2] dispensari *R C μ* [3] in] in ipso *R μ*

[4] gaudeamus] *in P K (hic explicit praefatio incipiunt libri) Lond. hic explicit prooemium*

[5] omnis] *in P K Lond. hic incipit lib. I*

---

[7] Five loaves, Matthew 14:17–21; seven, 15:34–38.

[8] Reading *disputari*; the alternative reading gives "be bestowed" (*dispensari*).

[9] First use of the term *doctrina*, or "education," but never (in this period) "doctrine." "Knowledge" (the end-product of teaching) is another possible translation.

[10] This looks like a simple contrast between concrete and abstract; but the distinction between concrete and abstract, or symbol and referent, or literal and metaphorical, is a foundation on which to construct a protosemiotics.

[11] This refers to things that have no metaphorical or tropological meaning, which therefore signify nothing except them-

seven, before they began to be shared among the hungry; but then the distribution began, and thus many thousands of people had enough to eat, and they filled up baskets and containers.[7] (3) Just as that bread increased in quantity, therefore, even as it was being broken, so too those materials that the Lord has already provided for us to set about this task will be multiplied when we begin to discuss[8] them, and the Lord himself will be the supplier. As a result, in this ministry of ours we should not only refuse to admit to any lack of material, we should in fact celebrate the extraordinary abundance of it.

2. (4) All teaching[9] consists of things or signs,[10] but the things are learned by means of the signs. Strictly speaking, in this context I have used the term "thing" to apply to what is not required for being a sign for anything else:[11] for example "wood," "stone," "livestock,"[12] and so on. This does not include that[13] special wood that we have read about Moses throwing into the bitter waters to make them free from bitterness;[14] or that stone that Jacob had set down for himself, to rest his head;[15] nor that ram that Abraham sacrificed in place of his son.[16] For these too are

selves. A cat, e.g., in or out of a box, is just a cat, and not (yet) a paradox.

[12] It is not clear until the next sentence (in which *pecus* must be translated "ram") that Augustine is thinking of a single animal.

[13] Triple anaphora of the pronoun (*ille/illud*) to make the shift from general to specific. [14] Exodus 15:25. Typology was a common form of text interpretation. [15] Genesis 28:11.

[16] Genesis 22:13; the story, known as the *Aqedah*, or "binding" of Isaac, is interpreted as a type of the sacrifice of Christ (Hebrews 11:17; James 2:21).

Abraham. Hae namque ita res sunt, ut aliarum etiam signa sint rerum.

(5) Sunt autem alia signa quorum omnis usus in significando est, sicuti sunt verba. Nemo enim utitur verbis nisi aliquid significandi gratia. Ex quo intellegitur quid appellem signa: res eas videlicet quae ad significandum aliquid adhibentur. Quam ob rem omne signum etiam res aliqua est; quod enim nulla res est, omnino nihil est. Non autem omnis res etiam signum est. (6) Et ideo in hac divisione rerum atque signorum, cum de rebus loquemur, ita loquemur ut etiamsi earum aliquae adhiberi ad significandum possint, non impediant partitionem, qua prius de rebus, postea de signis disseremus; memoriterque teneamus id nunc in rebus considerandum esse, quod sunt non quod aliud etiam praeter seipsas significant.

3. (7) Res ergo aliae sunt quibus fruendum est, aliae quibus utendum, aliae quae fruuntur et utuntur. Illae quibus fruendum est nos beatos faciunt. Istis quibus utendum est, tendentes ad beatitudinem adiuvamur et quasi adminiculamur, ut ad illas quae nos beatos faciunt, pervenire atque his inhaerere possimus. Nos vero, qui fruimur et

---

[17] Augustine is grappling with existential questions about nouns, but strictly as a means of opening up the matter of how texts (scripture in particular) mean things.

[18] In rhetorical theory and in philosophy *partitio* (Greek, *diairesis*), the division of subject matter into sections. Cicero discusses it at length in his dialogue *Part. or*: it is a subsection of "definition" (see *TT* 13.43; Cic. *Top.* 28–30).

[19] The Roman moral take on this opposing pair is exemplified in a comment on the aftermath of the battle of Cannae, "when Hannibal could have made use of his victory, he preferred to

things, but in such a way that they are also signs of other things.

(5) There are other signs whose entire purpose is to signify—words are signs of this kind. No one uses words except in order to signify something. This is how I understand what I should refer to as "signs": obviously they are those things that we call into service to signify something. Therefore every sign is also a kind of thing, because what is not a thing is nothing whatsoever.[17] It is not the case, though, that every thing is also a sign. (6) So in this distinction between things and signs, when we talk about things, we shall do so in such a way that even if some of those things can be used for signifying, that does not get in the way of our division of material,[18] according to which we shall discuss things first, and signs afterward. For the time being we must bear in mind that our theme is things, and what they are. It is not what else they may signify besides themselves.

3. (7) Some things exist for us to enjoy them, and some are to be useful;[19] while others are both enjoyable and useful. Those things that are for our enjoyment make us happy. Those that are useful enable us to strive for happiness, and as it were[20] support us, so that we can attain to those things that make us happy, and cleave to them. Those of us who gain both enjoyment and usefulness are

enjoy it": Flor. *Epit.* 1.22.21. Augustine is more subtle; his understanding of the "joy" in "enjoyment" is theological.

20 This modifier is added because the verb (*adminiculo*) evokes a distinctive metaphor: *adminiculum* (noun) is a prop or support in viticulture.

utimur inter utrasque constituti, si eis quibus utendum est frui voluerimus, impeditur cursus noster et aliquando etiam deflectitur, ut ab his rebus, quibus fruendum est, obtinendis vel retardemur vel etiam revocemur inferiorum amore praepediti.

4. (8) Frui est enim amore inhaerere alicui rei propter seipsam. Uti autem, quod in usum[6] venerit ad id quod amas obtinendum referre, si tamen amandum est. Nam usus illicitus abusus potius vel abusio nominanda[7] est. Quomodo ergo, si essemus peregrini, qui beate vivere nisi in patria non possemus, eaque peregrinatione utique miseri et miseriam finire cupientes, in patriam redire vellemus, opus esset vel terrestribus vel marinis vehiculis quibus utendum esset ut ad patriam, qua fruendum erat, pervenire valeremus; quod si amoenitates itineris et ipsa gestatio vehiculorum nos delectaret, conversi ad fruendum his quibus uti debuimus, nollemus cito viam finire et perversa suavitate implicati[8] alienaremur a patria, cuius suavitas faceret beatos: (9) sic in huius mortalitatis vita peregrinantes a domino, si redire in patriam volumus, ubi beati esse possimus, utendum est hoc mundo, non fruen-

[6] usu *K P*
[7] nominandus *μ*
[8] implicati *K*[1] *Lond. P*: implacati *K*

---

[21] An example that preoccupied Augustine elsewhere (*Conf.* 9.14–15, 10.49–50) would be singing and music in worship. It ought to delight hearers by teaching them about God; but the sensual pleasure of music can become an end in itself.

[22] In Latin, an unwieldy sentence from here to the end of §9.

located somewhere between the two: if we want to get enjoyment from something that ought to be useful, our progress is hindered and sometimes even diverted. As a result, we are hampered or even stopped from obtaining things meant for enjoyment, because we are entangled in our love of lesser things.[21]

4. (8) "Enjoying" means cleaving to something for its own sake, out of love. But "using" means turning what you have available for your use to the obtaining of something that you love—always supposing it is something worth loving. Inappropriate use should really be called *ab*use or *mis*use. In the same way,[22] if we were foreigners, who could not live a happy life except in our homeland, and if, because of our time spent in foreign parts, we were thoroughly wretched, and eager to put an end to our wretchedness, we would want to return to that homeland. We would need to use some transport either by land or sea, to give us the power to reach that homeland, so as to have the enjoyment of it. But if we were delighted by the pleasantness of the journey, and the ride in our conveyance, that would transform us into people finding enjoyment in what ought to be useful. We would not want a speedy end to our journey, and we would be ensnared by saccharine sweetness, and thus estranged from our homeland—even though its genuine sweetness would have made us truly happy. (9) This is how, in this mortal life, we are estranged from the Lord. If we want to return to our homeland, where we can be happy,[23] we should use this world, not enjoy it, so that we can glimpse and understand the unseen

[23] At this point the term *beati* (previously translated as "happy") begins to shift toward its Christian meaning of "blessed."

dum, ut invisibilia dei, per ea quae facta sunt, intellecta conspiciantur, hoc est, ut de corporalibus temporalibusque rebus aeterna et spiritalia capiamus.

5. (10) Res igitur quibus fruendum est, pater et filius et spiritus sanctus, eademque trinitas, una quaedam summa res, communisque omnibus fruentibus ea; si tamen res et non rerum omnium causa, si tamen et causa. Non enim facile nomen quod tantae excellentiae conveniat, inveniri potest, nisi quod melius ita dicitur trinitas haec, unus deus ex quo omnia, per quem omnia, in quo omnia. (11) Ita pater et filius et spiritus sanctus et singulus quisque horum deus, et simul omnes unus deus et singulus quisque horum plena substantia, et simul omnes una substantia. Pater nec filius est nec spiritus sanctus, filius nec pater est nec spiritus sanctus, spiritus sanctus nec pater est nec filius, sed pater tantum pater et filius tantum filius et spiritus sanctus tantum spiritus sanctus. (12) Eadem tribus aeternitas, eadem incommutabilitas, eadem maiestas, eadem potestas. In patre unitas, in filio aequalitas, in spiritu sancto unitatis aequalitatisque concordia. Et tria haec unum omnia propter patrem, aequalia omnia propter filium, connexa omnia propter spiritum sanctum.

---

[24] A thing's being a thing depends on the ultimate model of God the holy "Threeness." There are echoes of Platonism in the view that all things are imperfect except the originator-thing, which is God.

[25] In a philosophical sense, encapsulating the idea of creator, origin, and even reason.

[26] The Latin word *nomen* (from which the English "noun" derives) suggests both "name" and "description." In *TC* and *TT* it is translated "name-word" to keep this range of meaning in view.

things of God, by means of the things that he has created; in other words, so that we grasp what is eternal and spiritual by means of physical and earthly things.

5. (10) The things that are the proper object of human enjoyment are the Father, the Son, and the Holy Spirit, who constitute the Trinity[24]—one identical supreme thing accessible to all who enjoy it (if, that is, it really is a thing, rather than the cause of all things; and if it really is a cause[25]). It is not easy to find a name-word[26] befitting such greatness, unless this Trinity is something better described as one God by whom, and through whom, and in whom, all things have their being.[27] (11) So the Father, and Son, and Holy Spirit are all individually God, and at the same time they are all one God, and each one of them has its integrity of substance, and at the same time they are all of one substance.[28] The Father is not a Son or a Holy Spirit; the Son is not a Father or a Holy Spirit; the Holy Spirit is not a Father or a Son. Instead, the Father is solely the Father; and the Son is solely the Son; and the Holy Spirit is solely the Holy Spirit. (12) These three possess the same eternity, the same immutability, the same sovereignty, the same power. The Father possesses unity, the Son equality; the Holy Spirit possesses the harmony between unity and equality. All three of them are one through the Father, equal through the Son and bound together through the Holy Spirit.

27 Romans 11:36; Acts 17:28. Cf. Colossians 1:17; evocative of the eucharistic doxology.

28 The Latin Trinity was defined as three "persons" (*personae*), one "substance" (*substantia*). Unluckily, the Greek for "person" is *hypostasis*, verbally equivalent to *substantia*.

6. (13) Diximusne aliquid et sonuimus aliquid dignum deo? Immo vero nihil me aliud quam dicere voluisse sentio; si autem dixi, non hoc est quod dicere volui. Hoc unde scio, nisi quia deus ineffabilis est? Quod autem a me dictum est, si ineffabile esset, dictum non esset. Ac per hoc ne ineffabilis quidem dicendus est deus, quia et hoc cum dicitur, aliquid dicitur et fit nescio qua[9] pugna verborum, quoniam si illud est ineffabile, quod dici non potest, non est ineffabile, quod vel ineffabile dici potest! Quae pugna verborum silentio cavenda potius quam voce pacanda est. (14) Et tamen deus, cum de illo nihil digne dici possit, admisit humanae vocis obsequium, et verbis nostris in laude sua gaudere nos voluit. Nam inde est et quod dicitur deus. Non enim re vera in strepitu istarum duarum syllabarum ipse cognoscitur, sed tamen omnes Latinae linguae socios,[10] cum aures eorum sonus iste tetigerit, movet ad cogitandam excellentissimam quandam immortalemque naturam.

7. (15) Nam cum ille unus cogitatur deorum deus, ab his etiam, qui alios et suspicantur et vocant et colunt deos

[9] quae *G[1] P[1] B D K Lond. M S L Q Bam. RGr.*
[10] socios *L P K Gr. Mart. RGr.*: scios *codd. rec.* *μ*

---

29 Expressing the gap between intention and outcome, like a painter who has a perfect vision of what they want to paint but not the skill or tools to effect it.

30 In Latin, *de-us*, a role-description, not a personal name. God's personal name is disclosed at Exodus 3:14.

31 Disputed text: *scios* gives "those who know Latin," and *socios*, "those who associate together by their use of the Latin language." W. Green remarks, "as the harder reading, *scios* seems to

6. (13) Have we now spoken and proclaimed something that is worthy of God? To be honest, I feel that I have done nothing more than want to speak. But if I have spoken, this is not what I wanted to say.[29] How do I know this, other than because God is beyond expression? But what I have said could not have been said, if it really were inexpressible. By this means even God should not be called "beyond expression," because as soon as anyone describes him as "inexpressible," they have expressed something about him! So a kind of battle of words arises: for if we call something "inexpressible" when it cannot be put into words, then it is not in fact inexpressible, precisely because the term "inexpressible" can be used of it. Such a battle of words is better silently avoided rather than silenced by speech. (14) And even though we cannot worthily say anything about him, still God has made the human voice acceptable in his service, and wanted us to delight in praising him with our own words. For this is also why he is called "God": it is not in the sounding of those two syllables[30] that he is truly recognized, but rather, when that sound reaches their ears, it prompts everyone who is allied[31] by their use of the Latin language to recognize his particular supreme and eternal nature.

7. (15) When he, the only God, is thought of as god of gods by people who suppose that other gods exist (either

command instant favor. Though a rare word, it makes good sense. But the agreement of *C* [= Leningradensis] with all extant manuscripts written before 1100 seems to me to settle the question. The archetype in Hippo must have read *socios*" ("Textual Notes," 227–28).

sive in caelo sive in terra, ita cogitatur, ut aliquid, quo nihil sit melius atque[11] sublimius, illa cogitatio conetur attingere. Sane quoniam diversis moventur bonis, partim eis quae ad corporis sensum, partim eis quae ad animi intellegentiam pertinent, illi qui dediti sunt corporis sensibus, aut ipsum caelum aut, quod in caelo fulgentissimum vident, aut ipsum mundum deum deorum esse arbitrantur: aut, si extra mundum ire contendunt, aliquid lucidum imaginantur idque vel infinitum vel ea forma, quae optima videtur, inani suspicione constituunt aut humani corporis figuram cogitant, si eam ceteris anteponunt. (16) Quod si unum deum deorum esse non putant et potius multos aut innumerabiles aequalis ordinis deos, etiam eos tamen prout cuique aliquid corporis videtur excellere, ita figuratos animo tenent. Illi autem qui per intellegentiam pergunt videre quod deus est, omnibus eum naturis visibilibus et corporalibus, intellegibilibus vero et spiritalibus, omnibus mutabilibus praeferunt. Omnes tamen certatim pro excellentia dei dimicant, nec quisquam inveniri potest qui hoc deum credat esse quo est aliquid melius. Itaque omnes hoc deum esse consentiunt quod ceteris rebus omnibus anteponunt.

8. (17) Et quoniam omnes qui de deo cogitant, vivum aliquid cogitant, illi soli possunt non absurda et indigna

[11] nihilque *C K P*: sit atque *μ*

---

[32] Not physically, but mentally or spiritually, in a mystical vision (cf. *Conf.* 9.10.24). [33] Looking forward to Anselm's ontological argument, *Pros.* 2 (AD 1078): "we believe that you are that thing than which nothing greater can be conceived." On the definition of God, see *MBM*, 463–71.

in heaven or on earth), and who invoke them and worship them, he is nevertheless thought of in a way that tries to encapsulate what is better, and more sublime, than anything else. Undoubtedly such people are motivated by different types of good—some by those related to physical senses, others by those related to the mind and its understanding. So people who capitulate completely to their physical senses think that either the heaven itself or whatever shines brightest in heaven, or even the world itself, is the god of gods. If they strive to advance beyond the world,[32] they picture something luminous and in their delusive fantasy establish it as either infinite, say, or having a perfection of shape, or (if that is what they value above all else) they think it has a human form. (16) But if they believe not in one god of gods, but rather in many, even countless, gods of equal importance, they will still keep an ideal image of them in mind, in accordance with whatever each considers to be physical perfection. But those who are intent on using their intelligence, to perceive what God is, set him above all visible and physical, fathomable and spiritual natures, above everything that is subject to change. Yet everyone fights fiercely over God's perfection, and no one can be found who would believe that God is one who can be surpassed by anything. Everyone agrees, therefore, that this is what God is: the one who surpasses everything else.[33]

8. (17) Everyone who thinks of God thinks of something that is a living being. So only those who are thinking

existimare de deo, qui vitam ipsam cogitant. Et quaecumque illis forma occurrerit corporis, eam vel[12] vivere vel non vivere statuunt, et viventem non viventi anteponunt, eamque ipsam viventem corporis formam, quantalibet luce praefulgeat, quantalibet magnitudine praemineat, quantalibet pulchritudine ornetur, aliud esse ipsam, aliud vitam qua vegetatur intellegunt; eamque illi moli quae ab illa vegetatur et animatur dignitate incomparabili praeferunt. (18) Deinde ipsam vitam pergunt inspicere, et si eam sine sensu vegetantem invenerint, qualis est arborum, praeponunt ei sentientem, qualis est pecorum; et huic rursus intellegentem, qualis est hominum. Quam cum adhuc mutabilem viderint, etiam huic aliquam incommutabilem coguntur praeponere, illam scilicet vitam quae non aliquando desipit, aliquando sapit, sed est potius ipsa sapientia. (19) Sapiens enim mens, id est, adepta sapientiam, antequam adipisceretur non erat sapiens; at vero ipsa sapientia nec fuit umquam insipiens, nec esse umquam potest. Quam si non viderent, nullo modo plena fiducia vitam incommutabiliter sapientem commutabili vitae antepo-

[12] vel *coni. RGr.*: vitam *Mart.*: vita L^1 *P* B^1 *D K Lond. C* μ *Gr.*

---

[34] Following R. P. H. Green's conjecture. But "*vitam vivere*" is found elsewhere in Augustine (e.g., *Ep.* 120.4.18; *Mus.* 4.6).

[35] *sapientia* is very early identified as Christ the Word, e.g., John 1:1 with Proverbs 8:22; John 9:1; 1 Corinthians 2:7. But the Latin noun and its Greek equivalent (*sophia*) are both grammatically feminine, which imposes a difficult choice between English pronouns. See also 1.11.23, where masc. is preferred because the predominant idea is Christ the *incarnate* Word.

of life itself are capable of evaluating God in a way that is neither irrational nor unworthy. Whatever physical form they imagine, they decide that it is either[34] alive or not alive, and they prefer a living to a nonliving form. As for that actual living physical form, however brilliantly it shines, however massive is its predominance, however beautiful its ornamentation, they understand that such characteristics are one thing, and that the life that animates it is something else; and they prize that life infinitely more than the physical bulk that it animates. (18) Then they are eager to investigate that same living entity; and if they find it alive yet lacking any capacity for perception (like trees for example), they give the preference to what has sense perception (such as animals); and ahead of that category they prefer what has the capacity for rational thought (such as human beings). When they see that this type of life is still subject to change, they are obliged to give the preference to another type of life that is not subject to change—that life, surely, that is not foolish one minute and wise the next, but that is wisdom[35] itself instead. (19) For the wise mind[36] (the mind that has achieved wisdom, in other words) was not wise before achieving it. Whereas wisdom itself never has been foolish, and never can be. If they did not see this, there is no way they could—with complete confidence—treat life that is unchanging in its wisdom as superior to life that does change.

36 *mens* here, not *animus*.

nerent. Ipsam quippe regulam veritatis, qua illam clamant esse meliorem, incommutabilem vident; nec uspiam nisi supra suam naturam vident, quandoquidem se mutabiles vident.

9. (20) Nemo est enim tam impudenter[13] insulsus qui dicat, "unde scis incommutabiliter sapientem vitam mutabili esse praeferendam?" Id ipsum enim quod interrogat, unde sciam, omnibus ad contemplandum communiter atque incommutabiliter praesto est. Et hoc qui non videt, ita est quasi caecus in sole, cui nihil prodest ipsis locis oculorum eius tam clarae ac praesentis lucis fulgor infusus. (21) Qui autem videt et refugit, consuetudine umbrarum carnalium invalidam mentis aciem gerit. Pravorum igitur morum quasi contrariis flatibus ab ipsa patria repercutiuntur homines posteriora atque inferiora sectantes quam illud, quod esse melius atque praestantius confitentur.

10. (22) Quapropter, cum illa veritate perfruendum sit quae incommutabiliter vivit, et in ea trinitas deus, auctor et conditor universitatis, rebus quas condidit consulat,[14] purgandus est animus, ut et perspicere illam lucem valeat et inhaerere perspectae. Quam purgationem quasi ambulationem quandam et quasi navigationem ad patriam esse

[13] inpudenter *P K Lond.*: inprudenter *B D F S Bam.*
[14] consolat *L Cam.*

---

[37] The "rule of truth" (*regula veritatis* [sometimes *fidei*, "of faith"]) evokes Plotinus *Enn.* 1.3.5 but also has roots in Latin theology: e.g., Irenaeus (d. ca. AD 200) *Haer.* 1.9.4, 2.28.1, 4.69.

[38] *purgatio*, like Greek *catharsis*, is a matter of physical excretion, then by extension a mental or spiritual purification.

In fact, they see that the rule of truth[37] (by which they proclaim that such a life is better) is itself unchanging; and they see it as superior to their own nature in every way, insofar as they see themselves as subject to change.

9. (20) No one is so shockingly absurd as to ask the question, "On what grounds do you know that an unchangingly wise life is preferable to a changeable one?" For that very point that is challenged, "On what grounds do I know?" is there for all to scrutinize collectively and inalterably. Anyone who does not see this, therefore, is like a blind man in sunshine: even the brilliance of a very bright light, right in front of him, beaming onto his eye sockets, has no impact on him. (21) As for those who do see it, yet shrink from it, they give their thoughts an unsound direction because they are at home with the dark shadows of the flesh. So human beings are driven away from their true homeland by—as it were—conflicting winds of distorted behavior, pursuing what is secondary and inferior rather than what they themselves admit is better and more worthwhile.

10. (22) For this reason, since we should enjoy to the full that truth in which is life unchanging, and since God the Trinity, founder and creator of the universe, in that truth has a care for the things he has created, our minds must be cleansed,[38] to give them the capacity to perceive that light, and, having perceived it, to cleave to it. We should think of this cleansing as a kind of progress and voyage to our homeland. Not that we are progressing, in

arbitremur. Non enim ad eum qui ubique praesens est locis movemur, sed bono studio bonisque moribus.

11. (23) Quod non possemus, nisi ipsa sapientia tantae etiam nostrae infirmitati congruere dignaretur et vivendi nobis praeberet exemplum non aliter quam in homine, quoniam et nos homines sumus. Sed quia nos, cum ad illam venimus, sapienter facimus, ipsa, cum ad nos venit, ab hominibus superbis quasi stulte fecisse putata est. Et quoniam nos cum ad illam venimus, convalescimus, ipsa cum ad nos venit, quasi infirma existimata est. Sed quod stultum est dei, sapientius est hominibus, et quod infirmum est dei, fortius est hominibus. Cum ergo ipsa sit patria, viam se quoque nobis fecit ad patriam.

(24) Et cum sano et puro interiori oculo ubique sit praesens, eorum qui oculum illum infirmum immundumque habent, oculis etiam carneis apparere dignata est. Quia enim in sapientia dei non poterat mundus per sapientiam cognoscere deum, placuit deo per stultitiam praedicationis salvos facere credentes.

12. (25) Non igitur[15] per locorum spatia veniendo, sed in carne mortali mortalibus apparendo, venisse ad nos dicitur. Illuc ergo venit ubi erat, quia in hoc mundo erat et mundus per eam factus est. Sed quoniam cupiditate fruendi pro ipso creatore creatura homines configurati huic mundo et mundi nomine congruentissime vocati non eam cognoverunt, propterea dixit evangelista, "et mundus

15 ergo *B D*

---

39 Here, Christ. 40 John 14:6. 41 1 Corinthians 1:21.

42 John 1:10. The pronoun (*eam*) in Latin is feminine, to agree with *sapientia* (still indicating Christ).

terms of our physical location, toward him who is present in all places; but rather in terms of good intentions and good character.

11. (23) We could not achieve this, unless Wisdom himself[39] deigned to accommodate our weakness, and offer us a paradigm for living—and in human form, no less, since we too are human beings. But because we are acting wisely when we come to him, when he came to us, people who were arrogant thought that he was committing an act of folly. And because when we came to him, we regained our health and strength, when he came to us he was judged to be weak. But what is foolishness in God is wiser than humankind; and what is weakness in God is stronger than humankind. So because he himself is our homeland, he has also made himself the way for us to that homeland.[40]

(24) Also, although he is present everywhere to the inner vision that is pure and sound, he has even deigned to appear to the physical sight of those whose inner vision is weak and unclean. For because "in God's wisdom the world was unable to recognize God by means of wisdom, it was God's will to save those who believe by the foolishness of the proclamation."[41]

12. (25) We are told that he came to us not by making his way through physical space, but by appearing, in mortal flesh, to mortals. So he made his way to a place where he was already, since he was in the world and the world was made through him.[42] But human beings conformed themselves instead to this world, because of their craving to enjoy the creation instead of its Creator, and so it was very appropriate to describe them by the term "the world": they did not recognize him, as the evangelist remarked:

eam[16] non cognovit." Itaque in sapientia dei non poterat mundus per sapientiam cognoscere deum. Cur ergo venit cum hic esset, nisi quia placuit deo per stultitiam praedicationis salvos facere credentes?

(26) Quomodo venit, nisi quod verbum caro factum est et habitavit in nobis? Sicuti cum loquimur, ut id quod animo gerimus in audientis animum per aures carneas illabatur, fit sonus verbum quod corde gestamus, et locutio vocatur. Nec tamen in eundem sonum cogitatio nostra convertitur, sed apud se manens integra,[17] formam vocis qua se insinuet auribus, sine aliqua labe suae mutationis assumit. Ita verbum dei non commutatum, caro tamen factum est ut habitaret in nobis.

13. (27) Sicut autem[18] curatio via est ad sanitatem, sic ista curatio peccatores sanandos reficiendosque suscepit. Et quemadmodum medici cum alligant vulnera, non incomposite sed apte id faciunt, ut vinculi utilitatem quaedam pulchritudo etiam consequatur, sic medicina sapientiae per hominis susceptionem nostris est accommodata vulneribus, de quibusdam contrariis curans et de quibusdam similibus. (28) Sicut etiam ille qui medetur vulneri

16 eum *D* μ Kn.
17 integram *G P D K Lond.*
18 autem ista *Lond.*

---

43 A shift from perfect to imperfect tense in Latin sharpens this point.

44 John 1:14.

45 See *Conf.* 10.8.14 for memory as a physical location.

46 *vox*: "voice." not *verbum*, "word."

47 The analogy with the eternal Word and Wisdom (Christ)

"and the world did not know him." This is how "in God's wisdom the world was unable to recognize God by means of wisdom." After all, why did he come, when he was here already,[43] unless because it was God's will to save those who believe by the foolishness of the proclamation?

(26) By what means, other than this, did he come—that "the Word was made flesh and dwelt among us"?[44] In the same way, when we speak, to make what we have in mind slide into the mind of a listener through their physical ears, the word that we hold in our heart becomes a sound, and is called "speech." Yet our thought is not changed into the same sound: it remains intact in its own place,[45] even as it takes on a spoken form[46] so as to worm its way into our ears, without undergoing the slightest trace of alteration. Likewise, the Word of God underwent no alteration, even though he was made flesh so as to dwell among us.[47]

13. (27) Just as good care in general is the way to health, so this particular type of care has undertaken the healing and restoration of sinners. When doctors bind up wounds they do so neatly, not haphazardly, so that a kind of beauty[48] results from the process of binding. In the same way, the remedy that is Wisdom, by undertaking to become a human being, adapted himself to our wounds. Thus he healed them, some by applying allopathic, others by homeopathic remedies. (28) Anyone who treats a

explains the insistence that thoughts are not changed by being spoken.

[48] Beauty and order are close allies in Augustine's mind. For Aristotle, order and symmetry are necessary to beauty (*Metaph.* 1078a36); for Plato, beauty requires unity (*Symp.* 210a–11d; cf. Plotinus *Enn.* 1.6).

corporis adhibet quaedam contraria, sicut frigidum calido vel humido siccum vel si quid aliud eiusmodi, adhibet etiam quaedam similia, sicut linteolum vel rotundo vulneri rotundum vel oblongum oblongo ligaturamque ipsam non eandem membris omnibus, sed similem similibus coaptat; sic sapientia dei hominem curans seipsam exhibuit ad sanandum, ipsa medicus, ipsa medicina. Quia ergo per superbiam homo lapsus est, humilitatem adhibuit ad sanandum. Serpentis sapientia decepti sumus, dei stultitia liberamur. (29) Quemadmodum autem illa sapientia vocabatur, erat autem stultitia contemnentibus deum, sic ista quae vocatur stultitia, sapientia est vincentibus diabolum. Nos immortalitate male usi sumus ut moreremur, Christus mortalitate bene usus est ut viveremus. Corrupto animo feminae ingressus est morbus, integro corpore feminae processit salus. Ad eadem contraria pertinet, quod etiam exemplo virtutum eius vitia nostra curantur. (30) Iam vero similia quasi ligamenta membris et vulneribus nostris adhibita illa sunt, quod per feminam deceptos per feminam natus, homo homines, mortalis mortales, morte mortuos liberavit. Multa quoque alia diligentius considerantibus,

---

49 "The Fall" (*lapsus*) is a Christian interpretation of Genesis 3:1–7; it sees the action of the first humans in terms of a descent from a condition of goodness, hence this eisegetical translation.

50 In Vulg. not *sapiens* but *callidus* (crafty, shrewd, cunning): *serpens erat callidior cunctis animantibus terrae* (Genesis 3:1$^{\text{Vulg.}}$); other (VL) versions use *sapiens* or *prudens*.

51 *salus*: also "salvation."

52 The theological idea is "recapitulation," *anacephalaiōsis* in Greek. Irenaeus extends the Adam-Christ typology of Paul (Romans 5:12–21; 1 Corinthians 15:22) into a parallelism between Eve and Mary: *Haer.* 5.19.1.

53 The expression mimics the homeopathy: *homo homines*

bodily wound makes use of certain contrasting materials—cold for heat, dry for wet, and such like; but also uses certain similar ones—a round dressing for a round wound, or a square one for a square wound, and bandages that are not all the same regardless of the limb involved, but the right type of bandage for each body part. In the same way, out of his concern for humankind, the Wisdom of God offered himself for healing, being both doctor and remedy. Because it was through pride that human beings fell from grace,[49] he made use of humility to heal them. We were deceived by the serpent's wisdom[50] but liberated by the foolishness of God. (29) Just as he was called Wisdom, but was foolishness to those who reject God, so also his so-called foolishness is in fact wisdom to those who conquer the Devil. We made a wrong use of our immortality, and as a result we were dying, but Christ put his mortality to good use, so that we would live. The disease entered us through one woman's corrupted mind: the cure[51] emerged through another woman's inviolate body.[52] It is also relevant to these allopathic principles that our vices are cured by the example of his virtues. (30) Indeed such homeopathic principles as bandages for parts of our bodies and for our wounds have already been mentioned: thus what was born of a woman liberated those who were deceived by a woman; what was human liberated other humans, what was mortal liberated other mortals—by death he liberated the dead.[53] To those who are carefully pondering

mortalis mortales morte mortuos. Liberation of the dead could refer to those physically alive (but spiritually dead), or to the "harrowing of hell," a belief expressed in the Apostles' Creed according to which Christ "descended to the dead" (cf. 1 Peter 3:19–20).

quos instituti operis peragendi necessitas non rapit, vel a contrariis vel a similibus medicinae christianae apparet instructio.

14. (31) Iam vero credita domini a mortuis resurrectio et in caelum ascensio magna spe fulcit fidem nostram. Multum enim ostendit quam voluntarie pro nobis animam posuerit, qui eam sic habuit in potestatem resumere. Quanta ergo se fiducia spes credentium consolatur, considerans quantus quanta pro nondum credentibus passus sit! Cum vero iudex vivorum atque mortuorum exspectatur e caelo, magnum timorem incutit neglegentibus, ut se ad diligentiam convertant, eumque magis bene agendo desiderent, quam male agendo formident.

(32) Quibus autem verbis dici aut qua cogitatione capi potest praemium, quod ille in fine daturus est, quando ad consolationem huius itineris de spiritu suo tantum dedit, quo in adversis vitae huius fiduciam caritatemque tantam eius, quem nondum videmus habeamus, et dona unicuique propria ad instructionem ecclesiae suae, ut id quod ostendit esse faciendum, non solum sine murmure sed etiam cum delectatione faciamus.

15. (33) Est enim ecclesia corpus eius, sicut apostolica doctrina commendat, quae coniunx etiam eius dicitur.

---

54 Meaning himself, writing this present work.

55 The ubiquity of antithesis as a figure of rhetoric in Augustine's writings is apparent, even without knowledge of Latin, to one who counts the instances of *vel . . . vel* in *TC* and other argumentative works.

56 *animam*: the "animating principle" or life force, as in John 10:18.

57 Expanded. In Latin, *fine*.

many other matters also, and who are not carried away by the obligation to finish writing a work they have begun,[54] it is clear that the pattern of Christian healing consists in either what is allopathic or what is homeopathic.[55]

14. (31) Now the Lord's resurrection from the dead and his ascension into heaven (which we believe) underpin our faith with a great hope. They show us plainly how willingly he laid down his life for us, and how he had it in his power to take it up again.[56] Therefore with what great confidence believers' hopes are comforted, considering how greatly his greatness suffered for those who were not yet believers! While we await the coming from heaven of the Judge of the living and the dead, he strikes terrible fear into those who show themselves indifferent to him, so that they turn to love of him instead: and so, through doing good deeds, come to desire him more, instead of fearing him more because of their wrongdoing.

(32) What words can be uttered, what thoughts can be conceived, to express the reward that he is going to bestow at the end of all things?[57] For he has given so greatly of his own spirit for comforting us in this journey of ours, so that in the difficulties of this life, we have great trust and love for him (though as yet we do not see him); and has given gifts to each of us appropriate for the ordering of his own Church, so that whatever he shows us needs doing, that we do—and not only without grumbling but even with delight.

15. (33) The Church is his body, as the apostolic teaching affirms;[58] she is also called his bride.[59] He binds to-

[58] He means Paul: Ephesians 1:23.
[59] Ephesians 5:24.

Corpus ergo suum multis membris diversa officia gerentibus, nodo unitatis et caritatis tamquam sanitatis adstringit. Exercet autem hoc tempore et purgat medicinalibus quibusdam molestiis, ut erutam de hoc saeculo in aeternum sibi copulet coniugem ecclesiam, non habentem maculam aut rugam aut aliquid eiusmodi.

16. (34) Porro quoniam in via sumus, nec via ista locorum est, sed affectuum, quam intercludebant quasi saepta quaedam spinosa, praeteritorum malitia peccatorum, quid liberalius et misericordius facere potuit, qui se ipsum nobis qua rediremus, substernere voluit, nisi ut omnia donaret peccata conversis et graviter fixa interdicta reditus nostri pro nobis crucifixus evelleret?

17. (35) Has igitur claves dedit ecclesiae suae, ut[19] quae solveret in terra, soluta essent et in caelo, quae ligaret in terra, ligata essent et in caelo,[20] scilicet ut quisquis in ecclesia eius dimitti sibi peccata non crederet, non ei dimitterentur; quisquis autem[21] crederet seque ab his correctus averteret, in eiusdem ecclesiae gremio constitutus, eadem fide atque correctione sanaretur. Quisquis enim non credit dimitti sibi posse peccata, fit deterior desperando, quasi

[19] ut] ut . . . debeat §43 deest fol. in *Lond.*

[20] quae ligaret in terra, ligata essent et in caelo *om.* *B D K (corr. i.m. K¹)* [21] autem] hoc *K*

---

[60] Romans 12:4. [61] Oxymoron.

[62] Ephesians 5:27. [63] *affectuum*: loving desires, either negative (e.g., *Spir. et litt.* 48, "in a human soul, the image of God has been eroded by sinful inclinations"), or positive ("devout longing, heartfelt reverence, faith, hope, love": *En. Ps.* 86.3).

[64] The pronoun is feminine both grammatically ("church" is a

gether his own body, therefore, with its different parts each performing different functions,[60] in a bond of unity and love, of wholeness, as it were. But at this point in time he is training her and cleansing her with certain remedial vexations,[61] to rescue her from this age and join her to himself for ever as his bride, the Church, without blemish, or flaw, or anything of that nature.[62]

16. (34) What is more, we are on a journey, and that journey is not about places, but what we set our heart on:[63] and it is obstructed by a kind of hedge of thorns, consisting of the evil of past sins. He was willing to put himself under our feet as the way for us to come home. What more liberating, more merciful action could he take than to forgive all the sins of those who turn to him; and, by being crucified for us, to tear down the deeply entrenched prohibitions on our homecoming?

17. (35) For this reason he gave these keys to his Church, so that what she[64] released on earth would also be released in heaven; and what she bound on earth would also be bound in heaven.[65] This was undoubtedly so that anyone in his Church who did not believe that their sins were forgiven would not have those sins forgiven: whereas anyone who did believe it, and so reformed themselves and turned from those sins was established in the bosom of that same Church, and was cleansed by the same faith and reformation. Anyone who does not believe that their sins can be forgiven dwindles into despair—as if there

feminine noun) and figuratively (continuing the "bride" metaphor). [65] Matthew 16:19 (cf. John 20:23): a proof text for ecclesiastical authority, particularly the exercise (or withholding) of forgiveness.

nihil illi melius quam malum esse remaneat, ubi de fructu suae conversionis infidus est.

18. (36) Iam vero sicut animi quaedam mors est, vitae prioris[22] morumque relictio quae fit paenitendo, sic etiam corporis mors est animationis pristinae resolutio. Et quomodo animus post paenitentiam, qua priores mores perditos interemit, reformatur in melius, sic etiam corpus post istam mortem, quam vinculo peccati omnes debemus, credendum et sperandum est resurrectionis tempore in melius commutari, ut non caro et sanguis regnum caelorum possideat, quod fieri non potest, sed corruptibile hoc induat incorruptionem et mortale hoc induat immortalitatem, nullamque faciens molestiam quia nullam patietur indigentiam[23] a beata perfectaque anima cum summa quiete vegetetur.

19. (37) Cuius autem animus non moritur huic saeculo neque incipit configurari veritati, in graviorem mortem morte corporis trahitur, neque ad commutationem caelestis habitudinis, sed ad luenda supplicia revivescit. (38) Hoc itaque fides habet atque ita se rem habere credendum est, neque animum neque corpus humanum omnimodum

[22] vitae prioris . . . corporis mors est *om. B*

[23] indulgentiam *P K*

---

[66] *anima* and *animus* are not synonyms: *animus* refers to the mind with its rational and moral faculties, *anima* to the soul, or animating principle.

[67] 1 Corinthians 15:50–53.

[68] Virtual oxymoron to express the contrast in heaven between a state of vitality and the eternal rest of the blessed.

[69] Cf. Romans 12:2[VL]; Augustine follows that version (*in no-*

were nothing left to them better than abiding in sin, when there is a lack of trust concerning the effects of repentance.

18. (36) Now then, just as there is a kind of death of the mind[66]—that giving up of a former life and behavior that comes about through repentance—so too the death of the body is the setting free of what once animated it. And in the same way as the mind is changed for the better after repentance, by which it does away with its former abandoned behavior, so also we should believe and hope that on the day of resurrection the body is changed for the better, after that death to which we are all liable because of the bond of sin. This is not so that flesh and blood can possess the kingdom of heaven (which is impossible) but so that what is corruptible may put on incorruptibility, and what is mortal may put on immortality.[67] Making no difficulty, because there is nothing that it lacks, it will be enlivened in perfect rest[68] by a soul that is blessed and complete.

19. (37) Anyone whose mind does not die to this world, and does not begin to be conformed to the truth,[69] is drawn into a worse kind of death when their physical body dies. They come to new life[70] not to change to a heavenly dwelling place, but to undergo punishment. (38) So faith holds to this, and this state of affairs is essential to belief: that neither the mind nor the human body undergoes

vitate mentis tuae instead of *in novitate sensus vestri*[Vulg.]) in *an. et or.* (also known as *de anima et eius origine*) 4.20.

70 *revivescit*: a verb common in Cicero. Augustine repurposes it for Christianity: see *Conf.* 12.10.10.

interitum pati, sed impios resurgere ad poenas inaestimabiles, pios autem ad vitam aeternam.

20. (39) In his igitur omnibus rebus illae tantum sunt quibus fruendum est, quas aeternas atque incommutabiles commemoravimus; ceteris autem utendum est ut ad illarum perfruitionem pervenire possimus. Nos itaque qui fruimur et utimur aliis rebus, res aliquae sumus. Magna enim quaedam res est homo, factus ad imaginem et similitudinem dei, non in quantum mortali corpore includitur, sed in quantum bestias rationalis animae honore praecedit.

(40) Itaque magna quaestio est, utrum frui se homines debeant an uti an utrumque. Praeceptum est enim nobis ut diligamus invicem, sed quaeritur, utrum propter se homo ab homine diligendus sit an propter aliud. Si enim propter se, fruimur eo; si propter aliud, utimur eo. Videtur autem mihi propter aliud diligendus. Quod enim propter se diligendum est, in eo constituitur beata vita, cuius etiamsi nondum res, tamen spes eius nos hoc tempore consolatur. Maledictus autem qui spem suam ponit in homine.

21. (41) Sed nec seipso quisquam frui debet, si liquide[24] advertas, quia nec seipsum debet propter se ipsum diligere, sed propter illum quo fruendum est. Tunc est quippe optimus homo, cum tota vita sua pergit in incommutabilem vitam et toto affectu inhaeret illi. Si autem se propter

[24] liquido μ: aliquid K^1

---

[71] Cf. Matthew 25:46; John 5:29. The point is that "resurrection" (Latin noun *resurrectio*, verb *resurgo*) applies to both saved and damned. [72] John 13:34. [73] Jeremiah 17:5.

complete annihilation—instead, the wicked rise again to unimaginable punishments, but the godly to eternal life.[71]

20. (39) In all these matters the only things that we ought to enjoy are those that we have recorded as being eternal and unchanging. Anything else is to be used in such a way that we can attain the complete enjoyment of those things. Accordingly, we who enjoy and use other things are a kind of thing ourselves. A human being is a great thing, a particular thing, made in the image and likeness of God; not inasmuch as it is enclosed in a mortal body, but inasmuch as it outstrips the animals in the dignity of its rational soul.

(40) It is a pressing question, therefore, whether human beings ought to enjoy one another, or make use of one another, or both. We have been given a commandment, to love one another:[72] but it is a moot point whether one human being should be loved by another for their own sake or for the same of something else. If it is for their own sake, we enjoy that person; but if it is for the same of something else, then we are using them. It seems to me that a person should be loved for the sake of something else; because this is what the blessed life consists in what must be loved for its own sake. Even if at this time we do not have the reality of this blessed life to comfort us, we do still have the hope of it. After all, "cursed is anyone who puts their hope in humankind."[73]

21. (41) If you observe carefully, no one ought to enjoy their own self, because they should not love themselves for their own sake, but rather for the sake of him whom they should really be enjoying. Surely then the best kind of person is the one whose entire life is a striving for the unchangeable life, and who cleaves to that with all their

se diligit, non se refert ad deum, sed ad se ipsum conversus non ad incommutabile aliquid convertitur. Et propterea iam cum defectu aliquo se fruitur, quia melior est cum totus haeret atque constringitur incommutabili bono, quam cum inde vel ad seipsum relaxatur.

(42) Si ergo teipsum non propter te debes diligere, sed propter illum ubi dilectionis tuae rectissimus finis est, non suscenseat alius homo, si etiam ipsum propter deum diligis. Haec enim regula dilectionis divinitus constituta est, "diliges," inquit, "proximum tuum tamquam te ipsum, deum vero ex toto corde, ex tota anima, ex tota mente," ut omnes cogitationes tuas et omnem vitam et omnem intellectum in illum conferas, a quo habes ea ipsa quae confers. (43) Cum autem ait "toto corde, tota anima, tota mente," nullam vitae nostrae partem reliquit quae vacare debeat et quasi locum dare ut alia re velit frui, sed quidquid aliud diligendum venerit in animum, illuc rapiatur quo totus dilectionis impetus currit. Quisquis ergo recte diligit proximum, hoc cum eo debet agere, ut etiam ipse toto corde, tota anima, tota mente diligat deum. Sic enim eum diligens tamquam se ipsum totam dilectionem sui et illius refert in illam dilectionem dei quae nullum a se rivulum duci extra patitur, cuius derivatione minuatur.

22. (44) Non autem omnia quibus utendum est dili-

heart. But if they love themselves for their own sake, they do not acknowledge God but instead turn toward themselves, rather than turning to what is unchangeable. So now when they enjoy themselves, they do so in a deficient way. This is because they are better when they wholly cleave and bind themselves to what is good and unchangeable, than when they free themselves from it in order to focus upon themselves.

(42) If, then, you ought to love yourself not for your own sake but for the sake of him in whom the supremely righteous object of your love consists, no one should be angry if you love them also, for God's sake. This is because the rule of love has been established by God, who says, "you shall love your neighbor as yourself; and love God with all your heart, all your soul, all your mind." This means that you attribute all your thoughts, and all your life, and all your understanding to him who bestowed these powers on you. (43) When he says, "with all your heart, all your soul, all your mind," he lets no part of our life be devoid of this duty and leaves no space—as it were—for desiring to enjoy some other thing. Instead, whatever else comes to mind as an object of our love is carried off in the same direction as that which the whole force of our love is moving toward. Whoever loves their neighbor in the right way, therefore, ought to do so together with their neighbor, so that they too love God with all their heart, all their soul, all their mind. Then, loving him as they love themselves, they attribute all their love for themselves and for others to that love of God, which does not permit any flow to be directed away from itself which, if diverted, might diminish it.

22. (44) Not everything that is useable is also lovable,

genda sunt, sed ea sola quae aut nobiscum societate quadam referuntur in deum, sicut est homo vel angelus, aut ad nos relata beneficio dei per nos indigent, sicut est corpus. Nam utique martyres non dilexerunt scelus persequentium se, quo tamen usi sunt ad promerendum deum. (45) Cum ergo quattuor sint diligenda, unum quod supra nos est, alterum quod nos sumus, tertium quod iuxta nos est, quartum quod infra nos est, de secundo et quarto nulla praecepta danda erant. Quantumlibet enim homo excidat a veritate, remanet illi dilectio sui et dilectio corporis sui. Fugax enim animus ab incommutabili lumine omnium regnatore id agit, ut ipse sibi regnet et corpori suo, et ideo non potest nisi et se et corpus suum diligere. 23. (46) Magnum autem aliquid adeptum se putat, si etiam sociis, id est aliis hominibus, dominari potuerit. Inest enim vitioso animo id magis appetere et sibi tamquam debitum vindicare, quod uni proprie debetur deo. Talis autem sui dilectio melius odium vocatur. Iniquum est enim, quia vult sibi servire quod infra se est, cum ipse superiori servire nolit, rectissimeque dictum est "qui autem diligit iniquitatem, odit animam suam." Et ideo fit infirmus animus et de mortali corpore cruciatur. (47) Necesse est enim ut illud diligat et eius corruptione[25] praegravetur. Immortalitas enim et incorruptio corporis de sanitate animi existit, sanitas autem animi est firmissime inhaerere potiori, hoc est incommutabili deo. Cum vero etiam eis qui sibi naturaliter

[25] correptione *D*

---

[74] 2 Timothy 2:18.
[75] Psalm 11:5 (10.6[Vulg.]).

but only what is associated with God by reason of a kind of affinity with us—such as another human being, or an angel; or what has been associated with us, and stands in need of God's blessing through our agency–such as our bodies. The martyrs, for example, certainly did not love the criminality of their persecutors, but still they made use of it, to win God's approval. (45) There are four categories for what we should love: the first, what is above us; next, what we ourselves are; the third, what is alongside us; and the fourth, what is beneath us: yet no commandments were needed concerning the second and the fourth categories. However far someone may fall from the truth,[74] there remains in them the love of self, and the love of their own body. The mind that flees from the unchanging light who reigns over all things does so in order to reign over itself, and over its own body. So it cannot fail to love both itself and its own body. 23. (46) But it thinks it has achieved something significant if it can exercise power over its associates, that is, over other human beings. It is characteristic of a corrupt mind to strive, and lay claim to (as its due) what is properly due to God alone. This kind of love of self is better described as hatred. It is wrong because it wants what is below it to be subject to it, yet it is itself unwilling to be subject to what is above it. How true is the saying, "Anyone who loves wrongdoing, hates their own soul."[75] Thus the mind becomes weak, and is tormented concerning its mortal body; (47) for it is inescapable that it loves its body, and is crushed by its corruptibility. Immortality and an incorruptible body are manifest fruits of integrity of the mind; but integrity of mind consists in determinedly cleaving to what is more powerful, namely God, who never changes. Pride, therefore, is altogether

pares sunt, hoc est, hominibus, dominari affectat, intolerabilis omnino superbia est.

24. (48) Nemo ergo se odit. Et hinc quidem nulla cum aliqua secta quaestio fuit. Sed neque corpus suum quisquam odit, verum est enim quod ait apostolus: nemo umquam carnem suam odio habuit. Et quod nonnulli dicunt, malle se omnino esse sine corpore, omnino falluntur. Non enim corpus suum, sed corruptiones[26] eius et pondus oderunt. (49) Non itaque nullum corpus, sed incorruptum et celerrimum corpus volunt habere, sed puta nullum corpus esse si tale fuerit, quia tale aliquid esse animam putant. Quod autem continentia quadam et laboribus quasi persequi videntur corpora sua, qui hoc recte faciunt, non id agunt ut non habeant corpus, set ut habeant subiugatum et paratum ad opera necessaria. (50) Libidines enim male utentes corpore, id est consuetudines et inclinationes animae ad fruendum inferioribus, per ipsius corporis laboriosam quandam militiam exstinguere affectant. Nam non se interimunt, sed curam suae valetudinis gerunt.

[26] corruptionem *P K*

---

[76] *secta* can embrace both Christian and philosophical schools; it is not confined to the negative resonance of the English "sect."

[77] Ephesians 5:29. The word for flesh, *carnem*, is a calque—a Latin word (a Greek one in the New Testament, *σάρκα*) with a Hebrew meaning. Augustine shows no awareness of body dysmorphia or anorexia.

[78] As with the English, so the Latin *corruptiones* encompasses both subjection to decay (physical) and immorality (metaphorical).

insupportable when it presumes to exercise power over those who are by nature its equals, which is to say, fellow human beings.

24. (48) So no one hates themselves. On this topic, surely, there has never been a dispute with any school of thought.[76] Neither does anyone hate their own body, for what the apostle says is true, "no one ever hated his own flesh."[77] When some people say that they would rather do without a body altogether, they are altogether deluded. For it is not the body that they hate, but its corruptions,[78] its being a burden. (49) Accordingly, they do not wish to have no body at all, but rather a body that is undecayed and alive:[79] but they reckon that a body like this would not be a body at all;[80] they reckon something of this kind must be a soul. As for the fact that they seem to afflict their body with a kind of asceticism, and hardships, those who do this appropriately do not do it as a way of having no body, but to keep the body under control,[81] prepared for all eventualities. (50) People who maltreat their body in this way are attempting to snuff out hedonistic desires (namely the soul's tendency and predilection for enjoying inferior things) by means of a kind of burdensome campaign against their own body. After all, they are not killing themselves, but taking care of their own well-being.

[79] *celerrimum corpus*: a "quickened" body (the term in English is slightly archaic).

[80] Perhaps recalling Porphyry's slogan, *omne corpus fugiendum*, "the body must be completely abandoned," quoted in *Civ.* 10.29.2; 12.26.

[81] 1 Corinthians 9:27.

25. (51) Qui autem perverse id agunt, quasi naturaliter inimico suo corpori bellum ingerunt. In quo fallit eos quod legunt: "caro concupiscit adversus spiritum et spiritus adversus carnem; haec enim invicem adversantur." Dictum est enim hoc propter indomitam carnalem consuetudinem, adversus quam spiritus concupiscit; non ut interimat corpus, sed ut concupiscentia eius, id est consuetudine mala edomita faciat spiritui subiugatum, quod naturalis ordo desiderat. (52) Quia enim hoc erit post resurrectionem, ut corpus omnimodo cum quiete summa spiritui subditum immortaliter vigeat, hoc etiam in hac vita meditandum est, ut consuetudo carnalis mutetur in melius nec inordinatis motibus resistat spiritui. Quod donec fiat, caro concupiscit adversus spiritum et spiritus adversus carnem, non per odium resistente spiritu, sed per principatum; quia magis quod diligit vult subditum esse meliori, nec per odium resistente carne, sed per consuetudinis vinculum, quod a parentum etiam propagine inveteratum naturae lege inolevit.

(53) Id ergo agit spiritus in domanda carne, ut solvat malae consuetudinis quasi pacta perversa et fiat pax consuetudinis bonae. Tamen nec isti qui falsa opinione depravati corpora sua detestantur, parati essent unum oculum

---

[82] Galatians 5:17. [83] *naturalis ordo*: a cover term for the perception of a fixed pattern in the cosmos, of order and hierarchy as a positive phenomenon (cf. *Qu.* 153).

[84] The theological problem with traducianism is twofold: the whole human race inherits the sin of the first human beings, which contradicts divine justice; and human free will and capacity to choose the good are undermined. Cf. *Div. quaest.* 1.1.10, written in 396, his first publication as a bishop.

25. (51) People who behave in this perverse way are forcing a war against their own body, as if it were—by nature, so to speak—the enemy. In this respect they misconstrue what they read: "what the flesh desires is against the spirit, and what the spirit desires is against the flesh; these two things are polar opposites."[82] This was stated on account of undisciplined habits of the flesh, to which the spirit's appetites are opposed, not so as to destroy the body, but rather to bring the body under the spirit's control by curbing its appetites, in other words its evil habits. This is what the order of nature[83] wants. (52) Because after the resurrection it will be the case that the body will be completely obedient to the spirit, wholly at peace as it flourishes everlastingly, it should also be a subject for reflection in this life, so that the habits of the flesh change for the better and do not oppose the spirit with undisciplined passions. Until that happens, the flesh has desires that are resistant to the spirit, and the spirit has desires that resist the flesh. The spirit is not resistant out of hatred, but by virtue of its superiority. This is because it prefers what it loves to be obedient to what is better. The flesh is not resistant out of hatred, but because it is fettered by habit, which has become ingrained through our forebears' procreation of offspring,[84] and has spread according to the law of nature.

(53) This is what the spirit does to control the flesh, so as to undo the corrupt confederacy of harmful habits and bring about the concord of good habits. Yet not even those who curse their bodies because they have been disfigured by erroneous beliefs would be prepared to lose a single

vel sine sensu doloris amittere, etiamsi in altero tantus cernendi sensus remaneret, quantus erat in duobus, nisi aliqua res quae praeponenda esset urgeret. Isto atque huiusmodi documentis[27] satis ostenditur eis qui sine pertinacia verum requirunt, quam certa sententia sit apostoli, ubi ait, "nemo enim umquam carnem suam odio habuit." Addidit etiam, "sed nutrit et fovet eam, sicut et Christus ecclesiam."

26. (54) Modus ergo diligendi praecipiendus est homini, id est quomodo se diligat ut prosit sibi. Quin autem se diligat et prodesse sibi velit dubitare dementis est; praecipiendum etiam quomodo corpus suum diligat, ut ei ordinate prudenterque consulat. Nam quod diligat etiam corpus suum idque salvum habere atque integrum velit, aeque manifestum est. (55) Aliquid itaque amplius diligere aliquis potest, quam salutem atque integritatem corporis sui. Nam multi et dolores et amissiones nonnullorum membrorum voluntarias suscepisse inveniuntur, sed ut alia quae amplius diligebant consequerentur. Non ergo propterea quisquam dicendus est non diligere salutem atque incolumitatem corporis sui, quia plus aliquid diligit. (56) Nam et avarus quamvis pecuniam diligat, tamen emit sibi panem; quod cum facit dat pecuniam quam multum diligit et augere desiderat, sed quia pluris aestimat salutem corporis sui, quae illo pane fulcitur. Supervacaneum est diutius de re manifestissima disputare, quod tamen plerumque nos facere cogit error impiorum.

[27] documento L^1 μ

eye—even if it was painless, and even if their remaining eye retained the power of sight to the same degree as formerly the pair possessed—unless some particular circumstances were to favor such a course. This example, and others like it, are enough to show those who seek the truth without constant effort that the opinion voiced by the apostle is right, when he says "no one ever held their own flesh in aversion." And he added "but they nourish and nurture it, just as Christ does the Church."

26. (54) Human beings ought to be taught the proper measure for their loving—in other words how to love themselves in a way that does themselves good. It is a mark of folly to doubt that they love themselves and would wish to do themselves good. They must be taught how they should love their body so as to give it proportionate and careful consideration. For the fact that they love their own body and wish to keep it in good health, unharmed, is just as obvious. (55) Likewise a person can love something more than the health and well-being of their own body. Many are known to have accepted pain, and the loss of one or more limbs, willingly, in order to achieve other things that they loved more. For this reason no one should be accused of not loving their own body's health and well-being just because there is something else they love more. (56) Even though an avaricious person loves money, for example, they still use it to buy bread. When they do so, they hand over the money that they love so much, and long to accumulate, precisely because they give a higher priority to the health of their body, which is dependent on that bread. There is no point arguing this obvious point at greater length, though the delusions of the ungodly often oblige us to do so.

27. (57) Ergo quoniam praecepto non opus est ut se quisque et corpus suum diligat, id est quoniam id quod sumus et id quod infra nos, ad nos tamen pertinet, inconcussa naturae lege diligimus, quae in bestias[28] etiam promulgata est (nam et bestiae se atque corpora sua diligunt) restabat ut et de illo quod supra nos est et de illo quod iuxta nos est, praecepta sumeremus. "Diliges," inquit, "dominum deum tuum ex toto corde tuo et ex tota anima tua et ex tota mente tua," et "diliges proximum tuum tamquam teipsum. In his duobus praeceptis tota lex pendet et omnes prophetae." (58) Finis itaque praecepti est dilectio, et ea gemina, id est dei et proximi. Quod si te totum intellegas, id est animum et corpus, et proximum totum, id est animum et corpus eius—homo enim ex animo constat et corpore—nullum rerum diligendarum genus in his duobus praeceptis praetermissum est. Cum enim praecurrat dilectio dei eiusque dilectionis modus praescriptus appareat, ita ut cetera in illum confluant, de dilectione tua nihil dictum videtur: sed cum dictum est, "diliges proximum tuum tamquam teipsum," simul et tui abs te dilectio non praetermissa est.

28. (59) Ille autem iuste et sancte vivit, qui rerum integer aestimator est. Ipse est autem qui ordinatam habet dilectionem, ne aut diligat quod non est diligendum, aut non diligat quod diligendum est, aut amplius diligat quod minus diligendum est, <aut minus diligat quod amplius diligendum est>[29] aut aeque diligat quod vel minus vel

[28] bestiis *P B D Lond. R*   [29] <aut . . . est> *suppl. RGr.*

---

[85] Christ.   [86] Matthew 22:37–40.   [87] 1 Timothy 1:5.
[88] O'Donovan, *Problem of Self-Love*, 25–32.

27. (57) So there is no need for anyone to be taught to love their own body. This is because what we are, and what is beneath us but is still relevant to us, we love, as if by an unalterable law of nature that has even been declared to the animal kingdom (for even animals love themselves and their bodies). There remains what is above us, and what is on a level with us, for us to draw lessons from. He[85] says "you shall love the Lord your God with all your heart and with all your soul and with all your mind," and "you shall love your neighbor as yourself. On these two teachings hang the whole Law and all the prophets."[86] (58) The goal of the teaching, then, is love,[87] and a double love at that—namely of God and neighbor. So if you understand yourself as a whole (that is, as a mind and a body), and understand your neighbor as a whole (that is, their mind and their body—for human beings are made up of a mind and a body) no category of thing deserving love is lacking from these two teachings. Although the love of God comes before all else, and the proper way to love him has evidently been stipulated in such a way that everything else flows together toward him, nothing has apparently been said about love of self. But when it is said, "you shall love your neighbor as yourself," your own love of yourself has not been overlooked.

28. (59) The person who lives a holy and righteous life is the one who makes a sound calculation of things. Such a person has love that is properly ordered.[88] As a result they do not love what is unlovely, nor do they fail to love what deserves to be loved. They do not love overmuch what deserves less love, or give equal love to what deserves

amplius[30] diligendum est, aut minus vel amplius quod aeque diligendum est. Omnis peccator in quantum peccator est, non est diligendus, et omnis homo in quantum homo est, diligendus est propter deum, deus vero propter seipsum. (60) Et si deus omni homine amplius diligendus est, amplius quisque deum debet diligere quam seipsum. Item amplius alius homo diligendus est quam corpus nostrum, quia propter deum omnia ista diligenda sunt et potest nobiscum alius homo deo perfrui, quod non potest corpus, quia corpus per animam vivit qua fruimur deo.

29. (61) Omnes autem aeque diligendi sunt. Sed cum omnibus prodesse non possis, his potissimum consulendum est qui pro locorum et temporum vel quarumlibet rerum opportunitatibus constrictius tibi quasi quadam sorte iunguntur. (62) Sicut enim si tibi abundaret aliquid, quod dare[31] oporteret ei qui non haberet, nec duobus dari potuisset,[32] si tibi occurrerent duo, quorum neuter alium vel indigentia vel erga te aliqua necessitudine superaret, nihil iustius faceres quam ut sorte legeres cui dandum esset quod dari utrique non posset, sic in hominibus quibus omnibus consulere nequeas, pro sorte habendum est, prout quisque tibi temporaliter colligatius adhaerere potuerit.

30 quod vel . . . amplius] quod minus ut amplius *Lond.*
31 dari K^1 *Lond.* R μ
32 posset P μ: possit K

---

89 The referent is unclear, perhaps "those bodies." It cannot be human beings *tout court*. 90 Covering both the universal (poverty) and the particular (personal connection).

91 If one person is more closely connected than another, that

either less or more love. Every sinner, insofar as they are a sinner, is undeserving of love; and every human being, insofar as they are human, deserves to be loved for God's sake; and God deserves to be loved for his own sake. (60) If, then, God deserves to be loved more than all human beings, each human being ought to love God more than themselves. Likewise, we should love other human beings more than our own body, because it is for God's sake that all those things[89] deserve love, and another person can experience full enjoyment of God with us—this is not something the body can experience, as the body lives because of the soul, through which we enjoy God.

29. (61) All people ought to be loved equally. But since you cannot do good to all, you must give particular thought to those whose particular fortune it is to have closer connections with you, according to the hazards of space, and time, and circumstance. (62) Imagine that you had a plentiful supply of something that ought to be given to a person who had none, and that could not be given to two people. If you came across two people, neither of whom predominated over the other either in terms of need, or of any relationship with yourself,[90] you could not act more fairly than by casting lots as the way to choose which should receive what could not be given to both. In the same way, when you cannot give full consideration to every person, you should treat it as a matter of happenstance, according to how closely, in worldly terms, each of them can be linked to you.[91]

fact of chance (*sors*: the simplest meaning is a "lot" cast to determine a choice) may also be a matter of fate or fortune (also *sors*) to legitimate the choice of that closer person.

30. (63) Omnium autem qui nobiscum frui possunt deo, partim eos diligimus quos ipsi adiuvamus, partim eos a quibus adiuvamur; partim quorum et indigemus adiutorio et indigentiae subvenimus, partim quibus nec ipsi conferimus aliquid commodi nec ab eis ut nobis conferatur attendimus. Velle tamen debemus ut omnes nobiscum diligant deum, et totum quod eos vel adiuvamus vel adiuvamur ab eis ad unum illum finem referendum est.

(64) Si enim in theatris nequitiae qui aliquem diligit histrionem et tamquam magno vel etiam summo bono eius arte perfruitur, omnes diligit qui secum eum diligunt, non propter illos, sed propter eum quem pariter diligunt; et quanto est in eius amore ferventior, tanto agit quibus modis potest, ut a pluribus diligatur et tanto pluribus eum cupit ostendere, et quem frigidiorem videt, excitat eum quantum potest laudibus illius. Si autem contravenientem invenerit, odit in illo vehementer odium dilecti sui, et quibus modis valet, instat ut auferat. Quid nos in societate dilectionis dei agere convenit, quo perfrui beate vivere est, et a quo habent omnes qui eum diligunt et quod sunt et quod eum diligunt, de quo nihil metuimus ne cuiquam possit cognitus displicere, et qui se vult diligi, non ut sibi aliquid, sed ut eis qui diligunt aeternum praemium conferatur, hoc est ipse quem diligunt?

---

[92] Augustine is critical of the effects of theater in *Conf.* 3.2.2; cf. *Sermo* 332.1, which also criticizes obsession with actors.

30. (63) Out of all those who can enjoy God with us, some we love whom we ourselves help, others we love who help us. Some we love whose help we need and whose wants we are supplying, others on whom we neither bestow any benefit, nor do we devote ourselves to them in the hope of receiving such a benefit. We ought to want everyone to love God with us; and the entirety of the help we give to them, and they to us, should be directed to that end.

(64) Imagine that someone adores a particular actor in some immoral theater production,[92] and enjoys his performance to the full, as if it were a great good, even the highest good of all. Next, imagine that this person loves everyone who likewise loves the actor (not on their own account, but on account of him whom they all love alike): and the more passionate they are in this love, the more they try by any means they can to make the actor be loved by more people; and the more eager they are to show him off to more people. If they notice that the actor is somewhat cool toward them, they fire him up as much as possible by praising him. But if they meet anyone who disagrees with them, they utterly detest that person for their hatred of the beloved, and are eager to do away with it by any means they can. So what is it appropriate for us to do in our fellowship of love for God, when total enjoyment of him is life itself? And when everyone who loves him has, as God's gift, the fact that they exist, and the fact that they love him? And when we have never been afraid that he could become known to anyone without delighting them? And when he wants himself to be loved, not for his own advantage but so that those who love him may receive an eternal reward—namely himself, whom they love?

(65) Hinc efficitur ut inimicos etiam nostros diligamus. Non enim eos timemus, quia nobis quod diligimus auferre non possunt, sed miseramur[33] potius, quia tanto magis nos oderunt, quanto ab illo quem diligimus separati sunt. Ad quem si conversi fuerint, et illum tamquam beatificum bonum, et nos tamquam socios tanti boni necesse est ut diligant.

31. (66) Oritur autem hoc loco de angelis nonnulla quaestio. Illo enim fruentes etiam ipsi beati sunt, quo et nos frui desideramus; et quantum[34] in hac vita fruimur vel per speculum vel in aenigmate, tanto eam[35] peregrinationem et tolerabilius sustinemus et ardentius finire cupimus. Sed utrum ad illa duo praecepta etiam dilectio pertineat angelorum, non irrationabiliter quaeri potest. (67) Nam[36] quod nullum hominum exceperit qui praecepit ut proximum diligamus, et ipse in evangelio dominus ostendit et apostolus Paulus. Namque ille cui duo ipsa praecepta protulerat atque in eis pendere totam legem prophetasque omnes dixerat, cum interrogaret eum dicens, "et quis est mihi proximus?" hominem quendam proposuit descendentem ab Hierusalem ad Iericho incidisse in latrones et ab eis graviter vulneratum saucium et semivivum esse derelictum. Cui proximum esse non docuit, nisi qui erga illum recreandum atque curandum misericors ex-

33 miramur *Par. Bam.*

34 quanto] *B* μ

35 etiam *Par. San. Cam.*: nostram *R* μ

36 non *K*

(65) This is the basis on which we should love even our enemies. We are not afraid of them, for they cannot deprive us of what we love. Instead we pity them, because they more they are set apart from him whom we love, the more they hate us. If they were converted to him, they would inevitably love him as that good who has power to bestow blessings, and us, as their companions in that great good.

31. (66) At this point a question of some significance arises, concerning angels. They too, are themselves blessed while they enjoy God (whom we too long to enjoy). To the extent that we enjoy him in this life, as a reflection in a mirror, or a mystical vision,[93] we are better prepared to endure this journey in a foreign land, and more eager in our desire to come to its conclusion. But it is not unreasonable to put the question whether love for angels is covered by those two commandments. (67) He who instructed us to love our neighbor made no exception among human beings; and in the gospel, the Lord himself made this plain, as did the apostle Paul. When the man to whom he had made known those same two commandments, and had declared that the whole law and all the prophets depended on them, asked him, "and who is my neighbor?" he told the story of a certain man going down from Jerusalem to Jericho, who fell among thieves who badly wounded him, and left him injured and barely alive. He taught that this man had no neighbor except for the person who appeared to be full of compassion toward him in his need for healing and recovery—and the man who had

93 William Tyndale (1529) captures the Latin, "Now we se in a glasse even in a darke speakynge" (1 Corinthians 13:12).

stitit, ita ut hoc qui interrogaverat interrogatus ipse fateretur. (68) Cui dominus ait, "vade et tu fac similiter," ut videlicet eum proximum esse intellegamus, cui vel exhibendum est officium misericordiae, si indiget, vel exhibendum esset, si indigeret.

Ex quo est iam consequens ut etiam ille a quo nobis hoc vicissim exhibendum est, proximus sit noster. Proximi enim nomen ad aliquid est, nec quisquam esse proximus nisi proximo potest. (69) Nullum autem exceptum esse cui misericordiae denegetur officium, quis non videat, quando usque ad inimicos etiam porrectum est, eodem domino dicente, "diligite inimicos vestros, benefacite eis qui vos oderunt"?

32. (70) Ita quoque Paulus apostolus docet cum dicit, "nam non adulterabis, non homicidium facies, non furaberis, non concupisces, et si quod est aliud mandatum, in hoc sermone recapitulatur: diliges proximum tuum tamquam te ipsum. Dilectio proximi malum non operatur." Quisquis ergo arbitratur non de omni homine apostolum praecepisse, cogitur fateri, quod absurdissimum et sceleratissimum est, visum fuisse apostolo non esse peccatum si quis aut non christiani aut inimici adulterarit uxorem, aut eum occiderit aut eius rem concupiverit. Quod si dementis est dicere, manifestum est omnem hominem proximum esse deputandum, quia erga neminem operandum est malum.

33. (71) Iam vero si vel cui praebendum vel a quo nobis praebendum est officium misericordiae, recte proximus dicitur, manifestum est hoc praecepto quo iubemur dili-

---

[94] The parable known as the "Good Samaritan," Luke 10:29; see also *TC* 1.36.77. [95] Matthew 5:44. [96] Romans 13:9–10.

asked the question, when questioned himself, admitted as much. (68) The Lord said to him "go and do as he did."[94] So we must understand that anyone is our neighbor to whom we must show a duty of compassion if they are in need, or ought to show it if ever they were in need.

From this it follows that that person who in turn owes an act of kindness to us is also our neighbor. After all, the word "neighbor" implies nearness to something, and no one can be a neighbor without also having a neighbor. (69) Who can fail to see that no one is excluded, by being denied that duty of compassion that is even offered to enemies, when the Lord says likewise "love your enemies, do good to those who hate you?"[95]

32. (70) The apostle Paul teaches the same when he says "for you shall not commit adultery, you shall not commit murder, you shall not steal, you shall not covet, and if there is any other command, it is summed up in this saying, You shall love your neighbor as yourself. The love of neighbor does no wrong."[96] Anyone who considers that the apostle was not issuing this teaching as applying to all humankind has to admit something utterly ridiculous and scandalous—that the apostle did not think it was a sin if a man were to commit adultery with the wife of someone who was a non-Christian, or an enemy, or to kill him, or covet his property. Only someone mad would say this. It is clear, therefore, that we ought to consider every human being as our neighbor, because we must never do any wrong to another person.

33. (71) If we should carry out our duty to show compassion to any person, or they to us, that person is rightly described as a "neighbor"; and it is clear that even the holy

gere proximum, etiam sanctos angelos contineri, a quibus tanta nobis misericordiae impenduntur officia, quanta multis divinarum scripturarum locis animadvertere facile est. Ex quo et ipse deus et dominus noster proximum se nostrum dici voluit. Nam et se ipsum significat dominus Iesus Christus opilatum esse semivivo iacenti in via afflicto et relicto a latronibus. (72) Et propheta in oratione ait "sicut proximum, sicut fratrem nostrum, ita conplacebam." Sed quoniam excellentior ac supra nostram naturam est divina substantia, praeceptum quo diligamus deum, a proximi dilectione distinctum est. Ille enim nobis praebet misericordiam propter suam bonitatem, nos autem nobis invicem propter illius, id est, ille nostri miseretur ut se perfruamur, nos vero invicem nostri miseremur ut illo perfruamur.

34. (73) Quapropter adhuc ambiguum videtur esse, cum dicimus ea re nos perfrui quam diligimus propter se ipsam, et ea re nobis fruendum esse tantum, qua efficimur beati, ceteris vero utendum. Diligit enim nos deus, et multum nobis dilectionem eius erga nos divina scriptura commendat. Quomodo ergo diligit? Ut nobis utatur an ut fruatur? (74) Sed si fruitur, eget bono nostro, quod nemo sanus dixerit. Omne enim nostrum bonum vel ipse vel ab ipso est. Cui autem obscurum vel dubium est, non egere lucem rerum harum nitore quas ipsa illustraverit? Dicit etiam apertissime propheta, "Dixi domino: dominus meus es tu,

---

[97] For example, 1 Kings 19:7; Matthew 4:11; Acts 5:19; Hebrews 1:14. [98] Psalm 35:14; the text varies widely in versions independent of Vulg. [99] For example, Romans 5:8; John 3:16. [100] Cf. James 1:17.

angels are included in this commandment that requires us to love our neighbor, because they fulfill a duty of compassion for us that is as great as one may easily observe from many passages in the holy scriptures.[97] Consequently even God himself and our Lord wanted to be called our neighbor. For the Lord Jesus Christ makes it known that he himself came to the aid of the man who was left in distress, half-dead upon the road, and abandoned by the robbers. (72) And a prophet says in prayer, "I showed compassion like a neighbor, like our brother."[98] But given that the divine substance is more perfect than our own nature, and superior to it, the commandment that we should love God is set apart from the love of neighbor. For God shows compassion for us because of his goodness, whereas we in our turn do so to one another on his account—that is, he has compassion on us so that we can enjoy him to the full, but we in turn have to show one another compassion so as to enjoy him to the full.

34. (73) It seems, therefore, that there is still a lack of clarity here when we say that we have complete enjoyment of a thing that we love for its own sake, and that we should enjoy only what makes us happy, but everything else we merely use. For God loves us, and holy scripture frequently emphasizes to us his love for us.[99] So how does he love? In such a way as to use us, or enjoy us? (74) But if he enjoys us, he has need of our well-being, and no sensible person would claim that. Our well-being as a whole either consists in him or comes from him.[100] Who can be ignorant, or in doubt, that light has no need of the illumination provided by those things that it does itself cast light on? The prophet even states this with perfect clarity, I said to the Lord "you are my Lord, for you have no need of my

quoniam bonorum meorum non eges." Non ergo fruitur nobis, sed utitur. Nam si neque fruitur neque utitur, non invenio quemadmodum diligat.

35. (75) Sed neque sic utitur ut nos, nam nos res quibus utimur ad id referimus ut dei bonitate perfruamur, deus vero ad suam bonitatem usum nostrum refert. Quia enim bonus est, sumus; et in quantum sumus, boni sumus. Porro autem quia etiam iustus est, non impune mali sumus; et in quantum mali sumus, in tantum etiam minus sumus. Ille enim summe ac primitus est, qui omnino incommutabilis est, et qui plenissime dicere potuit, "ego sum qui sum," et, "dices eis: qui est misit me ad vos." Et cetera quae sunt, et nisi ab illo esse non possint, et in tantum bona sint, in quantum acceperunt ut sint. (76) Ille igitur usus qui dicitur dei, quo nobis utitur, non ad eius sed ad nostram utilitatem refertur, ad eius autem tantummodo bonitatem. Cuius autem nos miseremur et cui consulimus, ad eius quidem utilitatem id facimus eamque intuemur, sed nescio quomodo etiam nostra fit consequens, cum eam misericordiam quam impendimus[37]

[37] sed nescio . . . impendimus *om. K Lond. suppl. K*[1] (facimus *pro* impendimus *K*[1])

---

101 Psalm 16:2. As in English, so in Latin "goods" (*bona*) can be abstract qualities or concrete property.

102 Exodus 3:14. In English the translated personal name of God, "I am," is the same in both parts of the verse "I am who I am (*ego sum qui sum*)/'I am' has sent me to you," but being a verb in Hebrew, Greek, and Latin, it changes to a third person singular form for the statement, "he is (*qui est*)," making the name appear different.

goods."[101] So he does not enjoy us, he uses us. For if he neither enjoys us nor uses us, I cannot see how he could possibly love us.

35. (75) Even so, he does not use us in the same way as we use things; for this is the standard we judge the things we use by, namely the complete enjoyment of God's goodness—whereas God judges his use of us by the standard of his own goodness. Because he is good, we exist; and only insofar as we exist are we good. Furthermore, because he is just, we cannot be evildoers with impunity; and insofar as we are evildoers, to the same extent our existence is diminished. He exists in the highest degree, aboriginally, and is wholly immutable, the one who was able to express it most fully, "I am who I am"; and, "I am" has sent me to you.[102] And other things that exist, and could not exist if they did not originate in him, are also good insofar as they have received their existence from him.[103] (76) That type of usage that is ascribed to God, according to which he uses us, is not judged by his usefulness but by ours; instead it is judged solely by his goodness. If we have compassion for someone, and are mindful of them, we do so to benefit[104] them, and that is what we focus on; but somehow a benefit to ourselves also results, since God does not leave unrewarded the compassion which we expend on the per-

103 Augustine needs an abstract noun for existence. Quintilian used the word *essentia* (*Inst.* 2.14.2, 3.6.23, 8.3.33: on the analogy of the Greek *ousia*), a coinage that Seneca attributed to Cicero (*Ep.* 58.6). Augustine does know it (*Mor.* 2.2.2; *Ep.* 166.2.4) but chooses not to use it here.

104 *utilitatem*.

egenti, sine mercede non relinquit deus. Haec autem merces summa est ut ipso perfruamur, et omnes qui eo fruimur nobis etiam invicem in ipso perfruamur.

36. (77) Nam si in nobis id facimus, remanemus in via et spem beatitudinis nostrae in homine aut in angelo collocamus. Quod et homo superbus et angelus superbus arrogant sibi atque in se aliorum spem gaudent constitui. Sanctus autem homo et sanctus angelus etiam fessos nos atque in se adquiescere et remanere cupientes, reficiunt potius, aut eo sumptu quem propter nos, aut illo etiam quem propter se acceperunt, acceperunt tamen. Atque ita refectos in illum ire compellunt, quo fruentes pariter beati sumus. (78) Nam et apostolus clamat, "numquid Paulus crucifixus est pro vobis? Aut in nomine Pauli baptizati estis?" et, "neque qui plantat est aliquid neque qui rigat, sed qui incrementum dat deus." Et angelus hominem se adorantem monet ut illum potius adoret, sub quo ei domino etiam ipse conservus est.

37. (79) Cum autem homine in deo frueris, deo potius quam homine frueris. Illo enim frueris quo efficeris beatus, et ad eum te pervenisse laetaberis, in quo spem ponis ut venias. Inde ad Philemonem Paulus, "ita, frater, inquit, ego te fruar in domino." Quod si non addidisset "in domino," et "te fruar" tantum dixisset, in eo constituisset

105 *via*. Possibly alluding to "the Way": see Acts 19:23, 24:14.

106 *beatitudo*. Encompasses "happiness" and "blessedness."

107 1 Corinthians 1:13.

108 1 Corinthians 3:7.

son who is in need. The highest such reward is the complete enjoyment of God, and all of us who do enjoy him in turn have complete enjoyment of one another in him.

36. (77) If we do this in one another, we remain on the right path,[105] and rest our hope of happiness[106] upon a human being or an angel. This is something that proud human beings and proud angels appropriate for themselves, and they are delighted by having others' hopes set upon them. But a holy human being and a holy angel are eager for us to find rest in them, and to abide there, when we are weary. Indeed they even restore us, by expending either what they have received on our account, or what they have received on their own account—though in both cases it is still something they have received. So once we have been restored, they urge us toward God; and when we enjoy him, we attain to happiness as well. (78) For the apostle also declares "surely Paul was not crucified for you? And you were surely not baptized in Paul's name?"[107] And "it is not the one who plants or the one who waters who matters, but God, who gives the growth."[108] And an angel warns the person who is worshiping him that he had better worship that Lord in whose service he, the angel, was but a fellow slave.

37. (79) When, however, you enjoy a human being "in God," it is God you are enjoying, rather than a particular person. This is because you do enjoy the one who makes you happy, and you will rejoice that you have finally found your way to him on whom you set your hope for finding that way. For this reason Paul says to Philemon, "So, brother, I shall enjoy you in the Lord." If he had not added the words "in the Lord," and had only said "I shall enjoy you," he would have rested his own hope of happiness on

spem beatitudinis suae. Quamquam etiam vicinissime dicitur frui cum dilectione uti. (80) Cum enim adest quod diligitur, etiam delectationem secum necesse est gerat. Per quam si transieris eamque ad illud ubi permanendum est rettuleris, uteris ea et abusive, non proprie diceris frui. Si vero inhaeseris atque permanseris, finem in ea ponens laetitiae tuae, tunc vere et proprie frui dicendus es. Quod non faciendum est nisi in illa trinitate, id est summo et incommutabili bono.

38. (81) Vide quemadmodum, cum ipsa veritas et verbum per quod facta sunt omnia caro factum esset ut habitaret in nobis, tamen ait apostolus, "et si noveramus Christum secundum carnem, sed iam non novimus." Ille quippe qui non solum pervenientibus possessionem, sed etiam viam se voluit praebere venientibus ad principium viarum, voluit carnem assumere. Unde est etiam illud, "dominus creavit me in principio viarum suarum," ut inde inciperent qui vellent venire. (82) Apostolus igitur, quamvis adhuc ambularet in via et ad palmam supernae vocationis sequeretur vocantem deum, tamen ea "quae retro sunt obliviscens, et in ea quae ante sunt extentus," iam principium viarum transierat, hoc est eo non indigebat a quo tamen aggrediendum et exordiendum iter est omnibus qui ad veritatem pervenire et in vita aeterna permanere deside-

---

[109] *abusi*: this meaning is uppermost in Church Latin; but it can also refer to use of figurative language (*abusio*, Latin; *catachrēsis*, Greek), though still with a pejorative edge.

[110] Both names of Christ, John 1:1–14, 14:6.

[111] Paul. [112] 2 Corinthians 5:16.

[113] Proverbs 8:22. [114] Philippians 3:13–14.

Philemon. Even so, to "enjoy" someone is almost synonymous with "using them with love." (80) When something we love is before us, it is inevitably accompanied by pleasure. If you treat pleasure as a means of going further, and apply it to the place of our abiding, you are misusing[109] it, and it is not correct to call this "enjoyment." But if you cleave to it and abide in it, setting it as the goal of your joy, then you can truly, literally, speak of "enjoying." This can only be done with reference to the Trinity, which is the supreme, immutable good.

38. (81) Consider this: although the Truth and Word,[110] through whom all things were created, became flesh so as to dwell among us, nevertheless the apostle[111] said, "even if we once knew Christ according to the flesh, that is not how we know him now."[112] Indeed he did not only want to belong to those who have reached their goal; he actually wanted to offer himself as the way for those who come to the beginning of the ways: and so he was willing to take on human flesh. This is referred to in the verse, "The Lord created me at the beginning of his ways,"[113] so that from there those who wanted to come could begin their journey. (82) Although he was still walking the way, therefore, and following the God who was calling him toward the prize of his higher calling, when the apostle "forgot all that was behind him, and reached forward to all that was before him,"[114] he had already moved beyond this "beginning of the ways." In other words, the apostle was not separated from him who is the starting point for all people who long to reach the truth, and abide in eternal life, to draw near and begin the journey. This is why he says, I am

rant. Sic enim ait, "ego sum via et veritas et vita," hoc est, "per me venitur, ad me pervenitur, in me permanetur." (83) Cum enim ad ipsum pervenitur, etiam ad patrem pervenitur, quia per aequalem ille cui est aequalis agnoscitur, vinciente et tamquam agglutinante nos sancto spiritu, quo in summo atque incommutabili bono permanere possimus. Ex quo intellegitur quam nulla res in via tenere nos debeat, quando nec ipse dominus, in quantum via nostra esse dignatus est, tenere nos voluerit, sed transire, ne rebus temporalibus, quamvis ab illo pro salute nostra susceptis et gestis, haereamus infirmiter, sed per eas potius curramus alacriter,[38] ut ad eum ipsum, qui nostram naturam a temporalibus liberavit et collocavit ad dexteram patris, provehi atque pervehi[39] mereamur.

39. (84) Omnium igitur quae dicta[40] sunt ex quo de rebus tractamus,[41] haec summa est, ut intellegatur legis et omnium divinarum scripturarum plenitudo et finis esse dilectio rei qua fruendum est, et rei quae nobiscum ea re frui potest, quia ut se quisque diligat praecepto non opus est. (85) Hoc ergo ut nossemus atque possemus facta est tota pro nostra salute per divinam providentiam dispensa-

38 sed . . . alacriter *om. L add. m. al. in mg.*
39 pervenire *P K*
40 praedicta *P K F*
41 omnia . . . trac{tamus} *litt. notabilior. P*

115 Exegesis, not quotation: see 1 Corinthians 8:6; Hebrews 2:10. 116 John 14:9.
117 By himself being both divine and human.
118 Romans 13:10; 1 Timothy 1:5.
119 In the sense of "entity/being/reality."

the way and truth and life: in other words, "All must come through me, all must come to me, all must abide in me."[115] (83) For anyone who comes to him, comes to the Father too.[116] This is because it is through the Father, his equal, that he who is the Father's equal is recognized: and the Holy Spirit binds us and—as it were—glues us together, so that we can abide in this supreme, unchanging good. As a result is it understandable that nothing ought to detain us on the way, since even the Lord himself, by deigning to become our Way, did not want us to be detained, but rather to cross over. Then we would not cling feebly to the things of this world (which he took upon himself and bore for our salvation). Instead we would race eagerly through the midst of them, aiming to deserve to be transported and carried all the way to him, who set our human nature free from earthly things, and placed it at the right hand of the Father.[117]

39. (84) Of everything, then, that has been said since we began our discussion of these matters, this one is the chief: that we understand that love is the fullness and purpose of the law, and of all of holy scripture[118]—love of the thing[119] we ought to enjoy, and love of any thing[120] that can share our enjoyment of that thing. After all, given that everyone loves themselves, there is no need for an instruction to that effect. (85) Through divine providence, the entire design of the world[121] has been arranged for our

[120] Any object or means that helps the person to reach the supreme *res*, which is God.

[121] *dispensationi*: "arrangement" or "administration," the Latin equivalent of *oikonomia*, God's arrangement of the world, stemming from *dispensatio sacramenti absconditi*, Ephesians 3:9.

tio temporalis, qua debemus uti non quasi mansoria quadam dilectione et delectatione, sed transitoria potius tamquam viae, tamquam vehiculorum vel aliorum quorumlibet instrumentorum (aut si quid congruentius dici potest); ut ea quibus ferimur propter illud ad quod ferimur[42] diligamus.

40. (86) Quisquis igitur scripturas divinas vel quamlibet earum partem intellexisse sibi videtur, ita ut eo intellectu non aedificet istam geminam caritatem dei et proximi, nondum intellexit. Quisquis vero talem inde sententiam duxerit ut huic aedificandae caritati sit utilis, nec tamen hoc dixerit quod ille quem legit eo loco sensisse probabitur, non perniciose fallitur nec omnino mentitur. Inest quippe in mentiente voluntas falsa dicendi, et ideo multos invenimus, qui mentiri velint; qui autem falli, neminem. (87) Cum igitur hoc sciens homo faciat, illud nesciens patiatur, satis apparet in una eademque re illum qui fallitur, eo qui mentitur esse meliorem, quandoquidem pati melius est iniquitatem quam facere. Omnis autem qui mentitur inique[43] facit, et si cuiquam videtur utile aliquando esse mendacium, potest videri utilem aliquando esse iniquitatem. Nemo enim mentiens, in eo quod men-

[42] propter . . . ferimur *om. P* [43] iniquitatem *μ*

---

[122] So authorial intention becomes a tool for biblical interpretation. A text must not be interpreted in a way that misrepresents the author's intention: he does not explain how to reconstruct that intention.

[123] *velint/voluntas*: standard terminology for the human will. On lying, which he calls a *magna quaestio*, see *Against Lying*, a

salvation, to give us knowledge and power. We ought to use it with the kind of love and delight that are not fixed in one place, but rather meant to help us on our way—such as a conveyance or another means of transport (or some more fitting turn of phrase); this is so that we love the things that transport us for the sake of the end they transport us to.

40. (86) If anyone, therefore, considers that they have understood the holy scriptures, or some part of them, but does so in a way that fails to build up that double love—of God and neighbor—then they have not yet understood it. Also, if anyone draws such an interpretation from their source as may be productive in building up that love, but nonetheless has not said what that person whose words they are reading demonstrably intended[122] at that point, theirs is not a fatal error, or an out-and-out lie. Surely when someone lies they make a choice[123] to deceive by what they say. We find that many choose to lie, but no one chooses to be deceived (87) As to the former, people do in full awareness; but the latter they endure unawares. Clearly, in one and the same situation the person who is deceived is better than the liar, since for it is better to endure wrong than to commit it. Everyone who tells lies commits an injustice, and if anyone thinks that it is sometimes proper[124] to tell lies, it can look as if injustice is sometimes proper too. No one who tells a lie is trustwor-

work that he describes as "obscure, longwinded and wholly laborious" (*Retr*. 1.27).

124 Latin *utile* has a broader range than English "useful," incorporating what is "profitable," or "advantageous." Augustine cannot be saying that it is never "useful" to tell lies.

titur, servat fidem. Nam hoc utique vult, ut cui mentitur fidem sibi habeat, quam tamen ei mentiendo non servat. Omnis autem fidei violator iniquus est. Aut igitur iniquitas aliquando est utilis, quod fieri non potest, aut mendacium semper inutile est.

41. (88) Sed quisquis in scripturis aliud sentit quam ille qui scripsit, illis non mentientibus fallitur. Sed tamen, ut dicere coeperam,[44] si ea sententia fallitur, qua aedificet caritatem, quae finis praecepti est, ita fallitur ac si quisquam errore deserens viam eo tamen per agrum pergat quo etiam via illa perducit. Corrigendus est tamen, et quam sit utilius viam non deserere demonstrandum est, ne consuetudine deviandi etiam in transversum aut peruersum ire cogatur.

(89) Asserendo enim temere quod ille non sensit[45] quem legit plerumque incurrit in alia quae illi sententiae contexere nequeat. Quae si vera et certa esse consentit, illud non possit verum esse quod senserat; fitque in eo (nescio quomodo) ut amando sententiam suam scripturae incipiat offensior esse quam sibi. Quod malum si[46] serpere siverit,[47] evertetur ex eo. Per fidem enim ambulamus, non per speciem; titubabit autem fides, si divinarum scripturarum vacillat auctoritas. Porro fide titubante caritas etiam ipsa languescit. (90) Nam si a fide quisque ceciderit, a caritate etiam necesse est cadat. Non enim potest diligere quod esse non credit. Porro si et credit et diligit, bene

[44] sed tamen . . . coeperam *om. K*
[45] sentit *P R*
[46] se *K*
[47] coeperit *K P*

---

[125] 2 Corinthians 5:7.

thy where that lie is concerned. For they clearly want the person to whom they tell the lie to trust them—even though by lying to them they have forfeited that trust. Everyone who is untrustworthy is thus unjust. Either injustice is sometimes proper, then—which is impossible—or telling lies is always improper.

41. (88) Anyone who perceives something in the scriptures that is different from the perception of the author is mistaken, but the scriptures themselves are not lying. As I said at the start, though, if their mistaken perception is one that would build up love (which is the purpose of the commandment), their blunder is like someone who accidentally leaves their path, but who—despite straying across country—is still heading in the same direction as the path. Such a person should be corrected. Show them that it is more appropriate not to stray from the path, in case they get into a habit of straying and find themselves forced into a diversion or even going the wrong way.

(89) When they recklessly allege something that the author they are reading did not mean, they commonly run up against other points that they cannot make fit with their personal opinion. If they agree that these points are definitely true, then their original view cannot be true. But it turns out—goodness knows how—that they love their own opinion so much that they are more annoyed with scripture than with themselves. If they allow a wrong like this to insinuate itself, it will be their downfall. For we walk by faith, not sight:[125] faith will totter if the authority of holy scripture wavers. What is more, if faith totters even love itself begins to dwindle. (90) After all, if anyone has fallen away from the faith they cannot avoid falling away from love as well. For they cannot love what they do not believe in. On the other hand, if they have both belief and love,

agendo et praeceptis morum bonorum obtemperando efficit ut etiam speret se ad id quod diligit esse venturum. Itaque tria haec sunt quibus et scientia omnis et prophetia militat: fides, spes, caritas.

42. (91) Sed fidei succedet species quam videbimus, et spei succedet beatitudo ipsa ad quam perventuri sumus; caritas autem etiam istis decedentibus augebitur potius. Si enim credendo diligimus quod nondum videmus, quanto magis cum videre coeperimus? Et si sperando diligimus quo nondum pervenimus, quanto magis cum pervenerimus? (92) Inter temporalia quippe atque aeterna hoc interest, quod temporale aliquid plus diligitur antequam habeatur, vilescet autem cum advenerit. Non enim satiat animam, cui vera est et certa sedes aeternitas. Aeternum autem ardentius diligitur adeptum quam desideratum. Nulli enim desideranti conceditur plus de illo existimare quam se habet, ut ei vilescat cum minus invenerit, sed quantum quisque veniens existimare potuerit, plus perveniens inventurus est.

43. (93) Homo itaque fide et spe et caritate subnixus eaque inconcusse retinens non indiget scripturis nisi ad alios instruendos. Itaque multi per haec tria etiam in solitudine sine codicibus vivunt. Unde in illis arbitror iam impletum esse quod dictum est, "sive prophetiae evacuabuntur, sive linguae cessabunt, sive scientia evacuabitur." (94) Quibus tamen quasi machinis tanta fidei et spei et

[126] *species* has a semantic range from "pretense" to "true reality." Here it is a Latin equivalent for Platonic forms (or "ideas"). Cf. *Div. quaest.* 46.1.29. [127] These three (faith, hope, and love, later known as the "theological virtues."

[128] Ascetics rather than groups of nonliterate Christians.

[129] 1 Corinthians 13:10.

with appropriate conduct, obeying the rules of good behavior, they can bring about the hope of reaching the object of their love. So these are the three things that all knowledge and prophecy press for: faith, hope, love.

42. (91) Yet faith will give way to the true reality[126] that we shall see; and hope will give way to the true blessedness that we shall come to at last; but when even faith and hope are gone, love will continue to increase. If, because of our belief, we love what we do not yet see, how much greater will our love be when we have begun to see? And if, through hope, we love what we have yet to attain, how much more will we love when we have attained it? (92) This is the difference between the temporal and the eternal. Anything temporal is loved more before it is obtained, and less afterward. It does not satisfy the soul, whose true and fixed abode is eternity. But what is eternal is loved more once it has been obtained than when it was an object of desire. There is no chance that someone who desires it esteems it more highly than it warrants, so that it seems cheap to them when they discover that it is something less. However great each person can imagine it to be as they make their way to it, it will be found to be greater still when they finally reach it.

43. (93) So a person who relies on faith, hope and love, and who is firmly dependent on them, does not need scripture, except for the purpose of teaching others. And so this is how many people live by these three virtues[127] alone without any books.[128] In my judgment such people are a fulfillment of the saying, "if there are prophecies, they will be made void, if there are tongues they will cease, if there is knowledge, it will be made void."[129] (94) Using this scaf-

caritatis in eis surrexit instructio, ut perfectum aliquid tenentes, ea quae sunt ex parte non quaerant, perfectum sane, quantum in hac vita potest. Nam in comparatione futurae vitae nullius iusti et sancti est vita ista perfecta. Ideo manent inquit, fides, spes, caritas, tria haec. Maior autem horum est caritas, quia et cum quisque ad aeterna pervenerit,[48] duobus istis decedentibus caritas auctior et certior permanebit.

44. (95) Quapropter, cum quisque cognoverit "finem praecepti esse caritatem de corde puro et conscientia bona et fide non ficta," omnem intellectum divinarum scripturarum ad ista tria relaturus, ad tractationem illorum librorum securus accedat. Cum enim diceret "caritas," addidit "de corde puro," ut nihil aliud quam id quod diligendum est diligatur. Conscientiam vero bonam subiunxit propter spem: ille enim se ad id quod credit et diligit perventurum esse desperat, cui malae conscientiae scrupulus inest. Tertio et fide inquit non ficta. (96) Si enim fides nostra mendacio caruerit, tunc et non diligimus quod non est diligendum, et recte vivendo id speramus, ut nullo modo spes nostra fallatur.

Propterea de rebus continentibus fidem, quantum pro tempore satis esse arbitratus sum, dicere volui, quia in aliis voluminibus sive per alios sive per nos multa iam dicta sunt. Modus itaque sit iste libri huius. Cetera de signis, quantum dominus dederit, disseremus.

48 pervenerit *hic fol. un. Lond. amiss.*

---

130 1 Timothy 1:5. 131 Paul, who was believed to be the author of 1 Timothy. 132 Romans 5:5.

133 Last referred to at §§4–5, hinting that much of Book 1 may be a digression.

folding, as it were, such an edifice of faith, hope, and love has been built up in them that they do not seek what is partial, because they already possess what is perfect. This is insofar as perfection is possible in this life, because no one, however righteous and holy, has such a life of perfection, in comparison with the life that is to come. So, it says, "there remain faith, hope love, these three. But love is greater than the other two," because when anyone reaches eternal life, the other two will fall away, whereas love will abide, greater and more firmly established than ever.

44. (95) When anyone has come to understand, therefore, that "the purpose of the commandment is love from a pure heart, and a good conscience, and unfeigned faith,"[130] they are going to relate every interpretation of the holy scriptures to those three virtues. Then they will be confident in their approach to handling those books. After all, when he[131] said "love," he added, "from a pure heart," to ensure that nothing is loved except for what deserves to be loved. He yoked the words "good" and "conscience" together for the sake of hope: anyone who abandons hope of ever attaining to what they believe and love is suffering the pricking of a bad conscience. Third, he said "and with faith unfeigned." (96) If our faith is free from deceit, then we simply do not love what does not deserve love; and by living rightly we hope for this: that our hope will never disappoint us.[132]

These are the reasons why I wanted to speak of the things of which our faith consists (as much as I judged adequate for the present); because I, and others, have already spoken at length on this subject in other writings. Here this book comes to an end. From now on, as much as the Lord permits, our discussion will be about signs.[133]

LIBER II

1. (1) Quoniam de rebus cum scriberem praemisi commonens ne quis in eis attenderet nisi quod sunt, non etiam si quid aliud praeter se significant, vicissim de signis disserens hoc dico, ne quis in eis attendat quod sunt, sed potius quod signa sunt, id est, quod significant. Signum est enim res, praeter speciem quam ingerit sensibus, aliud aliquid ex se faciens in cogitationem venire; sicut vestigio viso, transisse animal cuius vestigium est cogitamus et fumo viso ignem subesse cognoscimus, et voce animantis audita affectionem animi eius advertimus, et tuba sonante milites vel progredi se vel regredi, et si quid aliud pugna postulat, oportere noverunt.

2. (2) Signorum igitur alia sunt naturalia, alia data. Naturalia sunt quae sine voluntate atque ullo appetitu significandi praeter se aliquid aliud ex se cognosci faciunt, sicuti est fumus significans ignem. Non enim volens significare id facit, sed rerum expertarum animadversione et notatione cognoscitur ignem subesse,[1] etiam si fumus solus appareat. Sed et vestigium transeuntis animantis ad

[1] etiam] *hinc continuat Lond.*

---

[1] First reference to signifying (apart from a passing mention, 1.33.71) since it was highlighted as a future topic early in Book 1 (§§4–5).

[2] Here and below the verb *subeo* is used literally, for the

BOOK II

1. (1) When I was writing about things, I started by emphasizing that people should pay them attention only for what they are in themselves, even if they signify[1] anything else besides what they are. Now, on the other hand, I am discussing signs, and I say this: no one should pay attention to them for what they are in themselves, but rather for what they are signs of; in other words, for what they signify. A sign is a thing that, apart from the impression it makes on our senses, makes something other than itself come to mind. For example: when we see a footprint, it makes us think that the animal that made the footprint has passed this way. And when we see smoke, it makes us think of the fire that is below it;[2] and when we hear the voice of some living creature we observe what state of mind it is in; and when a trumpet sounds soldiers know that they must advance or retreat, or whatever else the engagement requires.

2. (2) Some signs are natural, others have meaning imposed on them. Natural signs have no will, no power to signify; but by themselves they make known something beyond themselves, for example, smoke that signifies fire. The smoke does not signify intentionally: but when we notice things that are familiar, and remark upon them, we

physical location of the fire, and metaphorically, for a factor that is "underlying."

hoc genus pertinet; et vultus irati seu tristis affectionem animi significat, etiam nulla eius voluntate qui aut iratus aut tristis est; aut si quis alius motus animi vultu indice proditur, etiam nobis non id agentibus ut prodatur. Sed de hoc toto genere nunc disserere non est propositum. Quoniam tamen incidit in partitionem nostram, praeteriri omnino non potuit, atque id hactenus notatum esse suffecerit.

3. (3) Data vero signa sunt quae sibi quaeque viventia invicem dant ad demonstrandos quantum possunt motus animi sui, vel sensa aut intellecta quaelibet. Nec ulla causa est nobis significandi, id est signi dandi, nisi ad depromendum et traiciendum in alterius animum id quod animo gerit qui signum dat. Horum igitur signorum genus, quantum ad homines attinet, considerare atque tractare statuimus, quia et signa divinitus data, quae scripturis sanctis continentur, per homines nobis indicata sunt qui ea conscripserunt. (4) Habent etiam bestiae quaedam inter se signa, quibus produnt appetitum animi sui. Nam et gallus gallinaceus reperto cibo dat signum vocis gallinae ut accurrat; et columbus gemitu columbam vocat vel ab ea vicissim vocatur, et multa huiusmodi animadverti solent. Quae utrum, sicut vultus aut dolentis clamor, sine voluntate significandi sequantur motum animi an vere ad significandum dentur, alia quaestio est, et ad rem quae agitur non pertinet. Quam partem ab hoc opere tamquam non necessariam removemus.

recognize that a fire lies beneath, even when only smoke is visible. The footprints of a passing creature are a sign of this type; the expression of someone who is angry, or sad, signifies their mood even when the person who is angry or sad does not wish it. Any other mental reaction is betrayed by the witness of our facial expression, though we ourselves do nothing to disclose it. I am not proposing, however, to discuss everything in this category. Since it falls within our parameters it could not be omitted entirely, and we have now given it enough of our attention.

3. (3) Now for signs that are "given." All living creatures give such signs to one another, to show as clearly as they can the reactions of their mind, or anything they have felt or thought. For us, the sole cause of signifying (which means "giving signs") is to produce in another's mind, and pass across to it, what the person giving that signal has in their mind. We have decided to examine and handle signs of this kind (insofar as they relate to humankind), because even signs of divine origin, such as those contained in the holy scriptures, have been disclosed to us by the human beings who wrote them. (4) Certain animals make use of signals among their kind, by which they express their mind's desire. When a cock finds food he gives a vocal signal to his hen to come to him quickly. The male dove makes his plangent call to the female, and she calls to him in turn. We can observe many examples of this kind. It is another matter whether such things as facial expressions or cries of pain are responses to mental stimulus, apart from any intention of signifying. That is not relevant to our present theme. So we are setting that element aside, as it is not essential to this work.

4. (5) Signorum igitur quibus inter se homines sua sensa communicant, quaedam pertinent ad oculorum sensum, pleraque ad aurium, paucissima ad ceteros sensus. Nam cum innuimus non damus signum nisi oculis eius quem volumus per hoc signum voluntatis nostrae participem facere. Et quidam motus manuum pleraque significant, et histriones omnium membrorum motibus dant signa quaedam scientibus et cum oculis eorum quasi fabulantur, et vexilla draconesque militares per oculos insinuant voluntatem ducum. Et sunt haec omnia quasi quaedam verba visibilia. (6) Ad aures autem quae pertinent, ut dixi, plura sunt, in verbis maxime. Nam et tuba et tibia et cithara dant plerumque non solum suavem, sed etiam significantem sonum. Sed haec omnia signa verbis comparata paucissima sunt. Verba enim prorsus inter homines obtinuerunt principatum significandi quaecumque animo concipiuntur, si ea quisque prodere velit. (7) Nam et odore unguenti dominus, quo perfusi sunt pedes eius, signum aliquod dedit, et sacramento corporis et sanguinis sui per gustatum significavit quod voluit, et cum mulier tangendo fimbriam vestimenti eius salva facta est, nonnihil significat. Sed innumerabilis multitudo signorum, quibus suas

---

[3] On sense perceptions and their spiritual significance, see *Conf.* 10.27.38–35.55. For the categorization of five senses, see Arist. *De an.* 3.424b. [4] The earliest modern study is J. Bulwer, *Cheirologia: Or the Naturall Language of the Hand* (London, 1644). [5] See *TC* 1.30.64. [6] *vexilla draconesque*. The usual term for a military standard, *signum*, would be confusing.

[7] *verba visibilia*. The oxymoron depends on words being conceived primarily as oral, not visual, in this period.

[8] See Proem 6.12. [9] *salva* means "safe," but from the

4. (5) Of all the signs that people use to impart their feeling to one another, a number relate to the faculty of sight; rather more to that of hearing; and only a few to the other senses.[3] When we nod our head we are giving a signal specifically to the eyes of the person whom we are inviting—by that signal—to share in our endeavor. Some people use hand gestures to send a number of different signals.[4] Actors[5] use movements of all their limbs to send particular signals to those who are in the know, and to communicate with their eyes, as it were. Banners and military standards[6] make known the will of commanders through the medium of eyesight. All things of this kind are, in a manner of speaking, "words we can see."[7] (6) As I have said, the signs related to hearing are numerous, especially when it comes to words. Trumpet, pipe and lyre generally make a sound that is not only pleasing but also communicates meaning; but all signs of this type are dwarfed in number when compared with words. Certainly among human beings words have earned predominance as signifiers of whatever entities our minds can imagine, should anyone wish to express them. (7) For example, the Lord gave one kind of sign through the scent of the ointment that was poured over his feet; and through the sacrament[8] of his own body and blood he gave a sign of what he willed through the sense of taste; and when a woman was restored to health[9] through the act of touching the fringe of his garment that too signified something. But words provide a countless abundance of signs for human

time of Cyprian (ca. AD 210–258) also has a technical Christian meaning, "saved."

cogitationes homines exserunt, in verbis constituta est. Nam illa signa omnia quorum genera breviter attigi potui verbis enuntiare, verba vero illis signis nullo modo possem.

5. (8) Sed quia verberato aere statim transeunt nec diutius manent quam sonant, instituta sunt per litteras signa verborum. Ita voces oculis ostenduntur, non per se ipsas, sed per signa quaedam sua. Ista signa igitur non potuerunt communia esse omnibus gentibus, peccato quodam dissensionis humanae, cum ad se quisque principatum rapit. Cuius superbiae signum est erecta illa turris in caelum, ubi homines impii non solum animos, sed etiam voces dissonas habere meruerunt.

6. (9) Ex quo factum est ut etiam scriptura divina, qua tantis morbis humanarum voluntatum subvenitur, ab una lingua profecta, qua opportune potuit per orbem terrarum disseminari, per varias interpretum linguas longe lateque diffusa[2] innotesceret gentibus ad salutem. Quam legentes nihil aliud appetunt quam cogitationes voluntatemque illorum a quibus conscripta est invenire et per illas voluntatem dei, secundum quam tales homines locutos credimus. {7.} (10) Sed multis et multiplicibus obscuritatibus et ambiguitatibus decipiuntur qui temere legunt, aliud pro

[2] diffusas *D K*[1]

---

[10] That is, the relationship between sign and thing, *signum* and *res*, is not mere equivalence or interchangeability.

[11] Genesis 11. The tower of Babel, a biblical etiology for language differentiation, was interpreted ethically as a divine judgment on human ambition.

beings to use for disclosing their own thoughts. After all, I have been able to express in words all those signs of the types I have briefly referred to; but there is no way I could express the words in terms of those signs.[10]

5. (8) Now because words pass swiftly once they strike the air, and last no longer than the time they take to sound, written characters were established to act as signs for words. This is how spoken words become apparent to our eyes, not by what they are in themselves, but the individual signs that are proper to each word. Those signs, then, could not be held in common by all peoples, on account of one specific sin—human propensity for conflict—when every people snatched at preeminence for itself. The sign of their pride was that tower that they built up to the sky,[11] when godless men got not only the conflicting hearts that they deserved, but the conflicting voices too.

6. (9) As a result of this, even holy scripture, which provides help for the serious defects of the human will, emerged from a single language,[12] which allowed it to be spread easily throughout the world, but only through the different languages of translators, dispersed far and wide, did it become known to nations for their salvation. When people read scripture, their sole aim is to find out the thoughts and intentions of those who wrote it, and, through them, the will of God; for we believe that such authors spoke according to his will.[13] {7.} (10) Anyone who reads it in a thoughtless way is led astray by its many complexi-

[12] One language per Testament (setting aside the Aramaic verses, about 250, in Ezra and Daniel).

[13] Augustine is distinctive in his time for making authorial intention one of his exegetical criteria (see 1.40.86n122).

alio sentientes. Quibusdam autem locis quid vel falso suspicentur non inveniunt: ita obscure dicta quaedam densissimam caliginem obducunt. Quod totum provisum esse divinitus non dubito, ad edomandam labore superbiam et intellectum a fastidio renovandum,[3] cui facile investigata plerumque vilescunt.

(11) Quid enim est, quaeso, quod si quisquam dicat sanctos esse homines atque perfectos, quorum vita et moribus Christi ecclesia de quibuslibet superstitionibus praecidit eos qui ad se veniunt, et imitatione bonorum sibimet quodammodo incorporat, qui boni fideles et veri dei servi deponentes onera saeculi ad sanctum baptismi lavacrum venerunt atque inde ascendentes conceptione sancti spiritus fructum dant geminae caritatis, id est, dei et proximi. Quid est ergo quod si haec quisque dicat, minus delectat audientem quam si ad eundem sensum locum illum exponat de canticis canticorum ubi dictum est ecclesiae, cum tamquam pulchra quaedam femina laudaretur, "dentes tui sicut grex detonsarum ascendens de lavacro, quae omnes geminos creant et sterilis non est in illis"? (12) Num aliud homo discit, quam cum illud planissimis verbis

3 revocandum μ

14 That is, they select one meaning when a range of legitimate interpretations may be present. 15 *fastidio*: indicates disgust or aversion. He is thinking of his original contempt for biblical Latin (cf. *Conf.* 3.5.9). 16 For this meaning of *perfectos* in Christian Latin, see Matthew 5:48[Vulg.].

17 *superstitio*: usually extreme, excessive, or inappropriate fear of divine power (in contrasted with proper fear, *religio*); Christians and "pagans" alike regarded it negatively.

ties, dark and ambiguous; they observe one thing, rather than another.[14] In some sections they cannot find material even for an incorrect speculation, so they cloak any obscure expressions in an impenetrable smog. I am convinced that this is entirely a matter of divine providence, so that we conquer our squeamishness[15] through hard work, and refresh our capacity for understanding (which tends to regard straightforward subjects as valueless).

(11) Imagine, if you will, that someone says there exist persons who are holy and righteous,[16] whose example of life and behavior the Church of Christ uses to tear those who approach her away from certain superstitious[17] practices; and somehow she incorporates them into herself[18] through their imitating of those good persons. Then suppose that these good, faithful, true slaves of God are laying down the burdens of this world, and have come to the holy washing of baptism; and that when they emerge from the water, the Holy Spirit causes them to conceive and bring forth fruit of a double love, that is, love of God and neighbor. Why is it, then, that if someone said this, it would give the listener less pleasure than if he expressed the same idea by interpreting a passage of scripture from the Song of Songs, which speaks of the Church as if she were being praised as a particular woman of beauty: "your teeth are like a flock of shorn sheep coming up from being washed, which all give birth to twin young, with not one barren ewe

[18] *incorporat*: refers to a person becoming part of the body of Christ, identified with the Church: Romans 12:4–5; 1 Corinthians 12:12, 27, etc.; also *Ev. Io. Tr.* 26.13. "Church" is grammatically feminine, but also personified as such: Ephesians 5:25; Revelation 19:7, 21.2, etc. See 1.17.35n64.

sine similitudinis huius adminiculo audiret? Et tamen nescio quomodo suavius intueor sanctos, cum eos quasi dentes ecclesiae video praecidere ab erroribus homines atque in eius corpus, emollita duritia, quasi demorsos mansosque transferre. Oves etiam iucundissime agnosco detonsas, oneribus saecularibus tamquam velleribus positis, et ascendentes de lavacro, id est de baptismate, creare omnes geminos, id est duo praecepta dilectionis, et nullam esse ab isto sancto fructu sterilem video.

8. (13) Sed quare suavius videam[4] quam si nulla de divinis libris talis similitudo promeretur, cum res eadem sit eademque cognitio, difficile est dicere et alia quaestio est. Nunc tamen nemo ambigit et per similitudines libentius quaeque cognosci et cum aliqua difficultate quaesita multo gratius inveniri. (14) Qui enim prorsus non inveniunt quod quaerunt, fame laborant; qui autem non quaerunt, quia in promptu habent, fastidio saepe marcescunt: in utroque autem languor cavendus est. (15) Magnifice igitur et salubriter spiritus sanctus ita scripturas sanctas modificavit, ut locis apertioribus fami occurreret, obscurioribus autem fastidia detergeret. Nihil enim fere de illis obscuritatibus eruitur, quod non planissime dictum alibi repperiatur.

[4] videas *B*

---

[19] The question is one of hermeneutics, the relationship between "literal" and "figurative" meaning. His reflection on the affect generated by such figurative language is more unusual.

[20] That is, rejecting what is simple as concomitantly cheap.

among them"? (12) Surely one does not learn any more than if one were to hear the statement in straightforward terms, without any reinforcement from a simile?[19] Yet I contemplate those holy men with a greater degree of pleasure when I visualize them as the teeth of the Church, tearing people away from their wrongdoing, and breaking down their hardness, bringing them into her body as if she had bitten and chewed them off. It is particularly delightful to picture the shorn sheep, as if the fleeces they have laid aside stand for the burdens of this world, coming up out of the water—emerging from their baptism, that is—and producing only twin young (which stand for the dual command to love), and I imagine that not one of them is barren, lacking that holy fruit.

8. (13) As for why I find this image more appealing than if no such analogy from the sacred books was being proposed, when the actual thing is the same, and the knowledge it conveys is the same, it is hard to say, and is a separate subject of inquiry. Still, no one is presently in any doubt that we find it more enjoyable to recognize things through imagery; or that anything that we find it difficult to inquire into gives far greater pleasure when we find the answer. (14) Those who fail to find immediately what they are looking for are burdened by hunger; whereas those who do not look (because it is already in plain sight) are often weakened by being hypercritical.[20] Both these types of weakness are to be avoided. (15) For this reason the Holy Spirit has formed the holy writings in such a splendid and salubrious way as to answer the hunger for meaning with more straightforward passages; and purge the punctilio evoked by the more obscure ones. There is virtually nothing excavated from those obscure passages that cannot be found elsewhere expressed in the simplest of terms.

9. (16) Ante omnia igitur opus est dei timore converti ad cognoscendam eius voluntatem, quid nobis adpetendum fugiendumque praecipiat. Timor autem iste cogitationem de nostra mortalitate et de futura morte necesse est incutiat et quasi clavatis carnibus omnes superbiae motus ligno crucis affigat.

(17) Deinde mitescere opus est pietate neque contradicere divinae scripturae sive intellectae, si aliqua vitia nostra percutit, sive non intellectae, quasi nos melius sapere meliusque praecipere possimus, sed cogitare potius et credere id esse melius et verius quod ibi scriptum est, etiam si lateat, quam id quod nos per nos ipsos sapere possumus.

10. (18) Post istos duos gradus timoris atque pietatis ad tertium venitur scientiae gradum, de quo nunc agere instituі. Nam in eo se exercet omnis divinarum scripturarum studiosus, nihil in eis aliud inventurus quam diligendum esse deum propter deum, et proximum propter deum; et illum quidem ex toto corde, ex tota anima, ex tota mente diligere; proximum vero tamquam seipsum, id est, ut tota proximi sicut etiam nostri dilectio referatur in deum. (19) De quibus duobus praeceptis, cum de rebus ageremus, libro superiore tractavimus. Necesse est ergo, ut primo se quisque in scripturis inveniat amore huius saeculi, hoc est temporalium rerum, implicatum, longe seiunctum esse a tanto amore dei et tanto amore proximi quantum scriptura praescribit. Tum vero ille timor quo cogitat de iudicio dei,

---

[21] Here begins a list of prerequisites for proper reading.

[22] Semantically dense vocabulary. "Devotion" (*pietas*) evokes good faith, duty, true religion; "gentle" (*mitescere*), mellowing, mildness, maturity, meekness (see Matthew 5:4).

9. (16) Above all, therefore, we need[21] the fear of God to orientate ourselves toward learning his will; what he commands us to seek, and what to shun. That fear has to inculcate an understanding of our own mortality, and of our future death. It has to fasten every impulse of pride to the wood of the cross, by nailing our flesh there, so to speak.

(17) Next we need a sense of devotion to make us gentle[22] and stop us from challenging holy scripture, whether because we have understood it when it attacks our vices, or because we have failed to understand it as if we could know better, and produce better teaching. Instead we should become familiar with it, and believe that what is written in it is better and truer—even if its meaning lies shrouded—than what we can offer as wisdom by our own efforts.

10. (18) After those two stages, fear and devotion, we come to the third stage of knowledge, which I propose to deal with now. Everyone who studies the holy scriptures is trained in this. In those scriptures they will find nothing but the necessity of loving God for his own sake, and loving our neighbor for God's sake; and loving God with all our heart, all our soul, all our mind, and our neighbor as ourself. In other words, we are to love in such a way that all our love of neighbor is to be related to God, just as our love of self is. (19) We have given an account of these two commandments in the first book, when we were discussing things. So it is vital that each person first of all finds in the scriptures that they themselves are ensnared by the love of this world (which is to say the world of earthly things), and that they are far from loving God and neighbor to the utmost, as scripture directs. That is when the

et illa pietas qua non potest nisi credere et cedere auctoritati sanctorum librorum, cogit eum seipsum lugere. (20) Nam ista scientia bonae spei hominem non se iactantem sed lamentantem facit; quo affectu impetrat sedulis precibus consolationem divini adiutorii, ne desperatione frangatur, et esse incipit in quarto gradu, hoc est fortitudinis, quo esuritur et sititur iustitia. Hoc enim affectu ab omni mortifera iucunditate rerum transeuntium sese extrahit et inde se avertens convertit ad dilectionem aeternorum, incommutabilem scilicet unitatem eandemque trinitatem.

11. (21) Quam ubi aspexerit, quantum potest, in longinqua radiantem suique aspectus infirmitate sustinere se illam lucem non posse persenserit, in quinto gradu, hoc est in consilio misericordiae, purgat animam tumultuantem quodam modo atque obstrepentem sibi de appetitu inferiorum conceptis sordibus. Hic vero se in dilectione proximi gnaviter[5] exercet, in eaque perficitur.

(22) Et spe iam plenus atque integer viribus, cum pervenerit usque ad inimici dilectionem, ascendit in sextum gradum, ubi iam ipsum oculum purgat quo videri deus potest, quantum potest ab iis qui huic saeculo moriuntur quantum possunt. Nam in tantum vident in quantum moriuntur huic saeculo, in quantum autem hic vivunt, non vident. Et ideo quamvis iam certior et non solum tolerabilior sed etiam iucundior species lucis illius incipiat appa-

[5] naviter *P K*: graviter *R*: *v. A. Cser, Journal of Linguistics 47 (2011): 65–85*

---

[23] Oxymoron: *mortifera iucunditas*; paronomasia: a simple, then compound verb, *vertit* and *convertit*.

fear that fills their reflections on God's judgment, and the devotion that compels them to believe—and yield to—the authority of the holy books, forces them to lament the state they are in. (20) That knowledge of proper hope makes a person full of contrition rather than boasting. With this mind-set they grasp hold of the comfort of divine help, through their ardent prayers; otherwise despair would shatter them. Thus they begin the fourth stage, namely courage. This is the stage of hungering and thirsting after righteousness. For in this state of mind they extricate themselves from all the deadly delight of transitory things. They turn from them; and instead turn themselves[23] toward the love of what is eternal. This is nothing less than the unchanging unity, Trinity itself.

11. (21) Once they have looked (as much as they can) upon the Trinity as it shines into far-off places, and see that because their own sight is weak they cannot endure its light, they are at the fifth stage. This consists of making mercy their objective: they cleanse their soul, which is in a kind of state of agitation, blaming itself for the squalid objectives it has accepted because of its appetite for what is worthless. Now they are intent on training themselves and perfecting their skills in loving their neighbor.

(22) At this point they are full of hope, and their strength is beyond reproach, so when they reach the stage of loving their enemy, they ascend to the sixth stage. Here they cleanse the vision that allows them to look upon God as far as is possible for those who—as best they can—die to this world. What they see is in direct proportion to their dying to this world; insofar as they live in this world, they have no vision. So it is that although the form of that light begins to appear more sure, not only easier to endure but

rere, in aenigmate adhuc tamen et per speculum videri dicitur, quia magis per fidem quam per speciem ambulatur, cum in hac vita peregrinamur, quamvis conversationem habeamus in caelis.

(23) In hoc autem gradu ita purgat oculum cordis, ut veritati ne ipsum quidem praeferat aut conferat proximum, ergo nec seipsum, quia nec illum quem diligit sicut seipsum. Erit ergo iste sanctus tam simplici corde atque mundato, ut neque hominibus placendi studio detorqueatur a vero nec respectu devitandorum quorumlibet incommodorum suorum quae adversantur huic vitae. Talis filius ascendit ad sapientiam, quae ultima et septima est, qua pacatus tranquillusque perfruitur. Initium enim sapientiae timor domini. Ab illo enim usque ad ipsam per hos gradus tenditur et venitur.

12. (24) Sed nos ad tertium illum gradum considerationem referamus, de quo disserere quod dominus suggesserit atque tractare instituimus. Erit igitur divinarum scripturarum solertissimus indagator, qui primo totas legerit notasque habuerit, et si nondum intellectu, iam tamen lectione, dumtaxat eas quae appellantur canonicae. Nam ceteras securius leget fide veritatis instructus, ne praeoccupent imbecillem animum et periculosis mendaciis atque phantasmatibus eludentes praeiudicent aliquid contra sanam intellegentiam. In canonicis autem scriptu-

24 2 Corinthians 5:7.
25 Philippians 3:20.
26 Proverbs 1.7[VL].
27 That is, from fear to wisdom.

even more delightful as well, nevertheless it is still said to appear in a kind of obscure reflection. This is because when we make our pilgrimage through this life, our walking is more by faith than by sight,[24] even though our true sphere of life is in the heavens.[25]

(23) But at this stage they cleanse the vision of their heart, so that they do not set their neighbor on the same level as truth—far less on a higher one—nor, given that they do not do so for those whom they love as themselves, do they do so *to* themselves. Now they will be holy, true-hearted, cleansed; so that no eagerness to please other people, no thought of avoiding any such inconveniences as tend to beset one in this life, will turn them from the truth. A child like this makes the ascent to wisdom, which is the seventh and final stage, and enjoys that wisdom to the full, in peaceful tranquility. After all, "the fear of God is the beginning of wisdom."[26] These are the steps that point the way and draw people all the way from the one to the other.[27]

12. (24) We must bring our thinking back to that third stage: on the subject of knowledge, we have decided to tackle a discussion of the material that the Lord has supplied. The most zealous investigators of the holy scriptures will be those who begin by reading them in full, and becoming familiar with them—if not yet in terms of what the texts mean, at least in terms of what they cover, as far as those we call "canonical" are concerned. It will be less risky for them to read other writings once they have been trained to have faith in the truth. This will prevent such writings seizing control of a weak mind, and deceiving it with dangerous lies and delusions, so as to prejudice it against a sound understanding. As to the canonical scrip-

ris ecclesiarum catholicarum quam plurium auctoritatem sequatur, inter quas sane illae sint, quae apostolicas sedes habere et epistolas accipere meruerunt. (25) Tenebit igitur hunc modum in scripturis canonicis, ut eas quae ab omnibus accipiuntur ecclesiis catholicis praeponat eis quas quidam non accipiunt. In eis vero quae non accipiuntur ab omnibus, praeponat eas quas plures gravioresque accipiunt, eis quas pauciores minorisque auctoritatis ecclesiae tenent. Si autem alias invenerit a pluribus, alias a gravioribus haberi, quamquam hoc facile invenire non possit, aequalis tamen auctoritatis eas habendas puto.

13. (26) Totus autem canon scripturarum in quo istam considerationem versandam dicimus, his libris continetur: quinque Moyseos, id est genesi, exodo, levitico, numeris, deuteronomio, et uno libro Iesu Nave, uno iudicum, uno libello qui appellatur Ruth, qui magis ad regnorum principium videtur pertinere; deinde quattuor regnorum et duobus paralipomenon, non consequentibus sed quasi a latere adiunctis simulque pergentibus.

(27) Haec est historia, quae sibimet annexa tempora continet atque ordinem rerum. Sunt aliae tamquam ex diverso ordine, quae neque huic ordini neque inter se connectuntur, sicut est Iob et Tobias et Esther et Iudith et Machabeorum libri duo et Esdrae duo, qui magis sub-

---

28 "Universal": not local or partisan.

29 Letters preserved in the New Testament.

30 That is, striving for a criterion that makes disputes about authority virtually impossible.

31 1 and 2 Samuel; 1 and 2 Kings.

32 That is, Ezra and Nehemiah.

tures of the catholic[28] churches, they should follow the opinion of the majority, particularly those churches that were worthy of having apostolic sees and receiving letters.[29] (25) They will stick to this approach for the canonical scriptures, so as to privilege those that all catholic churches recognize over those that some do not recognize. Indeed, regarding those scriptures that are not universally accepted, they ought to privilege the ones that the greater number of authorities recognize over those that are supported by fewer, less important, churches. But if they find some scriptures being accepted by the majority of churches, and others being accepted by those with greater authority (although such an eventuality is practically impossible), I consider that they should be accepted as having equal weight.[30]

13. (26) The complete canon of the scriptures that we consider as deserving close attention consists of the following books: five books of Moses—Genesis, Exodus, Leviticus, Numbers, Deuteronomy; one book—Joshua son of Nun; one book—Judges; one little book called Ruth, which apparently belongs more to the beginning of Kings; then four books of Kings,[31] and two of Chronicles: these do not form a sequential narrative, but proceed side by side, as it were, and cover the same ground.

(27) Those books form a history that contains within it periods it has linked together, and an ordered sequence of events. Other books of scripture form a different group not related to the historical sequence, nor related within itself. This includes Job, Tobias, Esther, and Judith, 1 and 2 Maccabees, and 1 and 2 Ezra;[32] and these are appar-

sequi videntur ordinatam illam historiam usque ad regnorum vel paralipomenon terminatam. Deinde prophetae, in quibus David unus liber psalmorum, et Salomonis tres: proverbiorum, cantici canticorum et ecclesiastes. Nam illi duo libri, unus qui sapientia et alius qui ecclesiasticus inscribitur, de quadam similitudine Salomonis esse dicuntur. Nam Iesus Sirach eos conscripsisse constantissime perhibetur; qui tamen quoniam in auctoritatem recipi meruerunt, inter propheticos numerandi sunt.

(28) Reliqui sunt eorum libri qui proprie prophetae appellantur, duodecim prophetarum libri singuli, qui conexi sibimet, quoniam numquam seiuncti sunt, pro uno habentur; quorum prophetarum nomina sunt haec: Osee, Ioel, Amos, Abdias, Ionas, Micha, Naum, Abacuc, Sophonias, Aggeus, Zacharias, Malachi. Deinde quattuor prophetae sunt maiorum voluminum: Isaias, Hieremias, Daniel, Hiezechiel. (29) His quadraginta quattuor libris testamenti veteris terminatur auctoritas; novi autem quattuor librorum evangelio: secundum Matthaeum, secundum Marcum, secundum Lucam, secundum Ioannem; quattuordecim epistolis apostoli Pauli: ad Romanos, ad

---

[33] *videntur*: Someone of his skill and sophistication in interpreting text could not state that these books are straightforward continuations.

[34] These ascriptions of authorship remained traditional until the time of the "higher criticism" that emerged in the eighteenth century and came to dominate biblical scholarship from the nineteenth century on.

[35] In Augustine's time these were known only in Greek, hence the question about their authorship. "I later learned that Jesus ben Sirach was probably not the author of Wisdom" (*Retr.* 2.4.2).

ently[33] a continuation of that sequential history that ended with Kings and Chronicles. Then come the prophets: one book of David—the Psalms; and three of Solomon—Proverbs, Song of Songs, and Ecclesiastes.[34] There are two books, one entitled Wisdom and the other Ecclesiasticus, which are said to be by Solomon on the grounds of a degree of similarity; but the firmest attribution ascribes their authorship to Jesus son of Sirach.[35] Even so, because they have had the honor of being accepted as canonical, they should be counted with the prophetic books.

(28) The rest of the books are written by authors who are most properly called prophets.[36] There are the individual books of the twelve prophets; these are linked with each other, and because they are never separated they are counted as a single book. These are their names: Hosea, Joel, Amos, Obadiah, Jonah, Micah, Nahum, Habakkuk, Zephaniah, Haggai, Zachariah, and Malachi. Then there are the four major prophets, whose books are longer: Isaiah, Jeremiah, Daniel, Ezekiel. (29) The authentic content of the Old Testament is confined to these forty-four books. That of the New is confined to the gospel, in four books—according to Matthew, according to Mark, according to Luke and according to John; fourteen letters of the apostle

[36] That is, according to the Christian Old Testament classification of the three principal prophets (Isaiah, Jeremiah [with Lamentations], and Ezekiel, plus Daniel (counted among the writings in the Hebrew Bible), and last, the Twelve, or "minor," prophets. In the threefold division of the Hebrew Bible into law, prophets, and writings, the deuteronomic history (Joshua–2 Kings) was counted as prophecy; as authors, Moses and David were both counted among the prophets.

Corinthios duabus, ad Galatas, ad Ephesios, ad Philippenses, ad Thessalonicenses duabus, ad Colossenses, ad Timotheum duabus, ad Titum, ad Philemonem, ad Hebraeos; Petri duabus; tribus Ioannis; una Iudae et una Iacobi; Actibus Apostolorum libro uno et Apocalypsi Ioannis libro uno.

14. (30) In his omnibus libris timentes deum et pietate mansueti quaerunt voluntatem dei. Cuius operis et laboris prima observatio est, ut diximus, nosse istos libros, etsi nondum ad intellectum, legendo tamen vel mandare memoriae vel omnino incognitos non habere. Deinde illa quae in eis aperte posita sunt, vel praecepta vivendi vel regulae credendi, solertius diligentiusque investiganda sunt; quae tanto quisque plura invenit quanto est intellegentia capacior. (31) In iis enim quae aperte in scripturis posita sunt, inveniuntur illa omnia quae continent fidem moresque vivendi, spem scilicet atque caritatem, de quibus libro superiore tractavimus.

Tum vero facta quadam familiaritate cum ipsa lingua divinarum scripturarum, in ea quae obscura sunt aperienda et discutienda pergendum est, ut ad obscuriores locutiones illustrandas de manifestioribus sumantur exempla et quaedam certarum sententiarum testimonia dubitationem incertis auferant. In qua re memoria valet plurimum, quae si defuerit, non potest his praeceptis dari.

15. (32) Duabus autem causis non intelleguntur quae

---

[37] In order of importance: gospels, Pauline corpus (Romans-Hebrews), apostolic writings. [38] Twin purpose: doctrinal principles and ethical instruction. [39] See *TC* 1.41.90–44.96. [40] Latin *sententiarum*: indicates here the outcome or conclusion of an argument.

Paul—Romans, 1 and 2 Corinthians, Galatians, Ephesians, Philippians, 1 and 2 Thessalonians, Colossians, 1 and 2 Timothy, Titus, Philemon, Hebrews; then 1 and 2 Peter; 1, 2, and 3 John; Jude; James; the Acts of the Apostles; and the Apocalypse of John.[37]

14. (30) In all these books, those who are god-fearing and gentle in their faith seek God's will. The first duty of this present work, is (as we have said) to become familiar with these books: even if not to the level of comprehension, at least by reading them so as the commit them to memory—or at least not to be entirely ignorant of them. This make it possible to explore more shrewdly and conscientiously what is stated clearly in those books, whether guidance for living or rules of belief;[38] the more each person discovers both types of material, the more their comprehension increases. (31) This is because in the parts that are set out plainly in scripture are found all those matters that consist of belief and ethics, hope and love (we explored these in the first book[39]).

Once a degree of familiarity with the distinctive idiom of the holy scriptures has been established, the next step is to go on to a detailed clarification of the impenetrable parts. This means taking examples from the clearer parts to throw light on those more impenetrable utterances; and using particular evidence from proven interpretations[40] to remove doubt from those that are ambiguous. Memory is of the utmost importance for this task: if memory is lacking, it cannot be achieved by means of these rules.

15. (32) There are two reasons why things that are

scripta sunt, si aut ignotis aut ambiguis signis obteguntur. Sunt autem signa vel propria vel translata. Propria dicuntur, cum his rebus significandis adhibentur, propter quas sunt instituta, sicut dicimus bovem, cum intellegimus pecus, quod omnes nobiscum Latinae linguae homines hoc nomine vocant. (33) Translata sunt, cum et ipsae res quas propriis verbis significamus, ad aliquid aliud significandum usurpantur, sicut dicimus bovem, et per has duas syllabas intellegimus pecus quod isto nomine appellari solet, sed rursus per illud pecus intellegimus evangelistam, quem significavit scriptura, interpretante apostolo, dicens "bovem triturantem non infrenabis."

16. (34) Contra ignota signa propria magnum remedium est linguarum cognitio. Et Latinae quidem linguae homines, quos nunc instruendos suscepimus, duabus aliis ad scripturarum divinarum cognitionem opus habent, Hebraea scilicet et Graeca, ut ad exemplaria praecedentia recurratur, si quam dubitationem attulerit Latinorum interpretum infinita varietas. Quamquam et Hebraea verba non interpretata saepe inveniamus in libris, sicut "amen" et "allelluia" et "racha" et "osanna" et si qua sunt alia. Quorum partim propter sanctiorem auctoritatem, quamvis interpretari potuissent, servata est antiquitas, sicut sunt "amen" et "alleluia," partim vero in aliam linguam trans-

---

[41] For the post-Classical meaning of *proprietas*, see Quintilian, "Propriety is relative not to the word, but to its semantic value, and is to be judged not by the ear but by the understanding" (*Inst.* 8.2.1–7).

[42] Quint. *Inst.* 8.6.5: "the commonest and . . . most beautiful of tropes, . . . *translatio* . . . is called *metaphora* in Greek."

written are not understood. The meaning is veiled by signs that are either unknown or ambivalent. Signs are either "proper"[41] or "figurative."[42] They are called "proper" when they are used to signify the things for which they were established: for example we say "ox" when we mean the animal—which is the word that all Latin-speaking people use. (33) They are called figurative when the actual things that we signify by proper terms are appropriated to signify something else: for example, when we say "oxen," by those two syllables[43] we understand the animals that are routinely referred to by that word; but on another occasion we use the word for an animal to refer to an evangelist.[44] This is what scripture signifies when Paul gives a reading of the phrase, "you shall not muzzle a threshing ox."[45]

16. (34) A knowledge of languages is one dependable remedy for unfamiliar signs used in a proper sense. Here we have undertaken the instruction of Latin speakers, who need two additional languages for a knowledge of the scriptures—Hebrew, obviously, and Greek. This makes it possible to refer back to earlier usages, if the countless variety of Latin translations gives rise to any ambiguity. All the same, we often find in the Bible books Hebrew words that have not been translated, such as "amen," "alleluia," "racha," and "hosanna," and others of that kind. The original form of some of them has been preserved on account of a degree of holy authority, even though they could have been translated: "amen" and "alleluia" for example. Oth-

[43] In Latin *bos* has two syllables in oblique cases as here, *bovem*. [44] *evangelista* Latinizes the Greek word for someone who communicates (Christian) good news.

[45] 1 Corinthians 9:9.

ferri non potuisse dicuntur, sicut alia duo quae posuimus. (35) Sunt enim quaedam verba certarum linguarum quae in usum alterius linguae per interpretationem transire non possint. Et hoc maxime interiectionibus accidit, quae verba motum animi significant potius quam sententiae conceptae ullam particulam. Nam et haec duo talia esse perhibentur; dicunt enim "racha" indignantis esse vocem, "osanna" laetantis. (36) Sed non propter haec pauca quae notare atque interrogare facillimum est, sed propter diversitates, ut dictum est, interpretum illarum linguarum est cognitio necessaria. Qui enim scripturas ex Hebraea in Graecam verterunt, numerari possunt, Latini autem interpretes nullo modo. Ut enim cuique primis fidei temporibus in manus venit codex Graecus et aliquantum facultatis sibi utriusque linguae habere videbatur, ausus est interpretari.

17. (37) Quae quidem res plus adiuvit intellegentiam quam impedivit, si modo legentes non sint neglegentes. Nam nonnullas obscuriores sententias plurium codicum saepe manifestavit inspectio, sicut illud Esaiae prophetae ‹cum›[6] unus[7] interpres ait "et domesticos seminis tui ne

[6] *add. Schaüblin*
[7] *om. P K*: alius P^1

---

[46] See Hammond, *Sound of the Liturgy*, 2–7; Crystal, "Some Current Trends in Translation Theory." Also M. Mohr, *Holy Sh*t: A Brief History of Swearing* (Oxford, 2013).

[47] The legend of the Seventy (actually seventy-two, conventionally abbreviated LXX) and the miraculous perfection of their Old Testament translation from Hebrew into Greek is recorded in Philo (*Moses* 2.37–43). The first Christian witness to the legend

ers. it is said, cannot be translated into another language, for example the other two words that we suggested. (35) Again, there are some words in particular languages that cannot pass by means of translation into the usage of any other language. This is especially the case with exclamations—words that signify emotion rather than any element of a rational concept.[46] Those other two words are assigned to this class: "*racha*" is said to be a word used when one is indignant, and "*hosanna*" *is* for when one is rejoicing. (36) It is not, however, because of those few words (which are incredibly easy to learn and interpret) that familiarity with those languages is necessary, but because of differences between translators. We can give a figure for the number who translated the scriptures from Hebrew into Greek,[47] but this is impossible for translators into Latin. In the early days of Christianity, whenever someone got hold of a book in Greek,[48] and they reckoned themselves to have a modicum of competence in both languages, they had the presumption to produce a translation.

17. (37) Provided that readers are careful, things of this kind are more of a help than a hindrance to understanding. For example, scrutiny of several books[49] has clarified quite a few difficulties of interpretation, like when one translator makes the prophet Isaiah say, "and do not despise your relations who dwell with you"– while another says "and do

is Justin, *Apol.* 31.1–5; for the shift from seventy-two to seventy, see *Dial. Tryph.* 71.1–2.

[48] *Codex* not *liber*, so a book of scripture.

[49] *Codicum*: meaning differing individual copies (likely to be by different hands).

despexeris," alius autem ait "et carnem tuam ne despexeris"; uterque sibimet invicem attestatus est. (38) Namque alter ex altero exponitur, quia et caro posset accipi proprie, ut corpus suum quisque ne despiceret se putaret admonitum; et domestici seminis translate christiani possent intellegi, ex eodem verbi semine nobiscum spiritaliter nati. Nunc autem collato interpretum sensu probabilior occurrit sententia proprie de consanguineis non despiciendis esse praeceptum, quoniam domesticos seminis cum ad carnem rettuleris, consanguinei potissimum occurrunt. Unde esse arbitror illud apostoli quod ait, "si quo modo ad aemulationem adducere potuero carnem meam, ut salvos faciam aliquos ex illis"; id est ut aemulando eos qui crediderant et ipsi crederent. (39) Carnem enim suam dixit Iudaeos, propter consanguinitatem.

Item illud eiusdem Esaiae, "nisi credideritis, non intellegetis," alius interpretatus est, "nisi credideritis, non permanebitis." Quis horum verba secutus sit, nisi exemplaria linguae praecedentis legantur, incertum est. Sed tamen ex utroque magnum aliquid insinuatur scienter legentibus. Difficile est enim ita diversos a se interpretes fieri ut non se aliqua vicinitate contingant. (40) Ergo quoniam intellectus in specie sempiterna est, fides vero in rerum temporalium quibusdam cunabulis quasi lacte alit

---

50 Isaiah 58:7: first LXX, then Vulg. 51 The first Christians called one another "brother" and "sister" even when not related: see Min. Fel. *Oct.* 31.8. 52 Romans 11:14.

53 Isaiah 7:9[VL] and Vulg., a favorite text.

54 Exegetical translation: *verba.* 55 He sidesteps the historical question of what the prophet originally said.

not despise your own flesh":[50] each one has corroborated the other in turn. (38) The one is explained by the other: for "flesh" could be taken in its proper sense, and considered a warning that no one should despise their own body; and "blood relatives who dwell with you" could be understood in a figurative way as meaning "fellow Christians," that is, those born from the same seed of the Word[51] as we are. But when the meaning of the translations is compared, the more likely sense that comes to mind is the proper one, the commandment not to despise your own blood relatives. This is because if you compare "your relations who dwell with you" to "flesh" the dominant meaning is "blood relatives." I believe that this is what the apostle meant by saying "if by some means I may persuade my own flesh to compete with me, so that I may save some of them"[52]—in other words that by striving to compete with those who had believed earlier, they themselves would come to believe too. (39) What he referred to as his own flesh was the Jewish people, because they were his people by blood.

Another example from Isaiah: a text that says either "unless you have believed, you will not understand" or, in another version, "unless you have believed, you will not stand firm."[53] Which one of these has followed Isaiah's original words[54] is unclear unless the versions in the source language are consulted. Still, to anyone who reads with a degree of knowledge, something can be gleaned from both versions. It is hard for translators to be so different from one another that that have no point of contact at all.[55] (40) As a result, because understanding subsists in the vision of eternity, while faith subsists in (as it were) the cradle of earthly time, nourishing us infants with its milk,

parvulos, nunc autem "per fidem ambulamus, non per speciem," nisi autem per fidem ambulaverimus, ad speciem pervenire non possumus quae non transit sed permanet, per intellectum purgatum nobis cohaerentibus veritati, propterea ille ait, "nisi credideritis, non permanebitis," ille autem, "nisi credideritis, non intellegetis."

18. (41) Et ex ambiguo linguae praecedentis plerumque interpres fallitur, cui non bene nota sententia est, et eam significationem transfert, quae a sensu scriptoris penitus aliena est, sicut quidam codices habent, "acuti pedes eorum ad effundendum sanguinem"; ὀξύς enim et acutum apud Graecos et velocem significat. Ille ergo vidit sententiam qui transtulit, "veloces pedes eorum ad effundendum sanguinem"; ille autem alius ancipiti signo in aliam partem raptus erravit. (42) Et alia quidem non obscura, sed falsa sunt. Quorum alia condicio est; non enim intellegendos, sed emendandos tales codices potius praecipiendum est. Hinc est etiam illud, quoniam "moschos" Graece vitulus dicitur, "moscheumata" quidam non intellexerunt esse "plantationes"; et "vitulamina" interpretati sunt. Qui error tam multos codices praeoccupavit ut vix inveniatur aliter scriptum. Et tamen sententia manifestissima est, quia clarescit consequentibus verbis; namque "adulterinae plantationes non dabunt radices altas," convenientius dicitur

---

56 2 Corinthians 5:7. 57 *Acuti*: Psalm 13:3[LXX].

58 *Veloces*: Psalm 13:3[Vulg.].

59 He means the word *oxus*, with its multiple meaning; but the term he chooses (showing that this work is not an essay on translation) is "sign," not "word."

60 μόσχος, μόσχευματα: Wisdom 4:3. The Latin is confus-

we walk, for the time being, by faith not sight.[56] If we have not walked by faith, we cannot attain to the vision that is eternal rather than transitory, with our understanding cleansed by our cleaving to the truth, and that is why one of them said: "unless you have believed you will not stand fast" while the other one said: "unless you have believed you will not understand."

18. (41) Many a translator unfamiliar with the subject matter is misled by an ambiguity in the source language. This leads them to introduce a meaning completely different from what the writer intended. For example, certain copies have the text, "their feet are sharp[57] to shed blood." Now the word *oxus* means both "sharp" and "swift" in Greek. Whoever translated it as "their feet are swift[58] to shed blood" discerned the right meaning; while the other translator was carried away by the ambiguity of the sign[59] and went astray. (42) There are also some cases that are not opaque but actually incorrect. In this alternative situation, we must direct that such books be corrected, not interpreted. Here is another case: a calf is called *moschos* in Greek, but certain translators did not understand that the meaning of *moscheumata* is "seedlings," and translated it as a "group of calves" instead.[60] This error has taken hold in so many books that scarcely any other reading can be found. And yet the meaning is crystal clear, because it becomes apparent in the words that follow: "false *seedlings* will not produce deep roots" is a much

ing: it suggests that *plantationes* and *vitulamina* mean different things, when in fact both mean "seedlings." The confusion stems from the Greek word *moschos* (μόσχος) having two meanings: (1) "calf"; (2) "young shoot."

quam "vitulamina," quae pedibus in terra gradiuntur, et non haerent radicibus. Hanc translationem in eo loco etiam cetera contexta custodiunt.

19. (43) Sed quoniam et quae sit ipsa sententia, quam plures interpretes pro sua quisque facultate atque iudicio conantur eloqui, non apparet, nisi in ea lingua inspiciatur quam interpretantur, et plerumque a sensu auctoris devius aberrat interpres, si non sit doctissimus. Aut linguarum illarum ex quibus in Latinam scriptura pervenit petenda cognitio est, aut habendae interpretationes eorum qui se verbis nimis obstrinxerunt, non quia sufficiunt, sed ut ex eis libertas vel error dirigatur[8] aliorum, qui non tam verba quam sententias interpretando sequi maluerunt. (44) Nam non solum verba singula, sed etiam locutiones saepe transferuntur, quae omnino in Latinae linguae usum, si quis consuetudinem veterum qui Latine locuti sunt tenere voluerit, transire non possint. Quae aliquando intellectui nihil adimunt, sed offendunt tamen eos qui plus delectantur rebus, cum etiam in earum signis sua quaedam servatur integritas. Nam "soloecismus" qui dicitur nihil est aliud quam cum verba non ea lege sibi coaptantur qua coaptaverunt qui priores nobis non sine auctoritate aliqua locuti sunt. Utrum enim inter homines an inter

[8] detegatur μ

---

[61] The distinction is between formal equivalence ("literal") and functional equivalence ("gist") translations.

[62] An error in either the construction of a sentence or the usage of a word: see Arist. *Soph. El.* 173b17.

[63] It is impossible to reproduce the solecism in English. The Latin error is to put the noun "men" in the wrong grammatical

more appropriate translation than "calves," because calves tread the ground with their feet, and do not stay fixed in it by roots. Other contextual elements preserve this translation of the passage.

19. (43) All the same, it is unclear what is the actual sense that so many translators are trying to express, according to their own competence and judgment, unless it is examined in the source language that they are translating. For this reason all but the most learned translators often make a mistake, diverging from the author's meaning. In consequence we should strive to learn those languages from which scripture in Latin has emerged; or make use of translations by those who confined themselves strictly to the wording—not because that is adequate in itself, but so these versions can be used as a check on the license or blunders of others who preferred to follow the ideas rather than the wording in their translations.[61] (44) Not only individual words but also passages are often translated, which cannot be converted into the idiom of Latin—at least not if one wishes to maintain the long-established usages of Latin speakers. People can regard something as an affront even when it causes no loss of understanding, if they are the type who take more pleasure in things when the sign used for those things preserves a degree of proper usage. When something is called a "solecism"[62] it means that words are not being joined together on the same principle as our predecessors used in speaking—and they had some authority in this matter. Whether one says "among men" or "among mans"[63] is ir-

case (ablative instead of accusative); the English forms the plural of "man" incorrectly.

hominibus dicitur, ad rerum non pertinet cognitorem. (45) Item barbarismus quid aliud est nisi verbum non eis litteris vel sono enuntiatum, quo ab eis qui ante nos Latine locuti sunt enuntiari solet? Utrum autem "ignoscere" producta an correpta tertia syllaba dicatur, non multum curat qui peccatis suis deus[9] ut ignoscat petit, quolibet modo illud verbum sonare potuerit. Quid est ergo integritas locutionis nisi alienae consuetudinis conservatio, loquentium veterum auctoritate firmatae?

20. (46) Sed tamen eo magis inde offenduntur homines quo infirmiores sunt, et eo sunt infirmiores quo doctiores videri volunt, non rerum scientia qua aedificamur, sed signorum, qua non inflari omnino difficile est, cum et ipsa rerum scientia saepe cervicem erigat, nisi dominico reprimatur iugo. Quid enim obest intellectori quod ita scriptum est, "quae est terra in qua isti insidunt super eam, si bona est an nequam; et quae sunt civitates in quibus ipsi inhabitant in ipsis?" (47) Quam locutionem magis alienae linguae esse arbitror quam sensum aliquem altiorem. Illud etiam quod iam auferre non possumus de ore cantantium populorum, "super ipsum autem floriet sanctificatio mea," nihil profecto sententiae detrahit. Auditor tamen peritior mallet hoc corrigi, ut non "floriet," sed "florebit"

[9] deum *P K Lond.*[1] *Mart.*

---

[64] Rather than signs. [65] As "for-gĭve" (to rhyme with "live," verb) or "for-gīve" (to rhyme with "hive," noun).

[66] 1 Corinthians 8:1. [67] Correctly. The doubled pronoun ("in which" and "in them," Numbers 13:19[LXX]) follows Hebrew.

[68] Psalm 131:18[Vulg.] reads *super ipsum autem efflorebit sanctificatio mea.* Some of the VL versions give the verb a third (*flo-*

relevant to anyone who is occupied with things.[64] (45) Again, what is a "barbarism," if not the expression of a word using letters or sounds other than those that our Latin-speaking forebears customarily employed? Whether you say the word "forgive" with a long or short second vowel[65] is of little significance to anyone asking God to forgive their sins, no matter how they pronounce the word. To conclude: what is correctness in speaking but the preservation of others' usages as supported by the tradition of speakers from earlier generations?

20. (46) Even so, the way people are displeased by such matters is directly commensurate with their weakness; and their weakness is commensurate with their eagerness to appear learned—not in the knowledge of things (which builds us up) but in the knowledge of signs, which all too easily makes us puffed up.[66] This is because even a knowledge of things makes us toplofty, unless our neck is bowed by the Lord's yoke. Now, what obstacle is in the interpreter's way in this text?—"what is the land in which they lie in wait for her, if she is good or worthless; and what are the states in which they themselves live in them?" (47) I consider this form of expression to be a matter of foreign idiom rather than containing some deeper meaning.[67] And what about that example we cannot deprive our congregations of when they sing?—"My holiness shall florish over him."[68] Its meaning certainly is not vitiated. Still, a listener with greater expertise would prefer this to be corrected to read "flourish" rather than "florish"—and there is nothing

riet) rather than a second (*florebit*) conjugation. This English version has been formed from a Latin noun stem (*flor-*) and an English verbal suffix (*-ish*).

diceretur, nec quidquam impedit correctionem, nisi consuetudo cantantium. Ista ergo facile etiam contemni possunt, si quis ea cavere noluerit, quae sano intellectui nihil detrahunt. (48) At vero illud quod ait apostolus, "quod stultum est dei, sapientius est hominibus, et quod infirmum est dei, fortius est hominibus," si quis in eo Graecam locutionem servare voluisset, ut diceret "quod stultum est dei, sapientius est hominum, et quod infirmum est dei, fortius est hominum," iret quidem vigilantis lectoris intentio in sententiae veritatem, sed tamen aliquis tardior aut non intellegeret aut etiam perverse intellegeret. Non enim tantum vitiosa locutio est in Latina lingua talis, verum et in ambiguitatem cadit, ut quasi hominum stultum vel hominum infirmum sapientius vel fortius videatur esse quam dei. Quamquam et illud "sapientius est hominibus" non caret ambiguo, etiamsi soloecismo caret. (49) Utrum enim his "hominibus" ab eo quod est "huic homini" an his "hominibus" ab eo quod est "hoc homine" dictum sit, non apparet nisi illuminatione sententiae. Melius itaque ita dicitur, "sapientius est quam homines," et "fortius est quam homines."

21. (50) De ambiguis autem signis post loquemur. Nunc de incognitis agimus, quorum duae formae sunt, quantum ad verba pertinet. Namque aut ignotum verbum facit haerere lectorem, aut ignota locutio. Quae si ex alie-

---

69 1 Corinthians 1:25.

70 Latin uses the ablative case for comparison, as in the first version; Greek uses the genitive, as in the second.

71 These Latin phrases have no precise English equivalent. Augustine means that the plural *hominibus* could be either dative or ablative, whereas in the singular, the words are distinct (dative:

to prevent that correction, apart from the singers' habitual practice. Such matters can easily be disregarded, if anyone is reluctant to avoid them, because they surely make no difference to comprehension. (48) It is another matter when the apostle says, "God's foolishness is wiser than humans, and God's weakness is stronger than humans."[69] If someone had wanted to preserve the Greek idiom in this text, by saying, "God's foolishness is wiser of mortals, and what is God's weakness is stronger of mortals," the attention of an alert reader would move straight to the correct meaning of the statement, but a slower-witted person would either fail to understand or—worse still—would misinterpret it.[70] An expression of this type is not only incorrect in Latin, but also prone to ambiguity, as if to say that human folly and human weakness are apparently wiser or stronger than God's. The phrase "is wiser than mortals," though it is free from error, still has an element of ambiguity. (49) Whether this phrase, "than humans" comes from what would, in the singular, indicate "to this human" or "by this human" is only apparent in the light of the rest of the sentence. So it is best to say "is wiser than humans," and "is stronger than humans."[71]

21. (50) We shall discuss ambiguous signs later. Now we are tackling unfamiliar signs; as far as words are concerned there are two types of these. What gives a reader pause is either an unrecognized word, or an unrecognized expression. If they arise from foreign languages, we must

homini; ablative: *homine*). He resolves the problem by choosing (instead of the Latin ablative for comparison) the adverb *quam* (than)—now both parts of the comparison stay in the same case, avoiding ambiguity.

nis linguis veniunt, aut quaerenda sunt ab earum linguarum hominibus aut eaedem linguae, si et otium et ingenium est, ediscendae aut plurium interpretum consulenda collatio est. Si autem ipsius linguae nostrae aliqua verba locutionesque ignoramus, legendi consuetudine audiendique innotescunt. (51) Nulla sane sunt magis mandanda memoriae, quam illa verborum locutionumque genera quae ignoramus; ut cum vel peritior occurrerit de quo quaeri possint, vel talis lectio quae vel praecedentibus vel consequentibus vel utrisque ostendat quam vim habeat, quidve significet quod ignoramus, facile adiuvante memoria possimus advertere et discere. Quamquam tanta est vis consuetudinis etiam ad discendum ut qui in scripturis sanctis quodammodo nutriti educatique sunt, magis alias locutiones mirentur easque minus Latinas putent quam illas quas in scripturis didicerunt, neque in Latinae linguae auctoribus reperiuntur. (52) Plurimum hic quoque adiuvat interpretum numerositas collatis codicibus inspecta atque discussa. Tantum absit falsitas, nam codicibus emendandis primitus debet invigilare sollertia eorum qui scripturas divinas nosse desiderant, ut emendatis non emendati cedant, ex uno dumtaxat interpretationis genere venientes.

22. (53) In ipsis autem interpretationibus Itala ceteris praeferatur, nam est verborum tenacior cum perspicuitate

---

[72] Eisegetically translated to clarify the paradox that biblical Latin, which he once considered barbaric, has become standard, while the classic writers of his pre-Christian days are now the oddities. [73] *numerositas*: later "rhythm, harmony" (*eurhythmia*); cf. *TC* 4.41.115, 4.56.147.

either ask people who speak that language about them, or learn the language if we have brains and leisure enough: or we need to consult a survey of various translations. But if some words and expressions in our native tongue are unfamiliar, we can get to know them by reading and listening. (51) Certainly there is nothing more important to commit to memory than the types of words and expressions we are unfamiliar with. This is so that when we encounter someone more expert whom we can ask about them, or the form of expression, through what precedes and follows it (or both), reveals an emphasis or meaning that we do not know, with the aid of our memory we can easily remark and learn it. The force of habit is so powerful, though, particularly where learning is concerned, that any students who have been nourished by a particular approach to holy scripture are quite surprised by certain expressions, and think their Latinity less good than what they have learned in scripture, even those expressions that have no warrant in the canon of Classical literature.[72] (52) Most helpful of all is a large number[73] of translations, with all the books scrutinized and analyzed together. But mistakes must be avoided; because those who want to know the holy scriptures need to have their wits about them right from the start, so that books that have been corrected take priority over uncorrected texts, so long as they come from a single type of translation.

22. (53) Among these translations the Itala[74] should be preferred to the rest as it sticks to the actual words as well

[74] *Itala*, *-ae*, fem.: before Jerome's Vulg., the predominant Latin version in Italy.

sententiae. Et Latinis quibuslibet emendandis Graeci adhibeantur, in quibus septuaginta interpretum, quod ad vetus testamentum attinet, excellit auctoritas, qui iam per omnes peritiores ecclesias tanta praesentia sancti spiritus interpretati esse dicuntur, ut os unum tot hominum fuerit. (54) Qui si, ut fertur, multique non indigni fide praedicant, singuli cellis etiam singulis separati cum interpretati essent, nihil in alicuius eorum codice inventum est quod non isdem verbis eodemque verborum ordine inveniretur in ceteris: quis huic auctoritati conferre aliquid, nedum praeferre audeat? Si autem contulerunt ut una omnium communi tractatu iudicioque vox fieret, ne sic quidem quemquam unum hominem qualibet peritia ad emendandum tot seniorum doctorumque consensum aspirare oportet aut decet. (55) Quam ob rem, etiamsi aliquid aliter in Hebraeis exemplaribus invenitur quam isti posuerunt, cedendum esse arbitror divinae dispensationi quae per eos facta est, ut libri quos gens Iudaea ceteris populis vel religione vel invidia prodere nolebat, credituris per dominum gentibus ministra regis Ptolomei potestate tanto ante proderentur. Itaque fieri potest ut sic illi interpretati sint quemadmodum congruere gentibus ille, qui eos agebat, et qui unum os omnibus fecerat, spiritus sanctus iudicavit.

(56) Sed tamen ut superius dixi horum quoque inter-

---

[75] See *Civ.* 18.43.

[76] Cakeism, acknowledging that the myth of LXX's generation may indeed be a myth.

[77] See p. 269, n. 121.

as preserving clarity of meaning. We turn to Greek translations for correcting the Latin ones; among these the version of the Seventy[75] has supreme authority as far as the Old Testament is concerned: this is because among all the more enlightened churches they are said to have translated by the direct influence of the Holy Spirit, by which so many persons became one voice. (54) It is said (and many people distinguished for their faith have affirmed this) that each of them was alone in a separate room when they all made their different translations; yet in vocabulary and word order, in each man's completed volume, there was found absolutely no difference from all the others' versions. Who would presume to compare anything with its authority– never mind to prefer another version? Even if they did confer together and a single voice emerged from the common efforts of them all,[76] it still would not be right for any single individual, however expert, to presume to correct the consensus of so many seasoned scholars. (55) For this reason, even if some discrepancy with what they established is found in Hebrew originals, it is my considered opinion that priority should be given to the sacred arrangement[77] brought about through the Seventy, by means of which the books that the Judean people were unwilling to share with other peoples (whether because of religious scruples or jealousy) were shared with peoples who—through the Lord—were to become believers, by the influential agency of King Ptolemy. The Holy Spirit was spurring them on, and it had made of them a single voice: so it is possible that they translated in the way that the Spirit had decided was best suited to those other nations.

(56) Nevertheless, as I said earlier, a comparison of

pretum qui verbis tenacius inhaeserunt, collatio non est inutilis ad explanandam saepe sententiam. Latini ergo, ut dicere coeperam, codices veteris testamenti si necesse fuerit Graecorum auctoritate emendandi sunt, et eorum potissimum qui, cum septuaginta essent, ore uno interpretati esse perhibentur. Libros autem novi testamenti, si quid in Latinis varietatibus titubat, Graecis cedere oportere non dubium est, et maxime qui apud ecclesias doctiores et diligentiores reperiuntur.

23. (57) In translatis vero signis si qua forte ignota cogunt haerere lectorem, partim linguarum notitia, partim rerum investiganda sunt. Aliquid enim ad similitudinem valet et procul dubio secretum quiddam insinuat Siloa piscina, ubi faciem lavare iussus est cui oculos dominus luto de sputo facto inunxerat. Quod tamen nomen linguae incognitae nisi evangelista interpretatus esset, tam magnus intellectus lateret. (58) Sic etiam multa, quae ab auctoribus eorundem librorum interpretata non sunt nomina Hebraea, non est dubitandum habere non parvam vim atque adiutorium ad solvenda aenigmata scripturarum, si quis ea possit interpretari. Quod nonnulli eiusdem linguae periti viri non sane parvum beneficium posteris contulerunt, qui separata de scripturis eadem omnia verba interpretati sunt; et quid sit Adam, quid Eva, quid Abraham, quid Moyses; sive etiam locorum nomina, quid sit Hierusalem vel Sion vel Hiericho vel Sina vel Libanus vel Iordanis et quaecumque alia in illa lingua nobis sunt incog-

---

[78] See 2.50.122 for *sententia* meaning philosophical proposition. At §53 it means "signification, meaning."

[79] John 9:7. The word "anoint" (from Latin; Greek χρῖεν) alludes to a baptismal ritual. John translates Siloam as "sent."

these translators who stick quite closely to the words is not without its uses when it comes to making sense of a sentence.[78] As I started to say, the Latin copies of the Old Testament had to be corrected when necessary from the witness of Greek versions; above all those who though seventy in number were still said to have translated with one voice. There is no doubt that if some error is detected in the books of the New Testament amid the range of Latin versions (particularly by those in the churches who are scholarly and conscientious), Greek versions should have priority.

23. (57) As for figurative signs, if they happen to be unfamiliar they give the reader pause; they need to be scrutinized, through knowledge partly of languages, and partly of things. For example, the phrase "pool of Siloam" has some kind of figurative force as a simile—indubitably a secret one—where the man was ordered to wash his face after the Lord anointed his eyes with mud made from saliva.[79] But still, if the evangelist had not translated the word that was in an unfamiliar language, its important meaning would remain hidden. (58) So also, when it comes to working out puzzles in the scriptures, many Hebrew words that have not been translated by the authors of those same books undoubtedly have a markedly positive impact if you can translate them. A number of people who are expert in that language have bestowed this significant benefit upon later generations. They picked out all the words of this kind from the scriptures and translated them, and told us the meaning of "Adam," "Eve," "Abraham," and "Moses"; and the names of places: "Jerusalem," "Zion," "Jericho," "Sinai," "Lebanon," "Jordan," and any other names in that language that are unfamiliar to us.

nita nomina. Quibus apertis et interpretatis multae in scripturis figuratae locutiones manifestantur.

24. (59) Rerum autem ignorantia facit obscuras figuratas locutiones, cum ignoramus vel animantium vel lapidum vel herbarum naturas aliarumve rerum, quae plerumque in scripturis similitudinis alicuius gratia ponuntur. Nam et de serpente quod notum est, totum corpus eum pro capite obicere ferientibus, quantum illustrat sensum illum, quod dominus iubet astutos nos esse sicut serpentes, ut scilicet pro capite nostro, quod est Christus, corpus potius persequentibus offeramus, ne fides christiana tamquam necetur in nobis si parcentes corpori negemus deum. (60) Vel illud, quod per cavernae angustias coartatus, deposita veteri tunica vires novas accipere dicitur, quantum concinit ad imitandam ipsam serpentis astutiam exuendumque veterem hominem, sicut apostolus dicit, ut induamur novo; et exuendum per angustias, dicente domino, "intrate per angustam portam!" Ut ergo notitia naturae serpentis inlustrat multas similitudines quas de hoc animante scriptura dare consuevit, sic ignorantia nonnullorum animalium, quae non minus per similitudines commemorat, impedit plurimum intellectorem.

---

[80] *similitudo*: or "simile/analogy."

[81] Matthew 10:16.

[82] Ephesians 4:15. The modern reader will not find this a compelling construe. But Augustine is following a standard approach: creative, imaginative exegesis.

[83] Literally, "tunic, clothing."

[84] *hominem*: literally, "person." Ephesians 4:22 AV translates this as putting off the old "man"; RSV, as "nature"; (*anthrōpos* is

Once they have been made accessible through translation, many figurative expressions in the scriptures become clear.

24. (59) Gaps in our knowledge make figurative expressions obscure, when we are uninformed about the natures of living creatures, rocks, plants and the like. In the scriptures these are frequently used to represent a comparison.[80] For example, it is well-known that, if you strike them, snakes will put forward their whole body rather than their head: how well that clarifies the meaning of the Lord's commanding us to be as crafty as snakes.[81] Obviously we ought to offer up our own bodies to persecutors, in place of our head, which is Christ.[82] This is to prevent our Christian faith being put to death should we protect our bodies and so deny God. (60) Another example: snakes can squeeze themselves through narrow spaces in a cave, and we say they have sloughed off their old skin[83] to get a new one; and that chimes with imitating the snake's craftiness and taking off the old way of being[84]—as the apostle says—in order to be clothed with a new one. As for their stripping it off by moving through narrow spaces, that chimes with the Lord saying, "enter through the narrow gate!"[85] Just as knowing the characteristics of snakes sheds light on many comparisons that scripture habitually provides concerning such creatures, so being ignorant of particular creatures that it refers to in comparisons holds back many an interpreter.

the Greek equivalent of *homo*, a "human being" undifferentiated by gender).

[85] Matthew 7:13.

Sic lapidum, sic herbarum, vel quaeque tenentur radicibus. (61) Nam et carbunculi notitia, quod lucet in tenebris, multa illuminat etiam obscura librorum, ubicumque propter similitudinem ponitur; et ignorantia berylli vel adamantis claudit plerumque intellegentiae fores. Nec aliam ob causam facile est intellegere pacem perpetuam significari oleae ramusculo quem rediens ad arcam columba pertulit, nisi quia novimus et olei lenem contactum non facile alieno humore corrumpi et arborem ipsam frondere perenniter. Multi autem propter ignorantiam ysopi, dum nesciunt quam vim habeat vel ad purgandum pulmonem vel, ut dicitur, ad saxa radicibus penetranda, cum sit herba brevis atque humilis, omnino invenire non possunt quare sit dictum, "asperges me ysopo, et mundabor."

25. (62) Numerorum etiam imperitia multa facit non intelligi translate ac mystice posita in scripturis. Ingenium quippe, ut ita dixerim, ingenuum non potest nisi movere quid sibi velit quod et Moyses et Elias et ipse dominus quadraginta diebus ieiunaverunt. Cuius actionis figuratus quidam nodus nisi huius numeri cognitione et consideratione non solvitur. Habet enim denarium quater tamquam

---

86 That is, scripture. Carbuncle is a red stone, usually identified with garnet. The belief that it sheds light persisted into medieval times.

87 Probably emerald or aquamarine.

88 From the Greek for "invincible" (ἀδάμας, *adamas*), the hardest gemstone, diamond. 89 See Genesis 8:14; Psalm 52:8, 128:3. The *Apocalypse of Moses* records a belief that the tree of life in Eden was an olive (9.3).

90 LXX, VL, and Vulg. all have "sprinkle": the Hebrew Bible says "purge." It is odd that Augustine speaks of hyssop as a purga-

It is the same with anything mineral or vegetable (things that are rooted in place). (61) For example, knowing that a carbuncle glows in the dark sheds light on many obscurities in the books,[86] anywhere that it is put for a comparison. Being ignorant about beryl[87] or adamant[88] often closes the gates of understanding. It is easy to understand the sprig of olive that the dove brought on her return to the ark as a sign of endless peace, precisely because we recognize that the smooth feel of oil is not easily mixed with a different kind of liquid, while the actual tree is always in leaf.[89] Many people, moreover, are ignorant about hyssop: they know nothing of its power to purge the lungs or, so they say, to break through rocks with its roots even though it is a humble plant, and low growing. So they are utterly mystified by the saying, "You will sprinkle[90] me with hyssop, and I shall be cleansed."[91]

25. (62) Ignorance about numbers makes many things that are set in scripture in a metaphorical or mystical way incomprehensible. Intelligence that is innate, so to speak,[92] cannot help wondering what the fact that Moses, Elijah, and the Lord himself all fasted for forty days means for itself.[93] There is certainly a knotty metaphor in that circumstance that can only be resolved through knowledge and contemplation of this number. It consists of ten

tive when his text describes it as applied externally. The verb *aspergo* can mean "to sprinkle (a liquid)" or "scatter (a solid)." See Numbers 19:18; John 19:29.

91 Psalm 51:9.

92 This modifying phrase nods to an untranslatable wordplay in *ingenium/ingenuum*.

93 Exodus 24:18; 1 Kings 19:8; Matthew 4:2.

cognitionem omnium rerum intextam temporibus. (63) Quaternario namque numero et diurna et annua curricula peraguntur: diurna matutinis, meridianis, vespertinis nocturnisque horarum spatiis; annua vernis, aestivis, autumnalibus hiemalibusque mensibus. A temporum autem delectatione, dum in temporibus vivimus, propter aeternitatem in qua vivere volumus abstinendum et ieiunandum est, quamvis temporum cursibus ipsa nobis insinuetur doctrina contemnendorum temporum et appetendorum aeternorum. (64) Porro autem denarius numerus creatoris atque creaturae significat scientiam: nam trinitas creatoris est, septenarius autem numerus creaturam indicat propter vitam et corpus. Nam in illa tria sunt, unde etiam toto corde, tota anima, tota mente diligendus est deus; in corpore autem manifestissima quattuor apparent quibus constat elementa. In hoc ergo denario dum temporaliter nobis insinuatur (id est, quater ducitur) caste et continenter a temporum delectatione vivere, hoc est quadraginta diebus ieiunare. (65) Hoc lex, cuius persona est in Moyse, hoc prophetia, cuius personam gerit Elias, hoc ipse dominus monet, qui tamquam testimonium habens ex lege et prophetis, medius inter illos in monte tribus discipulis videntibus atque stupentibus claruit.

---

[94] *Trinitas* (threeness) is used with special theological meaning from the time of Tertullian (ca. 155–ca. 220; *Prax.* 3) on.

[95] Deuteronomy 6:5: the Hebrew text lists heart, soul, and strength as the three qualities; Matthew 22:38 keeps a triad, but as heart, soul, and mind. Mark (12:30) and Luke (10:27) list four: heart, soul, mind, and strength. [96] Earth, air, fire, and water: these fundamental elements were formulated by Empedocles and later endorsed by Aristotle.

[97] That is, "forty."

times four, like the knowledge of all things interwoven with the times. (63) For example, both the daily and yearly cycles are completed in a fourfold whole: the daily one consists of morning, midday, afternoon, and nighttime hours, and the annual one consists of spring, summer, fall, and winter months. While we live in the world of time, we ought to practice abstinence and fasting from temporal pleasures for the sake of the eternity in which we long to live: even though that cycle of time is the means by which the actual instruction to spurn the world of time, and seek eternity instead, recommends itself to us. (64) Next, the number ten signifies knowledge of the creator and creation, for "trinity"[94] is associated with the creator, while the number seven points to creation with respect to life and the body: in the former there are three elements, from which comes the imperative to love God with all the heart, mind, and soul.[95] In the body, though, the corresponding elements are clearly four.[96] So while this tenfold pattern is recommended to us in terms of earthly times—specifically, multiplying by four[97]—as living in a chaste and self-controlled manner, separate from earthly pleasure, this represents our fasting for forty days.[98] (65) The law (represented by Moses), the prophets (represented by Elijah), and the Lord himself give this instruction. This was on the mountain when the Lord shone so brightly in the middle between the other two who, as it were, bore witness in accordance with the law and the prophets, while his three disciples looked on in astonishment.[99]

98 His creative exegesis begins from the importance of the number forty and works the calculation backward using knowledge of other significant numbers.

99 Matthew 17:1–4; Mark 9:2–6.

Deinde ita quaeritur, quomodo quinquagenarius de quadragenario numero existat, qui non mediocriter in nostra religione sacratus est propter pentecosten, et quomodo ter ductus propter tria tempora, ante legem, sub lege, sub gratia, et[10] propter nomen patris et filii et spiritus sancti, adiuncta eminentius ipsa trinitate, ad purgatissimae ecclesiae mysterium referatur perveniatque ad centum quinquaginta tres pisces, quos retia post resurrectionem domini in dexteram partem missa ceperunt. Ita multis aliis atque aliis numerorum formis quaedam similitudinum in sanctis libris secreta ponuntur, quae propter numerorum imperitiam legentibus clausa sunt.

26. (66) Non pauca etiam claudit atque obtegit nonnullarum rerum musicarum ignorantia. Nam et de psalterii et citharae differentia quidam non inconcinne aliquas rerum figuras aperuit, et decem cordarum psalterium non importune inter doctos quaeritur utrum habeat aliquam musicae legem quae ad tantum nervorum numerum cogat; an vero, si non habet, eo ipso magis sacrate accipiendus sit ipse numerus vel propter decalogum legis, de quo item numero si quaeratur, nonnisi ad creatorem creatu-

10 et *coni. Hill, Teaching Christianity, 164*: vel *MSS*

---

100 From the Greek word for fifty: a Jewish festival that, in Christianity, marked the pouring out of the Holy Spirit on the apostles: Acts 2.

101 The calculation, following Hill's conjecture, is (50 x 3) + 3 = 153: John 21:6–11.

102 Latin *numerorum*: Augustine is thinking of number symbolism, not mathematics.

103 Latin only says *quidam*, a coyness about naming that sup-

After this one can investigate how the number fifty proceeds from forty, and how it has a particularly sacred significance in our religion because of Pentecost.[100] Also, you can take it three times, to correspond with the three eras (before the law, under the law, and under grace), and then, by means of the threefold name (Father, Son, and Holy Spirit), you can add the Trinity itself, to make it more impressive still. This is a reference to the mystery of the Church, wholly purified, and matches the number of 153 fishes that the disciples caught when they let down the nets on the starboard side of their boat after the Lord's resurrection.[101] This is how particular secrets are placed in the holy books using many different types of numbers, and these are inaccessible to those readers who lack expertise in numerology.[102]

26. (66) Ignorance of some musical matters likewise makes for quite a few impenetrable obscurities. There is a scholar[103] who has disclosed some figurative meanings in things concerning the difference between the psaltery and the lyre, and rather elegantly so. As regards the ten-stringed psaltery,[104] experts not unreasonably question whether there is some musical principle that demands this number of strings; or whether (if there is not) the number ten should therefore be taken as having more of a religious meaning. This would be either because of the ten commandments (if that number is investigated, it can only be explained in terms of the creator and the creation) or in

ports Hill 1996's identification of Augustine's contemporary and fellow north African, the Donatist Tyconius (96–97, 165): see also *En. Ps.* 32.2.5, 56.16, 80.5.

[104] Psalm 32:2.

ramque referendus est, vel propter superius expositum ipsum denarium. (67) Et ille numerus aedificationis templi, qui commemoratur in evangelio, quadraginta scilicet et sex annorum, nescio quid musicum sonat et relatus ad fabricam dominici corporis propter quam templi mentio facta est, cogit nonnullos haereticos confiteri filium dei non falso, sed vero et humano corpore indutum. Et numerum quippe et musicam plerisque locis in sanctis scripturis honorabiliter posita invenimus.

27. (68) Non enim audiendi sunt errores gentilium superstitionum qui novem Musas Iouis et Memoriae filias esse finxerunt. Refellit eos Varro, quo nescio utrum apud eos quisquam talium rerum doctior vel curiosior esse possit. Dicit enim civitatem nescio quam, non enim nomen recolo, locasse apud tres artifices terna simulacra Musarum, quod in templo Apollinis donum poneret, ut quisquis artificum pulchriora formasset, ab illo potissimum electa emerent. (69) Ita contigisse ut opera sua quoque illi artifices aeque pulchra explicarent, et placuisse civitati omnes novem atque omnes esse emptas ut in Apollinis templo dedicarentur. Quibus postea dicit Hesiodum poetam im-

105 §§62–63. 106 Unqualified, the Jerusalem temple.

107 Hill 1991, 180n40, calls numerology an "ancient equivalent to the crossword puzzle." The verb (*sonat*) covers music and signifying.

108 See Mark 14:58; John 2:19 with Ezekiel 43:11 (*fabrica*).

109 *Haeretici*: from the Greek *hairesis*, a pejorative term in Christian Latin for adherents of an opposing (and therefore non-"catholic") party.

110 A heresy known as docetism taught that his body appeared human but was not.

terms of the number ten itself, as I explained earlier.[105] (67) Again, that number referring to the sum total of years it took to build the temple[106] (as the gospel records) is of course forty-six, which has some kind of musical resonance[107] linked to the building[108] that is the Lord's body, hence the mention of the temple. This compels some heretics[109] to admit that God's Son assumed a real, rather than a sham, human body.[110] Certainly we have found both number and music given an honorable mention in several places in the holy writings.

27. (68) We should not countenance the delusions of gentile superstitions that have fabricated nine "Muses" as the daughters of Jupiter and Memory.[111] Varro refutes them, and I doubt whether any scholar is more learned than he in such matters, or more diligent.[112] He says that a certain city (I do not remember its name) placed contracts with three sculptors, each for three likenesses of Muses to be placed as an offering in the temple of Apollo: they would select whichever sculptor's statues were the most beautiful of all and buy them from him. (69) When it came about that the three sculptors completed works that were equally beautiful, the city was delighted with all nine, and bought them all to be consecrated in the temple of Apollo. Afterward, says Varro, the poet Hesiod[113] gave

111 Arnobius, a fourth-century apologist of Berber origin, may have been Augustine's source for this: *Adversus gentes* (or *nationes*) 3.37. Gellius refers to personified Memoria, equivalent to the Greek Mnemosyne (*NA* 13.8.3).

112 Augustine takes *curiosus* in a positive sense here, but see *Confessions* (3.3.2, 10.35.54). On his use of Varro, see Hagendahl, 2:627–30.

113 Late eighth–early seventh-century BC.

posuisse vocabula. Non ergo Iuppiter novem Musas genuit, sed tres fabri ternas creaverunt. (70) Tres autem non propterea illa civitas locaverat, quia in somnis eas viderat, aut tot se cuiusquam illorum oculis demonstraverant, sed quia facile erat animadvertere omnem sonum, quae materies cantilenarum est, triformem esse natura. Aut enim voce editur, sicuti eorum est qui faucibus sine organo canunt, aut flatu, sicut tubarum et tibiarum, aut pulsu, sicut in citharis et tympanis et quibuslibet aliis quae percutiendo canora sunt.

28. (71) Sed sive ita se habeat quod Varro rettulit sive non ita, nos tamen non propter superstitionem profanorum debemus musicam fugere, si quid inde utile ad intellegendas sanctas scripturas rapere potuerimus, nec ad illorum theatricas nugas converti, si aliquid de citharis et de organis quod ad spiritalia capienda valeat disputemus. (72) Neque enim et litteras discere non debuimus quia earum deum[11] dicunt esse Mercurium, aut quia Iustitiae Virtutique templa dedicarunt, et quae corde gestanda sunt in lapidibus adorare maluerunt, propterea nobis iustitia virtusque fugienda est. Immo vero quisquis bonus verus-

[11] earum deum] repertorem μ

---

[114] *Theog.* 77–79: Euterpe, Polyhymnia, Calliope, Clio, Terpsichore, Urania, Melpomene, Thalia, and Erato.

[115] Augustine is making the point that they were not real divinities but idols (man-made objects in receipt of cult: see Isaiah 40:18–20).

[116] *Theatricus* is a transliteration from Greek, perhaps a coinage by Augustine: see *Civ.* 6.6; *Mus.* 1.4.8, 6.11 (classical Latin uses *theatralis*).

each of them their names.[114] In this version, Jupiter did not beget nine Muses: rather three sculptors created three each.[115] (70) But that city had not placed contracts for the three of them because it had seen them in dreams, or because they had disclosed to one of the citizens that they were three in number; but because it is noticeable that every sound of which song consists, has a threefold nature. It is either produced by the voice, as is the case with persons who use their mouth and throat for singing (rather than an instrument); or by wind instruments like trumpets and pipes; or by percussion, such as stringed instruments and drums and other instruments that resound on being struck.

28. (71) Whether or not this took place in the way Varro has reported, if we can grasp from music something useful for interpreting the holy scriptures, we ought not to shun it just because of the irrational beliefs of non-Christians. Nor can we be converted to the frivolities of theater shows[116] just because we are investigating something connected with lyres and instruments that helps us to understand spiritual matters. (72) After all, we have not been obliged to forgo learning our letters just because people say that the god[117] of the alphabet is Mercury. And just because people have consecrated temples to Justice and Virtue, and have chosen to worship in stone what they ought to be carrying in their heart, we must not shun justice and virtue on that account. On the contrary, anyone

[117] The Maurist emendation (or variant, *mss prope omnes earum deum dicunt*: Migne) makes Mercury the inventor of writing: Hill 1996 (165n69) remarks that, "as a sheer emendation . . . it is certainly very bold."

que christianus est, domini sui esse intellegat, ubicumque invenerit veritatem quam conferens et agnoscens etiam in litteris sacris superstitiosa figmenta repudiet, doleatque homines atque caveat qui cognoscentes deum non ut deum glorificaverunt aut gratias egerunt, sed evanuerunt in cogitationibus suis et obscuratum est insipiens cor eorum; dicentes enim se esse sapientes stulti facti sunt et immutaverunt gloriam incorruptibilis dei in similitudinem imaginis corruptibilis hominis et volucrum et quadrupedum et serpentium.

29. (73) Sed ut totum istum locum, nam est maxime necessarius, diligentius explicemus, duo sunt genera doctrinarum quae in gentilibus etiam moribus exercentur. Unum earum rerum quas instituerunt homines, alterum earum quas animadverterunt iam peractas aut divinitus institutas. Illud quod est secundum institutiones hominum partim superstitiosum est, partim non est.

30. (74) Superstitiosum est[12] quidquid institutum est ab hominibus ad facienda et colenda idola pertinens vel ad colendam sicut deum creaturam partemve ullam creaturae vel ad consultationes et pacta quaedam significationum cum daemonibus placita atque foederata, qualia sunt molimina magicarum artium, quae quidem commemorare potius quam docere assolent poetae. Ex quo ge-

[12] superstitiosum (§73) . . . superstitiosum (§74) est] *K Lond.*: superstitiosum est partim non est superstitiosum] *P* K^1

---

[118] Romans 1:21–23.

[119] Here, "gentile" must refer to "heathens/pagans," not Christians as contrasted with Jews.

who is a genuinely good Christian must understand that they are the Lord's. Wherever they find truth that they bring together and acknowledge in the holy scriptures also, they will spurn the fictions of superstition. They will lament and avoid people who know God but have not glorified him as God, or given him thanks, but who have frittered away their lives on their own opinions, their hearts blinded by folly, who by claiming to be wise have made themselves fools, and exchanged the glory of the everlasting God for the likeness of images that will perish—human beings, birds, animals, and snakes.[118]

29. (73) It is absolutely imperative that we unfold this whole subject with the utmost care. There are two types of teaching that are followed even in gentile[119] practices. One is to do with things established by human beings; the other to do with what they have observed to be already enacted or established, and which is of divine origin. Anything that is established as of human origin is partly, but not entirely, a matter of superstition.

30. (74) A superstition is anything that has been established by human beings as connected with the manufacture and worship of idols, whether this involves worship of the creation—or any part of the creation—as if it were God, or consulting of oracles and particular pacts agreed in concert with evil spirits[120] about the meanings of things, such as attempts at practicing magic arts, the kind of thing that poets are more often in the habit of recounting than

[120] *Daemonibus*: beings with an intermediate place between gods and mortals (see *Civ.* 8.14). Christianity applies the term to malevolent interstitial creatures: see Tert. *Apol.* 22; Min. Fel. *Oct.* 26–27.

nere sunt, sed quasi licentiore vanitate, haruspicum et augurum libri. (75) Ad hoc genus pertinent omnes etiam ligaturae atque remedia, quae medicorum quoque disciplina condemnat, sive in praecantationibus sive in quibusdam notis quos caracteres vocant, sive in quibusque rebus suspendendis atque illigandis vel etiam saltandis[13] quodammodo, non ad temperationem corporum, sed ad quasdam significationes aut occultas aut etiam manifestas; quae mitiore nomine physica vocant, ut quasi non superstitione inplicare, sed natura prodesse videantur, sicuti sunt inaures in summo aurium singularum, aut de strutionum ossibus ansulae in digitis, aut, cum tibi dicitur singultienti ut dextera manu sinistrum pollicem teneas.

31. (76) His adiunguntur millia inanissimarum observationum, si membrum aliquod salierit, si iunctim ambulantibus amicis lapis aut canis aut puer medius intervenerit. Atque illud quod lapidem calcant tamquam diremptorem amicitiae minus molestum est quam cum

[13] saltandis ϕ: aptandis μ Migne: salutandis S.A.

---

[121] *Haruspicum et augurum*: religious professionals who discern the divine will by (1) inspecting the entrails of sacrificed creatures; (2) observing movements of birds. Their books (*libri*) have not survived (see Cic. *Har. resp.* 18; Val. Max. 1.1).

[122] A *character* is an imprinted mark like a brand. Augustine may be drawing on Ambrose, who refers to "the occult form of a certain mark representing a superstitious symbol, to which the ancients attributed miraculous power" (*Sermo* 24.6).

[123] The manuscript history almost unanimously reads "things for dancing": a single manuscript adopted by μ (according to Migne from a codex from Rheims) gives "things for applying." S.

teaching. The books of seers and augurs[121] fall into this category, as a rather more outrageous form of counterfeit. (75) Relevant to this category are all the amulets and charms that medical science denounces: these can consist of protective incantations, or particular marks that they call symbols,[122] or things that are for hanging up, or tying on, or even for dancing in some kind of way.[123] This latter is done not to compose the body, but for the purposes of some prognostication, whether occult or even overt. All of this they refer to by a more palatable name, calling them natural science.[124] This is so that they appear to be naturally beneficial, rather than being entangled in superstition such as having earrings on the lobes of each ear, or rings of ostrich bone[125] on the fingers, or like when you tell someone who has hiccups to hold their left thumb with their right hand.[126]

31. (76) We can add thousands of ridiculous observances to these; for example, if one of your limbs happens to jerk, or if friends are walking arm in arm and a stone, or dog, or slave comes between them. The action of kicking a stone as if it had broken up the friendship does less damage than boxing the ears of a blameless slave if he runs

Atkinson emends to "things for greeting" (*salutandis*). Ritual apotropaic dancing is not in itself unlikely (see, e.g., Plut. *Vit. Thes.* 21, the *geranos*): but a word may have dropped out or been corrupted.

[124] See *Civ.* 8.6: natural science or natural philosophy tends to perceive the invisible divine via visible nature.

[125] Perhaps chosen as an exotic material, rather than with reference to its specific properties: see Jer. *Comm. Iob* 30.

[126] An example chosen to make superstitions sound ridiculous.

innocentem puerum colapho percutiunt, si pariter ambulantibus intercurrit. Sed bellum est quod aliquando pueri vindicantur a canibus. Nam plerumque tam superstitiosi sunt quidam ut etiam canem qui medius intervenerit ferire audeant, non impune; namque a vano remedio cito ille interdum percussorem suum ad verum medicum mittit! (77) Hinc sunt etiam illa: limen calcare cum ante domum suam transit; redire ad lectum si quis dum se calceat sternutaverit; redire domum si procedens offenderit; cum vestis a soricibus roditur, plus tremere suspicionem futuri mali quam praesens damnum dolere. Unde illud eleganter dictum est Catonis, qui cum esset consultus a quodam qui sibi a soricibus erosas caligas diceret, respondit non esse illud monstrum, sed vere monstrum habendum fuisse si sorices a caligis roderentur!

32. (78) Neque illi ab hoc genere perniciosae superstitionis segregandi sunt, qui genethliaci propter natalium dierum considerationes, nunc autem vulgo mathematici vocantur. Nam et ipsi, quamvis veram stellarum positionem cum quisque nascitur consectentur, et aliquando etiam pervestigent,[14] tamen quod inde conantur vel actiones nostras vel actionum eventa praedicere, nimis errant et vendunt imperitis hominibus miserabilem servitu-

[14] praevestigent *E H*

---

[127] *Mathematici.* He claims that *mathematicus* once meant, "one who scrutinizes the movements of heaven and the stars" (*Div. quaest.* 83, 45.1, with *Conf.* 4.3.4). Some "pagans" also scorned divination and prognostication (Juv. 3.42–5).

[128] That is, the requirement for accurate detail implies integrity. Hill 1996 suspects the text and suggests an Augustinian coin-

between two of you walking side by side. But it is rather neat if you ever see the slaves being avenged by the dogs—for certain people are often so superstitious that they recklessly lash out at a dog that has got between them, and not without paying the price, for occasionally this futile countermeasure results in the dog actually sending its attacker to the doctor! (77) These too are of a piece: treading on your threshold when you walk past your own house; going back to bed if you sneeze while putting your shoes on; going back home if you trip on your way out; being more frightened of impending evil than lamenting the loss before your eyes when mice have nibbled your clothing. On this subject, Cato uttered a *bon mot* when someone told him that mice had been gnawing their boots, and asked him what to make of it: he replied that that did not count as an omen—but he should certainly take it as an omen if his boots starting nibbling mice!

32. (78) Concerning this type of deadly superstition, we must make no exception for those who are called horoscopists, or popularly known now as "astrologers"[127] on account of the way they investigate birthdays. This is despite the fact that they do scrupulous research into the correct position of stars when a person is born, and sometimes even track it down precisely:[128] because they try to predict from that either our actions, or the outcomes of those actions, they are nonetheless completely deluded, as they peddle to the naïve a wretched enslavement.

age, *praevestigent*. But if the first verb, *consectentur*, means "research," the second, *pervestigent* (also at *Conf*. 13.23.34; with *mathematici*, *Div. quaest.* 41), could have an intensifying or conclusive force.

tem. (79) Nam quisque liber ad huiusmodi mathematicum cum ingressus fuerit, dat pecuniam ut servus inde exeat aut Martis aut Veneris vel potius omnium siderum; quibus illi qui primi erraverunt erroremque posteris propinaverunt, vel bestiarum propter similitudinem vel hominum ad ipsos homines honorandos imposuerunt vocabula. Non enim occulto est cum etiam propioribus recentioribusque temporibus sidus, quod appellamus luciferum, honori et nomini Caesaris Romani dicare conati sunt. (80) Et fortasse factum esset atque isset in vetustatem, nisi avia eius Venus praeoccupasset hoc nominis praedium, neque iure ullo ad heredes traiceret, quod numquam viva possederat aut possidendum petiverat. Nam ubi vacabat locus neque alicuius priorum mortuorum honore tenebatur, factum est quod in rebus talibus fieri solet. Pro Quintili enim et Sextili mensibus Iulium atque Augustum vocamus de honoribus hominum Iulii Caesaris et Augusti Caesaris nuncupatos, ut facile qui voluerit intellegat etiam illa sidera prius sine his nominibus caelo vagata esse: mortuis autem illis, quorum honorare memoriam vel coacti sunt homines regia potestate vel placuit humana vanitate, nomina eorum

---

129 *Siderum.* Augustine either does not know that Mars and Venus are planets or does not consider it relevant to his argument.

130 A reference to the twelve zodiacal constellations, named (with the exception of the scales) after animals (ram, bull, crab, lion, scorpion, goat, fish) or humans (twins, virgin, archer, boy [identifying Aquarius with Ganymede]).

131 *Lucifer* refers to the planet Venus under its morning aspect. Julius Caesar claimed descent from Venus via Iulus, son of Aeneas: see Suet. *Jul.* 6; Vell. Pat. 2.41.

(79) Any time a free man makes an approach to one of these astrologers, he is paying good money for the privilege of departing as a slave—either of Mars or Venus or maybe of all the celestial bodies:[129] those who first went astray, and bestowed their shibboleths on those who came after, imposed on them the names of animals, on the grounds of some perceived resemblance, or of people, to honor those individuals.[130] Now this is hardly remarkable, given that even in closer and more recent times the Romans attempted to dedicate the star that we call "light bearer"[131] to the honored name of Caesar. (80) Perhaps this would have taken place, and gone down in history, but for the fact of Venus, his progenitrix, already being in possession of that familial inheritance. She could not, after all, legally bequeath it to her heirs—because she had never been alive so that she could own it or seek to own it.[132] For when an office of distinction was vacant, and was not already filled by being awarded to someone who had died first, what happened was what usually happens in such cases. Instead of calling two months Quintilis and Sextilis we call them July and August, in honor of two human beings, Julius Caesar and Augustus Caesar: likewise anyone who is so inclined easily gets the point that in time past those celestial bodies still traversed the heavens even back when they had no name. But after the deaths of men whose names people were either coerced by imperial power or spurred on by human vanity into giving to those celestial bodies, it was evident to those same people that

[132] Because—being a pagan goddess—she at no time existed; though even if she had been real, the law was for mortals, and could not apply to her.

imponentes sideribus, eos ipsos sibi mortuos in caelum levare videbantur.

(81) Sed quodlibet vocentur ab hominibus, sunt tamen sidera, quae deus instituit et ordinavit, ut voluit, et est certus motus illorum, quo tempora distinguuntur atque variantur. Quem motum notare, cum quisque nascitur, quo modo se habeat, facile est per eorum inventas conscriptasque regulas, quos sancta scriptura condemnat, dicens, "si enim tantum potuerunt scire, ut possent aestimare saeculum, quomodo eius dominum non facilius invenerunt?"

33. (82) Sed ex ea notatione velle nascentium mores, actus, eventa praedicere, magnus error et magna dementia est. Et apud eos quidem qui talia dediscenda didicerunt, sine ulla dubitatione refellitur haec superstitio. Constellationes enim quas vocant notatio est siderum, quomodo se habebant cum ille nasceretur de quo isti miseri a miserioribus consuluntur. Fieri autem potest ut aliqui gemini tam sequaciter fundantur ex utero, ut intervallum temporis inter eos nullum possit apprehendi et constellationum numeris annotari. (83) Unde necesse est nonnullos geminos easdem habere constellationes, cum paria rerum, vel quas agunt vel quas patiuntur, eventa non habeant, sed plerumque ita disparia ut alius felicissimus, alius infelicissimus vivat, sicut Esau et Iacob geminos accepimus natos, ita ut Iacob, qui posterior nascebatur, manu plantam praecedentis fratris tenens inveniretur.

---

133 Wisdom 13:9.

134 *constellatio* is not a fixed group of stars in which the shape of a person or thing is detected.

they were paying divine honors to men who were, in reality, dead.

(81) Stars, then, are stars, no matter what people call them. God has ordained and constituted them in accordance with his will. They have their determined courses, which demarcate movements and shifts of time. When anyone is born, it is easy to make a record of this course, and of its circumstances, by means of the methodology they have dreamed up and codified, but holy scripture denounces people who do this, saying, "Now if they were able to know so much that they could weigh up this world, how did they not find its lord more easily?"[133]

33. (82) Wanting to predict people's character, actions, and fortune when they are born is completely mistaken, indeed it is utter insanity. Among those who have learned to unlearn such matters, this superstition is proven beyond doubt to be false. What they call an "astral configuration"[134] is a record of what the arrangement of the stars was when there took place the birth of a person about whom the desperate consult people yet more desperate than themselves. But it can happen that some twins are expelled from the womb in such quick succession that no difference of time can be detected between them, and no difference in astral configuration can be numerically recorded. (83) Inevitably some twins have identical astral configurations, but they do not have the same fortune in their affairs (either actively or passively): rather, they are often so different that one has the happiest of lives, the other a life that is utterly wretched. This was what we have learned about the birth of the twins Esau and Jacob: that he who was born second was found with his hand clutching the foot of the twin who came out first. (84) Undoubtedly

(84) Horum certe dies atque hora nascentium notari aliter non posset, nisi ut amborum constellatio esset una. Quantum autem intersit inter amborum mores, facta, labores atque successus, scriptura testis est, iam ore omnium gentium pervagata.

34. (85) Neque enim ad rem pertinet, quod dicunt ipsum momentum minimum atque angustissimum temporis, quod geminorum partum disterminat, multum valere in rerum natura atque caelestium corporum rapidissima velocitate. Etsi enim concedam ut plurimum valeat, tamen in constellationibus a mathematico inveniri non potest, quibus inspectis se fata dicere profitetur. (86) Quod ergo in constellationibus non invenit, quas necesse est unas inspiciat, sive de Iacob sive de eius fratre consulatur, quid ei prodest si distat in caelo quod temere securus infamat, et non distat in tabula quam frustra sollicitus intuetur? Quare istae quoque opiniones, quibusdam rerum signis humana praesumptione institutis, ad eadem illa quasi quaedam cum daemonibus pacta et conventa referendae sunt.

35. (87) Hinc enim fiet ut occulto quodam iudicio divino, cupidi malarum rerum homines tradantur illudendi et decipiendi pro meritis voluntatum suarum, illudentibus eos atque decipientibus praevaricatoribus angelis, quibus ista mundi pars infima, secundum pulcherrimum ordinem rerum, divinae providentiae lege subiecta est. Quibus illusionibus et deceptionibus evenit, ut istis superstitiosis et

the day and hour of their birth could only be recorded in such a way as to give them both the same astral configuration. Yet scripture witnesses to the great divide between them in terms of character, actions, hardships, and posterity, and this has been made widely known to all the nations.

34. (85) There is no relevance in any of them saying that the infinitesimal fraction of time that separates the birth of twins is of great importance when it comes to the nature of the physical world, and the extraordinarily swift movement of heavenly bodies. Even if I were to admit that it was highly significant, no astrologer can discover it in these astral configurations that he examines, before claiming to be predicting the future. (86) When he fails to discover this distinction, therefore, in those astral configurations—which he must examine as a single whole, whether it is Jacob or his brother being scrutinized—what use is it to him if, thinking himself secure, he rashly blasphemes what is far off in heaven, yet stays glued to his star chart that he scans with fruitless anxiety? This is why these beliefs too, which human arrogance has categorized as particular signs of things, must be classed together with those kind of agreements and deals with demons.

35. (87) Hence it will often happen that (by some hidden divine decree) people who are enamored of things that are evil are consigned to be mocked and deceived, just as their wills deserve. It is the transgressor angels who are mocking and deceiving them, those who have sovereignty over that lowest part of the world by a divine providence befitting the splendid scheme of things. As a result of these mockeries and deceits many matters, past and future, get affirmed in accordance with those damnable

perniciosis divinationum generibus multa praeterita et futura dicantur, nec aliter accidant quam dicuntur, multaque observantibus secundum observationes suas eveniant, quibus implicati curiosiores fiant et sese magis magisque inserant multiplicibus laqueis perniciosissimi erroris. (88) Hoc genus fornicationis animae salubriter divina scriptura non tacuit, neque ab ea sic deterruit animam, ut propterea talia negaret esse sectanda quia falsa dicuntur a professoribus eorum, sed etiam "si dixerint vobis, inquit, et ita evenerit, ne credatis eis." Non enim quia imago Samuelis mortui Saul regi vera praenuntiavit, propterea talia sacrilegia, quibus imago illa praesentata est, minus exsecranda sunt, aut quia in actibus apostolorum ventriloqua femina verum testimonium perhibuit apostolis domini, ideo Paulus apostolus pepercit illi spiritui, ac non potius feminam illius daemonii correptione atque exclusione mundavit.

36. (89) Omnes igitur artes[15] huiusmodi vel nugatoriae vel noxiae superstitionis, <et>[16] ex quadam pestifera societate hominum et daemonum, quasi pacta infidelis et dolosae amicitiae constituta, penitus sunt repudianda et fugienda christiano, "non quod idolum sit aliquid," ait apostolus, "sed quia quae immolant, daemoniis immolant et non deo; nolo autem vos socios daemoniorum fieri." (90) Quod autem de idolis et de immolationibus, quae

[15] artifices *L G P B Gr. RGr.*

[16] *Suppl. Schaüblin lac. maior. susp. RGr.*

---

[135] See also *TC* 3.9.20, with *Conf.* 1.13.21, "the love of this world is a physical infidelity to you."

[136] Deuteronomy 13:2–3.

forms of superstitious fortune-telling, which then turn out as predicted. When many of these matters turn out, for those who observe them, in accordance with their observations, they get entangled and become even more inquisitive, and enmesh themselves further and further in manifold snares of damnable delusion. (88) For the sake of our well-being, holy scripture has not remained silent about this type of prostitution of the soul.[135] It did not discourage the soul from it by saying that such practices ought not to be followed because those who professed them were telling lies, but rather, "even if they say something to you and it comes to pass, do not believe them."[136] The fact that what the ghost of the dead Samuel prophesied to king Saul was true did not make the use of such sacrilegious rituals to summon up his ghost any less deplorable. Likewise in Acts, just because a woman who told fortunes[137] gave witness to the Lord's apostles that was true, Paul did not spare the spirit that possessed her and instead cleansed the woman of that evil demon by reproving and expelling it.

36. (89) Therefore Christians must completely renounce and shun all arts of this kind whether trivial or dangerous, which have been established through particular deadly confederacies of humans and demons, as if they were an unholy alliance of false friendship, "not because an idol stands for something real," says the apostle, "but because what they sacrifice, they sacrifice to demons, not to God; I do not want you to be allied with demonic

137 *Ventriloqua* (*engastrimuthos* in Greek). See also Acts 16:16–18; Tert. *Prax.* 19.4, *Mar.* 4.25. Ventriloquists were seen as false prophets, or even as demon-possessed.

honori eorum exhibentur, dixit apostolus, hoc de omnibus imaginariis signis sentiendum est, quae vel ad cultum idolorum vel ad creaturam eiusque partes tamquam deum colendas trahunt vel ad remediorum aliarumque observationum curam pertinent; quae non sunt divinitus ad dilectionem dei et proximi tamquam publice constituta, sed per privatas appetitiones rerum temporalium corda dissipant miserorum. In omnibus ergo istis doctrinis societas daemonum formidanda atque vitanda est, qui nihil cum principe suo diabolo nisi reditum nostrum claudere atque obserare conantur. (91) Sicut autem de stellis, quas condidit et ordinavit deus, humanae et deceptoriae coniecturae ab hominibus institutae sunt, sic etiam de quibusque nascentibus vel quoquo modo divinae providentiae administratione exsistentibus rebus multi multa humanis suspicionibus quasi regulariter coniectata litteris mandaverunt, si forte insolite acciderint, tamquam si mula pariat aut fulmine aliquid percutiatur.

37. (92) Quae omnia tantum valent quantum praesumptione animorum quasi communi quadam lingua cum daemonibus foederata sunt. Quae tamen plena sunt omnia pestiferae curiositatis, cruciantis sollicitudinis, mortiferae servitutis. Non enim quia valebant animadversa sunt, sed

---

[138] 1 Corinthians 10:19–20. [139] For a detailed survey, see Tert. *Mar.* 2.10. [140] Latin, *coniectura*: the "casting together" of disparate items into a unity, making things "add up to" a whole. Augustine means that what God created, humankind interprets, and to it attributes significance.

[141] A rare meaning for Latin *suspicio:* "notion/conjecture." Augustine may be remembering Cic. *Nat. d.* 1.23.62.

[142] Epexegetic of *quae omnia*.

forces."[138] (90) What the apostle said, though, about idols and sacrifices that are carried out in their honor is what we should believe where all these imaginary signs are concerned, whether they inveigle us into the cult of idols, or into worshipping creation and its parts as if they were god, or whether they have to do with a preoccupation with antidotes and other ritual observances. These are not of divine origin. They are not established to further the love of God and neighbor as if for the common good, but instead, by means of their own personal ambition for the things of this world, they overthrow the hearts of the forlorn. In all those teachings, alliances with demons must be feared and shunned, for their whole purpose, with their leader the Devil,[139] is to close the door to our return, and bolt it. (91) Think of the stars: God created them and set them in their places, whereas human beings established interpretations of signs[140] even though they were of human origin and prone to mislead. In the same way, when it comes to all kinds of things being born or in some way coming into existence by the exercise of divine providence, many people have committed many things to writing in a way that looked, by human notions,[141] like matters of scientific method, even if they happened by chance and unpredictably: for example, if a mule were to foal, or if some object were to be struck by lighting.

37. (92) As a result of false mental assumptions, these kinds of beliefs and practices[142] have a power that is commensurate with their alliance with demons, based on a type of shared language. Nonetheless, they are teeming with lethal inquisitiveness, excruciating anxiety, and

animadvertendo atque signando factum est ut valerent. Et ideo diversis diverse proveniunt secundum cogitationes et praesumptiones suas. Illi enim spiritus qui decipere volunt talia procurant cuique qualibus eum irretitum per suspiciones et consensiones eius vident.

(93) Sicut enim, verbi gratia, una figura litterae, quae decussatim notatur, aliud apud Graecos, aliud apud Latinos valet, non natura, sed placito et consensione significandi: et ideo qui utramque linguam novit, si homini Graeco velit aliquid significare scribendo, non in ea significatione ponit hanc litteram in qua eam ponit cum homini scribit Latino; et beta uno eodemque sono apud Graecos litterae, apud Latinos holeris nomen est; et cum dico, lege, in his duabus syllabis aliud Graecus, aliud Latinus intellegit.

(94) Sicut ergo hae omnes significationes pro suae cuiusque societatis consensione animos movent, et quia diversa consensio est, diverse movent; nec ideo consenserunt in eas homines, quia iam valebant ad significationem, sed ideo valent quia consenserunt in eas. Sic etiam illa signa, quibus perniciosa daemonum societas comparatur, pro cuiusque observationibus valent. (95) Quod manifes-

---

143 In Greek a letter of the alphabet, X ("ch-"); in Latin a numeral, X (10). 144 The second letter of the alphabet, equivalent to "b" (β). 145 Augustine uses the single adjective *Latinus*, where in English we distinguish between Latin (language) and Roman (people). 146 Latin *lege* is a two-syllable imperative meaning "read/choose!" Greek *lege* (λέγε) means "say!" It neatly shows that Augustine, even when writing, thinks by hearing: to the eye, but not the ear, Latin *lĕge* is indistinguishable from *lēge* (meaning "by law").

deadly enslavement. It was not because they had any real influence that people took notice of them, but rather because they took notice, and treated them as signifying something, that they came to be influential. And so they come to matter in different ways to different people, in accordance with their own reflections and assumptions. For those spirits who are intent on deceiving provide for each individual exactly what they see will have them ensnared, corresponding to their beliefs, both personal and shared.

(93) Take this example: a single written symbol, which is made by crossing two lines, means one thing in Greek, another in Latin.[143] This is not a matter of nature. It happens because of people's cooperation and agreement over what something signifies. Thus if someone who knows both languages wanted to signify something in writing to a Greek, they would not write down this letter as having the same signifying force as when they write it for someone Roman. Again, the word "beta" has one and the same sound in Greek—where it means a letter[144]—and in Latin—where it is the word for "vegetable."[145] And again: when I say, "read,"[146] Greeks understand onc thing by those two syllables, and Romans another.

(94) So all these ways of signifying prompt mental responses in accordance with what is consensus in each person's community; and because there are varieties of consensus, people respond to them in different ways. People have not come to a consensus about such things because the things already had that significatory power; rather, they had a significatory power because people established such a consensus. Likewise also those signs through which people achieve their damnable confederacy with demons

tissime ostendit ritus augurum, qui et antequam observent et posteaquam observata signa tenuerint, id agunt ne videant volatus aut audiant voces avium, quia nulla ista signa sunt, nisi consensus observantis accedat.

38. (96) Quibus amputatis atque eradicatis ab animo christiano, deinceps idendae sunt institutiones hominum non superstitiosae, id est, non cum daemonibus, sed cum ipsis hominibus institutae. Namque omnia quae ideo valent inter homines, quia placuit inter eos ut valeant, instituta hominum sunt; quorum partim superflua luxuriosaque instituta sunt, partim commoda et necessaria. (97) Illa enim signa, quae saltando faciunt histriones, si natura, non instituto et consensione hominum valerent, non primis temporibus saltante pantomimo praeco praenuntiaret populo Carthaginis quid saltator vellet intellegi. Quod adhuc multi meminerunt senes, quorum relatu haec solemus audire. Quod ideo credendum est, quia nunc quoque, si quis theatrum talium nugarum imperitus intraverit, nisi ei dicatur ab altero quid illi motus significent, frustra totus intentus est. (98) Appetunt tamen omnes quandam similitudinem in significando, ut ipsa signa, quantum possunt, rebus quae significantur similia sint. Sed quia multis modis simile aliquid alicui potest esse, non constant talia signa inter homines nisi consensus accedat.

39. (99) In picturis vero et statuis ceterisque huiusmodi

[147] Not corporate entities but elements of a foundation, arrangement, or education.

have power according to each person's pet practices. (95) The rituals of augurs are ample proof of this. Both before they are to make their observations and after they have completed and verified them, they act in a way that avoids seeing the flights of birds or hearing their cries, because these are not treated as any kind of sign unless they secure the agreement of the person conducting the observation.

38. (96) Now that we have pruned and eradicated such practices from the mind of a Christian, the next step is to scrutinize human institutions[147]—not the superstitious ones, namely those associated with demons, but those that human beings have instituted for themselves. For all the things that matter among mortals—on the grounds that they have agreed among themselves that they should matter—are institutions of human origin: some of them are excessive and indulgent, others appropriate and requisite. (97) Take the kind of signs that actors create by their dancing: if these had meaning that was natural, not established by human agreement, then back in the beginning when a ballet dancer performed there would not be a herald telling the people of Carthage in advance what meaning the dancer intended to convey. But there are still older men aplenty who remember this, and we often hear them talking of it. This ought to be believed, because even now if someone new to such fripperies goes to the theater, unless another person explains to them what the gestures signify, their rapt attention will all be for nothing. (98) Still, everyone strives for some degree of resemblance when they want to signify something, and as a result, signs themselves are as similar as possible to the things that they signify. But because one item can be like another in a number of ways, such signs are not consistent between one person and another, unless they agree to concur.

simulatis operibus, maxime peritorum artificum, nemo errat, cum similia viderit, ut agnoscat quibus sint rebus similia. Et hoc totum genus inter superflua hominum instituta numerandum est, nisi cum interest quid eorum, qua de causa et ubi et quando et cuius auctoritate fiat. Milia denique fictarum fabularum et falsitatum, quarum mendaciis homines delectantur, humana instituta sunt. Et nulla magis hominum propria, quae a se ipsis habent, existimanda sunt, quam quaeque falsa atque mendacia.

(100) Commoda vero et necessaria hominum cum hominibus instituta sunt, quaecumque in habitu et cultu corporis ad sexus vel honores discernendos differentia placuit, et innumerabilia genera significationum sine quibus humana societas aut non omnino aut minus commode geritur; quaeque in ponderibus atque mensuris, et nummorum impressionibus vel aestimationibus, sua cuique civitati et populo sunt propria, et cetera huiusmodi, quae nisi hominum instituta essent, non per diversos populos varia essent, nec in ipsis singulis populis pro arbitrio suorum principum mutarentur.

40. (101) Sed haec tota pars humanorum institutorum, quae ad usum vitae necessarium proficiunt, nequaquam est fugienda christiano, immo etiam quantum satis est intuenda memoriaque retinenda. {40.} (102) Adumbrata enim quaedam et naturalibus utcumque similia hominum

---

148 Hill 1996 suggests mosaic as another category.

149 His last example: literary narratives. Hill 1996 notes that despite the puritanical tone, "the bark of his bigotry . . . was much more severe than its bite" (166n89).

150 *Memoria retinenda* is unlikely to mean that human institutions should be "committed to memory."

39. (99) Certainly when it comes to paintings and statues and other imitative works of this kind,[148] especially those created by the most skilled artists, no one who observes the likenesses mistakes what things they are likenesses of. This entire category should be reckoned among unnecessary institutions of human origin, except for when it makes a difference to the institutions why, and where, and when, and by whose authority they came into being. Lastly, thousands of made-up stories and fabrications are human institutions, and human beings take pleasure in the lies they tell.[149] Nothing, then, is more truly the preserve of human beings than to prize what they themselves have made, which is therefore fake and deceitful.

(100) There do exist institutions created by, and for, human beings that are worthwhile and appropriate: such as differences of dress and adornment for the body to mark distinctions between the sexes, or classes, and countless types of significations without which human civilization would fail to function altogether, or at least would go on less straightforwardly. Examples would be weights and measures, and coinage designs and values: each of these is adapted to its own polity and people, and there are other institutions of this kind which, if they had not been human creations, would be all alike across different nations, rather than being changed in each individual nation in accordance with the whim of their rulers.

40. (101) Christians must not altogether shun those human institutions that are indispensible to a productive way of life. Up to a point, in fact, we should pay attention to them, and be mindful of them.[150] {40.} (102) Certainly some things instituted by human beings have a sketchy

instituta sunt. Quorum ea quae ad societatem, ut dictum est, daemonum pertinent, penitus repudianda sunt et detestanda; ea vero quae homines cum hominibus habent, assumenda, in quantum non sunt luxuriosa atque superflua, et maxime litterarum figurae sine quibus legere non possumus, linguarumque varietas quantum satis est, de qua superius disputavimus. (103) Ex eo genere sunt etiam notae, quas qui didicerunt proprie iam notarii appellantur. Utilia sunt ista nec discuntur illicite nec superstitione implicant nec luxu enervant, si tantum occupent, ut maioribus rebus, ad quas adipiscendas servire debent, non sint impedimento.

41. (104) Iam vero illa quae non instituendo, sed aut transacta temporibus aut divinitus instituta investigando, homines prodiderunt, ubicumque discantur, non sunt hominum instituta existimanda. Quorum alia sunt ad sensus corporis, alia vero ad rationem animi pertinentia. Sed illa quae sensu corporis attinguntur, vel narrata credimus vel demonstrata sentimus vel experta conicimus.

42. (105) Quidquid igitur de ordine temporum transactorum indicat ea quae appellatur historia, plurimum nos adiuvat ad libros sanctos intellegendos, etiamsi praeter ecclesiam puerili eruditione discatur. Nam et per olympiadas et per consulum nomina multa saepe quaeruntur a

---

151 *litterarum figurae*, "shapes of letters."

152 §50.

153 See *Conf.* 10.27.38.

likeness to those found in nature. Among these, those that tend to involve associating with demons must be utterly rejected and denounced, as I said before. But we can adopt those in which human beings associate with one other, as long as they involve no excessive self-indulgence. Above all this means letters of the alphabet,[151] without which reading is impossible; and different languages according to need, as we have already discussed.[152] (103) In the same category are shorthand symbols, and people who have learned them are correctly called stenographers. Institutions like these are useful: there is nothing wrong with learning them, and they neither entangle people in superstition nor corrupt them with self-indulgence, provided that they take up only such time as does not detract from more important matters that they should be helping them to master.

41. (104) Now for those phenomena that human beings have produced, not by instituting them, but instead discovering them—either events in human time or those instituted by divine providence. Wherever these are learned, they ought not to be considered as institutions of human origin. Some of them relate to the physical senses,[153] others to the capacity for rational thought. Those that pertain to the physical senses we either believe when we are told about them, or we experience them when shown them, or we discuss them when we have experienced them.

42. (105) What we call "history," therefore, points to whatever has to do with events taking place in a temporal sequence. It is most advantageous in helping us to interpret the holy books, even if such history is learned outside the context of faith, and at a rudimentary level. For we

nobis; et ignorantia consulatus, quo natus est dominus et quo passus est, nonnullos coegit errare, ut putarent quadraginta sex annorum aetate passum esse dominum, quia per tot annos aedificatum templum esse dictum est a Iudaeis, quod imaginem dominici corporis habebat. (106) Et annorum quidem fere triginta baptizatum esse retinemus auctoritate evangelica; sed postea quot annos in hac vita egerit, quamquam textu ipso actionum eius animadverti possit, tamen ne aliunde caligo dubitationis oriatur, de historia gentium collata cum evangelio, liquidius certiusque colligitur. Tunc enim videbitur non frustra esse dictum quod quadraginta sex annis templum aedificatum sit, ut cum referri iste numerus ad aetatem domini non potuerit, ad secretiorem instructionem humani corporis referatur, quo indui propter nos non dedignatus est unicus dei filius, per quem facta sunt omnia.

43. (107) De utilitate autem historiae, ut omittam Graecos, quantam noster Ambrosius quaestionem solvit, calumniantibus Platonis lectoribus et dilectoribus, qui dicere ausi sunt omnes domini nostri Iesu Christi sententias, quas mirari et praedicare coguntur, de Platonis libris

---

[154] These are the best known methods of date calculation in Classical Greece (starting from the first Olympiad, in 776 BC) and Rome, respectively. Eusebius of Caesarea (d. 339 BC) was the first Christian chronographer (as well as historian): his *Chronological Canons* did for dating systems what Origen's *Hexapla* had done for Bible versions a century before.

[155] See above, §67. Another calculation put his age at forty-nine because of John 8:57: see Iren. *Haer.* 2.22.4–6, with Devin L. White, "Jesus at Fifty: Irenaeus on John 8:57 and the Age of Jesus," *JThS* 71 (2020): 158–63.

often research many matters by means of Olympiads and names of consuls.[154] It was ignorance of consular dating that led some to mistake the dates when the Lord was born, and when he suffered; so they believed that the Lord suffered when he was forty-six[155] years old, because the Jews claimed that as the number of years it took to build the temple,[156] and the temple was a symbol of the Lord's body. (106) We have it on gospel authority[157] that he was about thirty years of age when he was baptized. As for how many years his life continued after that, we could work it out from the actual course of his actions: but still to avoid any fog of doubt arising from some other source, this is more clearly and accurately deduced from comparing Classical historiography with the gospel. That will show that it was not a mistake to state that the temple was built in forty-six years. So, as that number could not be correlated with the Lord's age, it must instead be correlated with some more abstruse teaching to do with the human body which he, the only Son of God, by whom all things were made, did not regard as beneath him to assume on our account.[158]

43. (107) As for the practical advantages of history (setting aside Greek historical writers) our own Ambrose solved a really knotty problem when readers and supporters of Plato laid false information by having the cheek to claim that all the propositions[159] of our Lord Jesus Christ,

156 John 2:20. 157 Luke 3:23.

158 John 1:3, the "incarnation," or *enanthropesis*, with an echo of the Nicene Creed in "by whom all things were made."

159 *Sententias*. The term can also mean "decision" or "opinion." See 2.22.56n78.

eum didicisse, quoniam longe ante humanum adventum domini Platonem fuisse negari non potest. (108) Nonne memoratus episcopus, considerata historia gentium, cum reperisset Platonem Hieremiae temporibus profectum fuisse in Aegyptum, ubi propheta ille tunc erat, probabilius esse ostendit quod Plato potius nostris litteris per Hieremiam fuerit imbutus, ut illa posset docere vel scribere quae iure laudantur? Ante litteras enim gentis Hebraeorum, in qua unius dei cultus eminuit,[17] ex qua secundum carnem venit dominus noster, ne ipse quidem Pythagoras fuit, a cuius posteris Platonem theologiam didicisse isti asserunt. Ita consideratis temporibus fit multo credibilius istos potius de litteris nostris habuisse quaecumque bona et vera dixerunt, quam de Platonis dominum Iesum Christum, quod dementissimum est credere.

44. (109) Narratione autem historica cum praeterita etiam hominum instituta narrantur, non inter humana instituta ipsa historia numeranda est, quia iam quae transierunt nec infecta fieri possunt, in ordine temporum habenda sunt, quorum est conditor et administrator deus. Aliud est enim facta narrare, aliud docere facienda. Historia facta narrat fideliter atque utiliter, libri autem harus-

[17] eminuit *P* γ: emicuit *K Lond. R* μ

---

160 A potentially serious charge. Authenticity is bound up with antiquity, so this, combined with the intellectual prestige of Plato, was a challenge that needed refuting, even by means of historical fabrication.

161 Augustine does not acknowledge that Jeremiah was a Jewish writer, he simply appropriates him.

162 See *Civ.* 6.5: Augustine quotes Varro on three types of

which they cannot help admiring and propagating, were cribbed from the Platonic canon—just because it is undeniable that Plato lived long before the Lord came in human form.[160] (108) Didn't the aforementioned bishop look into world history, and discover that Plato had gone to Egypt in the days when Jeremiah the prophet was there, and then demonstrate that in all likelihood Plato had been steeped in our[161] literature under the influence of Jeremiah, which gave him to ability to produce those teachings and writings that are rightly applauded? Not even Pythagoras antedates the writings of the Hebrew people, in which worship of the one God has been so remarkable, and from which came our own Lord according to the flesh—and Plato's followers insist that he learned his theology[162] from Pythagoras' successors. Once we have looked into the chronology of events, it is far more likely that those people got from the writings that belong to us whatever they affirmed to be good and true, than that the Lord Jesus Christ got it from Plato's. To believe that would be the height of madness.

44. (109) When human institutions from the past are chronicled in a historical narrative, that history ought not to be counted as a human institution. This is because what has already happened and cannot be undone exists in a temporal sequence whose creator and governor is God. It is one thing to narrate past deeds, and quite another to teach people what they should do. History narrates past deeds in a way that can be trusted, and that bears practical

theology (using the Latinized Greek term, *theologia*): as evident from stories, poetry, and myths; from the physical world; and from the religious practices of institutions like the state.

picum et quaeque similes litterae facienda vel observanda intendunt docere, monitoris audacia, non indicis fide.

45. (110) Est etiam narratio demonstrationi similis, qua non praeterita sed praesentia indicantur ignaris. In quo genere sunt quaecumque de locorum situ naturisque animalium, lignorum, herbarum, lapidum aliorumve corporum scripta sunt. De quo genere superius egimus eamque cognitionem valere ad obligatione scripturarum solvenda docuimus, non ut pro quibusdam signis adhibeantur, tamquam ad remedia vel machinamenta superstitionis alicuius; nam et illud genus iam distinctum ab hoc licito et libero separavimus. Aliud est enim dicere: tritam istam herbam si biberis, venter non dolebit, et aliud est dicere: istam herbam collo si suspenderis, venter non dolebit. Ibi enim probatur contemperatio salubris, hic significatio superstitiosa damnatur. (111) Quamquam ubi praecantationes et invocationes et caracteres non sunt, plerumque dubium est utrum res quae alligatur aut quoquo modo adiungitur sanando corpori, vi naturae valeat, quod libere adhibendum est, an significativa quadam obligatione proveniat, quod tanto prudentius oportet cavere christianum, quanto efficacius prodesse videbitur. Sed ubi latet qua causa quid valeat, quo animo quisque utatur interest,

---

163 A method of divination by means of examination of internal organs of sacrificed animals, especially the liver.

164 Augustine does not mean that history says nothing of the past, but that its purpose is to educate the present. 165 §59.

166 The first mention of "signs" proper since §98.

167 *Contemperatio* is a coinage from *temperatio* (well-balanced mixture).

fruit, whereas books of haruspicy[163] and similar works of literature, set out to teach people what action to take and what signs to monitor; but with foolhardy counsel, not trustworthy directions.

45. (110) Historical narrative is like a presentation, which reveals, to those who are uninformed, not past but present events.[164] We include within this literary category writings on geography, zoology, botany, geology, or other physical phenomena.[165] We have mentioned this category above, and argued that it improves our understanding of how to solve conundrums in the scriptures; but not so that we receive them like some sort of signs,[166] as if they were cures or stratagems drawn from some superstition. We have set that category apart and distinguished it from what is permissible and unrestricted. It is one thing to say, "if you drink this powdered herb, your stomach will stop hurting." But it is quite another to say, "If you hang this herb around your neck, your stomach will stop hurting." In the former case, a healthy concoction[167] is approved; in the latter, a superstitious signifier is condemned. (111) Although in the absence of charms, invocations, and magical symbols, it is mostly doubtful whether something one ties on to the body or attaches to it in some other way with the aim of restoring bodily health, has any physical effect, such a practice can be employed without restriction. But if it produces an improvement through what the act of binding signifies, this is something that, the more effective it appears, the more Christians would be wise to shun it. Where the reason why a thing works is unclear, the attitude of the user makes a difference insofar curing the

dumtaxat in sanandis vel temperandis corporibus sive in medicina sive in agricultura.

46. (112) Siderum autem cognoscendorum non narratio sed demonstratio est, quorum perpauca scriptura commemorat. Sicut autem plurimis notus est lunae cursus, qui etiam ad passionem domini anniversarie celebrandam sollemniter adhibetur, sic paucissimis ceterorum quoque siderum vel ortus vel occasus vel alia quaelibet momenta sine ullo sunt errore notissima. (113) Quae per se ipsa cognitio, quamquam superstitione non alliget, non multum tamen ac prope nihil adiuvat tractationem divinarum scripturarum et infructuosa intentione plus impedit; et quia familiaris est perniciosissimo errori fatua fata cantantium, commodius honestiusque contemnitur. Habet autem praeter demonstrationem praesentium etiam praeteritorum narrationi simile aliquid, quod a praesenti positione motuque siderum, et in praeterita eorum vestigia regulariter licet recurrere. Habet etiam futurorum regulares coniecturas, non suspiciosas et ominosas, sed ratas et certas; non ut ex eis aliquid trahere in nostra facta et eventa temptemus, qualia genethliacorum deliramenta sunt, sed quantum ad ipsa pertinet sidera. (114) Nam sicut is qui computat lunam, cum hodie inspexerit quota sit et ante quotlibet annos quota fuerit et post quotlibet annos quota futura sit, potest dicere, sic de unoquoque siderum,

---

168 See below, §115. 169 Pasch, or Easter, is a Christian festival tied to both lunar and solar time: following the Council of Nicaea in 325, Easter is calculated as the first Sunday after the first full moon after the vernal equinox.

170 Augustine had been interested in possible methods of predicting the future: *Conf.* 4.3.4–6; 7.6.8–9.

body or restoring it to harmony is concerned. This is true in medicine and agriculture.[168]

46. (112) Knowledge of the stars, however, is something we have pointed out to us, rather than being told it as a story, and scripture hardly mentions them at all. Almost everyone notices the phases of the moon, and we even make use of them for the solemn annual celebration of the Lord's passion;[169] but very few people are likewise sufficiently well-versed in the rising or setting or other types of movements of the stars to avoid making mistakes. (113) Although such expertise does not of itself implicate people in superstition, it is not much help—virtually none at all—when it comes to dealing with the holy writings; instead this is hindered by such fruitless fixation. Since this witless wittering about fate goes hand-in-hand with deadly error, it is safer and more prudent to censure it. Besides indicating the present time, this expertise has something in common with the narration of past events: namely that from the position and movement of stars in the present, it is also possible for the traces of their past movements to recur in a methodical pattern. This makes reliable interpretations of future events possible.[170] Instead of being dubious and foreboding, they are reasonable and definite; not to make us try and extract anything from them to apply to our own actions and future outcomes—that way lie the ravings of horoscopists—but insofar as they relate specifically to the stars. (114) Take the case of those who make lunar calculations: when they have observed the moon's dimensions today, they can reckon what those same dimensions were, as many years in the past, and as many years in the future, as you like. In the same way, pick any

qui ea perite computant, respondere consuerunt. De qua tota cognitione, quantum ad usum eius attinet, quid mihi videretur aperui.

47. (115) Artium etiam ceterarum quibus aliquid fabricatur, vel quod remaneat post operationem artificis ab illo effectum, sicut domus et scamnum et vas aliquod atque alia huiuscemodi, vel quae ministerium quoddam exhibent operanti deo, sicut medicina et agricultura et gubernatio, vel quarum omnis effectus est actio, sicut saltationum et cursionum et luctaminum; harum ergo cunctarum artium de praeteritis experimenta faciunt etiam futura conici. Nam nullus earum artifex membra movet in operando, nisi praeteritorum memoriam cum futurorum exspectatione contexat. (116) Harum autem cognitio tenuiter in ipsa humana vita cursimque usurpanda est, non ad operandum, nisi forte officium aliquod cogat, de quo nunc non agimus, sed ad iudicandum, ne omnino nesciamus quid scriptura velit insinuare, cum de his artibus aliquas figuratas locutiones inserit.

48. (117) Restant ea quae non ad corporis sensus, sed ad rationem animi pertinent, ubi disciplina regnat disputationis et numeri; sed disputationis disciplina ad omnia genera quaestionum quae in litteris sanctis sunt penetranda et dissolvenda, plurimum valet. Tantum ibi cavenda est libido rixandi et puerilis quaedam ostentatio deci-

---

171 Or "government"; Latin *gubernatio*.

172 Repeated fine motor skills (e.g., practicing sport or music), colloquially known as "muscle memory."

173 A process of reasoning, rather than a dispute.

star you like: people who have the skill to calculate these things are well-versed in getting the answer right. I have now disclosed, I believe, as much as is relevant for practical purposes about this whole area of expertise.

47. (115) There are other skills used for constructing things—this could be something concrete that the maker has completed and that goes on existing after their work is done, such as houses or benches or implements or anything of that kind; or the kind of things that offer a service of some kind to God as he is about his work, such as medicine and agriculture and navigation;[171] or things that are entirely to do with types of movement, like dancing, running, and wrestling. Where all these skills are concerned, future instances can be deduced from past ones, for every expert practitioner, at their work, disposes their limbs in a way that meshes the memory of past actions with the anticipation of future ones.[172] (116) In the lives of mortals, however, only a slight, cursory degree of expertise in these matters need be acquired. For we are not making a point here about how to perform those skills (unless perhaps compelled by some obligation), but about exercising judgment, so that we do not completely miss the point that scripture means to make known to us, when it adopts particular metaphorical language derived from these skills.

48. (117) We still have to deal with matters pertaining not to our physical senses but to our mental reasoning. Here the disciplines of argument[173] and mathematics reign supreme. But the discipline known as argument is most valuable for fathoming and solving all kinds of problems in the sacred texts. All the same we must beware of taking pleasure in bickering, and that childish showing-off

piendi adversarium. Sunt enim multa quae appellantur sophismata, falsae conclusiones rationum et plerumque ita veras imitantes, ut non solum tardos, sed ingeniosos etiam minus diligenter attentos decipiant. (118) Proposuit enim quidam, dicens ei cum quo loquebatur, "Quod ego sum, tu non es." At ille consensit, verum enim erat ex parte, vel eo ipso quod iste insidiosus, ille simplex erat. Tum iste addidit, "ego autem homo sum." Hoc quoque cum ab illo accepisset, conclusit dicens "tu igitur non es homo." Quod genus captiosarum conclusionum scriptura, quantum existimo, detestatur illo loco, ubi dictum est, qui sophistice loquitur odibilis est. Quamquam etiam sermo non captiosus, sed tamen abundantius quam gravitatem decet, verborum ornamenta consectans, sophisticus dicitur.

49. (119) Sunt etiam verae conexiones ratiocinationis falsas habentes sententias, quae consequuntur errorem illius cum quo agitur, quae tamen ad hoc inferuntur a bono et docto homine, ut in his erubescens ille cuius errorem consequuntur, eundem relinquat errorem; quia, si in eodem manere voluerit, necesse est etiam illa quae damnat tenere cogatur. Non enim vera inferebat apostolus cum

---

[174] Latin (from Greek) *sophismata*: a *sophisma* is originally any kind of trick or device, later one with a pejorative nuance, "quibble, sophism," in contrast with a valid argument.

[175] Latin *proposuit*: the verb can mean the first premise or the main theme of an argument. "Syllogism" is usually a form of reasoning from generals to particulars.

[176] Ecclesiasticus 37:20; 2 Timothy 2:16.

[177] *Ratiocinationis*: logic.

at duping one's antagonist. For what we call fallacies[174] are commonplace, both arguments with invalid conclusions and those that on the whole mimic true ones: as a result they dupe not only the slow-witted, but also clever people who are not paying proper attention. (118) There was a man who began a syllogism[175] by saying to his interlocutor, "What I am, you are not." But when the latter agreed (it was true to some extent, if only because one of them was crafty, the other naïve), the former moved to the next logical step, "But I am a human being"; and when the other agreed to that also, the first person clinched the argument, saying, "Therefore you are not a human being." In my opinion, scripture abhors this type of misleading conclusion to a syllogism, in the verse that says, "whoever speaks in a sophistical way is detestable."[176] All the same, we use the word "sophistical" not just when speech is misleading, but also when it is more florid than the seriousness of an occasion demands or tries too hard for elaborate vocabulary.

49. (119) Examples occur in reasoning[177] of consequences[178] that are valid:[179] but that are based on false propositions; these follow on from a mistake made by one's interlocutor. All the same, those conclusions are deduced by the good and the learned to this end: namely to make interlocutors (those whose mistake they are following) blush for their mistake and abandon it. This is because if they insist on not budging they are obliged to uphold what they condemn also. For example: the apostle Paul was not

[178] *Conexiones*, steps in a logical sequence.
[179] *Verae*. Augustine uses it for "true" and "valid."

diceret, "neque Christus resurrexit," et illa alia, "inanis est praedicatio nostra, inanis est et fides vestra"; et deinceps alia: quae omnino falsa sunt, quia et Christus resurrexit, et non erat inanis praedicatio eorum qui hoc annuntiabant, nec fides eorum qui hoc crediderant. Sed ista falsa verissime conectebantur illi sententiae, qua dicebatur non esse resurrectionem mortuorum. (120) Istis autem falsis repudiatis, quoniam vera erant,[18] si mortui non resurgunt, consequens erit resurrectio mortuorum. Cum ergo sint verae conexiones, non solum verarum, sed etiam falsarum sententiarum, facile est veritatem conexionum etiam in scholis illis discere, quae praeter ecclesiam sunt. Sententiarum autem veritas in sanctis libris ecclesiasticis vestiganda est.

50. (121) Ipsa tamen veritas conexionum non instituta, sed animadversa est ab hominibus et notata, ut eam possint vel discere vel docere, nam est in rerum ratione perpetua et divinitus instituta. Sicut enim qui narrat ordinem temporum, non eum ipse componit, et locorum situs aut naturas animalium vel stirpium[19] vel lapidum qui ostendit, non res ostendit ab hominibus institutas; et ille qui demonstrat sidera eorumque motus, non a se vel ab homine aliquo rem institutam demonstrat; sic etiam qui

[18] erant *P K*: erunt *L B Bam.*

[19] stirpium *K*[1] *Lond. M*: serpentium *P K*

---

[180] 1 Corinthians 15:13–14.

[181] *Verae.*

[182] Perhaps his most controversial conclusion so far: that Classical philosophy can be put to Christian use. Arguing in the next

making a true deduction by saying, "neither has Christ risen," and that other remark, "our preaching is worthless; worthless also is your faith,"[180] and so on. These remarks are wholly false, both because Christ did rise again, and because the preaching of those who brought tidings of the fact was not worthless, nor was the faith of those who had believed it. But those false remarks were a logical consequence of that proposition in which it was stated that there is no resurrection of the dead. (120) Once those falsehoods are rejected, since they were true if the dead do not rise, then the outcome must be that the resurrection of the dead is true. So although there are valid[181] logical steps from false propositions as well as from true ones, it is easy, even in those philosophical schools that are outside the Church, to learn what is true in logical reasoning.[182] We must, however, pursue the truth of propositions in the Church's holy books.

50. (121) Still, that same true logical reasoning was not established by human beings. Instead they observed it and took note of how they could teach or learn it; for there exists, in the reasoning nature of things, truth that is eternally established, and of divine origin. People who write history in a temporal sequence are not themselves history's composer; while those who reveal the facts of geography, or zoology, or botany, or geology, are not revealing things that are of human origin; and those who identify the stars and their movements are not identifying anything that they themselves (or anyone else) have established. In just the same way, when a person states that when a con-

section that this kind of knowledge is not a human creation helps him to avoid seeing a positive in "pagan" higher education.

dicit, cum falsum est quod consequitur, necesse est ut falsum sit quod praecedit, verissime dicit neque ipse facit ut ita sit, sed tantum ita esse demonstrat.

(122) Ex hac regula illud est quod de apostolo commemoravimus; praecedit enim non esse resurrectionem mortuorum, quod dicebant illi quorum errorem destruere volebat apostolus. Porro illam sententiam praecedentem, qua dicebant non esse resurrectionem mortuorum, necessario sequitur, neque Christus resurrexit. Hoc autem quod sequitur falsum est; Christus enim resurrexit. falsum est ergo et quod praecedit. Praecedit autem non esse resurrectionem mortuorum; est igitur resurrectio mortuorum. (123) Quod totum breviter ita dicitur: si non est resurrectio mortuorum, neque Christus resurrexit; Christus autem resurrexit, est igitur resurrectio mortuorum. Hoc ergo, ut consequenti ablato auferatur etiam necessario quod praecedit, non instituerunt homines, sed ostenderunt. Et haec regula pertinet ad veritatem conexionum, non ad veritatem sententiarum.

51. (124) Sed in hoc loco de resurrectione cum ageretur, et regula conexionis vera est, et ipsa in conclusione sententia. In falsis autem sententiis conexionis veritas est isto modo: faciamus aliquem concessisse: si animal est cochlea, vocem habet. Hoc concesso, cum probatum fuerit vocem cochleam non habere, quoniam consequenti ablato illud quod praecedit aufertur, concluditur non esse animal cochleam. Quae sententia falsa est, sed ex concesso

---

[183] That is, a "consequent"; the counterpart to an "antecedent."

sequence is false its premise must be false too, that person is speaking the absolute truth: of themselves they are not making it so, but are simply indicating that it is so.

(122) From this principle comes what we have mentioned about the apostle Paul: his premise was that there is no resurrection of the dead, which was what the people whose error the apostle wished to demolish used to say. On the other hand, it must follow from that earlier proposition, which stated that there is no resurrection of the dead, that Christ has not arisen either. The later step in the argument is false, for Christ has arisen. So what preceded it, namely the argument that there is no resurrection of the dead, must be false too. Therefore the resurrection of the dead is really true. (123) This precept can be summarized thus: if there is no resurrection of the dead, then Christ has not arisen either; but Christ has arisen, therefore there is a resurrection of the dead. Thus if a point that follows on[183] is dismissed, its antecedent also must be dismissed; and this is not something that human beings have established, they have merely pointed it out. This principle applies to the truth of a logical sequence, not to the truth of propositions.

51. (124) On this point, however, when the resurrection was under discussion, if the method of the logical sequence is true, the proposition in the actual conclusion is too. When it comes to false propositions, the truth of a logical sequence is like this: let us hypothesize that someone has granted this point: "if a snail is an animal, it has a voice." On this hypothesis, once it has been proved that a snail has no voice, it must be concluded that a snail is not an animal; because once a consequent has been dismissed its antecedent is dismissed too. The proposition is false,

falso vera conclusionis conexio. (125) Veritas itaque sententiae per se ipsam valet, veritas autem conexionis ex eius cum quo agitur opinione vel concessione consistit. Ideo autem, ut supra diximus, infertur vera conexione quod falsum est, ut eum cuius errorem corrigere volumus paeniteat sensisse[20] praecedentia, quorum consequentia videt esse respuenda. Iam hinc intellegere facile est, sicut in falsis sententiis veras, sic in veris sententiis falsas conclusiones esse posse. Fac enim aliquem proposuisse: "si iustus est ille, bonus est," et esse concessum; deinde assumpsisse: "non est autem iustus"; quo item concesso, intulisse conclusionem: non est igitur bonus. (126) Quae tametsi vera sint omnia, non est tamen vera regula conclusionis. Non enim sicut ablato consequenti aufertur necessario quod praecedit, ita etiam ablato praecedenti aufertur necessario quod consequitur. Quia verum est cum dicimus: si orator est, homo est, ex qua propositione si assumamus: "non est autem orator," non erit consequens cum intuleris:[21] "non est igitur homo."

52. (127) Quapropter aliud est nosse regulas conexionum, aliud sententiarum veritatem. In illis discitur quid sit consequens, quid non consequens, quid repugnans. Consequens est: si orator est, homo est; inconsequens: si

[20] sensisse ϕ: concessisse *F R* μ
[21] intuleris *Lond.*: intulerimus *P B D F K*

---

[184] In logic, *assumere* is used of the adding of a secondary proposition to a syllogism. Augustine may have drawn his terminology from Cicero.
[185] Or "deduction."

but from a false hypothesis the logical sequence leading to the conclusion is valid. (125) The truth of a proposition, therefore, has its own validity, whereas the truth of a logical sequence depends on what an interlocutor believes or concedes. There is a purpose, as we just noted, in drawing a false inference from a valid logical sequence: to make the person whose mistake we want to correct sorry for having given assent to initial propositions, now that the need to reject the conclusions that follow from them is apparent. That makes it easy to understand that just as there can be true conclusions to false propositions, so there can also be false conclusions to true propositions. Suppose that someone makes a proposition: "if that man is just, he is good"; and that point gains assent. Then a supplementary proposition is added:[184] "but he is not just." If this is agreed to, the inference leads to a conclusion, "therefore he is not good." (126) Even though each of the points made is true, the method for reaching a conclusion is still not valid. It is one thing when, after a consequence is abandoned, all that precedes it is necessarily abandoned too; but quite another if, after an antecedent point is abandoned, you necessarily abandon the consequent. For example: it is true when we say, "if he is an orator, he is a human being"; but if we add in another point, "but he is not an orator," it will not follow to draw the inference, "therefore he is not a human being."

52. (127) This is why it is one thing to know the rules for logical sequences, and another the know the truth of propositions. Regarding the latter, we have to learn the meaning of the terms, "valid inference,"[185] "invalid inference," and "illogicality." This is a valid inference: "if he is an orator, he is a man." This is an invalid inference: "if he

homo est, orator est; repugnans: si homo est, quadrupes est. Hic ergo de ipsa conexione iudicatur. In veritate autem sententiarum ipsae per se sententiae, non earum conexio consideranda est; sed veris certisque sententiis, cum incertae vera conexione iunguntur, etiam ipsae certae fiant necesse est. (128) Quidam autem sic se iactant, cum veritatem conexionum didicerint, quasi sententiarum ipsa sit veritas. Et rursus quidam plerumque retinentes veram sententiam male se contemnunt quia leges conclusionis ignorant; cum melior sit qui novit esse resurrectionem mortuorum quam ille qui novit consequens esse ut, si resurrectio mortuorum non est, "neque Christus resurrexerit."

53. (129) Item scientia definiendi, dividendi atque partiendi, quamquam etiam rebus falsis plerumque adhibeatur, ipsa tamen falsa non est neque ab hominibus instituta, sed in rerum ratione comperta. Non enim, quia et fabulis suis eam poetae et opinionibus erroris sui vel falsi philosophi vel etiam heretici, hoc est falsi Christiani, adhibere consuerunt, propter ea falsum est neque in definiendo neque in dividendo aut partiendo aliquid complectendum esse quod ad rem ipsam non pertinet, aut aliquid quod

is a man, he is an orator." This is an illogicality: "if he is a man, he is a quadruped." In this instance we have to make a judgment about the logical sequence. When it comes to the truth of propositions, though, it is the propositions themselves, not the logical sequence linking them that must be taken into account; but in the case of true and indisputable propositions, when they are joined to one that is disputed (though in a valid logical sequence), even those propositions themselves inevitably become indisputable. (128) There are people who brag of having learned the validity of a logical sequence, as if that were the same as the validity of propositions. There are also people who, on the whole, uphold a true proposition, but unfairly upbraid themselves because they do not know the rules for drawing logical conclusions—although anyone is better off knowing that there is a resurrection of the dead than someone who knows to call the statement, "if there is no resurrection of the dead, then neither has Christ has arisen," a logical sequence.

53. (129) So it is that although knowledge of definition, classification, and categorization is also often employed for deceitful purposes, it is not of itself deceitful. Nor is it something established by human beings; rather, it is embedded in the coherence of the universe. Just because poets have been in the habit of employing it in their own mythical stories, and both philosophers and heretics (that is to say false Christians) have been in the habit of employing it for their own mistaken beliefs, it is not, on that account, something false. Nor is it something to be eschewed for the purposes of defining, classifying, or categorizing, on the grounds that it is irrelevant to a particular matter, or that it is relevant but it would be improper

pertinet praetereundum. Hoc verum est, etiam si ea quae definiuntur aut distribuuntur vera non sint. (130) Nam et ipsum falsum definitur, cum dicimus falsum esse significationem rei non ita se habentis, ut significatur, sive alio aliquo modo; quae definitio vera est, quamvis falsum verum esse non possit. Possumus etiam dividere, dicentes duo esse genera falsi: unum eorum quae omnino esse non possunt, alterum eorum, quae non sunt, quamvis esse possint. (131) Nam qui dicit septem et tria undecim esse, id dicit, quod omnino esse non potest; qui autem dicit Kalendis, verbi gratia, Ianuariis pluisse, tametsi factum non sit, id tamen dicit quod fieri potuerit. Definitio ergo et divisio falsorum potest esse verissima, quamvis falsa ipsa utique vera non sint.

54. (132) Sunt etiam quaedam praecepta uberioris disputationis quae iam eloquentia nominatur, quae nihilominus vera sunt, quamvis eis possint etiam falsa persuaderi; sed quia et vera possunt non est facultas ipsa culpabilis, sed ea male utentium perversitas. Nam neque hoc ab hominibus institutum est, ut caritatis[22] expressio conciliet auditorem, aut ut facile quod intendit insinuet brevis et aperta narratio, et varietas eius sine fastidio teneat intentos; et ceterae huiusmodi observationes, quae sive in falsis sive in veris causis verae sunt tamen in quan-

[22] caritatis ϕ γ: veritatis μ Kn.

---

[186] Latin *significatio*: Augustine begins to tie his general argument about philosophical method to the specific case of signifying. [187] A momentary glimpse of Augustine the pre-Christian professor of rhetoric.

[188] That is, *captatio benevolentiae*.

to use it. This remains true, even if the subjects of the definition or classification are not true. (130) We do in fact define falsehood itself, when we call "false" the signification[186] of something that is not in reality what it is signified as being (or some similar definition like that); that definition is true, but the actual falsehood cannot be so. Again, we can classify it, by declaring that there are two types of falsehood: one of which is things that are completely impossible, the other is things that are not in fact true, but theoretically could be. (131) For example: someone who says that seven and three make eleven is saying what is altogether impossible. But someone who says that on the first of January (for example) it rained, is saying something that could have happened, even though in fact it did not. The definition and classification of falsehoods, therefore, can have everything to do with the truth, even though the falsehoods themselves contain no truth whatsoever.

54. (132) There is another kind of discourse, a more rewarding[187] one, which has its particular rules: we call it eloquence. Its rules are true, even though they may be used to persuade people of what is false; but because they can also be true, eloquence is not of itself a blameworthy ability—unlike the wrongheadedness of those who misuse it. It was not established by human beings to function in such a way that an expression of regard would win over a listener,[188] or a concise and clear explanation would easily impart what it aimed to; or a mixed style would hold the attention without becoming boring; or other observations of this kind. Whether what prompts them is false or true, these observations are themselves true, insofar as they bring it to pass that knowledge or belief is imparted, or

tum vel sciri vel credi aliquid faciunt, aut ad expetendum fugiendumve animos movent, et inventae potius quod ita se habeant quam ut ita se haberent institutae.

55. (133) Sed haec pars cum discitur, magis ut proferamus ea quae intellecta sunt quam ut intellegamus adhibenda est. Illa vero conclusionum et definitionum et distributionum plurimum intellectorem adiuvat: tantum absit error, quo videntur sibi homines ipsam beatae vitae veritatem didicisse cum ista didicerint; (134) quamquam plerumque accidat ut facilius homines res eas assequantur propter quas assequendas ista discuntur, quam talium praeceptorum nodosissimas et spinosissimas disciplinas. Tamquam si quispiam dare volens praecepta ambulandi, moneat non esse levandum posteriorem pedem, nisi cum posueris priorem, deinde minutatim quemadmodum articulorum et poplitum cardines oporteat movere, describat. Vera enim dicit, nec aliter ambulari potest; sed facilius homines haec faciendo ambulant quam animadvertunt cum faciunt, aut intellegunt cum audiunt. (135) Qui autem ambulare non possunt, multo minus ea curant, quae nec experiendo possunt attendere. Ita plerumque citius ingeniosus videt non esse ratam conclusionem quam praecepta eius capit, tardus autem non eam videt, sed multo minus, quod de illa praecipitur.

Magisque in his omnibus ipsa spectacula veritatis saepe delectant, quam ex eis in disputando aut iudicando

---

189 This parity of intellectual integrity between philosophy and rhetoric is important to Augustine's defense of education in classical scholarly disciplines, but it is not much to modern taste.

190 Rhetoric.

191 An exemplary summary of how to teach motor skills.

they move the spirit either to press on or to retreat. It has been discovered that they work in this way; they have not been humanly established with this end in view.[189]

55. (133) When we learn this subject,[190] we use it more for communicating what we have understood rather than for understanding things. That subject, philosophy, is particularly helpful to someone who wants to understand conclusion, definition, and arrangement: only they must avoid making the mistake of seeing themselves as people who have learned the truth about a blessed life, just because they have learned those philosophical topics. (134) All the same it often happens that people achieve the object that they had in view when they learned those subjects more easily than they do the knotty, thorny discipline of such rules; as if some person, say, wanted to give instructions for walking, by advising you not to lift up your back foot until your front foot was placed on the ground, and then going into minute detail about how you should move your toe and knee joints. Their account is accurate, and this is the only way in which walking is possible; but human beings find it easier to walk by doing these things than by noticing how they are done, or understanding them by hearing about them.[191] (135) People who are unable to walk, though, take very little interest in motions that they cannot achieve even if they try. So someone intelligent is quicker at perceiving that a conclusion does not add up than they are at grasping the theory behind it; whereas someone dull-witted sees nothing of the truth of the conclusion, far less the underlying theory.

Where all these rules are concerned, actual perceptions of truth are often more pleasing to us than the help they provide us with for constructing arguments and

adiuvamur, nisi forte quod exercitatiora reddunt ingenia, si etiam maligniora aut inflatiora non reddant, hoc est, ut aut decipere verisimili sermone atque interrogationibus ament, aut aliquid magnum, quo se bonis atque innocentibus anteponant, se assecutos putent qui ista didicerint.

56. (136) Iam vero numeri disciplina cuilibet tardissimo clarum est quod non sit ab hominibus instituta, sed potius indagata et inventa. Non enim sicut primam syllabam Italiae, quam brevem pronuntiaverunt veteres, voluit Vergilius et longa facta est, ita quisquam potest efficere cum voluerit ut ter terna aut non sint novem aut non possint efficere quadratam figuram, aut non ad ternarium numerum tripla sint, ad senarium sescupla, ad nullum dupla, quia intellegibiles numeri semissem non habent. (137) Sive ergo in se ipsis considerentur sive ad figurarum aut ad sonorum aliarumve motionum leges numeri adhibeantur, incommutabiles regulas habent, neque ullo modo ab hominibus institutas, sed ingeniosorum sagacitate compertas.

---

[192] Evangeliou, "Man as the Most Mimetic Animal," 3:175–86. [193] *Aen.* 1.2. [194] Verg. *Aen.* 4.361, *Italiam non sponte sequor.* In Latin poetry, each syllable can have a naturally short vowel, like the "I" in the English name "Ĭtaly," or a naturally long one, like the "o" in "Rome." But unlike English poetry, it also has vowels that are short by nature but are sounded as long because they are followed by two consonants. [195] By arranging three rows of three dots, ergo, a "square number."

[196] Latin *intellegibiles*: the sense demands this translation, but that usage, not found elsewhere, is itself called "unintelligible" (Hill 1996, 167n114). It may be a colloquial usage, rooted in the difficulty of expressing fractions in the Roman numeral system

drawing conclusions—except, perhaps, for the training that gets our wits into better shape.[192] But it had better not make us too malicious or cocky: by which I mean having fun fooling people with spurious disputation and syllogisms, or thinking that we have achieved something impressive by learning those techniques, to make ourselves superior to good and decent people.

56. (136) It is now evident even to the meanest intelligence that the study of numbers is not something of human origin, but rather something that has been ferreted out and discovered. It is not the same as Virgil[193] wanting the first syllable of "Italy," which people of old pronounced with a short vowel, to be taken as long:[194] no one can make it happen that three threes are not nine, or do not create a square shape,[195] or are not three times what three is, or one and a half times six, and not double another integer (because odd[196] numbers are not divisible by two). (137) So whether we scrutinize numbers as they are in themselves, or whether we use them to formulate laws of geometry or music or other motions, their principles are immutable,[197] and they have certainly not been established by human beings, but instead have been discovered by the sharp thinking of notably clever people.

(which had no decimal point). On the problem of infinite divisibility, see *Ep.* 3.2; *De lib. arb.* 2, 8, 22.

[197] Varro uses (perhaps coins) this word with reference to unchanging principles of language, *omnia verbi principia incommutabilia, Ling.* 9.99; see also Cic. *Har. resp.* 2.57.33. *Incommutabilis* is rare in Classical Latin, but Augustine uses it repeatedly here (see also *Retr.* 1.9; *Ep.* 3.3; *Trin.* 7.1), perhaps following Ambrose (*De. fug. saec.* 1.6.35).

57. (138) Quae tamen omnia quisquis ita dilexerit ut iactare se inter imperitos velit, et non potius quaerere unde sint vera, quae tantummodo vera esse persenserit, et unde quaedam non solum vera, sed etiam incommutabilia, quae incommutabilia esse comprehenderit, ac sic a specie corporum usque ad humanam mentem perveniens, cum et ipsam mutabilem invenerit, quod nunc docta, nunc indocta sit, constituta tamen inter incommutabilem supra se veritatem, et mutabilia infra se cetera, ad unius dei laudem atque dilectionem cuncta convertere, a quo cuncta esse cognoscit, doctus videri potest, esse autem sapiens nullo modo.

58. (139) Quam ob rem videtur mihi studiosis et ingeniosis adulescentibus et timentibus deum beatamque vitam quaerentibus, salubriter praecipi ut nullas doctrinas, quae praeter ecclesiam Christi exercentur, tamquam ad beatam vitam capessendam secure sequi audeant, sed eas sobrie diligenterque diiudicent; et si quas invenerint ab hominibus institutas, varias propter diversam voluntatem instituentium et ignotas propter suspiciones errantium, maxime si habent etiam cum daemonibus initam societatem per quarundam significationum quasi quaedam pacta atque conventa, repudient penitus et detestentur; alienent etiam studium a superfluis et luxuriosis hominum institutis. Illa vero instituta hominum, quae ad societatem conviventium valent, pro ipsa vitae huius necessitate non

---

[198] A reference to esoteric language, rites, and meaning: this stern warning encourages the reader to accept that other forms of "pagan" learning can safely be distinguished and used.

57. (138) Some people take such delight in these matters that they are eager to boast about themselves in the company of the uneducated, rather than to investigate how things are true, when all they have is an impression that they are true; and how certain things are not only true but also immutable, once they have grasped that they are immutable. So then they leave behind the appearance of physical objects and come to the human mind, and find this too to be mutable (because it has understanding at one moment, and ignorance the next), in a position between immutable truth above themselves, and everything else, which is mutable, beneath them. But they do not turn all these things to praise and love of the one God, from whom they know that all things have their origin. These people can appear learned, but by no means can they be wise.

58. (139) I believe that it is beneficial, therefore, to instruct young people who are diligent and intelligent, and who fear God and seek the blessed life, that they cannot safely take the risk of seeking that life of bliss by adopting any teachings that fall outside the Church of Christ. On the contrary, they should weigh them up with care and caution, and if they find that any of those teachings are of human origin—diverse because the wills of those who established them were not all alike, unreliable because of the conjectures of those in error—most of all if they involve making a pact with demons through some kind of deal or contract about special ways of signifying,[198] they should utterly renounce and abominate them. Moreover, they should keep the focus of their studies away from anything of human origin that is unnecessary and decadent. But they need not discount human institutions that are a force for social cohesion by supplying the necessaries of this life.

neglegant. (140) In ceteris autem doctrinis, quae apud gentes inveniuntur, praeter historiam rerum vel praeteriti temporis vel praesentis ad sensus corporis pertinentium, quibus etiam utilium artium corporalium experimenta et coniecturae annumerantur, et praeter rationem disputationis et numeri, nihil utile esse arbitror. In quibus omnibus tenendum est, "ne quid nimis," et maxime in his quae ad corporis sensus pertinentia volvuntur temporibus et continentur locis.

59. (141) Sicut autem quidam de verbis omnibus et nominibus Hebraeis et Syris et Aegyptiis, vel si qua alia lingua in scripturis sanctis inveniri potest, quae in eis sine interpretatione sunt posita, fecerunt ut ea separatim interpretarentur; et quod Eusebius fecit de temporum historia propter divinorum librorum quaestiones, quae usum eius flagitant; quod ergo hi fecerunt de his rebus, ut non sit necesse christiano in multis propter pauca laborare; sic video posse fieri, si quem eorum qui possunt benignam sane operam fraternae utilitati delectet impendere, ut quoscumque terrarum locos quaeve animalia vel herbas atque arbores sive lapides vel metalla incognita speciesque

---

199 See Proem 5.13n.

200 Latin *historia rerum*: what we call history would be *historia rerum gestarum*. In Christian Latin, *historia* can mean a non-allegorical account. He has already described the usefulness of narrative history (§§109–10).

201 Or "speculation": *coniectura*. See §§91, 119. Elsewhere, he uses the term both positively (*coniectura placidae voluntatis*, *Civ.* 14.26) and negatively (*non prophetico spiritu, sed coniectura mentis humanae*, *Civ.* 18.52).

202 Ter. *An.* 1.61. See Wilkins, "ΜΗΔΕΝ ΑΓΑΝ," 144–48.

(140) As for other types of learning that are found among the pagans,[199] apart from straightforward accounts[200] of physical reality (either contemporary or past) that have to do with the bodily senses, in which we include the practice and theory[201] of useful physical skills, I judge them (except for logical reasoning and mathematics) to contain nothing of value. In all such matters, most of all those to do with the physical senses, involved in the world of time and space, our rule must be, "Nothing to excess."[202]

59. (141) There are people who have made a separate study of all the words and names in Hebrew, Aramaic,[203] and Egyptian[204] (or any other language that may be found in the holy writings) that are set there without being translated. There is also what Eusebius[205] produced on historical chronology, to assist with questions at issue in the sacred books, which is essential reading. With respect to these subjects, such people have rendered it unnecessary for the Christian to do a lot of spadework for modest returns: and so I see it as possible that, if any of them with the ability were generous enough to go to the trouble of so kind a service to brotherly convenience, whatever geographical locations, or animals, or plants and trees, or stones and metals, were unknown, and whatever topics

203 From "Aram," an ancient name for Syria. The later form of Aramaic (a Semitic language related to Hebrew) is called Syriac. Augustine does not mention Greek because it is not an obscure language for him (but cf. *Conf.* 1.13.20).

204 He may be thinking of names or titles, such as "pharaoh" (*pharao* in Latin: from the Egyptian meaning "great house"), "Susannah" ("lily"), or Potiphar (*Putipher*: from the Egyptian "he whom the sun gives."

205 See above, §105, n. 154.

quaslibet scriptura commemorat, ea generatim digerens, sola exposita litteris mandet. (142) Potest etiam de numeris fieri ut eorum tantummodo numerorum exposita ratio conscribatur, quos divina scriptura meminit. Quorum aliquid aut omnia iam forte facta sunt, sicut multa quae a bonis doctisque christianis elaborata et conscripta non arbitrabamur, invenimus; sed sive propter turbas neglegentium sive propter invidorum occultationes latent. (143) Quod utrum de ratione disputandi fieri possit ignoro; et videtur mihi non posse, quia per totum textum scripturarum colligata est nervorum vice; et ideo magis ad ambigua solvenda et explicanda, de quibus post loquemur, legentes adiuvat, quam ad incognita signa cognoscenda, de quibus nunc agimus.

60. (144) Philosophi autem qui vocantur, si qua forte vera et fidei nostrae accommodata dixerunt, maxime Platonici, non solum formidanda non sunt, sed ab eis etiam tamquam ab iniustis possessoribus in usum nostrum vindicanda. Sicut enim Aegyptii non tantum idola habebant et onera gravia, quae populus Israhel detestaretur et fugeret, sed etiam vasa atque ornamenta de auro et de argento et vestem, quae ille populus exiens de Aegypto sibi potius

---

206 In Latin, the whole of §141 is a single (convoluted) sentence, possibly a mark of incomplete revision.

207 *Nervorum* includes ligaments, tendons, and nerves.

208 The meaning of the term in Greek, which makes the role description ("philosophers") palatable to a Christian readership sensitive to the taint of "pagan" learning.

209 Zeugma: idols for their own religion, and the burden of the making of bricks without straw imposed on the Israelites (Exodus 5:18).

scripture records, they could order and classify them, explaining them individually and committing them to writing.[206] (142) This could also be done for numbers, composing a methodical record of only those numbers that sacred scripture mentions. Some part, or perhaps even all, of these tasks have been accomplished already, like the many painstaking works we have found that we were not aware that good and learned Christians had written. These remain obscure, either because the common crowds overlook them, or because they suppress them out of envy. (143) But whether this could be done for logical reasoning I do not know. Indeed it seems to me that it is not possible, because it is interwoven with the whole text of the scriptures, like the sinews of a body.[207] Therefore it is of more help to readers in clarifying and explaining ambiguities (which we shall discuss later) than coming to understand unknown signs, to which we turn now.

60. (144) There are men who are called "lovers of wisdom,"[208] particularly those of the school of Plato, who may happen to speak truths that are consonant with our faith. Not only is there no reason to fear those teachings of theirs, but we should in fact be reappropriating them for our own use, like property returned to its rightful owners. Think of the Egyptians. They had idols and heavy burdens[209] that the people of Israel abominated and shrank from; but they also had vessels and decorative objects made of gold and silver, and fine[210] robes, and when the Israelites departed from Egypt they secretly appropriated

[210] Implied, not stated: see, e.g., Ezekiel 16:3; Revelation 18:12.

tamquam ad usum meliorem clanculo vindicavit, non auctoritate propria, sed praecepto dei, ipsis Aegyptiis nescienter commodantibus ea, quibus non bene utebantur. (145) Sic doctrinae omnes gentilium non solum simulata et superstitiosa figmenta gravesque sarcinas supervacanei laboris habent, quae unusquisque nostrum, duce Christo, de societate gentilium exiens, debet abominari atque devitare; sed etiam liberales disciplinas usui veritatis aptiores et quaedam morum praecepta utilissima continent: deque ipso uno deo colendo nonnulla vera inveniuntur apud eos. Quod eorum tamquam aurum et argentum, quod non ipsi instituerunt sed de quibusdam quasi metallis divinae providentiae quae ubique infusa est, eruerunt, et, quo perverse atque iniuriose ad obsequia daemonum abutuntur, cum ab eorum misera societate sese animo separat, debet ab eis auferre christianus ad usum iustum praedicandi evangelii. Vestem quoque illorum, id est, hominum quidem instituta, sed tamen accommodata humanae societati, qua in hac vita carere non possumus, accipere atque habere licuerit in usum convertenda christianum.

61. (146) Nam quid aliud fecerunt multi boni fideles nostri? Nonne aspicimus quanto auro et argento et veste suffarcinatus exierit de Aegypto Cyprianus et doctor suavissimus et martyr beatissimus? Quanto Lactantius?

---

211 See *En. Ps.* 104.28 on Psalm 104.37$^{\text{Vulg.}}$ (= 105.37^{MT}); also *Div. quaest.* 53. 212 Gold, silver, and fine linen (clothing) are collectively emblematic of worldly riches: see Ezekiel 16:10; Zechariah 14:14; Revelation 18:12. 213 In earlier Latin, *suffarcinatus* was an uncomplimentary word meaning "stuffed." Augustine repurposed it, perhaps following Jerome (*Ep.* 58.2).

them for themselves as if for a nobler purpose. This was not on their own initiative, but in obedience to a divine decree. What is more, the Egyptians themselves unwittingly supplied those objects that they had made no good use of.[211] (145) So the teachings of the gentiles as a whole contain not just sham and imaginary superstitions, and a heavy burden of futile endeavor—which every single one of us who are under Christ's leadership, and have abandoned fellowship with gentiles, ought to denounce and spurn—but also enlightened teachings that serve the purposes of truth and contain beneficial moral precepts. We find in them, moreover, a number of truths about worshiping only one god. For them this is like treasures of gold and silver that they did not create but dug up from some mines, so to speak, of the divine providence that is all around us. In their outrageous wickedness, they misuse it for their worship of demons: though Christians ought instead to separate themselves in their minds from fellowship with such wretches, and to appropriate that treasure from them, repurposing it for a righteous service, namely preaching the gospel. There is also their fine clothing,[212] in other words the institutions of human origin that befit human society, and that—in this life—we cannot do without. It is permissible to adopt and maintain these, adapting them to a Christian purpose.

61. (146) What else, after all, have many of our good and faithful believers done? Surely we can see how that most appealing of teachers, that most blessed of martyrs, Cyprian, came out of Egypt laden[213] with great piles of silver and gold and fine clothing? And Lactantius, Victori-

Quanto Victorinus, Optatus, Hilarius, ut de vivis taceam? Quanto innumerabiles Graeci? Quod prior ipse fidelissimus dei famulus Moyses fecerat, de quo scriptum est quod eruditus fuerit omni sapientia Aegyptiorum. (147) Quibus omnibus viris superstitiosa gentium consuetudo, et maxime illis temporibus cum Christi recutiens iugum christianos persequebatur, disciplinas quas utiles habebat numquam commodaret si eas in usum colendi unius dei, quo vanus idolorum cultus excinderetur, conversum iri suspicarentur. Sed dederunt aurum et argentum et vestem suam exeunti de Aegypto populo dei, nescientes quemadmodum illa quae dabant, in Christi obsequium redderentur. Illud enim in exodo factum sine dubio figuratum est, ut hoc praesignaret, quod sine praeiudicio alterius aut paris aut melioris intellegentiae dixerim.

62. (148) Sed hoc modo instructus divinarum scripturarum studiosus, cum ad eas perscrutandas accedere coeperit, illud apostolicum cogitare non cesset: "scientia inflat, caritas aedificat." Ita enim sentit, quamvis de Aegypto dives exeat, tamen nisi pascha egerit salvum se esse non posse. Pascha autem nostrum immolatus est Christus, nihilque magis immolatio Christi nos docet quam illud quod ipse clamat, tamquam ad eos quos in Aegypto sub Pharaone videt laborare, "venite ad me, qui laboratis et

---

214 Doignon, "Nos bons hommes de foi," 795–805. The nonappearance of Ambrose in this list, Martin argues, gives a *terminus ante quem* of April 397 for this section of *TC* 2.

215 Acts 7:22.

216 1 Corinthians 8:1. See 2.20.46n66.

217 1 Corinthians 5:7.

218 *Immolatio*, pointing to the Christian eucharistic sacrifice.

nus, Optatus, Hilary[214]—to say nothing of those still living? And countless Greek writers? This was what Moses himself, God's most faithful servant, had been the first to do; and it was written of him that he was learned in all the wisdom of the Egyptians.[215] (147) The pagans, with their superstitious ways—more than ever in those days when they threw off the yoke of Christ and started persecuting Christians—would never have made those branches of their learning that they considered useful available to all these men if they had suspected that they were going to be redirected toward the practice of worshipping a single god, thus obliterating the vain worship of idols. Yet they bestowed their own gold and silver and fine clothing on the people of God as they were leaving Egypt, little suspecting how what they bestowed would be converted to the service of Christ, which undoubtedly took place at the exodus as a prophetic sign action, foreshadowing this act of appropriation. I must declare that this is without prejudice to any other interpretation, either equal or better.

62. (148) Even so, when a person who is trained in this method, and devoted to the holy writings, begins to approach them in detail, they should keep constantly in mind that saying of the apostle: "knowledge puffs up, love builds up."[216] Although someone may get out of Egypt with their treasures, they are aware that they cannot be saved unless they celebrate the Passover. But the Passover sacrificed for us is Christ,[217] and beyond everything else the sacrifice of Christ[218] teaches us the meaning of what he himself declares (as if speaking to those he sees laboring in Egypt in subjection to Pharaoh): "Come to me, you who are la-

onerati estis, et ego vos reficiam. Tollite iugum meum super vos et discite a me, quoniam mitis sum et humilis corde, et invenietis requiem animis vestris. Iugum enim meum lene est et sarcina mea levis est": quibus, nisi mitibus et humilibus corde, quos non inflat scientia, sed caritas aedificat? (149) Meminerint ergo eorum qui pascha illo tempore per umbrarum imaginaria celebrabant; cum signari postes sanguine agni iuberentur, ysopo fuisse signatos. Herba haec humilis et mitis est, et nihil fortius et penetrabilius eius radicibus, ut in caritate radicati et fundati possimus comprehendere cum omnibus sanctis quae sit latitudo et longitudo et altitudo et profundum, id est, crucem domini. Cuius[23] latitudo dicitur in transverso ligno, quo extenduntur manus; longitudo, a terra usque ad ipsam latitudinem, quo a manibus et infra totum corpus affigitur; altitudo, a latitudine sursum usque ad summum, quo adhaeret caput; profundum vero, quod terrae infixum absconditur. (150) Quo signo crucis omnis actio christiana

23 (§149) cuius . . . (§150) plenitudinem *om.* Eug.

---

219 Matthew 11.28-30: close to Vulg. but not identical.

220 The dative and ablative plural of *anima* (soul) is regularly *animis* up to the time of Vulg. (not *animabus*, as in Vulg. and later Latin).

221 Latin *quibus*, following from the verb "declares" before the quotation.

222 Latin *per umbrarum imaginaria*, literally, "through the representations of shadows."

223 Latin *signari*: Augustine brings forward figurative language in scripture, the subject matter of book three.

224 Exodus 12:22.

boring and overburdened, and I will refresh you.[219] Take my yoke upon you, and learn from me, since I am mild and humble of heart, and you will find rest for your souls.[220] For my yoke is easy, and my baggage is light." Who else is he speaking to[221] if not to the mild and humble of heart, whom knowledge does not puff up, but rather love builds up? (149) They ought to remember the people who were celebrating the Passover in those days by means of shadowy reflections:[222] who, when they were commanded to make a sign[223] on their doorposts with the blood of a lamb, were themselves signed with hyssop.[224] It is a humble and mild plant, and nothing is stronger or more penetrating than its roots, with the result that we have been rooted and grounded in love, so that we can grasp (with all the saints[225]) what is the breadth and length and height and depth, in other words, the Lord's cross.[226] Its breadth relates to the crossbeam, upon which his hands are outstretched; its length to the upright, from the earth to the crossbeam, to which his whole lower body from the hands down is nailed; the height is from the crossbeam all the way to the top, where his head rests; and of course the depth is that part fixed into the ground out of sight. (150) On that sign, the cross, every Christian act is represented:

225 Ephesians 3:18. "Saints" (*sancti*) is a regular term for ordinary Christians.

226 The nexus of meaning he detects is not obvious to a modern reader, being more creative and imaginative than historical or logical. In this period the meaning of the cross was transitioning from gallows (negative) to spiritual icon (positive). From here to the sentence of §150 ending with *omnem plenitudinem* is omitted by one of the earliest textual witnesses, Eugippius.

describitur: bene operari in Christo et ei perseveranter inhaerere, sperare caelestia, sacramenta non profanare. Per hanc actionem purgati valebimus cognoscere etiam supereminentem scientiae caritatem Christi, qua aequalis est patri, per quem facta sunt omnia, ut impleamur in omnem plenitudinem dei. Est etiam in ysopo vis purgatoria, ne inflante scientia de divitiis ab Aegypto ablatis, superbe aliquid pulmo tumidus anhelet: "asperges me," inquit, "ysopo et mundabor, lavabis me et super nivem dealbabor. Auditui meo dabis exsultationem[24] et laetitiam." Deinde consequenter annectit ut ostendat purgationem a superbia significari ysopo: exsultabunt ossa humiliata.

63. (151) Quantum autem minor est auri argenti vestisque copia, quam de Aegypto secum ille populus abstulit, in comparatione divitiarum quas postea Hierosolymae consecutus est, quae maxime in Salomone rege ostenduntur, tanta fit cuncta scientia quae quidem est utilis, collecta de libris gentium, si divinarum scripturarum scientiae comparetur. Nam quidquid homo extra didicerit si noxium est ibi damnatur; si utile est ibi invenitur. Et cum ibi quisque invenerit omnia quae utiliter alibi didicit,

[24] exsultationem *P Lond.*: gaudium *K Vulg.*

---

[227] Hyssop was used as a purgative; it developed a spiritual meaning ("purify").

[228] John 1:3; but the precise wording draws on the Latin version of the Nicene Creed. See also *Civ.* 9.9.

[229] See Ephesians 1:10, 1:23, 3:19, 4:13.

[230] The psalmist (traditionally identified as King David).

to devote oneself to Christ and steadfastly cleave to him; to set one's hope on heavenly things; not to desecrate the sacraments. Doing this will cleanse[227] us, and give us strength to recognize the love of Christ that makes him equal to the Father through whom all things were made,[228] so that we may be filled with all the fullness[229] of God. Hyssop has a purgative quality to it that prevents the lungs from breathing in and becoming swollen with pride because of knowledge puffing up over those treasures carried away from Egypt: "You will sprinkle me," he[230] says, "with hyssop and I shall be cleansed, you shall wash me, and I shall be whiter than snow."[231] You will make me hear rejoicing and gladness. Then he links in sequence what ensues, to show that hyssop signifies being cleansed from pride—then the bones that have been abased will rejoice.

63. (151) The amount of gold, silver, and fine clothing which the Hebrews carried away with them from Egypt, was just as modest, in comparison with the riches that they acquired later at Jerusalem (which reached their height in the time of King Solomon),[232] as was all the knowledge (the useful part anyway) gathered from the books of the gentiles, in comparison with the knowledge of the holy writings. This is because anything that someone learns from elsewhere, if it is dangerous, is condemned; while if it is useful, it will be found there. And when someone has found, in scripture, all the things that they can usefully learn elsewhere, they will also find there, in superabun-

[231] Psalm 51:9–10.
[232] 1 Kings 10:14–27.

multo abundantius ibi inveniet ea quae nusquam omnino alibi, sed in illarum tantummodo scripturarum mirabili altitudine et mirabili humilitate discuntur.

Hac igitur instructione praeditum cum signa incognita lectorem non impedierint, mitem et humilem corde, subiugatum leniter Christo et oneratum sarcina levi, fundatum et radicatum et aedificatum in caritate quem scientia inflare non possit, accedat ad ambigua signa in scripturis consideranda et discutienda, de quibus iam tertio volumine dicere aggrediar, quod dominus donare dignabitur.

dance, things that are to be found absolutely nowhere else, but that we learn only in the wonderful exaltation and wonderful humility of those scriptures.

So when unknown signs have not caused stumbling, because readers are mild and humble of heart, having submitted calmly to Christ's yoke, and shouldered his baggage with ease; when they are founded and rooted and built up in that love, knowledge cannot puff them up; then they must advance, equipped with this training, to the studying and scrutiny of ambiguous signs in scripture. For I shall now proceed to explain, in the third volume of this work, whatever the Lord is kind enough to entrust to me on this subject.

LIBER III

1. (1) Homo timens deum voluntatem eius in scripturis sanctis diligenter inquirit. Et ne amet certamina pietate mansuetus; praemunitus etiam scientia linguarum, ne in verbis locutionibusque ignotis haereat, praemunitus etiam cognitione quarumdam rerum necessariarum, ne vim naturamve earum, quae propter similitudinem adhibentur, ignoret; adiuvante etiam codicum veritate, quam sollers emendationis diligentia procuravit, veniat ita instructus ad ambigua scripturarum discutienda atque solvenda.

(2) Ut autem signis ambiguis non decipiatur, quantum per nos instrui potest—fieri autem potest ut istas vias, quas ostendere volumus, tamquam pueriles vel magnitudine ingenii, vel maioris illuminationis claritate derideat—sed tamen, ut coeperam dicere, quantum per nos instrui valet, qui eo loco animi est ut per nos instrui valeat, sciat ambiguitatem scripturae aut in verbis propriis esse aut in translatis, quae genera in secundo libro demonstravimus.

2. (3) Sed cum verba propria faciunt ambiguam scrip-

---

[1] Luke 15:8.

[2] For the idea that faith dispels conflict, see Iren. *Haer.* 2.27.

[3] Classical Latin literature does not use *discutio* in the sense of its English derivative "discuss," but it is common in ecclesiastical Latin. [4] A hefty dollop of irony here.

BOOK III

1. (1) Anyone who fears God searches diligently[1] for his will in the holy scriptures. Devotion makes them gentle, with no love for conflict.[2] They must be fortified by their knowledge of languages, so as not to get stuck over unfamiliar words and expressions. They must also be fortified by expertise in certain essential things, so as not to be uninformed about their force and nature when they are used for comparative purposes. The accuracy of the books, which expert and diligent textual criticism have secured, will be their helper. Then let them come, fully trained, to discuss[3] and untangle ambiguities in the scriptures.

(2) To avoid their being fooled by ambiguous signs (insofar as we are able to train them)—after all it could happen that they scorn those paths that we wish to show them as childish (because they are so immensely clever or brilliantly perspicacious[4])—still, as I was just beginning to say, insofar as we have the power to train them and they are in a fit state of mind to embrace our training, they ought to know that ambiguity in scripture consists in words used either literally or metaphorically. We indicated these types in our second book.

2. (3) When words used in their literal sense[5] make

[5] Applied to words, the adjective *proprius* indicates an original, concrete, root, or literal (to use four figurative terms) meaning, not a tropical, or figurative, usage. See Gell. *NA* 2.6.5, 9.1.8.

turam, primo videndum est ne male distinxerimus aut pronuntiaverimus. Cum ergo adhibita intentio incertum esse perviderit quomodo distinguendum aut quomodo pronuntiandum sit, consulat regulam fidei, quam de scripturarum planioribus locis et ecclesiae auctoritate percepit; de qua satis egimus cum de rebus in libro primo loqueremur. (4) Quod si ambae vel etiam omnes, si plures fuerint partes ambiguitatis, secundum fidem sonuerint, textus ipse sermonis a praecedentibus et consequentibus partibus, quae ambiguitatem illam in medio posuerunt, restat consulendus, ut videamus cuinam sententiae, de pluribus quae se ostendunt, ferat suffragium eamque sibi contexi patiatur.

3. (5) Iam nunc exempla considera. Illa haeretica distinctio, "in principio erat verbum et verbum erat apud deum et deus erat,"[1] ut alius sit sensus: verbum hoc erat in principio apud deum, non vult deum verbum confiteri. Sed hoc regula fidei refellendum est qua nobis de trinitatis aequalitate praescribitur, ut dicamus "et deus erat verbum," deinde subiungamus "hoc erat in principio apud deum."

4. (6) Illa vero distinctionis ambiguitas neutra parte resistit fidei et ideo textu ipso sermonis diiudicanda est, ubi ait apostolus, "et quid eligam ignoro. Compellor autem

[1] deus erat verbum] *P K Mon. S Par.* Kn.

---

[6] In this period, layout and punctuation of written texts were rudimentary and inconsistent.

[7] On the "rule of faith," see p. 224, n. 37.

[8] John 1:1.

[9] The "threeness" of God is first expressed in Greek, *trias*, by

scripture ambiguous, however, the first thing to see to is whether we have arranged the phrasing or punctuation incorrectly.[6] Then, when a closer look has confirmed that it is still unclear how to phrase or punctuate it, readers should consult the rule of faith,[7] as discerned from more straightforward passages of scripture, and from the authority of the Church. We dealt sufficiently with this when we discussed things in the first book. (4) But if both meanings, or even all meanings (if there are multiple elements of ambiguity) are consonant with the faith, we are obliged to make reference to the actual context, the preceding and following sections that have that ambiguity set in their midst: then let us see which interpretation, out of the many that present themselves, gets our vote and allows itself to be integrated into the passage.

3. (5) Consider the following examples. There is that heretical phrasing: "in the beginning was the Word and the Word was with God and was God."[8] It was done to give an alternative meaning: "this Word was in the beginning with God," shows reluctance to declare that the Word is God. But the rule of faith ought to refute this, for it dictates to us the equality of persons in the Trinity,[9] so that we say, "and the Word was God," then add, "he was in the beginning with God."

4. (6) There is that ambiguity of phrasing in which neither division into sections is at odds with the faith, which must therefore be decided on the actual context of what is said, such as when the apostle says, "and I do not know what to choose. I feel the force of both options, hav-

Theophilus of Antioch (d. ca. 184), *Apology to Autolycus* 2.15. On the Latin equivalent, see p. 326, n. 94.

ex duobus, concupiscentiam habens dissolvi et esse cum Christo—multo enim magis optimum—manere in carne necessarium propter vos." Incertum est enim utrum, "ex duobus concupiscentiam habens," an, "compellor autem ex duobus," ut illud adiungatur, "concupiscentiam habens dissolvi et esse cum Christo." (7) Sed quoniam ita sequitur, "multo enim magis optimum," apparet eum eius optimi dicere se habere concupiscentiam, ut cum ex duobus compellatur, alterius tamen habeat concupiscentiam, alterius necessitatem; concupiscentiam scilicet esse cum Christo, necessitatem manere in carne. Quae ambiguitas uno consequenti verbo diiudicatur, quod positum est "enim." Quam particulam qui abstulerunt interpretes, illa potius sententia ducti sunt, ut non solum compelli ex duobus, sed etiam duorum habere concupiscentiam videretur. (8) Sic ergo distinguendum est, "et quid eligam ignoro. Compellor autem ex duobus," quam distinctionem sequitur, "concupiscentiam habens dissolvi et esse cum Christo." Et tamquam quaereretur quare huius rei potius habeat concupiscentiam, "multo enim magis optimum," inquit. Cur ergo e duobus compellitur? Quia est manendi necessitas, quam ita subiecit, "manere in carne necessarium propter vos."

5. (9) Ubi autem neque praescripto fidei neque ipsius sermonis textu ambiguitas explicari potest, nihil obest

---

[10] Philippians 1:22–24.

[11] Modern punctuation, in this case the comma in the first quotation of Philippians 1:23–24, solves the difficulty efficiently. It also disguises what would have been real problems of interpre-

ing a longing to be set free and be with Christ—for that is much the best thing—but to remain in the flesh for your sakes is my duty."[10] It is not clear whether the phrasing is, "having a longing for both options" or "I feel the force of both options," so that the next part is joined with that, "having a longing to be set free and be with Christ."[11] (7) But given that the passage continues, "for that is much the best thing," it is evident that he is saying he has a longing for that best option. Thus although he feels the force of both options, he feels longing regarding one option, but a duty regarding the other: without doubt his longing is to be with Christ, but his duty is to remain in the flesh. The right judgment of this ambiguity is confirmed by the single word that follows, "for." Translators who have removed this particle[12] have been persuaded by the view that Paul not only felt the force of both options, but also longed for both options. (8) So this is how we should phrase it: "and I do not know what to choose. I feel the force of both options," (after this phrase he goes on), "having a longing to be set free and be with Christ." Then, as if someone were asking him why he has more of a longing for the one thing, he says, "for that is much the best thing." Why, therefore, does he feel the force of two options? Because he has an obligation to remain alive, which he has added as follows: "to remain in the flesh for your sakes is my duty."

5. (9) When an ambiguity cannot be ironed out, however, either by the faith's instruction or by the context of

tation in the texts Augustine had to read from, his explanations of which seem ponderous in what follows.

[12] Quintilian uses *particula* of a clause in a sentence; Gellius gives the sense here, a grammatical particle (e.g., *NA* 5.12.9).

secundum quamlibet earum quae ostenduntur sententiam distinguere. Veluti est illa ad Corinthios, "has ergo promissiones habentes, carissimi, mundemus nos ab omni coinquinatione carnis et spiritus, perficientes sanctificationem in timore dei. Capite nos, nemini nocuimus." Dubium est quippe utrum, "mundemus nos ab omni coinquinatione carnis et spiritus," secundum illam sententiam, "ut sit sancta et corpore et spiritu," an, "mundemus nos ab omni coinquinatione carnis," ut alius sit sensus, "et spiritus perficientes sanctificationem in timore dei capite nos." Tales igitur distinctionum ambiguitates in potestate legentis sunt.

6. (10) Quaecumque autem de ambiguis distinctionibus diximus, eadem observanda sunt et in ambiguis pronuntiationibus. Nam et ipsae nisi lectoris nimia vitientur incuria, aut regulis fidei corriguntur aut praecedentis vel consequentis contextione sermonis: aut si neutrum horum adhibetur ad correctionem, nihilominus dubiae remanebunt, ut quolibet modo lector pronuntiaverit, non sit in culpa. (11) Nisi enim fides revocet, qua credimus deum non accusaturum adversus electos suos et Christum non condemnaturum electos suos, potest illud sic pronuntiari, "quis accusabit adversus electos dei?" ut hanc interrogationem quasi responsio consequatur, "deus qui iustificat," et item interrogetur, "quis qui condemnat?" et respondeatur, "Christus Iesus qui mortuus est." Quod credere quia

---

[13] 2 Corinthians 7:1–2. [14] 1 Corinthians 7:34.

[15] "Elect" refers to those foreknown and predestined by God to be his chosen: see J. Rist, "Augustine on Free Will and Predestination," *JThS* 20, no. 2 (1969): 420–47.

[16] Romans 8:33–34.

the passage, it is entirely acceptable to phrase according to whichever interpretation of those available one prefers. Take the example from the letter to the Corinthians: "therefore having these promises, my dear people, let us cleanse ourselves from the taint of flesh and spirit, bringing sanctification in the fear of God to perfection. Make us welcome; we have not harmed anyone."[13] It is certainly unclear whether, "let us cleanse ourselves from the taint of flesh and spirit" concurs with that interpretation, "that she may be holy in both body and spirit,"[14] or, "let us cleanse ourselves from all taint of flesh and spirit," giving a different sense, "and receive us who are bringing to perfection sanctification of the spirit in the fear of God." Such ambiguities of phrasing, therefore, are the reader's responsibility.

6. (10) All that we have said, then, about ambiguities of phrasing is also apparent in matters of ambiguous pronunciation. For these too are corrected either by the rules of faith or by the context that precedes or follows the passage—provided that they are not corrupted by a reader's carelessness. But if neither of these factors is of use in making the correction, doubts about pronunciations will persist, so that whichever pronunciation the reader uses, it will not be at fault. (11) For example: if faith did not deter us from believing that God will bring no accusation against his own elect,[15] and that Christ would not condemn his own elect, it is possible that this passage could be pronounced as follows: "Who will make an accusation against God's elect?" so that an apparent reply would follow, "God who makes righteous," and then it would be asked "who is there who condemns?" and the response would come, "Christ Jesus who died."[16] Because it would

dementissimum est, ita pronuntiabitur, ut praecedat percontatio, sequatur interrogatio. (12) Inter percontationem autem et interrogationem hoc veteres interesse dixerunt, quod ad percontationem multa responderi possunt, ad interrogationem vero aut "non" aut "etiam." Pronuntiabitur ergo ita, ut post percontationem qua dicimus, "Quis accusabit adversus electos dei?" illud quod sequitur sono interrogantis enuntietur, "deus qui iustificat?" ut tacite respondeatur, "non"; et item percontemur, "quis qui condemnat?" rursusque interrogemus, "Christus Iesus qui mortuus est, magis autem qui resurrexit, qui est in dextera dei, qui et interpellat pro nobis?" ut ubique respondeatur, "non." (13) At vero illo in loco ubi ait, "quid ergo dicemus? quia gentes quae non sectabantur iustitiam, apprehenderunt iustitiam," nisi post percontationem qua dictum est, "quid ergo dicemus?" responsio subiciatur, "quia gentes quae non sectabantur iustitiam, apprehenderunt iustitiam," textus consequens non cohaerebit. Qualibet autem voce pronuntietur illud quod Nathanael dixit, "a Nazareth potest aliquid boni esse?" sive affirmantis, ut illud solum ad interrogationem pertineat quod ait, "a Nazareth?" sive totum cum dubitatione interrogantis, non video quo modo discernatur. Uterque autem sensus fidem non impedit.

7. (14) Est etiam ambiguitas in sono dubio syllabarum, et haec utique ad pronuntiationem pertinens. Nam quod

---

[17] See Quint. *Inst.* 9.2.6 ("We use the two terms indiscriminately, although *percontatio* is designed to obtain information and *interrogatio* to prove a point"). See Schindel, "Textkritisches zu lateinischen Figurenlehren," 5–114, esp. 103.

[18] Romans 9:30. [19] John 1:46. [20] *sono dubio*: as in the English heteronym, "does" (*dŭz*, verb; *dōze*, plural noun).

be utter madness to believe this, it is instead pronounced first with an inquiry, then with questioning. (12) Scholars of old have stated that there is a distinction between the terms "inquiry" and "questioning":[17] that there can be many responses to an inquiry, but to questioning the response is either "no" or "yes indeed." So it will be pronounced in such a way that after the inquiry in which we say, "who will bring an accusation against God's elect?" the phrase that follows must be expressed with the inflection of a questioner, "is it God who makes righteous?" to which the tacit reply is, "no." The same when we make an inquiry, "who is there who condemns?" and again we must question, "is it Christ Jesus, who died, and still more who was resurrected, who is at God's right hand, who also makes intercession on our behalf?" Again the universal answer is, "no." (13) Yet in that place where it says, "What then are we to say? That the gentiles, who did not pursue righteousness, seized hold of righteousness,"[18] the context that follows will not be coherent unless, following the inquiry that asked, "what then are we to say?" this response is supplied, "because the gentiles who did not pursue righteousness, seized hold of righteousness." As for what Nathanael said, "Can anything good come from Nazareth?"[19] in whatever way one pronounces it—asserting either that only the part where he says, "From Nazareth?" is part of the questioning, or that the whole phrase expresses the doubt of the questioner, I see no way of determining. Neither meaning presents an obstacle to faith.

7. (14) There is certainly ambiguity when the length of a syllable[20] is uncertain.[21] This is especially relevant when

[21] Again drawing on Quintilian: *Inst.* 7.9.13, 9.3.69.

scriptum est, "non est absconditum a te os meum, quod fecisti in abscondito," non elucet legenti utrum correpta littera "os" pronuntiet an producta. Si enim corripiat, ab eo quod sunt ossa, si autem producat, ab eo quod sunt ora, intellegitur numerus singularis. (15) Sed talia linguae praecedentis inspectione diiudicantur, nam in Graeco non "stoma" sed "oston" positum est. Unde plerumque loquendi consuetudo vulgaris utilior est significandis rebus quam integritas litterata. Mallem quippe cum barbarismo dici, "non est absconditum a te ossum meum," quam ut ideo esset minus apertum, quia magis Latinum est. Sed aliquando dubius syllabae sonus etiam vicino verbo ad eandem sententiam pertinente diiudicatur, sicut est illud apostoli, "quae praedico vobis, sicut praedixi, quoniam qui talia agunt, regnum dei non possidebunt." (16) Si tantummodo dixisset "quae praedico vobis" neque subiunxisset "sicut praedixi," nonnisi ad codicem praecedentis linguae recurrendum esset, ut cognosceremus utrum in eo quod dixit, "praedico," producenda an corripienda esset syllaba media. Nunc autem manifestum est producendam esse; non enim ait "sicut praedicavi," sed "sicut praedixi."

---

22 Psalm 139:15.

23 The signs used here, breve and macron respectively, were not available to Augustine.

24 *ŏs*, *ŏssis* (pl., *ŏssa*), "a bone"; *ōs*, *ōris* (pl. *ōra*), "a mouth": both neuter.

25 *ostoun* (Attic contraction for *osteon*), not *stoma*.

26 In Latin, he invents an incorrect back-formation (*ossum*) of the singular from the plural, somewhat akin to an incorrect English singular like "a mice" instead of "a mouse."

speaking aloud. Takes the verse of scripture, "My *os*, which you have made in secret, is not hidden from you":[22] it does not clarify for reader whether to say "ŏs" with a short vowel letter, or "ōs" with a long one.[23] If readers shorten the vowel, it is understood to be the singular of the word "bones," but if they lengthen it, it is the singular of the word meaning "mouth."[24] (15) Matters of this kind are determined by a scrutiny of the original language; for in Greek the word "bone,"[25] not "mouth," has been used. Thus a normal conversational idiom is usually more useful than purely correct writing when it comes to signifying things. In fact, I would rather things were spoken with a solecism, such as "my bowne is not hidden from you,"[26] than that the meaning should be less plain because it is in better Latin.[27] Sometimes we can decide whether the vowel in a syllable is long or short by the use of an adjacent word in the same sentence, for example when the apostle says, "I warn you, as I have warned you already, that those who do such things will not possess the kingdom of God."[28] (16) Had he written only "what I *praedico* you," without adding "as I have warned you already," we would have had to resort to a Greek text to discover whether the penultimate syllable should be long or short. But as it is, the syllable is definitely long, for he uses the perfect tense that means "I have warned," not "I have preached."

[27] This may suggest that the incorrect singular *ossum* was a common or typical error.

[28] Galatians 5:21. The first use of the verb, could be "I warn/foretell," from the third conjugation (*praedīco, praedīcere*), or "I preach," from the first (*praedĭco, praedĭcare*). The repetition of the verb using the perfect tense confirms that it is the former.

8. (17) Non solum autem istae, sed etiam illae ambiguitates quae non ad distinctionem vel ad pronuntiationem pertinent, similiter considerandae sunt; qualis illa est ad Thessalonicenses, "propterea consolati sumus fratres in vobis." Dubium enim utrum, "O fratres," an "hos fratres": neutrum autem horum est contra fidem. Sed Graeca lingua hos casus pares non habet et ideo illa inspecta renuntiatur vocativus, id est, "O fratres." (18) Quod si voluisset interpres dicere, "propterea consolationem habuimus, fratres, in vobis," minus servitum esset verbis, sed minus de sententia dubitaretur, aut certe adderetur: nostri. Nemo enim fere ambigeret vocativum casum esse, cum audiret "propterea consolati sumus, fratres nostri, in vobis." Sed iam hoc periculosius permittitur. Ita factum est in illa ad Corinthios, cum ait apostolus, "Quotidie morior, per vestram gloriam, fratres, quam habeo in Christo Iesu." (19) Ait enim quidam interpres, "quotidie morior, per vestram—iuro—gloriam," quia in Graeco vox iurantis manifesta est sine ambiguo sono. Rarissime igitur et difficillime inveniri potest ambiguitas in propriis verbis, quantum ad

---

29 *distinctio*: a marked pause or sign of punctuation. See Quint. *Inst.* 11.3.37, 39, 52.

30 1 Thessalonians 3:7. The verb "console" could be deponent instead of passive, which admits of ambiguity to complicate translation.

31 Vocative and accusative, respectively.

32 The Latin uses verb + direct object; the English uses punctuation to make the phrase unambiguous.

33 The Authorized Version of the Bible (1611), sensitive to adding words to scripture, used italics to indicate any word with no direct equivalent in the source languages.

34 1 Corinthians 15:31.

8. (17) We must give similar consideration not only to these ambiguities but also to those that are not about punctuation[29] or reading aloud, such as that one in Thessalonians, where it is not clear whether he means, "O brothers" in the vocative ("therefore we have been consoled, O brothers, in you") or "these brothers" as the object of the verb ("therefore we have consoled these brothers in you"); neither of which is incompatible with the faith.[30] But in the Greek language these two grammatical cases[31] are not alike, so after consulting that version it is confirmed to be the vocative, namely, "O brothers." (18) But if the translator had chosen to say, "therefore we have received consolation, brothers,[32] in you," they would have made a less accurate job of the wording, but there would be less doubt about the meaning. Or they could, of course, have added the word "our": for virtually no one would be in doubt that this was a vocative case on hearing, "therefore we have been consoled, our brothers, in you." All the same, to allow this practice is risky.[33] It has been done in that passage of Corinthians[34] where the apostle says, "I die daily, by your glory, brothers, which I have in Christ Jesus": (19) for one particular translator says, "I die daily, I swear by your glory," because in Greek it is clearly the wording of someone making an oath, and lacks any trace of ambiguity.[35] So when words are used in their literal meanings, it is difficult (if not impossible), where the texts

[35] The preposition *per* has a wide semantic range, only one element of which is the addressing of oaths (e.g., *per deos immortales*!, "by the immortal gods") with ellipse of the verb. The Greek text has the emphatic affirmative particle *nē* (but like Latin using the accusative) of the divinity invoked.

libros divinarum scripturarum spectat, quam non aut circumstantia ipsa sermonis, qua cognoscitur scriptorum intentio, aut interpretum collatio aut praecedentis linguae solvat inspectio.

9. (20) Sed verborum translatorum ambiguitates, de quibus deinceps loquendum est, non mediocrem curam industriamque desiderant. Nam in principio cavendum est ne figuratam locutionem ad litteram accipias. Et ad hoc enim pertinet quod ait apostolus, "littera occidit, spiritus autem vivificat." Cum enim figurate dictum sic accipitur, tamquam proprie dictum sit, carnaliter sapitur. Neque ulla mors animae congruentius appellatur, quam cum id etiam quod in ea bestiis antecellit, hoc est intellegentia, carni subicitur sequendo litteram. (21) Qui enim sequitur litteram, translata verba sicut propria tenet, neque illud quod proprio verbo significatur refert ad aliam significationem: sed si "sabbatum" audierit, verbi gratia, non intellegit nisi unum diem de septem, qui continuo volumine repetuntur; et cum audierit "sacrificium," non excedit cogitatione illud quod fieri de victimis pecorum terrenisque fructibus solet. Ea demum est miserabilis animi[2] servitus, signa pro rebus accipere, et supra creaturam corpoream oculum mentis ad hauriendum aeternum lumen levare non posse.

[2] animi *P K*: animae *R Lond.* μ

---

[36] Or "metaphorically," in contrast with "literally."

[37] Latin *desiderant*. Augustine uses this rare sense elsewhere: *rerum documenta desiderat* (*TC* 4.46.127).

[38] 2 Corinthians 3:6: two figurative verbs.

of the holy scriptures are concerned, to find ambiguity that cannot be resolved by scrutiny either of the context of what is said (which confirms the authorial intention), or by comparison of versions, or of the source language.

9. (20) But now it is time to speak of ambiguities in words that are used figuratively,[36] which require[37] no little diligence and endeavor. First you must ensure that you do not mistake figurative speech for literal. Relevant to this is the apostle's saying, "the letter deadens, but the spirit revitalizes."[38] For when a saying is taken as figurative even though it was said literally, it smacks of fleshly[39] meaning. The death of the soul is never more properly termed so, than when that faculty of the soul that lifts it above the merely animal—namely intelligence—is in thrall to the flesh through pursuing literal meaning. (21) Those who pursue the literal take figurative words as nonfigurative, and fail to associate what is signified nonfiguratively with any other signification: but if they hear the word "sabbath" (for example) they understand nothing more than one day out of seven, all of which come round continually; and when they hear "sacrifice" their understanding goes no further than what happens to sacrificial animals and agricultural produce.[40] In conclusion, it is a wretched enslavement of the intellect to take signs as being actual things, and fail to lift the eyes of the mind above the physical creation to drink in the eternal light.[41]

39 Or "physical." "Flesh" in early Christianity means "corporeal," but with the taint of death about it.

40 Or "fruits of the earth" (a biblical calque: Deuteronomy 26:2).

41 The Augustine of *Confessions* is glimpsed here.

10. (22) Quae tamen servitus in Iudaeo populo longe a ceterarum gentium more distabat, quandoquidem rebus temporalibus ita subiugati erant ut unus eis in omnibus commendaretur deus. Et quamquam signa rerum spiritalium pro ipsis rebus observarent, nescientes quo referrentur, id tamen insitum habebant, quod tali servitute uni omnium, quem non videbant, placerent deo. Quam custodiam tamquam sub paedagogo parvulorum fuisse scribit apostolus. (23) Et ideo qui talibus signis pertinaciter inhaeserunt, contemnentem ista dominum, cum iam tempus revelationis eorum venisset, ferre non potuerunt; atque inde calumnias, quod sabbato curaret, moliti sunt principes eorum populusque signis illis tamquam rebus astrictus, non credebat deum esse, vel a deo venisse, qui ea sicut a Iudaeis observabantur nollet attendere.

Sed qui crediderunt, ex quibus facta est prima ecclesia Hierosolimitana, satis ostenderunt quanta utilitas fuerit eo modo sub paedagogo custodiri, ut signa quae temporaliter imposita erant servientibus, ad unius dei cultum, qui fecit caelum et terram, opinionem observantium religarent. (24) Namque illi quia proximi spiritalibus fuerunt (in ipsis enim temporalibus et carnalibus votis atque signis, quamvis quomodo spiritaliter essent intellegenda nescirent, unum tamen didicerant venerari aeternum deum), tam capaces exstiterunt spiritus sancti, ut omnia sua venderent eorumque pretium indigentibus distribuendum ante

---

[42] That is, things to do with time and creation, not divine eternity. [43] Galatians 3:24. [44] A partial representation: Matthew 5:18. [45] This does not explain why some believed but others did not. [46] In the sense alluded to in 2 Corinthians 3:6.

10. (22) This enslavement nonetheless kept the Jewish people at a distance from the ways of other peoples, for even though they were in thrall to the things of this world,[42] it was in such a way that among them all there was agreement that God is one. Even though they saw signs of spiritual things instead of the things themselves, and did not understand what they were signs of, still by that enslavement to the one God of all (whom they were unable to see), they instinctively did what was pleasing to God. The apostle writes that this was like a teacher's guardianship of little ones.[43] (23) That is why they clung so tenaciously to those signs that the Lord had no value for. Although the time for their revelation had come at last, they could not bear him; and the leaders and people—hardened in their resolve by the signs that they took for things—heaped up malicious charges (such as that he was healing on the sabbath) and refused to believe that he, who paid no attention to Jewish observances of that sort,[44] either was God or had come from God.

Those who did believe, however, who made up the first Jerusalem church, were abundant proof of how useful it was to have a teacher's guardianship in this way, so that the signs imposed on them for a while, in the time of their enslavement, bound the belief of those who scrutinized them to worship of the one God who made heaven and earth.[45] (24) What is more, because they were so close to being spiritual,[46] (for in those earthly and fleshly prayers and signs, though they were ignorant of how to understand them spiritually, they had still learned to worship one eternal God) they were so receptive to the Holy Spirit that they sold everything they owned and laid the proceeds of

apostolorum pedes ponerent, seque totos dedicarent deo tamquam templum novum, cuius terrenae imagini, hoc est templo veteri, serviebant. 11. (25) Non enim hoc ullas ecclesias gentium fecisse scriptum est, quia non tam prope inventi erant, qui simulacra manufacta deos habebant.

(26) Et si quando aliqui eorum illa tamquam signa interpretari conabantur, ad creaturam colendam venerandamque referebant. Quid enim mihi prodest simulacrum, verbi gratia, Neptuni non ipsum habendum deum, sed eo significari universum mare vel etiam omnes aquas ceteras quae fontibus proruunt? Sicut a quodam poeta illorum describitur, si bene recolo, ita dicente:

> Tu, Neptune pater, cui tempora cana crepanti
> cincta salo resonant, magnus cui perpete mento
> profluit oceanus et flumina crinibus errant.

(27) Haec siliqua intra dulce tectorium sonantes lapillos quatit; non est autem hominum, sed porcorum cibus. Novit quid dicam qui evangelium novit. Quid ergo mihi prodest quod Neptuni simulacrum ad illam significationem refertur, nisi forte ut neutrum colam? Tam enim mihi statua quaelibet, quam mare universum, non est deus. Fateor tamen altius demersos esse, qui opera homi-

---

[47] Acts 4:32–35.

[48] A nexus of allusion. The "new temple" is the heavenly Jerusalem (Revelation 3:12); a building is a metaphor for an individual human body; the "old temple" stands for the Old Testament/covenant, which is the type of the New Testament (antitype).

[49] That is, idols, which the Jewish Christians of the Jerusalem church would continue to shun.

[50] The "pagans." The author is unknown (see Baehrens, *Frag-*

the sale at the apostles' feet, for distribution to the poor.[47] And they dedicated themselves completely to God, as a new temple, the earthly antitype of which is that old temple that once they used to serve.[48] 11. (25) For none of the other churches is recorded as having done this, and this is because they had been found to be less close, for they used to have gods that were made by human hands.[49]

(26) If ever some of them tried to understand those idols as signs, they used to compare them to something created to be worshipped and adored. But what good does it do me to take a likeness of Neptune (for example), to treat it not as a god but as a way of signifying the sea as a whole, or all the other waters too, the ones that flow out from springs? As one of their[50] poets puts it, saying (as best I can remember):

> You, father Neptune, whose white head echoes,
> girded with breaking spindrift; from whose beard
> great Ocean flows unceasing; from whose locks the
> rivers spout.

(27) This husk shakes up the rattling seeds within its tender casing: yet it is not food for people but for pigs. Anyone who knows the gospel knows what I mean.[51] So what good does it do me that a likeness of Neptune is associated with that kind of signifying (except perhaps to warn me off worshiping either the object or what it represents)? For me, neither any particular statue, nor the entirety of the sea, is God. I admit that people who think the works of human hands are gods are sunk even deeper than those

menta poetarum Romanorum, 388; Courtney, *Fragmentary Latin Poets*, 456). [51] Luke 15:16.

num deos putant, quam qui opera dei. Sed nobis unus diligendus et colendus deus praecipitur, qui fecit haec omnia, quorum illi simulacra venerantur vel tamquam deos vel tamquam signa et imagines deorum. (28) Si ergo signum utiliter institutum pro ipsa re sequi, cui significandae institutum est, carnalis est servitus, quanto magis inutilium rerum signa instituta pro rebus accipere! Quae si rettuleris ad ea ipsa, quae his significantur, eisque colendis animum obligaveris, nihilominus servili carnalique onere atque velamine non carebis.

12. (29) Quam ob rem christiana libertas eos quos invenit sub signis utilibus, tamquam prope inventos, interpretatis signis quibus subditi erant, elevatos ad eas res quarum illa signa sunt, liberavit. Ex his factae sunt ecclesiae sanctorum Israhelitarum. Quos autem invenit sub signis inutilibus, non solum servilem operationem sub talibus signis, sed etiam ipsa signa frustravit removitque omnia, ut a corruptione multitudinis simulatorum deorum, quam saepe ac proprie scriptura fornicationem vocat, ad unius dei cultum gentes converterentur; nec sub ipsis iam signis utilibus serviturae, sed exercitaturae potius animum in eorum intellegentia spiritali.

13. (30) Sub signo enim servit qui operatur aut veneratur aliquam rem significantem, nesciens quid significet. Qui vero aut operatur aut veneratur utile signum divinitus

---

[52] Mark 15:38; Hebrews 6:19, 10:20.

[53] Mark 12:34.

[54] The subject is still "freedom."

who think that God's works are gods. But we are taught to love and worship the one God who has made all these things, the likenesses of which all of them revere, either as gods or as signs and images of gods. (28) If a sign has been established with a worthwhile purpose, yet pursuing that sign, in place of the real thing that the sign was established to represent, is an enslavement to the physical, how much more so it is to take the signs of worthless things as the things themselves! If instead you refer those signs to the actual things that they signify, and commit your spirit to worshipping them, you still will not be free from the slavish burden of the physical, or from the veil.[52]

12. (29) Christian freedom, therefore, has liberated those whom it found under the sway of useful signs, as if they were found to be almost at their destination.[53] By giving the true meaning of the signs they were in thrall to, it lifted them up to the realities in place of those signs. The churches of the Israelite saints were made up of people like this. As for those whom it[54] found under the sway of worthless signs, it blocked and dismissed not only their slavish laboring under those signs but also the signs themselves. The result was the conversion of gentiles from the corruption of a bevy of false gods (which scripture frequently, and properly, calls a form of infidelity) to the worship of the one God—in subjection to the same worthwhile signs, which were no longer a mark of servitude, but rather of training the spirit to understand them in their spiritual sense.

13. (30) Anyone who makes use of some thing that is a signifier, or venerates it, but does not know what it signifies, is enslaved to that sign. On the other hand anyone who makes use of a worthwhile sign that comes from God,

institutum, cuius vim significationemque intellegit, non hoc veneratur, quod videtur et transit, sed illud potius quo talia cuncta referenda sunt. Talis autem homo spiritalis et liber est, etiam tempore servitutis, quo carnalibus animis nondum oportet signa illa revelari, quorum iugo edomandi sunt. (31) Tales autem spiritales erant patriarchae ac prophetae, omnesque in populo Israhel per quos nobis spiritus sanctus ipsa scripturarum et auxilia et solacia ministravit.

Hoc vero tempore posteaquam resurrectione domini nostri manifestissimum indicium nostrae libertatis illuxit, nec eorum quidem signorum, quae iam intellegimus, operatione gravi onerati sumus, sed quaedam pauca pro multis eademque factu[3] facillima et intellectu augustissima et observatione castissima ipse dominus et apostolica tradidit disciplina, sicuti est baptismi sacramentum et celebratio corporis et sanguinis domini. (32) Quae unusquisque cum percipit, quo referantur imbutus agnoscit, ut ea non carnali servitute, sed spiritali potius libertate veneretur. Ut autem litteram sequi et signa pro rebus, quae his significantur, accipere, servilis infirmitatis est; ita inutiliter signa interpretari, male vagantis erroris est. Qui autem non intellegit quid significet signum, et tamen signum esse intellegit, nec ipse premitur servitute. Melius est autem vel premi incognitis sed utilibus signis quam, inutiliter ea interpretando, a iugo servitutis eductam cervicem laqueis erroris inserere.

[3] factu *Lond.*: facta *P*

---

[55] See Proem 6.12.

or who venerates it, while understanding its power and significance, is not actually venerating the thing he sees (for that is temporal) but rather that to which all such signs should be related. Someone like that is spiritual and free, even in the present era of slavery when it is not yet right to reveal the meaning of those signs to spirits still ensnared in the flesh, who are not yet broken to the yoke. (31) The patriarchs and prophets were men of spirit in this sense, and so were all those of the people of Israel through whom the Holy Spirit has ministered to us the true help and comfort of the scriptures.

In our time, since the proof of our freedom has blazed brightly because of the resurrection of our Lord, we are no longer burdened by the cumbersome working of those signs, for now we understand them. So the Lord himself, and the teaching of the apostles, has bestowed on us a few particular signs in place of the many. These few are easy to accomplish, noble in meaning, hallowed in observance: namely the sacrament of baptism, and the celebration of the body and blood of the Lord.[55] (32) Once individuals grasp these and are inspired to acknowledge what they point to, they revere those signs not in the enslavement of the flesh, but rather with spiritual freedom. Just as it is slavish weakness to follow the letter and mistake signs for the things that they signify, so too giving signs an unprofitable meaning is a damaging diversion. If a person does not understand the meaning of a sign, but does understand that it is a sign, they are not burdened with a form of enslavement. Perhaps it is better to be burdened by signs one does not recognize but that are worthwhile, than to stick one's neck—just rescued from the yoke of enslavement—into the noose of pagan error, by taking them in a sense that is not worthwhile.

14. (33) Huic autem observationi, qua cavemus figuratam locutionem, id est translatam quasi propriam sequi, adiungenda etiam illa est, ne propriam quasi figuratam velimus accipere. Demonstrandus est igitur prius modus inveniendae locutionis, propriane an figurata sit. Et iste omnino modus est, ut quidquid in sermone divino neque ad morum honestatem neque ad fidei veritatem proprie referri potest, figuratum esse cognoscas. (34) Morum honestas ad diligendum deum et proximum, fidei veritas ad cognoscendum deum et proximum pertinet. Spes autem sua cuique est in conscientia propria, quemadmodum se sentit ad dilectionem dei et proximi cognitionemque proficere. De quibus omnibus primo libro dictum est.

15. (35) Sed quoniam proclive est humanum genus non ex momentis ipsius libidinis, sed potius suae consuetudinis aestimare peccata, fit plerumque ut quisque hominum ea tantum culpanda arbitretur, quae suae regionis et temporis homines vituperare atque damnare consuerunt; et ea tantum probanda atque laudanda quae consuetudo eorum cum quibus vivit admittit. Eoque contingit ut si quid scriptura vel praeceperit quod abhorret a consuetudine audientium, vel quod non abhorret culpaverit, si animum eorum iam verbi vinxit auctoritas, figuratam locutionem putent. (36) Non autem praecipit scriptura nisi caritatem, nec culpat nisi cupiditatem, et eo modo informat mores hominum. Item si animum praeoccupavit alicuius erroris opinio, quidquid aliter asseruerit scriptura, figuratum

---

56 Matthew 22:37–39. 57 See *Conf.* 1.12.19, 4.16.30, etc.

58 *mores*: habitual social behaviors commonly approved; they are qualitatively different from Christian "goods," such as faith, hope, and love.

14. (33) The precept by which we advised caution with respect to figurative expressions (not to pursue figurative expressions as if they were literal) now needs supplementing: we must resist taking what is literal as if it were figurative. First, we have to present a method for investigating whether an expression is literal or figurative. That method is simply this: anything in the divine discourse that cannot be applied literally to behavior that shows integrity, or to true faith, should be acknowledged as figurative. (34) Integrity of behavior has to do with the love of God and neighbor, true faith with coming to know God and neighbor.[56] As for hope, each person has that in their own conscience in accordance with how much progress they feel they are making in their love and knowledge of God and neighbor. All this was discussed in the first book.

15. (35) The human race, however, is prone to assess sins in accordance with its own customary behavior, rather than the circumstances of the actual physical gratification. As a result it often happens that each individual judges only those acts that people from the same place and culture habitually denounce and condemn as blameworthy; conversely, only acts that the customs of their society allow are praiseworthy and acceptable. This is why (as sometimes happens), when scripture insists on an action that is shocking to the ways of those who hear it, or condemns something that it uncontroversial to them, those people assume that it is using a figurative expression—that is, if the authority of the word has convinced them. (36) Yet scripture insists on nothing that is not love, and condemns nothing that is not appetite;[57] and this is how it molds human morality.[58] If some misguided conviction has taken control of their thinking, they will adjudge anything that

homines arbitrantur. Non autem asserit nisi catholicam fidem rebus praeteritis et futuris et praesentibus. Praeteritorum narratio est, futurorum praenuntiatio, praesentium demonstratio; sed omnia haec ad eandem caritatem nutriendam atque roborandam, et cupiditatem vincendam atque exstinguendam valent.

16. (37) Caritatem voco motum animi ad fruendum deo propter ipsum et se atque proximo propter deum; cupiditatem autem motum animi ad fruendum se et proximo et quolibet corpore non propter deum. Quod autem agit indomita cupiditas ad corrumpendum animum et corpus suum flagitium vocatur; quod autem agit ut alteri noceat, facinus dicitur. (38) Et haec sunt duo genera omnium peccatorum, sed flagitia priora sunt. Quae cum exinaniverint animum et ad quandam egestatem perduxerint, in facinora prosilitur, quibus removeantur impedimenta flagitiorum aut adiumenta quaerantur. Item quod agit caritas quo sibi prosit, utilitas est; quod autem agit ut prosit proximo, beneficientia nominatur. Et hic praecedit utilitas, quia nemo potest ex eo quod non habet prodesse alteri. Quanto autem[4] magis regnum cupiditatis destruitur, tanto caritatis augetur.

17. (39) Quidquid ergo asperum et quasi saevum factu dictuque in sanctis scripturis legitur ex persona dei vel sanctorum eius, ad cupiditatis regnum destruendum valet. Quod si perspicue sonat, non est ad aliud referendum

[4] enim *P B D Bam.*

---

[59] *eandem*: the special kind of love he has been describing.

[60] *flagitium*: could be translated "disgrace," encapsulating the social element in wrongdoing.

[61] *utilitas*.

scripture asserts to the contrary to be a figurative expression. But scripture proclaims nothing less than the catholic faith in past, present and future events: it tells the story of past history, it prophesies the future, it clarifies the present: and all this works to nurture and build up Christian[59] love, and to conquer desire and snuff it out.

16. (37) "Love" is what I call the mind's impulse to enjoy God for his own sake, and to enjoy one's neighbor because of God. "Desire" is what I call the mind's impulse to enjoy oneself, and one's neighbor, and any physical thing, but not because of God. Uncontrolled desire, which spurs the mind and its body to ruin is called "wrongdoing";[60] whereas what spurs them to harm someone else is called "crime." (38) These are the two types of sin; but wrongdoing comes first, for when it has worn the mind down, and inveigled it into a position of hardship, then it makes the leap into criminality. At this point what stands in the way of wrongdoing is set aside, or what maintains it is actively pursued. Likewise, what love does to benefit itself is said to be "self-advantage";[61] but what it does for the benefit of a neighbor is termed "kindness." In this case, self-advantage comes first, for no one can do a kindness to anyone else with what is not in their possession. But the more the reign of desire is broken down, the more the reign of love is built up.

17. (39) Anything about the character of God or of his saints, therefore, that we read in the holy writings that is harsh and verges on cruelty (in either deed or word), has the power to destroy the realm of desire. If it speaks clearly, it should not be made to relate to something else

quasi figurate dictum sit. Sicuti est illud apostoli, "thesaurizas tibi iram in die irae et revelationis iusti iudicii dei, qui reddet unicuique secundum opera sua: his quidem qui secundum sustinentiam boni operis, gloriam et honorem et incorruptionem quaerentibus, vitam aeternam; his autem qui ex contentione sunt et diffidunt veritati, credunt autem iniquitati, ira et indignatio. Tribulatio et angustia in omnem animam hominis operantis malum, Iudaei primum et Graeci." (40) Sed hoc ad eos, cum quibus evertitur ipsa cupiditas, qui eam vincere noluerunt. Cum autem in homine cui dominabantur, regna cupiditatis subvertuntur, illa est aperta locutio, "qui autem Iesu Christi sunt carnem suam crucifixerunt cum passionibus et concupiscentiis"; nisi quia et hic quaedam verba translata tractantur, sicuti est "ira dei," et "crucifixerunt." (41) Sed non tam multa sunt vel ita posita, ut obtegant sensum et allegoriam vel aenigma faciant, quam proprie figuratam locutionem voco. Quod autem Ieremiae dicitur, "Ecce constitui te hodie super gentes et regna, ut evellas et destruas et disperdas et dissipes," non dubium quin figurata locutio tota sit, ad eum finem referenda quem diximus.

18. (42) Quae autem quasi flagitiosa imperitis videntur, sive tantum dicta sive etiam facta sunt, vel ex dei persona vel ex hominum, quorum nobis sanctitas commendatur, tota figurata sunt. Quorum ad caritatis pastum enucleanda

---

[62] *incorruptionem.*

[63] Romans 2:5–9.

[64] Galatians 5:24.

[65] Jeremiah 1:10.

as if it were a figurative idiom. For example: the apostle's saying, "Store up wrath for yourself against the day of wrath and the revelation of the righteous judgment of God, who will pay back to each person according to their works: on those who, according to the endurance of a good work, seek glory and honor and the salvation of the body,[62] he will bestow eternal life. But on those who are quarrelsome and who despair of the truth, but who put their trust in wickedness, he will inflict his wrath and displeasure. Distress and anguish will come to every human soul that does wrong, first Jews, then Greeks."[63] (40) But this refers to those who are overthrown together with their desire, those who were unwilling to conquer it. When the realms of desire are overturned, though, in people whom once they ruled over, that saying speaks plainly, "Those who belong to Jesus Christ have crucified their own flesh with its passions and desires,"[64] except that even here certain terms should be treated as figurative, namely, "wrath of God" and "crucified." (41) Still, they are not so numerous, or so placed, that they obscure the meaning and generate an allegory or a puzzle (those are what I call proper figurative expressions). Jeremiah's saying, on the other hand, "Behold, this day I have established you above the nations and kingdoms, to tear down and destroy, to scatter and disperse,"[65] is undoubtedly purely figurative, so should be referred to that purpose that we mentioned above.

18. (42) When things look like wrongdoing to the untrained eye, whether they are merely said or also enacted in the person either of God, or of human beings whose holiness recommends them to us, they are entirely figurative. Their secrets must be extracted in such a way that

secreta sunt. Quisquis autem rebus praetereuntibus restrictius utitur, quam sese habent mores eorum cum quibus vivit, aut temperans aut superstitiosus est; quisquis vero sic eis utitur ut metas consuetudinis bonorum inter quos versatur excedat, aut aliquid significat aut flagitiosus est. (43) In omnibus enim talibus non usus rerum, sed libido utentis in culpa est. Neque ullo modo quisquam sobrius crediderit, domini pedes ita unguento pretioso a muliere perfusos, ut luxuriosorum et nequam hominum solent, quorum talia convivia detestamur. Odor enim bonus fama bona est, quam quisquis bonae vitae operibus habuerit, dum vestigia Christi sequitur, quasi pedes eius pretiosissimo odore perfundit. (44) Ita quod in aliis personis plerumque flagitium est, in divina vel prophetica persona magnae cuiusdam rei signum est. Alia est quippe in perditis moribus, alia in Oseae prophetae vaticinatione coniunctio meretricis. Nec, si flagitiose in conviviis temulentorum et lascivorum nudantur corpora, propterea in balneis nudum esse flagitium est!

19. (45) Quid igitur locis et temporibus et personis conveniat, diligenter attendendum est ne temere flagitia reprehendamus. Fieri enim potest ut sine aliquo vitio cupediae vel voracitatis, pretiosissimo cibo sapiens utatur; insipiens autem foedissima gulae flamma in vilissimum ardescat. Et sanius quisque maluerit more domini pisce

---

66 *libido*: characteristically locating wrongness in the motivation/will of the wrongdoer, not the act of wrongdoing. See §46 below. 67 John 12:3. 68 *est*: a strong way of expressing the representation or signifying that he detects.

69 Hosea 1:2: the prophet personifies Israel as an unfaithful wife. 70 Luke 24:43.

they foster love. Someone who uses the passing things of this world more sparingly than is customary in the community where they live is either self-restrained or superstitious; whereas someone who goes beyond the boundary of the norms of the decent people they live among is either signifying something or behaving outrageously. (43) In both cases it is not the actual uses of things, but the inordinate urges[66] of the user, that are blameworthy. Decent people will never believe that the woman poured expensive perfume over the Lord's feet[67] in the same way as that self-gratifying depravity shown by the kind of people whose degenerate partying we abominate. For the fine fragrance stands for[68] a good reputation, and everyone who possesses such, through the actions of a good life while following in Christ's footsteps, is figuratively soaking his feet with the most expensive perfume. (44) Thus what is frequently wrongdoing in other persons, in the divine person or in a prophet is a sign of some great thing. For example: "uniting oneself with a prostitute" is one thing among those lost to all morality, but something else in the prophesying of the prophet Hosea.[69] Again, it may be scandalous for people to bare their bodies at drunken parties, but that does not make it scandalous to strip off and have a bath!

19. (45) We should pay careful attention to what is appropriate to particular places, times and persons, so as not to be rash in criticizing instances of wrongdoing. It may be the case that a wise person, without any taint of lickerish greediness, partakes of very expensive delicacies; whereas a fool is aflame with quite disgusting cravings for junk food. One person, too, might have a healthy preference for eating fish (as the Lord used to do[70]) rather than pot-

vesci quam lenticula more Esau nepotis Abraham, aut hordeo more iumentorum. (46) Non enim propterea continentiores nobis sunt pleraeque bestiae, quia vilioribus aluntur escis. Nam in omnibus huiuscemodi rebus, non ex earum rerum natura quibus utimur, sed ex causa utendi et modo appetendi vel probandum est vel improbandum quod facimus.

20. (47) Regno terreno veteres iusti caeleste regnum imaginabantur et praenuntiabant. Sufficiendae prolis causa erat uxorum plurium simul uni viro habendarum inculpabilis consuetudo. Et ideo unam feminam maritos habere plurimos honestum non erat; non enim mulier eo est fecundior, sed meretricia potius turpitudo, vel quaestum vel liberos vulgo quaerere. (48) In huiuscemodi moribus quidquid illorum temporum sancti non libidinose faciebant, quamvis ea facerent, quae hoc tempore nisi per libidinem fieri non possunt, non culpat scriptura. Et quidquid ibi tale narratur, non solum historice ac proprie, sed etiam figurate ac prophetice acceptum, interpretandum est usque in finem illum caritatis sive dei sive proximi sive utriusque. (49) Sicut enim talares et manicatas tunicas habere apud Romanos veteres flagitium erat, nunc autem honesto loco natis, cum tunicati sunt, non eas habere flagitium est, sic animadvertendum est in cetero quoque usu rerum abesse oportere libidinem, quae non solum ipsa eorum, inter quos vivit, consuetudine nequiter abutitur, sed etiam saepe fines eius egressa, foeditatem suam, quae

---

[71] Genesis 25:34.

[72] Perhaps echoing Verg. *G* 3.65.

tage like Esau[71] (the grandson of Abraham) or barley like livestock. (46) Most animals feed on cheaper foodstuffs, but they are not, on that account, more self-restrained than we humans; for in all matters of this kind it is not the nature of the things we make use of, but what motivates our use, and the means by which we seek them, that make them praiseworthy or blameworthy.

20. (47) The righteous used to picture the heavenly realm as being like an earthly kingdom, and that was how they prophesied about it. The reason why one man would have several wives was to ensure enough offspring:[72] a practice that calls for no criticism. That is why it was not proper for one woman to have a large number of husbands; for that does not enable a woman to have more children; and in fact striving for profit or progeny is more like the degradation of offering sex for money. (48) Scripture does not condemn anything that holy men and women practice without the taint of sensuality, even though what they were doing would nowadays be attributable to nothing but sensual indulgence. Anything of that kind that scripture relates should be taken as figurative and prophetic, not simply as historical and literal; it should be understood in terms of how it is directed toward love, either of God, or neighbor, or both. (49) Among the Romans of old it was wrong to wear tunics that were full-length, or long-sleeved, but now it is wrong for well-bred people, when they are dressed in a tunic, not to wear them long: similarly, I must remark that in all other such use of physical things there should be no sensuality, for it not only taints and misuses the customs of those among whom one lives, but also frequently transgresses them altogether,

inter claustra morum sollemnium latitabat, flagitiosissima eruptione manifestat.

21. (50) Quidquid autem congruit consuetudini eorum cum quibus vita ista degenda vel necessitate imponitur vel officio suscipitur, a bonis et magnis hominibus ad utilitatem et beneficientiam referendum est, vel proprie sicut et nos debemus, vel etiam figurate sicut prophetis licet. 22. (51) In quae facta legenda cum incurrunt indocti alterius consuetudinis, nisi auctoritate reprimantur, flagitia putant; nec possunt animadvertere totam conversationem suam, vel in coniugiis vel in conviviis vel in vestitu ceteroque humano victu atque cultu, aliis gentibus et aliis temporibus flagitiosum videri.

(52) Qua varietate innumerabilium consuetudinum commoti quidam dormitantes, ut ita dicam, qui neque alto somno stultitiae sopiebantur, nec in sapientiae lucem poterant evigilare, putaverunt nullam esse iustitiam per se ipsam, sed unicuique genti consuetudinem suam iustam videri; quae cum sit diversa omnibus gentibus, debeat autem incommutabilis manere iustitia, fieri manifestum nullam usquam esse iustitiam. Non intellexerunt, ne multa commemorem, "quod tibi fieri non vis, alii ne feceris," nullo modo posse ulla eorum gentili diversitate variari. (53) Quae sententia cum refertur ad dilectionem dei, omnia flagitia moriuntur, cum ad proximi, omnia facinora.

---

73 Hill 1996: "I have to confess that I really have no idea what he is talking about in this sentence" (198). Augustine is not the last person to wonder why a garment may be fashionable at one time yet ridiculous at another.

74 Tobit 4:15; Matthew 7:12; etc.

and explodes into flagrant obscenity, which used to lurk unseen within the bounds of customary morality.[73]

21. (50) Whatever fits in with the customs of the people with whom one spends one's life, either imposed by need or accepted as a duty, people of good standing should ascribe to usefulness and benevolence. This can be of a literal kind, such as our obligations, or it can be figurative, as is fitting for the prophets. 22. (51) When uneducated people, with different customs, encounter actions of this kind in the course of their reading, they consider them to be wrong unless an authority figure directs them otherwise. They cannot understand that their own entire way of life—marriage, table fellowship, clothing, and other aspects of human necessaries and social norms—look wrong to other peoples in other historical eras.

(52) There are even people who are so disturbed by the sheer variety of customs and practices, and so slow-witted, as it were, that they were neither lulled by the deep sleep of stupidity nor able to awaken into the light of wisdom: they thought that there is no such thing as actual righteousness; but that each nation's customs seemed righteous to them. Yet although righteousness is different among different nations, it ought in itself to remain unchanging; so they thought it obvious that righteousness, as a result, clearly does not exist. To take just one example, they have failed to understand that "do not do to others what you do not want to happen to you,"[74] can by no means be modified by the variety of practices among the gentiles. (53) When this saying is applied to the love of God, all wrongdoing perishes. When it is applied to the love of neighbor, all criminal activity perishes. No one wants their

Nemo enim vult corrumpi habitaculum suum, non ergo debet corrumpere habitaculum dei, se ipsum scilicet. Et nemo vult sibi a quoquam noceri; nec ipse igitur cuiquam nocuerit.

23. (54) Sic eversa tyrannide cupiditatis caritas regnat iustissimis legibus dilectionis dei propter deum, sui et proximi propter deum. Servabitur ergo in locutionibus figuratis regula huiusmodi, ut tam diu versetur diligenti consideratione quod legitur, donec ad regnum caritatis interpretatio perducatur. Si autem hoc iam proprie sonat, nulla putetur figurata locutio.

24. (55) Si praeceptiva locutio est aut flagitium aut facinus vetans, aut utilitatem aut beneficientiam iubens, non est figurata. Si autem flagitium aut facinus videtur iubere, aut utilitatem aut beneficentiam vetare, figurata est. "Nisi manducaveritis," inquit, "carnem filii hominis et sanguinem biberitis, non habebitis vitam in vobis." Facinus vel flagitium videtur iubere: figura ergo est, praecipiens passioni dominicae esse communicandum et suaviter atque utiliter recondendum in memoria, quod pro nobis caro eius crucifixa et vulnerata sit.

(56) Ait scriptura, "si esurierit inimicus tuus, ciba illum; si sitit potum da illi." Hic nullo dubitante beneficientiam praecipit. Sed quod sequitur, "hoc enim faciens carbones ignis congeres super caput eius," malivolentiae

---

75 *habitacula*: a dwelling place of God, or (as here) of the soul. See Ephesians 2:22$^{\text{Vulg.}}$. 76 A passive form of Socrates' paradox that no one willingly does wrong. 77 This gave rise to anti-Christian polemic. See Justin, *Apol.* 1.26; Tert. *Apol.* 8.2; see also Wagemakers, "Incest, Infanticide, and Cannibalism," 337–54. 78 John 6:54. 79 Romans 12:20.

own dwelling place[75] to be defiled, so we ought not to defile the dwelling place of God—in other words, ourselves. Also no one consents to their own harm;[76] so we should do no harm to anyone else.

23. (54) Once the tyranny of desire has been overthrown, love rules by the most righteous laws of all: devotion to God for God's sake, and devotion to self and neighbor for God's sake. For this reason we shall stick to a rule of this kind when it comes to figurative expressions: that we should mull over in our minds what we read, giving it our devout attention, until our interpretation of it brings us home to love's domain. But if such a saying already has a literal resonance, it must not be considered as a figurative expression.

24. (55) If an expression takes the form of instruction, and is forbidding wrongdoing and crime, or demanding what is advantageous and beneficial, it is not figurative. If, however, it is apparently demanding wrongdoing or crime, or forbidding advantage or benefit, it is figurative. Jesus says, "Unless you eat the flesh of the Son of man[77] and drink his blood, you will have no life in you."[78] What he demands seems to be wrong, or criminal: so it is a figurative expression, teaching us that the fact his flesh was crucified and wounded for us is a means of sharing in the Lord's passion, and consigning it safely to our memory to lighten care and do us good.

(56) Scripture says, "If your enemy is hungry, feed him; if he is thirsty, give him a drink." This is undoubtedly an instruction to do something good. But when there follows, "by doing this you will heap coals of fire on his head,"[79]

facinus putes iuberi. Ne igitur dubitaveris figurate dictum. Et cum possit dupliciter interpretari, uno modo ad nocendum, altero ad praestandum; ad beneficientiam te potius caritas revocet, ut intellegas carbones ignis esse urentes paenitentiae gemitus, quibus superbia sanatur eius qui dolet se inimicum fuisse hominis a quo eius miseriae subvenitur.

(57) Item cum ait dominus, "qui amat animam suam, perdet eam," non utilitatem vetare putandus est qua debet quisque conservare animam suam, sed figurate dictum "perdat animam," id est, perimat atque amittat usum eius, quem nunc habet, perversum scilicet atque praeposterum, quo inclinatur temporalibus, ut aeterna non quaerat. Scriptum est, "da misericordi, et ne suscipias peccatorem." Posterior pars huius sententiae videtur vetare beneficientiam. Ait enim, "ne suscipias peccatorem"; intellegas ergo "peccatorem" figurate positum pro peccato, ut peccatum eius non suscipias.

25. (58) Saepe autem accidit ut quisquis in meliori gradu spiritalis vitae vel est vel esse se putat, figurate dicta esse arbitretur quae inferioribus gradibus praecipiuntur; ut verbi gratia si caelibem amplexus est vitam, et se "castravit propter regnum caelorum," quidquid de uxore diligenda et regenda sancti libri praecipiunt, non proprie sed translate accipi oportere contendat; et si quis statuit ser-

---

[80] John 12:25.

[81] Sirach 12:4.

[82] This remark shows the latitude he allows himself in applying his criterion of love.

[83] Matthew 19:12.

you may be thinking that a crime of malice is being demanded of you. Make no mistake: this is being said figuratively. And even though there are two ways of taking it, one that does harm, the other offering help, let love call you back rather to what is beneficial. Then you will understand that the "coals of fire" are the burning cries of penitence, which cleanse the person's pride as they grieve that they were once hostile to the person who has healed their affliction.

(57) Likewise, when the Lord says, "anyone who loves their own life will lose it,"[80] you should not think of this as prohibiting the pragmatism that leads us all to defend our own life from harm. In fact, the words are said figuratively, "let them lose their life," in other words, let them annul and abandon the way they are using it at present, namely being inclined to what is ephemeral, thus precluding what is eternal. That is undoubtedly perverse and wrongheaded. It is written, "give to the merciful and do not support a sinner." The second part of the sentence looks like it is forbidding being kind, for it states, "do not support a sinner";[81] so you should take it that the word, "sinner" has been put figuratively for "sin," so that it is sin that you do not support.[82]

25. (58) It often happens that persons who either are on a higher level of the spiritual life, or think that they are, decide that instructions that apply at lower levels have been said figuratively. For example, if a man has embraced living as a celibate, and has "castrated himself for the sake of the kingdom of heaven,"[83] he may argue that anything prescribed by the holy books in terms of having to love one's wife, or control her, ought not to be taken literally but metaphorically. So too if a man has decided to keep

vare innuptam virginem suam, tamquam figuratam locutionem conetur interpretari qua dictum est, "trade filiam, et magnum opus perfeceris." (59) Erit igitur etiam hoc in observationibus intellegendarum scripturarum, ut sciamus alia omnibus communiter praecipi, alia singulis quibusque generibus personarum, ut non solum ad universum statum valetudinis, sed etiam ad suam cuiusque membri propriam infirmitatem medicina perveniat. In suo quippe genere curandum est, quod ad melius genus non potest erigi.

26. (60) Item cavendum est ne forte quod in scripturis veteribus pro illorum temporum condicione, etiamsi non figurate, sed proprie intellegatur, non est flagitium neque facinus, ad ista etiam tempora quis putet in usum vitae posse transferri. Quod nisi dominante cupiditate, et ipsarum quoque scripturarum quibus evertenda est satellitium quaerente, non faciet; nec intellegit miser ad hanc utilitatem illa esse sic posita ut spei bonae homines salubriter videant et consuetudinem quam aspernantur posse habere usum bonum, et eam quam amplexantur esse posse damnabilem, si et ibi caritas utentium et hic cupiditas attendatur.

27. (61) Nam si multis uxoribus caste uti quisquam pro tempore potuit, potest alius una libidinose. Magis enim

---

[84] Precisely quoting 1 Corinthians 7:37. *Virgo* means a young woman without further qualification; or one who has not had sexual intercourse; or one who is not married. Celibate marriage was practiced as a Christian virtue in Augustine's time.

[85] Sirach 7:25.

[86] *satellitium*: a rare word, but Augustine liked to use it. See *Conf.* 6.15.25.

the young woman he is betrothed to unmarried,[84] he should try to take the saying, "give your daughter in marriage, and you will have accomplished a great object,"[85] as a figurative expression. (59) Here is another factor in our remarks upon interpreting the scriptures: that we know some commands are laid upon us all alike, while others are for individuals or groups of people. This lets a remedy have its effect both on our general state of health and on the particular ailments of our individual parts. To be sure, anything that cannot be promoted to a higher level needs to be cured at its own level.

26. (60) When something in the Old Testament is neither a disgrace nor a crime, even if taken literally, not just figuratively (according to the circumstances of those days) we must take care not to assume that it can be transplanted into this day and age and applied to our lives. No one will do so unless desire has taken control, and is looking for protection[86] from those same scriptures whose purpose is its overthrow. Meanwhile the poor wretch does not understand that those episodes were set there with this practical objective: that people of conviction may benefit from seeing that a practice that they repudiate can have a worthwhile purpose, and then that one that they hold dear can be abhorrent. This is provided that we take into account the love exercised by the former; and the desire exercised by the latter.

27. (61) For example: whereas in the past one man could make use of[87] many wives without impropriety according to the standards of the time, another man can

[87] Stressing that motivation is critical recalls his *utor/frui* distinction (see 1.3.7).

probo multarum fecunditate utentem propter aliud quam unius carne fruentem propter ipsam. Ibi enim quaeritur utilitas temporum opportunitatibus congrua, hic satiatur cupiditas temporalibus voluptatibus implicata. Inferiorisque gradus ad deum sunt, quibus secundum veniam concedit apostolus carnalem cum singulis coniugibus consuetudinem propter intemperantiam eorum, quam illi qui plures singuli cum haberent, sicut sapiens in cibo et potu nonnisi salutem corporis, sic in concubitu nonnisi procreationem filiorum intuebantur. (62) Itaque si eos in hac vita invenisset domini adventus, cum iam non mittendi sed colligendi lapides tempus esset, statim se ipsos castrarent propter regnum caelorum. Non enim est in carendo difficultas, nisi cum est in habendo cupiditas. Noverant quippe illi homines etiam in ipsis coniugibus luxuriam esse abutendi intemperantiam. Quod Tobiae testatur oratio, quando est copulatus uxori. Ait enim, "Benedictus es, domine patrum nostrorum, et benedictum nomen tuum in omnia saecula saeculorum. Benedicant te caeli et omnis creatura tua. Tu fecisti Adam et dedisti illi adiutorium Evam. Et nunc, domine, tu scis quoniam non luxuriae causa accipio sororem meam, sed ipsa veritate, ut miserearis nostri, domine."

---

88 *secundum veniam*: quoted from 1 Corinthians 7:6^{VL} not Vulg. 89 1 Corinthians 7:2.

90 *adventus* refers to the second coming of Christ (Matthew 24:30), rather than the season of preparation for Christmas.

91 Ecclesiasticus 3:5: he means the gathering in of the faithful (Matthew 25:31–46). 92 Matthew 19:12.

93 Hebrew says "man" and woman," but the nouns were read as proper in Greek and then Latin, generating the personal names "Adam" and "Eve." See Genesis 2:20.

nowadays make use of just the one, but in a way that is driven by desire. I prefer to commend a man who makes use of many women's capacity for childbearing to some purpose, rather than one who takes pleasure in the body of just one woman, for the sake of the flesh alone. The former is pursuing something useful, which is compatible with the standards of the time; while in the latter case, desire is entangling itself in fleeting pleasures, and gorging on them. Also, the men to whom the apostle granted, as a concession,[88] the practice of marital intercourse with one wife[89] (because of their lack of self-restraint) were at a lower level before God than the men who each had several wives and who nonetheless—like a wise person regarding food and drink as being for bodily health—regarded copulation as being only for the procreation of children. (62) If, then, the Lord had returned[90] and found them still living now that the time for gathering stones together was at hand,[91] they would immediately castrate themselves for the kingdom of heaven's sake.[92] For it is only difficult to do without something when you have a desire to possess it. Those men certainly knew that there can be sinful indulgence in the misuse of intercourse even within marriage. The words of Tobias, when he coupled with his wife, bear witness to this. He said, "Blessed are you, Lord of our fathers, and blessed is your name for ever and ever. Let the heavens and all your creation bless you. You have made man and have given him woman as his helpmeet.[93] And now, Lord, you know that I do not take my own kinswoman[94] for sinful gratification's sake, but in genuine honesty, so that you have mercy upon us."

[94] *sororem*: see Tobit 7:11, 8:7–10.

28. (63) Sed qui effrenata libidine vel per multa stupra diffluentes evagantur, vel in ipsa una coniuge, non solum excedunt ad liberorum procreationem pertinentem modum, sed etiam inhumanioris intemperantiae sordes inverecunda omnino licentia servilis cuiusdam libertatis accumulant. Non credunt fieri potuisse ut temperanter multis feminis antiqui uterentur viri, nihil servantes in usu illo nisi congruum tempori propagandae prolis officium. Et quod ipsi laqueis libidinis obstricti vel in una non faciunt, nullo modo in multis fieri posse arbitrantur.

29. (64) Sed isti possunt dicere nec honorari quidem atque laudari oportere viros bonos et sanctos, quia ipsi cum honorantur atque laudantur, intumescunt superbia; tanto avidiores inanissimae gloriae, quanto eos frequentius atque latius lingua blandior ventilaverit. Qua ita leves fiunt ut eos rumoris aura, sive quae prospera sive quae adversa existimatur, in quaslibet invehat voragines flagitiorum, aut in facinorum etiam saxa collidat. Videant ergo quam sibi arduum sit atque difficile, nec laudis esca illici, nec contumeliarum aculeis penetrari, et non ex se alios metiantur.

(65) Credant potius apostolos nostros nec cum suspicerentur ab hominibus inflatos fuisse, nec cum despi-

---

95 *servilis libertatis*: oxymoron.

96 He means polygamy, not merely multiple liaisons.

28. (63) But those who stray from the path in their unbridled passion (whether deviating far and wide across multiple shocking liaisons or inflicting them on their spouse only) do not only go beyond the confines of what is required for the procreation of children. They also pile up the filth of their bestial dissipation, completely shameless and dissolute in a degree of slavish laxity.[95] They do not believe that the men of old were able to make use of many women[96] in a self-controlled way, paying no attention to that purpose except with respect to their duty of begetting offspring, as was appropriate in those days. Also, because they are so entrapped by the snares of seduction, they judge it impossible to achieve with many wives what they themselves are incapable of achieving even with only one.

29. (64) But those same men are able to claim that even the good and holy should not be honored and praised, and this because when they themselves are honored and praised, they swell with pride. The greedier they are for glory that is utterly worthless, then, the more broadly and constantly flattering tongues sway them. This makes them so lacking in dignity that a whisper of rumor (whether people think it is favorable or unfavorable) carries them off into a maelstrom of every kind of wrongdoing, or even dashes them on the rocks of criminality of every kind. So they ought to observe how hard it is, how demanding, for themselves to be neither seduced by their hunger for praise, nor wounded by the darts of hostile criticism: and not to measure others according to the standards they themselves live by.

(65) They would do better to believe that our apostles were not puffed up when people looked up to them, or deflated when people looked down on them. Both types

cerentur elisos. Neutra quippe temptatio defuit illis viri. Nam et credentium celebrabantur praeconio et persequentium maledictis infamabantur. (66) Sicut ergo isti pro tempore utebantur his omnibus et non corrumpebantur, sic illi veteres, usum feminarum ad sui temporis convenientiam referentes, non patiebantur eam dominationem libidinis, cui serviunt qui ista non credunt.

30. (67) Et ideo isti nullo modo sese cohiberent ab inexpiabili odio filiorum a quibus vel uxores vel concubinas suas attemptatas aut attrectatas esse cognoscerent, si eis forte tale aliquid accidisset. (68) Rex autem David cum hoc ab impio atque immani filio passus esset, non solum ferocientem toleravit, sed etiam planxit exstinctum. Non enim carnali zelo irretitus tenebatur, quem nullo modo iniuriae suae, sed peccata filii commovebant. Nam ideo, si vinceretur, eum occidi prohibuerat, ut edomito servaretur paenitendi locus; et quia non potuit, non orbitatem doluit in eius interitu, sed noverat in quas poenas tam impie adultera et parricidalis anima raperetur. Namque alio prius filio qui innocens erat, pro quo aegrotante affligebatur, moriente laetatus est.

31. (69) Et hoc maxime apparet qua moderatione ac temperantia illi viri feminis utebantur, quod cum in unam

---

97 Absalom: 2 Samuel 18:33.

98 *parricidalis*: Augustine conflates Absalom's murder of his half-brother Amnon with the attempted murder of his father.

99 The verb (*laetatus est*) may be taken as internal (David felt delight) or, better, external (David behaved in a way characteristic of happiness). Either is a fourth-century AD take on 2 Samuel 12:20–23.

of temptation assailed them: for believers trumpeted their fame, while their persecutors' slanders attacked their reputations. (66) So just as the apostles made use of all these things, in ways that were appropriate in those days, yet were not corrupted, so too those men of old made their treatment of women conform to their own time. They did not allow that tyranny of unbridled desire that enslaves all who are not believers.

30. (67) This is why, had they discovered that their sons had either tried to assault their wives or concubines, or had actually succeeded—if anything of the kind had taken place—they would be incapable of restraining themselves from irredeemably hating them. (68) Yet King David, when he endured just that at the hands of that wild, ungodly son of his, not only put up with his unruly behavior but even wept for him once he was dead.[97] He was not caught in the snare of his own human jealousy, for it was the sins of his son that troubled him, not by any means the offenses committed against himself. This is why David had given orders that Absalom was not to be killed if he was vanquished: to secure an opportunity for him to repent after his defeat. When this proved to be impossible, he did not lament the loss he suffered in the death of his son, but he knew the punishments that such a soul, ungodly, adulterous, and murderous[98] was hurtling toward. And after all, there was another son before that, who was innocent, for whom David was distraught while the child was ill; yet at its death he rejoiced.[99]

31. (69) The moderation and self-control exercised by men in those days in their treatment of women[100] stands

100 A selective presentation: Absalom had killed Amnon for raping Tamar (2 Samuel 13).

illicite irruisset rex idem, aestu quodam aetatis et temporalium rerum prosperitatibus abreptus, cuius etiam maritum occidendum praeceperat, accusatus est per prophetam, qui cum ad eum venisset convincendum de peccato, proposuit ei similitudinem de paupere qui habebat ovem unam, cuius vicinus multas cum haberet, ad adventum hospitis sui unicam potius vicini sui pauperis oviculam exhibuit epulandam. (70) In quem commotus David occidi eum iussit et quadruplicari ovem pauperi, ut se nesciens condemnaret qui peccaverat sciens. Quod cum ei manifestatum esset et divinitus denuntiata vindicta, diluit paenitendo peccatum.

Sed tamen in hac similitudine stuprum tantummodo designatum est de ove vicini pauperis. De marito autem mulieris interempto, hoc est de ipso paupere, qui unam ovem habebat occiso, non est per similitudinem interrogatus David, ut in solum adulterium diceret sententiam damnationis suae. (71) Ex quo intellegitur quanta temperantia multas mulieres habuerit, quando de una in qua excessit modum, a se ipso puniri coactus est. Sed in isto viro immoderatae huius libidinis non permansio, sed transitus fuit; propterea etiam ab arguente propheta ille illicitus appetitus "hospes" vocatus est. Non enim dixit eum regi suo, sed hospiti suo vicini pauperis ovem ad epulandum exhibuisse. (72) At vero in eius filio Salomone

---

101 *per*: prophets speak not their own words but God's.

102 That is, Nathan the prophet never denounced David for the death of Uriah the Hittite (which the king had intended, and facilitated, but not directly caused). See 2 Samuel 11–12.

103 Not the most convincing defense of David.

104 *hospes*: following VL. Vulg. has *peregrinus*.

out clearly in the following case. That same king, in the heat of his youthful passion, carried away with material successes, unlawfully ravished a woman after giving orders for her husband to be cut down: but he was then denounced by[101] the prophet. That prophet had come to convict David of sin, and so set out for him a parable, about a poor man who had one ewe, but whose neighbor had many. Yet when a guest of his arrived, the neighbor provided the poor man's little ewe lamb for the feast. (70) David was outraged against the neighbor and gave orders for him to be killed, and for the poor man to be repaid fourfold in sheep. Thus he who had sinned knowingly was condemning himself unknowingly. When the business was revealed to him, and under divine guidance the sentence of punishment was declared, David washed away his sin by his repentance.

In this parable, though, only the sexual sin is represented by the ewe belonging to the poor neighbor. As for the husband of the woman, who was got rid of, and who was represented by the poor man with one ewe, after he was killed David was not challenged about him through the parable, since he passed the sentence of his own condemnation for adultery only.[102] (71) From this we understand what self-control he exercised in possessing his many women, insofar as he was driven to punish himself over just one, in whose case he had behaved immoderately.[103] Not that this unbridled passion found an abiding home in David. It was a passing moment. Hence when the prophet made his case, he referred to that unlawful desire as a "passing guest."[104] After all, he said that the neighbor had served up the ewe at a feast for his guest, not for his king. (72) Unbridled passion was no passing guest, though,

non quasi hospes transitum habuit, sed regnum ista libido possedit; de quo scriptura non tacuit, culpans eum fuisse amatorem mulierum. Cuius tamen initia desiderio sapientiae flagraverunt; quam cum amore spiritali adeptus esset, amisit amore carnali.

32. (73) Ergo quamquam omnia vel paene omnia quae in veteris testamenti libris gesta continentur, non solum proprie, sed etiam figurate accipienda sint, tamen etiam illa quae proprie lector acceperit, si laudati sunt illi qui ea fecerunt, sed ea tamen abhorrent a consuetudine bonorum qui post adventum domini divina praecepta custodiunt: figuram ad intellegentiam referat, factum vero ipsum ad mores non transferat. Multa enim sunt quae illo tempore officiose facta sunt, quae modo nisi libidinose fieri non possunt.

33. (74) Si qua vero peccata magnorum virorum legerit, tametsi in eis aliquam figuram rerum futurarum animadvertere atque indagare potuerit, rei tamen gestae proprietatem ad hunc usum assumat, ut se nequaquam recte factis suis iactare audeat et prae sua iustitia ceteros tamquam peccatores contemnat, cum videat tantorum virorum et cavendas tempestates, et flenda naufragia. (75) Ad hoc enim etiam peccata illorum hominum scripta sunt ut apostolica illa sententia ubique tremenda sit, cum ait, "quapropter qui videtur stare, videat ne cadat." Nulla enim fere pagina est sanctorum librorum in qua non sonet quod "deus superbis resistit, humilibus autem dat gra-

---

105 2 Samuel 12:13–15.

106 1 Kings 5:12.

when it came to David's son Solomon: it took over the kingdom. Scripture did not remain silent about it, but instead censured him as a lover of women.[105] Solomon began by being aflame with desire for wisdom,[106] but although he won her by spiritual love, he lost her through physical love.

32. (73) Although all the action, therefore (or almost all of it) that is contained in the books of the Old Testament is to be taken figuratively as well as literally, there will be things that the reader takes as literal if the doers of those actions are praised, which are nonetheless repellent to the practices of those good men who safeguard the divine teachings from the period after the Lord's coming. Then the reader should refer them for figurative interpretation, and not incorporate such actions into their own morality. For many such actions were perfectly proper in those days; but now they cannot be practiced except as a means to self-gratification.

33. (74) Certainly, if someone has read about some sins committed by great men, even if they can detect in them some sort of prefiguring of future events, still they must adopt the literal sense of every deed in this way: when they see what dreadful storms these great men have to steer past, and what shipwrecks they have to regret, the reader must not boast of their own deeds with reckless impropriety, and condemn others as sinners in comparison with their own righteousness. (75) For this purpose the sins of such people were recorded in writing: to make that saying of the apostle universally portentous, namely, "therefore, let anyone who aims to stand take care not to fall." For there is scarcely a page of the holy books in which that principle does not resound: "God resists the proud, but

tiam." (76) Maxime itaque investigandum est utrum propria sit an figurata locutio quam intellegere conamur. Nam comperto quod figurata sit, adhibitis regulis rerum quas in primo libro digessimus, facile est eam versare omnibus modis, donec perveniamus ad sententiam veritatis, praesertim cum usus accesserit pietatis exercitatione roboratus. Invenimus autem utrum propria sit an figurata locutio, illa intuentes quae supra dicta sunt.

34. (77) Quod cum apparuerit, verba quibus continetur aut a similibus rebus ducta invenientur, aut ab aliqua vicinitate attingentibus.

35. (78) Sed quoniam multis modis res similes rebus apparent, non putemus esse praescriptum ut quod in aliquo loco res aliqua per similitudinem significaverit, hoc eam semper significare credamus. Nam et in vituperatione posuit fermentum dominus cum diceret, "cavete a fermento Pharisaeorum," et in laude cum diceret, "simile est regnum caelorum mulieri quae abscondit fermentum in tribus mensuris farinae donec totum fermentaretur."

36. (79) Huius igitur varietatis observatio duas habet formas. Sic enim aliud atque aliud res quaeque significant, ut aut contraria aut tantummodo diversa significent. Contraria scilicet, cum alias in bono alias in malo res eadem per similitudinem ponitur, sicut hoc est quod de fermento supra diximus. Tale est etiam quod leo significat Christum,

---

[107] James 4:6.

[108] Hill 1996: "this whole section [is] pure flannel—something he would surely either have cut out or given some substance to, had he really revised the work" (199n53).

[109] Matthew 16:11.

[110] Luke 13:21. The last paragraph of the first edition is §78. The earliest MS, L, also stops here. See *Retr.*

gives grace to the lowly."[107] (76) This is why we must examine thoroughly whether what we are trying to understand is a literal expression or a figurative one. Once we have used the rules that we discussed in book one to ascertain that it is figurative, it is easy to reflect upon it using various approaches, until we reach an accurate judgment, particularly when experience is underpinned by devotional practices. We discover whether an expression is literal or figurative by scrutinizing those factors mentioned above.

34. (77)[108] Once this is clear, you will find that the words in which is it expressed are drawn from some similar case, or touch on some parallel example.

35. (78) Since particular instances appear to be alike in many respects, we should not consider it a firm rule that what something signifies by analogy in one particular place we should believe has always that same meaning. For the Lord meant it as a negative when he said, "beware of the leaven of the Pharisees";[109] but as a positive when he said, "the kingdom of heaven is like a woman who covered leaven with three measures of flour until the whole batch was leavened."[110]

36. (79) Scrutiny of this divergence takes two forms. This is how all individual things have one significance or another: they either signify things that are the opposite, or things that are merely different. They are certainly opposites when the same thing is used as an analogy for something good in one place, and something bad in another, as in the case of the leaven we just mentioned. Another such instance is the fact that a lion signifies

ubi dicitur, "vicit leo de tribu Iuda," significat et diabolum, ubi scriptum est, "adversarius vester diabolus tamquam leo rugiens circuit, quaerens quem devoret." (80) Ita serpens in bono est, "astuti ut serpentes," in malo autem, "serpens Evam seduxit in astutia sua." In bono panis, "ego sum panis vivus qui de caelo descendi," in malo panis, "panes occultos libenter edite." Sic et alia plurima. Et haec quidem quae commemoravi, minime dubiam significationem gerunt, quia exempli gratia commemorari nonnisi manifesta debuerunt. Sunt autem quae incertum sit in quam partem accipi debeant, sicut, "calix in manu domini vini meri, plenus est mixto." (81) Incertum est enim utrum iram dei significet non usque ad novissimam poenam, id est usque ad faecem; an potius gratiam scripturarum a Iudaeis ad gentes transeuntem, quia "inclinavit ex hoc in hoc," remanentibus apud Iudaeos observationibus quas carnaliter sapiunt, quia "faex eius non est exinanita." Cum vero res eadem non in contraria, sed tantum in diversa significatione ponitur, illud est in exemplo, quod aqua et populum significat, sicut in Apocalypsi legimus, et spiritum sanctum, unde est illud, "flumina aquae vivae fluent de ventre eius," et si quid aliud atque aliud, pro locis in quibus ponitur, aqua significare intellegitur.

---

[111] Scripture. [112] Revelation 5:5. [113] 1 Peter 5:8.
[114] Matthew 10:16. [115] 2 Corinthians 11:3.
[116] John 6:51. [117] Proverbs 9:17. See *Conf.* 3.6.11, *panes occultos libenter edite*, quoting his preferred VL, not *panis absconditus suavior*, Vulg. [118] Psalm 75:8. LXX and Latin versions call the wine both "mixed" (*mixto*) and "unmixed" (*meri*). Wine was regularly drunk diluted: see *Conf.* 9.8.18.
[119] *gratia* is still acquiring its technical sense of God's undeserved favor. [120] Revelation 17:15. [121] John 7:38.

Christ, when it[111] says, "the lion of the tribe of Judah,"[112] but it signifies the Devil where it is written, "your adversary the Devil as a roaring lion goes here and there, seeking someone to devour."[113] (80) Again, the snake is taken as good in, "be clever as snakes,"[114] but as evil in, "the snake in its craftiness beguiled Eve."[115] Bread is good in, "I am the bread of life who came down from heaven,"[116] but bad in, "loaves of bread eaten out of sight are pleasurable."[117] There are countless such examples. The ones that I have mentioned have very little ambiguity about what they signify, because only clear instances should be mentioned when giving examples. Of course, there are instances where it is unclear whether they should be taken as negative or positive, for example, "in the hand of the Lord is a cup of pure wine, filled up by mixed wine."[118] (81) It is not clear whether it signifies God's wrath (though not right to the uttermost penalty, which is to say all the way down to the dregs), or rather the free gift[119] of the scriptures passing from the Jews to the gentiles, because "it changed from the one to the other," as the Jews went on maintaining their observances (which they understand according to the flesh inasmuch as they "did not drink down to the dregs"). To be sure, when one example is used not with an opposite signification, but merely one that is different (as in the case that water signifies a people, which we read in Revelation,[120] but also the Holy Spirit, as in, "rivers of living water flow from the core of them,"[121] this is in addition to anything else at all that water is understood as signifying, depending on the context in which it is mentioned.

37. (82) Sic et aliae res non singulae, sed unaquaeque earum non solum duo aliqua diversa, sed etiam nonnumquam multa significat, pro loco sententiae, sicut posita reperitur.

(83) Ubi autem apertius ponuntur, ibi discendum est quo modo in locis intellegantur obscuris. Neque enim melius potest intellegi quod dictum est deo, "apprehende arma et scutum et exsurge in adiutorium mihi," quam ex loco illo ubi legitur, "domine, ut scuto bonae voluntatis tuae coronasti nos." Nec tamen ita ut iam ubicumque scutum pro aliquo munimento positum legerimus, non accipiamus nisi bonam voluntatem dei. Dictum est enim et "scutum fidei, in quo possitis, inquit, omnes sagittas maligni ignitas exstinguere." Nec rursum ideo debemus in armis huiuscemodi spiritalibus scuto tantummodo fidem tribuere, cum alio loco etiam lorica dicta sit fidei, "induti, inquit, loricam fidei et caritatis."

38. (84) Quando autem ex eisdem scripturae verbis non unum aliquid, sed duo vel plura sentiuntur, etiam si latet quid senserit ille qui scripsit, nihil periculi est, si quodlibet eorum congruere veritati ex aliis locis sanctarum scripturarum doceri potest, id tamen eo conante qui divina scrutatur eloquia, ut ad voluntatem perveniatur auctoris per quem scripturam illam sanctus operatus est spiritus; sive hoc assequatur, sive aliam sententiam de illis verbis quae fidei rectae non refragatur exsculpat, testimonium habens a quocumque alio loco divinorum eloquiorum. (85) Ille

[122] Psalm 35:2. [123] Psalm 5:12. [124] Ephesians 6:16. [125] 1 Thessalonians 5:8. [126] See Introduction to *TC*, p. 171. [127] Latin *divina eloquia*: here and at the end of this paragraph, referring to scripture. [128] §84 is one long Latin sentence.

37. (82) There are multiple examples too that, taken in isolation, signify not just two differing options but sometimes even a number of them, depending on the context within which the example is mentioned.

(83) When they are used more straightforwardly, that is where we learn how to make sense of the less obvious usages. There is no better way to understand what God says, "seize weapons and shield and arise to help me,"[122] than that passage that reads, "Lord, you have crowned us with the shield of your favor."[123] That is not to say that now, whenever we happen to read the word "shield" standing for some type of protection, we are only to take it as meaning God's favor. Also mentioned is "the shield of faith, by which you have power to quench all the fiery darts of the wicked one."[124] Again, this is not a reason why, in this type of instance of spiritual weaponry, we must associate faith solely with a shield, for another passage mentions a breastplate of faith, saying, "put on the breastplate of faith and love."[125]

38. (84) When you detect, though, not one meaning but two or more from those same scriptures, even if the meaning intended by the writer[126] is obscure there is no risk involved where any one of them can be shown (by comparison with other passages of the holy writings) to be in harmony with the truth. This depends on the person who is examining the divine communications[127] doing their utmost to get to the intention of the author through whom the Holy Spirit produced that particular scripture, whether they succeed in that aim, or whether they carve out another sense from those words, which does not contradict the true faith because it is corroborated by another passage in the divine communications.[128] (85) The author

quippe auctor in eisdem verbis quae intellegere volumus, et ipsam sententiam forsitan vidit et certe dei spiritus, qui per eum haec operatus est, etiam ipsam occursuram lectori vel auditori sine dubitatione praevidit, immo ut occurreret, quia et ipsa est veritate subnixa, providit. Nam quid in divinis eloquiis largius et uberius potuit divinitus provideri, quam ut eadem verba pluribus intellegantur modis, quos alia non minus divina contestantia faciant approbari?

39. (86) Ubi autem talis sensus eruitur, cuius incertum certis sanctarum scripturarum testimoniis non possit aperiri, restat ut ratione reddita manifestus appareat, etiam si ille cuius verba intellegere quaerimus eum forte non sensit. Sed haec consuetudo periculosa est; per scripturas enim divinas multo tutius ambulatur. Quas verbis translatis opacatas cum scrutari volumus, aut hoc inde exeat quod non habeat controversiam, aut si habet, ex eadem scriptura ubicumque eius inventis atque adhibitis testibus terminetur.

40. (87) Sciant autem litterati modis omnibus locutionis, quos grammatici Graeco nomine "tropos" vocant, auctores nostros usos fuisse, et multiplicius atque copiosius quam possunt existimare vel credere qui nesciunt eos et in aliis ista didicerunt. Quos tamen tropos qui noverunt agnoscunt in litteris sanctis eorumque scientia ad eas intellegendas aliquantum adiuvantur. Sed hic eos ignaris

---

[129] Capitalized as a name for Christ (John 14:6). He makes the point that divine inspiration is not only in the writer but also in the receiver, of the scriptures. [130] See *TC* 2.15.32.

[131] "Our authors" means Christian writers; "other texts" means classical writings.

himself, in fact, perhaps saw the same sense in those very words that we want to interpret; certainly the Holy Spirit did, for it achieved its purpose through the author, and it undoubtedly anticipated that actual meaning's presenting itself to a reader or hearer, and what is more, made provision for it to occur, for it is founded upon the Truth.[129] After all, what more abundant and fruitful purpose in the divine communications could be furnished by divine providence than for the same words to be understood in a variety of ways that other equally inspired witnesses serve to validate?

39. (86) When a meaning is elicited, the ambiguity of which cannot be clarified beyond doubt by witnesses from the holy scriptures, there is still the option to make the sense clear through applying reason, even if the author whose words we are trying to understand did not perceive that meaning. But this is a risky practice. We must take the utmost care as we make our way through the divine scriptures. When we wish to examine texts of scripture that have been obscured by words not used in their literal sense, the conclusion needs to be beyond dispute. But if it is disputed, let the answer be determined from the same text wherever witnesses to it can be found and applied.

40. (87) Educated people ought to know that our authors have made use of every kind of expression that teachers of grammar describe by a Greek term, "tropes,"[130] and have done so in many more ways and places than people who know nothing of those authors, and who have learned such figures of speech from other texts.[131] Yet people who understand these tropes recognize them in sacred texts, and their knowledge of these will help them to understand, at least to some extent. This is not the right

tradere non decet, ne artem grammaticam docere videamur. Extra sane ut discantur admoneo, quamvis iam superius id admonuerim, id est in secundo libro, ubi de linguarum necessaria cognitione disserui. (88) Nam litterae, a quibus ipsa grammatica nomen accepit ("grammata" enim Graeci litteras vocant), signa utique sunt sonorum ad articulatam vocem qua loquimur pertinentium. Istorum autem troporum non solum exempla, sicut omnium, sed quorundam etiam nomina in divinis libris leguntur, sicut allegoria, aenigma, parabola. Quamvis paene omnes hi tropi qui liberali dicuntur arte cognosci, etiam in eorum reperiantur loquellis qui nullos grammaticos audierunt, et eo quo vulgus utitur sermone contenti sunt. (89) Quis enim non dicit, "sic floreas?" Qui tropus "metaphora" vocatur. Quis non dicit, "piscinam," etiam quae non habet pisces, nec facta est propter pisces, et tamen a piscibus nomen accepit? Qui tropus "catachresis" dicitur.

41. (90) Longum est isto modo ceteros persequi, nam usque ad illos pervenit vulgi locutio qui propterea mirabiliores sunt quia contra quam dicitur significant, sicuti est quae appellatur "ironia" vel "antiphrasis." Sed ironia pronuntiatione indicat quid velit intellegi, ut cum dicimus homini mala facienti, "res bonas facis"; antiphrasis vero,

---

132 *TC* 2.19.43.

133 Approximating to modern linguistics or philology.

134 The blooming (*florere*) of flowers (*flores*) applied to a human being.

135 Latin *piscina*: Augustine's point works better in French than in English (*piscine*, swimming pool).

136 Quint. *Inst.* 8.6: "we are right to translate this as 'abuse' [or 'abnormal use']." He means use of a word in an abnormal

place, though, to be passing on knowledge of tropes to the uneducated: we must not look as if we are teaching language skills. Of course, I encourage people to learn them in another context: although I have already encouraged this above, in my second book, where I discussed the importance of knowledge of languages.[132] (88) For letters, from which grammar[133] takes its name (for the Greeks call letters "grammata") are undeniably signs for the sounds related to the articulate speech we use when talking. Not only are there examples of these tropes (as there are of everything), but for some of them the actual name-words are there for us to read in the sacred books. For example, "allegory," "enigma," "parable." Although almost all these tropes are ones that are said to be learned in a liberal education, they are also detectable in the speech of people who have never had a grammar lesson, and who are quite happy with the vulgar tongue. (89) Who has never said, "are you flourishing?" That trope is called "metaphor."[134] Who has never said, "fishpond,"[135] even when the pond has no fish, or was not even designed for fish, but still derives its name from fish? This trope is called "catachresis."[136]

41. (90) It is too long a job to describe all figures of speech in this way, for even common speech has got as far as using figures that are all the more remarkable because they signify the opposite of what they say. We call this "irony" or "antiphrasis." Irony, though, uses pronunciation to make clear what it wants to be understood, as when we say to someone doing something wrong, "that's a good job

sense, giving the example of *parricida*, "parricide," for one who kills his mother or brother, as well as his father (see §68, above).

ut contraria significet, non voce pronuntiantis efficitur, sed aut verba habet sua, quorum origo e contrario est, sicut appellatur lucus, quod minime luceat; aut consuevit aliquid ita dici, quamvis dicatur etiam non e contrario, velut cum quaerimus accipere quod ibi non est, et respondetur nobis, abundat; aut adiunctis verbis facimus ut a contrario intellegatur quod loquimur, velut si dicamus, cave illum, quia bonus homo est. (91) Et quis talia non dicit indoctus nec omnino sciens qui sint vel quid vocentur hi tropi? Quorum cognitio propterea scripturarum ambiguitatibus dissolvendis est necessaria quia cum sensus ad proprietatem verborum si accipiatur absurdus est, quaerendum est utique ne forte illo vel illo tropo dictum sit quod non intellegimus; et sic pleraque inventa sunt quae latebant.

42. (92) Ticonius quidam qui contra Donatistas invictissime scripsit, cum fuerit donatista, et illic invenitur absurdissimi cordis, ubi eos non omni ex parte relinquere voluit, fecit librum quem "Regularum" vocavit, quia in eo quasdam septem regulas exsecutus est, quibus quasi clavibus divinarum scripturarum aperirentur occulta. Quarum primam ponit de domino et eius corpore; secundam,

---

137 *lucus* (grove)/*lux* (light).

138 *RGr.* suggests as a modern equivalent "no problem" (for what will be troublesome).

139 For example, calling John Little "little John" in the Robin Hood legends. "Antiphrasis is a form of speech signifying by means of the opposite, as we call what is not wonderful (*bonum*) a 'war' (*bellum*), and call a 'grove' a place where there is little light . . . It differs from irony (which uses pronunciation and delivery to signify meaning) whereas antiphrasis uses a change of terminology": Diomedes Grammaticus, *Ars grammatica* 2.462 Keil,

you're doing." Antiphrasis, though, signifies an opposite meaning but not by the sound of the voice speaking. Either it has individual words that exhibit it, which originally had an opposite meaning; for example when we call a place a "grove" (for there is scarcely any light[137] there); or it is usual that something is said in a certain way, though it can be said without a contrary meaning, as when we want to get something that is not there, and we are told, "there's plenty,"[138] or we add extra words so that the opposite of what we say is being understood, for example if we said, "watch out for him, for he is a good man."[139] (91) Who does not say things like this, even if they are uneducated, completely ignorant of what these "tropes" are, or what they are called? This is why knowledge of tropes is vital for resolving ambiguities in the scriptures: when the meaning is absurd if words are taken literally, it is absolutely essential to investigate whether what we do not understand has been said using some trope or other. More often than not, this is how we find out what was formerly obscure.

42. (92) There is a man called Ticonius whose writings against the Donatists are unbeatable, though he has himself been a Donatist. That fact proves the utter folly of his feelings when he was unwilling to abandon them completely. He composed a book that he called his "Rules" because he set out in it seven specific rules that could be used as keys to unlock the secrets of the holy scriptures, as follows: first, "the Lord and his body"; second, "the dual

probably late fourth century; the parallel may hint that Augustine had read the work.

de domini corpore bipartito; tertiam, de promissis et lege; quartam, de specie et genere; quintam, de temporibus; sextam, de recapitulatione; septimam, de diabolo et eius corpore.

(93) Quae quidem considerata, sicut ab illo aperiuntur, non parvum adiuvant ad penetranda quae tecta sunt divinorum eloquiorum. Nec tamen omnia quae ita scripta sunt ut non facile intellegantur, possunt his regulis inveniri, sed aliis modis pluribus, quos hoc numero septenario usque adeo non est iste complexus, ut idem ipse multa exponat obscura in quibus harum regularum adhibet nullam, quoniam nec opus est. (94) Neque enim aliquid illic tale versatur aut quaeritur, sicut in Apocalypsi Ioannis quaerit, quemadmodum intellegendi sint angeli ecclesiarum septem, quibus scribere iubetur, et ratiocinatur multipliciter et ad hoc pervenit ut ipsos angelos intellegamus ecclesias. In qua copiosissima disputatione nihil istarum est regularum, et utique res illic obscurissima quaeritur. Quod exempli gratia satis dictum sit, nam colligere omnia nimis longum et nimis operosum est, quae ita obscura sunt in scripturis canonicis ut nihil istorum septem ibi requirendum sit.

43. (95) Iste autem cum has velut regulas commendaret, tantum eis tribuit, quasi omnia quae in lege, id est in divinis libris, obscure posita invenerimus, his bene cognitis atque adhibitis intellegere valeamus. Ita quippe exorsus est eundem librum ut diceret, "necessarium duxi ante omnia quae mihi videntur libellum regularum scribere et

---

[140] See Galatians 3:21.

[141] Revelation 1:20.

nature of the Lord's body"; third, "the promises and the Law";[140] fourth, "species and genus"; fifth, "times"; sixth, "recapitulation"; seventh, "the Devil and his body."

(93) If we give thought to these, as he discloses them, they are no small help when it comes to fathoming parts of the divine communications that have been obscured. This is not to say that everything written in such a way as to be understood only with difficulty can be discovered using these rules: some require a number of other means, which he did not include in his sevenfold scheme. As a result he himself explains many difficulties to which he applies none of his rules, because they are unnecessary there. (94) So nothing of the kind is tried out or explored, for example in the Revelation of John when he explores how to understand the angels of the seven churches that he has been ordered to write to.[141] He uses different ways of reasoning, coming to the conclusion that we must understand those same angels as being churches. In all his lengthy calculations, there is no trace of those rules: and the matter under investigation there is certainly very obscure. I have said enough in terms of examples, and anyway it would be too time-consuming, too labor-intensive, to gather together everything in the canonical writings that is so abstruse that none of his seven rules can be turned to for help.

43. (95) When Ticonius was promoting all these as rules, he gave them staunch backing: if we got to know them and applied them, we would have the capacity to understand everything in the Law (which is to say, in the holy books) that we found was obscurely written. This book he began in the following fashion: "I considered it most pressing, among those subjects that occur to me, to

secretorum legis veluti claves et luminaria fabricare. Sunt enim quaedam regulae mysticae quae universae legis recessus obtinent, et veritatis thesauros aliquibus invisibiles ‹visibiles›[5] faciunt. Quarum si ratio regularum sine invidia, ut communicamus, accepta fuerit, clausa quaeque patefient et obscura dilucidabuntur, ut quis prophetiae immensam silvam perambulans his regulis quodammodo lucis tramitibus deductus ab errore defendatur."

(96) Hic si dixisset, "sunt enim quaedam regulae mysticae quae nonnullos legis recessus obtinent," aut certe, "quae legis magnos recessus obtinent," non autem quod ait, "universae legis recessus"; neque dixisset, "clausa quaeque patefient," sed "clausa multa patefient," verum dixisset, nec tam elaborato atque utili operi suo plus quam res ipsa postulat dando in spem falsam lectorem eius cognitoremque misisset. (97) Quod ideo dicendum putavi, ut liber ipse et legatur a studiosis, quia plurimum adiuvat ad scripturas intellegendas, et non de illo speretur tantum quantum non habet. Caute sane legendus est, non solum propter quaedam in quibus ut homo erravit, sed maxime propter illa quae sicut donatista haereticus loquitur. Quid autem doceant vel admoneant istae septem regulae, breviter ostendam.

44. (98) Prima de domino et eius corpore est. In qua

[5] invisibiles ‹visibiles› μ *Mart.*

---

142 Ticonius, *Praefatio.*

write a short book of rules, fashioning them as keys, and lamps, for the Law's hidden truths. For there are certain mystic rules that govern the furthest corners of the universal Law, and they make the invisible treasures of truth visible—to some of us. If the underlying schema of the rules is going to be received—just as we are sharing them—without resentment, each one of them will open up what was closed off, and clarify what was unclear, so that a person who traverses the boundless thickets of prophecy will be led by these rules as if by paths of light and will be preserved from error."[142]

(96) If only he had said at the start, "there are certain mystical rules that govern some of the Law's furthest corners," or indeed, "which govern vital corners of the Law," instead of, "the corners of the whole Law." If only he had not said, "each one of them will open up what was closed off," but instead, "much that has been closed off will be opened up." Then he would have been speaking the truth: he would not have drawn his readers and defenders into a false hope by investing that painstaking and productive work of his with unfulfillable promise. (97) The reason why I thought this needed saying is that his book is being read by eager students because it is extremely helpful for understanding the scriptures. But they should not be hoping that it will deliver more than it realistically can. Yes, it should be read, but with care, and not just because on certain points he was prone to human error; but most of all because it mentions those points from a Donatist heretic's perspective. Now I shall briefly set out those seven rules, what they instruct us to do, and what they caution us against.

44. (98) The first rule concerns the Lord and his body.

scientes aliquando capitis et corporis (id est Christi et ecclesiae) unam personam nobis intimari (neque enim frustra dictum est fidelibus, "ergo Abrahae semen estis," cum sit unum semen Abrahae quod est Christus), non haesitemus quando a capite ad corpus vel a corpore transitur ad caput, et tamen non receditur ab una eademque persona. (99) Una enim persona loquitur dicens, "sicut sponso imposuit mihi mitram et sicut sponsam ornavit me ornamento." Et tamen quid horum duorum capiti, quid corpori, id est, quid Christo, quid ecclesiae conveniat, utique intellegendum est.

45. (100) Secunda est de domini corpore bipertito, quod quidem non ita debuit appellari: non enim re vera domini corpus est, quod cum illo non erit in aeternum, sed dicendum fuit, de domini corpore vero atque permixto, aut vero atque simulato, vel quid aliud, quia non solum in aeternum, verum etiam nunc hypocritae non cum illo esse dicendi sunt, quamvis in eius esse videantur ecclesia. Unde poterat ista regula et sic appellari, ut diceretur, de permixta ecclesia.

(101) Quae regula intellectorem vigilantem requirit,

---

[143] Galatians 3:29. [144] *Personae* is used in Latin theology for the three "persons" of the Trinity (*substantia* refers to their single essence, or substance). [145] Isaiah 61:10.

[146] Isaiah 61:10 begins with a change of subject from God (61:8–9) and uses male and female similes for a single [or corporate] object of God's generosity. Unheralded switches of grammatical subject are common in prophetic texts and psalms.

[147] In Christian Latin from Tertullian on, the term has its modern meaning, someone who pretends to be what they are not. This derives from classical usage: one who acts out the gestures of a speaking actor on stage.

In this, we know that sometimes he is disclosed to us as a single person with a head and a body (these are Christ and the Church respectively). There was a purpose to telling the faithful, "so you are the seed of Abraham,"[143] although there is but one seed of Abraham, and that is Christ. So we should not be at a loss when the text jumps from head to body or from body to head, while still referring to one and the same person.[144] (99) For example one person says, "he has placed a crown on my head like a bridegroom, and like a bride he has adorned me with finery."[145] Here it is vital to understand what of these two refers to the head, and what to the body; or in other words, what refers to Christ and what refers to the Church.[146]

45. (100) The second rule concerns the dual nature of the Lord's body, though that is an inappropriate description, because what will not be with him for ever is not in reality the body of the Lord. It should say, "concerning the true and the mixed body of the Lord," or "the true and the feigned," or something like that: because right now, as well as for eternity, we should not say that hypocrites[147] are with him, even though they are noticeable in his Church.[148] So this rule could also be called (as I mentioned), "on the mixed Church."

(101) This rule demands that the interpreter[149] be

148 Here, "the body of Christ" refers to the Church, not the fullness of Christ's humanity. How the Church consisted of a mixture of good and evil was a current issue for Augustine as he was finishing *Civ.* in AD 426, as well as *TC*.

149 Augustine seems to have borrowed the word *intellector* from Irenaeus (e.g., *Haer.* 3.21.2). He uses it in the proem to *TC*, 5.9.

quando scriptura cum ad alios iam loquatur, tamquam ad eos ipsos ad quos loquebatur videtur loqui, vel de ipsis cum de aliis iam loquatur, tamquam unum sit utrorumque corpus, propter temporariam commixtionem et communionem sacramentorum. Ad hoc pertinet in cantico canticorum, "fusca sum et speciosa ut tabernacula Cedar, ut pelles Salomonis." Non enim ait, fusca fui ut tabernacula Cedar et speciosa sum ut pelles Salomonis, sed utrumque se esse dixit propter temporalem unitatem intra una retia piscium bonorum et malorum. Tabernacula enim cedar ad Ismaelem pertinent, qui non erit heres cum filio liberae.

(102) Itaque cum de bona parte dicat deus, "ducam caecos in viam quam non noverunt, et semitas quas non noverunt calcabunt, et faciam illis tenebras in lucem et prava in directum: haec verba faciam et non derelinquam eos," mox de alia parte, quae mala permixta est, dicit, "ipsi autem conversi sunt retro," quamvis alii iam significentur his verbis. Sed quoniam nunc in uno sunt, tamquam de ipsis loquitur de quibus loquebatur: non tamen semper in uno erunt. Ipse est quippe ille servus commemoratus in evangelio, cuius dominus cum venerit dividet eum et partem eius cum hypocritis ponet.

46. (103) Tertia regula est de promissis et lege, quae alio modo dici potest de spiritu et littera, sicut eam nos

---

[150] Hill 1996: "a most peculiar sentence" (200n66).

[151] Song of Songs 1:5. Quoting from VL, which preserves the Hebrew connective, unlike Vulg., which substitutes an adversative, *nigra sum sed formosa.* [152] Matthew 13:47–48.

[153] Isaiah 42:16–17. [154] Not a very clear way of saying that the grammatical subject has changed. [155] Matthew 24:51.

vigilant, when scripture, although it is now speaking to one group of people, seems to be addressing the same people it was speaking to before, or about those same people when it talks about others, as if both groups were as one, thanks to their earthly mingling and fellowship in the sacraments.[150] There is an example of this in the Song of Songs, "I am dark and beautiful, like the tents of Kedar, like the yurts of Solomon."[151] She does not say, "I have been dark like the tents of Kedar, and I am now beautiful like the yurts of Solomon." Rather, she said that both these things hold at the same time, because time is the same as far as the one net containing both good and bad fish is concerned.[152] For the tents of Kedar relate to Ishmael, who will not inherit together with the son of the freeborn woman.

(102) So although God says about the element that is good, "I shall lead the blind onto a road that they do not know, and they will tread on unknown paths, and I will make their shadows into light, and their crooked ways I will make straight: I shall perform what I speak, and I will not abandon them," he immediately says of the other element, the bad component that has been mixed among them, "but they will turn back"[153]—but now these words refer to a different group of people.[154] All the same, since they are all now a single whole, he speaks of them as if he was speaking of the first group: yet they will not always be a single whole. In fact they are that slave celebrated in the gospel, whose lord, when he comes, will separate him out and assign him a place with the hypocrites.[155]

46. (103) The third rule concerns the law and the promises, which could alternatively be said to be on "the spirit and the letter," which is the name we ourselves gave

appellavimus, cum de hac re librum scriberemus. Potest etiam sic dici, de gratia et mandato. Haec autem magis mihi videtur magna quaestio quam regula, quae solvendis quaestionibus adhibenda est. Haec est quam non intellegentes Pelagiani vel condiderunt suam haeresem vel auxerunt. Laboravit in ea disserenda Ticonius bene, sed non plene. (104) Disputans enim de fide et operibus, opera nobis dixit a deo dari merito fidei, ipsam vero fidem sic esse a nobis ut nobis non sit a deo. Nec attendit apostolum dicentem, "pax fratribus et caritas cum fide a deo patre et domino Iesu Christo." Sed non erat expertus hanc haeresem quae nostro tempore exorta multum nos, ut gratiam dei quae per dominum nostrum Iesum Christum est, adversus eam defenderemus, exercuit; et secundum id quod ait apostolus, "oportet haereses esse ut probati manifesti fiant in vobis," multo vigilantiores diligentioresque reddidit, ut adverteremus in scripturis sanctis quod istum Ticonium minus attentum minusque sine hoste sollicitum fugit, etiam ipsam scilicet fidem donum esse illius qui eius mensuram unicuique partitur.

(105) Ex qua sententia quibusdam dictum est, "vobis donatum est pro Christo, non solum ut credatis in eum, verum etiam ut patiamini pro eo." Unde quis dubitet utrumque esse dei donum, qui fideliter atque intellegen-

[156] In AD 412. [157] Heretics in "catholic" eyes. Their leader Pelagius denied original sin and had a positive view of human volition, which Augustine opposed (AD 412–418).

[158] A theological crux even within the New Testament: e.g., Romans 4:1–5; James 1:22–2:26. [159] Ephesians 6:23.

[160] 1 Corinthians 11:19. [161] Romans 12:3.

[162] Philippians 1:29.

it, when we were writing a book on this subject.[156] It can also be called, "on grace and commandment," but this seems to me to be an important matter for debate, rather than a rule, which is something we employ for resolving debates. This is what the Pelagians[157] failed to understand, both when they established their heresy and when they propagated it. Ticonius made a good job of disseminating it, but he did not complete the task. (104) When he debated faith and works[158] he stated that God gave to us our works according to the merits of our faith, but that faith itself was from us, and was not, therefore, from God. He paid no heed to the apostle's greeting, "peace to the brothers, and love, with faith from God the Father and the Lord Jesus Christ."[159] But Paul had had no experience of this heresy, for it has emerged in our time, and has constantly preoccupied us as we defend the grace of God through our Lord Jesus Christ against it. In accordance with the apostle's saying, "there must be heresies among you, so that it is clear who is tried and tested,"[160] we are become more vigilant and careful , with the result that we noticed in the holy scriptures something that escaped Ticonius' notice (for having no one to challenge him in debate made him less observant, and less punctilious): that without a doubt even faith itself is a gift of God, who distributes it proportionately to every person.[161]

(105) In accordance with this axiom some have been told, "For Christ's sake, it has been granted to you not only to believe in him, but also to suffer for him."[162] Going by this, can anyone who hears—with faith and understanding—that both these things have been bestowed doubt

ter audit utrumque donatum? Plura sunt et alia testimonia quibus id ostenditur, sed hoc nunc non agimus. Alibi autem atque alibi saepissime ista egimus.

47. (106) Quarta Ticonii regula est de specie et genere. Sic enim eam vocat, volens intellegi speciem partem, genus autem totum, cuius ea pars est quam nuncupat speciem. Sicut unaquaeque civitas pars est utique universitatis gentium, hanc ille vocat speciem, genus autem omnes gentes. Neque hic ea discernendi subtilitas adhibenda est, quae a dialecticis traditur, qui inter partem et speciem quid intersit acutissime disputant. (107) Eadem ratio est, si non de unaquaque civitate, sed de unaquaque provincia vel gente vel regno tale aliquid in divinis reperiatur eloquiis. Non solum enim verbi gratia de Hierusalem vel de aliqua gentium civitate, sive Tyro sive Babylonia sive alia qualibet dicitur aliquid in scripturis sanctis quod modum eius excedat et conveniat potius omnibus gentibus, verum etiam de Iudaea, de Aegypto, de Assyria et quacumque alia gente in qua sunt plurimae civitates, non tamen totus orbis sed pars eius est, dicitur quod transeat eius modum et congruat potius universo, cuius haec pars est vel, sicut iste appellat, generi cuius haec species est. (108) Unde et in notitiam vulgi verba ista venerunt, ut

---

163 Not with the same sense as modern biological taxonomy: closer to "subtype and type." Augustine knew and used Aristotle's *Categories*: see *Conf.* 4.16.28.

164 Latin *species* (cf. verb *specio*, "look at") suggests categorization based on appearance. *Genus* (from Greek *gignō*) implies plurality.

165 Latin *civitas*: often translated as "state" or even "city" (e.g., *civitas dei*, "City of God"). See p.159, n. 8.

that both of them are gifts from God? Plenty of other passages make the same point; but this is not what we are currently concerned with. We have dealt with these matters elsewhere, and dealt with them repeatedly.

47. (106) Ticonius' fourth rule concerns species and genus.[163] That at any rate is what he calls his rule, and wants it to be understood thus: "species" is the individual instance, "genus" is the collective whole, any single part of which consists of what he calls an instance.[164] For example: each and every polity[165] is certainly a part of the whole collective of nations, and Ticonius calls this individual polity a "species," while all the nations together form a "genus." Not that there is any need to employ the fine distinctions made by logicians, who debate in minute detail the distinction between species and genus. (107) If something like this is found in the divine communications that is not about an individual polity, but about an individual province or nation or kingdom, the schema is the same. For example: something is said in the holy writings that is not only about Jerusalem, or any of the polities of the gentiles (whether Tyre or Babylon or any other polity), which goes beyond its boundaries and is more applicable to all the nations. But it is also said about Judaea, Egypt, Assyria and any other nation consisting of large numbers of polities, which still is not the entire world, only a part of it. Then it is said that it transcends its boundaries and becomes more like a whole, though it is only a part of one (or, as Ticonius says, it becomes like that genus of which it is a species.[166] (108) These terms have now become

166 From "For example" to "species" is a single unwieldy sentence in Latin.

etiam idiotae intellegant quid specialiter, quid generaliter in quocumque praecepto imperiali sit constitutum. Fit hoc etiam de hominibus; sicut ea quae de Salomone dicuntur excedunt eius modum et potius ad Christum vel ecclesiam, cuius ille pars est, relata clarescunt.

48. (109) Nec species semper exceditur. Saepe enim talia dicuntur quae vel ei quoque vel ei fortasse tantummodo apertissime congruant. Sed cum a specie transitur ad genus, quasi adhuc de specie loquente scriptura, ibi vigilare debet lectoris intentio, ne quaerat in specie quod in genere potest melius et certius invenire. (110) Facile est quippe illud quod ait propheta Hiezechiel, "domus Israhel habitavit in terra, et polluerunt illam in via sua et in idolis suis et peccatis suis; secundum immunditiam menstruatae facta est via eorum ante faciem meam. Et effudi iram meam super eos, et dispersi illos inter nationes, et ventilavi eos in regiones. Secundum vias eorum et secundum peccata eorum iudicavi eos." Facile est, inquam, hoc intellegere de illa domo Israhel, de qua dicit apostolus, "Videte Israhel secundum carnem," quia haec omnia carnalis populus Israhel et fecit et passus est.

(111) Alia etiam quae sequuntur eidem intelleguntur populo convenire. Sed cum coeperit dicere, "et sanctificabo nomen meum sanctum illud magnum, quod pollutum est inter nationes, quod polluistis in medio earum; et

---

167 Adjective cognate with *species* (individual instance).

168 Adjective cognate with *genus* (whole group).

169 Ezekiel 36:17–19.

170 Biblical idiom for "in my presence."

171 1 Corinthians 10:18: the actual, historical, house of Israel.

172 A reference to Israel's apostasy during the exile.

common knowledge, so that even ordinary people understand what is a specific[167] pronouncement and what is a generic[168] one, in any imperial injunction. This also applies to people: for example, there are things said about Solomon that go beyond the individual person, and become clear when we apply them to Christ or the Church, of which Solomon is a part.

48. (109) We do not always overstep the boundaries of species. Often what is said is consonant with it, or perhaps applies to it alone. But when scripture goes on referring to species while a transition from species to genus is taking place, then the reader must concentrate and be alert, so as not to seek in a species what can be better and more firmly identified in a genus. (110) The prophet Ezekiel says,[169] "The house of Israel dwelt in the land, and they have defiled it by their own way, and with their own idols, and their own sins; before my face,[170] their way has become like the uncleanness of a woman who is menstruating. And I have poured out my wrath upon them and I have dispersed them among the nations, and scattered them to every region. According to their ways and according to their sins I have judged them." It is easy—easy, I say—to understand this as that house of Israel, which the apostle referred to, saying, "Look at the house of Israel according to the flesh,"[171] because all these things are what the physical people of Israel did, and endured.

(111) Also, some things that follow are understood as applying to the same people. But when he begins to say, "And I shall sanctify my name, which is holy and great, which has been defiled among the nations, which you have defiled in the midst of them;[172] and the nations will know

scient gentes quoniam ego sum dominus" iam intentus debet esse qui legit, quemadmodum species excedatur et adiungatur genus. Sequitur enim et dicit, "dum sanctificabor in vobis ante oculos eorum et accipiam vos de gentibus et congregabo vos ex omnibus terris et inducam vos in terram vestram, et aspergam vos aqua munda et mundabimini ab omnibus simulacris vestris et mundabo vos, et dabo vobis cor novum et spiritum novum dabo in vos, et auferam cor lapideum de carne vestra, et dabo vobis cor carneum, et spiritum meum dabo in vos, et faciam ut in iustitiis meis ambuletis, et iudicia mea custodiatis et faciatis, et habitabitis in terra quam dedi patribus vestris, et eritis mihi in populum et ego ero vobis in deum, et mundabo vos ex omnibus immunditiis vestris."

(112) Hoc de novo testamento esse prophetatum, ad quod pertinet non solum una gens illa in reliquiis suis, de quibus alibi scriptum est, "si fuerit numerus filiorum Israhel sicut harena maris, reliquiae salvae fient," verum etiam ceterae gentes, quae promissae sunt patribus eorum, qui etiam nostri sunt, non ambigit quisquis intuetur et lavacrum regenerationis hic esse promissum, quod nunc videmus omnibus gentibus redditum. Et illud quod ait apostolus, cum testamenti novi gratiam commendaret, ut in comparatione veteris emineret, "epistola nostra vos estis, scripta non atramento, sed spiritu dei vivi; non in tabulis lapideis, sed in tabulis cordis carnalibus," hinc esse

---

[173] Ezekiel 36:23. [174] Ezekiel 36:24–29. The polysyndeton is an imitation of Hebrew idiom rather than a figure of rhetoric. [175] Those remaining alive after the exile.

[176] Isaiah 10:22; Romans 9:27. [177] 2 Corinthians 3:2–3.

that I am the Lord,"[173] then readers ought to watch out for the reference going beyond the species and bordering on the genus. For he goes on to say, "while I shall be sanctified among you before their eyes, and I shall take you out of the nations and gather you from all the lands and shall lead you into your own land, and I shall sprinkle you with clean water, and you will be cleansed of all your images, and I shall make you clean; and I shall give you a new heart and give you a new spirit; and I shall take away the heart of stone from your body, and give you a heart of flesh, and I will set my spirit within you, and I shall make you walk in my ways of righteousness, and you will keep my judgments and do them, and you shall live in the land that I gave to your ancestors, and you will be my people, and I shall be your God, and I shall cleanse you from all your uncleannesses."[174]

(112) This was a prophecy of the new covenant, and through its remnants[175] it applies to more than just that one nation of which this has been written elsewhere: "if the number of the children of Israel were as the grains of sand in the sea, a remnant shall be preserved":[176] it also applies to the other nations that were promised to their ancestors, who are ours too. There is no doubt that everyone can observe the water of regeneration being promised here, which we now see has been given to all the nations. Also there is what the apostle says, when he was endorsing the grace of the new covenant so that by comparison it eclipsed the old, "you are our letter, written not with ink, but with the spirit of the living God; not on tablets of stone, but upon the fleshly tablet that is the human heart":[177] this looks back from here, and perceives a con-

respicit et perspicit ductum ubi iste propheta dicit, "et dabo vobis cor novum et spiritum novum dabo in vos; et auferam cor lapideum de carne vestra, et dabo vobis cor carneum." (113) Cor quippe carneum, unde ait apostolus, "tabulis cordis carnalibus," a corde lapideo voluit vita sentiente discerni, et per vitam sentientem significavit intellegentem. Sic fit Israhel spiritalis, non unius gentis, sed omnium quae promissae sunt patribus in eorum semine, quod est Christus.

49. (114) Hic ergo Israhel spiritalis ab illo Israhele carnali, qui est unius gentis, novitate gratiae, non nobilitate patriae, et mente non gente distinguitur. Sed altitudo prophetica dum de illo vel ad illum loquitur, latenter transit ad hunc; et cum iam de isto vel ad istum loquatur, adhuc de illo vel ad illum videtur loqui, non intellectum scripturarum nobis quasi hostiliter invidens, sed exercens medicinaliter nostrum.

(115) Unde et illud quod ait, "et inducam vos in terram vestram," et paulo post tamquam id ipsum repetens, "et habitabitis," inquit, "in terra quam dedi patribus vestris," non carnaliter sicut carnalis Israhel, sed spiritaliter sicut spiritales Israhel debemus accipere. Ecclesia quippe "sine macula et ruga" ex omnibus gentibus congregata atque in aeternum regnatura cum Christo, ipsa est terra beatorum,

---

[178] Latin *ductus*: see Quint. *Inst.* 4.2.53 on *ductus* as a type of pattern or connective structure.

[179] In the sense of offspring or stock.

[180] A neat conceit, combining assonance and alliteration (*novitate/nobilitate*), eye rhyme (*gratiae/patriae*), and rhyme (*mente/gente*).

[181] Teaching fleshly Israel the truth of the spiritual Israel,

tinuity of sequence,[178] in that prophet's saying, "and I shall give you a new heart and give you a new spirit; and I shall take away the heart of stone from your body, and give you a heart of flesh." (113) Certainly he wanted the heart of flesh (from which the apostle speaks of "fleshly tablets of the heart") to be distinguishable from the heart of stone by its being living and sentient; and its qualities of being living and sentient signified understanding. So the spiritual Israel came into being, consisting not of one nation, but of all those nations that were promised to the patriarchs through their seed,[179] which is Christ.

49. (114) Here, then, the spiritual Israel is distinguished from the fleshly Israel (which is a single nation), by newness of grace, not the fame of a fatherland, and by rationality, not nationality.[180] But even as this sublime prophetic utterance speaks about the former, or to the former, it quietly shifts to the latter; and when it is already speaking of, or to, this latter, it still give the impression of referring to the former, or addressing it. It is not envying us our understanding of the scriptures, as if it were our enemy. It is giving our understanding some remedial training.[181]

(115) For this reason, we must take what the prophet says, "and I shall lead you into your land," and, a little later, almost repeating the idea, "and you will dwell in the land that I have given to your fathers," in a way that is not fleshly, like the fleshly Israel, but in a spiritual way, like the spiritual Israel. Certainly the Church, which has been gathered—without spot or wrinkle[182]—out of all the nations, and will reign for ever with Christ, is herself the land

while helping spiritual Israel to see itself in the context of divine providence. 182 2 Corinthians 3:2–3.

"terra viventium." Ipsa intellegenda est patribus data, quando eis certa et immutabili dei voluntate promissa est, quoniam ipsa promissionis vel praedestinationis firmitate iam data est, quae danda suo tempore a patribus credita est, sicut de ipsa gratia quae sanctis datur scribens ad Timotheum apostolus ait, "non secundum opera nostra, sed secundum suum propositum et gratiam, quae data est nobis in Christo Iesu ante saecula aeterna, manifestata autem nunc per adventum salvatoris nostri." (116) Datam dixit gratiam quando nec erant adhuc quibus daretur, quoniam in dispositione ac praedestinatione dei iam factum erat quod suo tempore futurum fuerat, quod ipse esse dicit manifestatum. Quamvis haec possint intellegi et de terra futuri saeculi, quando erit caelum novum et terra nova, in qua iniusti habitare non poterunt. Et ideo recte dicitur piis quod ipsa sit terra eorum quae ulla ex parte non erit impiorum, quia et ipsa similiter data est, quando danda firmata est.

50. (117) Quintam Tyconius regulam ponit quam de temporibus appellat, qua regula plerumque inveniri vel conici possit latens in scripturis sanctis quantitas temporum. Duobus autem modis vigere dicit hanc regulam, aut tropo synecdoche aut legitimis numeris.

---

[183] Psalm 27:13.

[184] 2 Timothy 1:9–10.

[185] See p. 269, n. 121; *Gen. litt.* 5.22.43, *regimen providentiae*.

[186] That is, "revealed" rather than coming into being at that moment.

[187] Revelation 21:1.

of the blessed, the "land of the living."[183] That land, that Church, should be understood as a gift to the patriarchs, when it was promised to them by God's sure and unchanging will: for what the patriarchs believed was to be bestowed on them in God's good time was already bestowed by a constancy of promise or predestination. This is like what the apostle said when he wrote to Timothy about the grace that is given to the saints, "not according to our works, but according to his own design, and grace that was given to us in Christ Jesus before the eternal ages, and is manifested now through the coming of our savior."[184] (116) He said that grace had been given when as yet there was no one to give it to, since what was going to unfold in the time God had created had already, in God's providential design,[185] taken place; which is why he said it was "manifested":[186] all the same, this can also be understood as a reference to the land of the age to come, when there will be a new heaven and a new earth,[187] in which the unrighteous will not be able to abide. For this reason it is rightly said to the devout that this is their land, and not a fraction of it is for the ungodly; for in the same way the giving of it was effected when the design of giving it was established.

50. (117) Tyconius posits a fifth rule, which he calls "on times." Using this rule can frequently enable us to discover or conjecture arcane measurements of time. He states that this rule functions in two ways: either using the figure synecdoche[188] or by using numbers with their normal meanings.

188 For example, saying "motor" or "wheels" for "car." A figure of rhetoric.

Tropus synecdoche aut a parte totum aut a toto partem facit intellegi, sicut unus evangelista post dies octo factum dicit, quod alius post dies sex, quando in monte discipulis tantum tribus praesentibus facies domini fulsit ut sol et vestimenta eius ut nix. (118) Utrumque enim verum esse non posset, quod de numero dierum dictum est, nisi ille qui dixit "post dies octo," intellegatur partem novissimam diei ex quo id Christus praedixit futurum, et partem primam diei quo id ostendit impletum, pro totis diebus duobus atque integris posuisse; eum vero qui dixit, "post dies sex," integros omnes et totos, sed solos medios computasse. Hoc modo locutionis, quo significatur a parte totum, etiam illa de resurrectione Christi solvitur quaestio. (119) Pars enim novissima diei quo passus est, nisi pro toto die accipiatur, id est adiuncta etiam nocte praeterita, et nox in cuius parte ultima resurrexit nisi totus dies accipiatur, adiuncto scilicet die illucescente dominico, non possunt esse tres dies et tres noctes, quibus se in corde terrae praedixit futurum.

51. (120) Legitimos autem numeros dicit quos eminentius divina scriptura commendat, sicut septenarium vel denarium vel duodenarium et quicumque alii sunt, quos legendo studiosi libenter agnoscunt. Plerumque enim numeri huiusmodi pro universo tempore ponuntur, sicut, "septies in die laudabo te," nihil est aliud quam, "semper

---

[189] Matthew 17:1–2 (six days); Mark 9:1–2 (six days); Luke 9.28 (about eight days): the "transfiguration."

[190] Matthew 12:40: inclusive time reckoning is needed to bring the number of days up to three, though we would naturally reckon this span of time as two days.

The figure synecdoche makes us understand something either by using part for a whole, or whole for a part. Take the time when the face of the Lord shone like the sun, and his clothing was snow-white, when just three of the disciples were with him on the mountain:[189] one of the evangelists says this happened after eight days, but another after six days. (118) Those statements about the number of days could not both be true, unless we interpret this as the one who said "after eight days" including the final part of the day after which Christ foretold that this would happen, and the beginning of the day on which he revealed that it would be fulfilled, reckoning both these days as whole and complete. Then the one who said "after six days" counted only all the whole and complete days in between. This use of language, in which the whole is signified by a part, gives us the solution to a question about the resurrection of Christ. (119) For unless we take the part of the last day on which he suffered as standing for a whole day, in other words joining it to the night before; and unless we take the final night, in some moment of which he was resurrected, as a whole day—and we certainly have to add in the dawning of the Lord's day—there cannot be three days and three nights in which he predicted that he would be in the heart of the earth.[190]

51. (120) Tyconius refers to numbers with their normal meanings as those that divine scripture holds in highest esteem: say the number seven, or ten, or twelve, and any and all others that scholars recognize without difficulty when reading. These kind of numbers usually stand for units of time as they are commonly understood: for example, "seven times a day I will praise you" means exactly

laus eius in ore meo." (121) Tantundem valent et cum multiplicantur, sive per denarium, sicut septuaginta et septingenti (unde possunt et septuaginta anni Hieremiae pro universo tempore spiritaliter accipi, quo est apud alienos ecclesia), sive per se ipsos, sicut decem per decem centum sunt, et duodecim per duodecim centum quadraginta quattuor, quo numero significatur universitas sanctorum in Apocalypsi. Unde apparet non solas temporum quaestiones istis numeris esse solvendas, sed latius patere significationes eorum et in multa proserpere. Neque enim numerus iste in Apocalypsi ad tempora pertinet, sed ad homines.

52. (122) Sextam regulam Tyconius recapitulationem vocat, in obscuritate scripturarum satis vigilanter inventam. Sic enim dicuntur quaedam, quasi sequantur in ordine temporis vel rerum continuatione narrentur, cum ad priora quae praetermissa fuerant, latenter narratio revocetur; quod nisi ex hac regula intellegatur, erratur. (123) Sicut in Genesi, "et plantavit," inquit, "dominus deus paradisum in Eden ad orientem, et posuit ibi hominem quem formavit, et produxit deus adhuc de terra omne lignum

---

[191] Psalms 119:164, 34:1.

[192] Jeremiah 25:11.

[193] Revelation 7:4, 14:3.

[194] This technical term in Latin theology, drawn from scripture (*anacephalaiōsis* in Greek: see Romans 13:9; Ephesians 1:10), was developed by Irenaeus: see *Haer*. 3.16.6, 3.18.1, 3.18.7; 4 *praef*. 2.22.8) and later Augustine (e.g., *Civ*. 15.21). It was a theological idea centered on Christ as a second Adam recapitulating the deeds of the first Adam so as to reverse them. Augustine's take on it is not mainstream.

the same as "his praise is ever on my lips."[191] (121) They mean exactly the same when we multiply them, for example by tens, like seventy and seven hundred: this is how Jeremiah's "seventy years"[192] can be taken, in a spiritual sense, for the whole period of time in which the Church was among foreign peoples; or when we multiply them by themselves, like ten tens making a hundred, and twelve twelves making a hundred and forty-four (a number that signifies the whole assembly of the saints in Revelation).[193] This shows that questions about times are not the only kind that numbers, used normally, can resolve. Their significations extend more broadly and insinuate themselves into all sorts of places. In any case, the number 144 in Revelation refers not to times, but to persons.

52. (122) Tyconius calls his sixth rule "recapitulation."[194] With his remarkably watchful approach, he found the term hidden away in the scriptures. Certain things are mentioned as if they follow in historical sequence or are narrated in a continuous account of events, even though the narration covertly reverts to earlier matters that had previously been omitted. Unless we understand such a case in accordance with this rule, we will go astray. (123) For example: it says in Genesis, "the Lord God planted a garden[195] in Eden facing east, and there he placed the man whom he had formed, and moreover God brought forth from the earth all kinds of trees that were beautiful and

[195] *paradisum*: a loanword from Greek *paradeisos* (park, pleasure ground). Hebrew has "garden"; LXX has παράδεισον; Vulg. has *paradisum voluptatis* (Genesis 2:8): Augustine consistently quotes this verse according to VL, i.e., without the gloss *voluptatis* (pleasure).

speciosum et bonum in escam," ita videtur dictum tamquam id factum sit posteaquam factum posuit hominem in paradiso, cum breviter utroque commemorato—id est, quod "plantavit deus paradisum et posuit ibi hominem quem formavit"—recapitulando redeat et dicat quod praetermiserat, quomodo scilicet paradisus fuerit plantatus, quia "produxit deus adhuc de terra omne lignum speciosum et bonum in escam."

(124) Denique secutus adiunxit, "et lignum vitae in medio paradisi, et lignum scientiae boni et mali." Deinde flumen, quo paradisus irrigaretur, divisum in quattuor principia fluviorum quattuor explicatur; quod totum pertinet ad institutionem paradisi. Quod ubi terminavit, repetivit illud quod iam dixerat, et re vera hoc sequebatur, atque ait, "et sumpsit dominus deus hominem quem finxit, et posuit eum in paradiso," et cetera. (125) Post ista enim facta ibi est positus homo, sicut nunc ordo ipse demonstrat; non post hominem ibi positum facta sunt ista, sicut prius dictum putari potest, nisi recapitulatio illic vigilanter intellegatur, qua reditum est ad ea quae fuerant praetermissa.

53. (126) Itemque in eo libro, cum commemorarentur generationes filiorum Noë, dictum est, "hi filii Cham in tribubus suis secundum linguas suas in regionibus suis et in gentibus suis." Enumeratis quoque filiis Sem dicitur, "hi filii Sem in tribubus suis secundum linguas suas in regio-

[196] *factum*: the translation is exegetical for clarity.

[197] Genesis 2:8–9. [198] Genesis 2:15.

[199] Referring to the revisiting or renewing of a figure in this form of theological typology. It is perhaps unavoidable when composing by dictation. [200] Genesis 10:10.

good for food." So it seems to state that bringing forth the trees[196] happened after God made the man and set him in paradise: although both actions were briefly recorded (namely that "God planted a garden and there he placed the man whom he had made"), Genesis goes back on itself to recapitulate and state what it had omitted, surely the matter of how paradise had been planted, that "moreover God brought forth from the earth all kinds of trees that were beautiful and good for food."[197]

(124) Lastly it followed this by adding, "and the tree of life was in the middle of paradise, and the tree of knowledge of good and evil." Next, the flowing water that was to water paradise is set out; it was divided into four heads of rivers. This whole passage concerns the establishment of paradise. When Genesis finished it, it repeated what it had already said (and what in reality came here in the sequence of events) and remarked, "and the Lord God took the man who he had formed, and set him in paradise"[198] and so on. (125) For it was after those actions that the man was placed there, and the actual order of narration here confirms the fact. It is not the case that the rest happened after the man was set there—although we might have thought it previously said so, had we not been alert to spot recapitulation, which effects a return to matters that had previously been omitted.[199]

53. (126) There is another instance when Genesis records the generations of the sons of Noah, and states, "these are the sons of Ham in their own tribes, according to their own languages, in their own territories and their own nations."[200] Then, after listing the sons of Shem, it states, "these are the sons of Shem in their own tribes, according to their own languages, in their own territories

nibus suis et in gentibus suis." Et annectitur de omnibus, "hae tribus filiorum Noë, secundum generationes eorum secundum gentes eorum. Ab his dispersae sunt insulae gentium super terram post diluvium. Et erat omnis terra labium unum et vox una omnibus."

(127) Hoc itaque quod adiunctum est, "et erat omnis terra labium unum et vox una omnibus," id est, una lingua omnium, ita dictum videtur tamquam eo iam tempore, quo dispersi fuerant super terram etiam secundum insulas gentium, una fuerit omnibus lingua communis. Quod procul dubio repugnat superioribus verbis, ubi dictum est, "in tribubus suis secundum linguas suas." Neque enim dicerentur habuisse iam linguas suas singulae tribus, quae gentes singulas fecerant, quando erat omnibus una communis. (128) Ac per hoc recapitulando adiunctum est, "et erat omnis terra labium unum et vox una omnibus," latenter narratione redeunte, ut diceretur quomodo factum sit, ut ex una omnium lingua fuerint divisi per multas. Et continuo de illa turris aedificatione narratur, ubi haec eis iudicio divino ingesta est poena superbiae, post quod factum dispersi sunt per terram secundum linguas suas.

---

201 Genesis 10:31.

202 *insulae*: a *difficilior lectio*. Augustine uses VL, which follows LXX *nēsoi*. Vulg. omits it. Blaise, *Dictionnaire latin-français*, glosses it as "isolated group/area/region/people," but cites only this passage in support. Spurrell, *Notes on the Hebrew Text*, 102, remarks on Genesis 10:5 that the Hebrew word in question "denotes regularly 'the islands and coastlands' of the Mediterranean."

203 Apparently, an attempt to answer the question of how the world was repopulated after the flood.

and their own nations."[201] Next it adds about them all, "these are the tribes of the sons of Noah, according to their generations, according to their nations. From them, the faraway habitations[202] of the nations were scattered over the earth after the flood.[203] And the whole earth was one language, and one voice was common to all."[204]

(127) So that phrase that is added at the end, "and all the earth was one language, and one voice was common to all," meaning that there was a single language for everyone, seems to have been said as if there was still one language common to all, at the time when they had been scattered over the earth, along the coastlands of the nations. Unquestionably this contradicts the earlier words, which stated, "in their own tribes according to their own languages." Those individual tribes, which formed individual nations, would not be described as having their own languages at a time when there was one language, common to all. (128) By recapitulation the words "and the whole earth was one mouth and there was one voice common to all" have been added through this, as the narrative unobtrusively goes back on itself, to give an explanation of how it happened that after everyone had a single language they were divided into many. Immediately after this it recounts the building of the tower, when that division was inflicted upon them by divine decree as a punishment for pride.[205] After that happened, they were distributed over the earth in accordance with their particular languages.

204 Genesis 10:32, 11:1.
205 Babel, Genesis 11:9.

54. (129) Fit ista recapitulatio etiam obscurius, sicut in evangelio dicit dominus, "die quo exiit Loth a Sodomis pluit ignem de caelo et perdidit omnes: secundum haec erunt dies filii hominis, quo revelabitur. Illa hora, qui erit in tecto, et vasa eius in domo, non descendat tollere illa; et qui in agro, similiter non revertatur retro. Meminerit uxoris Loth." Numquid cum dominus fuerit revelatus, tunc sunt ista servanda, ne quisque retro respiciat, id est vitam praeteritam cui renuntiavit inquirat? Et non potius isto tempore ut, cum dominus fuerit revelatus, retributionem pro eis quae quisque servavit vel contempsit, inveniat? (130) Et tamen quia dictum est, "in illa hora," tunc putantur ista servanda cum dominus fuerit revelatus, nisi ad intellegendam recapitulationem sensus legentis invigilet, adiuvante alia scriptura quae ipsorum apostolorum adhuc tempore clamavit, "filii, novissima hora est." Tempus ergo ipsum quo evangelium praedicatur, quousque dominus reveletur, hora est in qua oportet ista servari, quia et ipsa revelatio domini ad eandem horam pertinet, quae die iudicii terminabitur.

55. (131) Septima Ticonii regula est eademque postrema de diabolo et eius corpore. Est enim et ipse caput impiorum, qui sunt eius quodam modo corpus, ituri cum illo in supplicium ignis aeterni, sicut Christus caput est ecclesiae, quod est corpus eius futurum cum illo in regno et gloria sempiterna. Sicut ergo in prima regula, quam

---

[206] Genesis 19:26; Luke 17:29–32. [207] 1 John 2:18.
[208] Romans 2:5, 13:11.
[209] *caput*: both "leader" and "origin," as well as body part.
[210] Matthew 25:41.

54. (129) This technique of recapitulation may be even more tricky, as when the Lord says in the gospel, "On the day when Lot departed from Sodom, it rained fire from heaven and dispatched them all: this is what the day when the Son of Man is revealed will be like. On that day, if someone is on the roof, and their baggage is in the house, they must not go down to fetch it; while if someone is outdoors, they also should not turn back. They should remember Lot's wife."[206] Surely it is not after the Lord is revealed that we need to follow that advice not to look back (meaning we should not delve into the past life that has been abandoned)? Is it not rather in this time? So that once the Lord has been revealed, each person discovers the payback for what they have upheld or rejected? (130) All the same, because it was said, "in that hour," people think that the time for following that advice is the moment when the Lord has been revealed—unless the reader's understanding is on the alert to recognize recapitulation. Help comes from another passage of scripture, which declared even in the lifetime of the apostles themselves, "Sons, the final hour is at hand."[207] The proper time for preaching the gospel, then, up until the time when the Lord will be revealed, is the hour when that advice has to be followed: because the actual revealing of the Lord also relates to the same hour that will end with the day of judgment.[208]

55. (131) Ticonius' seventh rule, which is the last, is on the Devil and his body. He himself is the head[209] of the wicked, while they, in a way, are his body, destined to go with him into the punishment for perpetual fire;[210] just as Christ is the head of the Church, which is his body, to be with him in the eternal glory of his kingdom. Just as in the

vocat "de domino et eius corpore," vigilandum est ut intellegatur, cum de una eademque persona scriptura loquitur, quid conveniat capiti, quid corpori, ita et in ista novissima aliquando in diabolum dicitur quod non in ipso, sed potius in eius corpore possit agnosci, quod habet non solum in eis qui manifestissime foris sunt, sed in eis etiam qui, cum ad ipsum pertineant, tamen ad tempus miscentur ecclesiae, donec unusquisque de hac vita exeat vel a frumento palea ventilabro ultimo separetur.

(132) Quod enim scriptum est apud Esaiam, "quomodo cecidit de caelo Lucifer mane oriens," et cetera, quae sub figura regis Babyloniae de eadem persona vel ad eandem personam dicta sunt, in ipsa contextione sermonis, de diabolo utique intelleguntur. Et tamen quod ibi dictum est, "contritus est in terra qui mittit ad omnes gentes," non totum ipsi capiti congruit. Nam etsi mittit ad omnes gentes diabolus angelos suos, tamen in terra corpus eius, non ipse, conteritur; nisi quia ipse est in corpore suo, quod contritum fit pulvis quem proiciet ventus a facie terrae.

56. (133) Hae autem omnes regulae, excepta una quae vocatur "de promissis et lege," aliud ex alio faciunt intellegi, quod est proprium tropicae locutionis, quae latius patet quam ut possit, ut mihi videtur, ab aliquo universa comprehendi. Nam ubicumque velut aliud dicitur ut aliud

211 Luke 3:17.
212 Isaiah 14:12.
213 Psalm 1:4.

first rule, which he calls "on the Lord and his body," readers must be alert to understand, when scripture speaks of one and the same person, what refers to the head, and what to the body, so too in this final rule; when something is ascribed to the Devil that can be recognized as referring to his body rather than himself, which is the case not only in those who are beyond all doubt outsiders but also in those who, although they belong to the Devil, are still mixed in with the Church for the present time, until each and every person departs this life and is like chaff separated from wheat in the final winnowing.[211]

(132) It is written in Isaiah, "how Lucifer, who rises in the morning, has fallen from heaven,"[212] and so on: what is said about the same person, or to the same person, has used the imagery of the king of Babylon, but going by the context of the actual words spoken, it undoubtedly refers to the Devil. Even so, what has been said there, "he who sends to all the nations has been ground down on the earth," does not fit perfectly with the head himself. For even if the Devil sends his own angels to all the nations, it is still his body that is ground down on the earth, not he himself; unless it is the case that he himself is in his own body, which, after it has been ground down, becomes dust, which the wind will expel from the face of the earth.[213]

56. (133) Now all these laws, except for the one entitled, "on the promises and the law," use one thing to make some other thing understood. This is the proper function of the metaphorical mode of expression, and that is so broad and wide-open a category that I do not think any one person capable of giving a complete analysis of it. Thus whenever one thing is said in such a way that something else is understood, even if we do not find the term

intellegatur, etsi nomen ipsius tropi in loquendi arte non invenitur, tropica locutio est. Quae cum fit ubi fieri solet, sine labore sequitur intellectus; cum vero ubi non solet, laboratur ut intellegatur, ab aliis magis ab aliis minus, sicut magis minusve dona dei sunt in ingeniis hominum, vel adiutoria tribuuntur.

(134) Proinde sicut in verbis propriis, de quibus superius disputavimus, ubi res ut dicuntur intellegendae sunt, sic in translatis quae faciunt tropicas locutiones, ubi aliud ex alio intellegendum est, de quibus huc usque quantum visum est, satis egimus. Non solum admonendi sunt studiosi venerabilium litterarum ut in scripturis sanctis genera locutionum sciant, et quomodo apud eas dici aliquid soleat, vigilanter advertant memoriterque retineant, verum etiam, quod est praecipuum et maxime necessarium, orent ut intellegant. In eis quippe litteris, quarum studiosi sunt, legunt quoniam "dominus dat sapientiam, et a facie eius scientia et intellectus," a quo et ipsum studium, si pietate praeditum est, acceperunt.

(135) Sed haec satis etiam de signis, quantum ad verba pertinet, dicta sint. Restat ut de proferendis eis quae sentimus, sequenti volumine, quae dominus donaverit, disseramus.

for the actual figure as given in the theory of rhetoric, it is still figurative speech. When this occurs in a familiar way, understanding comes without effort. But when it is unfamiliar, it takes an effort—sometimes a little, other times a lot—to understand it. This is like God's distributing of gifts of human intelligence (here more, there less), or the way his divine assistance is bestowed.

(134) It follows from this that by now we have given what feels like a sufficient treatment of words being used literally (which we discussed earlier), as when things are to be understood with the plain meaning of the term used; and likewise now words used figuratively, to form metaphorical expressions, in which one thing is understood by means of another. Those who study our revered texts must be reminded of the need to know the kinds of speech contained within the holy scriptures, and how they customarily refer to things. They must pay careful attention and have a retentive memory, but also—this is the most vital thing of all—they must pray for understanding. Certainly in these texts that they are studying they read that "the Lord gives wisdom, and knowledge and understanding come from his being";[214] and it is from him that they have taken their devotion to study, if it is enriched with devotion.

(135) But we have said enough now about signs in relation to words. It now remains to discuss, in the next book, the presentation of what we understand, the Lord being our helper.

214 Proverbs 2:6.

LIBER IV

1. (1) Hoc opus nostrum quod inscribitur de doctrina christiana, in duo quaedam fueram prima distributione partitus. Nam post proemium, quo respondi eis qui hoc fuerant reprehensuri, "duae sunt res," inquam, "quibus nititur omnis tractatio scripturarum: modus inveniendi quae intellegenda sunt, et modus proferendi quae intellecta sunt. De inveniendo prius, de proferendo postea disseremus." (2) Quia ergo de inveniendo multa iam diximus et tria de hac una parte volumina absolvimus, adiuvante domino, de proferendo pauca dicemus, ut si fieri potuerit, uno libro cuncta claudamus totumque hoc opus quattuor voluminibus terminetur.

2. (3) Primo itaque exspectationem legentium, qui forte me putant rhetorica daturum esse praecepta, quae in scholis saecularibus et didici et docui, ista praelocutione cohibeo,[1] atque ut a me non exspectentur admoneo; non quod nihil habeant utilitatis, sed quod si quid habent, seorsum discendum est, si cui fortassis bono viro etiam haec vacat discere, non autem a me vel in hoc opere vel in aliquo alio requirendum.

[1] cohibeo *E Col. Mon. San. Cam. μ Gr. RGr.*: prohibeo *P K Sull. Mart.*

---

[1] *TC* 1.1.1.

[2] *liber* (a word derived from tree bark used as a writing surface) refers, by synecdoche, to a whole work, *volumen*, to papyrus

BOOK IV

1. (1) In my original plan, I had divided this work, entitled "Teaching Christianity," into two distinct sections; for after the proem, in which I answered critics who would have been likely to censure it, I state, "All handling of scripture depends on two factors: how to find out what needs to be understood; and how to present it once it has been understood. We shall consider discovery first, and presentation afterward."[1] (2) So as we have already spoken at length about discovery, and have completed three volumes on this first section, we must now say a few words—the Lord being our helper—about presentation. We ought, if possible, to conclude the whole with this book, thus confining the entire work to four volumes.[2]

2. (3) At the start, therefore, I am using this preamble to rein in readers' expectations, in case they think that I am going to offer them the principles of rhetoric which once I learned, and taught, in the schools of pagan education: I advise them not to expect this of me. This is not because such stuff has no use, but because, if it has any, it should be a separate educational subject for any worthy person who has the free time to learn it. They should not ask it of me, either in this work or in any other.[3]

sheets glued and rolled. Martial is the earliest literary witness to the new form known as *codex* (Mart. 1.2.1–4).

[3] He will not return to his old life as a professor of rhetoric: a proleptic reassurance to readers.

3. (4) Nam cum per artem rhetoricam et vera suadeantur et falsa, quis audeat dicere adversus mendacium in defensoribus suis inermem debere consistere veritatem, ut videlicet illi qui res falsas persuadere conantur noverint auditorem vel benevolum vel intentum vel docilem proemio facere, isti autem non noverint? Illi falsa breviter, aperte, verisimiliter et isti vera sic narrent ut audire taedeat, intellegere non pateat, credere postremo non libeat? Illi fallacibus argumentis veritatem oppugnent, asserant falsitatem, isti nec vera defendere nec falsa valeant refutare? Illi animos audientium in errorem moventes impellentesque dicendo terreant, contristent, exhilarent, exhortentur ardenter, isti pro veritate lenti frigidique dormitent? Quis ita desipiat ut hoc sapiat? (5) Cum ergo sit in medio posita facultas eloquii, quae ad persuadenda seu prava seu recta valet plurimum, cur non bonorum studio comparatur, ut militet veritati, si eam mali ad obtinendas perversas vanasque causas in usus iniquitatis et erroris usurpant?

4. (6) Sed quaecumque sunt de hac re observationes atque praecepta, quibus, cum accedit in verbis plurimis ornamentisque verborum linguae[2] sollertissima consue-

[2] linguae *K (ante 5 fere litt. eras. P)* γ: exercitationis *Lond. Sull.*

---

[4] A masterly rhetorical *apologia* for harnessing rhetoric to Christian teaching.

3. (4) Given that the art of rhetoric is used to persuade people of both truths and falsehoods, who would be so rash as to state that when truth makes its stand—amid those who would defend it—against deceit, it should do so with no weapons in its hand? Even though it would surely mean that those who try to convince people of what is false will know how deliver an opening that gets the listener on their side, or paying attention, or that makes them open to persuasion, while those of us who are on the other side have no such knowledge? And that those speakers would tell their lying tales crisply, clearly, and apparently candidly; while we would tell the truth—but in a way that was boring to listen to, hard to follow, and that listeners would be disinclined to believe? And that they would contend against truth with specious reasoning, asserting what is false, while we would have no power either to defend what is true or to reject what is false? And that they would spur the hearts of listeners into error, using their powers of speech to drive them headlong, making them frightened, dismayed, elated, worked up; while we who are on the side of truth would be acquiescent, heedless and disengaged? Who is so stupid as to see any sense in that?[4] (5) As it is, a talent for persuasive speech sits between these extremes, having immense power to persuade, for good or ill. So, given that evildoers are appropriating it for devious and worthless purposes in pursuit of wickedness and wrong, why not let people of integrity acquire it through study, so that it can be valiant for truth?

4. (6) Whatever the prevailing principles and practice in this field, once someone has acquired supreme artistry in speech, including a breadth of vocabulary and verbal ornamentation, it gives rise to that talent that we call elo-

tudo, fit illa quae facundia vel eloquentia nominatur, extra istas litteras nostras, seposito ad hoc congruo temporis spatio, apta et convenienti aetate, discenda sunt eis qui hoc celeriter possunt. (7) Nam et ipsos Romanae principes eloquentiae non piguit dicere quod hanc artem nisi quis cito possit numquam omnino possit perdiscere. Quod utrum verum sit, quid opus est quaerere? Non enim, etiam si possint haec a tardioribus tandem aliquando perdisci, nos ea tanti pendimus ut eis discendis iam maturas vel etiam graves hominum aetates velimus impendi. (8) Satis est ut adulescentulorum ista sit cura, nec ipsorum omnium quos utilitati ecclesiasticae cupimus erudiri, sed eorum quos nondum magis urgens, et huic rei sine dubio praeponenda necessitas occupavit, quoniam si acutum et fervens adsit ingenium, facilius adhaeret eloquentia legentibus et audientibus eloquentes, quam eloquentiae praecepta sectantibus.

(9) Nec desunt ecclesiasticae litterae, etiam praeter canonem in auctoritatis arce salubriter collocatum, quas legendo homo capax, etsi id non agat, sed tantummodo rebus quae ibi dicuntur intentus sit, etiam eloquio quo dicuntur, dum in his versatur, imbuitur, accedente vel maxime exercitatione sive scribendi sive dictandi, postremo etiam dicendi, quae secundum pietatis ac fidei regulam sentit.

---

[5] Cic. *De or.* 3.36.89, 146. [6] *adulescentulorum*: so Cicero describes himself aged twenty-seven (*Orat.* 30), and Caesar is described (Sall. *Cat.* 49) in his mid-thirties.

[7] A Greek word: *kanōn* means a stick used as a standard of measurement. By the fourth century it had a technical meaning, identifying writings that counted as holy scripture.

quence or fluency. Independently of these writings of mine, anyone with the capacity to learn fast, when they have reached an appropriate maturity, should set aside a proper period of time for mastering this subject. (7) For the leading figures in Roman eloquence were not backward in asserting that unless a person could master the skill swiftly, they could never master it at all.[5] Not that we need ask whether this is true: for even if people who are less acute could master it in the long run, we do not regard it so highly that we would wish people of mature or advanced years to devote their time to learning it. (8) If those who are younger[6] devote themselves to it, that is enough; and not all of them, whom we want to see educated for the Church's benefit, but only those who are not yet engrossed by some more pressing duty that has to come before rhetoric. This is because when people have sharp and keen intelligence, they will accumulate eloquence by reading and hearing practitioners of eloquence more than by striving to learn principles of eloquence.

(9) We are not short of Christian literature, even outside the canon,[7] which, for our benefit, has a place on the highest pinnacle of authority. Even if it is not their aim, someone talented, who reads it with a focus only on the content of the texts, is still steeped in the eloquence of that style of writing: and they may even approach supreme skill in their writing, or dictating, and finally even in their speaking,[8] on matters they perceive to be in accordance with the rule of devotion and faith.

[8] *scribendi . . . dictandi . . . dicendi*: a progression to public speaking as the highest level.

(10) Si autem tale desit ingenium, nec illa rhetorica praecepta capiuntur nec, si magno labore inculcata quantulacumque ex parte capiantur, aliquid prosunt; quandoquidem etiam ipsi qui ea didicerunt et copiose ornateque dicunt, non omnes ut secundum ipsa dicant, possunt ea cogitare cum dicunt, si non de his disputant. Immo vero vix ullos eorum esse existimo qui utrumque possint, et dicere bene et ad hoc faciendum praecepta illa dicendi cogitare cum dicunt. (11) Cavendum est enim ne fugiant ex animo, quae dicenda sunt, dum attenditur ut arte dicantur. Et tamen in sermonibus atque dictionibus eloquentium impleta reperiuntur praecepta eloquentiae, de quibus illi ut eloquerentur vel cum eloquerentur non cogitaverunt, sive illa didicissent sive ne attigissent quidem. Implent quippe illa, quia eloquentes sunt, non adhibent ut sint eloquentes.

5. (12) Quapropter, cum ex infantibus loquentes non fiant, nisi locutiones discendo loquentium, cur eloquentes fieri non possunt, nulla eloquendi arte tradita, sed elocutiones eloquentium legendo et audiendo et, quantum assequi conceditur, imitando? Quid, quod ita fieri ipsis quoque experimur exemplis? Nam sine praeceptis rhetoricis novimus plurimos eloquentiores plurimis qui illa didice-

---

9 *infantibus*: from the verb *fari* (to speak) plus the inseparable negativing particle. See *Conf.* 1.8.13.

(10) If they have not the natural talent, though, they cannot grasp the principles of rhetoric, nor—if they make a supreme effort to cram them, and so grasp just a small fraction—will it do them any good. Not even all the people who have learned them, and who speak with an attractive fluency, can keep these principles in mind while they are speaking, so as to make sure that their speech is consistent with them (the exception is when these very principles are being discussed). It is my view that hardly any of them can do both, namely speaking well, and (with that end in view) reflecting on those rhetorical principles. (11) They must be careful not to forget what it is they should be speaking about, while they are preoccupied with speaking in an elegant manner. Meanwhile, we can find the principles of eloquence fully realized in the style of speech and delivery of those who are eloquent, though they were not thinking about such matters in order to speak well, or while they were speaking; this is true whether they had learned them formally, or had never so much as touched on them. In fact, it is because they possess eloquence that they can fulfill these principles. They do not call upon the principles as a way to make themselves eloquent.

5. (12) Since articulate speakers, therefore, do not grow from inarticulate babies[9] unless they learn from speakers how to speak, why can they not become eloquent themselves, by reading and hearing the utterances of the eloquent and by imitating it insofar as opportunity allows, rather than by being taught the skill of eloquence? What of the fact that there are actual instances when we experience this happening? For we know that that there are plenty of people who lack a foundation in rhetoric yet are more eloquent than the many who have learned those

runt, sine lectis vero et auditis eloquentium disputationibus vel dictionibus neminem. (13) Nam neque ipsa arte grammatica, qua discitur locutionis integritas, indigerent pueri, si eis inter homines, qui integre loquerentur, crescere daretur et vivere. Nescientes quippe ulla nomina vitiorum, quidquid vitiosum cuiusquam ore loquentis audirent, sana sua consuetudine reprehenderent et caverent, sicut rusticos urbani reprehendunt, etiam qui litteras nesciunt.

6. (14) Debet igitur divinarum scripturarum tractator et doctor, defensor rectae fidei ac debellator erroris, et bona docere et mala dedocere atque in hoc opere sermonis conciliare aversos, remissos erigere, nescientibus quid agatur quid exspectare debeant intimare. Ubi autem benevolos, intentos, dociles aut invenerit aut ipse fecerit, cetera peragenda sunt, sicut postulat causa. Si docendi sunt qui audiunt, narratione faciendum est, si tamen indigeat, ut res de qua agitur innotescat. (15) Ut autem quae dubia sunt certa fiant, documentis adhibitis ratiocinandum est. Si vero qui audiunt movendi sunt potius quam docendi, ut in eo quod iam sciunt agendo non torpeant et rebus assensum quas veras esse fatentur accommodent, maioribus dicendi viribus opus est. Ibi obsecrationes et increpationes, concitationes et coercitiones et quaecumque alia valent ad commovendos animos, sunt necessaria.

---

[10] *debellator*: an echo of Virgil (*Aen.* 6.853, 7.651). See *Cont.* 3.7 (*bellatores virtutum debellatoresque vitiorum*); *C. Jul. imp.* 3.21.44.

[11] The idea of unteaching may be echoing Cicero (*Fin.* 1.20; *De or.* 2.72).

principles: but not one such person who has not read and listened to the arguments and delivery of the eloquent. (13) Children would not need expertise in grammar, which teaches faultless speech, if they were allowed to live and grow up among people who spoke faultlessly. Of course they would be ignorant of the labels we give to solecisms, but when they heard something incorrect from the mouth of a person speaking, their own faultless habits would tell them what to criticize and avoid, in the same way as urbanites—even unlettered ones—criticize provincials.

6. (14) Anyone who handles and teaches the holy writings, therefore, must defend true faith and vanquish[10] error, teaching what is good and unteaching[11] what is evil; and through their work on discourse they must reconcile opponents, motivate slackers, and reveal to those who are ignorant of the subject under discussion what they ought to expect. But when they either find people well-disposed, attentive, amenable, or make them so, then there are other things to accomplish, depending on the particular case. If those listening need instruction, the facts must be set out in chronological sequence as and when necessary, so as to impart information about the matter in hand. (15) If it is a matter of confirming matters that are unclear, examples must be produced to facilitate decision making. If it is a matter of stirring the emotion of an audience, rather than instructing it, greater oratorical powers are required, to ensure that listeners are not slow to respond to a matter they are already aware of, and to vouchsafe their assent to things that they agree are true. In that case, they need appeals, rebukes, incitement, intimidation, and anything else that has the power to motivate minds.

7. (16) Et haec quidem cuncta quae dixi omnes fere homines in his quae eloquendo agunt, facere non quiescunt. (17) Sed cum alii faciant obtunse, deformiter, frigide, alii acute, ornate, vehementer, illum ad hoc opus unde agimus iam oportet accedere, qui potest disputare vel dicere sapienter, etiamsi non potest eloquenter, ut prosit audientibus, etiamsi minus, quam prodesset si et eloquenter posset dicere. Qui vero affluit insipienti eloquentia, tanto magis cavendus est quanto magis ab eo in his quae audire inutile est, delectatur auditor et eum quoniam diserte dicere audit, etiam vere dicere existimat. (18) Haec autem sententia nec illos fugit qui artem rhetoricam docendam putarunt: fassi sunt enim sapientiam sine eloquentia parum prodesse civitatibus, eloquentiam vero sine sapientia nimium obesse plerumque, prodesse numquam. Si hoc ergo illi, qui praecepta eloquentiae tradiderunt, in eisdem libris in quibus id egerunt, veritate instigante coacti sunt confiteri, veram, hoc est supernam quae a patre luminum descendit sapientiam nescientes, quanto magis nos non aliud sentire debemus, qui huius sapientiae filii et ministri sumus?

(19) Sapienter autem dicit homo tanto magis vel minus, quanto in scripturis sanctis magis minusve profecit: non dico in eis multum legendis memoriaeque mandandis, sed bene intellegendis et diligenter earum sensibus indagan-

---

[12] *frigide* is a Ciceronian term for oratory that fails to stir an audience (*Brut*. 48, 178; *QFr*. 3, 3, 3).

[13] See Cic. *Inv. rhet*. 1.1.

[14] That is, pagan rhetorical theorists.

[15] James 1:17.

7. (16) Virtually everyone, in matters effected through the power of speech, makes constant use of all these factors that I have mentioned. (17) But some people do so in a way that is dull, contorted, lukewarm,[12] while others are sharp, polished, passionate; so for the task we have in hand, we must approach someone who can debate and speak wisely, even if he cannot do so eloquently; and this will benefit the listeners, though less so than if he were also capable of eloquence in speaking. We must be even more careful about fluent and eloquent speakers who nonetheless lack wisdom: when it comes to them listening to matters that are irrelevant, a listener may find it enjoyable, and thinks that because he is easy to listen to, he is also speaking truly. (18) Even people who believed that the art of rhetoric can be taught did not miss this conviction: they admitted that wisdom without eloquence was insufficiently beneficial to polities, whereas eloquence without wisdom was positively obstructive, and never beneficial.[13] So if this is what truth has goaded the people who have passed on those principles of eloquence[14] (in the same books in which they dealt with these matters) into declaring—even though they know nothing of the true wisdom that is on high, coming down from the father of lights[15]—how much more should we, who are offspring and servants of this wisdom, be in complete agreement with this opinion?

(19) A person speaks more or less wisely in proportion to their proficiency in the sacred writings: I am not talking about how often they have read them, or how much they have memorized them, but how well they have understood them, how carefully they have tracked down their meanings. For there are people who read them but do not take

dis. Sunt enim qui eas legunt et neglegunt: legunt ut teneant, neglegunt ne intellegant. (20) Quibus longe sine dubio praeferendi sunt qui verba earum minus tenent et cor earum sui cordis oculis vident. Sed utrisque ille melior qui et cum volet eas dicit et sicut oportet intellegit.

8. (21) Huic ergo qui sapienter debet dicere, etiam quod non potest eloquenter, verba scripturarum tenere maxime necessarium est. Quanto enim se pauperiorem cernit in suis, tanto eum oportet in istis esse ditiorem, ut quod dixerit suis verbis probet ex illis, et qui[3] propriis verbis minor erat, magnorum testimonio quodammodo crescat. Probando enim delectat qui minus potest delectare dicendo. (22) Porro qui non solum sapienter, verum etiam eloquenter vult dicere, quoniam profecto plus proderit, si utrumque potuerit, ad legendos vel audiendos et exercitatione imitandos eloquentes eum mitto libentius quam magistris artis rhetoricae vacare praecipio; si tamen hi qui leguntur et audiuntur, non solum eloquenter, sed etiam sapienter dixisse vel dicere veraci praedicatione laudantur.

(23) Qui enim eloquenter dicunt, suaviter, qui sapienter, salubriter audiuntur. Propter quod non ait scriptura, multitudo eloquentium, sed, "multitudo sapientium sanitas est orbis terrarum." Sicut autem saepe sumenda sunt

[3] quod *Hill (1996; v. p. 241)*

---

[16] *proprius*: not here referring to literal meaning.

[17] *praedicatione*: covers proclamation, praise, prophecy, and preaching.

[18] Wisdom 6:26.

them to heart: they read them to memorize them, but they do not take them to heart, and so do not understand them. (20) Beyond doubt, by far the better course is to memorize the words of scripture less, but instead to see into their heart with the eyes of one's own heart. But better than both of these is someone who can quote them at will, and who also understands them properly.

8. (21) To those, then who, precisely because they cannot speak eloquently, ought to speak wisely, it is of the highest importance to keep in mind the words of the scriptures. The poorer they see themselves as being in terms of their own words, the more it matters for them to be rich in words of scripture, so that they will corroborate from scripture what they say in their own words; then those who used to lack distinction in their own[16] use of words will somehow grow in stature thanks to the witness of the great. Those who are less able to delight audiences with their speaking still delight them by corroborating a case. (22) Then again, regarding those who wish to speak not only wisely but eloquently too—for it is certainly more constructive if they can do both—I would much rather send them off to the eloquent, to read, or hear, or practice imitating them, than tell them to find the time for teachers of the art of rhetoric. This is if those whom they read or hear are praised for having spoken, or speaking, not just eloquently but also wisely, who are genuinely proclaiming the word.[17]

(23) Listening to those who speak eloquently brings us enjoyment, whereas those who speak wisely have a wholesome effect. This is why scripture says, "a multitude of the wise is healthy for the world," and not "a multitude of the eloquent."[18] This is like nasty-tasting cures, which need to

et amara salubria, ita semper vitanda est perniciosa dulcedo. Sed salubri suavitate vel suavi salubritate quid melius? Quanto enim magis illic appetitur suavitas, tanto facilius salubritas prodest. (24) Sunt ergo ecclesiastici viri qui divina eloquia non solum sapienter, sed eloquenter etiam tractaverunt, quibus legendis magis non sufficit tempus quam deesse ipsi studentibus et vacantibus possunt.

9. (25) Hic aliquis forsitan quaerit utrum auctores nostri, quorum scripta divinitus inspirata canonem nobis saluberrima auctoritate fecerunt, sapientes tantummodo an eloquentes etiam nuncupandi sint. Quae quidem quaestio apud me ipsum et apud eos qui mecum quod dico sentiunt, facillime solvitur. Nam ubi eos intellego, non solum nihil eis sapientius, verum etiam nihil eloquentius mihi videri potest. Et audeo dicere omnes qui recte intellegunt quod illi loquuntur, simul intellegere non eos aliter loqui debuisse. (26) Sicut est enim quaedam eloquentia quae magis aetatem iuvenilem decet, est quae senilem, nec iam dicenda est eloquentia si personae non congruit eloquentis; ita est quaedam, quae viros summa auctoritate dignissimos planeque divinos decet. Haec illi locuti sunt, nec ipsos decet alia nec alios ipsa. Ipsis enim congruit; alios autem, quanto videtur humilior, tanto altius non ventositate, sed soliditate transcendit.

---

[19] English "sweet" often has diminutive or patronizing resonance; Latin has *suavitas* and *dulcedo*, both commonly used metaphorically of pleasures but without that resonance.

[20] Referring to scripture as *divina eloquia* implies that eloquence is an acceptable tool for teachers of Christianity.

[21] The Latin is epigrammatic, but the sense is clear.

[22] Oxymoronic. It rises up because it is heavy, not light.

be taken often, even as deadly confections must at all times be shunned. But what is better than healthy pleasure or pleasant health? The more we seek what is pleasurable, the easier it is to promote what is good for us.[19] (24) That is why there are Christian men who have handled the divine communications[20] not just wisely, but eloquently too. It is more the case that there is not time enough for reading them than that those with leisure for study cannot access them.

9. (25) At this point, someone may ask whether Christian authors, whose writings, by divine inspiration, have fashioned for us a canon possessed of supreme salvific authority, are wise only, or should also be declared to be eloquent. This question is simplicity itself to resolve, for me personally, and for those who agree with what I am saying. For when I understand those authors, it seems to me that there is nothing more wise, and also nothing more eloquent. I even dare to say that everyone who understands aright what those authors are saying also understands that it was never an option for them to have spoken in some other way. (26) Just as there is one sort of eloquence more appropriate in one's youth, so too there is a kind that is more appropriate in old age (though it should not be called "eloquence" if it is inappropriate to the character of the speaker); and it is this type that befits men who deserve the highest authority, and who are clearly divinely inspired. What they have spoken, they have spoken:[21] and it would be improper for them to speak otherwise, and for others to say what they said. It is peculiar to them: the more humble it appears, the more it soars supreme above others, and this is because of its weightiness, not because it is full of hot air.[22]

(27) Ubi vero non eos intellego, minus quidem mihi apparet eorum eloquentia, sed eam non dubito esse talem, qualis est ubi intellego. Ipsa quoque obscuritas divinorum salubriumque dictorum tali eloquentiae miscenda fuerat, in qua proficere noster intellectus, non solum inventione, verum etiam exercitatione deberet.

10. (28) Possem quidem, si vacaret, omnes virtutes et ornamenta eloquentiae, de quibus inflantur isti qui linguam suam nostrorum auctorum linguae non magnitudine, sed tumore praeponunt, ostendere in istorum litteris sacris, quos nobis erudiendis, et ab hoc saeculo pravo in beatum saeculum transferendis, providentia divina providit. (29) Sed non ipsa me plus quam dici potest, in illa eloquentia delectant, quae sunt his viris cum oratoribus gentilium poetisve communia. Illud magis admiror et stupeo, quod ista nostra eloquentia ita usi sunt per alteram quandam eloquentiam suam, ut nec deesset eis nec emineret in eis, quia eam nec improbari ab illis nec ostentari oportebat. Quorum alterum fieret si vitaretur, alterum putari posset si facile agnosceretur. (30) Et in quibus forte locis agnoscitur a doctis, tales res dicuntur, ut verba quibus dicuntur, non a dicente adhibita, sed ipsis rebus velut sponte subiuncta videantur, quasi sapientiam de domo sua, id est, pectore sapientis intellegas procedere et tam-

---

[23] The “divine difficulty” hypothesis. See p. 185.

[24] *gentilium*: Christian appropriation of a Jewish term for non-Jews to distinguish themselves from (non-Jewish) non-Christians. See p. 198, n. 13.

(27) So when I do not understand these authors, their eloquence is harder for me to recognize, but I have no doubt that it is of the same quality as what I do understand. Indeed, this very obscurity in sacred and salvific pronouncements had to be mixed in with a commensurate amount of eloquence, which was necessary for the good of our understanding, which obliges us not only to discover meaning, but also to wrestle with it.[23]

10. (28) If there was time, I could present all the strengths and embellishments of eloquence in the holy writings of these men: though such qualities evoke conceit in those who favor their own use of language (which is distinguished by bombast rather than stature) over that of the Christian authors whom divine providence has prepared for our education, to transfer us from the wickedness of the present age to the age of bliss. (29) It is not, however, what these men have in common with pagan[24] orators or poets that delights me more than I can say about their eloquence. What amazes and astonishes me is this: that they used this eloquence of ours by means of that different kind of eloquence that was all their own, so that it was neither deficient in them nor too conspicuous, because it was important that they did not disapprove of it or make a spectacle of it. The former would be the case if they avoided eloquence altogether; the latter could be imputed if the eloquence was too noticeable. (30) If, moreover, experts do find it noticeable in places, the subject matter is related in such a way that the vocabulary used seems not to be a conscious choice by the author, but to have arisen naturally from the events themselves. You could understand it as being like wisdom emerging from her own house (in other words from the breast of someone

quam inseparabilem famulam etiam non vocatam sequi eloquentiam.

11. (31) Quis enim non videat quid voluerit dicere et quam sapienter dixerit apostolus, "gloriamur in tribulationibus, scientes quia tribulatio patientiam operatur, patientia autem probationem, probatio vero spem, spes autem non confundit; quia caritas dei diffusa est in cordibus nostris per spiritum sanctum qui datus est nobis"? Hic si quis, ut ita dixerim, imperite peritus artis eloquentiae praecepta apostolum secutum fuisse contendat, nonne a Christianis doctis indoctisque ridebitur? (32) Et tamen agnoscitur hic figura, quae "climax" Graece, Latine vero a quibusdam est appellata "gradatio," quoniam scalam dicere noluerunt, cum verba vel sensa conectuntur alterum ex altero; sicut hic ex tribulatione patientiam, ex patientia probationem, ex probatione spem conexam videmus. Agnoscitur et aliud decus, quoniam post aliqua pronuntiationis voce singula finita, quae nostri "membra" et "caesa," Graeci autem "cola" et "commata" vocant, sequitur ambitus sive circuitus, quem "periodon" illi appellant, cuius membra suspenduntur voce dicentis, donec ultimo finiatur.

---

[25] A play on two compounds of the same verb (*confundo/confundit*; *diffundo/diffusa*), translated here as "discompose/spread abroad," is noticeable in the Latin. There is no such wordplay in the Greek of Romans 5:3–5.

[26] What follows is a distinctively innovative analysis of a biblical text in literary-critical terms.

[27] Drawing attention to his oxymoron.

[28] Augustine uses this latter term, e.g., *En. Ps.* 109.5.

wise) while eloquence, like a constant attendant who does not have to be summoned, follows after her.

11. (31) Who can fail to see what the apostle wanted to say, and how wisely he said, "we boast in our misfortunes, knowing that misfortune produces endurance; and endurance, affirmation; and affirmation, hope; and hope does not discompose us, because the love of God has been spread abroad in our hearts[25] through the Holy Spirit who has been given to us."[26] If some inexpert expert (so to speak)[27] were to insist that the apostle had followed the principles of the art of eloquence, surely learned and unlearned Christians alike would laugh at him? (32) Even so, we recognize here a rhetorical figure, which is called *klimax* in Greek (in Latin some label it, "ascent"[28] because they do not intend to refer to a ladder[29]), when words or experiences are linked together each one to the next in sequence: so as here we see the linking of "misfortune" to "endurance," of "endurance" to "affirmation," of "affirmation" to "hope." There is another flourish too, since after the expression of individual utterances is completed (which we call "sections" and "clauses," and the Greeks *kōla* and *kommata*) a periodic sentence emerges[30] (which the Greek call *periodos*): the vocal control of a speaker keeps the sections of a periodic sentence hanging, until they are completed by the final clause.

[29] The Greek *klimax* means "ladder"; the Latin *gradatio* means "staircase": both, metaphorically, can mean "ascent."

[30] *Ambitus vel circuitus* (a loop or circuit). In a periodic sentence, a number of elements are subordinated, in dependent clauses, to a main verb—a jewel of golden Latin prose, but a headache for learners. See Cic. *Brut.* 162; Quint. *Inst.* 9.4.22.

(33) Nam eorum quae praecedunt circuitum, membrum illud est primum "quoniam tribulatio patientiam operatur," secundum "patientia autem probationem," tertium "probatio vero spem." Deinde subiungitur ipse circuitus, qui tribus peragitur membris, quorum primum est, "spes autem non confundit," secundum, "quoniam caritas dei diffusa est in cordibus nostris," tertium, "per spiritum sanctum qui datus est nobis." At haec atque huius modi in elocutionis arte traduntur. Sicut ergo apostolum praecepta eloquentiae secutum fuisse non dicimus, ita quod eius sapientiam secuta sit eloquentia non negamus.

12. (34) Scribens ad Corinthios, in secunda epistola redarguit quosdam qui erant ex Iudaeis pseudapostoli eique detrahebant. Et quoniam se ipsum praedicare compellitur, hanc sibi velut insipientiam tribuens quam sapienter dicit quamque eloquenter! Sed comes sapientiae, dux eloquentiae, illam sequens, istam praecedens et sequentem non respuens.

(35) "Iterum dico," inquit, "ne quis me existimet insipientem esse; alioquin velut insipientem suscipite me, ut et ego modicum quid glorier. Quod loquor, non loquor secundum deum, sed quasi in stultitia, in hac substantia gloriae. Quoniam quidem multi gloriantur secundum car-

---

31 Latin *subiungitur* (whence, "subjunctive"): his usual choice for the subordinate clause in an oblique mood. Cf. §42.

32 This quotation does not match the fuller version in §31, using *quoniam* in place of *quia* (a *lectio difficilior* resisting assimilation to Vulg.).

33 2 Corinthians 11:16–30.

34 *Praedicare.* The switch to the historic present tense, followed by exclamation, marks a degree of emotion in Augustine's response to this passage.

(33) Of the clauses that precede the completion of the period, the first is, "since misfortune produces endurance," the second is, "patience produces affirmation," the third is, "affirmation produces hope." Then the period is added to complete the whole,[31] concluding with three sections: the first part is, "hope does not discompose us," the second, "since[32] the love of God has been spread abroad in our hearts," and the third is, "through the Holy Spirit who has been given to us." This, however, and this sort of thing, are passed on through learning eloquence. So just as we do not say that the apostle followed the principles of eloquence, so also we do not deny that eloquence was a product of his wisdom.

12. (34) When he wrote to the Corinthians, in his second letter[33] he countered certain Jewish people, false apostles, who were disparaging him. Since he is forced to preach himself,[34] he attributes to himself this apparent folly; yet how wisely, how eloquently he speaks! He waits upon wisdom, a commander of eloquence: following the former, leading the latter, not spurning the eloquence that follows him:[35]

(35) "Again I say," he remarks, "let no one judge me to be a fool; or else receive me as a fool, so that I too may boast a little. What I speak, I do not speak according to God, but as if in absurdity amid the reality of glory. Since there are many who boast according to the flesh, I too will boast. For you suffer fools gladly, seeing that you your-

[35] The language is military; the apostle is in the middle rank, serving wisdom but commanding eloquence, yet (the point of the argument) not regarding eloquence as beneath him.

nem, et ego gloriabor. Libenter enim sustinetis insipientes, cum sitis sapientes. Toleratis enim si quis vos in servitutem redigit, si quis devorat, si quis accipit, si quis extollitur, si quis in faciem vos caedit. Secundum ignobilitatem dico, quasi nos infirmati simus. In quo autem quis audet (in insipientia dico), audeo et ego. Hebraei sunt? Et ego. Israhelitae sunt? Et ego. Semen Abrahae sunt? Et ego. Ministri Christi sunt? (insipiens dico), super ego: in laboribus plurimum, in carceribus abundantius, in plagis supra modum, in mortibus saepius. A Iudaeis quinquies quadraginta una minus accepi. Ter virgis caesus sum, semel lapidatus sum, ter naufragium feci; nocte et die in profundo maris fui; in itineribus saepe, periculis fluminum, periculis latronum, periculis ex genere, periculis ex gentibus, periculis in civitate, periculis in deserto, periculis in mari, periculis in falsis fratribus; in labore et aerumna, in vigiliis saepius, in fame et siti, in ieiuniis saepius, in frigore et nuditate; praeter illa quae extrinsecus sunt, incursus in me cotidianus, sollicitudo omnium ecclesiarum. Quis infirmatur, et ego non infirmor? Quis scandalizatur, et ego non uror? Si gloriari oportet, in his quae infirmitatis meae sunt, gloriabor." Quanta sapientia ista sint dicta vigilantes vident, quanto vero etiam eloquentiae concurrerint flumine, et qui stertit advertit.

---

[36] *saepius*: *TC* preserves an alternative to Vulg. *frequenter*. Note the *variatio* in *plurimum*, *abundatius*, *supra modum*, *saepius*. [37] Deuteronomy 25:2–3. Omission of the fortieth blow was precautionary, to avoid exceeding the commandment.

[38] Another, earlier, north African bishop, Cyprian, uses the verb *facio* of the undergoing of martyrdom (*facienda martyria*: *Ep*. 57.2–3; 61.2). [39] An English-language equivalent for Hebrew *midbār* and Greek *erēmos*.

selves are wise. You put up with it if someone reduces you to slavery, if they consume you, if they accept you, if they aggrandize themselves, if anyone strikes you in the face. I am speaking in terms of dishonor, as if we are weak. But in this matter, where others are bold (I am speaking in terms of folly) I too am bold. Are they Hebrews? So am I. Are they Israelites? So am I. Are they of the seed of Abraham? So am I. Are they servants of Christ? Speaking in terms of folly, I am more so: in countless endeavors, more often imprisoned, more severely beaten, more frequently[36] in deadly dangers. Five times the Jews subjected me to forty lashes save one.[37] Three times I was beaten with rods. Once I was stoned. Three times I endured[38] shipwreck. I spent a day and a night in the deep of the sea. I was constantly on the road: in peril from rivers, in peril from robbers, in peril from my own people, in perils from gentiles, in perils in communities, in peril in the wilderness,[39] in peril on the sea, in peril from turncoat Christians; with hard labor, constant sleep deprivation, hunger and thirst, unremitting poverty, cold and exposure. Besides those things, which are external, bearing down upon me daily is my responsibility for all the churches. Who is weak while I am not weak? Who stumbles on the way, without it touching my emotions?[40] If it is proper to boast, then boast I shall—but in the sins of my weakness." Readers who are on the alert see how wisely he says all this, and not even people who snore can ignore[41] how his words pour out in a torrent of eloquence.

[40] Latin *uror*: of heated emotion, but not anger with the one who has stumbled.

[41] Latin *stertit advertit*: the conspicuous rhyme has a bathetic effect.

13. (36) Porro autem qui novit, agnoscit quod ea caesa quae "commata" Graeci vocant, et membra et circuitus, de quibus paulo ante disserui, cum decentissima varietate interponerentur, totam istam speciem dictionis et quasi eius vultum, quo etiam indocti delectantur moventurque, fecerunt. (37) Nam unde coepimus hunc locum inserere, circuitus sunt. Primus minimus, hoc est bimembris; minus enim quam duo membra circuitus habere non possunt, plura vero possunt. Ergo ille primus est, "iterum dico, ne quis me existimet insipientem esse." Sequitur alius trimembris, "alioquin velut insipientem suscipite me, ut et ego modicum quid glorier." (38) Tertius qui sequitur membra habet quattuor, "quod loquor, non loquor secundum deum, sed quasi in stultitia, in hac substantia gloriae." Quartus duo habet, "quoniam quidem multi gloriantur secundum carnem, et ego gloriabor." Et quintus duo, "libenter enim sustinetis insipientes, cum sitis sapientes." Etiam sextus bimembris est, "toleratis enim si quis vos in servitutem redigit." Sequuntur tria caesa, "si quis devorat, si quis accipit, si quis extollitur." (39) Deinde tria membra, "si quis in faciem vos caedit, secundum ignobilitatem dico, quasi nos infirmati simus." Additur trimembris circuitus, "In quo autem quis audet (in insipientia dico), audeo et ego."

Hinc iam singulis quibusque caesis interrogando positis singula itidem caesa responsione redduntur, tria tribus, "Hebraei sunt? Et ego. Israhelitae sunt? Et ego. Semen Abrahae sunt? Et ego." Quarto autem caeso simili inter-

---

[42] The division between parts of the sentence given here by Augustine does not match the necessary sense division in §35.

13. (36) Then again, anyone who is in the know will admit that those divisions that the Greeks call *kommata*, and the clauses and periods that we discussed just now, have been set out with a really well-balanced range of expressions, achieving that perfect arrangement of phraseology, so that its expressive countenance (as it were) can delight and stir even people of no education. (37) For example, where I began to quote this passage, there are periodic sentences. The first is very short, consisting of two parts: and periods cannot have fewer than two parts, but obviously they can have more. This, then, is the first period: "Again I say, let no one judge me to be a fool." Next comes another period, in three parts: "or else receive me as a fool, so that I too may boast a little." (38) Next comes the third, in four parts: "What I speak, I do not speak according to God, but as if in absurdity, amid the reality of glory." The fourth has two, "Since there are many who boast according to the flesh, I too will boast." The fifth also has two: "For you suffer fools gladly, seeing that you yourselves are wise." And again the sixth is in two parts: "You put up with it if someone reduces you to slavery." Then follow three phrases: "if they consume you, if they accept you, if they aggrandize themselves." (39) Next come three parts: "if anyone strikes you in the face—I am speaking in terms of dishonor, as if we are weak."[42] A three-clause period is joined to this: "But in this matter, where others are bold (I am speaking in terms of folly) I too am bold."

From here on, each individual phrase set as a question has its individual phrase in reply, three against three: "Are they Hebrews? So am I. Are they Israelites? So am I. Are they of the seed of Abraham? So am I." But the fourth

rogatione posito, non alterius caesi, sed membri oppositione respondet, "ministri Christi sunt? (insipiens dico) super ego." (40) Iam caesa quattuor sequentia, remota decentissime interrogatione funduntur, "in laboribus plurimum, in carceribus abundantius, in plagis supra modum, in mortibus saepius." Deinde interponitur brevis circuitus, quoniam suspensa pronuntiatione distinguendum est, a "Iudaeis quinquies," ut hoc sit unum membrum, cui connectitur alterum, "quadraginta una minus accepi."

(41) Inde reditur ad caesa et ponuntur tria, "ter virgis caesus sum, semel lapidatus sum, ter naufragium feci." Sequitur membrum, "nocte et die in profundo maris fui." Deinde quattuordecim caesa decentissimo impetu profluunt, "in itineribus saepe, periculis fluminum, periculis latronum, periculis ex genere, periculis ex gentibus, periculis in civitate, periculis in deserto, periculis in mari, periculis in falsis fratribus; in labore et aerumna, in vigiliis saepius, in fame et siti, in ieiuniis saepius, in frigore et nuditate." (42) Post haec interponit trimembrem circuitum, "praeter illa quae extrinsecus sunt, incursus in me quotidianus, sollicitudo omnium ecclesiarum." Et huic duo membra percontatione subiungit, "quis infirmatur, et ego non infirmor? Quis scandalizatur, et ego non uror?" Postremo totus iste quasi anhelans locus bimembri circuitu terminatur, "si gloriari oportet, in his quae infirmitatis meae sunt gloriabor."

---

[43] It is not clear to a modern reader that this separation of subject and verb creates two clauses. Perhaps performance within worship suggests to him a dramatic pause before the revelation of what the "baddies" of the New Testament have done to the apostle. [44] In Christian Latin, *desertum* can refer to a wild, uninhabited region as well as a sandy, waterless one.

phrase, though likewise formulated as a question, he answers not with a counterphrase but with a clause in response: "Are they servants of Christ? Speaking as a fool, I am more so." (40) At this point he leaves off the question-and-answer form at the perfect moment, to pour out a sequence of four phrases: "more in terms of endeavors, more often imprisoned, more severely beaten, more frequently in deadly dangers." Then he inserts a brief period that we have to mark with a pause in delivery: "Five times the Jews"—making this one clause, to which he links the other—"subjected me to forty lashes save one."[43]

(41) Next he returns to phrases, giving us three: "Three times I was beaten with rods. Once I was stoned. Three times I endured shipwreck." After this comes a clause, "I spent a day and a night in the deep of the sea." After this, fourteen phrases gush out in a perfect flood: "I was constantly on the road: in peril from rivers, in peril from robbers, in peril from my own people, in peril from gentiles, in peril in inhabited places, in peril in the wilderness,[44] in peril on the sea, in peril from turncoat Christians; with hard labor, constant sleep deprivation, hunger and thirst, unremitting poverty, cold and exposure." (42) After this he inserts a period consisting of three clauses: "Besides those things, which are external, bearing down upon me daily is my responsibility for all the churches." To this he appends two clauses in question form: "Who is weak while I am not weak? Who stumbles on the way, without it touching my emotions?" Finally, the whole passage, with its breathless delivery, draws to a close with a two-clause period: "If it is proper to boast, then boast I shall—but in the sins that reveal my weakness."

(43) Quod vero post hunc impetum interposita narratiuncula quodammodo requiescit et requiescere auditorem facit, quid decoris, quid delectationis habeat, satis dici non potest. Sequitur enim dicens, "deus et pater domini nostri Iesu Christi scit, qui est benedictus in saecula, quia non mentior." Ac deinde quomodo periclitatus fuerit et quomodo evaserit, brevissime narrat.

14. (44) Longum est cetera persequi vel in aliis sanctarum scripturarum locis ista monstrare. Quid, si etiam figuras locutionis quae illa arte traduntur, in his saltem quae de apostoli eloquio commemoravi, ostendere voluissem? Nonne facilius graves homines me nimium quam quisquam studiosorum sibi sufficientem putarent? (45) Haec omnia, quando a magistris docentur, pro magno habentur, magno emuntur, magna iactatione venduntur. Quam iactationem etiam ego redolere vereor, dum ista sic dissero. Sed male doctis hominibus respondendum fuit, qui nostros auctores contemnendos putant, non quia non habent, sed quia non ostentant, quam nimis isti diligunt eloquentiam.

15. (46) Sed forte quis putat tamquam eloquentem nostrum elegisse me apostolum Paulum. Videtur enim ubi ait, "etsi imperitus sermone, sed non scientia," quasi concedendo obtrectatoribus sic locutus, non tamquam id verum agnosceret confitendo. Si autem dixisset, "imperitus quidem sermone, sed non scientia," nullo modo aliud pos-

---

[45] *narratiuncula* is a rare word. See Quint. *Inst.* 1.9.6, "Short narratives found in the poets should, in my view, be taught for general knowledge, not for developing eloquence." In the younger Pliny, *narratiuncula* means an anecdote (*Ep.* 6.33.8).

[46] 2 Corinthians 11:6.

(43) As for the way in which he inserts a short intervening narrative[45] after the flurry of words, somehow calming himself down and calming his listeners, there are no words to express how perfectly and delightfully he effects this. For he follows it up with, "the God and Father of our Lord Jesus Christ, who is blessed for ever, knows that I am not lying." And then he gives a very short report of how he was in danger, and how he escaped.

14. (44) It is a long task to follow up the rest of these features, or to demonstrate them in others of the holy writings as well. What if I wanted to display the figures of rhetoric that skillful speaking passes onto us, even just in these instances where I have drawn attention to the apostle's eloquence? Undoubtedly, rather than any individual scholars concluding that I was providing enough information to suit them, serious people would quickly conclude that I was giving too much. (45) When teachers instruct us in all these aspects, we regard them as important, we pay a high price for them, we peddle them vaingloriously. For my part I dread reeking of such vainglory while I explain these matters. But I had to respond to those ill-educated people who believe that Christian authors are contemptible, not because of their lack of that eloquence to which those people are themselves so attached, but because they do not show it off.

15. (46) Perhaps someone reckons that I chose the apostle Paul as if he were our example of a man of eloquence. For where he said, "though unskilled in speaking, I am not without knowledge,"[46] it looks like he has said it as if he was making a concession to his detractors, not like he was admitting it as if it were really true. But if he had said, "I am unskilled in speaking, but not in knowledge,"

set intellegi. Scientiam plane non cunctatus est profiteri, sine qua esse doctor gentium non valeret. (47) Certe si quid eius proferimus ad exemplum eloquentiae, ex illis epistolis utique proferimus, quas etiam ipsi obtrectatores eius, qui sermonem praesentis contemptibilem putari[4] volebant, graves et fortes esse confessi sunt.

(48) Dicendum ergo mihi aliquid esse video et de eloquentia prophetarum, ubi per tropologiam multa obteguntur. Quae quanto magis translatis verbis videntur operiri, tanto magis cum fuerint aperta dulcescunt. Sed hoc loco tale aliquid commemorare debeo, ubi quae dicta sunt non cogar exponere, sed commendem tantum quomodo dicta sint. Et ex illius prophetae libro potissimum hoc faciam, qui se pastorem vel armentarium fuisse dicit atque inde divinitus ablatum atque missum, ut dei populo prophetaret, non autem secundum septuaginta interpretes, qui etiam divino spiritu interpretati, ob hoc aliter videntur nonnulla dixisse, ut ad spiritalem sensum scrutandum magis admoneretur lectoris intentio, unde etiam obscuriora nonnulla quia magis tropica sunt eorum, sed sicut ex Hebraeo in Latinum eloquium presbytero Hieronymo utriusque linguae perito interpretante, translata sunt.

16. (49) Cum igitur argueret impios, superbos, luxurio-

[4] parere *Lond.*

---

47 1 Timothy 2:7.
48 2 Corinthians 10:10.
49 *exponere*: regularly used of explaining a biblical text.
50 Amos: not named in the Latin.
51 Amos 7:14–15.
52 Of the Septuagint. See note on *TC* 2.16.36.

his statement could have only one meaning. Certainly he has not hesitated to claim knowledge, without which he would not have the capacity to be the teacher of the gentiles.[47] (47) To be sure, if we are putting forward something of his for an example of eloquence, of course we put it forward from those letters that even his detractors (who were eager for the speeches he made in person to be considered contemptible) have admitted are weighty and forceful.[48]

(48) So I see that I must say something about the eloquence of the prophets too, though they veil many of their utterances in figurative kinds of speech. The more they appear to conceal behind figurative words, the more delightful they are when their meaning is disclosed. But at this point I need to give an example of such a text, for which I am not obliged to give an exegesis[49] of its contents, but simply a positive endorsement of its style. The most effective way for me to do this is by using the book of that prophet who tells us that he was a shepherd or herdsman,[50] and then by divine inspiration was carried away, and sent to prophesy to God's people[51]—but not in the version of the seventy translators[52] who also translated by divine inspiration, and who seem, on that account, to have expressed some things differently, so that the reader's attention would be more firmly directed to scrutinize the spiritual meaning (this accounts for some of what they say being more obscure because it is more figurative). I shall use instead the translation that the priest Jerome, an expert translator of both languages, made from Hebrew into Latin.

16. (49) When, therefore, he was denouncing the ungodly, the proud, hedonists, and those who were utterly

sos et fraternae ideo neglegentissimos caritatis, rusticus vel ex rustico iste propheta exclamavit, dicens, "Vae qui opulenti estis in Sion, et confiditis in monte Samariae, optimates capita populorum, ingredientes pompatice domum Israhel! Transite in Chalanne et videte et ite inde in Emath magnam et descendite in Geth Palaestinorum et ad optima quaeque regna horum, si latior terminus eorum termino vestro est. Qui separati estis in diem malum et appropinquatis solio iniquitatis, qui dormitis in lectis eburneis et lascivitis in stratis vestris, qui comeditis agnum de grege et vitulos de medio armenti, qui canitis ad vocem psalterii. Sicut David putaverunt se habere vasa cantici, bibentes in phialis vinum, et optimo unguento delibuti, et nihil patiebantur super contritione Ioseph." (50) Numquidnam isti, qui prophetas nostros tamquam ineruditos et elocutionis ignaros veluti docti disertique contemnunt, si aliquid eis tale vel in tales dicendum fuisset, aliter se voluissent dicere, qui tamen eorum insanire noluissent?

17. (51) Quid enim est quod isto eloquio aures sobriae plus desiderent? Prima ipsa invectio quasi sopitis sensibus ut evigilarent, quo fremitu illisa est! "Vae vobis qui opulenti estis in Sion, et confiditis in monte Samariae, opti-

---

[53] Doubling of verbs of saying is a biblical idiom.

[54] An exclamation or denunciation (Hebrew *hōy*; Greek *ouai*; Latin *vae*: see Matthew 23:15–29), distinctive of prophecy. Amos' application of a "woe" to Judah, the South Kingdom, was meant to be shocking.

[55] A figurative use of *vox*.

[56] *psalterio*: a stringed instrument, either with a sound box (like a lute) or without (like a lyre).

[57] King David, the traditional author of Psalms: see 2.13.27.

heedless of brotherly love, the peasant prophet (at least he was from peasant stock) cried aloud, saying,[53] "Woe[54] to you who are rich in Sion, who trust in the mountain of Samaria, the nobles, the leaders of the peoples, making your entrance into the house of Israel with pomp and circumstance! Cross over into Calneh and see; and go from there into mighty Hamath, and make your way down to Palestinian Gath, and to all the finest of their kingdoms, if their boundaries are wider than your boundaries. You who have been set apart for the evil day and draw near to the seat of iniquity, who sleep on beds of ivory and sate your appetites between the sheets, who fill your bellies with a lamb from the flock and calves from the midst of the herd, who sing to the sound[55] of the lyre.[56] They thought that they possessed musical instruments like David,[57] drinking their wine from bowls and plastering themselves with perfume. They cared nothing at all for the sorrow of Joseph."[58] (50) Do these men—as if presuming themselves to be expert and discriminating—scorn our prophets as if they were illiterate, and ignorant of how to speak in public? And, if they found themselves with anything similar to say, to a similar audience, would they have wanted to say any of it differently (I mean those of them unwilling to appear deranged)?

17. (51) Now what more could serious listeners[59] wish for than eloquence like this? That first assault, what a crashing cacophony, as if stirring sleepy senses! "Woe to you who are rich in Sion, who trust in the mountain of

[58] Amos 5:6, 6:1–6. The name of Joseph stands for the North Kingdom, ethnically cleansed in the eighth century BC by the Assyrian king Tiglath-Pileser III. [59] *aures*: synecdoche.

mates capita populorum, ingredientes pompatice domum Israhel!" Deinde, ut beneficiis dei, qui eis ampla spatia regni dedit, ostendat ingratos, quoniam confidebant in monte Samariae, ubi utique idola colebantur, "transite," inquit, "in Chalanne et videte et ite inde in Emath magnam et descendite in Geth Palaestinorum et ad optima quaeque regna horum, si latior terminus eorum termino vestro est." (52) Simul etiam cum ista dicuntur, locorum nominibus tamquam luminibus ornatur eloquium, quae sunt Sion, Samaria, Chalanne, Emath magna et Geth Palaestinorum. Deinde verba quae his adiunguntur locis decentissime variantur, "opulenti estis, confiditis, transite, ite, descendite."

18. (53) Consequenter denuntiatur futura sub iniquo rege appropinquare captivitas, cum adiungitur, "qui separati estis in diem malum et appropinquatis solio iniquitatis." Tunc subiciuntur merita luxuriae, "qui dormitis in lectis eburneis et lascivitis in stratis vestris; qui comeditis agnum de grege et vitulos de medio armenti." Ista sex membra tres bimembres circuitus ediderunt: (54) non enim ait, "qui separati estis in diem malum, qui appropinquatis solio iniquitatis, qui dormitis in lectis eburneis, qui lascivitis in stratis vestris, qui comeditis agnum de grege, qui vitulos de medio armenti." Quod si ita diceretur, esset

---

60 A figure, paraprosdokia. Christians would expect "put their trust in mount Sion" (Psalm 125:1). 61 *variatio*: a rhetorical figure. 62 Omitted from the list are "making your entrance" (as a participle it has adjectival as well as verbal force) and "see" (because it is not attached to a place-name). 63 Which was to encompass enslavement, mass displacement, and oppression.

Samaria, the nobles, the leaders of the peoples, making your entrance into the house of Israel with pomp and circumstance!" Then he shows how thankless they were for the benefits bestowed by God, who gave them a kingdom broad and far, while they put their trust in the mountain of Samaria,[60] where idols were certainly being worshiped. "Cross over into Calneh," he said, "and see; and go from there into mighty Hamath, and make your way down to Palestinian Gath, and to all the finest of their kingdoms, if their boundaries are wider than your boundaries." (52) At the same time as he says all this, he adorns his eloquence, like lights, with those exotic place-names: to be specific, Sion, Samaria, Calneh, Hamath and Palestinian Gath. Then he displays a fine use of variation[61] in the verbs attached to all these place-names: "you who are rich," "who trust," "cross over," "go," "make your way down."[62]

18. (53) This leads to a declaration that impending captivity[63] is drawing near under the unjust king who is to come, when he adds, "You who have been set apart for the evil day and draw near to the seat of iniquity." Then he appends the price to be paid for their hedonism, "who sleep on beds of ivory and sate your appetites between the sheets, who fill your bellies with a lamb from the flock and calves from the midst of the herd." Those six clauses are arranged in three two-clause periods: (54) for he does not say, "You who have been set apart for the evil day, who draw near to the seat of iniquity, who sleep on beds of ivory, who sate your appetites between the sheets, who fill your bellies with a lamb from the flock, who fill your bellies with calves from the midst of the herd." If he had in fact

quidem et hoc pulchrum ut ab uno pronomine repetito omnia sex membra decurrerent et pronuntiantis voce singula finirentur. Sed pulchrius factum est ut eidem pronomini essent bina subnexa, quae tres sententias explicarent; unam ad captivitatis praenuntiationem, "qui separati estis in diem malum et appropinquatis solio iniquitatis"; alteram ad libidinem, "qui dormitis in lectis eburneis, et lascivitis in stratis vestris"; ad voracitatem vero tertiam pertinentem, "qui comeditis agnum de grege et vitulos de medio armenti," ut in potestate sit pronuntiantis, utrum singula finiat et membra sint sex, an primum et tertium et quintum voce suspendat et secundum primo, quartum tertio, sextum quinto conectendo, tres bimembres circuitus decentissime faciat: unum quo calamitas imminens, alterum quo lectus impurus, tertium quo prodiga mensa monstratur.

19. (55) Deinde luxuriosam remordet aurium voluptatem. Ubi cum dixisset, "qui canitis ad vocem psalterii," quoniam potest exerceri sapienter a sapientibus musica, mirabili decore dicendi, invectionis impetu relaxato, et non ad illos sed de illis iam loquens, ut nos musicam sapientis a musica luxuriantis distinguere commoneret, non ait, qui canitis ad vocem psalterii, et sicut David putatis vos habere vasa cantici, (56) sed cum illud ad illos dixisset, quod luxuriosi audire deberent, "qui canitis ad vocem

---

[64] Like the professor of rhetoric he once was, Augustine imagines how best to deliver Amos' words. Written punctuation, as a guide to performance, was then vestigial and inconsistent, and it was looked down upon by theorists like Cicero (*De or.* 3.173).

[65] Augustine was ambivalent about the power of music (cf. *Conf.* 10.33.49): see *TC* 1.3.7, n. 21.

said it thus, then it would have been a fine speech because of the way it rushed through all six clauses with repetitions of a single pronoun, each one marked off by the speaker's vocal modulation.[64] But what makes it even finer is the way that each pair of clauses is subjoined to the same pronoun as it unfurls the three sentences: one predicting the captivity, "you who have been set apart for the evil day and draw near to the seat of iniquity"; the second on immorality, "who sleep on beds of ivory and sate your appetites between the sheets,"; and the third taking aim at gluttony, "who fill your bellies with a lamb from the flock and calves from the midst of the herd." This way it is a decision for the reader whether to pronounce each of the clauses separately, giving a total of six, or whether to use vocal inflection to keep the first, third, and fifth clauses hanging, then to hook up the second to the first, the fourth to the third, and the sixth to the fifth, making a perfect set of three two-clause periods: the first to indicate looming disaster, the second, sexual immorality, and the third, lavish consumption.

19. (55) Then he snaps at the hedonistic pleasure of the ears.[65] Since music can be wisely practiced by the wise, when he had said, "who sing to the sound of the lyre," he slackened the force of his critique, with a remarkably attractive style of speech, and, speaking about those people rather than to them, so as to warn us to distinguish the music of the wise from the music of the hedonist, he did not say, "you who sing to the sound of the lyre, and believe that you possess musical instruments like David"; (56) but when he had said to them (because the hedonists needed to hear that) "who sing to the sound of the lyre," somehow

psalterii," imperitiam quoque eorum aliis quodammodo indicavit, adiungens, "sicut David putaverunt se habere vasa cantici, bibentes in phialis vinum, et optimo unguento delibuti." Tria haec melius pronuntiantur si suspensis duobus prioribus membris circuitus tertio finiantur.

20. (57) Iam vero quod his omnibus adicitur, "et nihil patiebantur super contritione Ioseph," sive continuatim dicatur ut unum sit membrum, sive decentius suspendatur, "et nihil patiebantur," et post hanc distinctionem inferatur, "super contritione Ioseph," atque sit bimembris circuitus, miro decore non dictum est, "nihil patiebantur super contritione fratris," sed positus est pro fratre "Ioseph," ut quicumque frater proprio significaretur eius nomine, cuius ex fratribus fama praeclara est, vel in malis quae pendit, vel in bonis quae rependit. (58) Iste certe tropus ubi Ioseph quemcumque fratrem facit intellegi, nescio utrum illa quam didicimus et docuimus, arte tradatur. Quam sit tamen pulcher et quemadmodum afficiat legentes atque intellegentes, non opus est cuiquam dici, si ipse non sentit.

21. (59) Et plura quidem quae pertineant ad praecepta eloquentiae, in hoc ipso loco, quem pro exemplo posuimus, possunt reperiri. Sed bonum auditorem non tam si diligenter discutiatur instruit, quam si ardenter pronuntietur accendit. Neque enim haec humana industria composita, sed divina mente sunt fusa et sapienter et eloquen-

[66] A change of object: instead of addressing the wrongdoers, Amos addresses his listeners/readers. See p. 468, n. 146.

[67] Perhaps implying that technical vocabulary is not essential for recognizing figures.

he also indicated to others[66] how ignorant they were, by adding, "they thought that they possessed musical instruments like David, drinking their wine from bowls and plastering themselves with perfume." These three clauses are best delivered by leaving the first two suspended, and resolving the period with the third clause.

20. (57) Now for what is added after these clauses; "they cared nothing at all for the sorrow of Joseph." This can be said in a single utterance as if it is one clause, or (as is preferable) with a pause, "they cared nothing at all—" and, after the separation, bringing in "—for the sorrow of Joseph," so making a two-clause period. It was particularly elegant that it avoids saying, "they cared nothing for the sorrow of their brother," but instead of "brother" puts "Joseph": in this way any brother at all could be signified by the particular name of the most famous brother of them all, whether in the evils dealt to him or the good things he dealt in return. (58) To be sure, I do not know whether this figure, which uses the name "Joseph" to mean any brother you like, is something that the skill that once we learned and taught communicates.[67] Still, as for how attractive it is, and how it makes an impression on those who read and understand it, there is no point telling anyone who does not notice it for themselves.

21. (59) There is more material relevant to the principles of eloquence that can be found in this same passage that we have set as an exemplar. But it is not so good at instructing well-intentioned listeners when carefully analyzed, as it is at kindling their enthusiasm when it is passionately performed. For these words were not composed by human labor; rather, they were poured forth from the prophet's divinely-inspired mind with wisdom and elo-

ter, non intenta in eloquentiam sapientia, sed a sapientia non recedente eloquentia.

(60) Si enim, sicut quidam disertissimi atque acutissimi viri videre ac dicere potuerunt, ea quae oratoria velut arte discuntur, non observarentur et notarentur et in hanc doctrinam redigerentur, nisi prius in oratorum invenirentur ingeniis, quid mirum si et in istis inveniuntur quos ille misit qui fecit ingenia? Quapropter et eloquentes quidem, non solum sapientes canonicos nostros auctores doctoresque fateamur tali eloquentia qualis personis eiusmodi congruebat.

22. (61) Sed nos etsi de litteris eorum quae sine difficultate intelleguntur, nonnulla sumimus elocutionis exempla, nequaquam putare debemus imitandos nobis eos esse in his quae, ad exercendas et elimandas quodammodo mentes legentium, et ad rumpenda fastidia atque acuenda studia discere volentium, celandos[5] quoque, sive ut ad pietatem convertantur sive ut a mysteriis secludantur, animos impiorum utili ac salubri obscuritate dixerunt. (62) Sic quippe illi locuti sunt, ut posteriores, qui eos recte intellegerent et exponerent, alteram gratiam, disparem quidem, verumtamen subsequentem in dei ecclesia reperirent. Non ergo expositores eorum ita loqui debent, tamquam se ipsi exponendos simili auctoritate proponant, sed

[5] velandos *coni. Hill*

---

[68] "These eloquent and percipient men could doubtless be reduced to Cicero and Quintilian" (Hill 1996, 242).

[69] *ingenium* (inborn talent), often contrasted with *ars* (taught skill). See Cic. *De or.* 1.146.

[70] *canonicos*: see n. 7, above.

quence together. So this is not wisdom that strives for eloquence, but rather eloquence that does not shrink from wisdom.

(60) Some of the most cultured and perceptive of men[68] have been able to see, and state, that the techniques we learn as skills for public speaking would not be apparent, or recorded, and turned into a formal subject for study, had they not first been discovered in the natural abilities[69] of public speakers. Why is it surprising, then if they are also found in those people sent out on their mission by the One who has created those abilities? For this reason, we should confess that they were indeed eloquent, as well as wise, those biblical[70] authors and teachers of ours, and possessed that kind of eloquence that was consonant with their character.

22. (61) Even if we adopt a number of examples of expression from the writings of authors that are easy to understand, we must by no means regard those authors as suitable for us to imitate in respect of certain elements: these they have spoken to train and somehow refine the minds of readers, and to break up the boredom and sharpen the enthusiasm of those who want to learn, and also to veil the spirit of the ungodly with a fitting and wholesome obscurity (whether this is to turn them to godliness or to keep them away from the mysteries). (62) To be sure, they spoke in such a way that later generations (who understood them aright and interpreted them) found another kind of grace, admittedly unlike the first but following on from it in the Church of God. It is not right, therefore, for those who interpret them to speak as if offering themselves for interpretation as if they had the same degree of authority. Instead they must strive first and

in omnibus sermonibus suis primitus ac maxime ut intellegantur elaborent, ea[6] quantum possunt perspicuitate dicendi, ut aut multum tardus sit qui non intellegit, aut in rerum quas explicare atque ostendere volumus difficultate ac subtilitate, non in nostra locutione sit causa qua minus tardiusue quod dicimus possit intellegi.

23. (63) Sunt enim quaedam quae vi sua non intelleguntur aut vix intelleguntur, quantolibet et quantumlibet, quamvis planissime dicentis versentur eloquio; quae in populi audientiam vel raro, si aliquid urget, vel numquam omnino mittenda sunt. In libris autem, qui ita scribuntur ut ipsi sibi quodammodo lectorem teneant cum intelleguntur, cum autem non intelleguntur molesti non sint nolentibus legere, et in aliquorum collocutionibus non est hoc officium deserendum, ut vera quamvis ad intellegendum difficillima, quae ipsi iam percepimus, cum quantocumque labore disputationis ad aliorum intellegentiam perducamus, si tenet auditorem vel collocutorem discendi cupiditas nec mentis capacitas desit quae quoquo modo intimata possit accipere; non curante illo qui docet quanta eloquentia doceat, sed quanta evidentia.

24. (64) Cuius evidentiae diligens appetitus aliquando neglegit verba cultiora nec curat quid bene sonet, sed quid bene indicet atque intimet quod ostendere intendit. Unde ait quidam, cum de tali genere locutionis ageret, esse in

[6] et *P B D K Mart.*

---

[71] A direct reference to the teaching of Christianity that until now has been in the background.

[72] He is cautious about citing a "pagan" authority, namely Cicero (*Orat.* 75; Cf. §74).

foremost, in every sermon they preach, to be understood,[71] and—as far as possible—with such a clear way of speaking that either those who fail to understand are exceptionally slow-witted, or the reason why what we say can be less fully or less promptly understood lies in the complexity and subtlety of the matters that we want to explain and communicate, rather than in our style of speaking.

23. (63) The fact is, some things are in themselves incomprehensible or scarcely comprehensible, whatever way, and however much, and however clearly a speaker's eloquence ruminates upon them. Such things are for people to hear only occasionally, for some pressing reason, or (which is better) never at all. But books are written in such a way that when they are understood they fix their reader's attention somehow on themselves, while when they are not understood they do not bother people who have no wish to read them. Also, in dialogue with other people, we have a constant duty, however difficult truths may be to understand (as we ourselves have found already), to put maximum effort into our arguments to bring those truths to the understanding of others, if a longing to learn seizes our hearer or interlocutor, and they have the mental capacity to receive in any way what is being disclosed. Teachers must not be concerned with how eloquent their teaching is; but with how clearly convincing it is.

24. (64) A conscientious effort to be clear and convincing sometimes means setting aside more cultured speech, and not thinking of what will sound good, but what will communicate well and disclose what one means to express. This is why a certain person[72] says, when touching on this kind of public speaking, that it contains a kind of

ea quandam diligentem neglegentiam. Haec tamen sic detrahit ornatum ut sordes non contrahat. (65) Quamvis in bonis doctoribus tanta docendi cura sit, vel esse debeat, ut verbum quod nisi obscurum sit vel ambiguum, Latinum esse non potest, vulgi autem more sic dicitur ut ambiguitas obscuritasque vitetur, non sic dicatur ut a doctis, sed potius ut ab indoctis dici solet. Si enim non piguit dicere interpretes nostros, "non congregabo conventicula eorum de sanguinibus," quoniam senserunt ad rem pertinere, ut eo loco pluraliter enuntiaretur hoc nomen, quod in Latina lingua singulariter tantummodo dicitur, cur pietatis doctorem pigeat imperitis loquentem, ossum potius quam os dicere, ne ista syllaba non ab eo quod sunt ossa, sed ab eo quod sunt ora intellegatur, ubi Afrae aures de correptione vocalium vel productione non iudicant? (66) Quid enim prodest locutionis integritas quam non sequitur intellectus audientis, cum loquendi omnino nulla sit causa si quod loquimur non intellegunt, propter quos ut intellegant loquimur? Qui ergo docet, vitabit verba omnia quae non docent, et si pro eis alia integra, quae intellegantur, potest dicere, id magis eliget. Si autem non potest, sive quia non sunt sive quia in praesentia non occurrunt, utetur etiam

---

[73] Latin *diligentem neglegentiam*: oxymoron. See Cic. *Orat.* 78 (*quaedam etiam neglegentia est diligens*). [74] Contrasting compounds of the same verb: *detrahit/contrahat.*

[75] The Hebrew Bible/Old Testament has "offerings [plural] of blood [singular]"; LXX and Vulg. have "bloods" (presumably suggesting "blood offerings").

[76] A breve (˘) marks a vowel that sounds short when spoken; a macron (¯) marks a long vowel. The Latin for a "bone" is *ŏs* (to rhyme with English "boss"; plural *ŏssa*), which is visually (though

careful carelessness.[73] This admittedly excludes finesse, but does not go so far as to include flaws.[74] (65) Although good teachers take such pains with their teaching (or at any rate they ought to) that a word that cannot be Latin unless it is either obscure or ambiguous, yet in common usage it is pronounced in a way that avoids that obscurity and ambiguity, they should not pronounce it in the educated way, but rather in the way that uneducated people habitually say it. For example: Christian translators were not ashamed to say, "I will not gather their assemblies from bloods," for they realized that it made a difference to the matter that this noun was being articulated in that verse in the plural, though in the Latin language "blood" is only spoken in the singular.[75] So why should a devout teacher, when addressing beginners, be ashamed to say *ŏssum* as a singular, rather than *ŏs*,[76] to avoid the monosyllable being understood as coming not from *ŏs* but from *ōs*? Especially when African ears make no distinction between long vowels and short ones. (66) What is the point of correct speech when the understanding of listeners cannot follow it? Then there is no point whatever in speaking at all if the very people for whose benefit we are speaking, to help them understand, do not understand what we speak. Those who teach, therefore, will avoid every word that fails to teach, and if they can say other correct words in their place that are comprehensible, those are the ones they should select. But if that is impossible, because no such word exists, or because at that moment they cannot

not aurally) identical with *ōs* (to rhyme with English "gross"; plural *ōra*), meaning "mouth." The form *ossum* does not exist in good Latin; see 3.7.15n26.

verbis minus integris, dum tamen res ipsa doceatur atque discatur integre.

25. (67) Et hoc quidem non solum in collocutionibus, sive fiant cum aliquo uno sive cum pluribus, verum etiam et multo magis in populis quando sermo promitur, ut intellegamur instandum est, quia in collocutionibus est cuique interrogandi potestas, ubi autem omnes tacent ut audiatur unus et in eum intenta ora convertunt, ibi ut requirat quisque quod non intellexerit, nec moris est nec decoris, ac per hoc debet maxime tacenti subvenire cura dicentis. (68) Solet enim motu suo significare utrum intellexerit cognoscendi avida multitudo. Quod donec significet, versandum est quod agitur multimoda varietate dicendi; quod in potestate non habent qui praeparata et ad verbum memoriter retenta pronuntiant. Mox autem ut intellectum esse constiterit, aut sermo finiendus aut in alia transeundum est.

(69) Sicut enim gratus est qui cognoscenda enubilat, sic onerosus qui cognita inculcat, eis dumtaxat quorum tota exspectatio in dissolvenda eorum quae panduntur difficultate pendebat. Nam delectandi gratia etiam nota dicuntur, ubi non ipsa, sed modus quo dicuntur attenditur. Quod si et ipse iam notus est atque auditoribus placet,

---

[77] This section shows a glimpse of Augustine's understanding of the preacher's art, and how he "reads" his audience.

[78] He is now speaking as one teacher to other teachers.

think of any, they ought to use less correct words, provided that the matter in hand is being taught, and learned, correctly.

25. (67)[77] This hold true not only in conversations, whether with a single person or with more, but also, indeed far more, when preaching a sermon among the people, when it is imperative that we are understood.[78] This is because in conversations everyone has an opportunity to ask questions; but when everyone is silent in order to listen to a single person, and the faces turn and fix their attention on him, then it is not usual, or proper, for people to ask about anything they have not understood: for this reason speakers should take care to help those listening in silence as much as they can. (68) The crowd is hungry for knowledge, and usually signifies whether it has understood by the way it moves. Until it does show this sign of understanding, we must rack our brains for every imaginable style of speaking about the subject in hand; those who prepare a text beforehand, commit it word-for-word to memory, and deliver it aloud, are incapable of such flexibility. The moment it comes to a point of understanding, we should either conclude the sermon, or move on to another subject.

(69) Just as people are pleased with someone who demystifies what they need to know, so too they find a person who crams down their throat things that they know already annoying—at least it is to people who are completely focused upon solving a problem in the matter at issue. True, well-known points can be canvassed for the pleasure they bring, but we must be careful to restrict how long we speak of them. But if the preacher is familiar and popular with those listening, it hardly matters whether they are extem-

paene nihil interest utrum is qui dicit dictor an lector sit. (70) Solent enim et ea quae commode scripta sunt, non solum ab eis quibus primitus innotescunt iucunde legi, verum ab his etiam quibus iam nota sunt, neque adhuc illa de memoria delevit oblivio, non sine iucunditate relegi vel ab utrisque libenter audiri. Quae autem quisque iam oblitus est, cum commonetur, docetur.

Sed de modo delectandi nunc non ago; de modo quo docendi sunt qui discere desiderant loquor. (71) Is est autem optimus quo fit ut qui audit verum audiat et quod audit intellegat. Ad quem finem cum ventum fuerit, nihil tunc amplius de ipsa re tamquam diutius docenda laborandum est, sed forte de commendanda ut in corde figatur. Quod si faciendum videbitur, ita modeste faciendum est ne perveniatur ad taedium.

26. (72) Prorsus haec est in docendo eloquentia, qua fit dicendo, non ut libeat quod horrebat aut ut fiat quod pigebat, sed ut appareat quod latebat. Quod tamen si fiat insuaviter, ad paucos quidem studiosissimos suus pervenit fructus, qui ea quae discenda sunt, quamvis abiecte inculteque dicantur, scire desiderant. Quod cum adepti fuerint, ipsa delectabiliter veritate pascuntur, bonorumque ingeniorum insignis est indoles in verbis verum amare, non verba. (73) Quid enim prodest clavis aurea, si aperire quod

porizing or reading from a script. (70) If something has been well-written, for example, it is read with pleasure, not only by those coming to know it for the first time, but also by those who know it already, if forgetfulness has not yet wiped it from their memory; and rereading it is a source of pleasure too: while both groups enjoy listening to it. But when people have forgotten a thing, reminding them of it is a form of teaching.

I am not, however, discussing here how to delight people; I am speaking about how to teach them what they are longing to learn. (71) This is the best way to ensure that listeners are hearing what is true, and understanding what they hear. When that goal is accomplished, there is no need for further elaboration on this subject, as if one needed to go on and on teaching it; but perhaps there is a need to keep encouraging people to take it to heart. If it looks as if this is necessary, it must be done with restraint, so as not to end up boring people.

26. (72) To summarize, eloquence in teaching means using speech to bring about a result: not making something agreeable that used to be dreadful, or making something happen that was formerly rejected, but making plain what used to be obscure. If the learning process is disagreeable, its advantages will only reach a few, those who are most determined and committed, and who are eager to acquire knowledge in the subjects to be taught, even if they are communicated in a way that is mediocre and unsophisticated. Once they have acquired it, they delight in feeding on truth itself, for it is a mark of distinction in people whose nature is good to love the truth in words, not the words themselves. (73) After all, what use is a golden key if it cannot open what we want it to? And what

volumus non potest? Aut quid obest lignea, si hoc potest? Quando nihil quaerimus nisi patere quod clausum est. Sed quoniam inter se habent nonnullam similitudinem vescentes atque discentes, propter fastidia plurimorum, etiam ipsa sine quibus vivi non potest alimenta condienda sunt.

27. (74) Dixit ergo quidam eloquens, et verum dixit, ita dicere debere eloquentem ut doceat, ut delectet, ut flectat. Deinde addidit, "docere necessitatis est, delectare suavitatis, flectere victoriae." Horum trium quod primo loco positum est, hoc est docendi necessitas, in rebus est constituta quas dicimus, reliqua duo in modo quo dicimus. Qui ergo dicit cum docere vult, quamdiu non intellegitur, nondum se existimet dixisse quod vult ei quem vult docere; quia etsi dixit quod ipse intellegit, nondum illi dixisse putandus est a quo intellectus non est; si vero intellectus est, quocumque modo dixerit, dixit.

(75) Quod si etiam delectare vult eum cui dicit, aut flectere, non quocumque modo dixerit faciet, sed interest quomodo dicat, ut faciat. Sicut est autem ut teneatur ad audiendum, delectandus auditor; ita flectendus, ut moveatur ad agendum. Et sicut delectatur si suaviter loqueris, ita flectitur si amet quod polliceris, timeat quod minaris, oderit quod arguis, quod commendas amplectatur, quod

---

[79] *vescentes atque discentes*: assonance sharpens the analogy.

[80] Cic. *Orat.* 69.

[81] Because communication has been effected.

is wrong with a wooden one, if it can?—given that all we are aiming for is to open up what is closed off. But as there is a degree of likeness between eating and learning[79]—in that the vast majority of people are choosy—even the nourishment we cannot live without deserves its seasoning.

27. (74) This is why that man of eloquence has said, and said truly, that an eloquent person ought to speak with the aim of teaching, delighting, persuading. Next he added, "teaching is about being indispensable, delighting is about being engaging, and persuasion is all about changing people's thinking."[80] The first of these three aims—the requirement to teach—consists of the substance of our speaking; the other two aims consist of the modes in which we speak. When people speak with the intention of teaching, but are not understood, they should reckon that they have not yet spoken what they intend, to that person whom they want to teach. This is because even if they have said what they themselves understand, they should consider themselves as not yet having not yet addressed that person, given that they have not made themselves understood. If, in fact, they have made themselves understood, then whatever their style of speaking, true speaking is what it is.[81]

(75) If, however, they want to delight, or persuade, the person they are speaking to, speaking in any old way will not do, for the style of their speaking makes a difference to its effect. Just as you need to delight hearers to keep their attention so that they listen, so too you must persuade them in order to spur them into action. Also, just as you evoke delight when you speak attractively, so you effect persuasion if they like what you are promising, fear what you warn them against, hate what you take issue with,

dolendum exaggeras doleat, cum quid laetandum praedicas gaudeat, misereatur eorum quos miserandos ante oculos dicendo constituis, fugiat eos quos cavendos terrendo proponis; et quidquid aliud grandi eloquentia fieri potest ad commovendos animos auditorum, non quid agendum sit ut sciant, sed ut agant quod agendum esse iam sciunt.

28. (76) Si autem adhuc nesciunt, prius utique docendi sunt quam movendi. Et fortasse rebus ipsis cognitis ita movebuntur ut eos non opus sit maioribus eloquentiae viribus iam moveri. Quod tamen cum opus est, faciendum est; tunc autem opus est, quando cum scierint quid agendum sit, non agunt. Ac per hoc docere necessitatis est. Possunt enim homines et agere et non agere quod sciunt. Quis autem dixerit eos agere debere quod nesciunt? Et ideo flectere necessitatis non est, quia non semper opus est, si tantum docenti vel etiam delectanti consentit auditor. Ideo autem victoriae est, quia fieri potest ut et doceatur et delectetur et non assentiatur. (77) Quid autem illa duo proderunt, si desit hoc tertium? Sed neque delectare necessitatis est, quandoquidem cum dicendo vera monstrantur (quod ad officium docendi pertinet), non eloquio agitur neque hoc attenditur, ut vel ipsa vel ipsum delectet eloquium, sed per se ipsa, quoniam vera sunt, manifestata delectant. Unde plerumque delectant etiam falsa pate-

---

[82] Latin *commovendos*: the verb *moveo* can indicate physical movement, or, as here, the metaphorical movement that is emotion.

[83] A noble defense of, and justification for, Christian eloquence.

embrace what you support, deplore what you emphasize as deplorable, rejoice when you declare something is wonderful, pity the people whom—through your oratory—you conjure up before their eyes as pitiable, reject those whom you suggest ought to be shunned: and whatever else eloquence can effect to move[82] the hearts of listeners, not so that they know what to do, but so that once they know what needs to be done, they do it.[83]

28. (76) But if they still do not know, then they must certainly be taught first and moved afterward. It may be that once they understand the matters at issue, they will be so moved that they have no need of more forceful eloquence to move them. But when it is necessary, we must make use of it: for it is precisely when they know what needs to be done, but are not doing it, that it is required. This is why the teaching aspect is essential. For people can either act, or not act, upon what they know: yet who would say that they ought to take action, when they are still in a state of ignorance? And this is why persuasion is nonessential: because it is not always required, if listeners are in harmony with the person who teaches or delights them. As for winning them over, this is necessary because it can happen that they are taught, and delighted, but still do not yield to persuasion. (77) What use are those other two aims, if this third one is lacking? Not that giving delight is essential, since when truths are made known through speech (this is part of the work of teaching), this is not effected by eloquence, nor is this what people are looking for, that either the content or the style of speaking be delightful in itself; instead, once the actual content is made known, it is delightful—because it is true. This is how even falsehoods can often give pleasure once they are

facta atque convicta. Neque enim delectant quia falsa sunt, sed quia falsa esse verum est, delectat et dictio qua hoc verum esse monstratum est.

29. (78) Propter eos autem quibus fastidientibus non placet veritas, si alio quocumque modo, sed si eo modo dicatur, ut placeat et sermo dicentis, datus est in eloquentia non parvus etiam delectationi locus. Quae tamen addita non sufficit duris, quos nec intellexisse nec docentis elocutione delectatos esse profuerit. Quid enim haec duo conferunt homini, qui et confitetur verum et collaudat eloquium nec inclinat assensum, propter quem solum, cum aliquid suadetur, rebus quae dicuntur invigilat dicentis intentio?

(79) Si enim talia docentur quae credere vel nosse sufficiat, nihil est aliud eis consentire nisi confiteri vera esse. Cum vero id docetur quod agendum est, et ideo docetur ut agatur, frustra persuadetur verum esse quod dicitur, frustra placet modus ipse quo dicitur, si non ita discitur ut agatur. Oportet igitur eloquentem ecclesiasticum, quando suadet aliquid quod agendum est, non solum docere ut instruat et delectare ut teneat, verum etiam flectere ut vincat. (80) Ille quippe iam remanet ad consensionem flectendus eloquentiae granditate, in quo id non egit usque ad eius confessionem demonstrata veritas, adiuncta etiam suavitate dictionis.

exposed and proven. They do not give pleasure because they are false, but because it is a truth that they are false, and so our speaking can give pleasure when it has proven something to be true.

29. (78) There are finicky people, though, who will not be pleased by truth however it is spoken, but only if it is spoken in such a way that they approve of the speaker's style of discourse. This is why eloquence allows plenty of room for the element of delight. Even adding this is not enough for those tough characters who see no benefit in having understood their teacher's eloquence, or being delighted by it. What do these two qualities bestow on someone who both acknowledges the truth and praises the eloquence, but still withholds consent; even though the intention of the speaker is wholly focused on securing that consent when trying to persuade the person of something?

(79) For if it is enough to believe or know the things that you are teaching, the only thing they need to agree upon is admitting that they are true. Certainly, when you teach something that needs to be done, and so you teach in such a way that it does get done, there is no point persuading people that what you say is true, and there is no point saying it in a way that people enjoy, unless that teaches them to do the thing. So when a Christian orator persuades people of something that they ought to do, they ought to teach in a way that instructs those listening, and delight them in a way that keeps them listening; but they should also prevail upon the people, in order to convince them. (80) Undoubtedly there is a further category of persons who need to be persuaded to give their assent by eloquence in the grand style. Proven truth has not brought them to confess the faith, even after an agreeable style of speaking has been factored in.

30. (81) Cui suavitati tantum operae inpensum est ab hominibus, ut non solum non facienda, verum etiam fugienda ac detestanda tot et tanta mala atque turpia, quae malis et turpibus disertissime persuasa sunt, non ut eis consentiatur, sed sola delectationis gratia lectitentur. Avertat autem deus ab ecclesia sua quod de synagoga Iudaeorum Ieremias propheta commemorat dicens, "Pavor et horrenda facta sunt super terram. Prophetae prophetabant iniqua, et sacerdotes plausum dederunt manibus suis, et plebs mea dilexit sic. Et quid facietis in futurum?" (82) O eloquentia tanto terribilior quanto purior, et quanto solidior, tanto vehementior! O vere securis concidens petras! Huic enim rei simile esse verbum suum, quod per sanctos prophetas fecit, per hunc ipsum prophetam deus ipse dixit. Absit itaque, absit a nobis, ut sacerdotes plaudant iniqua dicentibus et plebs dei diligat sic. (83) Absit a nobis, inquam, tanta dementia; nam quid faciemus in futurum? Et certe minus intellegantur, minus placeant, minus moveant quae dicuntur, vera tamen dicantur, et iusta, non iniqua libenter audiantur. Quod utique non fieret, nisi suaviter dicerentur.

31. (84) In populo autem gravi, de quo dictum est domino,[7] "in populo gravi laudabo te," nec illa suavitas delectabilis est qua non quidem iniqua dicuntur, sed exigua et fragilia bona spumeo verborum ambitu ornantur, quali

[7] deo *F R K Lond. μ Gr. RGr.*

---

[84] A reference to the "immoral" qualities of classical literature, which Hill 1996 unfairly characterizes as "elegant pornography" (242). [85] Jeremiah 5:30–31. [86] Jeremiah 23:29, 46:22. [87] Psalm 35:18. [88] Recalling Cicero's "periodic collocations of words": *Brut.* 162.

30. (81) So much effort has been devoted to this agreeable style as to necessitate not only refraining from many profoundly vicious evils but also treating them as repulsive and abominable; for they are peddled to us so appealingly by those who are themselves immoral and vicious, not to win our assent but so that they are read and read again, solely for pleasure's sake.[84] God preserve his own Church from what Jeremiah the prophet relates of the synagogue of the Jews, saying, "Fear and terrors have taken place upon the earth. The prophets have prophesied iniquity, and the priests have applauded with their own hands, and my people have loved its being so. And what will you do in time to come?"[85] (82) What eloquence! As pure as it is petrifying, as fundamental as it is fierce! Surely this is the ax that splits the rocks![86] God himself, through this very prophet, has said that his own word—which he formed by the holy prophets—was a thing like this. Far be it from us, far indeed, that our priests applaud those who speak wickedness, and God's people love its being so. (83) Far be it from us, I say, this madness: for what shall we do in time to come? For certain, better that what we say be less comprehensible, less agreeable, less moving, if only it be true; and let justice, not iniquity, be heard with gladness. But that could not possibly be accomplished without the use of attractive speech.

31. (84) In a people of substance, such as the psalmist speaks of to God ("in a people of substance will I praise you")[87] that attractive style is not to their taste, because things spoken in that style, though admittedly not wicked, still embellish trivial and flimsy goods with a wordy froth of florid periods;[88] the kind of thing that should not prop-

nec magna atque stabilia decenter et graviter ornarentur. Est tale aliquid in epistola beatissimi Cypriani, quod ideo puto vel accidisse vel consulto factum esse, ut sciretur a posteris quam linguam doctrinae christianae sanitas ab ista redundantia revocaverit et ad eloquentiam graviorem modestioremque restrinxerit, qualis in eius consequentibus litteris secure amatur, religiose appetitur, sed difficillime impletur.

(85) Ait ergo quodam loco, "petamus hanc sedem: dant secessum vicina secreta, ubi dum erratici palmitum lapsus pendulis nexibus per arundines baiulas repunt, viteam porticum frondea tecta fecerunt." Non dicuntur ista nisi mirabiliter affluentissima fecunditate facundiae, sed profusione nimia gravitati displicent. (86) Qui vero haec amant, profecto eos qui non ita dicunt sed castigatius eloquuntur, non posse ita eloqui existimant, non iudicio ista vitare. Quapropter iste vir sanctus et posse se ostendit sic dicere, quia dixit alicubi, et nolle, quoniam postmodum nusquam.

32. (87) Agit itaque noster iste eloquens, cum et iusta et sancta et bona dicit (neque enim alia debet dicere) agit ergo quantum potest cum ista dicit, ut intellegenter, ut libenter, ut oboedienter audiatur. Et haec se posse, si potuerit et in quantum potuerit, pietate magis orationum

---

[89] Cypr. *Ep.* 3.12–14H.

[90] The near-triple alliteration (*affluentissima fecunditate facundiae*) pokes gentle fun at Cyprian's exuberance.

erly be used to embellish even important and serious matters. There is an example of this kind in a letter of blessed Cyprian, which makes me think it came there, or was deliberately put there, to teach later generations how wholesome Christian teaching has called our language away from superfluity of expression, and drawn it back to a more substantive and restrained eloquence, of the kind that it is safe to admire in his later letters, and reverent to imitate, but extremely difficult to achieve.

(85) For example: he says somewhere, "Let us seek this seat: the nearby hideaways offer a retreat, where wandering vines tumble down in a tangle of swags; through the laden trellis they worm their way, where foliaceous integuments make a bower of vines."[89] It is all said with remarkably fruitful facility for fluency, but its overblown excess is not pleasing to the serious-minded.[90] (86) People who like this stuff undoubtedly believe that those of us who do not speak like that, but instead use a more restrained style of speech, are unable to use florid eloquence, not that we make a judgment call by avoiding doing so. For this reason, that holy man first showed that he was able to use that style of speech, for he spoke that way on the one occasion; then showed that he chose not to, for he never did so again.

32. (87) Eloquent Christian speakers manage, therefore, when they are speaking of what is just and holy and good (and they should not be speaking of anything else), they manage, then (as much as is possible when they speak of those things) to be heard with understanding, with enthusiasm, with acquiescence. And they should have no doubt that if they are able—and insofar as they are able—to achieve this, they do so more by the devoutness of their

quam oratorum facultate non dubitet, ut orando pro se ac pro illis quos est allocuturus, sit orator antequam dictor. Ipsa hora iam ut dicat accedens, priusquam exserat proferentem linguam, ad deum levet animam sitientem, ut ructet quod biberit, vel quod impleverit fundat.

(88) Cum enim de unaquaque re, quae secundum fidem dilectionemque tractanda sunt, multa sint quae dicantur et multi modi quibus dicantur ab eis qui haec sciunt, quis novit quid ad praesens tempus vel nobis dicere vel per nos expediat audiri, nisi qui corda omnium videt? Et quis facit ut quod oportet et quemadmodum oportet dicatur a nobis, nisi in cuius manu sunt et nos et sermones nostri? (89) Ac per hoc discat quidem omnia quae docenda sunt, qui et nosse vult et docere, facultatemque dicendi, ut decet virum ecclesiasticum, comparet. Ad horam vero ipsius dictionis, illud potius bonae menti cogitet convenire quod dominus ait, "nolite cogitare quomodo aut quid loquamini; dabitur enim vobis in illa hora quid loquamini. Non enim vos estis qui loquimini, sed spiritus patris vestri qui loquitur in vobis." Si ergo loquitur in eis spiritus sanctus, qui persequentibus traduntur pro Christo, cur non et in eis qui tradunt discentibus Christum?

33. (90) Quisquis autem dicit non esse hominibus prae-

---

91 Despite his own argument, Augustine includes a play on two meanings of the word *orator*: (1) "public speaker"; (2) "person uttering a prayer"; perhaps to reinforce the same point he just made about florid speech in Cyprian.

92 *exserat*: indicating preparation for action. Petronius uses the same verb of lifting one's head for a kiss (*Sat.* 114.10).

93 Psalm 142:6.

prayers than the fluency of their public speaking. So by praying for themselves and for those whom they are about to address, they may be prayerful first, and eloquent afterward.[91] The moment when they arrive to speak, before they reveal[92] their ready tongue, let them lift up their thirsty soul to God,[93] so that they can blurt out what they have drunk in, or pour forth what they have filled it with.

(88) There is much to be said, after all, on any individual matter that is explored in accordance with faith and love, and many ways for people who know about such matters to say it. So who—except for him who sees the hearts of all—knows at any given moment, what it is best either for us to say or for others to hear from us? And who but the one who hold us, and our words,[94] in his hand makes it happen that we say what we ought to say, and in the way that we ought to say it? (89) This is why it is proper for Christian orators, who want both to know and to teach, to learn every kind of teaching they can access; and for them to acquire the ability to speak in public. At the time when they give their address, they must first think of what best becomes a good intellect, as the Lord says, "do not think about how or what you may say, for it will be given to you at the time when you are to say it. For it is not you who speak, but the spirit of your Father who speaks in you."[95] So if the Holy Spirit speaks in those who are handed over to persecutors for Christ's sake, how can it not do the same in those who pass on Christ to learners?

33. (90) Anyone who says that it is not for mortals to

[94] *sermones*: here not in its Christian sense, but alluding to Wisdom 7:16 (in Greek, *logoi*).

[95] Matthew 10:19–20.

cipiendum quid vel quemadmodum doceant, si doctores sanctus efficit spiritus, potest dicere nec orandum nobis esse, quia dominus ait, "scit pater vester quid vobis necessarium sit priusquam petatis ab eo," aut apostolum Paulum Timotheo et Tito non debuisse praecipere quid vel quemadmodum praeciperent aliis. Quas tres apostolicas epistolas ante oculos habere debet, cui est in ecclesia persona doctoris imposita: (91) nonne in prima ad Timotheum legitur, "annuntia haec et doce"? Quae autem sint, supra dictum est. Nonne ibi est, "seniorem ne increpaveris, sed obsecra ut patrem"? Nonne in secunda ei dicitur, "formam habe verborum sanorum, quae a me audisti"? Nonne ibi ei dicitur, "satis age, teipsum probabilem operarium exhibens deo, non erubescentem, verbum veritatis recte tractantem"? Ibi est et illud, "praedica verbum, insta opportune, importune; argue, hortare,[8] increpa in omni longanimitate et doctrina." (92) Itemque ad Titum nonne dicit episcopum iuxta doctrinam fidelis verbi perseverantem esse debere, "ut potens sit in doctrina sana et contradicentes redarguere"? Ibi etiam dicit, "tu vero loquere quae decet sanam doctrinam, senes sobrios esse," et quae sequuntur. Ibi et illud, "haec loquere et exhortare et increpa cum omni imperio. Nemo te contemnat. Admone illos principibus et potestatibus subditos esse," et cetera.

[8] obsecra *Vulg. R μ Sull. Mart.*

---

[96] Matthew 6:8. [97] 1 Timothy 4:11.
[98] 1 Timothy 5:1. [99] 2 Timothy 1:13.
[100] 2 Timothy 2:15. [101] 2 Timothy 4:2.
[102] Titus 1:9. [103] Titus 2:1–2.
[104] Titus 3:1.

give instructions on what or how to teach, if the Holy Spirit is the one who makes people into teachers, can likewise say that we ought not to pray, because the Lord said, "your Father knows what you need before you ask him";[96] or that the apostle Paul ought not to have given Timothy and Titus instructions on what and how they should instruct others. Anyone in the Church on whom the status of "teacher" is bestowed should have those three apostolic letters before their eyes: (91) do we not we read in the first letter to Timothy, "proclaim these things and teach them"?[97] He had said just before what "these things" were. Is this not also said there, "do not reprove those who are older than yourself, but entreat them as you would a father"?[98] And this, in the second letter, "keep the form of sound words that you have heard from me"?[99] And also this, in the same, "keep active, show God that you are a worthy laborer, free from shame, managing the word of truth well"?[100] And also, in the same, is "preach the word, appeal to it whether the moment is auspicious or inauspicious; make the case, encourage, criticize, exercising your patience and your teaching to the full."[101] (92) In the same way, he surely he says to Titus that a bishop ought to be persevering in accordance with the teaching of the word of faith, so as to be a master of sound doctrine who refutes opponents.[102] He also says there, "you must say what sound teaching requires: the older men should be sober,"[103] and so on. And again there, "speak these things and encourage and rebuke with full authority. Let no one disregard you. Warn them to be obedient to leaders and governments,"[104] and so on.

(93) Quid ergo putamus? Numquid contra seipsum sentit apostolus qui, cum dicat doctores operatione fieri spiritus sancti, ipse illis praecipit quid et quemadmodum doceant? An intellegendum est et hominum officia ipso sancto spiritu largiente, in docendis etiam ipsis doctoribus non debere cessare; et tamen "neque qui plantat est aliquid neque qui rigat, sed deus qui incrementum dat"?

(94) Unde ipsis quoque ministris sanctis hominibus vel etiam sanctis angelis operantibus nemo recte discit quae pertinent ad vivendum cum deo, nisi fiat a deo docilis deo, cui dicitur in psalmo, "doce me ut faciam voluntatem tuam, quoniam tu es deus meus." Unde et ipsi Timotheo idem dicit apostolus, loquens utique ad discipulum doctor, "tu autem persevera in his quae didicisti et tradita sunt tibi, sciens a quo didiceris." (95) Sicut enim corporis medicamenta quae hominibus ab hominibus adhibentur, nonnisi eis prosunt quibus deus operatur salutem, qui et sine illis mederi potest, cum sine ipso illa non possint, et tamen adhibentur (et si hoc officiose fiat, inter opera misericordiae vel beneficientiae deputatur) ita et adiumenta doctrinae tunc prosunt animae adhibita per hominem, cum deus operatur ut prosint, qui potuit evangelium dare homini, etiam non ab hominibus neque per hominem.

---

105 1 Corinthians 3:7.

106 Psalm 142:10.

107 2 Timothy 3:14.

108 After a scripture-based defense of rhetoric, he moves on to defense by analogy.

109 Or "good news": the content of the Christian message.

(93) Now what do we think? Surely the apostle is not making a judgment against himself simply because, when he states that people become teachers by the workings of the Holy Spirit, he himself gives them instructions on what to teach, and how? Rather, we must understand that even when the Holy Spirit itself is giving of its bounty, the human duty to teach teachers should not cease, despite the fact that "it is not the one who plants something, nor the one who waters it, but God who gives the growth."[105]

(94) So no one truly learns what is requisite for living with God, though his holy ministers and even the holy angels have their part to play, unless God brings it about that they are open to being taught by God: as it says in the psalm, "teach me to do your will, for you are my God."[106] So too the apostle speaks directly to Timothy, and says, as a teacher to his pupil, "you persevere in what you have learned, and what has been passed on to you, bearing in mind from whom you have learned it."[107] (95) For medicines for the body,[108] which one person recommends to another, only do good if God bestows a return to health; but God can effect a cure without such aids, and without him they have no power, though still we recommend them (and if this is done in a spirit of service it is counted as one of the works of mercy or kindness): and in the same way when people have recourse to teaching, it does good to the soul, since God effects that benefit. After all, he could bestow the gospel[109] on humankind without any human individual to pass it on, or to proclaim it.[110]

[110] On the question of why God does not operate through divine fiat, see Gregory of Nyssa, *Oratio catechetica* 31.

34. (96) Qui ergo nititur dicendo persuadere quod bonum est, nihil illorum trium spernens (ut scilicet doceat, ut delectet, ut flectat) oret atque agat ut, quemadmodum supra diximus, intellegenter, libenter, oboedienter audiatur. Quod cum apte et convenienter facit, non immerito eloquens dici potest, etsi non eum sequatur auditoris assensus. Ad haec enim tria, id est ut doceat, ut delectet, ut flectat, etiam illa tria videtur pertinere voluisse idem ipse Romani auctor eloquii, cum itidem dixit, "is erit igitur eloquens, qui poterit parva summisse, modica temperate, magna granditer dicere," tamquam si adderet illa etiam tria, et sic explicaret unam eandemque sententiam, dicens, is erit igitur eloquens, qui ut doceat poterit parva summisse, ut delectet modica temperate, ut flectat magna granditer dicere.

35. (97) Haec autem tria ille, sicut ab eo dicta sunt, in causis forensibus posset ostendere, non autem ‹in nostris›[9] hoc est in ecclesiasticis quaestionibus, in quibus huius quem volumus informare, sermo versatur. In illis enim ea parva dicuntur, ubi de rebus pecuniariis iudicandum est; ea magna, ubi de salute ac de capite hominum. Ea vero ubi nihil horum iudicandum est nihilque agitur ut agat sive decernat, sed tantummodo ut delectetur auditor, inter utrumque quasi media et ob hoc modica, hoc est

[9] *Suppl. Schaüblin sec. RGr.*: *post* autem *add* hic *Lond. μ Sull.*

---

[111] Cic. *Orat.* 100, paraphrased. [112] A love of numerical pattern overcomes the argument: the effect of associating teaching with what is lesser distracts from his theme.

[113] Reading the conjecture *nostris*. See C. Schaüblin, "Zum Text . . . ," *Wiener Studien* 87 (1974): 175–76.

34. (96) For this reason, as we said earlier, people who make an effort to use their speaking ability to persuade others of what is good, and who are not too proud to use those three aims (namely to teach, to please, to persuade) ought to pray, and do their utmost to make themselves heard with understanding, with enthusiasm, with acquiescence. When they do this properly and judiciously, it is appropriate to call them "eloquent," even if they do not secure their listener's approval. As well as this triad (to teach, to please, to persuade), the same Roman orator apparently wanted to factor in another triad, for he likewise said, "That man will be eloquent, therefore, if he is able to speak quietly of lesser matters, proportionately of routine matters, and powerfully of matters of significance."[111] It is as if he added this second triad, and so laid out a single complete judgment, saying, "people will therefore be eloquent if they can speak quietly of lesser matters in order to teach; proportionately of moderate matters in order to please; and powerfully of important matters in order to persuade."[112]

35. (97) He could have illustrated the triad that he has described using public legal cases, but not Christian[113] ones—in other words, not the ecclesial controversies that the person we want to sketch would be concerned with in his public discourse. In the former, we call "lesser matters" anything where a judgment is required in financial affairs. "Important matters" means when the well-being and life of a human being is at stake. Any case where nothing of this kind is being adjudicated, and nothing is happening to make anyone take action or make a decision, but the only purpose is to charm the listener, is in between the extremes, like an intermediate position that they de-

moderata dixerunt. Modicis enim modus nomen imposuit, nam modica pro parvis abusive, non proprie dicimus.

(98) In istis autem nostris, quandoquidem omnia, maxime quae de loco superiore populis dicimus, ad hominum salutem nec temporariam sed aeternam referre debemus, ubi etiam cavendus est aeternus interitus, omnia sunt magna quae dicimus, usque adeo ut nec de ipsis pecuniariis rebus vel acquirendis vel amittendis parva videri debeant quae doctor ecclesiasticus dicit, sive sit illa magna sive parva pecunia. (99) Neque enim parva est iustitia, quam profecto et in parva pecunia custodire debemus, dicente domino, "qui in minimo fidelis est, et in magno fidelis est." Quod ergo minimum est, minimum est; sed in minimo fidelem esse, magnum est. Nam sicut ratio rotunditatis, id est ut a puncto medio omnes lineae pares in extrema ducantur, eadem est in magno disco, quae in nummulo exiguo, ita ubi parva iuste geruntur, non minuitur iustitiae magnitudo.

36. (100) De iudiciis denique saecularibus (quibus utique nisi pecuniariis?) cum loqueretur apostolus, "audet quisquam vestrum, inquit, adversus alterum negotium habens, iudicari ab iniquis et non apud sanctos? An nesci-

---

[114] *modus* means an "amount" or "measure" (of space, action, sound, means, etc.). [115] The meaning of this sentence depends on Latin cognates that cannot be precisely paralleled in English. Augustine thinks in terms of fixed meaning ("proper" in the sense of "correct") rather than use determining meaning, as for Humpty-Dumpty in Lewis Carroll, *Through the Looking-Glass*, ch. 6, and Wittgenstein, *Philosophical Investigations* 43.

[116] He means both a raised place for the preacher to stand and a metaphorical position of authority. [117] Luke 16:10.

scribe as moderate. The noun *modus*[114] has given us the adjective "moderate"; so to say "moderate" when we mean "small" is not proper use of language but rather a misuse of it.[115]

(98) In our case, though, everything, especially what we say to people from a higher position[116] must refer to human salvation (eternal, not temporary), and we must also warn them against perishing eternally: for this reason everything we say counts as "important." The result is that what a Christian teacher says about financial affairs *per se*, or about acquiring or losing money should be seen as lesser matters, regardless of whether the sum of money involved be small or large. (99) For justice is never a little matter, and we certainly ought to safeguard it even when the sum involved is small; as the Lord says, "anyone who is faithful in a very small matter is also faithful in a big one."[117] A minimal matter is, well, minimal: but to be minimally faithful—that is a big matter. For example: the proportions of a circle are such that from the center point all the lines that reach to the edge are the same length; and this is the same for a large disk as for a tiny coin. Likewise when small matters are conducted with justice, their smallness does not diminish the dimensions of that justice.

36. (100) In conclusion, when the apostle was talking about civil judgments (and undoubtedly that means financial judgments), he says, "if you are in dispute with another person, does any one of you dare to be judged by the unrighteous and not among the saints? Or do you not know that the saints are to judge the world? And if the

tis quoniam sancti mundum iudicabunt? Et si in vobis iudicatur mundus, indigni estis qui de minimis iudicetis? Nescitis quia angelos iudicabimus, nedum saecularia? Saecularia igitur iudicia si habueritis, eos qui contemptibiles sunt in ecclesia, hos collocate ad iudicandum. Ad reverentiam vobis dico. Sic non est inter vos quisquam sapiens, qui possit inter fratrem suum iudicare? Sed frater cum fratre iudicatur et hoc apud infideles. Iam quidem omnino delictum est, quia iudicia habetis vobiscum. Quare non magis iniquitatem patimini? Quare non potius fraudamini? Sed vos iniquitatem facitis et fraudatis et hoc fratres. An nescitis quia iniusti regnum dei non haereditabunt?"

(101) Quid est quod sic indignatur apostolus, sic corripit, sic exprobrat, sic increpat, sic minatur? Qui d est quod sui animi affectum tam crebra et aspera vocis mutatione testatur? Quid est postremo quod de rebus minimis tam granditer dicit? Tantumne de illo negotia saecularia meruerunt? Absit! Sed hoc facit propter iustitiam, caritatem, pietatem, quae nulla sobria mente dubitante etiam in rebus quamlibet parvulis magna sunt.

37. (102) Sane si moneremus homines quemadmodum ipsa negotia saecularia vel pro se vel pro suis apud ecclesiasticos iudices agere deberent, recte admoneremus ut agerent tamquam parva summisse. Cum vero de illius viri disseramus eloquio, quem volumus earum rerum esse doctorem quibus liberamur ab aeternis malis atque ad

---

118 That is, "Christians." The Latin follows Vulg. *fratrem* (singular) after the preposition *inter* ("between").

119 1 Corinthians 6:1–9.

world is judged among you, will you be unworthy to pass judgment on little matters? Do you not know that we shall pass judgment on angels, to say nothing of civil disputes? So if you conduct civil judgments, the people you should assign to pass judgment should be those of lowest status in the Church. I say this to encourage you to take this seriously. Is there really no wise person among you who can judge between brothers?[118] As it is, brother goes to law against brother, and among unbelievers too. It is already a fault that there is a matter for judgment between you. Why do you not accept suffering injustice? Why would you not rather be cheated? But you commit injustice, and you cheat, and this is despite your being brothers. Or do you not know that the unrighteous will not inherit the kingdom of God?"[119]

(101) Why is the apostle so indignant? Why does he reproach them, accuse them, chide them, admonish them? Why is it that such frequent and harsh vocal modulations bear witness to his heartfelt emotion? And why, finally, does he speak in such exalted terms about such trivial matters? Did these civil lawsuits really deserve such treatment from him? By no means! But he acts as he does out of justice, love, devotion: and these, however trivial their specific substance, are undoubtedly matters of importance to a right-thinking individual.

37. (102) Certainly if we were advising people how to manage their own civil affairs, either on their own behalf or for their families, they ought to plead their case before Christian judges; we would be right to advise to make their plea quietly, as if it were a minor matter. But what of when we are discussing that man of eloquence whom we wish to be a teacher of those subjects that free us from everlasting

aeterna pervenimus bona; ubicumque agantur haec, sive apud populum sive privatim, sive ad unum sive ad plures, sive ad amicos sive ad inimicos, sive in perpetua dictione sive in collocutione, sive in tractatibus sive in libris, sive in epistolis vel longissimis vel brevissimis, magna sunt. (103) Nisi forte quoniam calix aquae frigidae res minima atque vilissima est, ideo minimum aliquid atque vilissimum dominus ait, quod eum qui dederit discipulo eius non perdet mercedem suam; aut vero quando iste doctor in ecclesia facit inde sermonem, parvum aliquid debet existimare se dicere; et ideo non temperate, non granditer, sed summisse sibi esse dicendum. Nonne quando accidit ut de hac re loqueremur ad populum et deus adfuit ut congrue diceremus, tamquam de illa aqua frigida quaedam flamma surrexit, quae etiam frigida hominum pectora ad misericordiae opera facienda, spe caelestis mercedis accenderet?

38. (104) Et tamen cum doctor iste debeat rerum dictor esse magnarum, non semper eas debet granditer dicere, sed summisse cum aliquid docetur, temperate cum aliquid vituperatur sive laudatur. Cum vero aliquid agendum est, et ad eos loquimur, qui hoc agere debent nec tamen volunt, tunc ea quae magna sunt, dicenda sunt granditer, et ad flectendos animos congruenter. Et aliquando de una eademque re magna et summisse dicitur si docetur, et temperate si praedicatur, et granditer si aversus inde animus ut convertatur impellitur.

---

[120] *tractatibus* can embrace "sermons." Augustine elsewhere refers to "addresses before the people, which Greeks call 'homilies'": *Haer.* 4 praef. [121] Matthew 10:42.

[122] 2 Maccabees 1:32.

evil, and bring us to everlasting joy? Wherever those subjects are at issue, they are important: in public or in private, to one person or to several, to friends or to enemies, in an uninterrupted speech or in a dialogue, in sermons or books,[120] in the longest of letters or the shortest of notes. (103) Unless, of course, because a cup of cold water is something trivial and of low value, then what the Lord said—that anyone who gives it to one of his disciples will not lose his reward[121]—is therefore also trivial and of low value; or unless when our teacher preaches on this in church, he ought to think that he is talking about something insignificant, and so should speak neither moderately nor powerfully but quietly. Was I not addressing the people once, on this subject, with God standing beside me to help me speak fittingly, when a flame seemed to leap up from that icy water[122]—a flame that set cold human hearts ablaze for doing works of mercy, in hope of a heavenly reward?

38. (104) Even though teachers ought to speak on great matters, they must not always speak about them in the grand style, but when they are teaching a subject they should speak calmly, and when using invective or praise they should speak with moderation. Now if some action must be taken, and they are talking to the people who should take that action, but who are reluctant to do so, then they must deliver their important speeches in the grand style, which is most conducive to persuading a change of heart. Sometimes their speech, though it is on a single serious topic, is in the plain style when it is a matter of teaching, in a moderate style for preaching, and in a grand one when there is a need to change hearts that are set against them.

(105) Quid enim deo ipso maius est? Numquid ideo non discitur? Aut qui docet unitatem trinitatis, debet nisi summissa disputatione agere, ut res ad dignoscendum difficilis, quantum datur, possit intellegi? Numquid hic ornamenta et non documenta quaeruntur? Numquid ut aliquid agat est flectendus auditor et non potius ut discat instruendus? (106) Porro cum laudatur deus sive de seipso sive de operibus suis, quanta facies pulchrae ac splendidae dictionis oboritur ei qui potest quantum potest laudare, quem nemo convenienter laudat, nemo quomodocumque non laudat! At si non colatur aut cum illo vel etiam prae illo colantur idola sive daemonia sive quaecumque creatura, quantum hoc malum sit atque ut ab hoc malo avertantur homines, debet utique granditer dici.

39. (107) Submissae dictionis exemplum est apud apostolum Paulum, ut planius aliquid commemorem, ubi ait, "dicite mihi, sub lege volentes esse legem non audistis? Scriptum est enim quod Abraham duos filios habuit, unum de ancilla et unum de libera, sed ille quidem qui de ancilla, secundum carnem natus est; qui autem de libera, per repromissionem. Quae sunt in allegoria. Haec enim sunt duo testamenta: unum quidem a monte Sina in servitutem

---

[123] *creatura* (*ktisis* in Greek) was originally equivalent to English "creation" (i.e., the whole created order, not an individual species as in the modern sense of the word "creature").

[124] Latin *repromissionem*: a "counterpromise"; cf. Cic. *QRosc.* 56. [125] "Covenant," in the Hebrew Bible/Old Testament, is a form of contract (Noahic, Abrahamic, Mosaic, etc) between God and his people. It becomes a shorthand for marking the division between the old covenant (or "testament") of Judaism and the new covenant of Christianity.

(105) What is greater than God himself? But surely we can still be taught about him? And what about someone who is teaching the unity of the trinity—surely they should only handle the matter with a discussion in the plain style, so that they can make the subject (with its tricky fine distinctions) comprehensible, to the best of their ability? Surely what we look for here is clear proofs, not rhetorical embellishments? Surely the listener needs to be instructed in order to learn something, rather than persuaded to do something? (106) Then again, when they praise God either on his own account or for his works, what a vision of lovely, luminous speech springs up in the speaking of those who can praise God to the utmost of their ability, though no one can praise him as he deserves, and no one can completely fail to praise him! But if he is not worshiped, or if idols, or demons, or any other created beings[123] are worshiped with him, or even in his place, then the grand style is undoubtedly required for expressing the gravity of the evil, and with the aim of turning people away from that evil.

39. (107) To state this even more plainly, there is an example of the plain style of speech in the apostle Paul, when he says, "tell me, you who want to be subject to the law, have you not heard the law? For it is written that Abraham had two sons, one by a slave woman and one by a woman who was freeborn: but he who was by the slave woman was born according to flesh, while he who was by the freeborn woman was born according to promise.[124] These women are an allegory. The two of them are the two covenants:[125] one, of course, produces offspring from

generans, quae est Agar. Sina enim mons est in Arabia, quae coniuncta est huic quae nunc est Hierusalem, et servit cum filiis suis. Quae autem sursum est Hierusalem, libera est, quae est mater nostra," et cetera.

(108) Itemque ubi ratiocinatur et dicit, "fratres, secundum hominem dico, tamen hominis confirmatum testamentum nemo irritum facit aut superordinat. Abrahae dictae sunt promissiones et semini eius. Non dicit, 'et seminibus,' tamquam in multis, sed tamquam in uno: 'et semini tuo,' quod est Christus. Hoc autem dico: testamentum confirmatum a deo, quae post quadringentos et triginta annos facta lex, non infirmat ad evacuandas promissiones. Si enim lege hereditas, iam non ex promissione; Abrahae autem per repromissionem donavit deus."

(109) Et quia occurrere poterat audientis cogitationi, "Utquid ergo lex data est, si ex illa non est hereditas?" Ipse sibi hoc obiecit atque ait velut interrogans, "quid ergo lex?" Deinde respondit, "transgressionis gratia proposita est, donec veniret semen cui promissum est, dispositum per angelos in manu mediatoris. Mediator autem unius non est, deus vero unus est." Et hic occurrebat, quod sibi ipse proposuit, "lex ergo adversus promissa dei?" Et respondit, "absit!" reddiditque rationem, dicens, "si enim data esset lex quae posset vivificare, omnino ex lege esset iustitia. Sed conclusit scriptura omnia sub peccato, ut pro-

---

[126] Galatians 3:15–22. [127] A calculation of the years between the times of Abraham and Moses the Hebrew nomothete.

[128] *transgressio* indicates an action that is unlawful, but without the volitional/metaphysical element suggested in "sin" (*peccatum*).

mount Sinai, for slavery. This is Hagar. For mount Sinai is in Arabia, which lies beside this earthly Jerusalem, and is in slavery with her offspring. But the Jerusalem that is above is free, which is our mother";[126] and so on.

(108) Again, when he is arguing, and says, "brothers, I am speaking in human terms: no one can invalidate a person's last will and testament, or add anything to it, once it has been proved. The promises were delivered to Abraham and his seed. It does not say 'and to his seeds,' as if they were many, but speaks as to one, 'to your seed'—and that means Christ. But I say this: the testament has been proved by God, and a law made four hundred and thirty years afterward[127] does not invalidate it so as to abrogate its promises. For if inheritance happens according to law, it does not happen according to the promise. yet God has granted it to Abraham by a promise."

(109) Even so, it might occur to his listener to think, "why was the law given, then, if it does not resolve the matter of inheritance?" Paul put this objection to himself and said, as if he was asking a question, "So what is the law for?" Then he replies, "the law has been established because of transgression;[128] until the coming of the seed to whom the promise was made; which has been assigned by angelic agency in the hand of a mediator. God, of course, is one; but a mediator is not single in that way." At this point he came up against an obstacle, which he put to himself: "is the law, therefore, against the promises of God?" And he replies, "Far from it!" and gives an explanation, saying, "If the law that was given were able to bring life, righteousness would undeniably come from the law. But scripture has gathered all things into the category of sin, so as to give a promise to those who believe, in ac-

missio ex fide Iesu Christi daretur credentibus" et cetera, vel si quid eiusmodi est.

(110) Pertinet ergo ad docendi curam non solum aperire clausa et nodos solvere quaestionum, sed etiam dum hoc agitur, aliis quaestionibus quae fortassis inciderint, ne id quod dicimus improbetur per illas aut refellatur, occurrere; si tamen et ipsa earum solutio pariter occurrerit, ne moveamus quod auferre non possumus. Fit autem ut, cum incidentes quaestioni aliae quaestiones et aliae rursus incidentibus incidentes pertractantur atque solvuntur, in eam longitudinem ratiocinationis extendatur intentio, ut nisi memoria plurimum valeat atque vigeat, ad caput unde agebatur disputator redire non possit. Valde autem bonum est ut quidquid contradici potest, si occurrerit, refutetur, ne ibi occurrat ubi non erit qui respondeat, aut praesenti quidem, sed tacenti occurrat et minus sanatus abscedat.

40. (111) In illis autem apostolicis verbis dictio temperata est, "seniorem ne increpaveris, sed obsecra ut patrem, iuniores ut fratres, anus ut matres, adulescentulas ut sorores." Et in illis, "obsecro autem vos, fratres, per miserationem dei, ut exhibeatis corpora vestra hostiam vivam, sanctam, deo placentem." Et totus fere ipsius exhortationis locus temperatum habet elocutionis genus; ubi illa pulchriora sunt in quibus propria propriis tamquam debita

---

[129] 1 Timothy 5:1–2.

[130] Romans 12:1. In classical Latin *hostia* refers to an animal sacrifice. By the third century it could refer to eucharistic sacrifice (Cypr. *Unit.* 17) or martyr self-sacrifice (Cypr. *Ep.* 31.5; 76.3).

cordance with their faith in Jesus Christ;" and so on (if there is anything more on this theme).

(110) This, therefore, is an aspect of the teacher's duty: not only to open up what has been shut down, and to untangle knotty questions, but also, at the same time as all this, to come to grips with other questions that they may perhaps encounter. This prevents what we say from being criticized or disproved by such questions; at any rate, it does if the actual solution to those questions comes to us at the same time. Otherwise we may start something that we cannot carry off. But it does happen that when they encounter one question, other questions crop up for them to get to grips with and resolve; and after those, they encounter more again: thus the thread of the argument becomes so long drawn out that unless their memory is in very good shape indeed, the speaker cannot bring the argument back to where it began. So it is especially valuable that anything that can be refuted is countered as soon as it crops up: otherwise it may crop up where no one will be available to give an answer, or when there is someone present, but they stay silent, so that the questioner departs without being completely healed.

40. (111) The middle style is used in those words of the apostle, "do not criticize an elder, but implore him like a father, and younger men like brothers, and elderly women like mothers, and young women like sisters."[129] And in these, "I implore you, brothers, by the mercy of God, that you present your bodies as a living sacrifice,[130] holy, pleasing to God." Almost the whole of this passage uses the restrained speaking style characteristic of exhortation, in which the more attractive elements are those in which each suitable element gives way to the next in a fitting way,

reddita decenter excurrunt, sicuti est, (112) "habentes dona diversa secundum gratiam quae data est nobis, sive prophetiam, secundum regulam fidei; sive ministerium, in ministrando: sive qui docet, in doctrina; sive qui exhortatur, in exhortatione; qui tribuit in simplicitate; qui praeest, in sollicitudine; qui miseretur, in hilaritate. Dilectio sine simulatione, odio habentes malum, adherentes bono, caritate fraternitatis invicem diligentes, honore mutuo praevenientes, studio non pigri, spiritu ferventes, domino servientes, spe gaudentes, in tribulatione patientes, orationi instantes, necessariis sanctorum communicantes, hospitalitatem sectantes. Benedicite persequentes vos, benedicite et nolite maledicere. Gaudere cum gaudentibus, flere cum flentibus, id ipsum invicem sentientes."

(113) Et quam pulchre ista omnia sic effusa bimembri circuitu terminantur, "non alta sapientes, sed humilibus consentientes!" Et aliquanto post, "in hoc ipso," inquit, "perseverantes, reddite omnibus debita: cui tributum, tributum; cui vectigal, vectigal; cui timorem, timorem; cui honorem, honorem." Quae membratim fusa clauduntur etiam ipsa circuitu, quem duo membra contexunt, "nemini quicquam debeatis, nisi ut invicem diligatis." Et post paululum, "nox praecessit," inquit, "dies autem appropinquavit. Abiciamus itaque opera tenebrarum et induamus nos arma lucis. Sicut in die honeste ambulemus, non in comessationibus et ebrietatibus, non in cubilibus et impudicitiis, non in contentione et aemulatione; sed induite dominum

---

131 Romans 12:6–15.

132 Romans 13:6–8.

like the proper payment of a debt, like this: (112) "having different gifts according to the grace that has been given to you, whether prophecy, in accordance with the rule of faith; or service, in serving; or those who teach, in teaching; or those who encourage, in encouragement; or those who are generous, in candor; or those in charge, through the exercise of responsibility; or those who are compassionate, in cheerfulness. Let love be genuine; hate what is evil, cleave to what is good, love one another with familial tenderness, surpassing one another in your mutual esteem, not slow to show enthusiasm, aflame with the Spirit, serving the Lord, rejoicing in hope, enduring misfortune, earnest in prayer, sharing in the needs of the saints, doing your utmost to show hospitality. Bless those who persecute you; bless, and do not curse them; rejoice with those who are rejoicing, weep with those who weep, sharing the same feelings with one another."[131]

(113) How attractively all these phrases flow on, ending with a period of two clauses, "do not be high-minded, but instead be in harmony with those who are humble!" And just after this he says, "continue in this way, and pay everyone what you owe them: taxes if you owe taxes, expenses if you owe expenses; reverence those who deserve reverence; respect those who deserve respect." This profusion of clauses is itself rounded off with a period formed from two interwoven clauses, "owe no one anything except for the love you have for one another."[132] Then just after this he says, "The night has passed, but the day has drawn near. Let us cast away works done in the shadows, and let us put on the armor of light. Let us walk with integrity as in daylight: not in partying and drunkenness, nor brazenly sleeping around, nor in competitive rivalry—but put on

Iesum Christum, et carnis providentiam[10] ne feceritis in concupiscentiis." (114) Quod si quisquam ita diceret, et carnis providentiam ne in concupiscentiis feceritis; sine dubio aures clausula numerosiore mulceret; sed gravior interpres etiam ordinem maluit tenere verborum. Quomodo autem hoc in Graeco eloquio sonet, quo est locutus apostolus, viderint eius eloquii usque ad ista doctiores; mihi tamen quod nobis eodem verborum ordine interpretatum est, nec ibi videtur currere numerose.

41. (115) Sane hunc elocutionis ornatum, qui numerosis fit clausulis, deesse fatendum est auctoribus nostris. Quod utrum per interpretes factum sit an (quod magis arbitror) consulto illi haec plausibilia devitaverint, affirmare non audeo, quoniam me fateor ignorare. Illud tamen scio, quod si quisquam huius numerositatis peritus illorum clausulas eorundem numerorum lege componat—quod

[10] curam *Vulg. P K*

---

[133] *providentiam*: Augustine usually quotes Romans 13:14 with *providentiam* rather than the *curam* of Vulg. The AV translation, by a cognate noun ("make [no] provision"), hints that this Latin may have influenced the 1611 translators.

[134] *concupiscentiis*: found only in Christian Latin: Romans 12:12–14. This text changed Augustine's life: see *Conf.* 8.12.29.

[135] Latin *clausula*: the "little close," or ending of a sentence, starting from the penultimate stressed syllable. The first version quoted ends with a six-syllable word, the second with one of four syllables: what he admires is the two-word *clausula* using 6 + 4 syllables. Multisyllabic endings in classical poetry can have a "tadah" force: Catull. 68.112 ends the whole second half of a pentameter with *Amphitryoniades*.

the Lord Jesus Christ, and do not make provision[133] for the flesh with its inordinate desires."[134] (114) If someone were to express it like this, "and do not make provision for the flesh with its desires that are inordinate," there is no doubt that the cadence[135] would be all the more delectable[136] for that rhythmic pattern. But the rather serious-minded translator has even preferred to keep the word order.[137] As for how this sounds in terms of the Greek rhetoric that the apostle employed, those who are more expert in such matters as eloquence of this kind will know. But to me that version that has been translated for us, using the same word order, does not seem to flow particularly rhythmically.

41. (115) I have to admit that our Christian authors are lacking in the rhythmic cadences that are an attractive feature of rhetorical delivery. I do not presume to pass judgment whether this was a decision on the part of translators, or whether (as I tend to think), the original authors deliberately avoided such charming elements. Frankly, I have no idea. But I do know this: if someone[138] skilled in the art of prose rhythms were to arrange the cadences of our Christian writers according to the rules of those

[136] R. P. H. Green notes that quantitatively there is little to choose between the cadence forms, which may suggest an accentual preference instead. See Oberhelman, "History and Development," 241–42. [137] Of the Greek original.

[138] He is thinking of himself, and his reappraisal of biblical Latinity. *Clausulae* are a matter of rhythm, which is felt by the body as much as heard by the ear: see Hammond, *Sound of the Liturgy*, 116. He must have endured disappointment at missed rhythmic opportunities when listening to scripture.

facillime fit mutatis quibusdam verbis, quae tantundem significatione valent, vel mutato eorum quae invenerit ordine—nihil illorum quae velut magna in scholis grammaticorum aut rhetorum didicit, illis divinis viris defuisse cognoscet et multa reperiet locutionis genera tanti decoris, quae quidem et in nostra, sed maxime in sua lingua decora sunt, quorum nullum in eis quibus isti inflantur litteris invenitur.

(116) Sed cavendum est ne divinis gravibusque sententiis, dum additur numerus, pondus detrahatur. Nam illa musica disciplina, ubi numerus iste plenissime discitur, usque adeo non defuit prophetis nostris ut vir doctus Hieronymus quorundam etiam metra commemoret, in Hebraea dumtaxat lingua; cuius ut veritatem servaret in verbis, haec inde non transtulit. (117) Ego autem ut de sensu meo loquar, qui mihi quam aliis et quam aliorum est utique notior, sicut in meo eloquio, quantum modeste fieri arbitror, non praetermitto istos numeros clausularum, ita in auctoribus nostris hoc mihi plus placet, quod ibi eos rarissime invenio.

42. (118) Grande autem dicendi genus hoc maxime distat ab isto genere temperato, quod non tam verborum

---

139 He never did, or at least no trace of such an experiment survives. His only extant effort at accentual rhythm was his "psalm against the Donatists," the chorus of which is a fair representation of the rhythmic whole: *vós qui gaudétis de páce/módo vérum iudicáte.*

140 In the prologue to his translation of Job, Jerome refers to dactyls and spondees in the verse portions of the text (*hexametri versus sunt, dactylo spondaeoque currentes*). Socrates of Con-

rhythms—which is easy to do if you change certain words that still keep the same signification, or if you change the existing word order—they would admit that nothing of the qualities that they learned as being great, in the schools of teachers of literature and rhetoric, was lacking in those holy men. Also, in those discourses they will find many types of features that are outstanding, and that are certainly attractive in our language—and most of all in their own tongue—none of which is found in the literature that puffs them up with pride.

(116) We must still make sure not to diminish the seriousness in that holy and weighty discourse if we factor rhythm in.[139] It is in the subject of music that matters of rhythm are covered most fully, and it was so abundant in the prophets that Jerome, that man of letters, even recounts the meters used by some of them, albeit in the Hebrew tongue;[140] though in order to preserve the integrity of the original words he did not reproduce these meters in his translation. (117) If I may speak, then, of my own perception—which I obviously know better than other people and their perceptions—just as in my own public speaking (as much as I consider shows proper restraint), I do not neglect these kind of rhythmic cadences, so when it comes to our Christian authors, the more rarely I find them there, the happier I am.

42. (118) Now the grand style of oratory is a very different thing from that moderate style, for instead of being

stantinople mentions a fourth-century father and son, both Apollinaris, as having translated biblical books into genres and meters of "pagan" Greek literature (*Hist. eccl.* 2.46, 3.16).

ornatibus comptum est, quam violentum animi affectibus. Nam capit etiam illa ornamenta paene omnia, sed ea si non habuerit, non requirit. Fertur quippe impetu suo et elocutionis pulchritudinem, si occurrerit, vi rerum rapit, non cura decoris assumit. Satis enim est ei propter quod agitur ut verba congruentia non oris eligantur industria, sed pectoris sequantur ardorem. (119) Nam si aurato gemmatoque ferro vir fortis armetur, intentissimus pugnae agit quidem illis armis quod agit, non quia pretiosa, sed quia arma sunt; idem ipse est tamen et valet plurimum, etiam cum "rimanti telum ira facit." Agit apostolus ut pro evangelico ministerio patienter mala huius temporis, cum solatio donorum dei, omnia tolerentur. Magna res est, et granditer agitur, nec desunt ornamenta dicendi: (120) "ecce," inquit, "nunc tempus acceptabile, ecce nunc dies salutis. Nullam in quoquam dantes offensionem, ut non reprehendatur ministerium, sed in omnibus commendantes nosmetipsos ut dei ministros, in multa patientia, in tribulationibus, in necessitatibus, in angustiis, in plagis, in carceribus, in seditionibus, in laboribus, in vigiliis, in ieiuniis, in castitate, in scientia, in longanimitate, in benignitate, in spiritu sancto, in caritate non ficta, in verbo veritatis, in vir-

---

141 *oris* (mouth): can mean "speech" in poetic and late Latin.

142 The verb, *sequantur*, suggests not a "spontaneous overflow of powerful feeling" but the imitation of one.

143 Latin *rimanti. Rimare* means "to root out/rummage"; Verg. *Aen.* 507–8, "anger makes a weapon of whatever each man rummages around for." Augustine had loved Virgil once, but it is surprising that here he allows himself to quote him.

144 Latin *acceptabile* (a Church word not found in classical Latin) translates the Greek *kairos*: AV and its successors have kept

stylish and neat, it has a powerful effect on people's state of mind. It embraces almost all of those artistic features, but if it happens not to have them, it does not go looking for them. In fact it is carried along by its own momentum, and carries off the beauty of its delivery—when that occurs—from the power of its subject matter rather than by attention to elegance of expression. For this it is enough that its words fit the subject at hand, and are not selected for a prepared speech,[141] but strive for[142] heartfelt emotion. (119) For example: if a man of valor were to arm himself with gilded weapons studded with gems, all his attention would be on the battle, where he does what he does with those weapons, not because they are valuable but because they are weapons. He himself is still the same mighty man of valor even when "anger makes him a weapon even as he gropes around for one."[143] The apostle is urging his readers, the sake of ministering the gospel, to endure all the evils of the present time, with the gifts of God to bring them consolation. It is a vital matter, and he presses it in the grand style, which still includes some rhetorical artistry: (120) "Look," he says, "now is the critical moment,[144] now is the day of deliverance. You must not give anyone cause for complaint, so that your ministry suffers no setback. But in everything you must make us acceptable as God's servants, in long-suffering, in misfortunes, in poverty, in dire straits, in injury, in imprisonment, in civil unrest, in travail, in watchfulness, in poverty, in pureness of living, in knowledge, in patience, in goodwill, in the Holy Spirit, in genuine love, in the word of

the translations "accepted/acceptable," but it is an obsolete sense in English.

tute dei; per arma iustitiae dextra et sinistra, per gloriam et ignobilitatem, per infamiam et bonam famam, ut seductores et veraces, ut qui ignoramur et cognoscimur, quasi morientes et ecce! vivimus, ut coerciti et non mortificati, ut tristes, semper autem gaudentes, sicut egeni, multos autem ditantes, tamquam nihil habentes et omnia possidentes." Vide adhuc ardentem, "os nostrum patet ad vos, o Corinthii, cor nostrum dilatatum est" et cetera, quae persequi longum est.

43. (121) Itemque ad Romanos agit, ut persecutiones huius mundi caritate vincantur, spe certa in adiutorio dei. Agit autem et granditer et ornate: "scimus," inquit, "quoniam diligentibus deum omnia cooperantur in bonum, his qui secundum propositum vocati sunt. Quoniam quos ante praescivit, et praedestinavit conformes imaginis filii sui, ut sit ipse primogenitus in multis fratribus. Quos autem praedestinavit, illos et vocavit; et quos vocavit, ipsos et iustificavit; quos autem iustificavit, illos et glorificavit. Quid ergo dicemus ad haec? Si deus pro nobis, quis contra nos? Qui filio proprio non pepercit, sed pro nobis omnibus tradidit eum, quomodo non etiam cum illo omnia nobis donavit? Quis accusabit adversus electos dei? deus qui iustificat: quis qui condemnat? Christus Iesus qui mortuus est, magis autem qui resurrexit, qui et est in dextera dei, qui et

---

145 This list transitions seamlessly between qualities of character, external pressures, and external strengths, with the preposition "in" working at full flexibility.

146 2 Corinthians 6:2–11.

147 *conformis*: another Christian Latin word.

148 Augustine composes a version of this Pauline patterning in

truth, in the power of God;[145] by the weapons of righteousness on the right hand and the left, by honor and dishonor, by renown and infamy; as if liars, though we are honest; as unknown, yet recognized; as if we were dead, yet look!—we are alive; as hemmed in yet not killed; as sorrowing, yet we always rejoice; as poor, yet enriching many; seeming to own nothing, yet possessing everything." See how his passion continues, "we have opened our mouth and spoken to you, people of Corinth, our tenderness toward you has grown," and so on (it would take too long to quote in full).[146]

43. (121) He also makes his case to the Romans that they ought to triumph over the persecutions of this world through their certain hope of God's help. He does so in a style that combines grandeur and artistry, saying, "we know that all things work together for good among those who love God, who have been called in accordance with his plan. This is because those he foreknew, he also predestined to be conformed[147] to the likeness of his Son, who would therefore be the firstborn amid many sons; but those whom he predestined, he also called; and those whom he called he also justified; and those whom he also justified, he also glorified.[148] What are we to say to that? If God is for us, who is against us? If God did not spare his own Son, but handed him over for our sakes, how can he not have bestowed all things on us, along with his Son? Who will bring a charge against God's chosen ones? It is God who justifies, so who can there be to condemn us? Is it Christ Jesus, who died, what is more who has risen from the dead, who is even at the right hand of God, who inter-

Conf. 7.10.16, "O everlasting Truth, and true Love, and beloved Eternity, you are my God."

interpellat pro nobis? Quis nos separabit a caritate Christi? Tribulatio? an angustia? an persecutio? an fames? an nuditas? an periculum? an gladius? Sicut scriptum est, 'quia propter te mortificamur tota die, aestimati sumus ut oves occisionis.' Sed in his omnibus supervincimus per eum qui dilexit nos. Certus sum enim quia neque mors neque vita neque angelus neque principatus neque praesentia neque futura neque virtus neque altitudo neque profundum neque creatura alia poterit nos separare a caritate dei, quae est in Christo Iesu domino nostro."

44. (122) "Ad Galatas" autem quamvis tota illa epistola summisso dicendi genere scripta sit nisi in extremis partibus ubi est eloquium temperatum, tamen interponit quendam locum eo motu animi, ut sine ullis quidem talibus ornamentis qualia sunt in his quae modo posuimus, non posset tamen nisi granditer dici. (123) "Dies," inquit, "observatis et menses et annos et tempora. Timeo vos, ne forte sine causa laboraverim in vos. Estote sicut et ego, quoniam et ego sicut vos. Fratres, precor vos, nihil me laesistis. Scitis quia per infirmitatem carnis iam pridem evangelizavi vobis, et temptationem vestram in carne mea non

---

149 *intercessio*: a form of prayer in which the one praying steps between God and the person on whose behalf the prayer is spoken. 150 *mortificati*: only in Christian Latin. A common verb in Vulg.

151 *occisionis*: rare in classical Latin; common in Vulg., e.g., Psalm 43:22.

152 *supervincimus*: a north African reading also found in Tertullian and Cyprian, it imitates the Greek, *hypernikōmen*. Vulg. has the less exotic *superamus*.

153 Romans 8:28–39; Psalm 44:22. Augustine attempts no in-

cedes[149] for us? Who will separate us from the love of Christ? Will misfortune? or hardship? or persecution? or hunger? or nakedness? or danger? or sword? As it is written, 'On your account we are being killed[150] all day long: we have been valued as sheep for the slaughter.'[151] But in all these things we are more than conquerors[152] through him who loved us. I am sure that neither death nor life nor angel nor principality nor things present nor things future nor power nor height nor depth nor any other creation will be able to separate us from the love of God, which is in Christ Jesus our Lord."[153]

44. (122) By contrast, the whole of his letter to the Galatians has been written in a subdued style of speech where his eloquence is moderate, except in the closing sections. Even so he inserts one passage of such animated emotion that even without any of those embellishments of the kind in the texts we have just laid out, it can only be said to be in the grand style.[154] (123) He says this: "you observe days and months and years and seasons. I fear for you, that it may turn out I have labored in vain for you. Be as I am, just as I am as you. Brothers, I promise you, you have done me no injury. You know that it was on account of a physical illness that I preached the good news to you long since, and you neither scorned not rejected the testing you experienced because of my physical state[155] but

depth rhetorical analysis, perhaps because categories of classical rhetorical theory fit Paul's rhetoric only imperfectly.

154 Galatians 4:10–20.

155 This passage stands out from the rest of the letter for its disjointed phrasing to create emotional tone: Schlier, *Der Brief an die Galater*, 208.

sprevistis neque respuistis, sed sicut angelum dei excepistis me, sicut Christum Iesum. Quae ergo fuit beatitudo vestra? Testimonium vobis perhibeo, quoniam si fieri posset, oculos vestros eruissetis et dedissetis mihi. Ergo inimicus factus sum vobis verum praedicans? Aemulantur vos non bene, sed excludere vos volunt, ut eos aemulemini. Bonum est autem aemulari in bono semper, et non solum cum praesens sum apud vos. Filioli mei, quos iterum parturio donec Christus formetur in vobis. Vellem autem nunc adesse apud vos et mutare vocem meam, quia confundor in vobis." (124) Numquid hic aut contraria contrariis verba sunt reddita aut aliqua gradatione sibi subnexa sunt aut caesa et membra circuitusve sonuerunt? Et tamen non ideo tepuit grandis affectus, quo eloquium fervere sentimus.

45. (125) Sed apostolica ista sic clara sunt ut et profunda sint, atque ita conscripta memoriaeque mandata ut non solum lectore vel auditore, verum etiam expositore opus habeant, si quis in eis non superficie contentus altitudinem quaerat. Quapropter videamus ista genera dicendi in eis qui istorum lectione ad rerum divinarum atque salubrium scientiam profecerunt eamque ecclesiae ministrarunt.

Beatus Cyprianus summisso dicendi genere utitur in eo libro ubi de sacramento calicis disputat. (126) Solvitur quippe ibi quaestio, in qua quaeritur utrum calix dominicus aquam solam an eam vino mixtam debeat habere. Sed exempli gratia aliquid inde ponendum est. Post princi-

---

156 Galatians 4:10–20. 157 *expositore* renders the Greek *exēgētēs*, "one who interprets or explains (usually scripture)."

158 *calix*, whence, "chalice."

rather you embraced me like an angel of God, like Jesus Christ himself. What then has become of the blessing you then received? This is my testimony to you: if it were possible, you would have plucked out your own eyes and given them to me. Is it for this that I have now become your enemy—for telling you the truth? They are zealous for you, and not in a good way. They want to shut you out, to make you zealous for them. True, zeal is a good thing when the end in view is good, and not just when I am present with you. Dear children, I am still laboring to bring you to birth until Christ takes shape in you. I wish I were now with you, and changing the tone of my speech, for I am perplexed about you."[156] (124) Is there any sign here of verbal antitheses, or buildup of clauses with auxesis? Have the phrases and clauses and periods been heard loud and clear? No. But despite this yet the power of his emotion is still ardent, which makes us feel his burning eloquence.

45. (125) These readings from the apostle, however, are so self-evident as to become profound too. They are written and memorized in such a way that they need not only a reader or listener, but also an exegete,[157] if someone is seeking profound meanings, rather than settling for what is on the surface. Let us therefore scrutinize these types of expression in those writers who have reached a degree of expertise in this sacred and salvific material, and have offered it for the Church's use.

Blessed Cyprian uses a plain style of speech in his book investigating the sacrament of the cup.[158] (126) This is, in fact, the place where he answers the question that asks whether the Lord's cup should contain only water or water mixed with wine. We need to quote a passage by way of example. So, after an introduction to the letter, he begins

pium ergo epistolae, iam solvere incipiens propositam quaestionem, "admonitos autem nos scias," inquit, "ut in calice offerendo dominica traditio servetur, neque aliud fiat a nobis, quam quod pro nobis dominus prior fecit, ut calix qui in commemoratione eius offertur mixtus vino offeratur. Nam cum dicat Christus, 'ego sum vitis vera,' sanguis Christi non aqua est utique, sed vinum. Nec potest videri sanguis eius, quo redempti et vivificati sumus, esse in calice, quando vinum desit calici quo Christi sanguis ostenditur, qui scripturarum omnium sacramento ac testimonio praedicetur. Invenimus enim in Genesi circa sacramentum Noë hoc idem praecucurrisse et figuram dominicae passionis illic exstitisse, quod vinum bibit, quod inebriatus est, quod in domo sua nudatus est, quod fuit recubans nudis et patentibus femoribus, quod nuditas illa patris a medio filio denotata est, a maiore vero et minore contecta, et cetera quae necesse non est exsequi, cum satis sit hoc solum complecti, quod Noë typum futurae veritatis ostendens, non aquam sed vinum biberit; et sic imaginem dominicae passionis expresserit. Item in sacerdote Melchisedech dominicum sacramentum praefiguratum videmus, secundum quod scriptura divina testatur et dicit, 'et Melchisedech rex Salem protulit panem et vinum.' Fuit autem sacerdos dei summi et benedixit Abraham. Quod autem Melchisedech typum Christi portaret,

---

159 John 15:1.

160 *sacramento*: of baptism, cf. *TC* 3.13.32.

161 Genesis 9:20–23. A fine example of the difference between ancient and modern exegesis. This reading is driven by the belief that Noah, saved for his righteousness, must prefigure

to answer the question he has been set, as follows: "You should know that we have been warned to preserve what the Lord handed down to us concerning the offering of the cup: we must not do anything other than what the Lord originally did on our behalf, namely that the cup that is offered in remembrance of him must be a cup in which wine is mixed. Since Christ says, 'I am the true vine,'[159] the blood of Christ cannot possibly be water: it has to be wine. There is no trace of his blood (which redeems us and restores us to life) in a cup when it lacks the wine that manifests Christ's blood, which is foretold in the sign[160] and witness of the Bible as a whole. Regarding such signs, we find in Genesis that Noah was a forerunner in this respect, and provided there a prefiguring of the Lord's passion; in that he drank wine; he became drunk, took off his clothes in his own house, lay on his back with his legs bare and spread apart; and in that his middle son pointed out his father's nakedness, while his eldest and youngest covered him up, and so on. There is no need to detail it all here. This on its own incorporates how Noah provided a type[161] of the truth that was to come: he drank wine, not water; and so formed a likeness of the Lord's passion. Again, in the priest Melchisedek we see the Lord's sign prefigured, in accordance with what holy scripture witnesses and states, 'and Melchisedek, king of Salem, brought bread and wine.' For he was the priest of the most high God, and blessed Abraham.[162] In the psalms, the Holy Spirit states that Melchisedek bore the imprint of

Christ. For Augustine the less exalted details of the passage do not disqualify it as a dominical type.

162 Genesis 14:18.

declarat in psalmis spiritus sanctus ex persona patris ad filium dicens, 'ante luciferum generavi te. Tu es sacerdos in aeternum secundum ordinem Melchisedech.'" Haec et alia quae sequuntur huius epistulae summissae dictionis modum servant, quod facile est explorare legentibus.

46. (127) Sanctus quoque Ambrosius cum agat rem magnam de spiritu sancto, ut eum patri et filio demonstret aequalem, summisso tamen dicendi genere utitur, quoniam res suscepta non ornamenta verborum aut ad flectendos animos commotionis affectum, sed rerum documenta desiderat. Ergo inter cetera in principio huius operis ait, "quo motus oraculo Gedeon, cum audisset quod deficientibus licet populorum milibus in uno viro dominus plebem suam ab hostibus liberaret, obtulit haedum caprarum, cuius carnem secundum praeceptum angeli et azima supra petram posuit et ea iure perfudit. Quae simul ut virgae cacumine quam gerebat angelus dei contigit, de petra ignis erupit atque ita sacrificium quod offerebatur absumptum est. Quo indicio declaratum videtur quod petra illa typum habuerit corporis Christi, quia scriptum est, 'bibebant de consequenti petra, petra autem erat Christus.' Quod utique non ad divinitatem eius, sed ad carnem relatum est, quae sitientium corda populorum perenni rivo sui sanguinis inundavit. Iam tunc igitur in

---

[163] In *On the Holy Spirit*, prologue 2–3.

[164] *oraculo*: repeatedly used in the Hebrew Bible/Old Testament of divine epiphanies; in this period it was applied to both "pagan" and Christian prophecies.

[165] Latin *iure*, from *ius, iuris*, n. visually identical with *ius* (law/right).

Christ, saying to the Son in the person of the Father, 'before the dayspring I have begotten you. You are a priest for ever, according to the order of Melchisedek.'" This passage, and what follows it in the letter, keep to the plain style of speech, which is easy for readers to make sense of.

46. (127) Saint Ambrose likewise, when dealing with the important subject of the Holy Spirit, uses the plain style of speech to prove that he is equal to the Father and the Son.[163] This is because the subject he tackles does not require elaborate language, or the stirring up of emotion to turn people's hearts, but factual proofs. For this reason, he states (among other things) at the beginning of this work, "When he heard that the Lord, even if a thousand of the people failed him, would liberate his own people from their enemies by a single man, that oracle[164] prompted Gideon to fetch a kid from his goats, to lay its flesh upon a rock together with unleavened bread as the angel instructed, and to pour broth[165] over it all. The moment the angel of God touched it with the tip of the rod he was carrying, fire burst from the rock and so the sacrifice he offered was completely consumed.[166] This seemed to be a token proving that the rock exemplified a type of the body of Christ, because it is written, 'they were drinking from the rock that followed them, yet the rock was Christ.'[167] Undoubtedly this refers not to his divinity but to his flesh, which flooded the hearts of thirsty peoples with the never-ending stream of his own blood. So it was

[166] Judges 6:11–21. Rods as instruments of supernatural effect appear elsewhere in the Bible (e.g., Exodus 7:11; Numbers 20:11); the ancestors of the "magic wand."

[167] 1 Corinthians 10:4.

mysterio declaratum est quia dominus Iesus in carne sua totius mundi peccata crucifixus aboleret, nec solum delicta factorum, sed etiam cupiditates animorum. Caro enim haedi ad culpam facti refertur, ius ad illecebras cupiditatum, sicut scriptum est, 'quia concupivit populus cupiditatem pessimam et dixerunt, quis nos cibabit carne?' Quod igitur extendit angelus virgam et tetigit petram, de qua ignis exiit, ostendit quod caro domini spiritu repleta divino peccata omnia humanae condicionis exureret. Unde et dominus ait: 'ignem veni mittere in terram,'" et cetera, in quibus rei docendae ac probandae maxime incumbit.

47. (128) De genere temperato est apud Cyprianum virginitatis illa laudatio: "nunc nobis ad virgines sermo est, quarum quo sublimior gloria est, maior et cura. Flos est ille ecclesiastici germinis, decus atque ornamentum gratiae spiritalis, laeta indoles laudis et honoris, opus integrum atque incorruptum, dei imago respondens ad sanctimoniam domini, illustrior portio gregis Christi. Gaudet per ipsas, atque in illis largiter floret ecclesiae matris gloriosa fecunditas; quantoque plus gloriosa virginitas numero suo addit, gaudium matris augescit." Et alio loco in fine epistulae, "quomodo portavimus, inquit, imaginem eius qui de limo est, sic portemus imaginem eius qui de caelo est. Hanc imaginem virginitas portat, portat integritas, sanctitas portat et veritas; portant disciplinae dei memores, iustitiam cum religione retinentes, stabiles in fide,

168 Numbers 11:4.
169 Luke 12:49.
170 Cypr. *Disc.* 3.23–24.
171 1 Corinthians 15:49.

made plain by this mystery that the Lord Jesus in his own flesh was nullifying the sins of the whole world by being crucified, and not only physical sins, but also sins of the mind and heart. The flesh of the kid corresponds to the substance of what is done, the broth to the lure of desires: as it is written, 'for the people coveted the worst of things to set their heart on, and said, who will give us flesh to eat?'[168] Therefore the angel stretched out his rod and touched the rock, and fire erupted from it, which shows that the flesh of the Lord is filled with the divine spirit to burn away all the sins of our human state. For this reason the Lord also said, 'I have come to send fire onto the earth;'"[169] and so, therein, devoting himself wholeheartedly to teaching and proving this view of the matter.

47. (128) Cyprian's work in praise of virginity is in the restrained, middle, style: "now we are addressing virgins, and the more exalted their glory, the more conscientious they are about it. It is the blossom on the Church's stem, an honor and adornment of spiritual grace, the joyful nature of praise and dignity, a wholly uncorrupted work, a likeness of God answering to the Lord's purity, the distinguished element in the flock of Christ. The bright fertility of mother Church rejoices through her virgins, and blossoms through them far and wide; the more her glorious virginity adds to her number, the more the joy of mother Church abounds."[170] In another passage, at the end of the letter, he says, "in the same way as we have borne the likeness of his earthly being, so shall we also bear the likeness of his heavenly self.[171] Virginity is the vessel of this likeness, and so are holiness and truth; they too are its vessels who are mindful of God's teaching, who maintain justice

humiles in timore, ad omnem tolerantiam fortes, ad sustinendas iniurias mites, ad faciendam misericordiam faciles, fraterna pace unanimes atque concordes. Quae vos singulae, o bonae virgines, observare, diligere, implere debetis, quae deo et Christo vacantes ad dominum cui vos dicastis, maiore et meliore parte praeceditis. Provectae annis iunioribus facite magisterium; minores natu, praebete comparibus incitamentum; hortamentis vos mutuis excitate, aemulis de virtute documentis ad gloriam provocate; durate fortiter, spiritaliter pergite, pervenite feliciter; tantum mementote tunc nostri, cum incipiet in vobis virginitas honorari."

48. (129) Ambrosius etiam genere dicendi temperato et ornato professis virginibus proponit, tamquam sub exempli forma, quod moribus imitentur, et dicit, "virgo erat non solum corpore, sed etiam mente, quae nullo doli ambitu sincerum adulteraret affectum; corde humilis, verbis gravis, animi prudens, loquendi parcior, legendi studiosior; non in incerto divitiarum, sed in prece pauperis spem reponens; intenta operi, verecunda sermone; arbitrum mentis non hominem, sed deum quaerere; nulli laedere os, bene velle omnibus; assurgere maioribus natu, aequalibus non invidere; fugere iactantiam, rationem sequi,

172 *vacantes* in Christian Latin is used of time for serving God: see Cypr. *Ep. ad Don.* 1.1–2.

173 1 Timothy 6:17.

174 Echoing Ter. *Ad.* 864.

in their devotion, who stand firm in faith, humble in reverence, with courage for every kind of endurance, gentle in bearing with every kind of harm, ready to act with mercy, of one mind united in brotherly peace. Each one of you good virgin women must do, must love, must fulfill all of this, for all your time is spent[172] on God and Christ, and ahead of us you make your way to the Lord, having dedicated yourselves to him in that greater and better way. You older virgins exercise your teaching ministry over the younger ones; you younger ones do service to the elder, and challenge those who are your own age. Stir one another up by your encouragement, urge one another on to glory by striving to outdo one another in goodness: be brave in enduring, going forward in the spirit, arriving in a state of joy. At that moment, though, remember us, as your virginity's reward begins."

48. (129) When he lays before professed virgins a kind of ideal scheme for them to imitate in terms of their behavior, Ambrose too uses the restrained, polished style of speech. He says, "She was a virgin in mind as well as body, for she never tainted a genuine attachment with any display of deceit; she was humble in heart, serious in conversation, sensible in her thinking, and as restrained in her talk as she was devout in her reading. She set her hope on the prayer of the poor, not on 'the uncertainty of riches.'[173] She concentrated on her work, she was shy about speaking out. She looked to God as the judge of her thoughts, not to any human being. She never spoke ill of anyone, she was well-intentioned toward everyone.[174] She stood up in the presence of her elders, she was not envious of her peer group. She avoided boasting, aiming to be reasonable, and valuing goodness. When has she ever upset her parents,

amare virtutem. Quando ista vel vultu laesit parentes? Quando dissensit a propinquis? Quando fastidivit humilem? Quando risit debilem? Quando vitavit inopem? Eos solos sollicita coetus virorum invisere, quos misericordia non erubesceret neque[11] praeteriret verecundia. Nihil torvum in oculis, nihil in verbis procax, nihil in actu inverecundum; non gestus fractior, non incessus solutior, non vox petulantior, ut ipsa corporis species simulacrum fuerit mentis et figura probitatis. Bona quippe domus in ipso vestibulo debet agnosci, ac primo praetendat ingressu nihil intus latere tenebrarum, tamquam lucernae lux intus posita foris luceat. Quid ergo exsequar ciborum parsimoniam, officiorum redundantiam; alterum ultra naturam superfuisse, alterum paene ipsi naturae defuisse? Illic nulla intermissa tempora, hic congeminati ieiunio dies, et si quando reficiendi successisset voluntas, cibus plerumque obvius qui mortem arceret, non delicias ministraret," et cetera.

(130) Haec autem propterea in exemplo huius temperati generis posui, quia non hic agit ut virginitatem voveant quae nondum voverunt, sed quales esse debeant quae iam votae sunt. Nam ut aggrediatur animus tantum ac tale propositum, grandi utique dicendi genere debet excitari et accendi. Sed martyr Cyprianus de habitu virginum, non

[11] ne quem] *P B D K R Gr. RGr.*

---

[175] Ambr. *Virg.* 2.2.7–8.

[176] The Latin equivalent of judging a book by its cover.

even by the look on her face? When has she quarreled with her neighbors? When was she disdainful toward someone humble? When has she laughed at someone with a disability? When has she passed the needy by on the other side? She took care to be in company with groups of men only when her compassion would not be put to the blush, and her modesty would not oblige her to neglect anyone. There was nothing wild in her eyes, nothing impertinent about her speech, nothing immodest in her behavior; no lack of grace in her movements, nothing sloppy in her carriage, nothing capricious in her voice.[175] As a result her physical appearance bore an exact resemblance to her mind, and the shape of her good character. After all, we should be able to tell a good house by its entrance:[176] as soon as we enter it should tell us that nothing shady lurks within, just like light from a lantern placed inside that casts its light outside. There is no need to run through her avoidance of gluttony, and her abundance of good works: in the former she consumed less than nature requires, while in the latter she far exceeded it. In the former she redoubled her times of fasting, in the latter she was busy every moment; and if ever the desire for refreshment seemed to have won, she partook of food to stave off death, not for feeding her own pleasure," and so on.

(130) I have quoted this as an example of this middle style, because he is not urging anyone to pledge their virginity if they have not already done so, only that they ought to live up to their vows. If the mind is to be urged to make such a momentous promise, it undoubtedly needs the grand style of speaking to kindle and embolden it. Cyprian, a martyr, wrote about the conduct of virgins, not about

de suscipiendo virginitatis proposito scripsit; iste vero episcopus etiam ad hoc eas magno accendit eloquio.

49. (131) Verum ex eo quod ambo egerunt, dictionis grandis exempla memorabo. Ambo quippe invecti sunt in eas quae formam pigmentis colorant vel potius decolorant. Quorum prior ille cum hoc ageret, ait inter cetera, "si quis pingendi artifex vultum alicuius et speciem et corporis qualitatem aemulo colore signasset; et signato iam consummatoque simulacro manus alius inferret, ut iam formata, iam picta quasi peritior reformaret, gravis prioris artificis iniuria et iusta indignatio videretur. Tu te existimas impune laturam tam improbae temeritatis audaciam, dei artificis offensam? Ut enim impudica circa homines et incesta fucis lenocinantibus non sis, corruptis violatisque quae dei sunt, peior adultera detineris. Quod ornari te putas, quod putas comi, impugnatio est ista divini operis, praevaricatio est veritatis. Monentis apostoli vox est, 'expurgate vetus fermentum ut sitis nova consparsio, sicut estis azimi. Nam pascha nostrum immolatus est Christus. Itaque festa celebremus, non in fermento veteri neque in fermento malitiae et nequitiae, sed in azimis sinceritatis et veritatis.' Num sinceritas perseverat et veritas, quando quae sincera sunt polluuntur et colorum adulterinis medicaminum fucis in mendacium vera mutantur? Dominus

177 *detineris*: perhaps a north African usage; it is common to Tertullian and Cyprian.

178 1 Corinthians 5:7–8.

undertaking a life of virginity. Ambrose the bishop used his utmost eloquence when encouraging them in this commitment.

49. (131) I shall, however, quote examples of the grand style on a subject that both of them spoke of. Certainly they both excoriated women who color their face with makeup—or rather, who *dis*color it. The earlier of the two, Cyprian, when he argued on the subject, said (among other things), "if a portrait artist had created a likeness of someone's face, and their appearance and the contours of their body, imitating their coloring; and another hand had applied itself to that completed representative likeness, as if it were more skillful, to reshape what was already formed and painted, that would appear to be a serious insult to the first artist, and a genuine provocation. Do you think that you can carry off such effrontery, such disgraceful recklessness with impunity, such an outrage against God the divine artist? Even though you may not be a trollop when in male company, or promiscuous when using your concealing blusher, by tinting and tainting what is God's work, you are accused of[177] being worse than an adulterer. What you see as prettifying yourself, doing your hair, is really an attack on a divine work, a sin against the truth. The voice of the apostle is warning you, 'clear away the old leaven; be like a new batch of dough, as you are unleavened. For Christ our Passover has been sacrificed. Therefore let us keep the feast, not with the old leaven, nor with the leaven of malice and wickedness, but with the unleavened bread of purity and truth.'[178] Surely purity and truth cannot endure when things that are pure have been tainted, and when things that are true have been changed into a lie by a counterfeited blush of unnatural color? Your Lord says,

tuus dicit, 'non potes facere capillum unum album aut nigrum,' et tu ad vincendam domini tui vocem vis te esse potiorem. Audaci conatu et sacrilego contemptu crines tuos inficis; malo praesagio futurorum capillos iam tibi flammeos auspicaris." Longum est inserere omnia quae sequuntur.

50. (132) Ille vero posterior ut in tales diceret: "hinc illa," inquit, "nascuntur incentiva vitiorum, ut quaesitis coloribus ora depingant, dum viris displicere formidant, et de adulterio vultus meditentur adulterium castitatis. Quanta hic amentia effigiem mutare naturae, picturam quaerere, et dum verentur maritale iudicium, prodere suum! Prior enim de se pronuntiat, quae cupit mutare quod nata est. Ita dum alii studet placere, prius ipsa sibi displicet. Quem iudicem, mulier, veriorem requiremus deformitatis tuae quam te ipsam, quae videri times? Si pulchra es, quid absconderis? Si deformis, cur te formosam esse mentiris, nec tuae conscientiae nec alieni gratiam erroris habitura? Ille enim alteram diligit, tu alteri vis placere, et irasceris si amet aliam, qui adulterare in te docetur. Male magistra es iniuriae tuae. Lenocinari refugit etiam quae est passa lenonem, ac licet vilis mulier, non alteri tamen, sed sibi peccat. Tolerabiliora propemodum in adulterio crimina sunt; ibi enim pudicitia, hic natura adulteratur."

---

[179] Matthew 5:36. [180] That is, to match the impending flames of hell (Cypr. *Disc.* 15). [181] *pictura* in this sense goes back as far as Plautus (*Mostell.* 263).

[182] *gratia*, in its classical, not its theological, sense.

[183] This careless estimate of a human being's value (*vilis* means "cheap") exposes the effect of people having monetary value in a slave-owning society. [184] Ambr. *Virg.* 1.6.2.

'you cannot make a single hair white or black,'[179] but you want to be mightier and prevail against the voice of your Lord. You have the brazen presumption and blasphemous lack of respect to dye your hair: what a foreboding evil for the future, that you adopt flame-red hair color."[180] What follows on is too much to include here.

50. (132) The later writer had this to say against such women: "this practice spawns temptations to immorality. Afraid of disappointing their husbands, they daub their faces with unnatural tints, and their thoughts turn from adulterating their appearance to adulterating their chastity. What madness, to change their natural appearance and turn to cosmetics,[181] and to surrender their own judgment, even while they fear that of their husband! A woman who wants to change her natural appearance is already announcing a guilty verdict upon herself. So all the time she is intent upon pleasing another, she is already displeased with herself. Woman, what truer judge of your disfigurement can we seek than you yourself, who are afraid of being seen? If you are beautiful, why would you hide yourself? If you are ugly, why deceive people into thinking you fair, when you will never win the good opinion[182] of your own conscience, or of someone else's mistaken evaluation? So he is in love with another woman, and you want to attract another man, yet you are angry if he loves another, but you were his teacher in the art of adultery. You are the one who taught him to tear your heart. Even a woman exploited by her pimp shrinks from exploiting herself, and however worthless[183] she may be, she is not sinning against another, but against herself. Charges of actual adultery are virtually preferable to this; for adultery corrupts chastity, but cosmetics corrupt nature."[184]

(133) Satis, ut existimo, apparet feminas ne suam fucis adulterent formam, et ad pudorem et ad timorem hac facundia vehementer impelli. Proinde neque[12] summissum neque temperatum, sed grande omnino genus hoc elocutionis agnoscimus. Et in his autem quos duos ex omnibus proponere volui, et in aliis ecclesiasticis viris et bona et bene, id est, sicut res postulat, acute, ornate ardenterque dicentibus, per multa eorum scripta vel dicta possunt haec tria genera reperiri et assidua lectione vel auditione, admixta etiam exercitatione, studentibus inolescere.

51. (134) Nec quisquam praeter disciplinam esse existimet ista miscere; immo quantum congrue fieri potest, omnibus generibus dictio varianda est. Nam quando prolixa est in uno genere, minus detinet auditorem. Cum vero fit in aliud ab alio transitus, etiamsi longius eat, decentius procedit oratio; quamvis habeant et singula genera varietates suas in sermone eloquentium, quibus non sinuntur in eorum qui audiunt frigescere vel tepescere sensibus. Verumtamen facilius summissum solum, quam solum grande diutius tolerari potest. (135) Commotio quippe animi quanto magis excitanda est, ut nobis assentiatur auditor, tanto minus in ea diu teneri potest, cum fuerit quantum satis est excitata. Et ideo cavendum est, ne, dum volumus altius erigere quod erectum est, etiam inde decidat quo fuerat excitatione perductum. Interpositis vero quae sunt dicenda summissius, bene reditur ad ea quae

[12] ne quem] *P B D K R Gr. RGr.*

(133) This, I reckon, is perfectly clear: women should not adulterate their appearance with cosmetics, and this fluent speech urges them toward modesty and fear. It is, therefore, neither plain nor moderate, but we notice that it is absolutely in the grand style of speaking. In these writers, then, whom I have chosen to put forward from among all the rest, and in other Christian authors who speak wisely and well (which is to say precisely, elegantly, passionately, according to circumstance) we can find these three styles of speaking in many of their works and words; by constant reading and listening, combined with some training also, students can become adept in their use.

51. (134) No one should think that it is against the rules to mix the three styles. Indeed, so long as it is appropriate to do so, one's style of speaking should vary by using all of them. If it goes on too long in one style, it begins to lose the audience. So when a shift takes place between one style and another, a speech proceeds more attractively, even if it is somewhat longer. Also each style has its own distinctive features in the delivery of the fluent public speaker, which prevent the attention of the listeners from cooling off or becoming lukewarm. All the same, it is easier to put up with the plain style than the grand style on its own. (135) The more we rouse and stir their minds, to make our listeners agree with us, the shorter the amount of time they can be kept in that state once they have reached the right level of excitement. This is why, while we want to rouse still further what we have aroused already, we must beware of their settling down from that pitch of excitement we originally led them to. If we insert an element delivered in the plain style, then we can return, to good effect, to matters that demand a grand style:

opus est granditer dici, ut dictionis impetus sicut maris aestus alternet. Ex quo fit ut grande dicendi genus, si diutius est dicendum, non debeat esse solum, sed aliorum generum interpositione varietur. Ei tamen generi dictio tota tribuitur, cuius copia praevaluerit.

52. (136) Interest enim quod genus cui generi interponatur vel adhibeatur, certis et necessariis locis. Nam et in grandi genere semper aut paene semper temperata decet esse principia; et in potestate est eloquentis ut dicantur nonnulla summisse, etiam quae possent granditer dici, ut ea quae dicuntur granditer, ex illorum fiant comparatione grandiora, et eorum tamquam umbris luminosiora reddantur.

In quocumque autem genere aliqua quaestionum vincula solvenda sunt, acumine opus est, quod sibi summissum genus proprie vindicat. (137) Ac per hoc eo genere utendum est et in aliis duobus generibus, quando eis ista incidunt: sicut laudandum aliquid vel vituperandum, ubi nec damnatio cuiusquam nec liberatio nec ad actionem quamlibet assensio requiritur, in quocumque alio genere occurrerit, genus adhibendum et interponendum est temperatum. In grandi ergo genere inveniunt locos suos duo cetera et in summisso similiter. (138) Temperatum autem genus non quidem semper, sed tamen aliquando summisso indiget, si, ut dixi, quaestio cuius nodus est solvendus, incurrat; vel quando nonnulla quae ornari possent ideo non ornantur, sed summisso sermone dicuntur, ut

this makes the force of our delivery like the ebb and flow of a tide. That is why, if we speak in the grand style for any length of time, we should not employ it alone, but should vary it by including passages in the other two styles. Still, the speech as a whole is assigned to whichever style predominates in terms of quantity.

52. (136) It makes a difference what individual style we employ to insert into another, in particular places where it is necessary. For example: with the grand style, it is always (or almost always) right to open the speech in the moderate style. A skilled speaker, moreover, has the capacity to deliver some sections in the plain style, even ones for which the grand style was an option: this makes what they do say in the grand style all the more grand in comparison with the rest, appearing all the brighter for that juxtaposition with the less brilliant passages.

Whatever the style used, when there are tangled questions to answer, we need insight, and the plain style claims this quality as its own property. (137) Because of this, that style should be used along with the other two whenever such matters are encountered. For example, there are cases where no one needs to be convicted or acquitted, or no determination on taking action needs to be made. Then whatever the style of the rest, the moderate style must be applied and included for any sections that are praising or criticizing something. The other two styles, therefore, can find a place for themselves within the grand style, and this is also true of the plain style. (138) This is not always the case with the moderate style, though sometimes it needs the plain style if it comes across a question that needs disentangling; or when certain parts that could be embellished are not embellished, but are delivered in the plain

quibusdam quasi toris ornamentorum praebeant eminentiorem locum. Grande autem genus temperata dictio non requirit; ad delectandos quippe animos, non ad movendos ipsa suscipitur.

53. (139) Non sane si dicenti crebrius et vehementius acclametur, ideo granditer putandus est dicere; hoc enim et acumina summissi generis et ornamenta faciunt temperati. Grande autem genus plerumque pondere suo voces premit, sed lacrimas exprimit. Denique cum apud Caesaream Mauritaniae populo dissuaderem pugnam civilem vel potius plus quam civilem, quam "catervam" vocabant; neque enim cives tantummodo, verum etiam propinqui, fratres, postremo parentes ac filii lapidibus inter se in duas partes divisi, per aliquot dies continuos certo tempore anni sollemniter dimicabant, et quisque ut quemque poterat occidebat; egi quidem granditer, quantum valui, ut tam crudele atque inveteratum malum de cordibus et moribus eorum avellerem pelleremque dicendo. Non tamen egisse aliquid me putavi, cum eos audirem acclamantes, sed cum flentes viderem. (140) Acclamationibus quippe se doceri et delectari, flecti autem lacrimis indicabant. Quas ubi aspexi, immanem illam consuetudinem a patribus et avis, longeque a maioribus traditam, quae pectora eorum hostiliter obsidebat vel potius possidebat, victam antequam re ipsa id ostenderent credidi; moxque

---

185 Echoing Verg. *Aen.* 9.324.

186 There were a number of settlements called Caesarea around the ancient Mediterranean. See G. Bonner, "Augustine's Visit to Caesarea in 418," in *Studies in Church History* 1, ed. C. W. Dugmore and C. Duggan (London, 1964), 104–13.

187 Echoing Luc. *BC* 1.1.

style so as to make other passages, with their decorative flourishes, stand out more. The grand style, though, has no need of the moderate style, for it is used to charm the mind, not to change it.

53. (139) We must not assume that because someone often wins enthusiastic acclaim when speaking in public they must be speaking in the grand style; the insights of the plain style and charm of the moderate style can do the same. All the same the grand style commonly silences voices[185] by its weight impressed, or by tears expressed. One last example: once when I was in Caesarea of Mauretania,[186] I was persuading the local people not to observe a battle between citizens, or rather a battle worse than that,[187] which they used to call "Squadron." It included not only citizens but also neighbors, brothers, even fathers and sons, divided into two camps. At a certain time of year, for a number of days, they used to fight with stones in ritual combat, and each man would kill anyone he could. I certainly pressed them in the grand style, using my powers of public speaking as best I could to tear this deep-seated barbarity from their hearts and habits and expel it. I did not think that I had achieved anything when I heard them cheering me, but only when they started sobbing. (140) Their cheering told me that I had taught them, and pleased them; but it was their tears that showed I had persuaded them. When I saw those tears, I believed that this monstrous observance of theirs, passed down from fathers and grandfathers and more distant forebears, which was like an enemy laying siege to their rational selves—or rather capturing it completely—had been vanquished, even before they made this apparent in reality. I quickly drew my speech to a close and turned their hearts

sermone finito ad agendas deo gratias corda atque ora converti. Et ecce iam ferme octo vel amplius anni sunt, propitio Christo, ex quo illic nihil tale temptatum est. Sunt et alia multa experimenta quibus didicimus homines, quid in eis fecerit sapientis granditas dictionis, non clamore potius quam gemitu, aliquando etiam lacrimis, postremo vitae mutatione monstrasse.

54. (141) Submisso etiam dicendi genere sunt plerique mutati, sed ut quod nesciebant scirent, aut quod eis videbatur incredibile crederent, non autem ut agerent quod agendum iam noverant et agere nolebant. Ad huiusmodi namque duritiam flectendam debet granditer dici. Nam et laudes et vituperationes quando eloquenter dicuntur, cum sint in genere temperato, sic afficiunt quosdam ut non solum in laudibus et vituperationibus eloquentia delectentur, verum et ipsi laudabiliter appetant fugiantque vituperabiliter vivere. Sed numquid omnes qui delectantur, imitantur, sicut in grandi genere omnes qui flectuntur, agunt, et in summisso genere omnes qui docentur, sciunt, aut credunt verum esse quod nesciunt?

55. (142) Unde colligitur illa duo genera quod efficere intendunt, hoc eis esse maxime necessarium, qui sapienter et eloquenter volunt dicere. Illud vero quod agitur genere temperato, id est, ut eloquentia ipsa delectet, non est propter se ipsum usurpandum, sed ut rebus quae utiliter

and voices to giving praise to God. And look—it is now almost eight years, perhaps more, thank the Lord, since anything of that sort was so much as attempted. There are also many other proofs by which we have learned that in the end people show what the grand power of wise speech may achieve in them, by their groans rather than their shouting, and sometimes by their tears as well, to change their lives.

54. (141) Many people have been changed by the plain style of oratory too, though it is a change from ignorance to knowledge, or from finding something unbelievable to giving it credence. It does not change them into doing what they already knew they ought to do but were nonetheless reluctant to. Turning people away from that kind of obduracy requires the grand style. This is because when praise and criticism are uttered with eloquence, even though it is done in the moderate style, the effect it has on certain people is that they take delight in that praise or criticism, but at the same time they actually long to live in a praiseworthy way, and to shun living in a way that deserves criticism. Surely, though, not everyone who enjoys a speech seeks to conform to it? Just as in the grand style not everyone who is persuaded acts upon that persuasion, and in the plain style not everyone who is taught acquires comprehension or believes something to be true that they do not comprehend?

55. (142) This leads to the conclusion that what those two latter styles of speech aim to achieve is the most vital quality of all for those who want to speak wisely and eloquently in public. After all, what is argued in the moderate style, that is, letting the actual eloquence create delight, should not be appropriated for its own sake, but only so

honesteque dicuntur, si nec docente indigent eloquio nec movente, quia et scientes et faventes auditores habent, aliquanto promptius ex delectatione ipsa elocutionis accedat vel tenacius adherescat assensus.

(143) Nam cum eloquentiae sit universale officium, in quocumque istorum trium genere dicere apte ad persuasionem, finis autem, id quod intenderis persuadere dicendo, in quocumque istorum trium genere dicit quidem eloquens apte ad persuasionem, sed nisi persuadeat, ad finem non pervenit eloquentiae. Persuadet autem in summisso genere vera esse quae dicit, persuadet in grandi ut agantur quae agenda esse iam sciuntur nec aguntur; persuadet in genere temperato pulchre ornateque se dicere. Quo fine nobis quid opus est? (144) Appetant eum qui lingua gloriantur et se in panegyricis talibusque dictionibus iactant, ubi nec docendus nec ad aliquid agendum movendus, sed tantummodo est delectandus auditor. Nos vero istum finem referamus ad alterum finem, ut scilicet quod efficere volumus cum granditer dicimus, hoc etiam isto velimus, id est, ut bona morum diligantur vel devitentur mala, si ab hac actione non sic alieni sunt homines ut ad eam grandi genere dictionis videantur urgendi, aut si iam id agunt, ut agant studiosius atque in eo firmiter perseverent. Ita fit ut etiam temperati generis ornatu

that if the audience do not need eloquence to teach or to move them (in matters that are the subject of useful and honest discussion) because they are already well-informed and well-disposed, they reach an agreement somewhat more promptly, or make it stick more firmly, when helped by the actual delight of the eloquence.

(143) Now since it is the universal duty of eloquence, using any one of the three styles, to speak in a way that is persuasive, the aim is to speak in a way that persuades people to go your way: whichever of the three styles is used, an eloquent speaker speaks in a persuasive way, though if their persuasion fails, they have not achieved the aim of their eloquence. But they use the plain style to persuade people that the things they say are true; the grand style to persuade them to do things that they already know need doing (but they are not doing them); they use the moderate style to persuade them that they are speaking beautifully, and elegantly—but what use is that to us? (144) Those people who boast of having a talented tongue, who show off their party-piece panegyrics, which do not aim to teach listeners, or stir them to action, but only to tickle their fancy: let those sort of people run after that. As for us, let us apply that aim to this, namely that what we want to achieve with speech in the grand style, we should also want to achieve in this one. In other words, to love right behavior, and loathe bad behavior, as when people are not so far removed from taking action that they seem to need to be pressed—in the grand oratorical style—to do so; or, if they are already taking action, they should do so more enthusiastically and should persevere with determination. In such a case, we may use the artistry of the moderate style in a way that it is shrewd instead of

non iactanter, sed prudenter utamur; non eius fine contenti, quo tantummodo delectatur auditor, sed hoc potius agentes, ut etiam ipso ad bonum quod persuadere volumus adiuvetur.

56. (145) Illa itaque tria, quae supra posuimus, eum qui sapienter dicit, si etiam eloquenter vult dicere, id agere debere ut intellegenter, ut libenter, ut oboedienter audiatur, non sic accipienda sunt tamquam singula illis tribus dicendi generibus ita tribuantur, ut ad summissum intellegenter, ad temperatum libenter, ad grande pertineat oboedienter audiri, sed sic potius ut haec tria semper intendat et quantum potest agat, etiam cum in illorum singulo quoque versatur. Nolumus enim fastidiri etiam quod summisse dicimus, ac per hoc volumus non solum intellegenter verum etiam libenter audiri. (146) Quid autem agimus, divinis testimoniis docendo, quod dicimus, nisi ut oboedienter audiamur, id est, ut credatur eis, opitulante illo cui dictum est, "testimonia tua credita facta sunt valde"? Quid etiam quaerit nisi credi, qui aliquid licet summisso eloquio discentibus narrat? Et quis eum velit audire, nisi auditorem nonnulla etiam suavitate detineat? Nam si non intellegatur, quis nesciat nec libenter eum posse nec oboedienter audiri?

(147) Plerumque autem dictio ipsa summissa, dum solvit difficillimas quaestiones et inopinata manifestatione

---

188 Psalm 93:5.

swaggering. This shows that we are not content with the aim of merely pleasing our audience, but rather we are actively desirous of helping to persuade them into some good purpose.

56. (145) Someone who speaks wisely, but is also keen to speak eloquently, needs to use those three styles we have articulated in a way that means they are listened to with understanding, with goodwill, and with obedience. But those three styles must not be adopted as if each one of them had its own characteristic, as if the plain style was associated with understanding, the moderate style with goodwill, and the grand style with obedience. Rather, they should pay attention to all three at all times, and make active use of them as much as possible; even when mostly engaged with just one of them. We do not want what we say in the plain style (for example) to become boring, which is why we want to be heard not only with understanding but with enjoyment too when we use it. (146) Why do we drive home what we say by using the sacred witnesses in our teaching, if it is not to make people listen obediently, meaning that they should believe those texts, the Lord (of whom scripture says, "your witnesses have been made surpassingly trustworthy"[188]) being our helper? When someone tells their pupils a story, even if it is in the plain style of eloquence, what is their aim, if not to be believed? And who would wish to listen to that someone, if they failed to hold the listener's attention with an attractive style of speech? After all, if they are incomprehensible, it is plain for all to see that no one is going to listen to them with goodwill or obedience either.

(147) As for the plain style of delivery, yes, it does solve the toughest of questions, and delineates them with re-

demonstrat, dum sententias acutissimas de nescio quibus quasi cavernis unde non sperabatur eruit et ostendit, dum adversarii convincit errorem et docet falsum esse quod ab illo dici videbatur invictum; maxime quando adest eius quoddam decus non appetitum, sed quodammodo naturale, et nonnulla non iactanticula, sed quasi necessaria atque, ut ita dicam, ipsis rebus exorta numerositas clausularum, tantas acclamationes excitat ut vix intellegatur esse summissa. (148) Non enim quia neque incedit ornata neque armata, sed tamquam nuda congreditur, ideo non adversarium nervis lacertisque collidit, et obsistentem subruit ac destruit membris fortissimis falsitatem. Unde autem crebro et multum acclamatur ita dicentibus, nisi quia veritas sic demonstrata, sic defensa, sic invicta delectat? Et in hoc igitur genere summisso iste noster doctor et dictor id agere debet ut non solum intellegenter, verum etiam libenter et oboedienter audiatur.

57. (149) Illa quoque eloquentia generis temperati apud eloquentem ecclesiasticum nec inornata relinquitur nec indecenter ornatur. Nec solum hoc appetit ut delectet, quod solum apud alios profitetur, verum etiam in his quae laudat sive vituperat, istis appetendis vel firmius tenendis, illis autem devitandis vel respuendis, vult utique oboedienter audiri. Si autem non auditur intellegenter, nec libenter potest. Proinde illa tria, ut intellegant qui audiunt, ut delectentur, ut oboediant, etiam in hoc genere agendum est, ubi tenet delectatio principatum.

---

[189] *iactanticula*: perhaps Augustine's coinage. He uses it elsewhere: *C. Jul. imp.* 3.32; *Con. Acad.* 3.8.17.

[190] A metaphor as effective as it is unexpected.

markable clarity; and it unearths and exposes the most perceptive judgments, as if from some hopelessly dark hollows. And all the while it is proving its opponent wrong, and teaching that their seemingly invincible argument is mistaken, especially when it comes with a certain artistry that is not contrived but somehow natural, and a rhythmical quality to the cadences that is not mere showing-off[189] but has the appearance of being appropriate, and, as it were, arising naturally from the subject matter: in these cases it gives rise to such enthusiastic acclaim that it hardly makes sense to call it "plain." (148) Precisely because it proceeds without adornment or equipment, but sheds its clothing to get to grips with an opponent, it needs no sinewy muscles to wrestle an opponent: but demolishes resistance and crushes falsehood with the strength of its bare hands.[190] How come those who speak in this style frequently win great acclaim, if not because it is wonderful to see truth proved, defended, still unconquered? This, therefore, is how our teacher and speaker should press their case, to ensure that they are heard not just with understanding but with goodwill and obedience as well.

57. (149) In the same way, the Christian orator's eloquence in the moderate style is not left bare, nor is it overdecorated. He does not only seek to delight his audience, which is all that other orators lay claim to; without doubt, when praising or condemning something, he also wants his hearers to be obedient, whether they seek, or hold more firmly to, what he praises; or whether they shun and repudiate what he condemns. Yet if they do not understand what they hear, they can feel no goodwill toward it either. As a result, the three aims—that audiences understand, feel goodwill, and obey what they hear—are still the purpose of this moderate style, though enjoyment predominates.

58. (150) Iam vero ubi movere et flectere grandi genere[13] opus est auditorem (quod tunc est opus, quando et veraciter dici et suaviter confitetur et tamen non vult facere quod dicitur), dicendum est procul dubio granditer. Sed quis movetur si nescit quod dicitur? Aut quis tenetur ut audiat si non delectatur? Unde et in isto genere ubi ad oboedientiam cor durum dictionis granditate flectendum est, nisi et intellegenter et libenter qui dicit audiatur, non potest oboedienter audiri.

59. (151) Habet autem ut oboedienter audiamur quantacumque granditate dictionis maius pondus vita dicentis. Nam qui sapienter et eloquenter dicit, vivit autem nequiter, erudit quidem multos discendi studiosos, quamvis "animae suae sit inutilis," sicut scriptum est.[14] Unde ait apostolus, "sive occasione sive veritate Christus annuntietur." Christus autem veritas est, et tamen etiam non veritate annuntiari veritas potest, id est, ut pravo et fallaci corde quae recta et vera sunt praedicentur. Sic quippe annuntiatur Iesus Christus ab eis qui sua quaerunt, non quae Iesu Christi.

(152) Sed quoniam boni fideles non quemlibet hominum, sed ipsum dominum oboedienter audiunt, qui ait,

[13] grandi genere *del. RGr. ("clearly inappropriate")*

[14] est] est: scribae et pharisaei in cathedra Moysi sederunt; quae dicunt facite, quae autem faciunt facere nolite. Dicunt enim et non faciunt] *ϕ (vid. infr. §152)*

---

191 Sirach 37:19.

192 Philippians 1:18.

193 John 14:6.

194 The verb (*praedicentur*) shows that he has preachers in

58. (150) It certainly requires the grand style to move and sway listeners: and this is needed when they admit that a speech contains truth and makes enjoyable listening, but still they have no desire to do what they are being told to. Unquestionably the grand style is required for such a speech. But who is moved if they do not know what the orator is saying? And who keeping on listening if there is no delight in it? This is why, when a hard heart needs a speech in the grand style to persuade it, that style cannot make the listener obedient unless the speaker is also listened to with understanding and goodwill.

59. (151) It still holds true that if we are to be heard and obeyed when speaking in public, however grand our delivery may be, the impact of our way of life carries the greater weight. For when a person speaks with wisdom and eloquence, but lives an immoral life, certainly they can teach many who are eager to learn, but it "does their own soul no good at all," as it is written.[191] That is why the apostle says, "whether truly or feignedly, let Christ be proclaimed."[192] But Christ himself is Truth,[193] so even Truth can be proclaimed in an untrue way; in other words, what is righteous and true can be preached[194] from a heart that is vicious and deceitful. This explains how Jesus Christ is proclaimed by those "who promote their own good, not that of Jesus Christ."[195]

(152) It is the Lord himself, rather than some mere mortal, that good and faithful people are listening obedi-

mind; here the parallelism between the classical orator (*vir bonus dicendi peritus*) and Augustine's preacher (*vir ecclesiasticus*) comes to the fore.

195 Philippians 2:21.

"quae dicunt, facite; quae autem faciunt, facere nolite; dicunt enim et non faciunt," ideo audiuntur utiliter, etiam qui utiliter non agunt. Sua enim quaerere student, sed sua docere non audent, de loco scilicet superiore sedis ecclesiasticae quam sana doctrina constituit. Propter quod ipse dominus priusquam de talibus quod commemoravi diceret, praemisit, "cathedram Moysi sedent." Illa ergo cathedra, non eorum sed Moysi, cogebat eos bona dicere, etiam non bona facientes. Agebant ergo sua in vita sua; docere autem sua cathedra illos non permittebat aliena.

60. (153) Multis itaque prosunt dicendo quae non faciunt, sed longe pluribus prodessent faciendo quae dicunt. Abundant enim qui malae vitae suae defensionem ex ipsis suis praepositis et doctoribus quaerant, respondentes corde suo, aut etiam si ad hoc erumpunt ore suo atque dicentes, "quod mihi praecipis, cur ipse non facis?" Ita fit ut eum non oboedienter audiant, qui se ipse non audit, et dei verbum quod eis praedicatur simul cum ipso praedicatore contemnant. (154) Denique apostolus scribens ad Timotheum, cum dixisset, "nemo adulescentiam tuam contemnat," subiecit unde non contemneretur, atque ait, "sed forma esto fidelium in sermone, in conversatione, in dilectione, in fide, in castitate."

---

[196] Matthew 23:2.

[197] The chair (*kathedra* in Greek) from which bishops delivered authoritative judgments.

[198] Matthew 23:2.

[199] 1 Timothy 4:12.

ently to, when he says, "what they say, do; but what they do, refrain from doing; for they say things that they do not do."[196] For this reason, listening to them is worthwhile, even if such individuals' behavior is not. For they eagerly pursue personal advantage, but they are not reckless enough to risk advocating personal advantage; not from the supposedly superior place of an episcopal seat[197] that wholesome teaching has established. For this reason before the Lord himself said what I have quoted on the subject of those sort of people, he first remarked, "they sit on the seat of Moses."[198] So that chair did not belong to them but to Moses, and it was forcing them to speak what was good, even though what they did was not good. In their own lives, then, they were promoting their own interest; but that chair belonged to another, and it was not allowing them to teach what was their own.

60. (153) So by what they preach but do not practice, they still benefit many: but they would benefit far more by practicing what they preach. We are not short of people who try to find a defense for their own wrong way of life in the lives of their leaders and teachers, who respond in their own minds or even burst out with it and say to their faces, "why are you telling me to do something you are not doing yourself?" The result of this is that they do not listen obediently to someone who is not listening to their own advice: and then they reject the word of God that is being preached to them, along with the preacher himself. (154) To conclude: the apostle wrote to Timothy and said, "no one should reject you because of your youth," and then added a reason for not rejecting him, saying, "in your preaching, your behavior, your loving, your faith, and your purity, set an example for the faithful."[199]

61. (155) Talis doctor ut oboedienter audiatur, non impudenter non solum summisse ac temperate, verum etiam granditer dicit, quia non contemptibiliter vivit. Sic namque elegit bonam vitam ut etiam bonam non neglegat famam, sed provideat bonam coram deo et hominibus quantum potest, illum timendo, his consulendo. In ipso etiam sermone malit rebus placere quam verbis, nec existimet dici melius nisi quod dicitur verius, nec doctor verbis serviat, sed verba doctori. Hoc est enim quod ait apostolus, "non in sapientia verbi, ne evacuetur crux Christi."

(156) Ad hoc valet etiam quod ait ad Timotheum, "noli verbis contendere; ad nihil enim utile est, nisi in subversione audientium." Neque enim hoc ideo dictum est ut adversariis oppugnantibus veritatem nihil nos pro veritate dicamus. Et ubi erit quod, cum ostenderet qualis esse episcopus debeat, ait inter cetera, "ut potens sit in doctrina sana et contradicentes redarguere?" Verbis enim contendere est non curare quomodo error veritate vincatur, sed quomodo tua dictio dictioni praeferatur alterius. (157) Porro qui non verbis contendit, sive summisse sive temperate sive granditer dicat, id agit verbis ut veritas pateat, veritas placeat, veritas moveat, quoniam nec ipsa quae praecepti finis et plenitudo legis est caritas, ullo

---

200 2 Corinthians 7:21.

201 1 Corinthians 1:17.

202 2 Timothy 2:14.

203 Titus 1:9.

204 1 Timothy 1:5; Romans 13:10.

61. (155) To ensure that he is heard and obeyed, this teacher should make no apology for using the grand style, as well as the plain and the moderate styles, in public speaking, precisely because his way of life is not contemptible. Thus he chooses a life of goodness that does not neglect a reputation for goodness; he looks after that good reputation with God and mortals[200] as best he can, by fearing the former and heeding the latter. When it comes to his preaching, he prefers that his actions, rather than his words, should be found pleasing: he regards nothing as being said better unless that means it has been said more truly. As a teacher he is not the servant of words; the words serve him, the teacher. This is what the apostle says, "not with words of wisdom, lest the cross of Christ be rendered null and void."[201]

(156) Another effective instance is what he says to Timothy, "do not engage in verbal disputation, which is no use for anything except undermining those who hear you."[202] Not that he said this to prevent us from speaking up for truth when our enemies attack it. Where would that leave what he said when he had to show what kind of man a bishop ought to be: (among other things) that he should be "effective in sound teaching, and in refuting those who argue against it"?[203] After all, verbal disputation is all about getting people to support your performance over someone else's, not about caring how error is overcome by the truth. (157) Furthermore, someone who says no to verbal disputation, whether they speak in the plain, the moderate or the grand style, is still using words to make a case so as to reveal truth, make truth acceptable, promote truth. For love itself, which is the real teaching of the law, and its fullest expression,[204] cannot possibly be righteous,

modo esse recta potest, si ea quae diliguntur non vera, sed falsa sunt. Sicut autem cuius pulchrum corpus et deformis est animus, magis dolendus est quam si deforme haberet et corpus, ita qui eloquenter ea quae falsa sunt dicunt magis miserandi, quam si talia deformiter dicerent.

(158) Quid est ergo non solum eloquenter, verum etiam sapienter dicere, nisi verba in summisso genere sufficientia, in temperato splendentia, in grandi vehementia, veris tamen rebus, quas audiri oporteat, adhibere? Sed qui utrumque non potest, dicat sapienter quod non dicit eloquenter, potius quam dicat eloquenter quod dicit insipienter. {61.} (159) Si autem ne hoc quidem potest, ita conversetur ut non solum sibi praemium comparet, sed et praebeat aliis exemplum et sit eius quasi copia dicendi forma vivendi.

62. (160) Sunt sane quidam qui bene pronuntiare possunt, quid autem pronuntient excogitare non possunt. Quod si ab aliis sumant eloquenter sapienterque conscriptum memoriaeque commendent atque ad populum proferant; si eam personam gerunt, non improbe faciunt. Etiam sic enim, quod profecto utile est, multi praedicatores veritatis fiunt nec multi magistri, si unius veri magistri idipsum dicant omnes et non sint in eis schismata. Nec deterrendi sunt isti voce Ieremiae prophetae, per quem deus arguit eos qui "furantur verba eius, unusquisque a prox-

205 1 Corinthians 1:10.
206 Jeremiah 23:30.

if that love is bestowed on things that are not true, but false instead. It ought to be more upsetting that someone has a misshapen mind in a shapely body, than if the body and the mind were both misshapen; in the same way as those who speak untruths with eloquence are more to be pitied than if their delivery were as misshapen as the content of their words.

(158) To speak not just with eloquence but with wisdom as well, we must make use of words that are adequate (for the plain style), vivid (for the moderate style), and powerful (for the grand style): and use them for subject matter that is true, and that people really need to hear. But if a person cannot manage both eloquence and wisdom, they should speak wisely where eloquence fails them, rather than speaking eloquently where wisdom fails them. {61.} (159) If they can manage neither of these, though, they ought to conduct themselves in a way that not only wins them their reward, but also provides an example to others, and to let the pattern of their life be itself an eloquent testimony, so to speak.

62. (160) Of course there are people who can deliver a speech well, but who cannot dream up their own subject matter. But if they take someone else's wise, eloquent composition and memorize it, then deliver it before the people, they are doing nothing improper in playing that role. There is also the fact (and this is a definite advantage) that many become preachers of truth but not many become teachers of it, provided that those teachers all speak alike of the one truth, and there is no discord among them.[205] They are not to be discouraged by the words of the prophet Jeremiah, by which God reproved those who "steal his words, each and every one, from his neighbor."[206]

imo suo." (161) Qui enim furantur, alienum auferunt, verbum autem dei non est ab eis alienum, qui obtemperant ei; potiusque ille dicit aliena qui, cum dicat bene, vivit male. Quaecumque enim bona dicit, eius excogitari videntur ingenio, sed ab eius moribus aliena sunt. Eos itaque dixit deus furari verba sua, qui boni volunt videri loquendo quae dei sunt, cum mali sint faciendo quae sua sunt. Nec sane ipsi dicunt bona quae dicunt, si diligenter attendas. Quomodo enim dicunt verbis quod negant factis? Non enim frustra de talibus ait apostolus, "confitentur se nosse deum, factis autem negant." Modo ergo quodam ipsi dicunt et rursus alio modo non ipsi dicunt, quoniam utrumque verum est quod veritas ait.

(162) De talibus enim loquens, "quae dicunt," inquit, "facite; quae autem faciunt, facere nolite." Hoc est, quod ex ore illorum auditis, facite; quod in opere videtis, facere nolite; "dicunt enim," inquit, "et non faciunt." Ergo quamvis non faciant, dicunt tamen. Sed alio loco tales arguens, "hypocritae, inquit, quomodo potestis bona loqui, cum sitis mali?" Ac per hoc, et ea quae dicunt, quando bona dicunt, non ipsi dicunt, voluntate scilicet atque opere negando quod dicunt. (163) Unde contingit ut homo di-

---

[207] Titus 1:16.

[208] That is, if it is said in scripture, it must contain truth (personified, as elsewhere; John 14:6).

[209] Truth personified, i.e., Christ.

[210] Matthew 23:3.

[211] *hypocritae*: see p. 468, n. 147.

[212] Matthew 12:34.

(161) Thieves take what is not their own, whereas the word of God belongs to those who obey him. The person who really speaks what does not belong to them is one who speaks well but lives badly. Whatever they say that is good seems to be the composition of their own intelligence, and is at odds with their actual behavior. This is why God has said that they have stolen his words, because they want to appear good by saying what is properly God's, though in reality they are bad because they do their own thing. And if you pay close attention, it is not actually they who are saying the good things that they say. For how can they be saying in words what they contradict by their actions? The apostle had a point when he said of such people, "they confess that they know God, but their actions contradict that claim."[207] In one way they are saying it; but in another way they are not saying it: for both these things that Truth has said are true.[208]

(162) He[209] spoke about such people, saying, "do what they say, but do not do what they do."[210] This means that you should do what you hear coming from their mouth, but not do what you see in their actions: for, he says, "they say but do not do." So although they do not do it, still they are saying it. Yet elsewhere he reproves them: "you hypocrites,[211] how can you speak what is good when you yourselves are bad?"[212] By this criterion, even when they say something that is good, it is not they who are saying it, precisely because their motivations[213] and actions cancel out what they say. (163) As a result, a skilled speaker who

213 *voluntas*: the faculty of intentional choice. See p. 270, n. 123.

sertus et malus sermonem quo veritas praedicetur dicendum ab alio non diserto sed bono ipse componat. Quod cum fit, ipse a seipso tradit alienum, ille ab alieno accipit suum. Cum vero boni fideles bonis fidelibus hanc operam commodant, utrique sua dicunt, quia et deus ipsorum est cuius sunt illa quae dicunt, et ea sua faciunt, quae non ipsi componere potuerunt, qui secundum illa composite vivunt.

63. (164) Sive autem apud populum vel apud quoslibet iam iamque dicturus, sive quod apud populum dicendum vel ab eis qui voluerint aut potuerint legendum est dictaturus, oret ut deus sermonem bonum det in os eius. Si enim regina oravit Esther, pro suae gentis temporaria salute locutura apud regem, ut in os eius deus congruum sermonem daret, quanto magis orare debet ut tale munus accipiat, qui pro aeterna hominum salute in verbo et doctrina laborat? (165) Illi vero qui ea dicturi sunt quae ab aliis acceperunt, et antequam accipiant orent pro eis a quibus accipiunt ut eis detur quod per eos accipere volunt, et cum acceperint orent ut bene et ipsi proferant et illi ad quos proferunt sumant, et de prospero exitu dictionis eidem gratias agant, a quo id se accepisse non dubitant, ut "qui gloriatur in illo glorietur" in cuius manu sunt et nos et sermones nostri.

---

[214] A play on two forms/senses of the verb *componere*: "compose" and "composed/orderly." [215] Esther 14:13: from the Septuagint additions to the Hebrew text of the book (verse numbering varies in different translations). [216] 1 Timothy 5:17.

[217] Plural in Latin (*illi*); but singularized in English to avoid confusion of pronouns.

[218] 1 Corinthians 1:31; Wisdom 7:16.

is immoral may compose a sermon that proclaims the truth, for someone less skilled, but more moral, to deliver. When this occurs, that skilled person is handing on from himself what is not his own, while the unskilled person receives what is truly their own from someone it does not belong to. Still, when good people of faith provide this service for other good people of faith, what both parties say is what belongs to them. This is because the things they say belong to their God, and what they themselves have been unable to compose, they make their own, by living in accordance with it, just as they ought.[214]

63. (164) When a person is just on the point of speaking before the people, or before some group, or when they are about to dictate something for speaking before the people, or for reading aloud by some willing and able person; they must ask God, in prayer, to put good speech into their mouth. For if Queen Esther prayed that God would give her the right words when she was about to speak before a king in defense of her own people's earthly well-being,[215] how much more is prayer required for such a gift of words from God when one is striving, by the words of one's teaching,[216] in defense of people's eternal salvation? (165) Certainly one[217] who is about to speak what others have given him should pray, before receiving it, for those people who are giving it to him, that what he wants to receive from them he does indeed receive. Then, when he has received it, he should pray for himself to deliver it well, and for those listening to adopt it; and give thanks to God for a successful conclusion to his speaking, for he is in no doubt that God is the source of this gift, so that "anyone who boasts, let them boast" in the one who "holds us, and our preaching, in his hand."[218]

64. (166) Longior evasit liber hic quam volebam quamque putaveram. Sed legenti vel audienti cui gratus est, longus non est. Cui autem longus est, per partes eum legat qui habere vult cognitum. Quem vero cognitionis eius piget, de longitudine non queratur. Ego tamen deo nostro gratias ago, quod in his quattuor libris non qualis ego essem, cui multa desunt, sed qualis esse debeat qui in doctrina sana, id est christiana, non solum sibi sed aliis etiam laborare studet, quantulacumque potui facultate disserui.

64. (166) This book has turned out longer than I was intending, or had expected. But if a person enjoys reading or hearing it, it is not long at all. Anyone who does find it long, but who wants to understand the subject, needs to read it in sections. But if someone cannot be bothered with understanding it, they should not grumble about how long it is. Nonetheless, I thank our God that in these four books I have used whatever ability I have, however modest it may be,[219] to explore not the kind of person I am, for I have many failings, but the kind of person one needs to be to dedicate oneself—not only for one's own good, but for others also—to work on sound teaching, in other words, on teaching Christianity.

219 A closing echo of Cicero, *quantulacumque est facultate* (*De or.* 1.135).

INDEX OF PERSONS AND PLACES

References to the Preface and the Introductions are by page number; references to the translation and notes for *The Teacher* are by chapter and paragraph number, and for *Teaching Christianity*, by book, chapter, and paragraph number.

Abraham, *TC* 1.2.4, 2.23.57, 3.19.45, 3.44.98, 4.12.35, 4.13.39, 4.39.107, 4.39.108n127, 4.48.126

Adam, *TC* 1.13.30n52, 3.27.62n93

Adeodatus, *TT passim*; 118

Africa/African, *TT* 2.4; 160, 171; *TC* 2.26.66n103, 4.12.35n38, 4.24.65, 4.43.121n152

Alypius, 5

Ambrose (bishop of Milan), xiii–xv; *TT* 4.8n39; 155, 175, 180; *TC* 2.30.75n122, 2.43.107, 2.56.137n197, 2.61.146n214, 4.46.127, 4.48.129–30

Anselm, *TC* 1.7.16n33

Antony of Egypt, 186; *TC* Pr.4.7

Aristophanes of Byzantium, 182

Aristotle, 153, 160, 162, 182; *TC* 1.13.27n48, 2.25.64n96, 3.47.106n163

Athens, 160, 162, 175

Carthage, xi, xv, 7, 188; *TC* Pr.5.11n14, 2.38.97

Cassiciacum, 5–6

Catiline, 178

Cato, 163

Christ. *See* Jesus

Cicero, xii, 3; *TT* 5.16; 153, 157, 159, 163–64, 174, 177–80, 182; *TC* 1.1.1n1, 1.2.5n18, 1.19.37n70, 1.35.75n103, 2.51.126n184, 4.4.8n6, 4.6.14n11, 4.7.17n12, 4.18.54n64, 4.21.60n68, 4.24.64n72, 4.31.84n88, 4.64.166n219

Cornelius, *TC* Pr.6.12

Cyprian, 180; *TC* Pr.5.11n14, Pr.6.12n18, 2.4.7n9, 2.61.146, 4.12.38n38, 4.31.84–85, 4.32.87n91, 4.43.121n152,

4.45.125, 4.47.128, 4.48.130, 4.49.131n177

David, *TC* 2.13.27, 2.62.150n230, 3.30.67–31.72, 4.16.49, 4.19.55–56

Epicurean/Epicureanism, 11; *TT* 13.41; *TC* Pr.5.11n14
Esau, *TC* 2.33.82, 3.19.46
Eugippius, 189; *TC* 2.62.149n226
Eve, *TC* 1.13.29n52, 3.27.62n93

Faustus, xiii–xiv

Greek (language/nationality), 2, 9, 11; *TT* 5.15–16, 6.18, 7.20n82; 152, 168n15, 182; *TC* Pr.5.9, 1.35.75n102–3, 2.15.33n42, 2.16.34–36, 2.18.41–42, 2.20.49, 2.22.53, 2.23.56–57, 2.28.71n116, 2.37.93, 2.43.107, 2.59.141n203, 2.61.146, 3.7.14–8.19, 3.17.39, 3.27.62n93, 3.40.87–88, 4.11.31–32, 4.13.36, 4.37.102n120, 4.40.114, 4.41.116n140

Hannibal, *TC* 1.3.7n19
Hippo, 4, 158, 188; *TC* 1.6.14n31
Homeric, 183

Irenaeus, *TC* 1.8.19n37, 1.13.29n52, 2.42.105n155, 3.45.101n149, 3.52.122n194
Isaac, *TC* 1.2.4n16

Jacob, *TC* 1.2.4, 2.33.83, 2.34.85
Jeremiah, 155, 175; *TC* 2.43.108, 3.17.41, 3.51.121
Jerome, 179–80; *TC* 2.60.145n213, 4.15.48, 4.41.116
Jerusalem, 160, 162, 175, 179; *TC* 1.31.67, 2.26.67n106, 2.63.151, 3.10.23, 3.10.24n48–11.25n49, 3.47.107, 4.39.107
Jesus, ix, 14; *TT* 1.2, 5.14, 11.38; 160, 166, 170, 175, 179; *TC* Pr.5.11, 1.1.1n2, 1.2.4n16, 1.8.17n34, 1.11.23n39, 1.12.26n47, 1.13.29–30, 1.25.53, 1.27.57n85, 1.33.72, 1.38.81, 2.6.11, 2.24.59, 2.43.107–8, 2.49.119, 2.50.122, 2.52.128, 2.58.139, 2.62.147–50, 3.4.6–6.12, 3.8.18, 3.17.40, 3.36.79, 3.44.98–99, 3.46.104, 3.47.108, 3.48.113, 3.49.115–18, 3.55.131, 4.12.35, 4.13.39, 4.13.43, 4.32.90, 4.39.108–9, 4.40.113, 4.43.121–23, 4.45.126–47.128, 4.49.131, 4.59.151, 4.61.155; as Teacher, 13, 16, 21; *TT* 1.2, 12.40
Jew/Jewish/Judean, 170; *TC* Pr.5.10n13, 2.17.39, 2.25.65n100, 2.29.73n119, 2.42.105, 2.43.108n161,

3.10.22–24, 3.17.40, 3.36.81, 4.10.29n24, 4.12.34–35, 4.13.39, 4.30.81
Julian of Eclanum, 156n6

Lucian, *TT* 3.6

Monnica, xi–xii, 5
Moses, *TC* Pr.7.15, 1.2.4, 2.13.26, 2.13.28n36, 2.16.36n47, 2.25.62, 2.25.65, 2.61.146, 4.39.108n127, 4.59.152

Noah, *TC* 3.53.126, 4.39.107n125, 4.45.126

Origen, 164, 170, 182–85

Paul (the apostle)/Pauline, *TT* 1.2, 5.14–15; 155, 180, 185; *TC* Pr.5.11–6.12, 1.25.53, 1.31.66, 1.32.70, 1.36.78, 1.38.81, 2.15.33, 2.35.88, 2.49.119, 2.50.122, 3.4.7, 3.46.105, 4.15.46, 4.33.90, 4.39.107, 4.39.109
Persius, *TT* 9.28
Peter, *TC* Pr.6.12
Philip (the apostle), *TC* Pr.7.14
Plato/Platonist, 3, 6–10, 14; *TT* 11.37n119, 13.43n135; 128, 153, 155, 157, 159–62, 175, 182; *TC* 1.5.10n24, 1.13.27.48, 1.42.91n126, 2.43.107–8, 2.60.144
Porphyry, *TC* 1.24.49n80
pseudo-Longinus, 163
Punic, *TT* 13.44

Quintilian, *TT* 1.1; 153, 163, 185n31, 187n33; *TC* 1.35.75.n103, 2.15.33n42, 3.6.12n17, 3.7.14n21, 3.8.17n29, 3.40.89n136, 3.48.112n178, 4.11.31n30, 4.13.43n45, 4.21.60n68

Satan (the Devil/ Enemy), 179; *TC* Pr.5.11, 1.13.29, 1.25.51, 2.36.91, 3.36.79, 3.42.92, 3.55.131–33
Socrates, 7, 10
Solomon, 155; *TC* 2.63.151, 3.31.72, 3.45.101, 3.47.108
Stoics/Stoicism, 11, 160–61

Tacitus, 153
Terence, *TT* 4.9
Tertullian, 160; *TC* 2.30.74n120, 2.35.88n137, 2.36.90n139, 3.24.55n77, 3.45.100n147, 4.43.121n152, 4.49.131n177
Ticonius, 156, 164, 171–72; *TC* 2.26.66n103, 3.42.92, 3.50.117, 3.51.120, 3.52.122
Tyndale, William, *TC* 1.31.66n93

Verecundus, 5
Verres, 178
Virgil, 12; *TC* 2.56.136, 4.6.14n10, 4.42.119n143

Wittgenstein, Ludwig, 2, 17, 186; *TC* 4.35.97n115

INDEX OF SUBJECTS

References to the Preface and the Introductions are by page number; references to the translation and notes for *The Teacher* are by chapter and paragraph number, and for *Teaching Christianity*, by book, chapter, and paragraph number.

actor(s). *See* pantomime
Aeneid, 12; *TT* 2.3n19
allegory, 168, 170–71; *TC* 2.58.140n200, 3.17.41, 3.40.88, 4.39.107
ambiguity, 12; *TT* 5.16n65, 8.22; 169, 171; *TC* 1.34.73, 2.7.10, 2.14.31, 2.16.34, 2.18.41, 2.20.48, 2.21.50, 2.59.143, 2.63.151, 3.1.1–2.4, 3.4.6–7, 3.5.9–6.10, 3.7.14, 3.8.17–9.20, 3.39.86, 3.41.91, 3.24.65
anacephalaiōsis. *See* recapitulation
angels, 168; *TC* Pr.6.12–7.14, 1.22.44, 1.31.66, 1.33.71, 1.36.77, 2.35.87, 3.42.94, 3.55.132, 4.33.94, 4.36.100, 4.39.109, 4.42.119, 4.43.121, 4.44.124, 4.46.127

Bible/biblical. *See* scripture(s)
book(s), as objects, 153–54, 161, 188; *TC* Pr.4.8, Pr.5.11n15, 2.16.35, 4.1.1n2
Book of Rules, 164, 172; *TC* 3.43.95

canon/canonical, *TT* 11.37n120; 155, 168, 173, 182; *TC* 2.12.24–27, 3.42.94, 4.4.9, 4.9.25, 4.21.60
catholic/catholicity xiii–xiv, 164; *TC* 2.12.24, 2.26.67n109, 3.15.36, 3.46.103n157
Catilinarian Orations, 177
Church, 155, 160, 164; *TC* 1.14.32–15.33, 1.17.35, 1.25.53, 2.6.11–12, 2.25.65, 2.49.120, 2.58.139, 3.2.3, 3.44.99–45.100, 3.47.108, 3.49.115, 3.51.121, 3.55.131, 4.22.61, 4.30.81, 4.33.90, 4.36.100, 4.47.128
City of God, 4n4, 15, 157, 159; *TC* 3.47.106

color(s), *TT* 3.5, 5.12, 7.19, 12.39; *TC* 4.49.131, 4.50.132
commemoration/remembrance, *TT* 1.1–2, 4.7, 7.19–20; *TC* 2.24.60, 2.26.67, 2.46.112, 3.45.102, 3.52.123, 4.30.81, 4.45.126
commentary, 13, 156, 183
Confessions, x–xv, 3, 5–6, 9, 13, 20; *TT* 10.31n105, 10.32n107; 152, 157, 163, 165, 186; *TC* 1.3.7n21, 1.7.15n32, 1.12.26n45, 1.19.37n70, 1.30.64n92, 2.4.5n3, 2.6.10n14, 2.32.78n127, 2.35.87n135, 2.40.102n153, 2.59.141n203, 3.15.35n57, 3.26.60n86, 3.36.80nn117–18, 3.47.106n163, 4.5.12n9, 4.19.55n65, 4.40.113n134, 4.43.121n148
content. *See* form/content
Contra academicos, 6
Cratylus, 182

definition, *TT* 8.24, 13.43; *TC* 1.2.5n18, 2.53.129–31, 2.55.133
delivery x, xiv, 152–53; *TC* 3.41.90n139, 4.4.11, 4.5.13, 4.13.40–14.41, 4.42.118, 4.51.134–35, 4.56.147, 4.58.150, 4.61.157
De musica, 11, 21; *TC* 1.8.17n34
De principiis, 164, 185n30
De pulchro et apto, 5
deaf persons, *TT* 3.5, 7.19, 13.44
dialogue, philosophical, 3, 5; *TT* 1.1, 3.5, 7.19, 8.22; 161; *TC* 1.2.6n18, 4.23.63, 4.37.102
difficulty hypothesis, 185; *TC* 4.9.27n23
discovery (*inventio*), 165; *TC* 1.1.1, 4.9.27
Div. quaest., *TC* 1.25.55n84, 1.41.91n126, 2.32.78n127, 2.60.144n211
Donatism/Donatist, 156; *TC* 4.41.116n139. *See also* Ticonius *in Index of Persons and Places*

eloquence, xii, xiv, 154, 162–63, 169, 172, 174, 176–78, 180–81; *TC* 2.54.132, 4.4.7–5.12, 4.7.16–18, 4.8.24n20, 4.9.26–12.35, 4.14.44–15.48, 4.17.51–52, 4.21.59–60, 4.23.63, 4.26.72, 4.27.74–29.80, 4.30.82, 4.31.84–32.87, 4.37.102, 4.40.114, 4.44.122–24, 4.48.130, 4.54.141–56.145, 4.57.149, 4.59.151, 4.61.157–58
enjoy/enjoyment, *TT* 12.40; 153, 165–66; *TC* 1.3.7–5.10, 1.20.39–21.41, 1.28.60, 1.30.64, 1.33.71–72, 1.35.75–37.80, 1.39.84, 2.11.23, 3.16.37
exegesis/exegetical, 156–57, 171, 173, 181, 183–84; *TC* 1.38.82n115, 2.24.59n82, 2.25.64n98, 4.15.48, 4.45.126n161

figurative language, 3–4, 17, 164, 167–68, 170–73, 184; *TC* 1.17.35n64, 1.37.80n109, 2.7.12n19, 2.15.33, 2.17.38, 2.23.57–24.59, 2.26.66, 2.62.149n223, 3.1.2n5, 3.9.20–21, 3.14.33–15.35, 3.17.39–18.43, 3.20.47, 3.21.50, 3.23.54–26.60, 3.32.73–76, 3.56.133–34, 4.15.48
form/content, 166–67, 173–74

gesture(s), *TT* 3.6, 4.7–8, 7.19, 10.32n111, 10.34; *TC* 2.4.5, 2.38.96

heresy/heretic, 160, 172; *TC* 2.26.67n110, 2.53.129, 3.3.5, 3.43.97, 3.46.103
hermeneutic/hermeneutical, 153, 155, 157, 164, 166, 171, 173, 183, 185; *TC* 2.7.12n19
history, literary/historical, *TT* 11.37, 162, 168, 171, 175; *TC* 2.13.27, 2.42.105–43.107, 2.44.109, 2.50.121, 2.58.140n200, 3.15.36
Hortensius, xii, 6, 163, 178

imitation, literary, 162, 166–67; *TC* 2.55.135n192, 4.42.142
intention, authorial, 171; *TC* 1.40.86, 1.41.89
inventio. *See* discovery

language(s), x, 2–5, 11, 17; *TT* 5.15–6.18, 13.44; 159, 164n11, 168–69, 171–72, 174, 179, 183–87; *TC* Pr.5.9–10, Pr.7.14, 1.37.80n109, 2.5.8n11, 2.6.9, 2.7.12n19, 2.16.34–36, 2.17.39, 2.18.41, 2.19.43, 2.21.50, 2.23.57–58, 2.37.92–93, 2.40.104, 2.47.116, 2.56.137n197, 2.59.141, 3.1.1, 3.7.15, 3.8.17, 3.9.19, 3.40.87, 3.50.118, 3.53.126–27, 4.10.28, 4.15.48, 4.24.65, 4.31.84, 4.46.127
learning, x–xv, 6, 9–10, 13, 15–17; *TT* 1.1–2, 10.29–11.37, 12.39–40, 13.43, 13.45–14.46; 153, 156, 160, 169, 175, 186; *TC* Pr.4.7, 2.9.16, 2.21.52, 2.58.139–40, 2.60.144n208, 2.61.147, 4.4.7, 4.11.33, 4.26.72–73
letter(s), of alphabet, xi; *TT* 4.7, 5.11, 5.14, 6.17n69, 7.20, 9.25; 167, 182–85; *TC* Pr.3.6–4.7, Pr.9.18, 2.19.45, 2.28.71, 2.37.93–94, 2.40.103n151, 3.7.14, 3.9.20, 3.13.30, 3.40.88, 3.46.103, 3.48.112
light (figurative), 15; *TT* 10.32, 11.38, 12.39–40; 179; *TC* 1.9.20, 1.22.45, 2.11.21–22, 2.14.31, 3.9.21, 3.21.52, 3.43.95, 3.45.102
literal, 156, 164n11, 168, 170, 182, 184; *TC* Pr.6.12n20, 1.2.4n10, 2.19.43n61, 3.2.3, 3.8.17, 3.9.20–21, 3.14.33, 3.20.47–21.50, 3.23.54, 3.25.58, 3.26.60, 3.32.73–33.76, 3.39.86, 3.41.91, 3.56.134

love, *TT* 8.21, 14.46; 153n1, 157–58, 166, 170; *TC* Pr.6.12, Pr.7.13, 1.3.7–4.8, 1.14.31–32, 1.15.33n63, 1.20.40–23.47, 1.25.51, 1.26.54–29.61, 1.30.63–34.74, 1.37.79–80, 1.39.85–40.86, 1.41.88

Manichaeism, xiii–xiv, 163
memory, 10; *TT* 5.12, 7.20, 12.39, 13.42–43; 155, 159; *TC* 1.12.26n45, 2.14.30–31, 2.21.51, 2.27.68
Meno, 7–9
metaphor/metaphorical, *TT* 1.2n15; 164, 167, 172, 182, 186; *TC* 1.2.4nn10–11, 1.3.7n20, 1.16.34n64, 2.15.32n42, 2.25.62, 2.47.116, 3.1.2, 3.25.58, 3.40.89, 3.56.133–34
mimesis. *See* imitation
motivation/motive, x, 166, 175, 186; *TC* 3.18.43n66, 3.19.46, 3.27.61n87, 4.62.162

name-word (noun), *TT* 4.8–6.18, 7.20, 8.23–9.28, 10.33, 11.36–37, 13.43; *TC* 1.5.10, 3.40.88
neighbor, *TC* 1.31.69–33.72

On the Sublime, 163

pagan/paganism, *TT* 9.28n102, 14.46n140; 152, 160, 169, 173–82; *TC* 2.6.11n17, 2.29.73n119, 2.32.78n127, 2.32.80n132, 2.49.120n182, 2.58.139n198, 2.58.140, 2.60.144n208, 2.61.147, 3.10.27n50, 3.13.32, 4.2.3, 4.7.16n14, 4.10.28, 4.24.64n72, 4.41.116n140, 4.46.127n164
pantomime, *TT* 3.5, 4.6, 7.19; *TC* 2.38.96
paradox, 8–10, 12, 16; *TT* 5.13n55, 5.14n60; *TC* 1.2.4n11, 3.22.53n76
Pelagian/Pelagianism, 156–57; *TC* 3.46.103
person, inner, 14–16; *TT* 1.2, 11.38–13.45; 152
philosophy, xiii; *TT* 8.22n88; 160–61, 174; *TC* 1.2.6n18, 2.49.120n182, 2.55.133
Platonism/Platonist, 6, 163, 167; *TC* 1.5.10n24, 2.43.107
Poetics, 162, 182
polity, 159; *TC* 2.39.100, 3.47.106–7
preach/preaching/preacher, 156, 158, 166, 173–74, 191; *TC* Pr.5.11, 3.54.130, 4.12.34, 4.22.62, 4.25.67–69, 4.33.91, 4.35.98n116, 4.37.103–38.104, 4.44.122, 4.59.151–61.155, 4.62.160, 4.63.165
proposition, *TT* 5.16, 7.20; 8.22n88; *TC* 2.22.56n78, 2.43.107, 2.49.119–20, 2.50.122–52.128

reason/reasoning, 12; *TT* 2.4n24, 4.9, 5.14–15, 6.18, 7.20, 8.24, 10.31, 12.39–40; 168–69; *TC* Pr.3.5n7,

1.5.10n25, 2.48.117, 2.49.119–50.121, 2.58.140, 2.59.143–60.144, 3.39.86, 3.42.93, 4.3.4
recapitulation (*anacephalaiōsis*), *TC* 1.13.29n52, 1.32.70, 3.42.92, 3.52.122–23, 3.54.129–30
Republic, of Plato, 159
Retractations, 6, 20–21, 154, 156–57, 188
revelation, 16, 153, 164; *TC* Pr.2.4, Pr.4.8, 3.10.23, 3.17.40
rhetoric, 17; *TT* 3.5n27; 152–54, 161–63, 165, 172–77, 180, 182; *TC* 1.1.1n1, 1.2.6n18, 1.13.30n55, 2.54.132, 3.48.111n174, 3.50.117n188, 3.56.133, 4.1.1 *passim*
Rhetoric, 182
rule of faith, 184; *TC* 1.8.19, 3.2.4–5, 4.40.112
rule of truth. *See* rule of faith

sacrament(s), 15, 170; *TC* Pr.6.12, 1.39.85n121, 2.4.7, 2.62.150, 3.13.31, 3.45.101, 4.45.125
sarabara, *TT* 10.33–35, 11.37
scripture(s), xii, 5, 14–15; *TC passim*
senses/sense perception, 17; *TT* 3.5, 4.7, 12.39; 162–63, 187; *TC* 1.7.15, 1.8.17, 2.1.1, 2.4.5–7, 2.41.104, 2.48.117, 2.58.140, 4.17.51, 4.41.115n138
sentence(s), *TT* 5.16; 185; *TC* 2.19.44n62, 2.20.49, 2.22.56, 3.4.7n12, 3.7.15, 3.24.57, 4.11.32, 4.13.36, 4.18.54, 4.40.114n135
signifiable, *TT* 4.8, 8.22
significate, *TT* 4.8
signs/signifying/signification, 2, 4, 6, 11–15; *TT* 1.2–11.37, 13.42–14.46; 156, 165, 167, 169, 184–87; *TC* 1.2.4–6, 1.44.95, Books 2–3 *passim*, 4.20.57, 4.25.67–68, 4.41.115, 4.45.126
singing, *TT* 1.1, 7.19, 13.42; *TC* 1.3.7n21, 2.27.70
sound, 11–12, 14; *TT* 1.1–2, 2.3, 3.5, 5.12–14, 6.17–18, 7.20, 8.22–23, 9.25, 10.34, 11.36–12.39, 13.44; 167; *TC* 1.6.14, 1.12.26, 1.28.59, 2.4.5, 2.19.44, 2.27.70, 2.37.93, 3.40.89, 3.41.90, 4.16.50, 4.19.55
soul, 15, 16n21; *TT* 1.2, 11.38, 13.41; *TC* Pr.7.15, 1.14.31n56, 1.16.34n63, 1.18.36, 1.20.39, 1.21.42–43, 1.22.46, 1.24.48–50, 1.27.57, 1.28.60, 1.42.91, 2.10.18, 2.11.21, 2.25.64, 2.35.88, 2.62.148, 3.9.20, 3.17.40, 3.22.54n75, 3.30.68, 4.32.87, 4.33.95, 4.59.151
styles, oratorical, xii, xiv, 180, 182; *TC* 2.54.132, 4.4.10, 4.15.48, 4.19.55, 4.22.62, 4.25.67, 4.27.74–75, 4.28.77–31.85, 4.38.104–39.107,

4.40.111, 4.42.118–58.150, 4.61.155–58

teacher, *TT* 5.13, 9.25–26, 10.29, 13.45–14.46; 177; *TC* 2.61.146, 3.10.22–23, 3.40.87, 4.8.22, 4.14.45, 4.15.48, 4.21.60, 4.23.63–25.67, 4.29.78, 4.33.90–94, 4.35.98, 4.37.102–38.104, 4.39.110, 4.41.115, 4.50.132, 4.56.148, 4.60.153, 4.61.155–62.160
teacher, inner (God/Christ), 9; *TC* Pr.8.17
theater, *TT* 3.5, 10.32; *TC* 1.30.64, 2.28.71, 2.38.97
theology/theological, 2, 6–7, 16–17, 153, 157–58, 166, 172–73, 183, 184; *TC* Pr.2.3n7, 1.3.7n19, 1.8.19n37, 1.13.29n52, 1.25.53n84, 2.25.64n94, 2.43.108, 3.44.98n144, 3.46.104n158, 3.52.122n194, 3.52.123n199, 4.50.132n182
things (contrasted with "signs"), 8, 10–13; *TT* 2.3–4, 3.6–4.9, 5.15, 7.19–20, 9.26–10.31, 12.39, 13.42–44; 156, 165, 185, 187; *TC* 1.2.4–5, Books 2–3 *passim*
Topica, *TC* 1.2.6n18
Trinity, 13, 166; *TC* 1.5.10–12, 1.10.22, 1.37.80, 1.38.83, 2.10.20–11.21, 2.25.63, 2.26.65, 3.3.5, 3.44.98n144, 4.38.105
trope(s), *TC* 2.15.33n42, 3.40.87–89, 3.41.91
truth, xiv, 10, 15–16; *TT* 7.20, 8.21, 10.31, 11.38–13.42, 13.45–14.46; *TC* Pr.7.15, Pr.8.17, 1.38.81–82, 2.11.23–12.24, 2.17.40, 2.28.72, 2.49.120–52.127, 2.53.131, 2.55.133–35, 2.57.138, 2.60.144–45, 3.38.84, 3.43.95–96, 4.3.4–5, 4.7.18, 4.23.63, 4.26.72, 4.28.77–29.80, 4.42.120, 4.44.123, 4.45.126, 4.47.128, 4.49.131, 4.56.148, 4.58.150–59.151, 4.61.156–57, 4.62.160–63
typology/ type(s), 170, 171n18; *TC* 1.2.4n14, 1.13.29n51, 3.52.125n199

use/using, 165–66; *TC* 1.1.2, 1.4.8, 1.20.39–40, 1.22.44, 1.26.54, 1.34.73, 1.35.75, 1.39.85, 3.27.61–28.63, 3.29.66

Verrines, *TT* 5.16; 177

wisdom, x, xii, 14; *TT* 11.38; 167, 174; *TC* 1.8.18, 1.11.23–24, 1.13.28, 2.9.17, 2.11.23, 2.60.144–45, 3.21.52, 3.31.72, 3.56.134, 4.7.17–18, 4.10.30, 4.11.33–12.34, 4.21.59, 4.59.151, 4.61.155–58
Word, as Logos/Christ, 12–13, 165; *TC* Pr.6.13, 1.8.19n35, 1.12.26–13.27, 1.38.81